P9-DCV-347

Dominican Republic

Gary Prado Chandler
Liza Prado Chandler

DAJABÓN (p212)
Haitian vendors and Dominican shoppers pour into this border town for an intriguing twice-weekly market

CABARETE (p191)
World-class kiteboarding and windsurfing and a boisterous nightlife to boot

LA VEGA (p236)
This nondescript town comes alive in February, throwing one of the country's best Carnival celebrations

PICO DUARTE (p230)
Catch sunrise from atop the Caribbean's highest peak, with views of the Atlantic and the Caribbean

BAHÍA DE LAS ÁGUILAS (p252)
A rustic and incredibly picturesque beach extending for miles and reachable only by boat

PENÍNSULA DE PEDERNALES (p246)
Off the beaten path, with unique white-stone beaches and a protected coastal lagoon offering excellent bird watching

Cap-Haïtien
Fort Liberté
HAITI
Hinche
Lac de Péligre
PORT-AU-PRINCE
Pétionville
Kenscoff
Forêt des Pins
Chaine de Vallières
Étang Saumâtre
Jimaní
Lago Enriquillo
Parque Nacional Sierra de Baoruco
Sierra de Baoruco
Péninsula de Pedernales
Pedernales
Parque Nacional Jaragua
Laguna de Oviedo
Isla Beata

Monte Cristi
Parque Nacional Monte Cristi
Dajabón
Sabaneta
Restauración
Comendador/ Elías Piña
Sierra de Neyba
Parque Nacional Isla Cabritos
Neyba
Parque Nacional Sierra de Baoruco
Barahona
Mao
Santiago
Moca
Puerto Plata
Sosúa
Cabarete
Salcedo
San Francisco de Macorís
La Vega
Jarabacoa
Parque Nacional Armando Bermúdez
Parque Nacional José del Carmen Ramírez
Pico Duarte (3175m)
San Juan de la Maguana
Cordillera Septentrional
Valle del
Presa de Hatillo
Bonao
Presa Alto Yuna
DOMINICAN REPUBLIC
Presa del Jigüey- Aguacate
Azua
Bani
Río Yaque del Sur
Valle de San Juan

72°W
71°W

45
1
29
20
31
18
16
5
25
21
1
23
233
5
45
109
305
3
3
121
307
3
306
47
2
50
48
46
44
44
44
102
102
1
1

ATLANTIC OCEAN

0 ——————————— 100 km
0 ——————————— 60 miles

RÍO SAN JUAN (p199)
As mellow as nearby
Cabarete is lively, with two
scenic beaches and great diving

**WHALE WATCHING
IN SAMANÁ (p149)**
See 30-ton humpbacks leap,
splash and jostle about in
one of the world's top
whale-watching spots

LAS GALERAS (p153)
Relax in a sleepy town
with great hiking, diving and
picturesque beaches

PLAYA LIMÓN (p142)
Deserted beach paradise
bordering a protected
lagoon, with thousands of
coconut trees and two hotels

**BÁVARO &
PUNTA CANA (p132)**
The Dominican Republic's beach
and all-inclusive resort capital
with stunning white-sand
beaches and blue-green seas

Río San Juan

5

Bahía
Escocesa

Nagua

132

Las
Terrenas

Las
Galeras

Península de Samaná

5 Samaná

Bahía de Samaná

Reserva Científica
Lagunas Redonda
y Limón

Playa Limón

Cibao

Cotuí

17

23

103

104

107

104

Cordillera Oriental

Parque Nacional
Los Haitises

Monte Plata

Hato Mayor

El Seibo

Higüey

Bávaro

Punta Cana

13

Río Ozama

23

4

4

4

Costa
del Coco

SANTO
DOMINGO

4

3

Boca
Chica

Juan
Dolio

San Pedro
de Macorís

3 La Romana

4

San Cristóbal

2

Parque
Nacional
Submarino
La Caleta

Isla
Catalina

Bayahibe

Parque
Nacional
del Este

Isla Saona

SANTO DOMINGO (p63)
A vibrant city of rich
historical sites, hip cultural
outlets, hopping nightlife and
beautiful sea views

BAYAHIBE (p122)
One-road beach town with
superb diving, nightly outdoor
parties and popular package
tours to Isla Saona

CARIBBEAN SEA

ELEVATION

2700m
2400m
2100m
1800m
1500m
1200m
900m
600m
300m
Sea Level

Destination Dominican Republic

The Dominican Republic is justly famous for its beaches – broad bands of white sand bounded by pastel waters and impossibly tall coconut trees. But the DR, as it is commonly called, has much more to offer than beaches. The North Coast is one of the best places in the world for windsurfing and kiteboarding and there's great whale watching off the Península de Samaná. The Dominican Republic has the Caribbean's highest peak (Pico Duarte at 3175m) and whether you climb it or not, the rugged area makes for fun hiking, biking and white-water rafting.

The Dominican Republic is home to many New World firsts – the first hospital, the first university, the first paved road. Perhaps most significantly, the first Catholic Mass in the New World was held in a settlement founded by Christopher Columbus on the North Coast. You can argue that the modern history of the Americas – and the unleashing of Earth-altering social, economic and political forces – began here. The Dominican Republic's modern history embodies the soaring triumph and searing tragedy that has followed those first steps.

It is a country of layers, of men playing dominoes on aluminum tables, wood frame houses painted bubblegum-pink, of cockfights and sweet coffee. And nowhere is baseball – by nature a mellow game – so imbued with the raucous spirit and celebration of its fans.

While there is no shame in spending time pampering yourself at one of the DR's famous all-inclusive resorts, this is a country of remarkable depth and grace, and well-worth exploring.

Highlights

WILLIAM J HEBERT/STONE/GETTY IMAGES

Fire up during Carnival (p236) in La Vega

Just one of the beautiful beaches waiting to be lounged on in La Romana (p118)

GREG JOHNSTON

GREG JOHNSTON

Take time to unwind in Bayahibe (p122)

Get a feel for New World history at Fortaleza Ozama, Santo Domingo (p75)

Sample some of the diverse wares on sale at Santo Domingo's markets (p95)

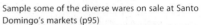

See how the other half lived at Casas Reales (p69), Santo Domingo

ALFREDO MAIQUEZ

Admire the painstaking restoration of the Museo Alcázar de Colón (p70), Zona Colonial, Santo Domingo

ALFREDO MAIQUEZ

Columbus' final resting place? See for yourself at Faro a Colón (p79), Santo Domingo

Lift your spirits in Santo Domingo's vibrant bar scene (p90)

STEPHEN ALVAREZ/NATIONAL GEOGRAPHIC/GETTY IMAGES

SCOTT DOGGETT

Mix with the locals in the Southwest (p254)

Might be time to grab a cocktail, La Romana (p118)

GREG JOHNSTON

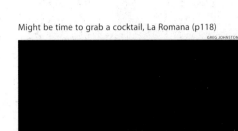

Do all of the watersports or just watch at Las Terrenas (p158)

ALFREDO MAIQUEZ

GREG JOHNSTON

We understand if you want to stay a while at La Romana (p118)

ALFREDO MAIQUEZ

Hiking is easier than you think when there's a beach waiting for you at the end (p155)

Get offshore and let the breeze take you, Bayahibe (p122)

GREG JOHNSTON

Watch the master cigar rollers at work (p95)

It's hard to resist a dip at Salto de Jimenoa (p226) – just check the water temperature first

Be charmed by colorful wooden houses found throughout the Dominican Republic (p148)

STUART WESTMORLAND/STONE/GETTY IMAGES

Samaná (p149) is one the world's top spots to see the amazing humpback whales

ALFREDO MAIQUEZ

The Dominican Republic is the world's best place to snap up some amber (p94)

Stop in the name of love: carnival is the time the country lets its hair down (p83)

ALFREDO MAIQUEZ

Shoot the rapids on Río Yaque del Norte river, near Jarabacoa (p226)

SCOTT DOGGETT

Baseball is the national sport of the Dominican Republic – checking out a lively match (p93) is a must during the season

EZRA SHAW/GETTY IMAGES

Try not to be too distracted by the stunning scenery while putting at Playa Grande (p201)

ANDREW MARSHALL & LEANNE WALKER

Regional Map Contents

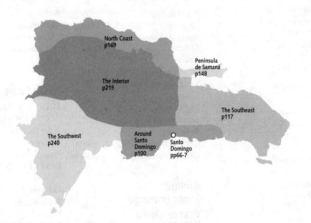

North Coast
p169

Península
de Samaná
p148

The Interior
p215

The Southeast
p117

The Southwest
p240

Around
Santo
Domingo
p100

Santo
Domingo
pp66-7

Contents

The Authors

GARY PRADO CHANDLER

Gary first went to the Dominican Republic in 1998, when he joined a friend for a family visit, and ended up staying two months. For this project, Gary and his wife and co-author Liza Prado Chandler were in the country even longer, staying for Carnival, Independence Day and Semana Santa, the DR's three main holidays. That made the research something of a challenge but gave Gary plenty of opportunities to improve his merengue moves – unfortunately it had no apparent effect. Gary is a graduate of UC Berkeley and Columbia Journalism School; this is his third assignment with Lonely Planet, after *Brazil* and *Central America*.

Our Favorite Things

In Santo Domingo, our favorite sights are Faro a Colón (p79), the Catedral Primada de América (p71), the Museo Mundo de Ambar (p70), wandering the Zona Colonial (p69) and baseball games (p92) at Estadio Quisqueya.

Of the DR's beaches, we love Playa Rincón (p154), Bávaro (p134), Playa Grande (p200) and for something different, Playa Los Patos (p250), a white-stone beach south of Barahona.

We haven't tried kiteboarding (p52) at Cabarete but it's obviously a rush. You gotta climb Pico Duarte (p230) at some point, but the hikes around Las Galeras (p154) are shorter and have beaches at the end!

Cabarete
Playa Grande
Pico Duarte
Las Galeras & Playa Rincón
Bávaro
Santo Domingo
Playa Los Patos

LIZA PRADO CHANDLER

Liza was working as a corporate attorney when she decided she'd had quite enough of all that steady income, high social standing and rapid career advancement, and became a travel writer instead. She co-authored two books to other Caribbean destinations – Cancun and the Yucatán Peninsula – before taking on one of her favorite places to travel, the Dominican Republic. A graduate of Brown University and Stanford Law School, she has traveled extensively in Latin America and Europe; this is her first assignment with Lonely Planet. After three years abroad and on the road, she and Gary now live in San Francisco.

LONELY PLANET AUTHORS

Why is our travel information the best in the world? It's simple: our authors are independent, dedicated travellers. They don't research using just the Internet or phone, and they don't take freebies in exchange for positive coverage. They travel widely, to all the popular spots and off the beaten track. They personally visit thousands of hotels, restaurants, cafés, bars, galle palaces, museums and more – and they take pride in getting all the details right, and how it is. For more, see the authors section on www.lonelyplanet.com.

Getting Started

The Dominican Republic (DR) is a year-round tourist destination. Any time of the year you can find great weather, beautiful beaches and interesting sporting and cultural activities. That's not to say some times aren't better than others, especially if you are coming for a specific reason beyond relaxing on the beach. Carnival, baseball, humpback whales, scuba diving and more – all big draws in the DR – are only available during certain months. If you have a particular interest, check the coverage in this book to be sure you go in the right season. There are also peak tourist seasons which can mean higher prices and larger crowds, and some months are rainier than others. These shouldn't be deal-breakers – the prices and weather don't vary *that* much – but are worth considering.

Although the Dominican Republic cannot be called a truly budget travel destination on backpacker terms, it is one of the most affordable places for all-inclusive resorts. With no hostels or camping, accommodation prices and, to a lesser degree, food costs can make shoestring travel a challenge. On the other hand, the public transportation system is excellent, and the Dominican Republic is small enough that travelers can cover the whole country in a single trip (and diverse enough to make doing so very rewarding).

WHEN TO GO

Except in the central mountains, temperatures don't vary much in the Dominican Republic, averaging a summery 28°C to 31°C (81°F to 87°F) in most places for most of the year. In the mountains, sunny days climb to 24°C (75°F) but can just as easily fall to single digits at night or on cloudy days. Tropical humidity can make the temperatures feel higher, though sea breezes help mitigate the effect. The rainy season is from May to October, though in Samaná and the North Coast it can last until December. The hurricane season is during August and September.

The main foreign tourist seasons are from December to February, July to August, and Semana Santa (the week before Easter). Expect higher prices and more crowded beaches during these times – Semana Santa is especially busy. Note that most water sports and activities, including

See Climate Charts (p261) for more information.

DON'T LEAVE HOME WITHOUT...

- Sunscreen: Vendors know you need it, and even small bottles can cost US$10 or more.
- Mosquito repellent: The DR had a minor malaria scare in 2005 – only a handful of people were infected, but you should bring repellent and check the Internet for updates.
- Passport and US cash: You'll need both to get in and out of the country.
- Flashlight: A flashlight comes in handy during frequent blackouts – just be sure to pack it in a place you can find in the dark!
- Good shoes: The DR is one Caribbean county where you'll be happy to have more than just flip-flops, whether for hiking or river rafting. If you like merengue, bring some dancing shoes too.
- Alarm clock: Few hotel rooms have clocks or a wake up service.
- Detergent and travel clothes line: Laundry can be expensive here, so it's nice to be able to do some handwashing.

scuba diving, jet-skiing, even kayaking are prohibited throughout the Dominican Republic during Semana Santa. Semana Santa is not a good time for that dive vacation you've been saving up for!

Several of the DR's most popular events and attractions can only be enjoyed at certain times of the year. Carnival is celebrated every weekend in February, sometimes stretching to the first week of March. February is also the best time for whale-watching in Samaná (p149), although the season officially stretches from mid-January to mid-March. If you're interested in baseball, the Dominican professional season runs from October to late January.

All in all, February and November are perhaps the best months to visit – both have great weather, thinner crowds and allow you to partake in either pro baseball, Carnival or whale-watching.

COSTS & MONEY

For independent travelers, the Dominican Republic can be a pretty expensive place. The big-ticket item is accommodation, which will cost at least US$20 per night, and not infrequently US$35 or more. There are no hostels, and very few hotels that offer budget rooms with shared bath. On top of that, many low-end hotels are basically revolving-door brothels – not exactly where most tourists want to spend the night.

Eating out can be expensive too, but at least you have more control over that. Going to restaurants every night will run at least US$10 per person per meal once drinks, taxes and tip are added in, and in many cases more. But by eating at street food vendors and cafeteria-style eateries, and by getting lunch or breakfast items at a grocery store instead of a restaurant, you can bring food costs down to US$6 per meal or less.

First-class bus tickets are never more than US$7.50 and most are much less (it's a small country after all). *Gua-guas* (small buses for local transportation) are even cheaper. *Motoconchos* (motorcycle taxis) and taxis vary in price, mostly having to do with location. Taxis in touristy areas can be exorbitant, but *motoconchos* are rarely more than a dollar or two. Of course, *motoconchos* are significantly less safe than taxis or buses – a shocking number of people, including tourists, have been hurt or killed in *motoconcho* accidents. A few do's and don'ts for safe riding: 1) Don't take a *motoconcho* in the rain or for long distances, especially if it means getting on the highway; 2) Don't share the *motoconcho* with another passenger; 3) Do be careful not to burn your leg on the muffler, especially when getting on or off; 4) Do be sure your feet are well-placed and your grip on the handholds is firm before setting off; and 5) Don't be afraid to ask the driver ¡*Más despacio, por favor!* (slow down!); if he doesn't slow down, ask *Déjame aquí, por favor*, to be let off.

For resort-goers, the story is very different. The Dominican Republic is famous for having affordable all-inclusive resorts, and rightly so. You can find some incredible bargains online and in newspaper travel sections. Deluxe all-inclusive resorts still tend to be in the US$150 to US$250 per-person-per-night range, but there are a number of very comfortable resorts where you can stay for US$75 per person per night. Lower-end places – where you lose a bit in terms of room and food quality, but usually still have a decent beach and pool – can go for an incredible US$35 per person per night, everything included.

Other costs to consider are car rental (per day including taxes and insurance US$45 to US$55), guided tours and excursions (typically per person US$35 to US$55) and Internet (per hour US$1 to US$3). Laundry is a cost that can be unexpectedly high as most *lavanderías* (laundries)

HOW MUCH?

Motoconcho ride US$1

Average hotel room US$30-40

Quality cigar US$4

Kiteboarding course (9hrs) US$350-400

Bleacher seats at Quisqueya Stadium US$1.50

charge by the piece. Rates will generally be in the region of US$0.75 to US$2 per piece. Laundries that charge per load are harder to find but typically charge US$8 to US$11 for up to 15lbs (7kg).

Budget travelers should expect to spend an average of US$20 to US$25 per room per day for accommodation, US$8 to US$15 per person per day on meals, and US$5 to US$10 per person per day on transport and incidentals, or a total of US$32 to US$50 per day. Sharing a bed will save you on lodging costs, as most hotels charge by the number of beds in a room, not the number of people. Be sure to budget for excursions, whether whale watching, diving or taking a kiteboarding class.

TOP TENS

Top 10 Spectator Events
Dominicans love spectator events, not only for the event itself but for the rambunctious atmosphere that always accompanies them. More really is merrier here, and travelers are always welcome to join in. The following are the best spectator events in the DR, from mega to mellow.

- Baseball game between Escojido and Licey at Estadio Quisqueya in Santo Domingo (p92).
- Carnival parade in La Vega (p236).
- Cockfight at Coliseo Gallístico Alberto Bonetti Burgos in Santo Domingo (p93).
- Master of the Ocean mixed water sports competition in Cabarete (p195).
- Baseball game at Estadio Tetelo Vargas in San Pedro de Macorís (p110).
- Wild and sometimes bloody Carnival celebrations in Monte Cristi (p209).
- Nightly softball games in Constanza (p235).
- Local basketball games in San Pedro de Macorís (p110).
- International Sand Castle Competition in Cabarete (p195).
- Tourist-friendly cockfights in Las Terrenas (p161).

Top 10 Merengue Hits
Get in the mood with some of these all-time favorites of Dominican music. El Conde promenade in Santo Domingo is lined with street-side music stands selling both genuine and bootleg copies of the most popular merengue albums.

- *Cumande* by Joseíto Mateo
- *La Muerte de Martín* by Johnny Ventura
- *Ojalá Que Llueva Café* by Juan Luís Guerra
- *La Agarradera* by Johnny Ventura
- *Abusadora* by Wilfrido Vargas
- *Déjame Volver* by Fernando Villalona
- *Guavaberry* by Juan Luís Guerra
- *Querido* by Alex Bueno
- *El Negrito del Batey* by Alberto Beltran
- *Madre* by Sergio Vargas

Top 10 Dominican Cigar Brands
The DR has hundreds of cigar makers, from tiny home-grown operations to factories producing tens of millions of cigars every year (p95). These are among the most sought-after Dominican brands.

- Arturo Fuente
- Romeo y Julieta 1875
- Cohiba Dominicana
- H Upmann
- Davidoff
- Montecristi
- Don Lino
- La Gloria Cubana
- La Aurora
- Macanudo Café

Midrange travelers will pay more for hotels, around US$45 to US$60 per room per night. Again, couples enjoy a considerable per-person savings by sharing a bed. Eating at midrange restaurants ranges from US$15 to US$25 per person per day. Excursion prices are the same, though many midrange travelers also choose to rent a car for several days or more. Total per person per day costs for midrange travelers are around US$75 to US$125.

Top-end travelers pay around US$80 to US$100 for a hotel, US$25 to US$45 per day on meals and typically rent a car for most of their trip, or even take a flight or two. Excursions booked through high-end hotels are often more personalized, but of course more expensive. In all, top-end travelers should expect to pay around US$125 to US$200 per day.

All-inclusive resorts have online specials starting at around US$40 per person per day, but are typically closer to US$75 to US$100, with an upper range of around US$250. Some packages also include discount airfares and transfer to and from the airport in addition to room, food and drinks.

ESSENTIAL LITERATURE

Fascinating, if somewhat preachy, *They Forged the Signature of God*, the first novel by Viriato Sencin, won the DR's national fiction prize but was denounced by Balaguer for its thinly veiled critique of his and Trujillo's regimes.

Azucar! The Story of Sugar, by Alan Cambeira, is a fascinating novel that portrays the human toll of sugar production in the DR. Though the story is fictional, much of the information, descriptions and events are based on real events and detailed research by the author.

In the Time of the Butterflies is an award-winning novel by Julia Álvarez about three sisters slain for their part in a plot to overthrow Rafael Trujillo. Also by Álvarez is *How the García Girls Lost Their Accents*.

Drown, by Junot Diaz, is a terrifically interwoven collection of short stories about growing up in the Dominican Republic and New Jersey. It is written in English but is liberally sprinkled with Dominicanisms.

Fiesta del Chivo is a fast-paced novel by Mario Vargas Llosas that weaves stories of a girl betrayed by her father to the dictator Trujillo, of the dictator himself and of the assassins who gun Trujillo down.

A sobering novel by a young Haitian-American woman, *The Farming of Bones* by Edwidge Danticat centers on the horrific slaughter of Haitians by Dominican soldiers in 1937.

For more reading please see the marginal book reviews in the Culture, History and Environment chapters.

INTERNET RESOURCES

There are a number of excellent websites providing general information about the Dominican Republic and traveling there.

Debbie's Dominican Republic Travel Page (www.debbiesdominicantravel.com) This site includes detailed first-hand reviews of various resorts around the country.

Dominican Republic One (www.dr1.com) Featured here is daily news developments in the DR, as well as travel and airline information pertaining to the country.

Hispaniola.com (www.hispaniola.com) Though companies pay to be featured here, this site's extensive listings and extra content – from a phrase book to local real estate brokers – make it extremely useful.

Lonely Planet (www.lonelyplanet.com) Our website features additional information and updates on travel in the DR, plus a traveler's chat room (The Thorn Tree) where travelers can post questions about specific routes, destinations etc.

República Dominicana (www.dominicana.com.do) The official website of the Dominican tourism board has surprisingly little information in English.

Itineraries

CLASSIC ROUTES

THE WHOLE COUNTRY   Three Weeks

This trip makes a large clockwise loop, starting and ending in Santo Domingo, and hitting Jarabacoa, Cabarete, the Samaná Peninsula, Bávaro and Punta Cana, and the southwest. It covers approximately 1000km (620 miles) and should take three weeks, accounting for travel time.

Fly into **Santo Domingo** (p63) and spend two days exploring – hit the Zona Colonial, the Faro a Colón and, if possible, a baseball game, cockfight, film or music performance and a night at a nightclub.

Day three, take a bus to **Jarabacoa** (p225). Visit the waterfalls in the afternoon, and sign up for whitewater rafting or canyoning the next day.

Head north to **Cabarete** (p191), which has world-class watersports and mountain biking. There's great diving and beaches in nearby **Sosúa** (p184) and **Río San Juan** (p199). Spend two to three days in the area.

Next you're off to the **Península de Samaná** (p147). If it's mid-January to mid-March, go whale watching. Otherwise take a boat trip to **Parque Nacional Los Haitises** (p146) to see the mangroves and cave paintings, or visit the waterfall near El Limón. Spend another two or three days hiking or boating to the beaches around **Las Galeras** (p153). For a bit more nightlife, base yourself in **Las Terrenas** (p158) instead.

Make your way to the southeast, famous for its beaches. Choose between rustic-and-deserted **Playa Limón** (p142) or manicured-and-gorgeous **Bávaro** and **Punta Cana** (p132).

Return to Santo Domingo and rent a car. Set off in the morning for a drive through the southwest. There's Taíno cave paintings in **San Cristóbal** (p111), a spectacular drive **south of Barahona** (p249) and crocodiles in **Lago Enriquillo** (p253). Spend a night or two, then head back to Santo Domingo.

BEACH-HOPPING
Two weeks

The previous itinerary spends a fair amount of time on the coast, but this one is for the dedicated beach hound.

Fly into the Puerto Plata airport and get a cab straight to Sosúa, where **Playa Alicia** (p186) is an attractive and amazingly underused beach right in town. From Sosúa, head east to **Cabarete** (p191), where sunbathers are entertained by hundreds of windsurfers and kiteboarders skimming and flying across the bay.

Next stop is Río San Juan, where cozy **Playa Caletón** (p200) and huge, rough **Playa Grande** (p200) are well worth visiting. If you dive or snorkel, there are some fun half- and full-day trips around there as well.

Further east is the Samaná Peninsula, where there's a mother lode of beaches in the sleepy town of Las Galeras. **Playa Rincón** (p154), with kilometers of nearly-white sand framed by huge coconut trees, was named one of the top 10 beaches in the Caribbean by *Conde Nast* magazine. That distinction could have easily gone to nearby Playa Madama or Playa Frontón, which are smaller and harder to get to than Rincón, but all the more isolated for it. Spend a few days and sample all three.

Catch a ferry across Samaná Bay and a local bus to **Playa Limón** (p142), just past the town of Miches. The beach is the staging ground for a popular resort tour through a nearby scientific reserve, but the beach is big enough that you won't even notice.

Close out your trip with the thick white sand and stunning blue waters at **Bávaro** and **Punta Cana** (p132). While Playa Rincón and Playa Limón offer a deserted-island feel, Bávaro and Punta Cana are best for relaxing and pampering yourself. Staying at one of the all-inclusive resorts here will maximize your sand-time, but even those at independent hotels have full access to the glorious coastline.

Fly home from Punta Cana.

This itinerary starts in Puerto Plata and sweeps east along the coast to Punta Cana. Stops include Sosúa, Cabarete, Las Galeras, Playa Limón and Bávaro. It covers only 400 km (250 miles) and spending two to three days at most spots, you can easily complete the tour in two weeks.

ROADS LESS TRAVELED

A LITTLE OF EVERYTHING (EXCEPT THE CROWDS)   Two weeks

This trip starts and ends in Santo Domingo, and includes less-traveled destinations like the southwest and Pico Duarte. Where it follows the tourist route, it's for less-common sights and activities. You'll cover up to 1100km (685 miles). You should be able to complete it in two weeks.

Arriving in **Santo Domingo**, veer immediately off the beaten path by renting a car and driving southwest to **Barahona** (p246), with a stop in San Cristóbal to see the Taíno **cave paintings** (p112). Spend the next day visiting **Laguna Oviedo** (p251) and/or **Bahía de las Águilas** (p252) – the drive alone is spectacular. The following day head to **Lago Enriquillo** (p253) – it's the lowest point in the Caribbean (and possibly the hottest!) and home to myriad iguanas and crocodiles.

Return the car in Santo Domingo and catch a bus to **Jarabacoa** (p225). Take a day for rafting or canyoning, but you're really here to climb **Pico Duarte** (p224), the highest peak in the Caribbean (3175m). The standard trip is three days, but consider arranging a side trip to beautiful **Valle del Tetero** (p233), which adds two days. (A less common five-day route is from San José de las Matas, southwest of Santiago)

From the mountains, head north and east along the coast to **Río San Juan** (p199) a small town that sees few tourists. There are two terrific beaches nearby and some of the best snorkeling and diving on the North Coast. Alternatively, consider stopping at **Cabarete** (p191), a beach town along the way to Río San Juan. While on the tourist route, Cabarete has more hotels, restaurants and outdoors options and a much livelier nightlife.

Leave early so you can get across the bay to Sabana de la Mar and **Parque Nacional Los Haitises** (p146) in one day. Visit the lodge at the entrance to the park for a tour featuring mangrove forests and Taíno paintings.

Your last stop should be **Playa Limón** (p142), an isolated beach and lagoon where you'll have kilometers of coastline to yourself. Return to Santo Domingo for your flight home.

TAILORED TRIPS

DOMINICAN REPUBLIC FOR KIDS

Spend a day or two in **Santo Domingo** (p63) where there's a great Children's Museum and a few kid-friendly sights, like the national aquarium, zoo and botanical garden; some of the forts and ruins make for fun exploring.

From Santo Domingo, make your way east along the coast. **Boca Chica** (p101) has a huge pretty beach with shallow, calm water that's ideal for youngsters. Just 30 minutes from Santo Domingo, this can also be a day trip from there. Further east, **Bayahibe** (p122) is a tiny town on the edge of a national park with a number of excursion options, from package tours of an island beach to more personalized snorkeling trips.

After a few days of exploring, close out your vacation at one of the many all-inclusive resorts at **Bávaro** and **Punta Cana** (p132) which offer go-karts, bowling, sailing trips, parasailing and an ecological park nearby. All resorts offer tours to local sights; for more independence, rent a car and use this book to explore on your own.

If your kids are up for more adventure, you can consider excursions elsewhere. One favorite is **whale-watching** (p149) in Samaná, possible between mid-January and mid-March. Or head to **Jarabacoa** (p225), where you can take the family whitewater rafting or horseback riding. For the especially adventurous, a number of windsurfing and kiteboarding schools in **Cabarete** (p191) offer special courses for children and teenagers.

All of these destinations can be reached either by bus or car from Santo Domingo.

NATIONAL PARKS & RESERVES

Head southwest from Santo Domingo to the town of **Barahona** (p246), a good base for bird-watching trips to Laguna Oviedo in **Parque Nacional Jaragua** (p251), and spotting crocodiles and iguanas at Lago Enriquillo in **Parque Nacional Isla Cabritos** (p253).

From here, head north to Jarabacoa, which serves as the gateway for **Parques Nacionales Armando Bermúdez and José del Carmen Ramírez** (p230). The two adjoining parks cover much of the DR's central mountain range, including Pico Duarte, the highest peak in the Caribbean (3175m).

From Pico Duarte continue northwest to **Parque Nacional Monte Cristi** (p209), which has pristine coral reefs and some rare manatees. Spend a day or two snorkeling and enjoying the park's beach.

From Monte Cristi, it's a long cross-country drive to **Parque Nacional Los Haitises** (p146), near Sabana de la Mar. Half-day boat tours of the park include visiting mangrove forests and seeing Taíno cave paintings.

There are more cave paintings in **Parque Nacional del Este** (p127) near Bayahibe, on the way back to Santo Domingo. Though Isla Saona – the main attraction – is over-touristed, the snorkeling and diving are superb.

Snapshot

On buses, over dominoes, at the hair and nail salons, the main topic of discussion in the Dominican Republic (DR) is the state of the peso (RD$), and how expensive everything has suddenly become. After holding steady at around 17 pesos to the US dollar for years, the national currency began devaluating in 2003 falling as low as RD$55 to the dollar before stabilizing at around RD$28 to the dollar. Shelf prices shot up but salaries did not, and Dominicans found themselves paying triple for everything from gasoline to a cup of coffee. Even after the exchange rate settled down, prices remained artificially high, as if no one had informed the supermarkets and utility companies that the peso had stabilized. Most Dominicans blamed then-president Hipolito Mejía, who presided over the peso's slide and who paid for it with a resounding defeat by Leonel Fernández, who had served as president just eight years earlier. Fernández's first election as president in 1996 was widely celebrated, marking the end of nearly 70 years of tyrannical rule by Rafael Trujillo and his disciple Joaquín Balaguer. There was a palpable sense of dejá vu this time around, and Dominicans have heaped admiration – and high expectations – on their returning hero.

Dominicans are also talking about another hero – an outfielder for the Anaheim Angels baseball team named Vladimir Guerrero. Guerrero, born and raised outside Baní, west of Santo Domingo, was voted the American League's Most Valuable Player in 2004, receiving 21 of the 28 first place votes cast. Guerrero, as much a gentleman as baseball has ever known, was quick to point out that three of the next four top vote-getters were also Dominican. For Dominicans, many of whom grow up playing with mitts made out of milk cartons or folded cardboard, Guerrero's spectacular play and unfailing graciousness evince a respect for the game of baseball that runs deep in the Dominican Republic but seems to be flagging in the US and elsewhere.

The US invasion and occupation of Iraq remains the subject of lasting discussion in the Dominican Republic. The DR sent a small contingent of soldiers – under no small pressure from the Bush administration – but quietly withdrew them as public support soured. The DR has been occupied by a half-dozen foreign powers over the years, and Dominicans are disinclined to support a larger nation invading a smaller one. At the same time, Dominicans know well what life is like under a dictatorship and are not deaf to the argument that tyrants cannot be removed without a fight.

Through it all, Dominicans are not ones to dwell on the negative. They find a great many reasons to be cheerful – Carnival, the start of baseball season, Semana Santa, summer, kids going back to school, the latest bachata hit – and these are the topics of everyday conversation as much as any other.

FAST FACTS

Population: 8.85 million

Life expectancy: women 70 years, men 64 years

Average monthly income of a farm worker: US$74

Average monthly income of Dominican players in the Major Leagues: US$222,000

Unemployment: 17%

Size of Dominican Republic: 48,734 sq km (larger than the Bahamas, Jamaica, Puerto Rico, the Virgin Islands and the French West Indies combined)

Length of coastline: 1572km

Number of tourists visiting the DR per year: 3.4 million

Number of cigars exported yearly to the United States and Europe: 350 million

History

FIRST ARRIVALS

The earliest-known inhabitants of Hispaniola were probably descendents of Amazonian peoples using huge dugout canoes to island-hop, over the course of many generations, from the southern tip of the Lesser Antilles (present-day Virgin, Leeward and Windward Island chains) north and west into the Greater Antilles (present-day Hispaniola, Cuba, Jamaica and Puerto Rico). That group was replaced by a second more advanced group, known as Saladoids, and they were replaced in turn by a still more advanced group, whose origin was probably either the Venezuelan Amazon or the Peruvian Andes. By AD 700, this third group – known as Taínos or 'friendly people' – occupied virtually all of the islands in the Caribbean basin.

TAÍNO LIFE

There were an estimated 400,000 Taínos on Hispaniola at the time of Columbus' arrival, living in villages of 1000 and 2000 people and loosely divided into local and regional chiefdoms. The Taínos cultivated root crops such as cassava and sweet potato using heaped mounds of earth called *conucos,* which slowed erosion and facilitated weeding and harvesting. They were skilled fishermen and caught fish with nets, spears, traps, hooks attached to lines and they even used a mild poison that slowed the reflexes of river fish, making them easy to grab. The Taínos also created extensive pictograms and petroglyphs in caves around the island, which can still be seen today in places like Reserva Antropológica El Pomier (p112), Parque Nacional del Este (p127) and Parque Nacional Los Haitises (p146).

The Dominican Republic: A National History by Frank Moya Pons is the most comprehensive book on the Dominican Republic's history.

Slave traders carried the Taínos' principal crop, cassava, to sub-Saharan Africa, where it was widely adopted. The Taínos also introduced Europe to the sweet potato, bean, squash and peanut, and to fruits such as guava, mamey and pineapple. They weren't the only native American group using canoes and hammocks (*canoa* and *hamaca* in Taíno), but it was on Hispaniola that Europeans first saw such innovations. Of course the Taínos' most famous contribution was a plant they called *tabaco,* which they prepared and smoked in much the same way cigars are today.

THE ADMIRAL

Columbus' first of four expeditions set sail from Palos, Spain, in 1492 carrying about 90 men and bound for Asia. Due to miscalculations of the Earth's circumference, Columbus expected to reach Japan by sailing 3860km to the west. Indeed, when he reached the New World, he mistook Cuba for Japan.

After stops at the small Bahamian island of Guanahaní and present-day Cuba, a mountainous landscape appeared before the explorers. Columbus named it La Isla Española, 'the Spanish Island,' which was later corrupted to Hispaniola. Days later, the fleet's flagship, the *Santa María* crashed into a coral reef and was doomed. Columbus had wood salvaged from the ship and used it to build a fort, which he named Villa La

2600 BC	AD 700
Earliest known human inhabitation of Hispaniola	Taíno indigenous people occupy all of the Greater Antilles except western Cuba (occupied by the Guanahatabeys)

THE SLAVE TRADE

The intercontinental slave trade was a well-established network that had been in place for 800 years before the first Europeans arrived in the New World. Starting in the 7th century, more than 15 million African people had been forced to cross the Sahara to toil in North Africa and the Middle East. Once Europeans on Hispaniola had wiped out the native Taíno population, it was an easy step to import slave labor from the west African coast.

It is estimated that more than half a million Africans were brought to Hispaniola between 1518 and 1801. It was a horrendous ordeal that began with African tribes kidnapping rival tribe members and selling them to European slave dealers established on the west African coast. After the sale, dealers would pack hundreds of men, women and children – often shackled in pairs by the wrist and leg – into the bowels of galleons that traveled to the New World.

The transatlantic trip, known as the Middle Passage, took three to six months. Up to a fifth of the enslaved people died en route, most from scurvy and amoebic dysentery stemming from malnutrition (slaves only received dried beans, corn and palm oil for food). Those that survived the trip faced devastating diseases like measles and smallpox, for which they had little or no natural resistance, and of course the horrors of slavery itself.

Once on Hispaniola, Africans were sold to European merchants and plantation owners for different purposes and prices depending on the age, gender and health of the person. Few records were kept regarding the origin of the Africans brought to Hispaniola or nearby islands, and it is all but impossible to trace the exact origins of most present-day African-Caribbeans. Yet it was through the sweat and blood of these kidnapped Africans – denied their language, history, even their names – that Hispaniola's mining and agricultural operations grew to prominence, as vital today as they were in colonial times.

Navidad, or Christmas Village, as they'd come ashore on December 25. Located near present day Cap-Haïtien, Haiti, it was the first settlement of any kind made by Europeans in the New World.

CONQUEST

Columbus left 39 men at Villa La Navidad and set off for Spain, where he was hailed as a hero. King Ferdinand and Queen Isabela bestowed upon him impressive titles, including 'Admiral of the Ocean Sea' and gave him 17 ships with which to return to the West Indies and bring back treasure.

But when Columbus returned to La Navidad in November 1493 he discovered everyone dead and the fort burned to the ground. He later learned that the men had taken to kidnapping and raping Taíno women, until the local Taíno chief ordered them killed.

Columbus sailed 110km east to a protected bay where he established another settlement, this one named La Isabela in honor of his royal patron. La Isabela is considered the first formal European settlement in the New World and the town's remains, including that of the church where the first Catholic mass in the Americas was held, can still be visited today (p206). However La Isabela was plagued with disease and disaster, and within five years the capital of the new colony was moved to the southern coast where it has remained.

But it was the Taínos who suffered the most those early years. Forced to work in mines, they died in great numbers of hunger, disease, accidents and Spanish brutality. Many committed suicide, usually by drinking poison,

1492	1494
Christopher Columbus arrives in the Caribbean	The New World's first Catholic Mass is held in La Isabela on the north coast of Hispaniola

and Spanish accounts tell of Taíno women killing their newborns to keep them out of slavery. In less than 30 years, the Taíno population on Hispaniola fell from 400,000 to less than 3000. Facing a labor shortage in its new colony, Spain turned to African slaves. The first arrived in 1520 and by 1568 the number had risen to about 20,000.

THE FRENCH GET A PIECE

France and England looked enviously at Spain's colony in the New World. Both countries paid pirates to hinder Spanish trade in the West Indies, while at the same time plotting to take over the island. In 1655 England sent 34 warships and 13,000 men to capture the island, but they were repelled by the colony's defenders.

The French took another tack that proved more effective. Instead of troops they sent hundreds of farmers and merchants – and thousands of enslaved Africans – to populate communities on the island's western side, shielded from Spanish rule by the massive central mountains. In 1677 there were 11 French villages on Hispaniola totaling more than 4000 settlers. Forty years later, Saint-Domingue – as the French colony was called – contained 30,000 free residents and 100,000 slaves, compared to a mere 18,400 inhabitants in the Spanish colony.

Why the Cocks Fight by Michele Wucker is a book that examines Dominican-Haitian relations through the metaphor of cockfighting.

Eventually Spain realized it would have to set a border or risk losing the colony all together. In 1771 the two countries agreed to a border following the path of two rivers in the western third of the island. The border is essentially the same today and border towns like Comendador (aka Elías Piña) and Dajabón still host intriguing twice-weekly markets.

HAITIAN INDEPENDENCE

Not long after the international border was established, Saint-Domingue's enslaved Africans rose up in bloody revolt. The Spanish – who had 60,000 slaves on their own – supported the revolt as a way of weakening France. The former slaves joined the Spanish in fighting the French, but then switched sides in September 1793 when France agreed to abolish slavery.

Spain ceded the island to France in October 1795 to end the fighting, agreeing to relocate all of its citizens within a year. But the Spanish colonists did not revel leaving their rich lands in Santo Domingo for inferior ones in Cuba; many refused to leave or to give up their slaves. As France and Spain haggled over the details, the deadline to relocate came and went. Finally in January 1801 the brilliant, self-trained leader of the rebel slave forces François Dominique Toussaint L'Ouverture (himself a former slave) could wait no longer; he marched his troops into Santo Domingo and, without French authority, declared that the abolition of slavery would be enforced throughout the island. The action elevated Toussaint in the eyes of his troops, but put him at odds with French leaders, who now viewed him as a loose cannon. Within a year, he was betrayed to the French who sent him in chains to France, where he died of neglect in a dungeon in April 1803.

Ironically, the French essentially abandoned their claims in the western hemisphere when Napoleon signed a treaty that allowed the purchase of Louisiana by the USA. On January 1, 1804, Haiti proclaimed its independence. Taking its name from one of the original Taíno names for the

1520	1795
First enslaved Africans brought to Hispaniola	Spain cedes the island of Hispaniola to France

island, Haiti was the first black republic in the New World, and only the second free republic in the Americas after the US. Jean-Jacques Dessalines, who had been one of Toussaint's chief lieutenants, crowned himself emperor of the Republic of Haiti. Sadly, he would be the first of many dictators the Haitian people would endure.

DOMINICAN INDEPENDENCE

Haiti was perfectly clear about its ambition of uniting Hispaniola under one flag. To prevent an invasion, Spanish colonists in Santo Domingo asked for, and were successful in being reincorporated into Spain. But Spain completely bungled its administration of Santo Domingo and on November 30, 1821, the colony declared its independence once again. Colonial leaders intended to join the Republic of Gran Colombia (a country that included present-day Ecuador, Colombia, Panama and Venezuela) but never got the chance – Haiti invaded and finally achieved its goal of a united Hispaniola.

Dominicans chaffed under Haitian rule for the next 22 years, and to this day both countries regard the other with disdain and suspicion. Resistance grew until February 27, 1844 – a day celebrated as Dominican Independence Day – when a separatist movement headed by Juan Pablo Duarte captured Santo Domingo in a bloodless coup. The Puerto del Conde in Santo Domingo marks the spot where Duarte entered the city.

In 1861 the Dominican Republic once again submitted to Spanish rule, partly to avoid reinvasion from Haiti. But ordinary Dominicans did not support the move and, after four years of armed resistance, succeeded in expelling Spanish troops in what is known as the War of Restoration. (Restauración is a common street name throughout the DR, and there are a number of monuments to the war, including a prominent one in Santiago; see p219). On March 3, 1865, the Queen of Spain signed a decree annulling the annexation and withdrew her soldiers from the island.

TOWARD A US PROTECTORATE

The newly independent Dominican Republic suffered one corrupt president after another. One, General Ulises Heureaux, known as Lilí, used violence and bribes to stay in power from 1882 until his assassination in 1899. He borrowed heavily from the US and Europe, running up national debt. Shortly before he was killed, Lilí closed the National Bank and replaced it with the US-owned and -operated San Domingo Improvement Company. Not only did he leave the treasury drained, but he placed control of the country's monetary system – even its key sugar industry – in the hands of Americans.

It soon became clear that the Dominican government was economically ruined and that it could not repay the debts. The San Domingo Improvement Company called on the US government to intervene, which it did in 1905 by taking control of the customs houses and guaranteeing repayment of all loans. However, the US Senate stopped short of ratifying a plan proposed by President Theodore Roosevelt that would have established a protectorate over the DR. The decision to seize and administer the customs offices marked the first of many times the US would intervene in Dominican politics.

In 1868, the United States proposed buying the Samaná Peninsula from the Dominican Republic for US$2 million to build a military base. After the Dominican government approved the sale, however, the US Senate rejected the plan. The base was eventually built at Guantanamo Bay, Cuba, where it remains today.

1804	1809
Former slaves defeat French troops and declare Haitian independence and sovereignty over the entire island	Dominican Republic reincorporated as Spanish Colony

EYES ON THE DOMINICAN REPUBLIC

The Dominican Republic has been the target of numerous plots and occupations, owing primarily to its strategic location as a portal to the Caribbean and Central and South America. Bahía de Samaná has been especially coveted, as its deep channel, eastward orientation and easy-to-defend mouth make it ideal for a naval installation. At least six different countries have either occupied the Samaná area or sought to do so, including Haiti, France, Spain, the US and Germany.

After gaining independence from its Spanish colonizers, the DR was taken over by Haiti, which controlled Hispaniola from 1822 to 1844. During this period Haiti invited more than 5000 freed and escaped slaves from the US to settle on the island. About half moved to the Samaná area.

During Haitian rule, France pressured its former colony to cede the Península de Samaná in return for a reduction in the debt Haiti owed it. (Incredibly, Haiti had been forced to pay restitution to France for land taken from French colonists in order to gain international recognition. Of course, France never paid restitution to former slaves for their ordeal.)

After Dominican independence from Haiti in 1844, the new Dominican government feared Haiti would reinvade and sought foreign assistance from France, England and Spain. The Dominican Republic eventually resubmitted to Spanish rule in 1861, and Spain immediately sent a contingent of settlers to the Samaná area and reinforced the military installations on Cayo Levantado, a large island (and present-day tourist destination) near the mouth of the bay.

The Dominican Republic regained independence in 1864, but the Península de Samaná remained a tempting prize for other countries. Beginning in 1868 the US, under President Ulysses S Grant, sought to purchase the Península de Samaná from the DR in order to build a naval base there. Dominican president and strongman Buenaventura Baéz agreed to the sale in order to obtain the money and weapons he needed to stay in power. However, the US Senate, under pressure from Dominican exile groups and strong opposition from France and the UK, rejected the proposal in 1871. A year later, Baéz arranged to lease the area to the US-based Samaná Bay Company for 99 years. To the relief of most Dominicans, the company fell behind on its payments and Baéz's successor, Ignacio María González, rescinded the contract in 1874. The US revisited the idea of annexing Samaná in 1897 as the Spanish-American war loomed, but the US quickly defeated Spain and decided to build its Caribbean base in Guantanamo Bay, Cuba, where it remains today.

German intentions toward the Península de Samaná are less clear, but US documents from the 1870s suggest Germany was also seeking to establish a military base in the Caribbean. In 1916, during WWI, the US occupied the DR in part because it feared Germany was seeking to establish itself in the Península de Samaná. The last foreign occupation of the country and the Península de Samaná was by the US from April 1965 to June 1966.

US OCCUPATION

Dominican politics remained chaotic and corrupt, spawning various bloody rebellions between 1911 and 1914. The US government eventually became convinced that unrest in the Caribbean posed a threat to US national security, and that only by managing the political and financial affairs of the region's countries could the area be stabilized. In 1916 Wilson sent the marines to the DR, ostensibly to help the president quell a coup plot but in fact remaining there to enforce US control there for the next eight years.

While respectful of most civil liberties, the US prohibited Dominicans from owning weapons. It also banned the publication or broadcast of anything anti-American. And most importantly, it controlled the Dominican

1821	1844
Fed up with Spanish mismanagement, Dominicans regain independence, only to be invaded by Haiti the following year	Dominican Republic declares independence from Haiti after 22 years of occupation

budget. Though deeply imperialistic, the US occupation did succeed in stabilizing Dominican politics and the economy.

By 1924 the American situation had changed considerably as well. Wilson was no longer president, WWI was over and the US, which had previously feared German attacks on the Panama Canal without an American military presence in the DR, was considerably less concerned with the republic's strategic importance. After fighting a war in Europe, America was looking inward. It was decided to bring the troops home – from Europe and from elsewhere, including the DR.

TRUJILLO'S RISE TO POWER

The years from 1924 to 1930 were good ones for most Dominicans, led by altruistic and progressive president Horacio Vásquez. During his administration major roads were built, creating access to the countryside; many schools were constructed; and irrigation programs and sanitation services were initiated.

However in 1930 Rafael Leonidas Trujillo, chief of the former Dominican National Police (renamed the National Army in 1928), forced Vásquez and his vice president to resign and held a sham election in which he – the sole candidate – was voted president. Within weeks of the election, Trujillo formed a terrorist band, La 42, which roamed the country, killing everyone who posed any threat to him. An egomaniac of the first degree, he changed the names of various cities – Santo Domingo became Ciudad Trujillo, for example – and lavished support on San Cristóbal, the small city west of the capital where he was born. There, a never-used palace Trujillo had built can still be visited. After the briefest of respites, tyranny had returned to the DR.

THE TRUJILLO ERA

Tossing aside democratic values and his country's constitution, Trujillo ruled the Dominican Republic with an iron fist from 1930 to 1947 and indirectly thereafter until his assassination in 1961. During these years, Trujillo used his government to amass a personal fortune by establishing monopolies that he and his wife controlled. By 1934 Trujillo was the richest man on the island.

The Dominican Republic has declared its independence three times, twice from Spain and once from Haiti.

Because his own personal wealth was directly linked to the wealth of his country, Trujillo carried out the most grandiose program of public works and construction ever realized in the DR. Seemingly everywhere there was a bridge, highway or irrigation canal being built, with peasant families settling on uncultivated lands donated by the state. Agricultural production soared. Trujillo also pressed for industrial progress, and during his rule scores of factories were opened. The economy flourished.

But Trujillo's repressive ways far outweighed the economic improvements he fomented. Anyone who criticized the dictator or his government faced imprisonment or death. The torture and murder of political prisoners was a daily event in Trujillo's DR. But Haitians were to suffer the most at the hands of the Dominican dictator, who in spite of being part black, was deeply racist and xenophobic. After hearing reports that Haitian peasants were crossing into the Dominican Republic, perhaps to steal cattle, Trujillo ordered all Haitians along the border to be tracked down and

1861	1865
Dominican President Santana Familias allows Spain to reannex the Dominican Republic despite public protests	Dominican Republic gains independence by defeating Spanish troops in War of Restoration

executed. Dominican soldiers used a simple test to separate Haitians from Dominicans – they would hold up a string of parsley (*perejil* in Spanish) and ask everyone they encountered to name it. French- and Creole-speaking Haitians could not properly trill the 'r' and were summarily murdered. Beginning on October 3, 1937 and lasting for several days, at least 15,000 – and some researchers say as many as 35,000 – Haitians were hacked to death with machetes and their bodies dumped into the ocean. (Guns would have too easily linked the massacre to the government, though there was never any doubt who had ordered it.) Trujillo never openly admitted a massacre had taken place, but in 1938, under international pressure, he and Haitian president Sténio Vicente agreed the Dominican Republic would pay a total of US$750,000 as reparation for Haitians who had been killed (a paltry US$50 per person). The Dominican Republic made an initial payment of US$250,000 but it's unclear if it ever paid the rest. What is clear is that none of the money went to the families of those killed.

DEMOCRATIZATION & WAR

At the time of Trujillo's assassination on May 30, 1961, puppet President Joaquín Balaguer was in office. As he was merely a figurehead used by Trujillo, Balaguer had neither a power base nor popular support. A groundswell of unrest following the assassination soon forced him to share power with a seven-member Council of State, which included two of the men who'd taken part in the roadside ambush that left Trujillo fatally wounded. The council guided the country until elections could be organized.

http://lanic.utexas.edu/la/ca/dr has detailed information about past and current Dominican leaders and politicians as well as basic economic information.

On December 20, 1962, the scholar and poet Juan Bosch Gaviño was elected president in the first free elections the Dominican Republic had seen in many years. His liberal government enacted land reform and created a new constitution that separated church and state, guaranteed civil and individual rights, and endorsed civilian control of the military.

The changes annoyed wealthy landowners and military leaders alike, and on September 25, 1963, Bosch was toppled in a military coup. In response, Bosch and a group of supporters who called themselves the Constitutionalists took to the streets and seized the National Palace. The military responded with tank assaults and bombing runs, but the Constitutionalists kept on fighting until the USA intervened in the civil war. A US force of 20,000 occupied the Dominican Republic until elections were organized.

PUPPET PRESIDENT NO MORE

The election of July 1, 1966, pitted Bosch the benevolent reformer against Balaguer, a throwback to the Trujillo era. Unfortunately for Bosch, most of the voters feared his victory would rekindle the civil war. Balaguer won handily, garnering 57% of the vote. He was reelected in 1970 and 1974, mostly by intimidation and bribes and by using the National Police to curtail opposition. But by the late 1970s plunging sugar prices and rising oil costs had brought the Dominican economy to a standstill, and Balaguer lost the 1978 election to a wealthy cattle rancher named Silvestre Antonio Guzmán.

Guzmán's administration was riddled with corruption, and he committed suicide shortly after leaving office. Guzmán was followed by Salvador

1916–24	1937
United States occupies the Dominican Republic	Dictator Rafael Trujillo orders the extermination of Haitians along DR–Haiti border; more than 15,000 are killed in a matter of days

Jorge Blanco who set about undoing the economic damage his predecessor had done. In negotiations with the International Monetary Fund (IMF), Blanco committed his country to a fiscal austerity plan that included a reduction in government salaries, a rise in prices and new restrictions on imports. Despite widespread anger at some parts of the austerity measures, Blanco adhered to them and slowly the economy picked up and inflation was brought under control.

Unfortunately, Blanco had alienated the military by firing more than 4000 officers (of a total force of just 22,000 at the time). In the presidential elections of 1986, the military supported the former president and Trujillo disciple Joaquín Balaguer. Though 80 years old, ailing and blind with glaucoma, Balaguer was once again elected to the country's top office.

BALAGUER'S RETURN

www.hispaniola.com is an excellent website with historical information and up-to-date travel listings.

From 1986 until the presidential election of 1994, Balaguer ran his government like a dictatorship and set about reversing everything that had been accomplished by the IMF/Blanco adjustment program. His efforts had the effect of devaluing the Dominican peso five-fold and causing the annual inflation rate to soar to 60%. Many Dominicans saw no choice but to leave the country and by 1990 almost 900,000 Dominicans, or 12% of the country's population, had moved to New York.

Reviled by his own people, Balaguer had to rig the 1990 and 1994 elections to stay in power. But by then the military had grown weary of Balaguer's rule and let him know in no uncertain terms. Balaguer agreed to cut his last term short and hold elections – amazingly enough, he did just that.

A PROGRESSIVE PRESIDENT

In 1996 Leonel Fernández, a 42-year-old lawyer who grew up in New York City, edged out three-time candidate José Francisco Peña Gómez in a runoff election for president.

In the first months of his presidency, Fernández shocked his nation by forcibly retiring two dozen generals, encouraging his defense minister to submit to questioning by the civilian attorney general and then firing the defense minister for insubordination – all in a single week. Dominicans braced for a military reaction. Nothing happened.

The DR needed to change, Fernández stated, and he was going to usher in those changes. In the four years of his presidency, he made good on his pledge, presiding over strong economic growth, privatization and reform that curbed waste and lowered inflation, unemployment and illiteracy.

THE BUBBLE POPS

A former tobacco farmer named Hipólito Mejía succeeded Fernández as president in 2000. Though he'd promised to expand social programs, one of Mejía's first acts as president was to cut spending and increase fuel prices by 30%. The faltering US economy and September 11 attacks ate into Dominican exports as well as cash remittances and foreign tourism. The Dominican peso began to devalue in October 2002, sinking as low at RD$52 to the US dollar before stabilizing at around RD$28 to RD$30 per dollar. It is a common joke that a month after the elections, you couldn't find a single person who'd admit to having voted for Mejía.

1961	1986
Rafael Trujillo is assassinated	Joaquín Balaguer, 80 years old and blind, is elected to his fifth term as president

LEONEL RETURNS

Leonel Fernandez returned to the national stage – he had never really left – by defeating Mejía by 25 percentage points in presidential elections held in May 2004. In September of that year, the DR was lashed by Hurricane Jeanne, a relatively weak storm that nevertheless caused tremendous destruction in the southeast. Many of the high-end resorts were closed and some guests had to be evacuated by helicopter. Rural areas north of the resorts suffered major crop loss, and months after the storm were still removing fallen trees and rebuilding collapsed roads and bridges. Destruction was much worse in Haiti, however, where more than a thousand people died in flooding and mudslides.

As the US economy regains footing, Dominicans are feeling the effect. Unfortunately, sticker prices – which had risen sharply as the peso devalued – have remained high, especially for utilities and gasoline. The effect is two-fold – raising the cost of living and stunting tourist spending. Still, spirits are high in the DR and were buoyed even more when Dominican outfielder Vladimir Guerrero of the Anaheim Angels was voted the American League's Most Valuable Player in 2004 – perhaps more amazing was that three of the other four top vote-getters were also Dominican.

GOVERNMENT & POLITICS

Over the years the Dominican Republic has had numerous constitutions; today it adheres to the one adopted in 1966.

The executive power is exercised by the president, who is elected (along with a vice president) for a four-year term. There is a National Congress, consisting of a Senate and a Chamber of Deputies, who also serve four-year terms. The judicial system is headed by a Supreme Court, which consists of at least nine judges elected by the Senate.

All three branches of government participate in the legislative process. Bills for consideration by the legislature may be introduced by members of either house, by the president, or by Supreme Court justices. There are three major parties: the Partido de la Liberación Dominicana (Dominican Liberation Party, or PLD); the Partido Reformista Social Cristiano (Social Christian Reformist Party, or PRSC); and the Partido Revolućionario Dominicano (Dominican Revolutionary Party, or PRD).

http://lcweb2.loc.gov /frd/cs/dotoc.html is the website of the US Library of Congress and has in-depth historical, political and economic information, plus a search engine for the library's holdings.

ECONOMY

Sugar revenue led the DR's economy until the early 1980s, when sugar prices hit a 40-year low, and the US – its chief export market – reduced its imports of sugar in response to lobbying efforts by domestic producers. The DR expanded mining operations, and within a decade gold, silver, ferronickel and bauxite exports constituted 38% of the country's gross domestic product. In the same period the number of hotels on the island quadrupled, and by the late 1990s tourism became the country's top source of income.

Another major revenue source is remittances from Dominicans living abroad. More than a million Dominicans live abroad, principally in New York and the eastern United States; collectively they send to the DR a whopping US$1 billion every year.

1996	2004
Leonel Fernández, a 42-year-old lawyer who grew up in New York City, elected president	Hurricane Jeane hits Hispaniola, causing extensive damage in the Dominican Republic and killing over 1000 people in Haiti

The Culture

THE NATIONAL PSYCHE

Most Dominicans are friendly and outgoing, and quick to offer assistance and hospitality. Many share a powerful sense of national pride, and friendliness and helpfulness are a way of showing, especially to a foreign tourist, that the Dominican Republic (DR) is not a Third World backwater but a place of refinement and class. It's not just a show for tourists; Dominicans are helpful and engaging to one another in a way found in few other places. For example, when making phone calls – whether to an acquaintance or a perfect stranger – it is considered impolite to simply start talking when the other party answers. Instead it is customary to ask the person's name, to tell them yours, and exchange a few niceties before getting to whatever business you called about – be it ordering a pizza or asking the price of a rental car.

Togetherness also ranks high in the minds of many Dominicans, who take great delight in parties, dancing and parades. But it would be naive to assume that there are no fractures in Dominican society and its psyche. Race – or more accurately color – is a powerful force in the DR; political and social standing often track color lines. People in the lower classes tend to have darker skin and most people in positions of power have light skin.

At the same time, Dominicans still tend to think of themselves as one group rather than many different ones. The same is not true regarding Haitians and Haitian-Dominicans, who are physically much darker than most native Dominicans and are widely viewed as violent or uncouth. Whether racism or national chauvinism, this is certainly the most disturbing feature of an otherwise rich and gracious society.

www.aquisantodomingo .com – this is the online version of a popular city guide covering cultural events in Santo Domingo.

LIFESTYLE

Dominican families are typically large and very close knit. The stereotype of the doting Latin American son and the fiercely loyal and slightly overbearing mother is not far off-base in the Dominican Republic. It is expected that children will stay close to home and help care for their parents as they grow older. That so many young Dominicans go to the United States creates a unique stress in their families. While Americans and Europeans commonly leave home to live and work in another city, this is still troubling for many Dominicans, especially in the older generation. It is no surprise that Dominicans living abroad send so much money

---

DOS & DON'TS

Politeness is a very important aspect of social interaction in the Dominican Republic. When beginning to talk to someone, it's proper to preface your conversation with a greeting – a simple 'Buenos días' or 'Buenas tardes' and a smile, answered by a similar greeting on the other person's part, gets a conversation off to a positive start.

Pay attention to your appearance when in the DR. Dominicans on the whole are very conscious of appearance, grooming and dress; it's difficult for them to understand why a foreign traveler, who is assumed to be rich, would go around looking scruffy when even poor Dominicans always do their best to look neat.

Shorts, tank tops and hats are not allowed – or at least strongly discouraged – in government buildings or churches.

home – along with tourism, foreign remittances rank as the country's most important source of income.

The DR is a Catholic country; though not to the degree practiced in other Latin American countries; the many churches are well maintained but often empty. It is not surprising, therefore, that most Dominicans have a fairly free attitude toward premarital and recreational sex. This does not extend to homosexuality though, which is still fairly taboo. Machismo is strong here but, like in merengue dancing, many Dominicans experience the traditional roles of men and women as more complimentary than confrontational. Indeed, Dominicans – both men and women – are often baffled by the strong negative reaction of foreign women toward men's 'appreciation' which usually includes passing comments like '*hola, preciosa*' (hi, beautiful) and not-so-subtle glances at one's backside. That is not to say that Dominican women are blind to discrimination, though theirs is an uphill battle. Inequality is most evident in business and political fields, where women hold relatively few top positions (see Women in the Dominican Republic, p38).

POPULATION

The Dominican Republic has roughly nine million residents. A little under three quarters are of mixed ethnic or racial ancestry, whether mulatto (mixed European and African descent, the most common) or mestizo (mixed European and indigenous descent). A minority of Dominicans are considered full Euro-Caucasian (16%) or of African (11%) ancestry. There are a sprinkling of other ethnic groups, including Chinese, Japanese, Arabic and Jewish (of mostly European descent).

More than a third of Dominicans earn less than US$400 per month, the official poverty line. (The minimum monthly salary in the DR is US$208 per month, except in the Free Trade Zones where it is a paltry US$152 per month.)

Almost a quarter of Dominicans live in Santo Domingo, which is without question the country's political, economic and social center. But beyond the capital, much of the DR is distinctly rural, and a large percentage of Dominicans still live by agriculture (or by fishing, along the coast). This is evident if you drive into the DR's vast fertile interior, where you'll see cows and horses grazing alongside the roads, tractors ploughing large fields, and trucks and *burros* loaded down with produce.

SPORTS

A number of sports and pastimes are popular in the Dominican Republic, including volleyball, basketball, soccer, and horseracing. But two sports – baseball and cockfighting – are far and away the most popular and both have long, rich traditions.

Baseball

The Dominican professional baseball league's season runs from October to January, and is known as the Liga de Invierno or Winter League. The country has six professional baseball teams: Licey and Escojido, both of Santo Domingo; the Águilas from Santiago; the Estrellas from San Perdo de Macorís; the Gigantes of San Francisco de Macorís; and the Azuqueros from La Romana. Because the US and Dominican seasons don't overlap, many Dominican players in the US Major Leagues (and quite a few non-Dominicans) play in the winter league in the DR as well. Needless to say, the quality of play in the Dominican professional league rivals that of the major leagues, and there is no doubt the top Dominican teams would do

Sugarball: The American Game, the Dominican Dream by Alan M Klein and *The Tropic of Baseball* by Rob Ruck are both excellent books examining the role of baseball in Dominican political and social life.

TOP TEN DOMINICAN BASEBALL PLAYERS

The Dominican Republic has sent over 300 players to the Major Leagues – far more than any other country after the US – and many more played in the Negro League or remained in the DR. These players are among the most notable over the years:

Juan Esteban 'Tetelo' Vargas – A legend in his own time who won the Dominican batting championship in 1953 at age 47.

Ozzie Virgil – First Dominican to enter the Major Leagues (1956).

Juan Marichal – Star pitcher for the San Francisco Giants known for his distinctive high-kicking windup; the first Dominican inducted into the Major League Baseball Hall of Fame (1983).

Julian Javier – Born in San Pedro de Macorís, Javier won three National League titles and two World Series with St Louis from 1964 to 1968.

Matty Alou – One of three Alou brothers in the majors; Matty batted .300 or better seven times, including a league-best .342 in 1966.

George Bell – Born in San Pedro de Macorís, Bell won the 1987 American League's most valuable player award.

Pedro Martinez – Born in San Pedro de Macorís, Martinez won a Cy Young pitching award once in the National League (1997) and twice in a row in the American League (1999, 2000).

Sammy Sosa – Also born in San Pedro de Macorís, Sosa hit 66 homeruns in 1998, which is the third-highest season tally of all time.

Miguel Tejada – Born in Baní, Tejada won the American League's most valuable player award in 2002.

Vladimir Guerrero – The latest Dominican superstar, Guerrero – born in Baní – won the American League's most valuable player award in 2004.

quite well in the US. If you are in the Dominican Republic during baseball season, ensure you make time to go to a game. Even if you are not a baseball fan, it's hard not to enjoy games in the DR, where fans dance merengue in the aisles between innings and every play is followed with tremendous anticipation and excitement.

Cockfighting

Even more than baseball, cockfighting is the traditional sport of the Dominican Republic. Almost every town and city in the DR has a *gallera* (cockfighting ring) where specially bred roosters are pitted against each other in bloody, to-the-death bouts. Gambling on fights is part of the sport, all conducted under a strict honor code. That said, some small-town rings are decidedly seedy and tourists should be alert for trouble. Santo Domingo has numerous cockfighting rings, but by far the most prestigious – and safe – is the Coliseo Gallístico Alberto Bonetti Burgos (p93), which regularly hosts international competitions.

It is impossible to argue that cockfighting is not a form of cruelty to animals – after all, the point is for one animal to kill the other, sometimes slowly and agonizingly, for the sake of entertainment and monetary gain. At the same time, it is an institution with such deep roots in Dominican culture and such strong support today that it cannot be dismissed merely as a relic of less-enlightened times. While detractors concentrate on the fact that the roosters are killed, aficionados focus on the clash itself – the roosters' strength, stamina, style and tactics, all of which can be truly remarkable. The majority die fighting, but not all – the toughest roosters retire after many fights to a life of comfort and high-price studding, revered in the same way Secretariat or Seabiscuit are by horseracing fans. Those that die are plucked and eaten, though many trainers will not eat their own roosters out of respect, superstition or both.

Perhaps it is no surprise that cockfighting – specifically the roosters' intensity and willingness to fight to the death – would resonate in a country that has endured so much civil strife and outside manipulation. Indeed, the fighting rooster is the symbol of a number of political parties and social organizations. For those reasons, many travelers see cockfighting as a window to Dominican culture. Others cannot reconcile a night at the *gallera* with the concept of responsible tourism. Both are justifiable points of view.

MULTICULTURALISM

Most Dominicans are classified under the single term 'mixed-race,' but the country's long history of immigration belies such simplistic description. Likewise, many of the DR's most vexing social issues stem from the movement of people in and out of the country.

The ethnic variety seen in this country is the result of various waves of immigrants. In addition to Spanish colonists and enslaved Africans, groups that have settled here over the centuries include Sephardic Jews from Curacao, Canary Islanders, Germans, Italians, Cubans, Puerto Ricans, Lebanese, Syrians, Palestinians, Jewish refugees from Germany, Japanese, Hungarians, freed slaves from the United States, and Protestant workers from Great Britain, the Netherlands and Denmark. Mainland Chinese came in small numbers in the early 20th century but by the 1980s, Chinese immigrants were the second fastest growing immigrant group in the Dominican Republic.

At www.ticketexpress.com.do you can buy tickets online to Dominican league baseball games and cultural events around the country.

But it is Haitians – long the largest and fastest-growing group of immigrants in the DR – who have defined the Dominican Republic's often rocky relationship with foreign immigration. Between a quarter and half a million Haitians live in the DR – the exact number is unknown – mostly working as farm workers on the DR's vast sugar cane, coffee and tobacco plantations. Many have assimilated into Dominican society, even advanced to supervisor positions in some cases, but the vast majority eke out difficult lives on the edge of society, openly discriminated against but absolutely essential to the economic vitality of their ambivalent host country.

Dominicans are themselves no strangers to the ups and downs of the immigrant experience. Close to a million Dominicans, or better than 10% of the population, live abroad, mainly in New York and New Jersey. Dominicans send home US$1 billion every year, equal to the annual income the DR generates from either tourism or agricultural exports. At the same time, Dominicans as a group are among the top utilizers of American welfare and assistance programs – one in four receive some form of government aid, one of the highest percentages of any immigrant group in the US.

Most Dominicans in the US are there legally, but those who can't get visas often hire professional people-smugglers to help them enter. The most common route is a risky 18-hour boat trip to Puerto Rico, usually departing from or around the town of Miches in eastern DR. The US Coast Guard closely patrols the straights between the two islands and intercepts around 4000 such would-be émigrés every year. For those who do make it to Puerto Rico, it's relatively simple to take a domestic flight to the mainland.

MEDIA

The Dominican Republic's two main newspapers – *Listín Diario* and *El Caribe* – are good sources of national news and events. For Dominican news in English, www.dr1.com is an excellent online resource.

RELIGION

Around 95% of Dominicans profess to be Roman Catholic. For a large majority though, religious practice is limited and formalistic. Few actually attend Mass regularly. As in many Latin American countries, evangelical Protestant Christianity has gained a strong foothold in Dominican culture, attracting adherents with dramatic faith healings and fiery sermons. Catholics tend to view evangelical churches with ill-disguised disdain, which of course feeds directly into the evangelical contention that the Catholic church is out of step with ordinary people and society. Many Haitian immigrants and their descendants are Catholic in name and identity, but continue to practice elements of traditional Vodou spiritualism. Such practices are generally done in secret, as the Dominican government, Catholic church and much of the public view Vodou as pagan or even evil.

WOMEN IN THE DOMINICAN REPUBLIC

Women have made significant strides toward social and economic equality in the Dominican Republic, but there is still a very long way to go. A higher percentage of women now receive high school and college degrees than men, but this has not yet translated into economic advancement, with women still earning about two-thirds as much as a man in the same position. And that is when women can even *get* the same position as men. Women make up less than a third of the DR's paid work force and the vast majority are employed as domestic workers or low-level office workers. Women are poorly represented in government and politics as well, making up just 10% to 15% of legislator and top or middle-level cabinet officer positions. Perhaps more troubling than the underrepresentation of women in the upper reaches of society are their overrepresentation in the very lowest. Almost 30% of women are single mothers, and make up one of the largest groups of people living in poverty.

Bachata: A Social History of Dominican Popular Music by Deborah Pacini Hernandez and *Merengue: Dominican Music and Dominican Identity* by Paul Austerlitz are academic examinations of the Dominican Republic's two most important musical contributions and obsessions.

ARTS
Music

Merengue is by far the most popular music in the Dominican Republic. From the minute you arrive in the DR until the minute you leave, merengue will be coming at you at full volume. At a restaurant, in public buses or taxis – it's there. At the beach or walking down the street – yet more merengue.

Merengue is the dance music of the Dominican Republic, and if you attend a dance club there and take a shine to the music, you may want to pick up some cassettes or CDs before leaving the country. There are many merengue bands in the DR; the nation's favorites include Johnny Ventura, Coco Band, Wilfredo Vargas, Milly y Los Vecinos, Fernando

---

THE GÜIRA

The *güira* is a popular musical instrument that is used to infuse a song with a rhythmical rasping sound. It was originally used by Hispaniola's indigenous people – the Taínos – who used dried, hollowed-out gourds and a forked stick to produce music for their *areítos* (ceremonial songs). Today, the *güira* has been modernized – but not by much. Instead of using vegetables, the modern *güira* is made of latten brass; it typically looks like a cylindrical cheese grater that is scraped with a long metal pick. The rasping sound is essentially the same – the modern-day instrument just lasts a little longer. The next time you hear a merengue or a *bachata* song, listen carefully – you're sure to hear this centuries-old sound.

Villalona, Joseito Mateo, Rubby Perez, Miriam Cruz and, perhaps the biggest name of all, Juan Luis Guerra.

Whereas merengue might be viewed as urban music, *bachata* is definitely the nation's 'country' music. This is the music of breaking up, of broken hearts, of one man's love for a woman or one woman's love for a man, about life in the country. Among the big names of *bachata* are Raulín Rodríguez, Antony Santos, Joe Veras, Luis Vargas, Quico Rodríguez and Leo Valdez.

Salsa, like *bachata*, is heard on many Caribbean islands, and it's very popular in the DR. If you like the music, it may interest you to know that the following individuals and groups enjoy particularly favorable reputations in the DR: Tito Puente, Tito Rojas, Jerry Rivera, Tito Gómez, Grupo Niche, Gilberto Santa Rosa, Mimi Ibara, Marc Anthony and Leonardo Paniagua.

Since 1986, merengue and *bachata* superstar Juan Luís Guerra has won almost every major music award possible, including a Grammy for his album *Bachata Rose,* three more Grammy nominations, three Latin Grammys for *Ni es lo mismo ni es Igual,* five Billboard Latin Music Awards for best tropical album and two *Premios Soberanos* from Premios Casa Dominican Republica in Santo Domingo.

Architecture

The quality and variety of architecture found in the Dominican Republic has no equal in the Caribbean. In Santo Domingo and in Santiago, you can see examples of Cuban Victorian, Caribbean gingerbread and art deco; in the Zona Colonial you'll also get an eyeful of the Gothic, which was popular in Europe during the colonial times. The buildings in Puerto Plata vary between the vernacular Antillean and the pure Victorian, sometimes English, sometimes North American. San Pedro de Macorís has late Victorian style buildings that were created with concrete (in fact, it was the first city in the Dominican Republic to use reinforced concrete in its construction). And rural clapboard homes have a charm all their own: small, square, single story and more colorful than a handful of jelly beans, you'll find yourself slowing down to take a longer look.

Literature

The Dominican Republic's literary history dates to the Spanish colonial period (1492–1795). It was then that Bartolomé de Las Casas, a Spanish friar, recorded the early history of the Caribbean and pleaded for fair treatment of the Taínos in his famous *Historia de las Indias* (History of the Indies). During the same era, Gabriel Téllez, a priest who helped to reorganize the convent of Our Lady of Mercy in Santo Domingo, wrote his impressive *Historia general de la Orden de la Mercéd* (General History of the Order of Mercy).

During the Haitian occupation of Santo Domingo (1822–1844), French literary style became prominent, and many Dominican writers who emigrated to other Spanish-speaking countries made names for themselves there. With the first proclamation of independence in 1844, Félix María del Monte created the country's principal poetic form – a short patriotic poem based on local events of the day.

During the late 19th and early 20th centuries, three literary movements occurred in the DR: *indigenismo, criollismo* and *postumismo. Indigenismo* exposed the brutalities the Taínos experienced at the hands of the Spaniards. *Criollismo* focused on the local people and their customs. And *postumismo* dealt with the repression that Trujillo's iron-fist leadership brought. Some writers, such as Manuel and Lupo Fernández Rueda, used clever metaphors to protest the regime. Juan Bosch, writing from exile, penned numerous stories that openly attacked Trujillo.

Most of the popular writing being done by Dominicans today comes from the expatriate community in New York City. Their work tends to focus on the hardships of life in the DR today, the frustration of the people, their dreams. In her 1991 book *How the García Girls Lost Their Accents,* novelist Julia Alvarez describes an emigrant Dominican family in New York. Junot Diaz is another Dominican writing from the US; his short-story collection *Drown* is written in English liberally sprinkled with Dominicanisms. Other well-known contemporary Dominican writers include José Goudy Pratt, Jeannette Miller and Ivan García Guerra.

Cinema

The Dominican Republic does not have a strong film industry of its own; only a handful of films made by Dominican directors have reached a wider audience. But more than 60 films and TV shows films ranging from *Miami Vice* to *Porno Holocaust* to *The Godfather: Part II* have been shot in full or in part in the Dominican Republic. Some of the more notable ones:

- *Jurassic Park*: Several scenes of the 1993 Steven Spielberg film were shot in the DR, including one at Salto Jimenoa Uno outside of Jarabacoa. The film is based on a Michael Crichton book about a scientist who extracts blood from a mosquito trapped in amber to clone dinosaurs. It is credited with reviving interest in amber and amber jewelry across the world. It is a fitting legacy, as the DR is home to some of the world's best amber, especially that containing insects and other inclusions.
- *Apocalypse Now:* Some of the famous river scenes in this 1979 classic by Francis Ford Coppola were filmed on the Río Chavón near La Romana.
- *1492: Conquest of Paradise*: Released to celebrate the 500th anniversary of Columbus' discovery of the New World, this big-budget film depicts some of the disastrous effects the Europeans had on the Taíno Indians.

Painting

The Dominican art scene today is quite healthy, thanks in no small part to dictator Rafael Trujillo. Although his 31 years of authoritarian rule in many ways negated the essence of creative freedom, Trujillo had a warm place in his heart for paintings, and in 1942 he established the Escuela Nacional de Bellas Artes (National School of Fine Arts). Fine Dominican artwork predates the school, but it really wasn't until the institution's doors opened that Dominican art underwent its definitive development.

The Eduardo León Jimenes Art Contest in Santiago began in 1964 and is the longest-running privately sponsored art competition in Latin America.

If the artwork looks distinctly Spanish, it's because the influence is undeniable. During the Spanish Civil War (1936–1939), many artists fled Franco's fascist regime to start new lives in the Dominican Republic. Influential artists include Manolo Pascual, José Gausachs, José Vela-Zanetti, Eugenio Fernández Granell and José Fernández Corredor.

The Dominican Republic also has produced many accomplished painters; if you visit any of the art galleries in Santo Domingo or Santiago (p94), keep an eye out for paintings by Adriana Billini Gautreau, who is famous for portraits that are rich in expressionist touches; the cubist forms of Jaime Colson emphasizing the social crises of his day; Luis Desangles, considered the forerunner of folklore in Dominican painting; Mariano Eckert, representing the realism of everyday life; Juan Bautista Gómez, whose paintings depict the sensuality of the landscape; and Guillo Pérez, whose works of oxen, carts and canfields convey a poetic vision of life at the sugar mill.

Also well represented is what's called 'primitive art' – Dominican and Haitian paintings which convey rural Caribbean life with simple and colorful figures and landscapes. These paintings are created by amateur

THE BEGINNINGS OF MERENGUE

There are many competing versions of the origin of the Dominican Republic's national dance. One is that it came from enslaved Africans who, chained at the ankle, were forced to drag one leg or walk with a distinctive hitch while cutting sugar cane.

Another version also gives merengue an African origin but that it grew from a dance practiced by the Bara people of Madagascar. In that story, the dance was dubbed the 'peg-leg' dance, partly for its jerky movements and partly because it was a common form of entertainment on pirate ships.

That is vaguely similar to yet another story, which begins with an anonymous man wounded in the leg while fighting in one of the DR's various revolutions. When he returned home, the people of his village threw him a party at which everyone danced with a limp out of respect and sympathy for the man's injury.

Perhaps the most likely explanation is that merengue is an adaptation of the Cuban music and dance called UPA, which was brought to the Dominican Republic via Puerto Rico in the mid-19th century.

painters – some would say skilled craftsmen – who reproduce the same painting hundreds of times. They are sold everywhere there are tourists; you're sure to get an eyeful regardless of the length of your trip.

Theater & Dance

The Dominican Republic does not have a strong tradition in classical dance, although the National Classical Ballet company does present enjoyable performances in Santo Domingo and other cities. Likewise, there is a national theatre in the capital (p92) but there isn't anything particularly notable about the Dominican stage.

What Dominicans *do* do well – better than anyone else in the world in fact – is dance merengue; they dance merengue with passion and flair. It follows a distinctive 2-2 and 2-4 beat pattern typically played with drums, an accordion like instrument known as a *melodeon,* and a *güira,* a metal instrument that looks a little like a cheese grater and is scraped using a metal or plastic rod. If you have a chance, go to a nightclub or dance hall where merengue is played. Even if you don't dance – something Dominicans will find very peculiar – you can't help but be impressed by the sheer skill and artfulness of even amateur dancers.

The Environment

THE LAND

If a nation's wealth could be measured by its landscape, the Dominican Republic would be the richest country in the Caribbean. With its high mountains, fertile valleys and diverse ecosystems, this is a dynamic place. Located near the center of the West Indies on the eastern two-thirds of the island of Hispaniola, with the turbulent Atlantic Ocean to the north and the Caribbean Sea to the south, the Dominican Republic is a melting pot of influences brought by ever-changing winds, tides and ocean currents. This is the second largest country in the Caribbean, after Cuba, with a landmass of 48,734 sq km (18,817 sq miles) and a spectacular coastline that wiggles and squiggles around rocky bluffs and hidden coves for 1572km (977 miles).

Having more in common with the Central American mainland to the west than its neighboring islands, the Dominican Republic boasts an astonishing assortment of precipitous mountain ranges. Primary among these is the Cordillera Central that runs from Santo Domingo into Haiti, where it becomes the Massif du Nord. All told, this mighty range makes up one-third of Hispaniola's landmass and divides the Dominican Republic into two distinct halves. The sheer size of this mountain range, which includes Pico Duarte, the highest peak in the Caribbean at 3175m (10,416ft), shuts off much of the rainfall coming from the northeast and makes the southwest corner of the Dominican Republic a rather arid place. Slightly more modest mountain ranges include the Cordillera Septentrional, noticed by windsurfers heading for Cabarete because its slopes rise dramatically from the coast; and the Cordillera Orientale, which trends like an enchanting East Asian landscape along the southern shoreline of Bahía de Samaná.

Between these ranges lie a series of valleys filled with plantations of coffee, bananas, cacao, rice, tobacco and many other crops. Generally, these valleys are lush and fertile like the Cibao, the valley that led Christopher Columbus to believe he had stumbled upon paradise when he visited the island. Valleys in the southwest tend to be arid and studded with cacti. Coastal plains perched on limestone plateaus dominate the southern and southeastern portions of the Dominican Republic, where they comprise the economically important landscape around Santo Domingo.

Many travelers to the Dominican Republic merely visit the country's justly famous shoreline. Here, a combination of white-sand beaches lined with palm trees and deluxe accommodations seem so perfect they are nearly impossible to leave. Adding a touch of the exotic are sea cliffs that create countless hidden beaches. Beneath the ocean's surface, however, the Dominican Republic offers many other surprises. The entire island of Hispaniola sits on top of a shallow underwater platform that extends far offshore (up to 50km along the north shore) and forms the foundation for bountiful coral reefs, multitudes of tiny islands and sheltered banks where humpback whales gather to breed. Large portions of this offshore platform would have been exposed during the last Ice Age when sea levels were 61m to 122m (200ft to 400ft) lower.

The unique landscape of the Dominican Republic and other islands of the West Indies can be traced back to a time about 90 million years ago when a large fragment of the earth's crust broke free and began drifting eastwards into the Atlantic Ocean. Grinding south past the North American Plate, this fragment (the Caribbean Plate) cracked and crumpled in a series of folds that formed the islands stretching from Cuba

Though written for the eastern Caribbean, Virginia Barlow's *The Nature of the Islands* is an excellent and highly readable introduction to the plants and animals of the entire region.

Limestone erodes readily in the presence of water to form caves, sinkholes, and dramatically sculpted formations – creating a landscape called 'karst' that is widespread in the Dominican Republic.

HURRICANE ALLEY

Caribbean hurricanes are born 3000km away off the west coast of Africa, where pockets of low-pressure draw high winds toward them and the Earth's rotation molds them into their familiar counter-clockwise swirl. The storms start small but grow in strength as they cross the Atlantic, fed by warm moist air, as they bear down on the Caribbean and the North American eastern shore.

Low-level storms are called tropical disturbances, which may then grow into a tropical depression. When winds exceed 64km/h, the system is upgraded to a tropical storm and is usually accompanied by heavy rains. The system is called a hurricane when wind speeds exceed 120km/h and intensify around a low-pressure center, the so-called eye of the storm. Hurricane systems can range from 80km in diameter to a devastating 1600km across. They travel at varying speeds, from as little as 10km/h to more than 50km/h.

The strength of a hurricane is rated from one to five. The mildest, Category One, has winds of at least 120km/h. The strongest and rarest hurricane, Category Five, packs winds that exceed 250km/h. There were back-to-back Category-Five hurricanes in 2003 and 2004 – Isabel and Ivan, respectively. Isabel swung north of the Caribbean, causing extensive damage in North Carolina in the US. Ivan swept right though the Caribbean – amazingly it missed most of the islands, but pummeled the places it did hit, including Grenada where up to 90% of the homes were destroyed. Other Category-Five storms include Hurricane Mitch, which killed more than 10,000 people in Central America in 1998, and a storm known simply as Hurricane Dominican Republic which killed 8000 in the DR in 1930.

A hurricane struck Hispaniola in 1979, killing more than a thousand people; in 1998, Hurricane Georges killed several thousand more and left parts of the island without electricity for several months. In 2004, Hurricane Jeanne was one of six hurricanes to sweep across the Atlantic. A relatively weak storm – it was upgraded from a tropical storm to Category-One hurricane just as it hit the Dominican Republic – Jeanne nevertheless caused major damage, knocking out power lines, destroying dozens of bridges and roadways, even causing an island in Laguna Limón to detach (it now meanders around the lake, pushed around by winds and currents). The storm also stranded thousands of people in southeastern DR, among them hundreds of tourists at all-inclusive resorts, some of whom had to be evacuated by helicopter. In Haiti, Jeanne caused flooding and mudslides that killed over a thousand people.

If you are near the coast when a hurricane is approaching, head inland, preferably to a large city where there are modern buildings and emergency services. If the storm is already hitting, or travel is unsafe, go to one of the large resorts, which have sturdy hurricane shelters and evacuation procedures. Stay away from the beach, rivers, lakes and anywhere mudslides are a risk. Avoid standing near windows, as flying debris and sudden pressure changes can shatter the glass.

For current tropical-storm information, go to the *Miami Herald*'s website (www.herald.com) or the website maintained by the US National Oceanic and Atmospheric Administration (www.esdim.noaa.gov/weather_page.html).

to Puerto Rico. Other collisions to the east, south and west formed the Lesser Antilles, the coastal mountains of Venezuela and much of Central America, so this single sliding plate obviously had a tremendous impact on the entire region. The Caribbean Plate still pushes eastwards at a rate of 1cm to 2cm (half an inch) or so per year, creating conditions for active volcanoes that plague parts of the Caribbean. This sliding motion also continues to slowly elevate Hispaniola. Samaná, for example, was a separate island 150 years ago but is now connected to the rest of the Dominican Republic due to uplift.

WILDLIFE

Although it is no easy matter for plants and animals to reach an isolated island across hundreds of kilometers of open ocean, Hispaniola has a remarkable diversity of life. Over 5600 species of plants and close to 500 vertebrate species have arrived one way or another and found a home on the island. Large numbers of plants and animals have become endemic to the island because once they arrived they evolved in isolation from the rest of the world. In historic times, European settlers added many new invasive species to the island.

Plants frequently reach islands by crossing the ocean as seeds or roots trapped in rafts of floating logs and vegetation. Reptiles, particularly lizards, may also survive for weeks as hitchhikers on these floating rafts while amphibians and mammals (who need daily water) don't fare as well. Reflecting this, the Dominican Republic has over 140 species of reptiles, but only 60 amphibians and 20 native land mammals (18 of which went extinct after the arrival of European settlers). The rest of the country's fauna is made up of a rich variety of birds, marine mammals and bats.

Adding to the Dominican Republic's natural diversity is the landscape's varied topography, vegetation and climate. There are two types of Caribbean islands (volcanic and coral) and the Dominican Republic has features of both – with lush volcanic peaks in the center of the island and flat dry soils characteristic of coral islands along the coast. This results in a mix of diverse habitats like thorny scrub forest and tropical rainforest that sometimes lie in close proximity to each other. Other unique habitats include mangrove swamps, and fresh- and saltwater lagoons.

Animals
BIRDS
Over 250 species of bird have been found in the Dominican Republic, including several dozen species found nowhere else in the world, making bird watching one of the foremost reasons (after beaches) that visitors travel to the country. Abundant, colorful species like the white-tailed tropicbird, magnificent frigatebird, roseate spoonbill and greater flamingo would alone be enough reason for a trip to the Dominican Republic, but unique endemic species like the Hispaniolan lizard-cuckoo, ashy-faced owl and Hispaniolan emerald (a hummingbird!) make this a highly sought after destination.

Travelers are most likely to encounter birds on beaches and coastal waterways – specifically herons, egrets, ibis, rails, pelicans and gulls. In remote areas, or around nesting colonies, these birds may number in the many thousands and make you feel like you're on safari. Some of the best spots for twitchers are Parque Nacional Jaragua, Parque Nacional Los Haitises, Parque Nacional Monte Cristi and Laguna Limón. More determined travelers taking the time to wander into some of the rich wildlife areas in the interior of the country can expect to encounter a tremendous variety of forest birds. Depending on the season and habitat, you will find a full range of North American warblers, or local birds like Hispaniolan trogons, woodpeckers, parakeets and parrots. Some of these are common and widespread, while others are highly secretive and require specialized knowledge or a guide to locate.

Favorites among birdwatchers include the national bird – the odd palmchat. Unrelated to other birds, the streaky brown palmchat is abundant and noisy, building large apartment-like nests in which each pair sleeps in its own chamber. Another bird, the splashy and cheerful yellow-bellied bananaquit, is a popular caged bird even though it readily frequents flower-filled yards and parks.

LAND MAMMALS
Hispaniola has never been home to a lot of land mammals, and most of those that once occurred here suffered terribly at the hands of European

---

Eugene Kaplan's twin volumes *A Field Guide to Coral Reefs: Caribbean and Florida* and *A Field Guide to Southeastern and Caribbean Seashores* can be used to identify many common species.

Bird lovers absolutely need *A Guide to the Birds of the West Indies* by Herbert Raffaele to answer all their bird questions.

The magnificent frigatebird is also known as the man o'war bird, because it hunts down other birds like a pirate to steal their food. During the breeding season, males inflate their red throat skin to impress females.

colonialists. Out of an estimated 20 native mammals, only two species remain and cling to survival in scattered pockets around the Dominican Republic. These are the hutia, a tree-climbing herbivore that looks like a large mole; and the solenodon, a primitive insectivore resembling a huge shriveled shrew with giant feet. Both are nocturnal and grow to about 30cm (1ft) long. The solenodon is an ancient and peculiar creature that hovers on the edge of extinction (if it is not already extinct).

Unfortunately, visitors are more likely to spot one of the superabundant introduced pests that now wreck havoc on the island. Foremost among these would have to be the mongoose, a slender brown animal that resembles a ferret. Introduced to control rodent populations (also introduced), the mongoose was an experiment that went seriously awry. It turns out they don't hunt at night when rodents are active but prefer to hunt during the day and eat native birds, mammals and reptiles – eliminating, or seriously impacting on, many unique local species.

MARINE MAMMALS

Hispaniola is world famous for its marine mammals, with manatees and humpback whales the star attractions. Travelers however, are more likely to see dolphins unless they arrive in the right season or make a special trip to the right habitat. Sailors once thought that manatees were mermaids (long sea voyages must have been really hard on sailors!), but these odd creatures more closely resemble a bulbous version of their distant relatives, the elephant. Weighing up to 590kg (1300lbs) and reaching 3.7m (12ft) in length, manatees are shy, docile creatures that live in still coastal waters, such as off Parque Nacional Monte Cristi, and move very languidly.

Several thousand humpback whales migrate south from frigid arctic waters to breed and calve in the tropical waters of the Dominican Republic each winter (peaking in January and February). This is considered one of the foremost places in the world to view whales, and it is one of few places where you can swim and snorkel (under supervision) with these magnificent creatures. Tourist boats make half-day excursions to the Banco de Plata (Silver Banks), just beyond the Bahía de Samaná, to view whales close up (p149).

FISH & MARINE LIFE

The shallow coastal waters and coral reefs that surround the Dominican Republic are home to a tremendous variety of sea life. So many species of tropical fish, crustaceans, sponges and corals can be found here that it takes a specialized field guide to begin to sort them out. Most visitors, however, will be content to simply snorkel or dive in awe rather than make the effort to identify these species. Where intact and unfished – such as at Sosúa (p186) and Monte Cristi (p210) – the reefs of the Dominican Republic are stupendously beautiful. Some of the more colorful Caribbean reef fish include fluorescent fairy basslet, queen angelfish, rock beauty and blue tang, but each visitor will quickly find their own favorites.

Among the real treasures of the Dominican Republic are its significant populations of five sea turtles: green, leatherback, hawksbill and loggerhead. From May to October, these turtles can be viewed coming ashore at night to lay their eggs on sandy beaches in places like Parque Nacional Jaragua. Snorkelers and divers may also have the incredibly moving experience of encountering these massive (up to 1.8m/6ft long) creatures underwater.

Humpback whales at birth are 4m to 5m (13ft to 16ft) long and weigh 900kg to 1800kg (1 to 2 tons).

Some reef shrimp set up 'cleaning stations' where fish line up and wait to be cleaned of external parasites and pieces of dead skin. If you find shrimp at their station offer your bare hand and they may climb aboard to look for morsels on your skin.

A colorful overview of Caribbean coral reefs can be found in the eye-opening *A Guide to the Coral Reefs of the Caribbean*, by Mark Spalding.

LAMBÍ

What Dominicans call *lambí* is known to scientists as *strombus gigas*, in Taíno as *cohobo* and in English *queen conch* – yet no matter what you call it, this hefty snail-like creature is the largest mollusk in the Caribbean (growing 35cm long and weighing up to 3 kg) and is a vital part of the underwater ecosystem and a staple of Dominican cuisine.

Conch (pronounced 'konk') live in shallow waters near coral reefs and are found throughout the Caribbean, as well as along the Mexico, Florida, Bahamas and Bermuda coastlines, and as far south as Brazil. They feed on algae that can asphyxiate coral if it's not kept in check.

Conch has been an important food source on Hispaniola and throughout the Caribbean for centuries. Archaeologists have uncovered piles of conch shells near ancient settlements, including on Isla Saona and Isla Catalinita in Parque Nacional del Este. Conch shells were used as a musical instrument (known as a *fututo*) and carved into fine necklaces and other jewelry, prized by ancient people for its durability and delicate pink or peach color. Taínos also ground up the shell to create, with other ingredients, a hallucinogenic powder used in religious ceremonies.

Lambí is found on almost every restaurant menu in the Dominican Republic; it is typically chopped into small morsels and served *al ajo* (in garlic) or *a la diabla* (in a spicy tomato sauce). Conch shells are still used in jewelry and other *artesanía* – particularly valued are conch pearls, which form in one out of every 10 thousand conch but, unlike oyster pearls, cannot be mass grown in underwater farms. The pearls come in various shapes and range from pale pink to fiery red.

Conch take three to five years to mature, and are easily caught, as they prefer clear shallow water. This is one reason that conch populations, though not yet endangered, have shrunk considerably in most areas of the Caribbean. Many experts are calling for stricter limits on their capture and consumption, including instituting a conch season and enforcing limits on the size and numbers caught.

REPTILES

Reptiles are one of the groups of animals that have successfully colonized the Dominican Republic. Expect to see lots of snakes, lizards, turtles, and crocodiles during your journey. These range from the endemic freshwater sliders, which are extremely abundant at Laguna Rincón in Cabral, to the American crocodile, which form one of the world's largest congregations in Lago Enriquillo (p253). There is also a Hispaniolan boa, though its numbers may be reduced due to mongoose predation. Most interesting of all has to be the Jaragua lizard, discovered in 1998, which is the world's smallest terrestrial vertebrate (adults measure only 2.8cm/1inch). At the other end of the scale, the unique rhinoceros iguana may weigh 10kg (22lbs) and reach 1.2m (47 inches) long.

With such a wealth of species it would be a shame not to consult *Amphibians and Reptiles of the West Indies* by Henderson and Schwartz to learn more about those scampering lizards and slithering snakes.

ENDANGERED SPECIES

All of the island's large animals, and many of its smaller ones, may be headed toward extinction. The following creatures appear on the World Conservation Monitoring Center's list of endangered species for Hispaniola: humpback whale, Pacific pilot whale, Caribbean monk seal, Atlantic spotted dolphin, Caribbean manatee, Antillean manatee, American crocodile, rhinoceros iguana, Hispaniola ground iguana, loggerhead turtle, green turtle, hawksbill turtle, three species of freshwater turtle and dozens of bird species. The list goes on and on.

A half dozen environmental groups have published pamphlets describing the slaughter and habitat destruction taking place on or near Hispaniola. Both Haiti and the Dominican Republic have outlawed practices that endanger protected species, but enforcement is minimal or absent. Except for the creation of national parks, next to nothing is being done to protect the animals listed above and many others too numerous to list here. Sadly, even in the national parks animals are not safe because no one is protecting the parks against poachers or other types of encroachment.

Plants

The Dominican Republic presents an overwhelming and bewildering assortment of plants. In every season there is something flowering, fruiting or filling the air with exotic fragrances, and it makes the place truly magical. The number of species – over 5600 with more than 30% unique to Hispaniola – is impressive, especially for a Caribbean island, but it's indicative of the island's diverse topography. Biologists divide the vegetation into more than 20 discrete zones, ranging from desert to subtropical forest to mangrove swamp.

Of these vegetation zones, by far the most prevalent is the subtropical forest, which blankets the slopes of many of the country's valleys and is found throughout the Samaná Peninsula. This is a majestic landscape, dominated by royal palms with large curving fronds, and native mahogany trees.

True tropical rainforest is rare in the Dominican Republic both because areas receiving enough rainfall are scarce in the country and because the grand trees of this mighty forest type have been extensively logged. Green-leaved throughout the year, these dense humid forests support a wealth of tree ferns, orchids, bromeliads and epiphytes. Examples can still be found in the Vega Real, which is located in the eastern end of the Valle de Cibao, adjacent to the Samaná region.

Above 1830m (6000ft) the habitat gives way to mountain forests characterized by pines and palms, in addition to ferns, bromeliads, heliconias and orchids. Although much of this has been felled for timber and to make room for cattle pastures and coffee plantations, large tracts still exist in Parques Nacionales Armando Bermúdez and José del Carmen Ramírez.

Thorn and cacti forests abound in the southwest corner of the Dominican Republic. Parque Nacional Jaragua, the country's largest protected area, consists largely of thorn forest and receives less than 700mm of rain a year. By anyone's reckoning this would count as a true desert, even though it's located in the tropics. Beautifully sculpted cacti, agaves and thorn trees predominate here.

Mangrove swamps deserve special mention because they are a characteristic feature along the coast around the Bahía de Samaná and other areas. Despite their scraggly and uninviting appearance, these are among the most important of all habitats for wildlife because they are the nurseries of the sea. Many fish and marine creatures have their young here, while huge colonies of water and sea birds nest among the impenetrable thickets. Mangrove stands also play a critical ecological role by buffering the coast from the erosive power of storms and tides.

In addition to these natural vegetation zones, there are countless introduced food and ornamental plants that thrive in the Dominican Republic. It's entirely possible to subsist largely on the bounty of the land (as many villagers do), with a steady harvest of mangos, bananas, papayas, passion fruit, coconuts and guavas, not to mention the fields of sugarcane, coffee, pineapple and melons. Lovely ornamental flowers grow profusely and bloom in every season.

NATIONAL & STATE PARKS

The Dominican Republic is home to some of the largest and most diverse parks in all the Caribbean. Over 10% of the country has been set aside in *parques nacionales* (national parks) and *reservas científicas* (scientific reserves) to prevent the stunning environmental devastation that has

The name heliconia means 'sun-loving' because these plants grow up to 3.7m (12ft) tall in sunny forest gaps where their bright colors attract hummingbirds.

Introduced from the Indian Ocean, coconut palms have huge leaves divided into narrow segments so they don't tear like cotton sheets in powerful tropical storms.

Living in salt water is a challenge for mangroves and some species require a healthy dose of freshwater at least once a year in order to survive. Their source – hurricanes.

wracked neighboring Haiti. This is one of few places in the Caribbean where visitors can undertake multi-day hikes into remote wilderness. Highlights of the country's park system include the highest and lowest points in the Caribbean (Pico Duarte at 3175m/10,416ft and Lago Enriquillo at 40m/131ft below sea level), as well as extensive mangrove swamps in Parque Nacional Los Haitises, fabulous coral reefs in Parque Nacional Monte Cristi and world famous humpback whale breeding grounds (p149). Hiking trails and amenities are generally scarce, and many sites are best accessed with a local guide and, in coastal areas, a boat.

So far it appears that these parks and reserves have done a reasonably good job of protecting local resources in the face of rampant development elsewhere in the country. This is especially important in coastal areas where beach resorts are devouring open spaces like they were candy and

THE DOMINICAN REPUBLIC'S NATIONAL PARKS

The Dominican Republic's 10 national parks feature most of the country's eco-systems and offer outdoor enthusiasts good options for adventure. A brief description of each follows; further details are found in related chapters.

Parque Nacional Armando Bermúdez (p230) Located in the Cordillera Central, this 766-sq-km park consists mostly of subtropical mountainous rain- and humid forest. It is blanketed in pine trees, tree ferns and palm trees and is home to the hawk-like Hispaniolan trogon.

Parque Nacional del Este (p127) This 430-sq-km park is in the southeastern part of the country. It consists of dry and subtropical humid forest with caves featuring Taíno pictographs and petroglyphs. Isla Saona, with its lovely white-sand beaches, also lies within the park. West Indian manatees and bottlenose dolphins are occasionally spotted near its beaches.

Parque Nacional Los Haitises (p146) Situated on the Bahía de Samaná, this 208-sq-km park contains lush hills that jut out of the ocean, mangroves, tawny beaches and several Taíno caves. The area also receives a lot of rainfall which permits bamboo, ferns and bromeliads to thrive. The Hispaniolan parakeet resides here.

Parque Nacional La Isabela (p206) Located on the north coast, this park was established in the 1990s to protect the site of the second European settlement in the New World (the first is La Navidad, Haiti). Today only a set of ruins and a cemetery remain of the settlement. An on-site museum however, contains many objects that were used by the earliest European settlers.

Parque Nacional Isla Cabritos (p253) In the southwest, this park is a 24-sq-km island surrounded by the saltwater lake, Lago Enriquillo. It is a refuge for crocodiles, iguanas, scorpions, flamingos, crows and cacti.

Parque Nacional Jaragua (p251) At 1400-sq-km, this is the largest park in the country. It is made up of an arid thorn forest, an extensive marine area, and the islands of Beata and Alto Velo. This southwestern park is also home to an impressive variety of birds: the American frigate bird, the roseate spoonbill, the little green heron, the black-crowned palm tanager and the flamingo. The park's beaches are nesting grounds for hawksbill turtles.

Parque Nacional José del Carmen Ramírez (p230) This 764-sq-km park is home to the Caribbean's tallest peak – Pico Duarte – and the headwaters of three of the DR's most important rivers: Yaque del Sur, San Juan and Mijo. Although there is occasional frost, the park is considered a subtropical humid mountain forest. Expect to see bamboo, ferns and juniper at the lower elevations and Creole pines higher up.

Parque Nacional Monte Cristi (p209) This 530-sq-km park in the republic's extreme northwest contains a subtropical dry forest, coastal lagoons and seven islets. It is home to many seabirds, including great egrets, brown pelicans and yellow-crowned night herons. American crocodiles also inhabit the park's lagoons.

Parque Nacional Sierra de Bahoruco (p252) Located in the southwest, this 800-sq-km park consists of desert lowlands that rise from just above sea level to large tracts of pine forest that are at elevations of 2000m. The result is vegetation that varies from cacti and thorn trees to forests of broadleaf and pine trees. More than 150 species of orchid have been identified in this park as have 49-bird species, including the endemic white-necked crow and the rare Hispaniolan parrot.

Parque Nacional Submarino La Caleta (p101) Only 22km from Santo Domingo, this 10-sq-km national park is one of the country's most visited. It contains several healthy coral reefs and two ship wrecks. The waters are warm and the visibility good, making this one of the top diving spots in the country.

destroying fragile coral reefs with huge numbers of tourists in the process. Enforcement has been less effective in the DR's central mountains, where logging and encroachment by farmers continues in many areas.

Parks also safeguard the forested watersheds that provide the country with much needed drinking water. Rich and diverse varieties of plants and animals that are disappearing elsewhere on the island now find their last remaining homes in these parks, while local villagers glean some income from the visitors who come to see these vanishing resources.

ENVIRONMENTAL ISSUES

The Dominican Republic, like all islands in the Caribbean, is ultimately a tiny isolated speck of land with limited space and resources. Place on it a growing local population and add millions of tourists each year, and you end up with a severely strained landscape. All types of problems arise from this toxic brew, but in the end it is the native plants, animals, rivers and mountains that suffer, not to mention delicate coral reefs and fragile marine ecosystems. Everyone wants to enjoy a tropical paradise, but even with the lightest of touches, their cumulative impact is detrimental.

But even before tourism became a booming business, centuries of human activity had forever altered the landscape of Hispaniola. One of the greatest errors was the assumption that fertile tropical soils could produce equally abundant crops, when in fact the wealth of these soils lay in the vegetation that was cut. Crops failed after only a few years and farmers moved on to clear new tracts of forest, while the abandoned fields eroded horribly. The full folly of this cycle is today evident in the devastated landscape of Haiti where all the topsoil has washed away with hardly a tree standing in what was once splendid tropical forest.

The Dominican Republic has been fortunate in seeing the errors of its close neighbor and is moving quickly to set aside pristine watersheds. However, parks and reserves remain chronically underfunded and illegal logging and agricultural encroachment are a problem in some areas, especially in the central highlands.

Early settlers and visitors also made some poor choices in introducing weedy plants and animals that have no natural predators on the island. Mongoose and wild boar are just two species that have wreaked havoc on native ecosystems, but there are countless other introduced species.

Modern environmental issues stem from both local residents and foreign visitors. Locals, for example, utilize rivers and waterways as garbage and sewage dumps, and many rivers and beaches are strewn with trash (especially plastic). Garbage is even a problem in urban areas, where trash bins are few and collection sporadic. Visitors bring with them their own insatiable appetite for disposable items, many of which end up in overflowing garbage pits or scattered elsewhere in the environment.

Coastal resorts and villages also have a tremendous impact on the very coral reefs that provide their livelihood. Pollution, runoff and other impacts caused by massive developments have destroyed many of the country's foremost reefs. Overfishing and the inadvertent destruction caused by careless humans, transform reefs into gray shadows of their former selves.

Fortunately, the plus side of all these impacts is that there is a growing awareness of the need to protect these diminishing resources. There is a new emphasis on low impact tourism and increased monitoring, while outside funding can help support critical infrastructure for ecotourism and parks. This hardly counters the rush to develop mega-resorts, but it's an improvement in just the last few years and hopefully the sentiment continues to grow.

Bloodwood is a common tree of swampy areas, where it has the local nickname *drago* because it's stilt-like roots rise like a dragon from the water while its red sap forms a medicine known as 'dragon's blood.'

Interested in making a significant contribution while having fun on your next dive? Check out REEF (www.reef.org), an organization of recreational divers who have conducted over 80,000 simple fish surveys to further scientific understanding of reef ecosystems.

The Center for the Conservation of Bahía de Samaná and its Surroundings offers a wide range of helpful information on its website, www.samana.org.do.

Outdoors

WALKING & HIKING

The most famous hike in the Dominican Republic (DR) is the ascent of Pico Duarte, at 3175m (10,416ft), the tallest peak in the Caribbean. It's a tough multi-day hike, but involves no technical climbing and most people hire mules to carry their supplies and equipment up the mountain. About 3000 hikers make it to the top every year; many wake up early on their summit day in order to be at the peak for sunrise, a truly sublime experience. There are three different routes to the top (p232) and several side trips you can take along the way, including hikes through two beautiful alpine valleys and up the Caribbean's second highest peak, La Pelona, not even 100m lower than Pico Duarte.

Pico Duarte was first climbed in 1944 as part of the 100th anniversary celebration of the Dominican Republic's independence from Haiti.

The most common starting point for climbing Pico Duarte is La Ciénaga, a small town just outside Jarabacoa in the central highlands. At least three tour operators – two in Jarabacoa (p227) and one based in Cabarete – offer organized trips up the mountain. Rates are roughly US$100 per person per day for three-, four- and five-day trips for an organized tour; less if you have a group of five or more. Alternatively, you can also hire a freelance guide in Jarabacoa for about US$275 for a three day trip, or hire local guides and mules right at the trailhead for about US$50 per day. Of course, the more you pay the less you have to arrange or worry about yourself.

Even if you're not keen on going all the way up the mountain, you can still enjoy some walks through the DR's impressive landscape. There are numerous waterfalls around Jarabacoa (p226) and the nearby town of Constanza (p235) that you can hike to. The Samaná Peninsula has some beautiful hikes near Las Galeras (p155) with picturesque deserted beaches as your reward at the end. In the southwest, the Parque Nacional Sierra de Bahoruco (p252) makes for a good day's hike, though trails and facilities are very primitive.

No matter what hike you take, it is a good idea to have sturdy shoes. For Pico Duarte they are absolutely essential – boots are even better – while some of the coastal hikes can be managed in good sandals with heel straps.

WINDSURFING

Not too long ago, Cabarete was a sleepy fishing village with a broad shallow bay. In 1985, a Canadian traveler and windsurfer named Jean Laporte was the first outsider to recognize the bay's windsurfing po-

---

RUBBISH

- Carry out *all* your rubbish. Don't overlook easily forgotten items, such as silver paper, orange peel, cigarette butts and plastic wrappers. Empty packaging should be stored in a dedicated rubbish bag. Make an effort to carry out rubbish left by others.

- Never bury your rubbish: digging disturbs soil and ground cover and encourages erosion. Buried rubbish is likely to be dug up by animals, who may be injured or poisoned by it. It may also take years to decompose.

- Minimize waste by taking minimal packaging and no more food than you will need. Take reusable containers or stuff sacks.

- Sanitary napkins, tampons, condoms and toilet paper should be carried out despite the inconvenience. They burn and decompose poorly.

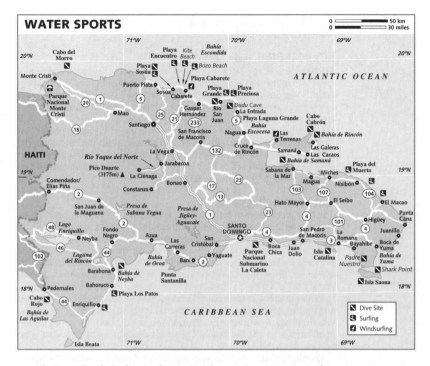

WATER SPORTS

tential. He evidently had a good eye, as Cabarete is now recognized as a world-class windsurfing location (p194). What neither he nor anyone else foresaw, however, was how the sport would transform Cabarete into the adventure-sport Mecca that it is today. Its one road, which was once a sandy track along the coast, is now crammed with hotels and resorts catering to wind-sport enthusiasts, restaurants and bars appealing to all tastes and budgets, and numerous rental and retail shops that also offer windsurfing lessons.

Cabarete's bay seems almost custom-made for windsurfing. A small coral reef on the bay's upwind side protects the bay from waves and currents, leaving a huge area of shallow flat water. With light morning winds and mellow seas, the bay is ideal for learning the basics: standing the board, lifting the sail out of the water and catching the wind. In the afternoon, thermal winds pick up, blowing east to west across the bay and reaching speeds of 25 to 40 km/h. During the summer, the conditions are perfect for high speed downsails and easy tacking. About a kilometer out, waves break over a second coral reef, and expert windsurfers head there to practice moves like 360-degree spins and end-over-end flips. From December to March, the waves are big enough to make even the inner bay a bit choppy. May, November and December have variable weather, gusty one day, windless the next. In general, windsurfing requires stronger winds than kiteboarding does.

The beach at Cabarete is lined with outfits, small and large, renting windsurf equipment and offering lessons for beginners. Renting a board and sail will cost about US$25 per hour, US$50 per day or US$250 per week. If you want to lean to windsurf, the same shops offer private and

www.activecabarete .com features listings, information and reviews about sporting activities in and around Cabarete.

group lessons, ranging from just one hour (US$40) to a complete four-session course (US$150).

KITEBOARDING Laurel Eastman

Kiteboarding is the latest evolution in high-flying, speed-racing water sports. Imagine surfing combined with wakeboarding and paragliding. Sounds like fun? It is, and there's no better proof than the sheer number of people learning kiteboarding every day in the Dominican Republic and around the world.

Like all sports, it can be as extreme as you make it – many people just like to get out and peacefully cruise, while others push the limits of aerial tricks and freestyle maneuvers. As a spectator sport it is impressive and entertaining, well worth a look while relaxing on the beach, even if you aren't keen to get in on the action yourself.

Best Kiteboarding Spots

The best place to learn kiteboarding is Cabarete (p193), the heart of the Dominican kiteboarding scene. A bustling one-street village based on water sports tourism (kiteboarding, surfing and windsurfing), Cabarete is extremely well set up for visitors from all over the globe. Cabarete is located a short distance east of Puerto Plata – about 25 minutes by car or taxi from the airport or an hour by bus from downtown Puerto Plata.

Kiteboarders perform tricks such as 'kitelooping,' 'back-side handle passes,' 'mobius' and 'slim chance.'

With excellent hotels, restaurants and bars, good Internet connections and many kiteboarding schools, Cabarete is quickly becoming the hottest kite destination in the world. Plus, if you've got room for more excitement after a day at the beach, Cabarete's raucous nightlife is easily the best on the North Coast.

Continue east along the winding North Coast for about 2½ hours, and you will find the town of Las Terrenas. Remote, tranquil and with a strong French influence, Las Terrenas has fewer kiteboarding outfits than Cabarete, but fewer people on the water as well. With lighter wind speeds and shallow water, it is a decent alternative when Cabarete is especially crowded.

Kiteboarding Schools

Choosing a kiteboarding school is an important decision. Beginners will do well to select the best possible school. The investment in lessons pays off handsomely in understanding safety procedures and accelerating the learning curve in this technical sport.

www.cabaretekite boarding.com and www.cabaretewind surfing.com focus on kiteboarding and windsurfing respectively with listings of schools, rental and retail outfits, plus reports on conditions and upcoming events.

Look for a professional organization with some years of experience, professionally trained instructors and an excellent safety track record. Within the organization, find an instructor who you understand clearly and with whom you feel a rapport. As cool as kiteboarding looks, it can be dangerous, and learning the right way will ensure your safe return home to kite another day.

DIVING & SNORKELING

The Dominican Republic is not known as a diving destination, but it has some great places for underwater exploring all the same. The warm Caribbean waters on the southern coast have pretty fields of coral and myriad tropical fish that make for fun easy dives. Two national parks east of Santo Domingo – Parque Nacional Submarino La Caleta (p101) and Parque Nacional del Este (p127) – can be reached with dive shops in Boca Chica (p102) and Bayahibe (p124), respectively. La Caleta is an

RESPONSIBLE DIVING

- Never use anchors on the reef and take care not to ground boats on coral.

- Avoid touching or standing on living marine organisms or dragging equipment across the reef. Polyps can be damaged by even the gentlest contact. If you must hold on to the reef, only touch exposed rock or dead coral.

- Be conscious of your fins. Even without contact, the surge from fin strokes near the reef can damage delicate organisms. Take care not to kick up clouds of sand, which can smother organisms.

- Practice and maintain proper buoyancy control. Major damage can be done by divers descending too fast and colliding with the reef.

- Take great care in underwater caves. Spend as little time within them as possible, as your air bubbles may be caught within the roof and thereby leave organisms high and dry. Take turns to inspect the interior of a small cave.

- Resist the temptation to collect or buy corals or shells or to loot marine archaeological sites (mainly shipwrecks).

- Ensure that you take home all your rubbish and any litter you may find as well. Plastics in particular are a serious threat to marine life.

- Do not feed fish.

- Minimize your disturbance of marine animals. *Never* ride on the backs of turtles.

underwater preserve covering just 10 sq km but is one of the country's most popular dive destinations. The main attraction is the *Hickory*, a 39m salvage ship with an interesting past (see p101) that was intentionally sunk in 1994. Parque Nacional del Este has a number of interesting dives too, including another wreck – a massive 89m cargo ship – and a site ominously called Shark Point (p124).

The DR's North Coast provides a very different diving experience. Facing the Atlantic, the water there is cooler and somewhat less transparent, but the underwater terrain is much more varied, making for challenging dives and unique profiles. There are a number of places with access to good diving – Río San Juan (p200) and Las Galeras (p155) are both tiny towns with just one dive shop apiece (a second may be opening in Las Galeras, however). At Río San Juan, you can dive the Seven Hills, a giant coral formation rising 50m nearly to the surface, or Crab Canon, a great channel dive with natural arches and swim-throughs. Las Galeras has easy access to Cabo Cabrón (Bastard Point) whose imposing walls are patrolled by huge fish making it one of the more memorable dives in the DR. Sosúa (p186) is the largest and most convenient for divers of the North Coast cities, with several recommended dive shops and at least 20 good dive sites. Las Terrenas (p160) has a wreck dive and most dive shops there can make special trips to Cabo Cabrón.

Off the beaten track, Monte Cristi (p210) and nearby Parque Nacional Monte Cristi (p209) has the country's best preserved coral reef and the remains of a colonial-era galleon, cannons and all, in 60m depths of water. There is no established dive center there as yet, but experienced divers with their own equipment sometimes dive here. Other off-the-beaten-track options are two diveable freshwater caves – Dudu Cave near Rio San Juan and Padre Nuestro near Bayahibe. Dudu, with two openings, three different tunnels and a spacious stalactite-filled chamber is one of the most memorable cave dives in the Caribbean and can be dived by

Divers exploring the waters near the Samaná Peninsula can sometimes hear humpback whales singing.

WHALE WATCHING

Between mid-January and mid-March more than 80% of the reproductively active humpback whales in the North Atlantic – some 10 to 12 thousand in all – migrate to the waters around the Samaná Peninsula to mate. The Bahía de Samaná is a favorite haunt of the whales, and one of the best places in the world to observe these massive, curious creatures. Most tours depart from the town of Samaná (p150), and you are all but guaranteed to see numerous whales surfacing for air, lifting their fins or tail, jostling each other in competition, and even breaching – impressive jumps followed by an equally impressive splash. Whale watching season coincides with Carnival (every weekend in February) and Independence Day (February 27) – major holidays here – so you should make reservations well in advance if you'll be visiting then.

experienced open-water divers. Located within the Parque Nacional del Este, Padre Nuestro is a challenging 290m tunnel that should be attempted only by trained cave divers. With the exception of the cave dives, most of the sites mentioned here also make for excellent snorkeling.

Dive prices vary from place to place, but average US$30 to US$40 for one tank, plus US$5 to US$10 for equipment rental (if you need it). Most people buy multi-dive packages, which can bring the per-dive price down to around US$25. You must have an Open Water certification card to dive with any of the shops recommended in this book; if you're new to the sport, all the dive shops also offer the Discover Scuba and Open Water certification courses. For snorkeling, trips cost around US$25 to US$40 per person.

There are at least two functioning decompression chambers in the Dominican Republic. They are located in **Santo Domingo** (☎ 809-593-5900; Base Naval 27 de Febrero, San Souci Pier, Av España) on the east side of Río Ozama, and **Puerto Plata** (☎ 809-586-2237; Hospital Dr Ricardo Limbardo, Av Manolo Taveres Busto 1 at Hugo Kundhart). The Santo Domingo chamber, though mainly used for military divers, is open to civilians and tourists in emergencies.

SURFING

As if the North Coast didn't have enough adventure sport possibilities, it is also the best place in the country for surfing. Once again, Cabarete (p194) is the center of the action, though there are a number of spots along the coast that can be quite good depending on the weather and swell.

Playa Encuentro (p193), 4km west of Cabarete, is an undulating beach where sand gives way to rock right at the water's edge. Waves break both right and left over a reef a short distance from shore, and vary from light rollers that are good for learning to 2½m monsters that thunder onto shore. The waves can get even bigger than that – up to 4m – but at that point you're better off heading west to Sosúa. There, the big waves roll in much cleaner, forming deep pipes perfect for those classic tube runs. Other popular places for surfing are Playa Grande (p200) and Playa Preciosa (p200), both near Río San Juan, and at Puerto Plata.

One of the opening scenes of Steven Spielberg's *Jurassic Park* was filmed in Salto Jimenoa Uno outside of Jarabacoa in the Central Highlands.

Surfing season tends to be the opposite of most other beach sports and activities, mainly because big waves are the product of bad weather, not good. Winter is the best season to surf, especially in September and October when hurricanes and tropical storms stir up swells that last for days or weeks. Big waves last well into spring before mellowing out during the summer, the best time for beginners to learn.

There are a number of surf shops in Cabarete and on Playa Encuentro itself where you can rent boards or take surfing lessons. Rentals cost from

US$10 to US$20 for half a day; courses vary from three hour introductory sessions (US$30 to US$40) to a full-blown five-day surf camp (per person US$110 to US$175). You can also rent surf boards at Playa Grande.

CYCLING

Some of the roads in the Dominican Republic are much better suited for a good mountain bike than the rickety buses and pickups trucks packed with humanity that ply their remote corridors. With a good map and a decent grasp of Spanish you could definitely ride around the backroads of the DR on your own. Or you can join a biking tour, which typically includes equipment, food, lodging, sag wagon, a guide to point out all the interesting things along the way and companions to share the experience with.

Not surprisingly, the Jarabacoa area (p228) is the best and most popular area for mountain bike riding. Tucked into the mountains, there are a number of dirt roads and single track trails offering challenging climbs and thrilling descents. The crisp air and cool climate make for ideal cycling and of course the scenery could hardly be more appealing, with thick forests and a number of waterfalls within easy reach. Near Jarabacoa, the town of Constanza is even higher – 1300m (4265ft) above sea level to Jarabacoa's 800m (2625ft) – and rides in the surrounding hillsides leave many riders sucking for air.

Las Galeras (p155), on the northern coast of the Samaná peninsula, also has memorable mountain biking opportunities. Most of the rides are on dirt roads and include exploring the area's craggy coast line. Several rides end up at scenic deserted beaches and have dramatic ocean views along the way. Elsewhere on the North Coast, Cabarete (p195) has a number of good rides and is home to the DR's best cycling tour operator (see below).

The southwest has the best road-bike options, with well-maintained highways and relatively little traffic. South from Barahona, Highway 44 winds and loops along the coast, with numerous vista points offering beautiful views of the turquoise Caribbean Sea and the area's intriguing white-stone beaches. West of Barahona, a well-maintained highway makes a long flat loop around Lago Enriquillo (p253), a saltwater lake that's the largest in the Greater Antilles as well as the Caribbean's lowest elevation at -40m. It is also one of the hottest areas in the country, and riders here should be extra careful to stay cool and hydrated. There are a few small towns along the way but almost no services, and the view of the lake is often blocked by a low scrub forest. Riders attempt this loop mostly for the challenge of it rather than the views. Be aware that Dominican drivers rarely offer the courtesy and elbow room you may be accustomed to getting from drivers elsewhere.

www.dominican republicpure.com is a comprehensive website of outdoor activities and tour operators throughout the Dominican Republic.

RIVER RAFTING

The Dominican Republic has one navigable white-water river, the Río Yaque del Norte (also the country's longest river). It is mostly a Class II- and III-river, with a couple of serious rapids, and the rest consists of fun little holes and rolls. The river winds through hilly countryside and makes for a nice half-day tour. The upriver areas where rafting takes place have some litter along the shore, but the water is pretty clean. It is more polluted downstream, as it winds through areas with more people and farmland. Be aware that the water is frigid – you'll be issued a wetsuit along with your life vest and helmet. River trips are offered by both main tour operators in Jarabacoa (p226) and cost around US$55 to US$65 per person.

CANYONING

Not for the faint at heart, this adventure sport involves jumping, rappelling and sliding down a slippery river gorge with a cold mountain river raging around you. Tour operators in Jarabacoa (p228) offer beginner and advanced tours, most lasting between three and four hours and costing US$50 to US$60. All make use of ropes, harnesses, helmets and other safety equipment, but good shoes and steady nerves are essential.

Several tour operators – especially one called Iguana Mama (p195) in Cabarete – offer highly recommended mountain bike tours ranging from half-day downhill rides to 12-day cross-country excursions. Iguana Mama is one of the best tour operators in the DR and their specialty is mountain bike rides, so you can hardly go wrong. It will also customize a trip to fit your interests, available time and experience level. In this book, you'll find listings for additional tour operators and independent guides in most of the towns mentioned above. Tour prices vary widely depending on the length of the ride, but begin at around US$30 per person for half-day trips.

GOLF

With so many all-inclusive resorts, it makes sense that the Dominican Republic has plenty of places to golf. The top courses all take advantage of the DR's dramatic coastline, with holes hugging high cliffs and offering golfers incredible views of the deep blue and turquoise seas, right along the fairway and greens. It's impossible to say which course is the best. The Casa de Campo (p120) mega resort near La Romana has two courses – 'Teeth of the Dog' and 'Links' – designed by Pete Dye. The former has been rated the number one golf course in the Caribbean and one of the top 25 in the world, and is the island's most exclusive course. It features seven holes so close to the water you'll feel like you're about to fall in. There's another Dye-designed course in Punta Cana, at the Punta Cana Resort and Club (p136). That course, called La Cana Golf Course, also offers ocean views from 14 holes, with four being especially dramatic.

Not to be out done, the 6265m Playa Grande Golf Course (p201), located on the North Coast near Río San Juan, was the last course designed by Robert Trent Jones Sr. Although he didn't live to see the final result, the course is classic RTJ style, with long sloping greens and 11 stunning sea-side holes. Here the sea can be quite rough, and the crashing waves and high streams of sea spray add to the course's appeal. Further west, the course at Playa Dorada (p180) is in the middle of a large manicured complex of all-inclusive resorts, a number of which offer attractive golf and lodging packages.

www.golfguide-do.com although updated somewhat infrequently, provides golf-related listings for the Dominican Republic including information on golf courses, clinics and convenient accommodations.

There are many more golf courses to choose from – more than 20 in fact – scattered over the country. Green fees vary widely – from US$200 at Teeth of the Dog and US$140 at La Cana down to just US$27 for two laps around the hilly Par 3 course at Jarabacoa Golf Club (p228), nestled among the pine trees in the DR's rugged central mountain range. Most courses require either a caddie or a golf cart, typically US$5 to US25 per round. All courses offer club rental and some offer private instruction from the resident golf pros.

Food & Drink

Eating and drinking is taken seriously in the Dominican Republic (DR), not so much for the food itself, but as a social activity. Families eat together, and it is custom to offer guests coffee, soda or water when they come into your home or business. Many businesses close for lunch, and lingering an hour or two over the midday meal is not uncommon. Dominican cuisine itself is not terribly complex, and doesn't contain the range of flavors and styles nor distinct regional variations that, say, Indian, Mexican or French food do. It has several major starches, including rice, potatoes, bananas, yucca and cassava, usually served in large portions – a Dominican meal is nothing if not extremely filling!

STAPLES & SPECIALTIES

Flavors and styles don't vary much around the country. Dinner is the biggest meal, though neither breakfast nor lunch are exactly light. All three meals usually consist of one main dish – eggs for breakfast, meat for lunch and dinner – served with one or more accompaniments, usually rice, beans, salad and/or boiled vegetables.

The most typically Dominican meal is known as *la bandera* (the flag); it consists of white rice, red beans *(habichuela)*, stewed meat, salad and fried green plantains, and is usually accompanied by a fresh fruit juice. It's not hard to see why it's so popular – it's good, cheap, easy to prepare and nutritionally balanced. Red beans are sometimes swapped for small *moros* (black beans), *gandules* (small green beans) or *lentejas* (lentils).

Bananas *(guineos)* are a staple of Dominican cuisine and served in a variety of ways, including boiled, stewed and candied. But the main way Dominicans eat bananas is boiled and mashed, like mashed potatoes. Prepared the same way, but with plantains, the dish is called *mangú*; with pork rinds mixed in, it is called *mofongo*. Both are very filling and can be served for breakfast, lunch or dinner, either as a side dish or as the main dish itself.

It should be no surprise that seafood is a central part of Dominican cuisine, especially along the coast where it is sure to be fresh. The most common plate is a fish fillet, usually *mero* (grouper) or *chillo* (red snapper), served in one of four ways: *al ajillo* (with garlic), *al coco* (in coconut sauce), *al criollo* (with a mild tomato sauce) or *a la diabla* (with a spicy tomato sauce). Other seafood like crab, octopus, shrimp, squid and *lambí* (conch) are prepared in the same sauces, as well as *al vinagre* (in vinegar sauce), a variation on seviche and for many people the tastiest of the lot.

Casabe (flat and round cassava bread) – a staple of the Dominican diet – dates back to the Taínos.

There are a number of dishes usually reserved for special occasions, but found on many restaurant menus. One is *sancocho de siete carnes* (seven-meat soup), made with sausage, chicken, beef, goat and several

---

VEGETARIANS NEED NOT APPLY

It's tough to say otherwise: the Dominican Republic is a meat-eating country. Without a doubt, *sancocho* – the hearty meat stew – is one of the DR's most treasured culinary delights. It is a time-consuming and complicated dish to prepare and, because of that, it is reserved for special occasions. Traditionally, *sancocho* is made only with beef, but chefs often prepare the dish with up to seven different types of meat. For *sancocho* and other Dominican recipes (including vegetarian dishes such as a tasty *crema de cepa de apio* – cream of celery root soup) check out www.dominicancooking.com.

CASABE

From ancient Taíno cooking fires to elegant presidential banquets, there is at least one common thread, a starchy bread known as *casabe*. High in carbs and low in fat – whatever would Dr Atkins say? – *casabe* is made from ground cassava roots (also known as manioc and a close relation to yucca). Cassava was one of the Taíno's principle crops, as it was for numerous indigenous peoples throughout the Caribbean and South America. Easy to plant – just bury a piece of the root or stalk into the ground – it also is fast growing. Europeans brought the hardy plant from the Caribbean to their colonies in Africa and Asia, where it was quickly and widely adopted. *Casabe* is still popular today, especially at traditional meals with soups and stews where it's great for soaking up every last drop. Rather tasteless on its own, *casabe* is best topped with butter, salt, tomato or avocado. A modern variation is the *catibía*, fried cassava flour fritters stuffed with meat.

pork parts, all combined with vegetables into a hearty stew. Goat meat is also extremely popular in the DR and is presented in many different ways. Two of the best are *pierna de chivo asada con ron y cilantro* (roast leg of goat with rum and cilantro) and *chivo guisado en salsa de tomate* (goat stewed in tomato sauce).

DRINKS
Nonalcoholic Drinks
One of the DR's favorite drinks, among locals and foreigners alike, are *batidas* (smoothies) which are made of crushed fruit, water, ice and several tablespoons of sugar. A *batida con leche* contains milk and is slightly more frothy. Though they can be made of just about any fruit, popular varieties include *piña* (pineapple), *papaya* (known as *lechoza*), *guineo* (banana), and *zapote* (sapote), some *batidas* have strange local names, such as *morir soñando* (literally, 'to die dreaming') made of the curious, but tasty, combination of orange juice and milk.

Juices (*jugos* or sometimes *refrescos*, although the latter also means carbonated soda) are typically made fresh right in front of you and are a great pick-me-up on a hot day. Popular flavors include *chinola* (passion fruit), *piña* (pineapple peel) and *tamarindo* (tamarind). Orange juice is commonly called *jugo de china,* although most people will understand you if you ask for *jugo de naranja.*

Other popular nonalcoholic Dominican drinks include *ponce de frutas* (fruit punch), *limonada* (lemonade) and *mabí,* a delicious drink made from the bark of the tropical liana vine.

Banana trees only give fruit once in their lifetime.

Alcoholic Drinks
When it comes to *ron* (rum), it's tough to beat the Dominican Republic for quality. It is known for its smoothness and its hearty taste, as well as for being less sweet than its Jamaican counterparts. The earliest form of rum was created by accident after colonists left molasses (a by-product of sugar production) in the sun for several days. Adding a little water, they realized that it fermented into a sweet drink with a kick. Homemade rum rapidly gained popularity in the New World and by the 1800s businessmen began perfecting its production. Today, over four million cases of rum are produced in the Dominican Republic every year.

Dozens of local brands are available, but the big three are Brugal, Barceló and Bermudez. Within these three brands, there are many varieties from which to choose, including *blanco* (clear), *dorado* (golden) and *añejo* (aged), which contains caramel and is aged in special wooden casks to mellow the taste.

Most travelers will recognize a *cuba libre* (rum and coke) but may not have tried a *santo libre* (rum and sprite) which is just as popular among Dominicans. *Ron ponche* (rum punch) is what you'd expect it to be – a blend of rum and sweet tropical juices – but is more often ordered by foreigners than by locals.

Whiskey is popular in the Dominican Republic and a number of familiar brands, plus a few Dominican variations, are available at most bars – purists will want a *trago de etiqueta roja* (Johnny Walker Red Label) or *trago de etiqueta blanca* (Dewar's White Label). You can also always order Bloody Marys, margarita, martini and Tom Collins, and white and black Russians.

There are a handful of locally brewed beers, including Presidente, Quisqueya, Bohemia and Soberante. The best and most popular way to enjoy a beer is to share a *grande* (large) with a friend or two. A tall 1.1 liter (40oz) beer is brought to your table in a sort of insulated sleeve, made from either wood or bamboo or from plastic and Styrofoam with a beer label emblazoned on the side, along with a small glass for each of you. There are few experiences more quintessentially Dominican than milking a couple of *Presidente grandes* at a plastic table on the sidewalk patio of a no-name restaurant.

WHERE TO EAT & DRINK

Restaurants are called just that – *restaurantes* – though more informal places may be called *comedores*. Most restaurants are open from 8am to 10pm every day, though a few are closed one day per week, typically Sunday, Monday or Tuesday. Reservations are rarely needed. There are very few places in the country where only tourists go, though certainly some cater more to foreigners (and their prices prove it) Most of the restaurants in this book are popular with locals and tourists alike, or even just locals.

Quick Eats

By far the most common snack in the DR – one served at nearly every celebration – is the *pastelito* or closely related empanada. Empanadas typically have ham or cheese in them, while *pastelitos* usually contain beef or chicken, that's first been stewed with onions, olives, tomatoes and a variety of seasonings, and then chopped up and mixed with peas, nuts and raisins.

www.theworldwide gourmet.com/countries /westindies/dominican-r /dominican-r.htm provides recipes as well as background on Dominican cooking, especially as it relates to other Caribbean cuisine.

TRAVEL YOUR TASTEBUDS

Dominican cuisine doesn't contain many surprises, whether a super-hot chili or strange meat or seafood. Anyone who has spent time in New York or Puerto Rico will recognize a number of dishes, due to Dominican immigrants readily reproducing food from back home.

Some of the more unique drinks and dishes you may come across include a *sapao de lambí,* a soupy rice and tomato dish made with conch (also served with shrimp, lobster or shellfish), *bacalao,* which is a salted cod fish, usually broiled and served in a tuna salad–like form (sans mayo) with tomato and onion. *Chivo al vino* is goat stewed in red wine, and *queso frito* consists of pan-fried thick slices of white cheese, which is sometimes accompanied by tomato and onion and served as a breakfast dish.

Mashed plantains are known as *mangú* and if pork rinds are added this becomes *mofongo*. *Sancocho de siete carnes* is a traditional stew usually served at celebrations and is made up of vegetables and seven different meats, from goat to pork rinds. *Tostones* are plantain slices fried like potato chips. The wonderfully named *morir soñando* (literally 'to die dreaming') is a drink made of milk and orange juice.

TAXES & TIPPING

The federal government required restaurants to add a 16% sales tax and 10% service tax to all bills. The latter is designed to go to the restaurant staff, though it's hard to gauge how much of that the workers actually see. It is also customary to leave an additional 10% tip for your waiter. If you're paying with a credit card, leave the tip in cash to make sure that your waiter gets it right away.

Whatever the filling, it is tucked into a patty of dough and fried in boiling oil. *Pastelitos* are a tradition enjoyed by generations of Dominicans, and are made at home as well as by street vendors whose carts are fitted with burners to keep the oil hot. Other traditional Dominican snacks include *frituras de batata* (sweet-potato fritters), *fritos maduros* (ripe plantain fritters), *tostones* (fried plantain slices) and *yaniqueques* (johnny cakes).

Because most Dominican street food is fried, you can be relatively confident it's safe to eat (your arteries may disagree, however.) A small step up from street vendors are tiny cafeteria-style eateries where food is kept in heated trays under glass. These places can be more risky than street vendors, as the food may have been prepared a long while ago, or even have been recycled from the previous day. If something looks like it's been out all day, it probably has and you're better off avoiding it. That said, some of these eateries are very conscientious about freshness and hygiene and are a great budget alternative to sit-down restaurants – you really have to judge each one separately. Follow the crowd – if a place is full, chances are the food is decent.

www.cookingwithcaro.bizhosting.com provides an excellent resource for Dominican and Creole recipes.

VEGETARIANS & VEGANS

Vegetarianism is not widely practiced in the Dominican Republic, and there are certainly a large number of Dominicans who view it as downright strange. Still, there are enough non-meat side dishes in Dominican cuisine – rice, salad, plantains, eggplant, yucca, okra and more – that vegetarians and even vegans shouldn't have too much problem finding something to eat. Beans are another tasty and easy to find staple, though they are often made using lard. Pizza and pasta restaurants are ubiquitous in the DR and there is always at least one vegetarian option (and if not, it's easy enough to request). Of course, for those vegetarians who make an exception for fish and seafood, there is no problem whatsoever. There is at least one vegetarian restaurant in the Dominican Republic – a place

THE DOMINICAN REPUBLIC'S TOP FIVE SMALL RESTAURANTS

- Ananda (Santo Domingo, p89) – Great freshly made Dominican fare that happens to be vegetarian.
- Hermanos Villar (Santo Domingo, p89) – Large sandwich and cafeteria-style eatery that's always packed with locals.
- Restaurant Agua Blancas (Constanza, p235) – A bit of class in a small-town setting, with popular lunch specials for under US$5.
- Restaurante El Almendro (Sosúa, p189) – Amid overpriced tourist traps, this hard to find hole-in-the-wall serves great home-style meals.
- Los Robles (Barahona, p248) – Tasty meat plates and hefty grilled sandwiches, to eat in or to go.

DOS & DON'TS

Dominican etiquette is pretty casual, with few of the strict rules you find elsewhere around the globe. Still, politeness and showing respect are important, and there are a few things you can do (or not do) to fit in a little better.

▪ Do tip at least 10% at restaurants.

▪ Do accept coffee or water when it's offered, especially in someone's home.

▪ Do spoon large quantities of sugar into your coffee – it's the Dominican way.

▪ Don't insist on knowing a person's last name – except in business settings, many people prefer not to give it.

---

called Ananda, in the Gazcue neighborhood of Santo Domingo – but virtually all the restaurants listed in this book will have at least some non-meat alternatives.

EATING WITH KIDS

Children are very welcome in restaurants in the Dominican Republic, where dining is traditionally a family affair. In fact, like in many Latin American countries, children are simultaneously *more* welcome at restaurants (and weddings, gatherings etc) here than they are in other countries, but *less* likely to be the center of all the adults' attention. Dominican food has few hidden surprises – like flaming-hot chilies or weird squishy textures – and is usually perfectly acceptable even to picky eaters. If your kid is a big milk drinker, he or she may not like Dominican milk which is ultra-pasteurized and often served only lukewarm. Otherwise, there are plenty of juices to pick from, including 'regular' ones like orange, lime, apple and pineapple. Large grocery stores in the DR carry a variety of baby foods, diapers and other products, and many of the same brands found in the US and Canada.

HABITS & CUSTOMS

Dominicans are as a rule very polite, but observe relatively very few strict rules of dining and etiquette. Though formal restaurants certainly exist, a casual atmosphere with loud conversation and lively background music are the norm, especially during lunch, the most boisterous of Dominican mealtimes. It is not considered rude to call out or even hiss to get the waiters attention. It *is* considered rude for a waiter to bring your bill before you've asked for it – the waiter isn't ignoring you, he's just being polite! This stems partly from the custom of lingering over meals, which are seen as much as a time to socialize as to fill one's stomach.

www.dominican cooking.com is a user-friendly website providing the history as well as the classic recipes of Dominican cuisine.

COOKING CLASSES

Cooking classes are occasionally offered to students at Spanish language schools (p262). Ask about them when you sign up for a language course.

EAT YOUR WORDS

Food is one area of traveling where hand signals and a healthy sense of adventure usually suffice. Still, knowing just a few terms will prevent you from ordering *guinea* (guinea hen) when you meant *guineo* (banana) or *mangú* (mashed plantains) when you really wanted mango. For pronunciation guidelines see p288.

Useful Phrases

The bill, please.
La cuenta, por favor.   la *kwen*-ta por fa-*vor*
Is the tip included?
¿La propina está incluída?   la pro-*pee*-na es-*ta* in-cloo-*wee*-da
Do you have a menu in English?
¿Tiene carta en inglés?   tye-ne *kar*-ta en een-*gle*
I'm vegetarian.
Soy vegetariano.   soy ve-khe-ta-ree-*ya*-no
May I have this dish without meat/chicken/ham?
¿Podría tener este plato sin   po-*dree*-ya te-*ner* es-te *pla*-to seen
carne/pollo/jamón?   *kar*-ne/po-yo/*kha*-mon
What does this dish contain?
¿Qué contiene este plato?   ke-con-*tye*-ne es-te *pla*-to
What do you have to drink?
¿Qué tiene de tomar?   que *tye*-ne de to-*mar*
What types of juice/soda/beer do you have?
¿Qué tipo de jugos/refrescos/cervezas hay?   ke *tee*-po de *khu*-gos/re-*fres*-cos/ser-*ve*-sas ai
We need more time.
Necesitamos más tiempo.   ne-se-see-*ta*-mos mas *tyem*-po
I haven't finished yet/I'm still eating
Todavía no he terminado.   to-da-*vee*-ya no e ter-mee-*na*-do
Would you bring me another fork/spoon/knife/napkin, please?
¿Me trae otro tenedor/cuchara/   me *tra*-ye o-tro te-ne-*dor*/koo-*cha*-ra/
cuchillo/servieta, por favor?   koo-*chee*-yo/ser-*vye*-ta por fa-*vor*
Very good/tasty.
Muy rico.   mooy *ree*-ko

Food Glossary

arroz con pollo	a-*ros* con *po*-yo	steamed rice with chicken
asopao de camarones	a-so-*pa*-o de ka-ma-*ro*-nes	soupy rice with tomatoes and shrimp; also made with *lambí* (conch) or *camarones al ajillo* (garlic shrimp)
camarones mariposa	ka-ma-*ro*-nes ma-ree-*po*-sa	butterflied shrimp
cazuela de mariscos	ka-*swe*-la de ma-*rees*-kos	seafood casserole
chillo al horno	*chee*-yo al *or*-no	oven-baked red snapper
chivo al vino	*chee*-vo al *vee*-no	goat cooked in wine
ensalada verde	en-sa-*la*-da *ver*-de	green salad
ensalada de camarones	en-sa-*la*-da de ka-ma-*ro*-nes	shrimp salad
filete a la parrilla	fee-*le*-te a la pa-*ree*-ya	broiled steak
guineas al vino	gee-*ne*-as al *vee*-no	guinea hen in wine
medallon de filete	me-da-*yon* de fee-*le*-te	beef medallions
mero a la plancha	*me*-ro a la *plan*-cha	grilled grouper
pechuga de pollo	pe-*choo*-ga de *po*-yo	breast of chicken, usually oven-baked
pulpo	*pool*-po	octopus
sopa de pescado	*so*-pa de *pes*-ka-do	fish soup
sopa de mariscos	*so*-pa de ma-*rees*-kos	seafood soup
sopa de vegetales	*so*-pa de ve-khe-*ta*-les	vegetable soup

Dominican Cookbook by María Ramírez de Carias is a comprehensive and beautifully presented book on the culinary delights of the Dominican Republic.

Santo Domingo

As in many Latin America countries, the Dominican Republic's political, economic and cultural energies are concentrated in its capital. And like its counterparts elsewhere, Santo Domingo (population 2.2 million) is a city of profound contrasts, where immense wealth and grinding poverty coexist in close quarters. It's a city of Catholics, yet it has no shortage of brothels; there are five-star hotels and frequent power outages; the heat is occasionally oppressive, but the people are optimistic and patient.

Santo Domingo is also a city of firsts: it contains the New World's first hospital, first university, first paved road and first two-story residence, as well as its oldest working church, the oldest monastery, and oldest surviving European fortress. In a very real sense, this is where Europe and the Americas first mingled. It is the very nexus from which earth-altering social, political and environmental events would grow.

And beyond all its historic gravity, Santo Domingo – or *la Capital* as Dominicans typically call it – is a terrifically fun place to visit. The city hosts the Dominican Republic's largest Carnival celebration, a merengue festival and a Latin music festival. Its dance clubs are packed with hipsters dancing till dawn, its cockfight arena and baseball stadium attract people from around the world and around the block, and its art scene is as rich as any in the Caribbean.

HIGHLIGHTS

- The **Faro a Colón** (p79) is the capital's homage to Christopher Columbus as well as being an intriguing and controversial sight and museum.

- Santo Domingo's **Catedral Primada de América** (p71) is the oldest working church in the New World.

- Baseball games are never boring at **Estadio Quisqueya** (p92), with dancing in the stands, chanting fans, and world-class players.

- Wander the quiet **backstreets of the Zona Colonial** (p69) to discover colonial homes and cobble-stone passageways.

- **Parque Colón** (p74) is perfect for sipping a tall Presidente beer after a long day of sightseeing.

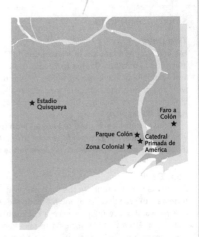

HISTORY

In a way it can be said that the founding of Santo Domingo was an act of desperation. Columbus' first settlement, Villa La Navidad in present-day Haiti, was burned to the ground and all settlers killed within a year. His second settlement, La Isabela, west of present-day Puerto Plata, lasted only five years and was beset from the beginning by disease and disaster. Columbus' brother Bartholomew, left in charge of La Isabela and facing rebellion from its disgruntled residents, pulled up stakes and moved clear around to the other side of the island. He founded Nueva Isabela on the east bank of the Río Ozama. The third time, evidently, was the charm as the city he founded, though moved to the west bank and renamed Santo Domingo, has remained the capital to this day.

That's not to say the city hasn't had its fair share of troubles. In 1586 the English buccaneer Sir Francis Drake captured the city and collected a ransom for its return to Spanish control. And in 1655 an English fleet commanded by William Penn attempted to take Santo Domingo but retreated after encountering heavy resistance. A century and a half later, a brazen ex-slave and Haitian leader by the name of Francois Dominique Toussaint L'Ouverture marched into Santo Domingo. Toussaint and his troops took control of the city without any resistance at all; the city's inhabitants knew they were no match for the army of former slaves and wisely didn't try to resist. During the occupation, many of the city's residents fled to Venezuela or neighboring islands. It was in Santo Domingo on February 27, 1844 that Juan Pablo Duarte – considered the father of the Dominican Republic (DR) – declared Dominican independence from Haiti, a day still celebrated today.

ORIENTATION

There are no buses to or from Aeropuerto Internacional Las Américas (the main airport) or Aeropuerto Internacional Herrera. From Las Américas, a taxi into the Zona Colonial costs US$25 to US$30, with very little room for negotiation. You may be able to get a cab to take you just to the *carretera* (highway), where you can catch a bus into town (US$7, plus US$0.75 per person for the bus fare), but only do this during the day. The fare from Herrera is more reasonable at US$10 – there's no permanent taxi stand there, but at least a couple of cabs meet every flight.

For travelers, the Zona Colonial – home to streets that were once strolled by Christopher Columbus and Sir Francis Drake – is the heart of Santo Domingo. This is where most of the museums, churches and other historical sites are located. It has a number of hotels and restaurants in various price

---

SANTO DOMINGO IN...

Two Days

Eat breakfast at **Plaza de la Hispanidad** (p74). Afterwards, visit the **Museo de las Casas Reales** (p69), **Fortaleza Ozama** (p75) and the **Cathedral** (p71). Eat lunch at **Parque Colón** (p74) and stroll along Arzobispo Portes and Padre Billini streets – these are attractive colonial lanes with churches, small parks and pedestrian alleyways. Check out the activity and bustle along El Conde. For an evening drínk or dinner head to **Mesón D'Bari** (p89) or **La Bodeguita de la Habana Vieja** (p89).

In the morning, take a taxi to **Faro a Colón** (p79). Return to the Zona Colonial for lunch and a visit to the **Amber or Larimar Museums** (p70). Later, take a cab to the **Jardín Botánico Nacional** (Botanical Gardens; p79), which is lovely in the late afternoon.

Four Days

Follow the two-day tour. On the third day, visit the Zona Colonial's less-visited sites, like **Monasterio de San Francisco** (p75) and **Mercado Modelo** (p95). Spend the evening among Dominicans at a **baseball game** (p93) or even a **cockfight** (p93). On your last day, browse the shops and galleries in Zona Colonial for gifts to take back home. Or take a bus to **Boca Chica** (p101), a small beach town just 33km away with a beautiful white sand beach.

ranges and offers easy access to Internet, ATMs, shops and more. Just west of the Zona Colonial is a residential area called Gazcue, which has a number of hotels that offer better value than you'll find in the Zona Colonial, plus good restaurants and some services. South of Gazcue is the beginning of the Malecón, a portion of Av George Washington that contains most of the city's high-rise hotels, nightclubs and casinos. The waterfront avenue runs the length of the city but the majority of activity takes place between Cambronal and Av Abraham Lincoln. On Sundays, the Malecón is closed to vehicular traffic and is a fun and popular place to spend the day for locals and tourists alike.

Maps

Mapas Gaar (Map pp72-3; ☎ 809-688-8004; www.mapas gaar.com.do in Spanish; Espaillat at El Conde; 🕙 8:30am-5:30pm Mon-Fri) is located on the 3rd floor of an aging office building and has the best variety and the largest number of maps in the Dominican Republic. Maps are designated by city or region (eg Santo Domingo and Environs, North, Central, South) and include a country map as well as several city maps on the back of each. Road atlases are also sold here.

Also in the Zona Colonial, the **Instituto Geográfico** (☎ 809-682-2680; Calle El Conde btwn Las Damas & Av del Puerto; 🕙 8am-6pm Mon-Fri) produces mostly commercial use maps, but does sell a handsome five-panel, 1m-by-1.5m map of the Dominican Republic for US$35.

INFORMATION
Bookstores

Editorial Duarte (Map pp72-3; ☎ 809-689-4832; Arzobispo Meriño at Mercedes; 🕙 8am-7pm Mon-Fri, 8am-6pm Sat) This dusty shop in the Zona Colonial has a good selection of Spanish-language fiction books, foreign-language dictionaries and maps.

Librería Pichardo (Map pp72-3; José Reyes at El Conde; 🕙 8am-7pm Mon-Thu, 8am-5:30pm Fri, 8am-1pm Sun) You used to be able to find loads of great old Spanish-language books here, but the owner says that since the 1990s the DR's supply of early and antique books has dwindled due to exportation and a lack of local preservation. There are a few good finds here still, mostly on colonial history and Latin American literature and poetry, plus some curios – we spotted a seven-language dictionary when we passed by. The owner is a friendly guy, but you may have to bargain hard to get a good price.

Cultural Centers

Casa de Italia (Italian House; Map pp72-3; ☎ 809-688-1497; Calle Hostos at General Luperón; admission free; 🕙 9:30am-7pm Mon-Sat) Regularly hosting art exhibits in its 1st-floor gallery, this center also doubles as an Italian language institute.

Casa de Teatro (Map pp72-3; ☎ 809-689-3430; www.arte-latino.com/casadeteatro; Arzobispo Meriño 110; admission varies; 🕙 9am-6pm, 8pm-3am Mon-Sat) Housed in a renovated colonial building, this fantastic arts complex features a gallery with rotating exhibits by Dominican artists, an open-air bar and performance space where music and spoken word shows are held every weekend, and a theatre that regularly hosts dance and stage productions. Call or stop by for a schedule of events.

Centro Cultural Español (Spanish Cultural Center; Map pp72-3; ☎ 809-686-8212; www.ccesd.org in Spanish; Av Arzobispo Meriño at Arzobispo Portes; admission free; 🕙 10am-9pm Mon-Sat) A cultural space run by the Spanish Embassy, this institute regularly hosts art exhibits, film festivals and musical concerts, all with a Spanish bent. It also has 15,000 items in its lending library with both Dominican and Spanish newspapers, magazines, fiction and art books. For a listing of events, stop by for a brochure.

Emergency

The **Politur** (Tourist Police; Map pp72-3; ☎ 809-689-6464; El Conde at José Reyes; 🕙 24hr) can handle most situations; for general police dial ☎ 911.

Internet Access & Fax

Abel Brawn's Internet World (Map pp72-3; ☎ /fax 809-333-5604; Plaza Lomba, 2nd fl; per hr US$1.40; 🕙 9am-9pm Mon-Sat, 10am-4pm Sat) Fast Internet access as well as international phone service (to USA US$0.30 per minute, Europe US$0.50 per minute), fax service (to USA US$0.50 per page, Europe US$0.75 to US$1 per page) and up-to-date computer accessories.

Caribae (Map pp72-3; ☎ 809-685-2142; General Luperón 106; per hr US$1.40; 🕙 9am-9pm Mon-Sat) Quiet Internet café.

Centro de Internet (Map p78; ☎ 809-238-5149; Av Independencia 201; per hr US$1; 🕙 8:30am-9pm Mon-Sat, 8:30am-3pm Sun) In Gazcue, come here for reasonably fast Internet and the cheapest international phone rates in town (to USA per min US$0.17, to Europe per min US$0.21).

Cyber Red (Map pp72-3; ☎ 809-685-9267; Sánchez 201; per hr US$1; 🕙 9am-9pm Mon-Sat) Just off El Conde, you can also make international calls here (to USA per min US$0.25, to Europe per min US$0.65).

Internet Café (Map pp72-3; ☎ 809-685-2083; José Reyes at Arzobispo Portes; per hr US$0.75; 🕙 10:30am-10pm Mon-Sat, noon-10pm Sun) The best price in town and on a pretty cobblestoned street to boot.

SANTO DOMINGO

SANTO DOMINGO

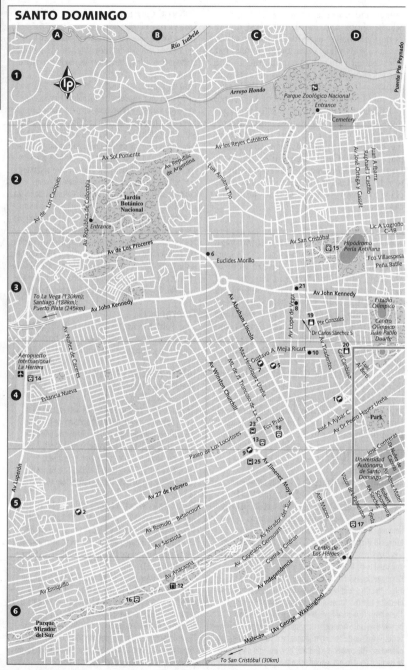

Río Isabela

Puente Pte Peynado

Arroyo Hondo

Parque Zoológico Nacional
Entrance

Cemetery

Av los Reyes Católicos

Av Sol Poniente

Av República
de Argentina

Av República de Colombia

Av de Los Caciques

Luis Amiama Tío

Juan A Ibarra
Raphael J Castillo
Av José Ortega y Gasset

Jardín
Botánico
Nacional

Entrance

Lic A Logroño
C-18

Av de Los Próceres

Av San Cristóbal

15

Hipódromo
Perla Antillana

6
Euclides Morillo

Fco Villaespesa

Peña Batlle

To La Vega (130km);
Santiago (188km);
Puerto Plata (245km)

Av John Kennedy

21

Av John Kennedy

Estadio
Olímpico

Av Abraham Lincoln

Av Lope de Vega

8

19
Pte Gonzales

Dr Carlos Sánchez S

Centro
Olímpico
Juan Pablo
Duarte

Aeropuerto
Internacional
La Herrera

14

Av Núñez de Cáceres

Max Henríquez Ureña

Gustavo A Mejía Ricart

ML de JS Troncoso de la C

Av Tiradentes

10

20

Luis F Barh

Cal Carlsbao

Estancia Nueva

Av Winston Churchill

5

1

José A Aybar C

Av Dr Pedro Hqvez Ureña

Park

José Contreras

Av Núñez de Cáceres

4

Fco Prats

23

18

13

Paseo de Los Locutores

9

25

Av Jiménez Moya

Universidad
Autónoma
de Santo
Domingo

Robert
Schomburg

R A Sánchez

Av Alma Mater

Av Lupéron

Av 27 de Febrero

Av Rómulo - Betancourt

Vizcao de Jasiantón

Tejeda

Av Sarasota

Av Mirador del Sur

17

Av Anacaona

Av Cayetano Germosen

Correa y Cidrón

Centro de
Los Héroes

4

2

12

Av Independencia

Av Enriquillo

16

Parque
Mirador
del Sur

Malecón (Av George Washington)

To San Cristóbal (30km)

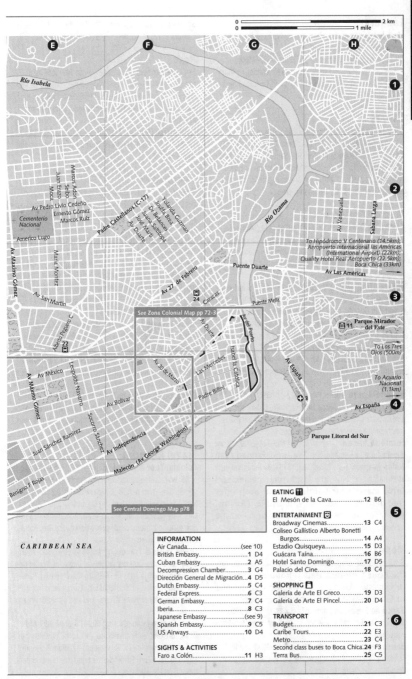

0 _____ 2 km
0 _____ 1 mile

Río Isabela

Av Pedro Livio Cedeño
Cementerio Nacional
Americo Lugo

Av Máximo Gómez

Marcos Adon
Selbo
Juan Erazo
Moca
Ernesto Gómez
Marcos Ruiz

María Montez

Av San Martín

Padre Castellanos (C-17)
Yolanda Guzmán
Josefa Brea
D. Rodriguez
Juana Saltitopa
José Martí
Av Duarte

Av 27 de Febrero

24 Caracas

See Zona Colonial Map pp 72-3

Av Duarte

Las Mercedes

Av 30 de Marzo

Isabel la Católica

Padre Billini

Av 22

Av México

Av Máximo Gómez

Leopoldo Navarro

Av Bolívar

Juan Sánchez Ramírez

Socorro Sánchez

Av Independencia

Malecón (Av George Washington)

Benigno F Rojas

See Central Domingo Map p78

Río Ozama

Av Venezuela

Sabana Larga

To Hipódromo V Centenario (14.5km);
Aeropuerto Internacional las Américas
(International Airport) (22km);
Quality Hotel Real Aeropuerto (22.5km);
Boca Chica (33km)

Av Las Américas

Puente Duarte

Puente Mella

Av del Puerto

Río Ozama

11 Parque Mirador
del Este

To Los Tres
Ojos (500m)

To Acuario
Nacional
(1.1km)

Av España

3

Av España

Parque Litoral del Sur

CARIBBEAN SEA

INFORMATION
Air Canada.............................(see 10)
British Embassy............................**1** D4
Cuban Embassy.............................**2** A5
Decompression Chamber.............**3** G4
Dirección General de Migración...**4** D5
Dutch Embassy.............................**5** C4
Federal Express............................**6** C3
German Embassy...........................**7** C4
Iberia..**8** C3
Japanese Embassy....................(see 9)
Spanish Embassy...........................**9** C5
US Airways..................................**10** D4

SIGHTS & ACTIVITIES
Faro a Colón...............................**11** H3

EATING 🍴
El Mesón de la Cava..................**12** B6

ENTERTAINMENT 🎭
Broadway Cinemas.....................**13** C4
Coliseo Gallístico Alberto Bonetti
    Burgos.....................................**14** A4
Estadio Quisqueya......................**15** D3
Guácara Taína............................**16** B6
Hotel Santo Domingo.................**17** D5
Palacio del Cine.........................**18** C4

SHOPPING 🛍
Galería de Arte El Greco.............**19** D3
Galería de Arte El Pincel............**20** D4

TRANSPORT
Budget..**21** C3
Caribe Tours...............................**22** E3
Metro..**23** C4
Second class buses to Boca Chica.**24** F3
Terra Bus....................................**25** C5

Laundry

Many hotels do laundry, though they typically charge per piece, which adds up real fast.

Lavandería Tin (Map pp72-3; ☎ 809-687-3400; Arzobispo Nouel btwn Espaillat & Palo Hinchado; ☿ 8am-6pm Mon-Sat) Washing and drying is US$4 per load, up to 14lbs (6.3kg).

Library

Biblioteca Nacional (National Library; Map p78; ☎ 809-688-4086; Plaza de la Cultura; Calle César Nicolás Penson 91; ☿ 9am-5pm Mon-Sat) Santo Domingo's best library. Memberships are limited to scholars and persons with residency status, but there are no restrictions pertaining to use of the library's books on-site.

Medical Services

Centro de Obstetricía y Ginoecología (Map p78; ☎ 809-221-7100; Av Independencia at José Joaquín Pérez; ☿ 24hr) This hospital specializes in gynecology and obstetrics, but has an emergency room and staff equipped to handle all emergencies.

Clínica Abreu (Map p78; ☎ 809-688-4411; Av Independencia at Burgos; ☿ 24hr) Widely regarded as the best hospital in the city, this is where members of the US, Japanese, German and other embassies go. Quite a few staff members received their training at American medical schools and speak excellent English.

Dra Rosalba Cabrera (☎ 809-482-4344; Av 27 de Febrero 481; ☿ 9am-6pm Mon-Fri) Comprehensive dental and orthodontic care.

Hospital Padre Billini (Map pp72-3; ☎ 809-221-8272; Av Sánchez btwn Arzobispo Nouel & Padre Billini; ☿ 24hr) The closest public hospital to the Zona Colonial, service is free here but expect long waiting lines.

Farmacia Vivian (Map p78; ☎ 809-221-2000; Av Independencia at Delgado; ☿ 24hr) and **Farmacia San Judas** (Map pp72-3; ☎ 809-685-8165; Av Independencia at Pichardo; ☿ 24hr) are large pharmacies and mini-marts near Clínica Abreu; both offer free delivery (medicines, hair dye, Doritos, whatever) to the Zona Colonial and Gazcue areas.

Money

Scotiabank and Banco de Reservas are in the Zona Colonial, Banco Popular is located in Gazcue. All have ATMs, though the one in Gazcue is not available after hours.

Banco de Reservas (Map pp72-3; ☎ 809-960-2108; Isabel la Católica at Las Mercedes; ☿ 8am-5pm Mon-Fri, 9am-1pm Sat)

Banco Popular (Map p78; ☎ 809-685-3000; inside Farmacia Carmina, Av Independencia at Pasteur; ☿ 9am-8pm Mon-Sat, 9am-1pm Sun)

Scotiabank (Map pp72-3; ☎ 809-689-5151; Isabel la Católica at Las Mercedes; ☿ 8:30am-4:30pm Mon-Fri)

Post

Federal Express (Map pp66-7; ☎ 809-565-3636, toll free ☎ 809-200-3138; www.fedex.com; Av de los Próceres at Camino del Oeste; ☿ 8:30am-5:30pm Mon-Fri, 8:30am-12:30pm Sat) Recommended for important shipments.

Post office (Map pp72-3; Isabel la Católica; ☿ 8am-5pm Mon-Fri, 9am-noon Sat) Facing Parque Colón in the Zona Colonial.

Telephone

Several of the listed Internet cafés (see Internet Access & Fax) also offer international phone service, some at even better rates than Verizon.

Verizon Centro de Comunicaciones (Map pp72-3; ☎ 809-221-4249; fax 809-221-4167; El Conde 202; ☿ 8am-9:30pm) Air-cooled and glaringly bright call center has international phone and fax service (to USA per min US$0.30, to Europe per min US$0.75).

Tourist Information

Secretaría de Estado de Turismo (State Tourism Office; Map pp72-3; ☎ 809-221-4660; www.dominicana .com.do; Av México at Av 30 de Marzo, 1st fl; ☿ 8am-4pm Mon-Fri) The staffers at the main tourist office are only marginally helpful but the selection of maps and brochures is good.

Tourist office (Map pp72-3; ☎ 809-686-3858; Isabel la Católica 103; ☿ 9am-3pm Mon-Fri) Located beside Parque Colón, this office has a handful of brochures and maps. English and French spoken.

Travel Agencies

Colonial Tour & Travel (Map pp72-3; ☎ 809-688-5285; www.colonialtours.com.do; Arzobispo Meriño 209; ☿ 8:30am-1pm & 2:30-5:30pm Mon-Fri, 8:30am-noon Sat) A few meters north of the El Conde promenade, this place has been around for years. Good for booking domestic and international plane tickets. English, Italian and French spoken.

Giada Tours & Travel (☎ 809-686-6994, 809-264-3704; giada@verizon.net.do; Hostal Duque de Wellington, Av Independencia 304; ☿ 8:30am-6pm Mon-Fri, 9am-2pm Sat) Friendly professional outfit arranges domestic and international plane tickets, and also condcuts area tours.

Turis Centro (Map p78; ☎ 809-688-6607, 809-689-2714; turiscentro@hotmail.com; Av George Washington 101 at Calle El Número; ☿ 8:30am-12:30pm & 2-6pm Mon-Fri, 9am-2pm Sun) Another reputable travel agency, located on the Malecón.

DANGERS & ANNOYANCES

Pick-pocketing, especially on buses or in clubs, is the main concern for visitors to Santo Domingo. Being alert to the people around you and careful with your wallet or purse (or even leaving them back at the hotel) is the best defense. Muggings are less common, especially of tourists, but they do happen occasionally. The Zona Colonial is generally very safe to walk around, day or night. The Malecón is safe as well, but be extra cautious if you've been drinking or are leaving a club or casino especially late. Gazcue is a residential area and quite mellow, but also very dark in places. As in any big city, the trick is not to be an easy target. Stick to well-lit and well-trafficked areas as much as possible, and definitely avoid flaunting (or openly fumbling with) cash, jewelry, or electronics like cameras or portable music players. If you have a long way to walk or are unsure of the neighborhood, play it safe and call or hail a cab; they're quite cheap.

SIGHTS & ACTIVITIES

Most of the sights in Santo Domingo are in the Zona Colonial and can easily be visited on foot. A few sites, including biggies like the Faro a Colón and the Jardín Botánico, are in the surrounding neighborhoods.

Zona Colonial

Listed as a Unesco World Heritage site, the Zona Colonial is a slightly hilly area on the west bank of the Río Ozama, where the deep river meets the Caribbean Sea. It is 11 city blocks from east to west and 11 city blocks from south to north, and its mix of cobblestoned and paved streets follow the classic European grid pattern.

Most of the structures in the Zona Colonial contain walls that were erected in the 16th century. Many of the buildings' facades have been altered, and in some instances floors have been added. As might be expected there have been changes in style, usage and materials – few of the buildings, for example, bear tile roofs as they initially did.

This is a great place to explore and linger. The western end of Arzobispo Portes street is especially attractive, a quiet leafy avenue with colonial homes, stone churches and pleasant parks. Throughout the Zona Colonial, keep your eyes open for the details and

AREA CODE SCAM

The Dominican Republic's area code – 809 – is at the heart of a scam that has victimized Americans and Canadians since 1996. Here's how it works: a message is sent via email, voicemail or post claiming that the recipient has either won a valuable prize or that a relative is in trouble. To collect the prize or to get information, the person must call an 809 telephone number. Since this only requires a 1 to be placed before it – like a domestic phone call – the caller has no idea that the call is an international one.

Once the victim calls, a series of recorded messages convinces him to stay on the line; for every minute he waits, he's charged US$25. A pricey call, even if it's just five minutes long! How do these scammers get away with it? The Dominican government permits companies to use its area code for pay-per-call services and foreign governments have no way of regulating that.

the little nooks and crannies – the church plaza, the small pedestrian alleys, men playing dominos at an aluminum folding table set on the street. These scenes, as much as the historical sites and buildings, make the Zona Colonial unique.

MUSEUMS

The Zona Colonial has a rich collection of museums. There are so many to choose from, you're bound to find one that interests you.

The **Museo de las Casas Reales** (Museum of the Royal Houses; Map pp72–3; ☎ 809-682-4202; Las Damas, near Plaza de la Hispanidad; adult/student US$1/0.15; ⏰ 9am-5pm, closed Mon), was built in the Renaissance style during the 16th century and was the longtime seat of Spanish authority for the entire Caribbean region, housing the Governor's office and the powerful Audiencia Real (Royal Court), among others. It showcases colonial-period objects including many treasures recovered from Spanish galleons that foundered in nearby waters. Each room has been restored according to its original style, and displays range from Taíno artifacts to dozens of hand-blown wine bottles and period furnishings. Also on display is an impressive antique weaponry collection acquired by dictator/president Trujillo from a Mexican general (ironically, during a 1955 world peace event); you'll see samurai swords, medieval armor, ivory-inlaid crossbows, and even a pistol/sword combo. This is a very worthwhile stop.

Designed in the Gothic-Mudéjar transitional style, the **Museo Alcázar de Colón** (Museum Citadel of Columbus; Map pp72-3; ☎ 809-682-4750; Plaza de la Hispanidad; admission US$1.75; 9am-5pm, closed Mon) was used as a residence by Columbus' son, Diego and his wife, Doña María de Toledo, during the early 16th century. Recalled to Spain in 1523, the couple left the home to relatives who occupied the handsome building for the next hundred years. It was subsequently allowed to deteriorate, then was used as a prison and a warehouse, before it was finally abandoned. By 1775 it was a vandalized shell of its former self and served as the unofficial city dump. Less than a hundred years later, only two of its walls remained at right angles.

The magnificent building we see today is the result of three restorations: one in 1957, another in 1971 and a third in 1992. Great pains were taken to adhere to the historical authenticity of its reconstruction and decor. Today it houses many household pieces said to have belonged to the Columbus family. The building itself – if not the objects inside – is definitely worth a look.

The **Museo Mundo de Ambar** (World of Amber Museum; Map pp72-3; ☎ 809-682-3309; www.amber worldmuseum.com; Arzobispo Meriño 452; admission US$2; 9am-6pm Mon-Sat, 9am-1pm Sun) has an impressive collection of amber samples from around the world. It explains the history of this fossilized resin, its prehistoric origins, its use throughout the ages, Dominican mining processes and its present-day value to the science and art worlds. The collection includes fine amber jewelry and various samples containing a wide array of critters and bugs – there is even an entire room dedicated to ants. Signage is in Spanish and English.

While not as impressive or thorough as its competitor, the **Museo de Ambar** (Map pp72-3; ☎ 809-221-1333; El Conde 107, on Parque Colón; admission free; 9am-6pm Mon-Fri, 9am-4pm Sat) has a decent exhibit. Dozens of high-quality samples are on display and a few signs in Spanish, English and German explain its origins. The museum also has a fine exhibit on Larimar – a blue mineral only found in the Dominican Republic.

On the 2nd floor of a jewelry shop, **Larimar Museum** (Map pp72-3; ☎ 809-689-6605; www.larimarmuseum.com; Isabel la Católica 54; admission free; 9am-6pm Mon-Sat, 9am-1pm Sun) is quite impressive, notwithstanding the fact that its main purpose is to get you to buy something at the store downstairs. It contains a remarkable display of the beautiful blue stone and relates just about everything there is to know about the subject. Signage is in English and Spanish.

Located in the Casa de Tostado – the beautifully restored 16th-century home of the writer Francisco Tostado – is the **Museo de la Familia Dominicana** (Museum of the Dominican Family; Map pp72-3; ☎ 809-689-5000; Padre Billini at Arzobispo Meriño; admission US$1.50; 9am-4pm, closed Sun). It is an architectural gem that features a double Gothic window over the front door – the only one of its kind in the Americas.

A PIECE OF EIGHT

Between the 16th and 18th centuries, the predominant currency on Hispaniola was the Spanish real, which was issued as silver and gold coins in various denominations. During the 17th century, one real was what a crewman aboard a Spanish galleon could expect to be paid for two days' hard work; it could buy a night at the best guest house in Santo Domingo.

The largest denomination – the eight-real coin or a 'piece of eight' – was pure silver and crudely made. The method was to pour a long narrow strip from a ladle of molten silver and then pound the strip flat with a hammer. From this strip, pieces of silver about six centimeters long were chiseled off and were rounded until the piece weighed one ounce. The coin maker would then stamp each side of the coin with a design, usually the king's coat of arms on one side and the Spanish Cross on the other.

Today, pieces of eight that have been salvaged from colonial shipwrecks can be purchased for about US$100 at the Museo de la Atarazana (opposite). The Dominican government allows the naval museum to sell the historic coins to pay the museum's utility bills.

Today the Casa de Tostado honors 19th-century Dominican life by displaying well-restored furnishings, kitchenware and other household objects from that time. Ask to go up the spiral mahogany staircase for a rooftop view of the Zona Colonial. Tours in Spanish only.

The small **Quinta Dominica** (Map pp72-3; Padre Bellini at 19 de Marzo; admission free; 9am-6pm Mon-Sat, 9am-2pm Sun) art gallery, located in a renovated colonial home, features ever-changing exhibits of colonial art. A shady courtyard in back with tables and chairs provides a great place to just sit back and relax. BYO snacks and drinks.

Though closed for renovations when Lonely Planet passed through, the **Museo de la Atarazana** (Map pp72-3; 809-682-5834; Vicente Celestino Duarte near La Atarazana; admission US$1; 9am-6pm, closed Wed) houses colonial-era items recovered from shipwrecks along the Dominican Republic's coastline. Special attention is paid to the wreck of the *Concepción*, which went down in the Bahía de Samaná in the 1500s and was at last discovered and salvaged some 400 years later. The collection includes cannons, crucifixes, silver coins, belt buckles, plates, silver spoons, swords, brandy bottles, pipes and silver bars. A vast amount of information about life aboard Spanish galleons is also presented. Signage is in English and Spanish.

The **Museo de la Artesanía Dominicana** (Dominican Handicrafts Museum; Map pp72-3; Arzobispo Meriño, next to Museo Mundo de Ambar) was in the works when Lonely Planet passed through but no inauguration date was set. Interesting in theory, it's worth a walk by to see if it's open.

CHURCHES

The influence of Catholicism in the New World is evident by the plethora of churches found throughout the Zona Colonial.

Diego Columbus, son of the great explorer, set the first stone of the **Catedral Primada de América** (Primate Cathedral of America; Map pp72-3; entrance faces Parque Colón; admission free; 9am-4pm) in 1514, but construction didn't begin in earnest until the arrival of the first bishop, Alejandro Geraldini, in 1521. From then until 1540, numerous architects worked on the church and adjoining buildings, which is why the vault is Gothic, the arches Romanesque and the ornamentation baroque. It's anyone's guess what the

planned bell tower would have looked like; a shortage of funds curtailed construction, and the steeple, which undoubtedly would have offered a commanding view of the city, was never built.

Although Santo Domingo residents like to say their cathedral was the first in the western hemisphere, in fact one was built in Mexico City between 1524 and 1532; it stood for four decades, until it was knocked down in 1573 and replaced by the imposing Catedral Metropolitano. It *can* be said that Santo Domingo's cathedral is the oldest cathedral in operation, which is something for sure, but its current interior is a far cry from the original – thanks to Drake and his crew of pirates, who used the basilica as their headquarters during their 1586 assault on the city. While there, they stole everything of value that could be carried away and extensively vandalized the church before departing.

Among the cathedral's more impressive features are its awesome vaulted ceiling and its 14 interior chapels. Signs in English and Spanish beside each chapel and other features describe their rich histories. Shorts and tank tops are strictly prohibited.

Built in 1510 by Charles V, the **Convento de la Orden de los Predicadores** (Convent of the Order of Preachers; Map pp72-3; Av Duarte at Padre Billini; admission free; varies) is the first convent of the Dominican order founded in the Americas. It also is where Father Bartolomé de las Casas – the famous chronicler of Spanish atrocities committed against indigenous peoples – did most of his writing. Be sure to take a look at the vault of the chapel; it is remarkable for its stone zodiac wheel, which is carved with mythological and astrological representations. On the walls are various paintings of religious figures, including Pope Saint Pius V.

The Gothic-style **Capilla de Nuestra Señora de los Remedios** (Chapel of Our Lady of Remedies; Map pp72-3; Las Damas at Las Mercedes; admission free; varies) was built during the 16th century by alderman Francisco de Avila and was intended to be a private chapel and family mausoleum. Early residents of the city are said to have attended Mass here under its barrel-vaulted ceiling. It was restored in 1884.

The **Iglesia de Nuestra Señora de las Mercedes** (Church of Our Lady of Mercy; Map pp72-3; Las Mercedes at José Reyes; admission free; varies), constructed

ZONA COLONIAL

INFORMATION
Abel Brawn's Internet World.......1 E4
American Airlines.............................2 E5
Banco de Reservas..........................3 G3
Caribae...4 F4
Casa de Italia..................................5 F4
Casa de Teatro................................6 G5
Centro Cultural Español...................7 G5
Colonial Tour & Travel....................8 G4
Cyber Red..9 E5
Editorial Duarte.............................10 G3
Farmacia San Judas.......................11 B6
French Embassy..............................12 G4
Hispaniola Academy.......................13 F3
Hospital Padre Billini....................14 E5
Instituto Geográfica.......................15 H4
Internet Café..................................16 F6
Lavandería Tin...............................17 D5
Librería Pichardo...........................18 E4
Mapas Gaar....................................19 D5
Politur..20 E4
Post Office......................................21 G4
Scotiabank.....................................22 G3
Tourist Office.................................23 G4
Trinidad & Tobago Embassy..........24 G3
Verizon Centro de
   Comunicaciones..........................25 F4

SIGHTS & ACTIVITIES
Capilla de la Tercera Orden
   Dominica.....................................26 F5
Capilla de Nuestra Señora de los
   Remedios.....................................27 G3
Casa de Francia......................(see 12)
Casa del Cordón.............................28 G3
Catedral Primada de América.......29 G4
Convento de la Orden de los
   Predicadores...............................30 G5
Fortaleza Ozama............................31 H4
Fuerte de Santa Bárbara...............32 G1
Hostel Nicolás de Ovando......(see 71)
Iglesia de la Regina Angelorum....33 F5
Iglesia de Nuestra Señora de las
   Mercedes.....................................34 E4
Iglesia de Nuestra Señora del
   Carmen.......................................35 E5
Iglesia de San Lázaro.....................36 D4
Iglesia de San Miguel.....................37 E3
Iglesia de Santa Bárbara................38 G1
Iglesia de Santa Clara....................39 G5
Larimar Museum............................40 G4
Monasterio de San Francisco.........41 F2

Museo Alcázar de Colón...............42 H2
Museo de Ámbar...........................43 G4
Museo de la Artesanía
   Dominicana.................................44 F2
Museo de la Atarazana..................45 G2
Museo de la Familia Dominicana..46 G5
Museo de las Casas Reales............47 G3
Museo Infantil Trampolín..............48 H4
Museo Mundo de Ámbar...............49 F2
Palacio Nacional............................50 A4
Panteón Nacional..........................51 G3
Puerta de San Diego......................52 H2
Puerta del Conde...........................53 C5
Quinta Dominica............................54 F5
Reloj del Sol...................................55 G3
Ruinas del Hospital San Nicolás de
   Bari...56 F3

SLEEPING
Antiguo Hotel Europa....................57 G2
Apart-Hotel Plaza Colonial............58 B5
Bettye's Exclusive Guest House..59 G4
Bettye's Galería.....................(see 59)
El Beaterío Guest House................60 F5
El Refugio del Pirata......................61 G3
Hostal Nicolás Nader.....................62 F4
Hotel Aida.....................................63 D5
Hotel Conde de Peñalba................64 G4
Hotel Doña Elvira..........................65 E5
Hotel Freeman...............................66 G4
Hotel Palacio.................................67 F4
Hotel Saint Amad..........................68 G2
La Residencia.................................69 A6
Sofitel Francés...............................70 G3
Sofitel Nicolás de Ovando.............71 H4

EATING
Baskin Robbins..............................72 E4
Café de las Flores..........................73 E5
Coco's Restaurant.........................74 G5
Comedor el Puerto........................75 G5
El Conde Restaurant...............(see 64)
El Taquito......................................76 G2
La Cafetera Colonial......................77 F4
La Crêperie....................................78 G2

La Dulcería....................................79 G3
Mesón D'Barí.................................80 F4
Nancy's Snack Bar.........................81 G4
Paco Cafetería...............................82 D5
Pasatiempo....................................83 G3
Restaurant & Bar Palmito
   Gourmet.....................................84 E6
Restaurant Café Français..............85 G4

DRINKING
Bobo's..86 G4
K-ramba Bar...................................87 G5
Tu Coche Bar.................................88 F4

ENTERTAINMENT
Aire Club..89 E4
Atarazana......................................90 G2
Centro Cultural Español Cinema..(see 7)
Murano..91 F3
Nowhere..92 F4
Red Zone.......................................93 F4
XXO...94 F3

SHOPPING
Ambar Maldo Gift Shop................95 G2
Artesanía Elisa..............................96 F5
Atelier Gallery...............................97 F6
Boutique del Fumador...................98 G4
De Soto Galería.............................99 F4
Encuentro Artesanal....................100 G2
Felipe & Co..................................101 G4
Flor Ambar Gift Shop...................102 G4
Galería de Arte María del
   Carmen.....................................103 G4
Mercado Modelo..........................104 D3
Museo del Tabaco..................(see 105)
Pulga de Antigüedades..........(see 59)
Swiss Mine...................................105 G4

TRANSPORT
Ferries del Caribe.........................106 H3
Second class buses to Baní
   & San Cristóbal.........................107 E1
Second class buses to Juan Dolío
   & San Pedro de Macorís..........108 E1

To Museo del Hombre Dominicano/
Museo de Arte Moderno (1km);
Guácara Taina (6.5km);
Aeropuerto de Herrera/Coliseo Gallístico (8km)

To State Tourism Office (800m);
Caribe Tours (1.5km);
Estadio Quisqueya (4km);
Metro (5km); Terra Bus (5.5km);
Zoo (6km); Jardín
Botánico (7.5km)

To second
class buses
to Higüey;
Puerto Plata;
La Romana;
Santiago;
Sosúa (15m)

Parque
Independencia

Altar de
la Patria

Cemetery

To Clínica Abreu (100m);
Gazcue (250m); Car
rental agencies (2km);
Malecón (2km)

See Central Santo Domingo Map p78

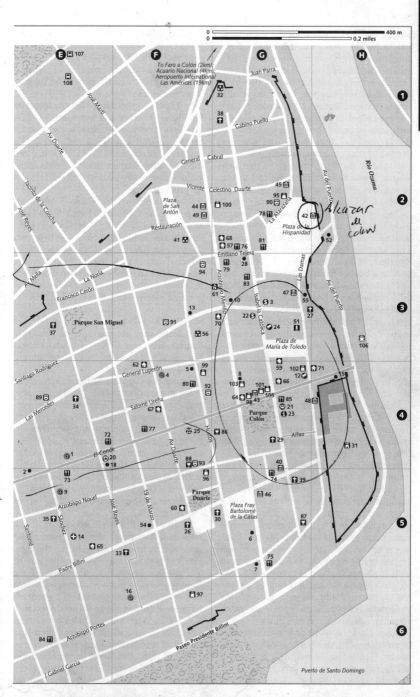

Alcazar del colon

during the first half of the 16th century, was sacked by Drake and his men and reconstructed on numerous occasions following earthquakes and hurricanes. The church is remarkable for its pulpit, which is sustained by a support in the shape of a serpent demon. The intricate baroque altarpiece is carved from tropical hardwood. Of the group of buildings that pay homage to the Virgin Mary, only the cloister adjacent to the church is in original condition.

Home to the first nunnery in the New World, **Iglesia de Santa Clara** (Map pp72-3; Padre Billini at Isabel la Católica; admission free; ☼ Sun mornings only) was built in 1552. Years after being sacked by Drake and his men (who apparently hated all things Catholic) it was rebuilt with funds from the Spanish Crown. This simple, discreet church has a severe Renaissance-style portal with a gable containing a bust of Saint Claire.

The baroque **Iglesia de Santa Bárbara** (Map pp72-3; Gabino Puello at Isabel la Católica; admission free; ☼ varies) was built in 1574 to honor the patron saint of the military. After being done over by Drake, however, the church was rebuilt with three arches – two are windowless and the third frames a remarkably sturdy door. These additions proved invaluable in protecting the building against pirates and hurricanes alike.

Paid for by a woman who donated her entire fortune to construct this monument for the cloistered Dominican Sisters, the **Iglesia de la Regina Angelorum** (Map pp72-3; Padre Billini at José Reyes; admission free; ☼ varies) was built toward the end of the 16th century. In addition to its imposing facade, the church is known for its elaborate 18th-century baroque altar, which is crowned with the king's coat of arms.

Completed in 1650, but altered several times since, **Iglesia de San Lázaro** (Map pp72-3; Santomé at Juan Isidro Pérez; admission free; ☼ varies) was erected beside a hospital that treated people with infectious diseases. The church was constructed to give the patients hope – a commodity that no doubt was in short supply for patients with tuberculosis, leprosy and other common diseases of colonial times.

Since 1596 the **Iglesia de Nuestra Señora del Carmen** (Map pp72-3; Sánchez at Arzobispo Nouel; admission free; ☼ varies) has served as a hospital, a jail and an inn, but is now famous for its carved-mahogany figure of Jesus, which is worshipped every Holy Wednesday during Easter Week. The small church, originally made of stone, was set aflame by Drake in 1586 and was rebuilt using bricks. During colonial times its small square was used to stage comedies.

In 1784, Spain ordered that the **Iglesia de San Miguel** (Church of Michael the Archangel; Map pp72-3; José Reyes at Juan Isidro Pérez; admission free; ☼ varies) be turned into a hospital for slaves. The decree, however, was never followed. Note the appealing juxtaposition of its rectangular stone doorway with the structure's curved exterior.

The Chapel of the Third Dominican Order, or the **Capilla de la Tercera Orden Dominica** (Map pp72-3; Av Duarte at Padre Billini) was built in 1729 and is the only colonial structure in Santo Domingo to reach the present fully intact. Today, the building is used by the office of the archbishop of Santo Domingo. It is not open to the general public but the graceful baroque facade is worth a look.

HISTORICAL SITES

Being the first colonial city in the New World, the Zona Colonial boasts several historical 'firsts,' including the first church, paved road and hospital.

Beside the Catedral Primasa de América is the historic Parque Colón, containing several shade trees and a large statue of Admiral Columbus himself. It is the meeting place for local residents and is alive with tourists, townsfolk, hawkers, guides, taxi drivers, shoeshine boys and tourist police all day long. El Conde Restaurant (p88), at the corner of Calles El Conde and Arzobispo Meriño, has seating inside and out and lends itself particularly well to people watching.

In front of the Alcázar de Colón, the **Plaza de la Hispanidad** has been made over many times, most recently during the early 1990s in honor of the 500th anniversary of Christopher Columbus' 'discovery' of the New World. The plaza is a large, open area that makes for a lovely stroll on a warm afternoon. Running along its northwest side is Calle La Atarazana, fronted by numerous restaurants and bars in buildings that served as warehouses through most of the 16th and 17th centuries. The street is occasionally closed to vehicular traffic and every afternoon much of it is lined with tables set up by the restaurants and bars. This is a popular place to have a drink around sunset and look out across the plaza to the Alcázar and beyond.

The **Fortaleza Ozama** (Map pp72-3; ☎ 809-686-0222; south end of Las Damas; admission US$0.50; ☼ 9am-6:30pm Mon-Sat, 9am-4pm Sun) is the oldest colonial military edifice in the New World. The site of the fort – at the meeting of the Ozama River and the Caribbean – was selected by Fray Nicolás de Ovando. Construction of the fortification began in 1502 under the direction of master builder Gómez García Varela and continued in various stages for the next two centuries. It served as a military garrison and prison until the 1970s, when it was opened to the public.

As soon as you walk into the site, you'll see the oldest of the buildings here – the impressive Torre del Homenaje (Tower of Homage). Its 2m-thick walls contain dozens of riflemen's embrasures and its roof-top lookout offers 360-degree views of the city. To its right, solid and windowless, stands El Polvorín – the Powder House – which was added in the mid-1700s; look for the statue of Saint Barbara over the door, the patron saint of the artillery.

Running along the riverside wall are two rows of cannons; the first dates from 1570, the second was added in the mid-1600s. Both served as the first line of defense for the city's port. The living quarters, now almost completely destroyed, were added along the cityside wall in the late 1700s. On the esplanade is a bronze statue of Gonzalo Fernández de Oviedo, perhaps the best-known military chronicler of the New World.

Near the door you'll find several guides, whose knowledge of the fort generally is quite impressive. Although the fee for a 20-minute tour is around US$3.50 per person, be sure to agree on a fee before you use their services. Tours are offered in Spanish, English and French and there is occasionally a guide who speaks German, Italian or even Japanese.

Originally constructed in 1747 as a Jesuit church the **Panteón Nacional** (National Pantheon; Map pp72-3; Las Damas; admission free; ☼ 9am-5pm, closed Mon) was also a tobacco warehouse and a theater before dictator Trujillo restored the building in 1958 for its current usage. Today many of the country's most illustrious persons are honored here, their remains sealed behind two marble walls. The

entire building, including its neoclassical facade, is built of large limestone blocks. As befits such a place, an armed soldier is ever present at the mausoleum's entrance. Located next to Plaza de María de Toledo, shorts and tank tops are discouraged.

Connecting Las Damas and Isabel la Católica, the **Plaza de María de Toledo** was named in honor of Diego Columbus' wife and is remarkable for two arches that were once part of the Jesuits' residence in the 17th century. Note the buttresses that support the Panteón Nacional; they are original, dating back to the construction of the Jesuit church in 1747, and a likely reason the building has survived the many earthquakes and hurricanes since.

Heading north and south in front of the fortress is **Las Damas** (Calle de las Damas, the Ladies' Street), the first paved street in the Americas. Laid in 1502, the street acquired its name from the wife of Diego Columbus and her lady friends, who made a habit of strolling the road every afternoon, weather permitting.

Across from the Museo de las Casas Reales, the **Reloj del Sol** (sundial; Map pp72-3) was built by Governor Francisco Rubio y Peñaranda in 1753 and positioned so that officials in the Royal Houses could see the time with only a glance from their eastern windows.

The **Monasterio de San Francisco** (Map pp72-3; Hostos, btwn E Tejera & Restauración) was the first monastery in the New World and belonged to the first order of Franciscan friars who arrived to evangelize the island. Dating from 1508, the monastery originally consisted of three connecting chapels. It was set ablaze by Drake in 1586, rebuilt, devastated by an earthquake in 1673, rebuilt, ruined by another earthquake in 1751 and rebuilt again. From 1881 until the 1930s it was used as an mental asylum until a powerful hurricane shut it down – portions of chains used to secure inmates can still be seen. The buildings were never repaired. Today the monastery is a dramatic set of ruins that is occasionally used to stage concerts and artistic performances.

Standing next to a bright, white Iglesia de la Altagracia are the **Ruinas del Hospital San Nicolás de Barí** (Map pp72-3; Hostos, near Las Mercedes), ruins of the New World's first hospital. They remain in place as a monument to Governor Nicolás de Ovando, who ordered the hospital built in 1503. So sturdy was the edifice that it survived Drake's invasion and centuries of earthquakes and hurricanes. It remained virtually intact until 1911, when after being devastated by a hurricane, public-works officials ordered much of it knocked down so that it wouldn't pose a threat to pedestrians. Even today, visitors can still see several of its high walls and Moorish arches. Note that the hospital's floor plan follows the form of a Latin cross.

The **Puerta del Conde** (Gate of the Count; Map pp72-3; west end of El Conde) owes its name to the Count of Peñalba, Bernardo de Meneses y Bracamonte, who led the successful defense of Santo Domingo against an invading force of 13,000 British troops in 1655. The gate is the supreme symbol of Dominican patriotism because right beside it, in February 1844, a handful of brave Dominicans executed a bloodless coup against occupying Haitian forces; their actions resulted in the creation of a wholly independent Dominican Republic. It also was atop this gate that the very first Dominican flag was raised. Just west of the gate look for the **Altar de la Patria**, a mausoleum that holds the remains of three national heroes: Juan Pablo Duarte, Francisco del Rosario Sánchez and Ramón Matías Mella.

Downhill from the Alcázar de Colón is the imposing **Puerta de San Diego** (Map pp72-3), built in 1571. For a time it was the main gate into the city. Beside it you still can see some of the original wall, which was erected to protect the city from assaults launched from the river's edge.

The Gate of Mercy, or **Puerta de la Misericordia** (Arzobispo Portes, near Palo Hincado) was erected during the 16th century, and for many decades served as the main western entrance to the city. The gate obtained its name after a major earthquake in 1842, when a large tent was erected beside it to provide temporary shelter for the homeless.

Said to be not only one of the first European residences in the Americas, but also one of the first residences in the western hemisphere with two floors, **Casa del Cordón** (House of the Cord; Map pp72-3; Isabel la Católica at E Tejera; 8:15am-4pm) was briefly occupied by Diego Columbus and his wife before they moved into their stately home down the street. Named after its impressive stone facade, which is adorned with the chiseled sash-

and-cord symbol of the Franciscan order, it is also believed to be the site where Santo Domingo's women lined up to hand over their jewels to Drake during the month he and his men held the city hostage. Today the structure is home to Banco Popular, and while you can go in to exchange money, visiting the house beyond the main lobby is not permitted.

The French House or **Casa de Francia** (Map pp72-3; Las Damas 42) was originally the residence of Hernán Cortés, conqueror of the Aztecs in what is today central Mexico. It was in this building that Cortés is believed to have organized his triumphant – and brutal – expedition. Built in the early 16th century and sharing many elements with the Museo de las Casas Reales, experts theorize that these buildings were designed by the same master; both have a flat facade and a double bay window in the upper and lower stories, repeating patterns of doors and windows on both floors, and top-notch stone rubblework masonry around the windows, doors and corner shorings.

Although the Casa de Francia served as a residence for nearly three centuries, it has had several incarnations since the beginning of the 19th century: a set of government offices, the Banco Nacional de Santo Domingo, a civil courthouse and the headquarters of the Dominican IRS. Today it houses the French Embassy. While visitors are not permitted past the lobby, this marvel of masonry is worth a walk by, if only to check out its facade.

Originally the residence of Governor Nicolás de Ovando, **Hostal Nicolás de Ovando** (Map pp72-3; Las Damas at General Luperón) is a handsome building with a Gothic facade that was built in 1509. Ovando is famous for ordering Santo Domingo rebuilt on the west bank of the Río Ozama following a hurricane that leveled most of the colony. Today it houses the posh Sofitel hotel (p84).

Fuerte de Santa Bárbara (Map pp72-3; Juan Parra at Av Mella), built during the 1570s, served as one of the city's main points of defense. It proved no match for Drake, however, who along with his fleet of 23 pirate-packed ships captured the fort in 1586. Today the fort lies in ruin at the end of a lonely street. There isn't much to see here anymore, mostly rooftops and occasionally, a cruise ship in the distance.

Plaza de la Cultura

Near the center of the city, the **Plaza de la Cultura** (Av Maxímo Gómez, btwn Avs México & Bolívar) is a large park-area with three museums, the national theater (p92) and the national library (p68). The land was once owned by the dictator Trujillo, and was 'donated' to the public after his assassination in 1961. At least two of the museums are worth visiting, though the plaza itself is rather underwhelming, and the theater and library will appeal to travelers with specific interests.

The most extensive of the museums is the **Museo del Hombre Dominicano** (Museum of the Dominican Man; Map p78; ☎ 809-689-4672; admission US$0.75; ✹ 10am-5pm Tue-Sun). Highlights here are the impressive collection of Taíno artifacts, including stone axes and intriguing urns and carvings, and the small but interesting section on Carnival with the masks and costumes used in various cities around the country. Other sections focus on slavery and the colonial period, African influences in the DR (including a small section on voodoo), and contemporary rural Dominican life, complete with a reconstructed thatched-roof home. Unfortunately, the explanations are all in Spanish and the displays very old-fashioned. English-speaking guides can be requested at the entry – the service is free, but small tips are customary.

The permanent collection at the **Museo de Arte Moderno** (Map p78; admission US$0.35; ✹ 10am-6pm Tue-Sun) is three floors up and includes paintings and a few sculptures by the Dominican Republic's best-known modern artists, including Luís Desangles, Adriana Billini, Celeste Woss y Gil, José Vela Zanetti, Dario Suro and Martín Santos. Though the collection has a number of excellent pieces, the temporary exhibits on the lower floors tend to be much fresher and more inventive than those upstairs – more installation and multimedia pieces, for starters – and will most likely be the highlight of your visit. Note that the entrance is on the 2nd floor – don't miss the artwork on the bottom level, accessed by a set of stairs just past the ticket counter.

Arranged in chronological order, the **Museo Nacional de Historia y Geografíca** (Map p78; ☎ 809-686-6668; admission US$0.20; ✹ 10am-5pm Tue-Sun) is divided into three wings, with each containing exhibits particular to a time period: 1822–61, 1861–1916 and 1916–61. The first wing focuses on the battles between Haitians and Dominicans; many weapons of the period are displayed, along with plenty of patriotic art. The second wing is mostly devoted to General Ulises Heureaux, the country's most prominent dictator during the 19th century. The third wing concentrates on Trujillo, the country's most prominent dictator during the 20th century, and the emphasis seems to be on his personal effects (his combs, razor, wallet etc are displayed with an air of great import). Probably not worth a visit were it not on the way between the Museo del Hombre Dominicano and the Museo de Arte Moderno.

The Dominican seat of government, the **Palacio Nacional** (Map pp72-3; ☎ 809-687-3191; Av México at Av 30 de Marzo) was designed by Italian architect Guido D'Alessandro and inaugurated in 1947. The palace is built of Samaná roseate marble in a neoclassical design and is outfitted in grand style with mahogany furniture, paintings from prominent Dominican artists, magnificent mirrors inlaid with gold, and a proportionate amount of imported crystal. Of special note is the Room of the Caryatids, in which 44 sculpted draped women rise like columns in a hall lined with French mirrors and Baccarat chandeliers.

The National Palace sits on most of a city block and is primarily used as an executive and administrative office building. It has never been used as the residence of a Dominican president, who is expected to live in a private home. Unfortunately, the Palace is not regularly open to the public, but you may be able to wrangle a VIP tour; they are offered free of charge and by appointment only on Monday, Wednesday and Friday. Dress appropriately – no flip-flops, shorts or T-shirts – if you are granted a tour.

Palacio de Bellas Artes (Palace of Fine Arts; Map p78; ☎ 809-687-9131; along Av Máximo Gómez, just north of Av Independencia) is an impressive beige building with a red tile roof that unfortunately, is used infrequently. Important exhibitions or performances are occasionally held here, but far fewer than either the building or the quality of Dominican art would suggest. When an event is scheduled, an announcement generally appears in the weekend edition of local papers.

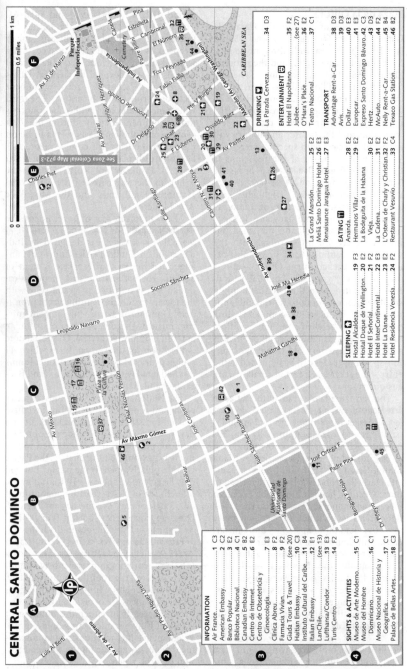

CENTRAL SANTO DOMINGO

Outlying Neighborhoods

Some very worthwhile sites are located just a cab ride away; if you've got the time, definitely check a couple of these out.

Certainly the most intriguing monument in Santo Domingo, both for its contents and history, is the imposing and controversial **Faro a Colón** (Map pp66-7; ☎ 809-592-1492, ext 251; Parque Mirador del Este; admission US$2.25; ☺ 9am-5:15pm Tue-Sun) or Columbus Lighthouse, on the east side of the Río Ozama. The Faro's massive cement flanks stretch nearly a block and stand some 10 stories high forming the shape of a cross. High power lights on the roof can project a blinding white cross in the sky, but are rarely turned on because doing so causes blackouts in surrounding neighborhoods.

At the intersection of the cross's arms is a tomb, guarded by stern white-uniformed soldiers, that purportedly contains Columbus' remains. Spain and Italy dispute that claim however, both saying *they* have the Admiral's bones. Inside the monument a long series of exhibition halls display documents (mostly reproductions) related to Columbus' voyages and the exploration and conquest of the Americas. The most interesting (though deeply ironic) displays are those sent by numerous Latin American countries containing photos and artifacts from their respective indigenous communities. A very worthwhile visit.

The lush grounds of the **Jardín Botánico Nacional** (National Botanical Garden; Map pp66-7; ☎ 809-385-2611; Av República de Colombia; admission US$1.25; ☺ 9am-6pm, ticket booth 9am-5pm) span 2 sq km and include vast areas devoted to aquatic plants, orchids, bromeliads, ferns, endemic plants, palm trees, a Japanese garden and much more. Great care is taken to keep the grounds spotless and the plants well tended, and it is easy to forget you are in the middle of a city of over two million people. The garden hosts a variety of events, including an orchid exhibition and competition in March and a bonsai exhibition in April. The onsite **Ecological Museum** (admission US$0.35; ☺ 9am-4pm, ticket booth 9am-5pm) exhibits and explains the major ecosystems found in the DR, including mangroves and cloud forests, plus a special display on Parque Nacional Los Haitises (p146). Once inside you can stay until 6pm. An **open-air trolley** (US$1.25; ☺ every 30 min until 4:30pm) takes passengers on a pleasant half-hour turn about the park and is especially enjoyable for children.

A taxi from the Zona Colonial costs around US$4; to get there by public transport, take a *público* (various types of cars used for public transport) or *gua-gua* (minibuses used for longer trips) west on Av Bolivar from Parque Independencia and ask to be let off at 'La Feria' and catch a long Ruta 11 bus north to the garden.

A long tree-filled corridor atop an enormous limestone ridge, **Parque Mirador Del Sur** (Southern Lookout Park; Map pp66-7; along Av Mirador del Sur) is riddled with caves, some as big as airplane hangars. One of the caves has been converted into a restaurant (p90), another into a dance club (p91). The park's seemingly endless paths are a popular jogging spot for thirty-something professionals, many of whom live in the middle- and upper-class neighborhoods north of the park. Av Mirador del Sur is closed to traffic from 6am to 9am and 4pm to 8pm every day, when it fills with men and women jogging, rollerblading and bicycling up and down the broad avenue, and mobile juice bars and snack stands for anyone who's hungry.

Consisting of three very humid caverns with still, dark lagoons inside and connected by stalactite-filled passages, **Los Tres Ojos** (The Three Eyes; Parque Mirador del Este; admission US$1.75; ☺ 9am-5pm) is a mildly interesting site frequented by organized tours. The caves are limestone sinkholes, carved by water erosion over thousands of years. The entrance is a long stairway down a narrow tunnel in the rock; once at the bottom, cement paths lead you through the caves or you can visit them by boat for another US$0.35. Unfortunately, the tranquility of the setting is usually upset by vendors aggressively hawking their postcards and jewelry to tourists at the entrance.

WALKING TOUR

There's a lot to see in the Zona Colonial. This walking tour makes two large loops, which you can do all at once or spread over two days.

Start by visiting beautiful **Catedral Primada de América (1**; p71), the oldest working church in the New World. From there, head north on Arzobispo Meriño two blocks and turn left (west) on General Luperón.

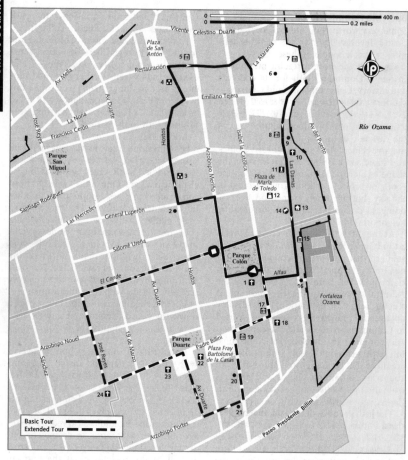

Start and Finish: Parque Colón

Basic tour: 3.6km
Duration: 2 hours

Extended tour: 6.4km
Duration: 4 hours

One block down, check out the **Casa de Italia** (**2**; p65), which often has interesting art exhibits. Turn north onto Hostos and in less than a block you'll see the **Ruinas del Hospital San Nicolás de Barí** (**3**; p75). Continuing north, Hostos climbs steeply past brightly colored clapboard houses to another co-

lonial ruin, the **Monasterio de San Francisco** (**4**; p75). A half-block further, turn right (east) on Restauración and walk a block to the **Museo Mundo de Ambar** (**5**; p70), on the corner.

The tour continues down Restauración to **Plaza de la Hispanidad** (**6**; p74), a large stone-paved plaza overlooking the Río Ozama, with the **Museo Alcázar de Colón** (**7**; p70) on the one side and the **Museo de las Casas Reales** (**8**; p69) and **Reloj del Sol** (**9**; p75) on the other. Plaza de la Hispanidad also has a number of pleasant outdoor restaurants for a snack or drink (What? Tired already?).

From there, walk down Calle Las Damas, where you'll pass the **Capilla de Nuestra Señora de los Remedios** (**10**; p71), the **Panteón Nacional**

(11; p75) and, if it's Sunday, a great **antiques flea market** (12; p95) at the Plaza de María de Toledo. Continuing south on Calle Las Damas, check out the lovely facades of the **Hostal Nicolás de Ovando** (13; p76) and the **Casa de Francia** (14; p76). If you have kids, stop in the **Museo Infantil Trampolín** (15; p82), located just after you cross El Conde. Next door to the museum is the entrance to the **Fortaleza Ozama** (16; p75).

Opposite the fort entrance is Alfau, a small pedestrian street that leads one block west to Isabel la Católica. At this point you're back where you started – that's the Cathedral in front of you – and this is where the basic tour ends. You can turn right and head back to Parque Colón.

To continue on the extended tour, turn south at the end of Alfau instead of north – within a block you'll see the **Larimar Museum** (17; p70) and a short distance further the simple **Iglesia de Santa Clara** (18; p74). Turn west on Padre Billini and walk a block to the **Museo de la Familia Dominica** (19; p70), with its famous Gothic window. Turn left (south) onto Arzobispo Meriño and you'll pass **Casa de Teatro** (20; p92), where you can check out an art exhibit or find out about upcoming performances.

Continue south to the corner of Arzobispo Portes, where you'll bump into the **Centro Cultural Español** (21; p65), which also has exhibits and a full calendar of events. Head west on Arzobispo Portes, one of the Zona Colonial's prettiest streets, with tidy colonial homes and plenty of shade trees. Turn right onto Av Duarte, which down here has cobble-stones and is for pedestrians only. Av Duarte opens into a plaza with two churches on either side – the spectacular **Convento de la Orden de los Predicadores** (22; p71) and the baroque **Capilla de la Tercera Orden Dominicana** (23; p74). Right in front is Parque Duarte, a pleasant and popular spot for locals and their families.

Turn left (west) onto Padre Billini and continue to José Reyes, where you'll see the **Iglesia de la Regina Angelorum** (24; p74), notable for its ornate facade and baroque-style altar. Go north on José Reyes to El Conde, the Zona Colonial's busy commercial walkway. Turn right and browse your way up to Parque Colón and the end of the tour. Relax over a beer or soda – you've earned it.

COURSES
Language
Santo Domingo makes a good place to study Spanish, not only because of the variety of schools but also because of the vibrant setting.

The **Instituto Intercultural del Caribe** (☎ 809-685-5826; www.edase.com; Aristides Fiallo Cabral 456, Zona Universitaria) was founded in 1994 and is the Spanish Department of Edase, a German-Dominican Language and Culture Institute. It offers Spanish courses of 20 and 30 hours per week in small classroom settings. There are more than a dozen price combinations, depending on the length and intensity of instruction and whether or not accommodations are included. Call for current course listings and prices. The institute also maintains a language school in Sosúa (p187).

Providing Spanish language instruction since 1982, **Entrena** (☎ 809-567-8990; entrena@verizon.net.do; Calle Virgilio Díaz Ordoñez 42, Ensanche Julieta) has a long list of former clients, ranging from Peace Corps volunteers to professional baseball players. Its base program is a four-week intensive Spanish and Dominican Culture course, which includes six hours of one-on-one instruction, competency-based language training and a homestay. Programs can also be coordinated on a per-hour basis allowing students to take as many or as few classes and hours as they wish.

Offering six levels of Spanish language instruction, the **Hispaniola Academy** (Map pp72-3; ☎ 809-688-9192; www.hispaniola.org; Hostos at Mercedes) is the only language school in the Zona Colonial. A week-long course – the shortest of the ones offered – consists of 20 lessons per week (ie four 50-minute classes per day) and your choice of accommodation. Prices begin at US$260 (with a family stay) and rise to US$580 (with hotel accommodations). Private classes available. Supplementary courses in cooking, dance and golf also offered.

SANTO DOMINGO FOR CHILDREN
Santo Domingo is not a bad place for children, but neither is it particularly kid-friendly. The children's museum in the Zona Colonial is truly remarkable and the aquarium and zoo are decent, but your options after that are just so-so. Perhaps more

difficult than the lack of age-appropriate sights is the lack of quiet parks and open green space – **Parque Duarte** (Av Padre Billini at Av Duarte) is a flagstone plaza with little passing traffic and really the only spot in the Zona Colonial where you can sit on a bench and let the kids romp about. Likewise, if you'd like to go out on the town, but the kids would rather jump on the hotel beds, high-end hotels often provide child care services.

If you're traveling with children, do not miss **Museo Infantil Trampolín** (Map pp72-3; ☎ 809-685-5551; www.trampolin.org.do in Spanish; Las Damas; adult/child US$3.50/1.75; ☟ 9am-6pm Tue-Fri, 10am-7pm Sat & Sun). Kids (and adults, if they like) are led through a high-tech, hands-on natural history, biology, science, ecology and social museum all wrapped up into one. The museum is divided into seven sections and includes rooms dedicated to the formation of Earth (complete with earthquake machines and volcano simulations), the human body (featuring skeletons, enormous eyes and brains, and even a body parts jungle gym, where children can slide down tongues and climb up noses), the national parks and ecosystems found on the island, and children's legal rights. Enthusiastic guides lead kids through the exhibits, keeping them captivated with explanations and interesting questions. Truly a place where learning is fun. Most tours in Spanish, but try asking for an English-speaking guide.

Showing its age, the **Acuario Nacional** (National Aquarium; ☎ 809-766-1709; Av España; admission US$1; ☟ 9:30am-5:30pm Tue-Sun) won't wow many adult travelers, but children are invariably delighted by the main attraction there – an enormous tank with a clear underwater walkway where you can watch sea turtles, stingray and huge fish pass on the sides and overhead. (With any luck you'll be there shortly after the plexiglass has been cleaned of algae; otherwise the view is somewhat obscured.) There's also a large shark tank and a pool where you can reach down and pet an endangered slider turtle, part of a breeding project. Many of the displays on shrimp, sea urchins and other marine creatures have small viewing windows built low to the ground so kids can really examine them. Your kids may also have fun playing in the yard with local school children who frequent the aquarium. Signs in Spanish only.

One of the largest in Latin America, the **Parque Zoológico Nacional** (Map pp66-7; ☎ 809-562-3149; Av los Reyes Católicos; admission US$1; ☟ 9am-6pm Tue-Sat) has a reasonably impressive collection of animals, from rhinos and chimps to flamingos and the endangered solenodon, an extremely rare, rat-like creature endemic to the island. Some of the enclosures are agreeable – the barless tiger compound for example – but others are disappointingly cramped. For a nominal fee you can cruise the large grounds by shuttle. The zoo is located in a somewhat seedy neighborhood in the northwest corner of the city, which may account for the dearth of visitors. It's also a bit hard to find; if you're driving, it's longer but much easier to take Av Argentina by the Botanical Garden up to Av los Reyes Católicos, which from there runs east for about 1.5km before crossing two bridges in a row. Look on your left for a steep downhill road with no sign *between* the two bridges leading to the zoo entrance – it's easy to miss. A taxi here from the Zona Colonial costs around US$5; be sure to arrange a return trip with the driver, as you won't find many cabs out there.

TOURS

Interesting and informative walking tours of the Zona Colonial are offered on a daily basis by a number of official guides. Tours cover the most important buildings in the zone and can be tailored to your specific interests. Walks typically last 2½ hours and cost between US$20 to US$30 depending on the language that the tour is given in (ie Spanish and English are less expensive). To find a guide, head to Parque Colón – you'll find a number of them sitting next to the Cathedral or hanging out under the trees. Guides are dressed in khakis and light blue dress shirts and have licenses with the official state tourism logo on it – ask to see it before you start your tour. Also be sure to agree upon a fee before setting out; some readers have reported being grossly overcharged at the end of their tours.

If you don't mind being grouped with a busload of tourists, an alternative is to hook up with one of the local agencies that provide city tours to guests of all-inclusive resorts. Popular agencies include **Prieto Tours** (☎ 809-685-0102; Av Francia 125), **Barceló Viajes** (☎ 809-685-6363; Av Máximo Gómez at Av 27 de Febrero) and **Omni Tours** (☎ 809-565-6591; Roberto Pastoriza 204).

FESTIVALS & EVENTS

For information on all the following events, contact the **Secretaría de Estado de Turismo** (State Tourism Office, p68). The office's website typically has the most up-to-date information on annual and upcoming events in Santo Domingo and around the country. Newspapers also carry reports and advertisements in the days and weeks leading up to most major festivals and celebrations.

Carnival (or *Carnaval,* in Spanish) is celebrated with great fervor throughout the country every Sunday in February, culminating in a huge blowout in Santo Domingo the last weekend of the month or first weekend of March. Av George Washington (the Malecón) is closed to cars and becomes an enormous party scene all day and night. The only vehicles allowed on the Malecón during this time are tractors pulling elaborate floats, and there are plenty of those, competing to be the year's best. Costumes, especially masks, are central to the celebration – groups that won prizes in their respective towns compete in Santo Domingo for top honors, though anyone can put on a mask and raise a ruckus. Costumes represent traditional and widely recognized Carnival characters; many of those found in celebrations around the country are also found in Santo Domingo. A few are unique to the south though, such as *Roba La Gallina* (literally Hen Thief), a man dressed like a woman with a gaudily painted face, his behind and breasts stuffed to exaggeration, wearing a wig and carrying an open umbrella.

The annual **Latin Music Festival** is held at the Olympic Stadium every June. This huge three-day event attracts the top names in Latin music – jazz, salsa, merengue and *bachata*. Salsa king Tito Rojas and merengue living legend Fernando Villalona are among the dozens of featured artists who regularly attend.

Santo Domingo's **Merengue Festival** is the largest in the country, a two-week celebration of the DR's favorite music held every year at the end of July and beginning of August. Most of the activity is on the Malecón, but there are related events across the city.

SLEEPING

Most of Santo Domingo's sights and restaurants are in and around the Zona Colonial, and that is where most independent travelers prefer to stay. There are some excellent mid- and upper-range options, some in attractive old colonial homes with high ceilings and thick stone walls. Budget travelers have surprisingly few options – there were no true hostels at the time of research (a real hole in this otherwise well-equipped city) and basic rooms with private bath and marginal charm start at around US$25 per night. If all the lower-priced rooms in the Zona Colonial are taken – there are few enough decent ones to make this a possibility – or if you just don't like what you see, consider staying in Gazcue (p85), a quiet residential area southwest of Parque Independencia. Prices there are about the same but you get better value. The drawback is you're a solid kilometer from the heart of the Zona Colonial. It's an easy enough walk, and *públicos* run east on Av Independencia, but it can still cramp your style. At night, consider taking a taxi. Of course, there are a number of high-rise hotels on the Malecón, which are best if you want to be near the nightclubs and casinos.

Zona Colonial
BUDGET

El Refugio del Pirata (Map pp72-3; ☎ 809-687-1572; www .refugiohotel.com; Arzobispo Meriño 356; r US$35; ⊠) Like most budget hotels in the Zona Colonial, this one has some good rooms and some awful ones, so definitely ask to see a few before plunking down your money. The Italian owner was refurbishing the hotel's 14 rooms one at a time when we passed through – with any luck, most will be done by the time you read this. *Habitaciónes remodeladas* (remodeled rooms) are small but have comfortable double beds, modern bathrooms and quaint stenciling on the walls; 2nd-floor units get more light, but you have to negotiate a narrow spiral staircase. Another good value is room 14, which is significantly larger than the rest and has a skylight to make up for the lack of windows – it can be a bit loud in the morning, though, as it's right over the reception area. The rest of the rooms really aren't worth the price. There is a tiny kitchen for guest use, but until it's remodeled and given regular cleaning, don't count on using it. All rooms have aircon, fan, cable TV and a small refrigerator. Call ahead if you will be arriving after 6pm, as the reception closes otherwise.

AUTHOR'S CHOICE

Hotel Doña Elvira (Map pp72-3; ☎ 809-221-7415; www.dona-elvira.com; Padre Billini 209; loft without/with aircon US$60/65, r without aircon US$80-90, with aircon US$90-100, suite without/with aircon US$100/110; P ☒ ☐ ☒) Located in a beautifully renovated colonial building, this small hotel offers 13 casually elegant rooms with exposed stone walls, Spanish tile floors and sumptuous linens. Rooms come in various sizes – from a small room with a loft to a spacious suite with an outdoor bathtub. A lush garden with a mosaic-tiled pool, a rooftop solarium and a comfortable reading room round out an already tranquil setting. Full breakfast for two is included in the rate. A gem of a hotel.

Bettye's Exclusive Guest House (Map pp72-3; ☎ 809-688-7649; bettyemarshall@hotmail.com; Isabel la Católica 103; dm per person US$22, r US$40) Opening onto Plaza de María de Toledo, this eclectic guesthouse mostly offers dormitory-style rooms filled to the brim with antique furnishings, chandeliers and modern art. Add to that sumptuous linens, a gleaming common kitchen and continental breakfast and you've got one-of-a-kind accommodations. Unfortunately, however, the dorms are reserved for groups of five but preferably 10. But all is not lost if you're traveling solo or in a pair; one private room – with similar decor – is offered. The toilet is in a *tiny* closet (if you're over 5'1", your legs may have a hard time fitting comfortably inside) and the door opens onto the street but it's a decent option if you can snag it. If it's low season, ask about staying in the dorms – the owner occasionally rents the whole place out to pairs. Reservations recommended.

Hotel Freeman (Map pp72-3; ☎ 809-689-3961; Isabel la Católica 155; s/d US$25/30; ☒) Just half a block from Parque Colón, this hotel gives you lots of bang for your buck. Once you get past the grim-looking front desk, you'll find six clean – though charmless – rooms with two queen-sized beds, private hot-water bath and cable TV. A breezy balcony at the top of the stairs provides a great lookout over the street.

Hotel Aida (Map pp72-3; ☎ 809-685-7692; fax 809-221-9393; Espaillat 254; r with fan/aircon US$27/32; ☒) Located near the El Conde promenade, this basic hotel offers windowless rooms that are showing wear but are acceptable for a night or two. Private hot-water bathrooms and 24-hour electricity are a plus.

MIDRANGE

Antiguo Hotel Europa (Map pp72-3; ☎ 809-285-0005; www.antiguohoteleuropa.com; Arzobispo Meriño at Emiliano Tejera; s/d/tw US$63/68/73; P ☒) Located just two short blocks from Plaza de la Hispani-

dad, this hotel offers 52 charming rooms all with Spanish tile floors, comfortable beds and modern amenities. About half of the rooms feature nice balconies – be sure to ask for one. Continental breakfast is included in the rate and is served in a classy rooftop restaurant with a spectacular view of the Zona Colonial.

El Beaterío Guest House (Map pp72-3; ☎ 809-687-8657; elbeaterio@netscape.net; Av Duarte 8; s/d US$50/60; s/d with aircon US$60/70; ☒) Originally a 16th-century nunnery, the Beaterío is now a small guesthouse offering 11 austere rooms. Each has wood-beamed ceilings, stone floors and 3m doors, and all are equipped with modern amenities. The setting is impressive but the rooms and bathrooms are a bit cramped for the price. The elegant reading room, however, makes a good place to relax. Breakfast is included in the rate.

Hotel Conde de Peñalba (Map pp72-3; ☎ 809-688-7121; www.condepenalba.com; El Conde at Arzobispo Meriño; s/d without windows US$60/70, s/d with windows US$65/75, tw US$80; ☒ ☐) Right on Parque Colón, this 20-room hotel has a stellar location. All rooms are comfortable with small bathrooms and cable TV. Many boast balconies overlooking the park, which is a major plus. The lack of an elevator may be inconvenient to some.

Hotel Saint Amad (Map pp72-3; ☎ 809-687-1447; Arzobispo Meriño 353; s/d US$50/55; ☒) This humble hotel offers small and sparsely decorated rooms in the center of the Zona Colonial. The accommodations need updating – the scruffy rugs should just be ripped out and the plastic flowers need to be tossed – but the modern amenities, quiet setting and key location keep it on the radar screen. Breakfast is included in the rate.

TOP END

Sofitel Nicolás de Ovando (Map pp72-3; ☎ 809-685-9955; www.sofitel.com; Las Damas near Plaza de María de Toledo; s US$220-336, d US$238-354; P ☒ ☐ ☒)

Located inside the historic Hostal de Ovando – the home of the first Governor of the Americas – this is among the city's finest hotels. Beautifully renovated into 107 luxurious rooms and suites, accommodations exude a simple elegance with high wood-beamed ceilings, original stone walls, and handcrafted iron-work furniture. In the common areas, guests will find a welcoming pool, a state-of-the-art fitness center, a comfortable library, and spectacular views of the Ozama River. An excellent buffet breakfast is included in the rate.

Hotel Palacio (Map pp72-3; ☎ 809-682-4730; www .hotel-palacio.com; Av Duarte 106; s US$80-90, d US$88-98; P ☒ ☐ ☒) This German-owned hotel occupies a huge 17th-century mansion (with some recent additions), featuring original stone walls, beautiful wood banisters, and several nooks and crannies outfitted with reading chairs. Thirty-four large rooms have thick beds, modern bathroom fixtures, cable TV, minibar, security box, and some even have motion-sensor lights and whirlpool baths. Some have small terraces opening onto leafy interior courtyards. There's a hot tub and small open-air exercise area on the roof. If you call for a reservation, the staff will turn on the aircon before you arrive, which clears the slight mustiness common in these old colonial structures. Discounts are available for stays of a week or more.

Hostal Nicolás Nader (Map pp72-3; ☎ 809-687-6674; General Luperón 151; d/tw US$80/90, tw with sofa bed US$110; ☒) All 10 rooms in this well-located colonial-style hotel are extremely spacious, with high ceilings and large shuttered windows. Beds are comfortable, some rooms have hefty armoires, and there is high-quality local artwork adorning the walls and common areas. Yet there is a somewhat cavernous feel to the place – the rooms are almost *too* big – exacerbated by the cold florescent lighting in many of the rooms. Also, the bathrooms are showing their age and could stand to be renovated. Not a bad option overall, but not the best one either.

Sofitel Francés (☎ 809-685-9331; www.accorhotels .com; Las Mercedes at Arzobispo Meriño; s/d US$150/170) Sister hotel to the Sofitel Nicolás de Ovando, rooms here follow the colonial mansion style, with high ceilings, stucco walls and thick beds with attractive wood headboards. Ask for rooms 207, 208 or 210,

which are more spacious and off the ground floor. The hotel's best feature may be its interior courtyard, where comfortable chairs and tables are set discretely about a sunny stone patio filled with tall potted plants. The **restaurant** (☒ breakfast, lunch & dinner; mains US$15-30) is quite good – try the goat marinated in red wine sauce or grilled dorado with potatoes and seafood reduction. Prices include a continental breakfast.

Gazcue
BUDGET
Hotel La Danae (Map p78; ☎ 809-238-5609; Calle Danae 18; r US$28-35; ☒) Of the three hotels on this street, this is probably the best value, offering 16 rooms all with aircon, fan, cable TV, mini-fridge and (best of all) a clean common kitchen for guest use. The cheaper rooms are in the original building, and some travelers prefer them for their high ceilings which lend a feeling of extra space. Of these, room 1 faces the front and gets more light than the rest, but also gets the most street noise (though it's generally a very quiet area). The more expensive rooms occupy the add-on in back – they don't have high ceilings, but the beds and bathrooms are more up-to-date and there's no street sound. All rooms have just one bed; the patio in front is nice for reading.

La Grand Mansión (Map p78; ☎ 809-682-2033; Calle Danae 26; r US$23, tw $28) This quiet hotel has the city's best rooms for under US$25, but you should look at a few before deciding as they vary considerably in size, light and decor. Some have freshly painted olive-green walls with high ceilings but no windows; others have two large banks of windows but somewhat ragged decor. The bathrooms in all are adequate but definitely aging. The most popular room is number 5, which is on the 2nd floor and has a small private terrace – the view is partially blocked by a snarl of power and telephone cables, but hey, it's all yours! The owners live on-site.

La Residencia (Map pp72-3; ☎ 809-412-7298; willianaresidencia@yahoo.com; Calle Danae 62; r with fan US$28, with aircon US$35, tw US$42; ☒) Good-sized, clean, comfortable rooms with fridges and large bathrooms explain the somewhat higher price tag here. There's also a common kitchen and a street-front terrace on each floor that are nice for relaxing. A potential drawback here is that the hotel, befitting its name, also rents rooms by the month – don't be surprised to find a number of older men whiling away the afternoon on the front porch when you arrive. The guests seemed harmless enough when we stopped in, but solo women may prefer the other hotels on this street.

MIDRANGE

Hostal Duque de Wellington (Map p78; ☎ 809-682-4525; www.hotelduque.com; Av Independencia 304; s US$48-68, d US$62-78; P ☒) A large hotel with a friendly, old-fashioned atmosphere, rooms here range from standard to suites, all with aircon, fan, telephone, cable TV and security box; suites are larger and the more expensive ones have balconies. The decor isn't exactly elegant but is definitely trying to be, with dark colors and interesting artwork in many rooms; 2nd-floor rooms have nice high ceilings. There is a restaurant and travel agency on-site, and other good eating options nearby. Av Independencia can be noisy, but an upside is that you can catch a cab or *público* to the Zona Colonial from right outside the hotel.

Hostal Alcaldeza (Map p78; ☎ 809-685-0825; Crucero Ahrens 2; r US$45-50) Though it doesn't look like much from the front, this family-run hotel offers small – make that cozy – well-appointed rooms that are good value. Of the 12 units, four have been remodeled, each with a small enclosed patio in addition to comfortable beds, spotless bathrooms, cable TV and minibar. There is no view – the hotel is all on one floor and boxed in by houses on either side – but the sliding-glass door to the patio affords the newer rooms natural light that the older ones lack.

Hotel El Señorial (Map p78; ☎ 809-687-4367; fax 809-687-0600; Pres Vicini Burgos btwn Avs Independencia & George Washington; s/d/tw US$51/56/63; ☒) The service here is ambivalent and the lobby and hallways could stand to be re-done, but the rooms themselves are decent-sized and hospital-room clean, and have crisp white linens, simple artwork on the walls, a mini-fridge, telephone and cable TV. Breakfast is included. The price feels high, but then again, that's the case all over Santo Domingo.

Studios

If you're staying for more than a week or so, or if you are traveling as a family or large group and don't like eating out all the time, the following hotels offer studios with plenty of space and in-room kitchens.

Apart-Hotel Plaza Colonial (Map p78; ☎ 809-687-9111; Julio Verne at Calle Pellerano; apt US$105-125; ☒ ☒ P) This huge hotel and apartment complex has a lot of seriously crappy rooms, which makes the two-bedroom/two-bath apartments all the more surprising. The spacious main room has a living area with sofas, TV and coffee table, a large dinner table and chairs and a full kitchen separated by a countertop. Down a hallway, both bedrooms have clean modern bathrooms – even bathtubs – and two queen beds in one and a queen and single in the other. Glass doors open onto to a terrace with a view of, well, mainly the parking lot, but it does allow for plenty of light and fresh air. The location may be a slight drawback for some – two blocks from Parque Independencia, it's closer to the Zona Colonial that it looks, but you do have to cross through the traffic and general hubbub around the park. There's an OK pool and so-so restaurant.

Hotel Residencia Venezia (Map p78; ☎ 809-682-5108; www.residence-venezia.com; Av Independencia 45; tw/ste US$60/67; ☒ P ☐) The lobby here is cool and sleek, with sofas, dim lighting and a café that looks more like a bistro. The long family rooms upstairs aren't nearly as chi-chi – kind of plain actually – but have two beds, a clean bathroom on one end, and a small, workable kitchen on the other. Suites are somewhat better-appointed, and some have a balcony looking onto the street. The hotel also rents standard single and double rooms if you have some spill-over, but they aren't great value.

Malecón

Santo Domingo's Malecón is closed to cars every Sunday, when it fills with locals, tourists, vendors and general revelry. All other days, the traffic is loud and fast, and the effect is decidedly less appealing. The high-rises aren't particularly unique, but staying there does put you an elevator-ride away from the main nightclubs and casinos. The Zona Colonial is somewhat distant, but easily reached by taxi or *público* on Av Independencia. All of the following hotels face the water – be sure to ask for an ocean-side room on an upper floor to get the best views. Not listed here is the Hilton, which was still under construction when we passed through, but will likely be Malecón's top hotel when completed.

TOP END

Hotel InterContinental (Map p78; ☎ 809-221-0000; www.intercontinental.com/santodomingo; Av George Washington 218; r US$190-210; ❄ ⚲ ✕ ℗ 🖳) With a beautiful lobby and hip bar-lounge area, the InterContinental oozes with cool class right from get go. Arguably the finest on the Malecón, rooms here are cozy and impeccably outfitted, and guests can make use of tennis courts, a fine swimming pool, spa services and even a karaoke bar. Like all the big hotels on the waterfront, the hotel also has a casino, popular both with tourists and the Dominican elite, especially on Fridays and Saturdays.

Meliá Santo Domingo Hotel (Map p78; ☎ 809-221-6666; www.solmelia.com; Av George Washington 365; s/d US$100/140; ❄ ⚲ ✕ ℗ 🖳) Another of the Malecón's top hotels, the Meliá has two recommended restaurants, an inviting lobby area and bar, and a great 2nd-floor swimming pool area. The rooms are comfortable and well-appointed, including in-room Internet access, though the decor is a tad dowdy. The rooms are priced, in part, according to how good the view is – all are supposed to have at least a partial ocean view, but you have to crane your neck in some rooms to see the water, especially those below the 5th floor. The hotel also has tennis courts, health spa, casino and popular dance club. Service is excellent.

Renaissance Jaragua Hotel (Map p78; ☎ 809-221-2222; www.renaissancehotels.com; Av George Washington 367; r US$130-150; ❄ ⚲ ✕ 🖳 ℗) You kind of have to mention the Jaragua here, if only because it's the best known of the high-rise hotels on the Malecón and still boasts the city's most popular nightclub, Jubilee (p91). The pool is appealing and the deluxe rooms and suites are quite nice, with sofa chairs and king-size beds, though somewhat dated decor. However the standard rooms are surprisingly bad – old furniture, crusty bathroom fixtures, saggy beds – and definitely not worth the price. The lobby area and restaurants could also use a facelift, and PDQ, before the hotel's vaunted reputation starts to suffer.

Airport

Quality Hotel Real Aeropuerto (☎ 809-549-2525; www.gruporeal.com; Autopista Las Américas Km 22.5; r US$87; ❄ ℗ ⚲ 🖳) Located just a five-minute drive from Aeropuerto Internac-ional Las Américas, rooms here are what you'd expect: comfortable, clean, and with modern amenities like aircon, cable TV and in-room telephone. A pool, gym and business center are added pluses. A good option if you have an early morning flight. A buffet breakfast is included in the rate. The hotel does not have courtesy shuttle; a cab there from the airport costs US$20.

EATING

Santo Domingo has a good selection of restaurants in various price ranges. The ones in the Zona Colonial are usually the most convenient, but there are some excellent options in Gazcue as well.

Overall, the quality of food is high – the DR is not known for the inventiveness or variety of its cuisine, but a strong tourist and business market and a number of expat restaurateurs make Santo Domingo a good place to go out for a nice meal. Seafood is always a reliable choice – waiters can usually tell you what came in fresh that day. For some truly local flavor, look for restaurants with outdoor tables or counter service, where conversation tends to be raucous, and the food inexpensive and filling. Whether it's for coffee during the day or tall Presidente beers at night, these are the eateries that Dominicans of all stripes especially enjoy.

Zona Colonial

BUDGET

La Cafetera Colonial (Map pp72-3; ☎ 809-682-7122; El Conde btwn Av Duarte & 19 de Marzo; mains US$2-5 ❄ breakfast, lunch & dinner) A classic Dominican greasy spoon, with a long bar and stools where you can order fried eggs and toast for US$1.50 and the espresso, served in tiny plastic cups to which aficionados add a heaping spoonful of sugar, could jolt you out of a coma. While a thoroughly male domain, the ambience is friendly and jocular and women travelers should feel entirely welcome.

Comedor el Puerto (Map pp72-3; ☎ 809-686-1669; Av Arzobispo Meriño at J Gabriel Garcia; mains US$2.50; ❄ lunch Mon-Fri) For classic Creole cooking in an entirely Dominican setting, head to this family-run joint. You'll have your choice of three types of meat dishes, two types of beans, a massive amount of rice and a small salad. Great for the food and even better for the experience.

Café de las Flores (Map pp72-3; ☎ 809-689-1898; El Conde btwn Sánchez & José Reyes; mains US$3-9; ❤ breakfast, lunch & dinner) With gaudy jungle scenes painted inside and several tables right on the walkway, you'd be forgiven for passing over this place as a tourist trap. Truth is, the food is quite good, the portions are large and the service, though occasionally brusque, is prompt and reliable. The *lambí a la criolla* (sliced conch in a tomato-based Creole sauce) is great over rice, while the *mofongo* (mashed plantains usually served with pork rinds but available here with shrimp) is served in a tall wooden cup. A 40oz Presidente beer, kept cool in a dried bamboo stalk, is perfect to share over dinner, and two or three can easily while the night away.

Paco Cafetería (Map pp72-3; El Conde at Palo Hincado; mains US$2-7; ❤ breakfast, lunch & dinner) This low-key, slightly unkempt eatery on a busy corner is often crowded with locals. Best for breakfast or lunch, where a plate of scrambled eggs and bowl of beans is less than US$3 and the *tortilla española* – here it's more like a potato-stuffed omelet – is served hot and tastes great all the same.

El Taquito (Map pp72-3; ☎ 809-687-1958; Emiliano Tejera 105; mains US$1.25-2.75; ❤ 9am-1am Mon-Thu, 9am-3am Fri & Sat, 5pm-1am Sun) This hole-in-the-wall is the place to go if you're in the mood for a burger, sandwich, or – as the name suggests – tacos (vegetarians will have to stick with chips here). Meals are made to order and are served up before you can reach for your wallet. Especially busy late night and on weekends, when locals use it as a pit stop between bars.

Baskin Robbins (Map pp72-3; El Conde near José Reyes; from US$2; ❤ 10am-10pm) A good spot if you just need to cool off, with good ice cream and outdoor tables cooled by huge paddle fans.

La Dulcería (Map pp72-3; ☎ 809-685-0785; Arzobispo Meriño at Emiliano Tejera; ❤ 7am-8:30pm Mon-Sat, 7am-1pm Sun) This is an excellent place to find traditional Dominican sweets like *alegrías* (sesame seed and molasses candy), *piñonates* (coconut bars) and *raspaduras de leche* (milk candy wrapped in royal palm bark). The rum is pretty good here too.

MIDRANGE

El Conde Restaurant (Map pp72-3; ☎ 809-688-7121; mains US$3-16; Hotel Conde de Peñalba, El Conde at Arzobispo Meriño; ❤ breakfast, lunch & dinner) This long-time restaurant serves a good variety

of dishes (think Cuban sandwiches, chow mein and filet mignon) at decent prices. Food is served quickly by a team of bow tie–clad waiters at tables that are either set up indoors in a fan-cooled room or outdoors on breezy Parque Colón. A great spot for people watching, El Conde is popular with travelers and locals alike.

La Crêperie (Map pp72-3; ☎ 809-221-4734; La Atarazana 11; mains US$4-12; ❤ 10:30am-1:30am Mon-Sat, 2pm-midnight Sun, closed Tue) One of the many eateries on Plaza de la Hispanidad, this is *the* place to go for crepes. Try a main like La Classique (ham and cheese; US$4) or La Caribe (conch, shrimp and crab prepared in cream of spinach; US$12) and – if you have room – follow it up with La Speciale (Nutella and almonds; US$6). If you're in the mood for something a little lighter, excellent salads are also served; La Montagnarde, with fresh lettuce, walnuts, prosciutto, blue cheese, tomato, croutons and a tangy vinaigrette (US$7), is a meal in itself. Pleasant outdoor seating provides a great view of the action on the Atarazana strip.

Nancy's Snack Bar (Map pp72-3; ☎ 809-685-1933; Plaza la Hispanidad; mains US$5-15; ❤ 8am-midnight) The most down-to-earth of the restaurants on this plaza, Nancy's has good grilled sandwiches – chicken, ham, *pierna* (leg of pork) with all the fixings – and comfortable seating both indoors and out. Look for specials on a chalkboard posted by the door: stewed chicken, fillet of fish, and grilled meats come with rice and beans at reasonable prices.

Restaurant & Bar Palmito Gourmet (Map pp72-3; ☎ 809-221-5777; Arzobispo Portes 401, at Santomé; mains US$9-14; ❤ lunch & dinner, closed Tue) A relaxed but classy restaurant, the Palmito Gourmet offers top-notch Creole food in an Old World setting. Traditional dishes such as *guinea al vino tinto* (hen in red-wine sauce) and *mondongo en salsa Criolla* (crushed plantains in a Creole sauce) are painstakingly prepared and presented with modern flair. Live music on weekend evenings (8:30pm to 11pm Friday and Saturday) makes this place a particularly enjoyable place for dinner.

Pasatiempo (Map pp72-3; ☎ 809-689-4823; Isabel la Católica 206; mains US$10-15; ❤ breakfast, lunch & dinner Mon-Sat) This dimly lit but pleasant restaurant offers tasty Italian dishes – the portions are on the small side but the meals are reliable.

AUTHOR'S CHOICE

Mesón D'Bari (Map pp72-3; ☎ 809-687-4091; Hostos at Salomé Ureña; mains US$6-12; ☺ lunch & dinner) Occupying a beautifully restored colonial home on a quiet corner in the Zona Colonial, the Mesón D'Bari manages to exude cool confidence and a warm welcome at the same time. A long-varnished wood bar with stools stretches most of the length of one wall, while smartly set tables occupy the rest of the dining area. On the walls hang excellent artwork, most by local artists and most for sale. (In fact some magazines also list the restaurant as an art gallery.) The *cangrejos guisados* (grilled crab) is the specialty, though the guinea hen in wine sauce (a highland favorite) is excellent, as are the steak and seafood dishes. Popular for the bar as much as the food service, Mesón D'Bari is usually quiet mid-week but can get crowded on weekends with upper-crust *capitalinos*. There's live music (jazz, Latin, some rock) on many weekend nights, played from a small stage in the back.

Restaurant Café Français (Map pp72-3; ☎ 809-687-4063; El Conde 60; mains US$8-14; ☺ 11am-2am) Just off Parque Colón, this outdoor restaurant offers good Dominican and French food. What distinguishes it from the pack – other than its stellar location – is that it offers *prix fixe* meals at killer prices: for US$10, diners receive a freshly made salad, choice of a fish, meat or chicken main with a side of rice and veggies, and seasonal fruit for dessert. Good value in a pricey part of town.

TOP END

Coco's Restaurant (Map pp72-3; ☎ 809-687-9624; Padre Billini 53; mains US$10-30; ☺ lunch & dinner, closed Mon) In this eclectic, chic restaurant, the British chef and co-owner serves up a creative menu that changes on a weekly basis. Meals are based on French and Thai foods but you can expect such taste treats as yucca pancakes with sour cream and caviar (US$8.50), sweet pear stuffed with blue cheese and walnuts (US$10), and beef and coconut curry with popadom, rice and chutney (US$16). As a nod to the motherland, roast beef with Yorkshire pudding is offered on Sunday (US$17.50).

Gazcue

These restaurants are convenient if you are staying in Gazcue, and are worth a special trip even if you aren't.

BUDGET

Ananda (Map p78; ☎ 809-682-7153; Casimiro de Moya 7; mains US$3-10; ☺ lunch & dinner Mon-Sat, lunch Sun) Run by the 'International Society of Divine Realization' and doubling as a yoga center, there is usually some enlightening reading material to accompany this restaurant's excellent and varied vegetarian food. The service and dining area are cafeteria-style, and dishes are mostly Dominican in flavor and ingredients – brown rice, roast beans, bananas and eggplant figure prominently. There are a few Indian options, but not as many as you might expect given the group's South Asian bent. Still, most find this a welcome and healthy change to typical Dominican eateries.

Hermanos Villar (Map p78; ☎ 809-682-1433; Av Independencia at Pasteur; mains US$2-9; ☺ breakfast, lunch & dinner) A big, busy, popular diner with cafeteria-style service in front and a bar and tables in back, the best reason to come here is for the sandwiches served on fresh baguettes, grilled hot and pressed flat, as is the Dominican custom. There are several dozen to choose from, with various combinations of ham, beef, chicken, turkey or *pierna*, several types of cheese, and lettuce, mayo, ketchup and other toppings. There are a few vegetarian options, and a number of Super and Extra Large sandwiches that can feed four people or more.

Groceries

La Cadena (Map p78; Yolanda Guzman btwn Av Independencia & Casimiro de Moya; ☺ 7:30am-10pm Mon-Sat, 9-2:30pm Sun) Fairly large supermarket with produce, dry goods, canned food, bottled water, a refrigerated section etc.

MIDRANGE

La Bodeguita de la Habana Vieja (Map p78; ☎ 809-476-7626; Av Independencia 302; mains US$7-12; ☺ noon-midnight Tue-Sun) There's an incarnation of this famous Cuban café/diner in dozens of cities around the Caribbean and Latin America. While many are hip bohemian spots where diners write their names and messages of proletarian revolution on the walls, this one is a bit more upscale, with mustard walls framed by heavy wooden beams, clothed tables and real wine glasses. Note that while you may not feel comfortable in shorts and a tank top here, the ambience is still casual and unassuming. Though the menu has a little of everything, Cuban dishes are the specialty here – for an appetizer, try *tamales Santiagueros*, a variation of the Mexican staple from Santiago de Cuba, and for a main the *ropa vieja* (literally 'old clothes'; shredded beef served in a tomato-based salsa) is a house favorite. There's live music – mostly mariachi, strangely enough – every night starting at 9pm.

L'Osteria de Charly y Christian (Map p78; ☎ 809-333-6701; Av George Washington 47; mains US$6-12; ☽ noon-2am) This small restaurant is popular with tourists, expats and Dominican professionals alike, specializing in homemade tagliatelle, penne and other pastas but serving a variety of quality Italian, French and other international dishes in a casual, lively setting. Right on the Malecón next to Hotel Napolitano, the dining area looks over the busy avenue to the ocean beyond. A full bar serves up fruit daiquiris and other mixed drinks and cocktails.

TOP END

Restaurant Vesuvio (Map p78; ☎ 809-221-1954; Av George Washington 521; mains US$12-17) One of the most highly regarded Italian restaurants in the capital, specializing in super-fresh seafood, quality beef and veal, and homemade pastas. A wheeled cart displays an impressive selection of cold and hot antipasti. For an appetizer try the kingfish carpaccio, then move onto the tricolor tallarin with a seafood sauce or the risotto prepared with a porcini-like mushroom found only in the Dominican Republic. The service is superb and the ambience decidedly upscale – you won't feel comfortable in shorts or sandals.

El Mesón de la Cava (Map pp66-7; ☎ 809-533-2818; Av Mirador del Sur; mains US$10-20; ☽ noon-1am) Built in a cave with craggy limestone walls and huge stalactites hanging from the ceiling, this is definitely one of the more unique restaurants you may ever eat at. It's actually two adjoining caverns – an elegant bar graces the first one and formally-set tables, attended by tuxedoed waiters, fill the

other. With a setting like this, the restaurant gets away with serving only average food – among the menu items are grilled salmon filet in a creamed sauce of charbroiled red bell peppers, veal cutlets in brandy and creamed porcini mushroom sauce, and fresh red snapper fillet in a medium-spicy tomato sauce served over linguini.

DRINKING

Santo Domingo has a lively bar and club scene, much of it located conveniently in the Zona Colonial.

Encuentro Artesanal (Map pp72-3; ☎ 809-687-1135; Arzobispo Meriño 407; ☽ 10am-8pm Mon-Sat) A great place to kick back and write a few postcards is this hipster juice bar in the back of a good handicrafts boutique (see p95). Set in a cozy and colorful room with a huge skylight, the drinks here will purportedly relieve such ailments as anxiety, arthritis, indigestion and fatigue. They'll even just quench your thirst. Coffee drinks are also served.

Bobo's (Map pp72-3; ☎ 809-689-1183; Calle Hostos 157; ☽ 11am-3pm & 6pm-2am Mon-Sat) An urban chic lounge with an Asian flair, this is the place to head if you want to dress up, drink a martini and immerse yourself in Dominican yuppyhood. Asian fusion dishes (US$10 to US$15) are served in a small dining area but the real reason to come here is the bar scene.

K-ramba Bar (Map pp72-3; ☎ 809-688-3587; Isabel la Católica 1; ☽ 10am-3am Mon-Sat) Near the southern end of the Zona Colonial, this Austrian-owned bar is a small place with indoor and outdoor tables. Drinks are served hard and fast and rock and roll is the music of choice. Popular with foreigners, this is a great place to meet expats and fellow travelers.

Tu Coche Bar (Map pp72-3; ☎ 809-682-0563; Arzobispo Nouel 55; ☽ 8am-midnight) A small, laid-back place with exposed brick walls and Spanish tile floors. Great for throwing back a couple of beers and playing cards. Live music on weekends starting at 9pm.

La Parada Cerveza (Map p78; Av George Washington at Sánchez; ☽ 8am-midnight) Advertising itself as a nightclub, restaurant, beauty salon and car wash, this open-air joint is mostly a place to drink beer and order plates of bar food as the night wears on. Right on the busy Malecón, the solution to the noise problem here is to play very loud music.

Somehow it all works though, and the bar has been, and remains, a very popular and appealing place.

ENTERTAINMENT

Santo Domingo has the country's best entertainment scene, from glitzy hotel nightclubs and casinos to small bars and dance spots. And lest you scoff, hotel nightclubs are hugely popular, especially among Santo Domingo's rich, young and restless. Merengue and *bachata* are omnipresent, but house, techno and American and Latin rock are popular as well. A number of clubs in town cater to gays and lesbians, or at least offer a welcoming mixed atmosphere. *Ocio* and *Aquí* magazines both have listings of bars and restaurants of all sorts – the former is definitely cooler, but both are useful. Look for them at the tourist office or shops in the Zona Colonial. Newspapers are another good place to find out about upcoming concerts and shows, and if your Spanish is good, radio stations hype the Capital's big events.

Nightclubs

The hotels on the Malecón have Santo Domingo's largest and most popular night clubs. The clubs attract the capital's wealthiest and hippest, and they dress up when they go dancing. Short-sleeve shirts, tennis shoes and jeans are not allowed. Admission is up to US$5 when there's a DJ (most nights) and US$10 when there's a band.

Jubilee (Map p78; Av George Washington 367; ☯ 9pm-4am Tue-Sat) This is Santo Domingo's swankiest and sweatiest nightclub, where the young and wealthy go to see and be seen – and to dance until dawn. The nightclub boasts the best light and sound shows in the city and the service is distinctly classy, especially for a disco. Drinks can run up a pretty steep bill, and raggedy clothes are definitely frowned upon. Bring some cash and your best threads and it's almost impossible not to have a great time.

El Napolitano (Map p78; ☎ 809-687-1131; www .hotelnapolitano.net; Av George Washington 101; admission US$3.50; ☯ 9pm-4am Thu-Sun) Much smaller than the Jubilee, the disco at this three-star hotel isn't much to look at – it's reminiscent of a rec room, in fact – but still gets packed with partiers every weekend. And located at the very top of the Malecón, it's the closest hotel nightclub to the Zona Colonial.

(Though walkable, you may still want to take a cab back to be safe.) The crowd is slightly less fabulous here than at the Jubilee – and the prices more accessible – but everyone still comes dressed to kill.

Guácara Taína (Map pp66-7; ☎ 809-533-0671; Av Mirador del Sur 655; admission US$9; ☯ 9pm-3am Thu-Sun) By far the most unique place to hear live merengue or salsa is in this giant club, located entirely inside a bat cave. It's so big that it can hold more than 2000 people, and in times past it has. Now it's primarily a tourist haunt – a stop of the cruise-ship crowd. The club is difficult to find, but every taxi driver in the city knows where it is. Admission price includes one drink.

Live Music

If these places fail to get your feet in the mood, have a look at our Drinking section (opposite) for some more places to exercise your ears.

Murano (Map pp72-3; ☎ 809-333-7033; Las Mercedes 155; admission free; ☯ 6pm-2am Mon-Sat) Located in a renovated colonial building, this chi-chi place caters to Santo Domingo's upper crust. An open-air mezzanine doubles as a dance floor and tables below are often peppered with young couples taking a merengue break. A long indoor lounge with overstuffed couches and dim lighting makes this a good place to socialize.

Atarazana 9 (Map pp72-3; ☎ 809-688-0969; Atarazana 9; admission free, Thu open bar US$7; ☯ 8pm-3am) Just off Plaza la Hispanidad, this bar and nightclub is in a safe and convenient location if you're staying in the Zona Colonial, and near a couple of other spots if you want to do some club hopping. Most of the action here takes place in the long front room, with a bar on one end, a stage on the other, and windows facing the street.

Nowhere (Map pp72-3; ☎ 809-877-6258; Calle Hostos 205; admission free; ☯ 9pm-4am Wed-Sat), which has a ladies' night on Thursdays, and **XXO** (Map pp72-3; ☎ 809-685-8103; Emiliano Tejera at Calle Hostos; admission free; ☯ 10pm-4am Wed-Sat), in front of the Monasterio de San Francisco ruins, offer music ranging from African drumming to French rock to Dominican dance music.

Cinemas

Palacio del Cine (Map pp66-7; ☎ 809-567-2960; tickets Mon-Thu US$2, Fri-Sun US$2.50) and **Broadway Cinemas** (Map pp66-7; ☎ 809-562-7171; Plaza Central

Mall; tickets Mon-Thu US$2, Fri-Sun US$2.50) both play recent Hollywood movies. These two cinemas are a couple of blocks apart on Av 27 de Febrero, between Abraham Lincoln and Winston Churchill.

Centro Cultural Español (Spanish Cultural Center; Map pp72-3; ☎ 809-686-8212; www.ccesd.org in Spanish; Av Arzobispo Meriño at Arzobispo Portes; admission free; 🕑 10am-9pm Mon-Sat) The center's periodic 'Cine en el Centro' series showcases alternative films, mostly by Spanish and Dominican filmmakers. The theatre is actually a gallery with a big white wall where DVDs are projected – unfortunately the acoustics aren't the best, so even good Spanish speakers may have trouble understanding some dialogue. Stop by the center for a current schedule.

Theater

Teatro Nacional (National Theater; Map p78; ☎ 809-682-7255; Plaza de la Cultura; tickets US$4-15) This 1600-seat theater hosts opera, ballet and symphonic performances. Tickets can be purchased in advance at the box office from 9:30am to 12:30pm and 3:30pm to 6:30pm every day. For show dates and times, call or check the weekend editions of local newspapers.

Gay & Lesbian Venues

Unfortunately, Santo Domingo – and the Dominican Republic in general – is home to few gay and lesbian businesses. Those that manage to open their doors often close or change names. At the time of research, the following were particularly popular:

Aire Club (Map pp72-3; ☎ 809-689-4163; Las Mercedes 313; club admission US$5.25 Fri & Sat, free Sun; 🕑 bar 6pm-2am Tue-Sun, club midnight-6am Fri-Sun) Considered the hottest club on the gay scene, Aire is a must for travelers looking to party. Located in a beautifully renovated colonial house with a lush courtyard, people come here to see and be seen. The place gets going around 11pm and stays full until closing. Top forty music rules the dance floor and drag shows are regularly featured. Lesbians and straights are very welcome.

O'Hara's Place (Map p78; ☎ 809-682-8408; Danae 3; admission free; 🕑 6:30pm-midnight) In Gazcue, this cool, cozy bar has a pool table and just a few tables inside, and a welcoming patio facing the street. Good music and a mellow atmosphere prevail. The manager's name is Scarlet, which may just be a coincidence.

Red Zone (Map pp72-3; ☎ 809-333-7002; Arzobispo Nouel 58; admission US$3.50-7; 🕑 closed Mon) A new kid on the block, this hopping place is known for its theme nights: Sugar (Tuesday), Cuban (Wednesday) and Tropical Fruits (Friday). On weekends, shows and competitions take the energy up a notch; among the most popular are the weekly transvestite shows (Friday and Saturday) and wet T-shirt and boxer competitions (Sunday).

Casinos

There are casinos at most of the large hotels on the Malecón, including the Inter-Continental (p87), **Hotel Santo Domingo** (Map pp66-7; ☎ 809-221-1511; Av Independencia at Av Abraham Lincoln) and **El Napolitano** (Map p78; ☎ 809-687-1131; Av George Washington 101). They generally open at 4pm and close at 4am. Bets may be placed in Dominican pesos or US dollars. Las Vegas odds and rules generally apply, though there are some slight variations; it doesn't hurt to ask the dealer what differences he or she is aware of before you start laying down money. All of the dealers at these casinos speak Spanish and English.

Sports
BASEBALL

Béisbol isn't just big in the Dominican Republic, it's huge. Dominican fans follow major league baseball in the US from April to October and then the 48-game Dominican winter league from mid-November until early February. Since the seasons don't overlap, many major league players – Dominicans and non-Dominicans alike – play for teams in the DR in winter, making games here as competitive as anywhere. If you are in the Dominican Republic during baseball season, definitely make time to go to a game or two.

Estadio Quisqueya (Map pp66-7; ☎ 809-540-5772; Av Tiradentes at San Cristóbal; tickets US$1.50-14; 🕑 game times 5pm Sun, 8pm Tue, Wed, Fri & Sat) is the home field of two of the DR's six professional teams, the Licey and Escojido, both of Santo Domingo. You can get tickets to most games by just showing up a little before game time; games between rivals Licey and Escojido or Licey and the Águilas sell out more quickly.

There is also a Liga del Verano (Summer League) if you're in the DR outside of regular season. Various major league franchises – the

San Francisco Giants, the Toronto Blue Jays, Arizona Diamondbacks, NY Yankees, to name a few – maintain farm teams in the DR, and summer league play is a semiformal tournament between these teams. Games are held at smaller stadiums around town.

COCKFIGHTING

While baseball has been the great Dominican national pastime for more than four decades, cockfighting is the traditional Dominican spectator sport. The **Coliseo Gallístico Alberto Bonetti Burgos** (Map pp66-7; ☎ 809-565-4038; Av Luperón across from Aeropuerto de Herrera; admission US$7-17.50; ☒ matches 6.30pm Wed & Fri, 3pm Sat) is the country's most prestigious *gallera* (cockfighting ring), its largest events drawing rooster handlers from as far away as Colombia, Brazil, Panama and Peru. Matches are held Wednesday and Friday at 6:30pm and Saturdays at 3pm. December to April is the busiest season (the roosters' plumage is fullest then) and a match could have 30 or 40 fights and last into the wee hours. Handler entry fees are higher on Saturdays, so the roosters tend be better and the stakes higher. Betting on cockfights is an intense and complex art – experts bet with dozens of people at high speed using only hand signals – but a good place to start is simply betting the guy next to you

which rooster will win. Opposing cocks are designated blue or white – colored tape is used to indicate which is which. There is always a favorite, so bets involve odds that can change even as the fight is in progress. Above all though, there is a powerful honor system that allows huge amounts of money to change hands peacefully with no oversight whatsoever. Those who renege on bets can be barred for life from the ring. Finally, it should be said that cockfighting is not for everyone. Fights are to the death – some are quick, others are torturous bloody affairs that can last up to 15 minutes (the official limit before a fight is called off).

HORSE RACING

Hippódromo V Centenario (☎ 809-687-6060; Autopista de las Américas Km 14.5; admission free; ☒ 3pm Tue, Thu & Sat) Located halfway between downtown Santo Domingo and the Las Américas international airport, the Centenario is the only horse track around.

SHOPPING

Santo Domingo has a good variety of shopping alternatives; you can choose among high-end boutiques, galleries, flea markets and kitschy gift shops. The easiest – and best – neighborhood to shop in is the Zona Colonial. Here you'll find row upon row of shops

IN THE STANDS

Steaming barbecue chicken, free-flowing rum, marimba breaks and bets shouted out at breakneck speed; watching a baseball game in Santo Domingo's Quisqueya Stadium is more than just a day at the park, it's an event reminiscent of a raging party, an off-track betting office and the World Series combined. It is one of the best places in the world to watch a baseball game.

As soon as you enter the 16,000-seat stadium, the experience begins. Vendors press through packed stands selling snacks and beer to eager fans. When a customer orders a drink, the vendor takes a bottle of beer and smashes a chunk of ice into a plastic cup. With a flip of the wrist, another bottle is poured into the cup and before you can say thank you, the vendor is moving on having started your bar tab for the game. He'll return periodically to make sure your cup is full and to give you the latest odds offered by bookies who cruise 'Wall Street' – the uppermost tier of the grandstand.

The bookies are hard to miss; they stand throughout the game, yelling out bets and having bets yelled to them. They'll accept wagers on almost anything – the next inning's score, the following pitch, the direction of the next hit – and they do it in a frenzy, shouting at the top of their lungs, each bookie trying to be heard over the others.

But whether they're betting or not, the most important people in the stands are the fans. Dominicans take baseball very seriously; they discuss innings effusively and know players' stats. They jump up excitedly and embrace the closest stranger when their team makes a good play; they also slump down in their seats when an error is made. And although opposing fans often sling insults at each other, fights rarely break out at Quisqueya. Excitement and fun rule the day.

offering locally made products at decent prices. The best of the lot are listed here.

Amber & Larimar

Considered national treasures, amber and larimar are sold widely throughout Santo Domingo. Typically these beauties are presented as jewelry but occasionally you'll find figurines, rosaries and other small objects. If you're considering buying something in amber or larimar (or both!), shop around – quality and price vary greatly. And don't worry about finding just the right piece, it's tough to find a shop in this town that doesn't sell a little of both. For a sure thing, try one of the following shops:

Swiss Mine (Map pp72-3; ☎ 809-221-1897; El Conde 101; ☺ 9am-6pm Mon-Fri, 10am-4pm Sat) On Parque Colón, this shop makes it hard to leave without buying a piece of jewelry. Not only does this boutique sell some of the finest quality amber and larimar around, but the design work is unsurpassed. English, French, Italian and German are spoken.

Ambar Maldo Gift Shop (Map pp72-3; ☎ 809-688-0639; La Atarazana; ☺ 10am-5pm Mon-Sat) One of the oldest stores in the Zona Colonial, this dusty shop has an eclectic selection of amber and larimar jewelry; some items are pretty junky while others are beautiful. It makes a great stop if you like to hunt for unique pieces. Prepare to bargain hard at this shop – prices have been marked up in anticipation of the ritual.

Flor Ambar Gift Shop (Map pp72-3; ☎ 809-687-3793; Las Damas 44; ☺ 9am-6pm) Among an unfortunate display of replica cave art and key chains, Flor Ambar offers a nice selection of

---

LARIMAR

Discovered in 1974 by Miguel Méndez and a Peace Corp volunteer, Norman Rilling, larimar is a blue pectolite the color of a summer sky. The two men discovered chunks of it while walking the beaches of Barahona and followed its traces up the Baharuco River before finding the mother lode deep in the southwestern mountains. It is the only place in the world that this mineral has been found. The name comes from a fusion of Méndez' daughter's name – Larisa – and the place it was first seen – *el mar* (the sea).

---

amber and larimar jewelry. Take your time at the display cases – this shop doesn't use the sales pitch and pressure that other shops in town are known for.

Art

Walking around Santo Domingo (and just about any city in the DR), you'll see plenty of Haitian works or 'primitive art,' characterized by simple, colorful depictions of rural life and landscapes. It is typically painted on large canvasses and sold fairly cheaply on the sidewalk or in small storefronts. Most of what you see on the street is pretty amateur, but you may find a few good pieces if you're up for searching; for top-notch Haitian art, head to Las Terrenas, which has one of the best Haitian art galleries in the country (p165). Santo Domingo's more formal galleries carry mostly Dominican art, ranging from portraits to modern sculptures. Quality varies, of course, but much of the artwork is quite respectable.

For a plethora of information on Dominican art and artists, get your hands on a copy of the *Enciclopedia de las Artes Plásticas Dominicanas* (Encyclopedia of Dominican Visual Arts) by Cándido Gerón. This book, contains 200 pages in Spanish followed by a direct translation into English, and is the bible of Dominican art. The book is currently out of print but may be found in the used bookstores of the Zona Colonial.

Bettye's Galería (Map pp72-3; ☎ 809-688-7649; Plaza de María de Toledo; Isabel la Católica 163; ☺ 9am-6pm, closed Tue) Owned by Bettye Marshall, a Tennessee-born transplant who has lived in the DR since the 1970s, this gallery is a good place to begin (and even end) the search for a unique work of art. If you like antiques, a fine selection of jewelry and furnishings can be found here as well.

Atelier Gallery (Map pp72-3; ☎ 809-688-7038; Arzobispo Portes 120; ☺ 10am-8pm Mon-Sat) Art displayed in this small gallery is of the sort you would expect to see in a fine modern art museum; the traditional work – paintings, sculpture, pottery – is top tier and experimental pieces are the norm. Stop in and take a look – you can't help but be impressed.

Swiss Mine (Map pp72-3; ☎ 809-221-1897; El Conde 101; ☺ 9am-6pm Mon-Fri, 10am-4pm Sat) Originally dealing only in high-end jewelry, the Swiss Mine now also has a spectacular selection of artwork by rising Dominican stars.

Galería de Arte María del Carmen (Map pp72-3; ☎ 809-682-7609; Arzobispo Meriño 207; ⊙ 9am-7pm Mon-Sat, 10am-1pm Sun) In business for over two decades, this place has been selling art long enough to attract a wide range of talented Dominican painters. Stop in for a look at some of their creations; the quality of the work may just tempt you to buy.

De Soto Galería (Map pp72-3; ☎ 809-689-6109; Hostos 215; ⊙ 9am-5:30pm Mon-Fri, 9am-noon Sat) This is a small gallery specializing in Dominican and Haitian painters. A rambling array of antiques is also for sale; you'll have to walk around and over the pieces to admire the fine collection of artwork on the walls.

Outside of the Zona Colonial are dozens of other galleries that feature Haitian and Dominican art. **Galería de Arte El Greco** (Map pp66-7; ☎ 809-562-5921; Av Tiradentes 16; ⊙ 8am-noon, 2-6pm Mon-Fri) and **Galería de Arte El Pincel** (Map pp66-7; ☎ 809-544-4295; Av Gustavo Mejía Ricart 24; ⊙ 8am-noon, 2-6pm Mon-Fri) are good options.

Cigars

Dominican cigars are considered to be among the finest in the world; some would argue they are the best. To decide for yourself, stop into one of the many cigar shops around Santo Domingo – you'll see several just strolling down Calle El Conde. Typically, prices vary from US$2 to US$6 per cigar and boxes can run as high as US$110.

If you want to see *tabacos* being rolled, drop by the **Boutique del Fumador** (Map pp72-3; ☎ 809-685-6425; El Conde 109; ⊙ 9am-7pm Mon-Sat, 10am-3:30pm Sun) or the **Museo del Tabaco** (Map pp72-3; ☎ 809-689-7665; El Conde 101; ⊙ 9:30am-8pm); both are located on Parque Colón and are owned by the same tobacco company – Monte Cristi de Tabacos. At either shop you can watch as one or two workers roll cigars in the shop window – a sampling of the 45 workers who roll away the day on the 2nd floor of the Boutique del Fumador. If you're lucky, the shopkeeper there will let you see the cedar aging room, where at any given time up to 400,000 cigars are maturing before they can be smoked. Montecristo, Cohiba and Caoba brand cigars are sold at both shops.

Handicrafts

Encuentro Artesanal (Map pp72-3; ☎ 809-687-1135; Arzobispo Meriño 407; ⊙ 10am-8pm Mon-Sat). Hands down, the best all-around selection of high-end Dominican handicrafts can be found at Encuentro Artesanal. At this urban chic shop, you'll find beautiful woodwork, paintings, kitchenware, hip clothing and unique jewelry. And if you work up a sweat shopping, the juice bar in back (p90) has a tasty variety of drinks and finger foods.

Artesanía Elisa (Map pp72-3; ☎ 809-682-9653; Arzobispo Nouel 54; ⊙ 9am-6pm Mon-Sat) Specializing in Dominican faceless dolls, this spacious shop sells the highest quality figurines in town. Dolls are handcrafted in-house and are made of porcelain; all are also dressed in late 18th–century garb. Prices vary according to the size and detail of each and run from US$10 to US$550.

Felipe & Co (Map pp72-3; ☎ 809-689-5812; El Conde 105; ⊙ 9am-8pm Mon-Sat, 10am-6pm Sun) On Parque Colón, this shop offers a wide range of Dominican handicrafts. You'll find colorful ceramics and handbags as well as decent Taíno cave art reproductions.

Markets

Mercado Modelo (Map pp72-3; Av Mella btwn Tomás de la Concha & Del Monte y Tejada; ⊙ 9am-5pm) Located in an aging two-story building just north of the Zona Colonial, this lively trading center offers some great buys if you are accomplished in the art of bargaining. Here you'll find a carnival of woodcarvings, Haitian paintings, amber jewelry, musical instruments, love potions and wicker art. You'll also find that the nicer you dress, the more expensive items become. Leave your Rolex at the hotel, wear a T-shirt and flip-flops, and come prepared to offer at least one third less than the asking price. Be sure to leave the neighborhood before dark; although it is bustling during the day, the area becomes somewhat sketchy after sunset.

Pulga de Antigüedades (Map pp72-3; Plaza de María de Toledo, Calle General Luperón btwn Isabel la Católica & Las Damas; ⊙ 9am-4pm Sun) If you like antiques or just poking around flea markets, head to this small open-air market held every Sunday. Here you'll find everything from platform shoes to antique jewelry. And remember to bargain – it's expected.

GETTING THERE & AWAY
Air

Santo Domingo has two airports: the main one, **Aeropuerto Internacional Las Américas** (☎ 809-549-0328, 809-947-2225), is 22km east of town. The smaller **Aeropuerto Internacional La**

Herrera (Map pp66-7; ☎ 809-567-7050) is near the west edge of the city and handles mostly domestic carriers and air taxi companies such as **Aerodomca** (☎ 809-567-1195), **Caribair** (☎ 809-542-6688) and **Take Off** (☎ 809-552-1333).

Most international flights come into and depart from Las Américas. The major carriers:

Air Canada (Map pp66-7; ☎ 809-541-2929; Av Gustavo Mejía Ricart 54)

Air France (Map p78; ☎ 809-686-8432; Plaza El Faro, Av Máximo Gómez 15); airport (☎ 809-549-0311)

American Airlines (Map pp72-3; ☎ 809-542-5151; El Conde near Sánchez); airport (☎ 809-549-0043)

Continental Airlines (☎ 809-549-0757; airport)

Copa (☎ 809-549-2672, reservations ☎ 809-472-2672; airport)

Iberia (Map pp66-7; ☎ 809-686-9191; Av Lope de Vega 63); airport (☎ 809-549-0205)

Jet Blue (☎ 809-549-1793; airport)

LanChile (Map p78; ☎ 809-689-2221; Malecón/Av George Washington 353)

Lufthansa/Condor (Map p78; ☎ 809-689-9625; Malecón/Av George Washington 353)

US Airways (Map pp66-7; ☎ 809-540-0505; Av Gustavo Mejía Ricart 54); airport (☎ 809-549-0165)

For more details on international air travel to and from the Santo Domingo area, see p273.

Boat

Ferries del Caribe (Map pp72-3; in Santo Domingo ☎ 809-688-4400, in Santiago ☎ 809-724-8771, in Mayagüez, PR ☎ 787-832-4400, in San Juan, PR ☎ 787-725-2643) offers the DR's only international ferry service, connecting Santo Domingo and Mayagüez, Puerto Rico. The ticket office and boarding area are on Av del Puerto opposite Fortaleza Ozama in Zona Colonial. The ferry departs Santo Domingo Sunday, Tuesday and Thursday at 8pm and returns from Mayagüez on Monday, Wednesday and Friday at 8pm. The trip takes 12 hours and costs around US$129/189 one-way/return in an airplane-style seat, or around per person s/d US$182/311 one-way or s/d US$295/474 return in a private cabin with an exterior window.

Bus

Santo Domingo has no central bus terminal. Instead, the country's two main bus companies – **Caribe Tours** (Map pp66-7; ☎ 809-221-4422; Av 27 de Febrero at Av Leopoldo Navarro) and **Metro** (Map pp66-7; ☎ 809-566-7126; Calle Francisco Prats Ramírez) – have individual depots west of the Zona Colonial. Caribe Tours has the most departures, and covers more of the smaller towns than Metro does. Both lines use large, comfortable and fairly modern passenger buses; some even have TVs and show movies. In any case, all but a few destinations are less than four hours from Santo Domingo. Metro is located behind Plaza Central mall, 50m east of Av Winston Churchill.

Fluctuations in fuel prices and in the Dominican peso have lent some unpredictability to bus services. Though things had settled down somewhat at the time of writing, it is still a good idea to call ahead to confirm the schedule and ticket price, and always arrive at least 30 minutes before the stated departure time. For more information on trip fares, duration and frequency, see the boxed text on opposite. Both bus lines also publish brochures (available at all stations) with up-to-date schedules and fares, plus the address and telephone number of their terminals throughout the country – handy if you'll be taking the bus often.

Expreso Santo Domingo Bávaro (Map p78; ☎ 809-682-9670; Juan Sánchez Ruiz at Máximo Gómez); Bávaro (☎ 809-552-0771) has a direct 1st-class service between the capital and Bávaro, with a stop in La Romana. Departure times in both directions are 7am, 10am, 2pm and 4pm (US$3.75, four hours).

There are four **2nd-class bus depots** near Parque Enriquillo in the Zona Colonial. All buses make numerous stops en route. Destinations include the following:

Baní (US$1.75, 1½hours, every 15 minutes, 5am to 10pm)

Boca Chica (caliente/expreso US$1/1.25, 30 minutes, caliente every 15 minutes, expreso every hour, 6am to 8pm)

Higüey (caliente/expreso US$4.25/5, 2½ hours, caliente every 20 minutes, expreso every hour, 6am to 7pm)

Juan Dolio (US$2.10, 45 minutes, every 30 minutes, 6am to 9:30pm)

La Romana (caliente/expreso US$2.75/3, two hours, caliente every 20 minutes, expreso every hour, 6am to 7pm)

Puerto Plata (US$5.25, 4½ hours, take any Sosúa bus)

San Cristóbal (US$1.40, 45 minutes, every 15 to 30 minutes, 6am-10pm)

San Pedro de Macorís (US$2.30, one hour, every 30 minutes, 6am to 9:30pm)

Santiago (US$2.80, two hours, take any Sosúa bus)

Sosúa (US$5.65, five hours, nine departures, 6:30am to 3:30pm)

FIRST-CLASS BUSES FROM SANTO DOMINGO

Caribe Tours (☎ 809-221-4422; Av 27 de Febrero at Leopoldo Navarro)

Destination	Distance (km)	Duration (hrs)	US$	Departures Per Day
Azua	120	1¼	4	8
Barahona	200	2	5.25	4
Castillo	150	1½	5.50	11
Dajabón	305	3	7.50	4
Guayacanes	39	25 min	6.75	4
Imbert	195	2	7	Hourly 6am-7pm
Jarabacoa	155	1½	5.25	4
La Vega	125	1¼	4	Every 30 min, 6am-8pm
Las Matas de Sta Cruz	250	2½	7.50	4
Monte Cristi	270	2¾	7.50	6
Nagua	180	1¾	6.50	11
Puerto Plata	215	2¼	7	Hourly 6am-7pm
Río San Juan	215	2¼	7	5
Samaná	245	2½	7.50	6
Sánchez	211	2	7.50	6
San Fco de Macorís	135	1¼	5.25	Every 30-60min, 7am-6pm
San J de la Maguana	163	1½	5.25	4
Santiago	155	1½	7.50	Every 30 min, 6am-8pm
Sosúa	240	2½	7.75	Hourly 6am-7pm

Metro (☎ 809-566-7126; Calle Francisco Prats Ramírez, east of Av Winston Churchill)

Destination	Distance (km)	Duration (hrs)	US$	Departures Per Day
Castillo	150	1½	5.75	4
La Vega	125	1¼	4.50	Take any Santiago bus
Nagua	180	1¾	6.50	4
Puerto Plata	215	2¼	7.50	9
San Fco de Macorís	135	1¼	5.25	5
Santiago (Caribe)	155	1½	7.50	every 30 min, 6:30am-8am, hourly 8am-7pm

To get to Haiti, Caribe Tours (opposite) and **Terra Bus** (Map pp66-7; ☎ 809-531-0383; Plaza Lama, Av 27 de Febrero at Av Winston Churchill) offer daily bus services to Port-au-Prince at 11am and 11:30am respectively. Both use comfortable, airconditioned coaches, and the trip takes about six hours and costs US$39. If possible, reserve at least two days in advance as the bus is frequently full.

Car
Numerous international and domestic car rental companies have offices in Santo Domingo proper and at Las Américas International Airport – most (but not all) have a booth just past customs. All are open every day roughly from 7am to 6pm in town

(sometimes later) and from 7am to 11:30pm at the airport. Rates average around US$55 per day for a compact car, including taxes and insurance, but there's room for negotiation in slow months or if you rent for more than a few days. Of course, it's worth checking the Internet for a better deal, especially if you prefer one of the larger companies. For more information about costs, rental requirements and so on, see p278.

Advantage Rent-a-Car (Map p78; ☎ 809-685-4000; Av Independencia btwn José Ma Heredia & Socorro Sánchez); airport (☎ 809-549-0536)

Avis (Map p78; ☎ 809-685-5095; Av Independencia at Socorro Sánchez); airport (☎ 809-549-0468)

Budget (Map pp66-7; ☎ 809-566-6666; Av John F Kennedy at Av Lope de Vega); airport (☎ 809-549-0351)

Dollar (Map p78; ☎ 809-221-7368; Av Independencia 366); airport (☎ 809-549-0738)

Europcar (Map p78; ☎ 809-688-2121; Av Independencia 354)

Hertz (Map p78; ☎ 809-221-5333; Av José Ma Heredia 1); airport (☎ 809-549-0454)

McAuto (Map pp72-3; ☎ 809-688-6518; Av George Washington at Peynado); airport (☎ 809-549-0373)

National (☎ 809-549-8303; airport)

Nelly Rent-a-Car (Map p78; ☎ 809-687-7997; Av Independencia 654); airport (☎ 809-549-0505)

Thrifty (☎ 809-549-0717; airport)

GETTING AROUND
To/From the Airport
The local taxi union has managed to prevent buses from connecting Santo Domingo to either of its two airports. From Las Américas, a taxi into town costs a whopping US$25 to US$30, with very little room for negotiation. (In their defense, the trip is a solid half hour.) You may be able to get a cabbie to drop you at the highway, about 2km away, where you can flag down a passing bus, but few are willing to give up their spot in line for such a small fare and it's not a good idea after dark. If there are any other travelers arriving when you do, try sharing a ride. Taxis are available at the airport 24 hours a day.

The fare from Herrera is more reasonable at US$10. There's no permanent taxi stand there, but at least one or two cabs meet every flight. If, for whatever reason, there are no taxis around when you arrive, call one of the companies mentioned in the following Taxi section.

Car
Driving can be difficult in Santo Domingo due to heavy traffic and aggressive drivers, especially taxis and buses. Drive with caution and whenever possible, have a passenger help you navigate the streets. Finding parking is not typically a problem, though if you are leaving your car out overnight, ask around for a parking lot. Many midrange and top-end hotels have parking with 24-hour guards. In any case, be sure not to leave any valuables inside your car.

Public Transportation
The Santo Domingo bus system is simple to use and very cheap – the cost of a bus ride from one end of the city to the other

is around US$0.25. Official public buses started using fixed bus stops in 1998, when a fleet of Brazilian-made buses was inaugurated and the president himself took the bus to work. Most stops are marked with a sign and the word *parada* (stop), but it took several years and a major public service campaign to get locals to actually use them. The routes tend to follow major thoroughfares – in the Zona Colonial, Parque Independencia is where Av Bolivar (the main westbound avenue) begins and Av Independencia (the main eastbound avenue) ends. If you're trying to get across town, just look at a map and note the major intersections along the way and plan your transfers accordingly.

Even more numerous than buses are the *públicos* – mostly beat-up minivans and private cars that follow the same main routes but stop anywhere someone flags them down. They are supposed to have *público* on their license plates, but drivers will beep and wave at you long before you can make out the writing there. Any sort of hand-waving will get the driver to stop, though the preferred gesture is to hold out your arm and point down at the curb in front of you. The fare is US$0.35 – pay when you get in. Speaking of getting in, be prepared for a tight squeeze – drivers will cram seven or even eight passengers into an ordinary two-door car.

Taxi
Taxis in Santo Domingo don't have meters, so you should always agree on the price before climbing in. The standard fare is a low US$3.50, even to the other side of the city. Within the Zona Colonial it should be even cheaper. Taxi drivers don't typically cruise the streets looking for rides; they park at various major points and wait for customers to come to them. In the Zona Colonial, Parque Colón and Parque Duarte are the best spots.

You can also call for a cab or ask the receptionist at your hotel to do so. Service is usually quick, the fare is the same, and you don't have to lug your bags anywhere. Many of the top hotels have cabs waiting at the ready outside, but expect to pay more for those. Reputable taxi agencies with 24-hour dispatches include **Apolo Taxi** (☎ 809-537-7771), **Super Taxi** (☎ 809-536-7014), **Taxi Express** (☎ 809-537-7777) and **Taxi Cacique** (☎ 809-532-3132).

Around Santo Domingo

There are a number of places around Santo Domingo that make for pleasant day or overnight trips. East of the capital is Boca Chica, the best beach within striking distance of the capital and a popular weekend escape for Santo Domingans. Further east, the beach and atmosphere at Juan Dolio isn't as attractive, but it was once a vacation hotspot and still has a number of loyal return visitors. Beyond that, San Pedro de Macorís is a big bustling city which in recent decades has produced more major league baseball players than any other city in the world.

West of Santo Domingo is a string of historic cities such as San Cristóbal, birthplace of dictator Rafael Trujillo and gateway to an anthropological reserve with Taíno cave paintings, and Baní, an agreeable city best known as the birthplace of Generalísimo Máximo Gómez y Báez, leader of Cuba's struggle for independence from Spain.

HIGHLIGHTS

- Marvel at the hundreds of Taíno cave paintings at **Reserva Antropológica El Pomier** (p112) outside San Cristóbal
- Poke around **Castillo del Cerro** (p111), a never-used fortress built by dictator Rafael Trujillo in San Cristóbal, his hometown.
- Relax on the white sand and mellow seas of **Boca Chica** (p101), the best of the beaches near Santo Domingo.
- Go to a **baseball game in San Pedro de Macorís** (p110) the baseball capital of the Dominican Republic
- Explore coral reefs and sunken ships in **Parque Nacional Submarino La Caleta** (p101)

Reserva Antropológica El Pomier ★
Castillo del Cerro ★
Parque Nacional Submarino La Caleta
Boca Chica ★
San Pedro de Macorís ★

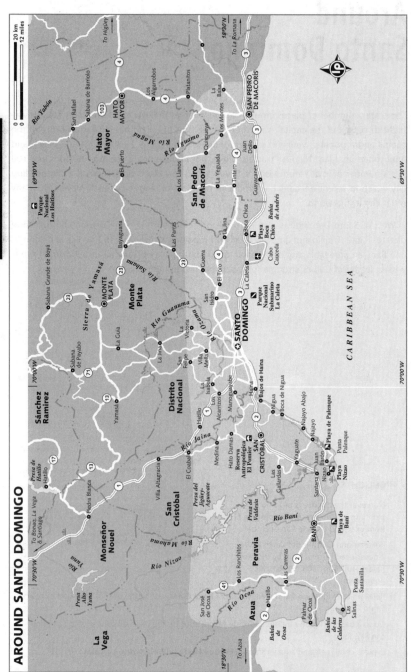

AROUND SANTO DOMINGO

EAST OF SANTO DOMINGO

From Santo Domingo, Hwy 3 runs east along the coast toward the beach towns of Boca Chica and Juan Dolio, and the sugarcane port of San Pedro de Macorís. The larger Hwy 4 runs the inland route.

PARQUE NACIONAL SUBMARINO LA CALETA

At 10 sq km, La Caleta is the smallest of the country's national parks. Located 22km southeast of Santo Domingo, however, it is one of the most frequented. Its main attraction is the coral reef that, although damaged by Hurricane Jean in 2004, remains home to a fair number of tropical fish and other underwater creatures. It is also the resting place of the *Hickory*, a salvage ship that was scuttled in 1984, the year that the park was founded (see boxed text above). Because the boat is in shallow, calm water, it's a fine site for beginner divers.

BOCA CHICA

Boca Chica has had its ups and downs; though they seem to be more about reputation and image than any actual changes

in the town itself. Just 33km east of Santo Domingo and the main airport, Boca Chica is no longer the 'in' destination that it once was, but neither is it the grimy over-commercialized town some make it out to be. It is simply a mid-size town with its fair share of kitschy shops, seaside restaurants and seedy areas. But it also has a great beach and some good-value accommodations, and makes a fine one-or-two day trip from Santo Domingo.

History

Located just 30km east of Santo Domingo, Boca Chica has been a popular weekend escape for residents of the capital city for more than 60 years. During dictator Trujillo's tenure, members of the moneyed class built vacation homes in the sleepy sugar-mill town and did much of their entertaining here. By the 1960s, a few bay side hotels were in place and Boca Chica was added to the expanding list of Caribbean party destinations.

With the development of Playa Dorada and Sosúa during the 1970s, however, Boca Chica lost much of its cachet. The once-bustling resort with its calm, shallow bay and its long white sandy beach, became a tranquil town again. It remained so for nearly 20 years, until a spate of hotel building in the early 1990s rekindled interest in

---

THE *HICKORY*'S COLORFUL PAST

For divers, the main attraction in the Parque Nacional Submarino La Caleta is the *Hickory*, a 39 meter-long steel ship that was scuttled in 1984. The *Hickory* was the primary vessel used in the recovery of artifacts from the Spanish galleons *Nuestra Señora de Guadalupe* and *El Conde de Tolosa*, both of which sank in the Bahía de Samaná on August 25, 1724.

Both of these galleons were en route to Mexico when a violent storm forced them away from the shore and towards a treacherous coral reef. The captains were unable to steer the galleons to safety and the ships were torn apart and sank, taking the lives of over 600 passengers.

The remains of the ships – and their cargo – were left untouched until 1976 when fishermen discovered the *Guadalupe*. Curious about the wreck, the Dominican government hired Tracy Bowden, president of the Caribe Salvage Company of Texas, to explore the sunken galleon using the *Hickory*.

Bowden and his crew spent over a year digging through the sediment that had accumulated over the galleon before recovering any artifacts. Spanish records also indicated that the *Tolosa* had sunk within hours of the *Guadalupe*; knowing it had to be nearby, the salvagers searched the Bahía de Samaná for six months before finding it just northwest of Miches.

Among the thousands of items discovered at the two wreck sites were hundreds of silver and gold coins minted in Spain during the early 18th century, a cache of jewelry and hundreds of crystal glasses. Many of these items, as well as dozens of photographs of the excavation, are on permanent display at the Museo de las Atarazanas in Santo Domingo (p71).

Boca Chica. Today, the town again appears on the radar screens of world travelers and Dominicans alike.

Orientation

Boca Chica follows a grid pattern that is easy to negotiate. It comprises a 10-by-15-block area between Hwy 3 and Bahía de Andrés, a bay so shallow and calm that it feels more like a lagoon than a large body of water. From the highway there are three main avenues – 24 de Junio, Juan Bautista Vicini and Caracol – that slope gently to the oceanfront streets of San Rafael and Duarte.

Information

EMERGENCY

Politur (☎ 809-523-5120; Calle Juanico Garcia btwn Av Duarte & Av San Rafael; ☷ 24hr)

INTERNET ACCESS & TELEPHONE

QK Internet Center (Av Duarte nr Calle Sanchez; ☷ 9am-10pm Mon-Sat, 9am-6pm Sun) Possibly the best international telephone rates in the country (to USA US$0.25 per minute, to Europe US$0.53 per minute) and decent Internet rates too (US$2.80 per hour).

Verizon Centro de Comunicaciones (Av San Rafael nr Av Caracol; ☷ 8am-10pm) International telephone service (to USA US$0.32 per minute, to Europe US$0.74 per minute) and the cheapest Internet connection in town (US$1.60 per hour). There are only two computers, so you may have to wait your turn. Despite the address, the main entrance is on Av Duarte.

MEDICAL SERVICES

Clinic Assist (☎ 809-412-2001 ext 2345; Av 20 de Diciembre at Av Juan Bautista Vicini; ☷ 24hr) Private medical clinic that offers house calls. English, French and German spoken.

Farmacia Boca Chica (☎ 809-523-4708; Av Duarte nr Av Juan Bautista Vicini; ☷ 8:30am-9pm Mon-Sat, 8:30am-8pm Sun)

MONEY

Banco Popular (Av Duarte at Av Juan Bautista Vicini; ☷ 8:15am-4pm Mon-Fri, 9am-1pm Sun) Opposite the southwest corner of Parque Central. One ATM.

BanReservas (Av San Rafael at Juanico Garcia; ☷ 8am-5pm Mon-Fri; 9am-1pm Sat) Behind Verizon. It has one ATM.

POST

Post Office (Av Duarte nr Av Juan Bautista Vicini; ☷ 8am-5pm Mon-Fri, 8am-noon Sat)

TOURIST INFORMATION

Tourist Office (☎ 809-523-5106; Calle Juanico Garcia; ☷ 9am-5pm Mon-Fri) Situated between Avs Duarte and San Rafael, this office gives lots of good maps and area pamphlets but not much in the way of personalized assistance. English and French spoken.

Sights

PLAYA BOCA CHICA

Boca Chica's only attraction – its beach – is the site of the town's main activities; splashing in the transparent and tranquil waters and sunning on the powdery white sand. Flanked by Av Caracol and Av 24 de Junio, Playa Boca Chica is one long stretch of beach that is lined with coconut palms and a string of food stands, restaurants and bars. It also, unfortunately, has a view of loading cranes and a sugar refinery in the distance; not exactly tropical, but a view that is pretty much forgotten as soon as you spend a little bit of time enjoying the surf and sand.

The beach is effectively divided into three sections: the eastern side is a lovely stretch of sand that is popular with children because of a jungle gym that is propped just a few meters from the water; the central area – which is the best place for sunbathing – begins as a thin band of sand but opens into one of the widest beaches in the country; and the western end which eventually gives way to a sandy parking lot and a row of food stalls selling cheap local food.

Most of the beach is lively, filled every day with locals and foreigners, vendors selling fruit from pushcarts and traveling musicians performing for a few dollars a song. About 100m from shore is a small shrub-covered island that you can wade out to. Towards the mouth of the Bahía de Andrés bay is a second, larger island that is privately owned.

Activities

Whereas diving in the north is known for its underwater features like canyons and swim-throughs, the south is famous for its coral reefs and abundance of colorful sea life. The water is warmer too – averaging 25°C – and the visibility ranges between 5m and 28m, depending on the season. There are over 25 dive sites in the area; most are located in the Parque Nacional Submarino La Caleta (p101) with its two shipwrecks and myriad coral heads. Dive trips to a

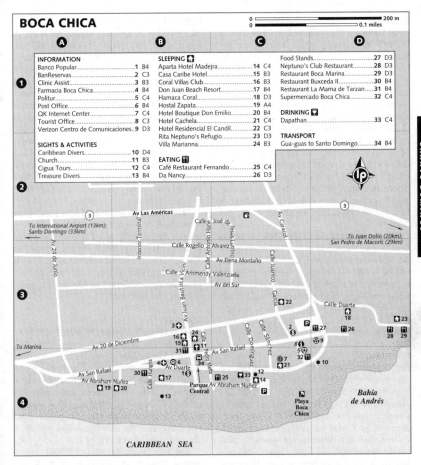

BOCA CHICA

0   200 m
0   0.1 miles

INFORMATION
Banco Popular.....................................1 B4
BanReservas.......................................2 C3
Clinic Assist...3 B3
Farmacia Boca Chica..........................4 B4
Politur...5 C4
Post Office..6 B4
QK Internet Center.............................7 C4
Tourist Office......................................8 C3
Verizon Centro de Comunicaciones..9 D3

SIGHTS & ACTIVITIES
Caribbean Divers...............................10 D4
Church...11 B3
Cigua Tours.......................................12 C4
Treasure Divers.................................13 B4

SLEEPING
Aparta Hotel Madejra........................14 C4
Casa Caribe Hotel.............................15 B3
Coral Villas Club...............................16 B3
Don Juan Beach Resort.....................17 B4
Hamaca Coral....................................18 D3
Hostal Zapata....................................19 A4
Hotel Boutique Don Emilio...............20 B4
Hotel Cachela....................................21 C4
Hotel Residencial El Candil...............22 C3
Rita Neptuno's Refugio.....................23 D3
Villa Marianna...................................24 B3

EATING
Café Restaurant Fernando.................25 C4
Da Nancy...26 D3

Food Stands.......................................27 D3
Neptuno's Club Restaurant...............28 D3
Restaurant Boca Marina.....................29 D3
Restaurant Buxceda II.......................30 B4
Restaurant La Mama de Tarzan.........31 B4
Supermercado Boca Chica.................32 C4

DRINKING
Dapathan...33 C4

TRANSPORT
Gua-guas to Santo Domingo.............34 B4

AROUND SAANTO DOMINGO

nearby cave are also offered as are trips to the waters near Bayahibe and Isla Catalina (p123). There are two reputable dive shops in town – **Treasure Divers** (☎ 809-523-5320, www.treasuredivers.de, on the beach nr Don Juan Beach Resort; ⏲ 8:30am-5pm) and **Caribbean Divers** (☎ 809-854-3483; www.caribbeandivers.de; on the beach, entrance at Av Duarte 28; ⏲ 8:30am-5pm). Dives average US$40 with equipment, but multi-dive packages bring the prices down a little. Padi courses are also offered. English, French and German are spoken at both.

Tours
Cigua Tours (☎ 809-523-6266; Av Duarte at Calle Domínguez; ⏲ 9am-noon & 4-6pm) Although it is operated out of a clapboard kiosk, this tour operator is actually affiliated with a well-established travel agency in Juan Dolio. Tours are slightly cheaper than its sister office and include trips to Santo Domingo (US$30 per person), Isla Saona (US$55 per person), Isla Catalina (US$59 per person) and Los Haïtises National Park (US$58 per person).

Sleeping
Boca Chica has a wide selection of hotels and apartments, offering a variety of options in different price ranges. If you plan to be here awhile, it makes sense to rent a place with a kitchen, although you might want to do your grocery shopping in Santo Domingo or San Pedro, as the stores in Boca Chica are quite expensive.

AROUND
SAANTO DOMINGO

BUDGET

Hotel Cachela (☎ 809 523-5454; Av Duarte 24; r/tw US$30/45; 🔀) Located in the heart of the action and across the street from the beach, the Cachela offers spacious, spotless and nicely appointed rooms. All have access to a pleasant balcony that overlooks Calle Duarte. Don't be turned off by the sketchy-looking stairway. This place is an excellent choice.

Casa Caribe Hotel (☎ 809-523-6724; Av Juan Bautista Vicini 12; r US$25; 🔀) Half a block north of Parque Central, the Casa Caribe is a homely hotel that offers seven clean and comfortable rooms with fans and cable TV. There is a good Italian restaurant on-site, which offers reasonably-priced dishes. A fine option, especially if you are on a tight budget.

Villa Marianna (☎/fax 809-523-4679; Av Juan Bautista Vicini 11; r without/with aircon US$20/45; studio US$35; 🔀 🖭) Across the street, the Villa Marianna offers acceptable though somewhat worn rooms: walls need a coat of paint, some beds are saggy and the decor hails from the early 80s. The rooms are clean though and the staff friendly. Aircon rooms aren't worth the extra price.

MIDRANGE

Rita Neptuno's Refugio (☎ 809-523-9934; Calle Duarte; neptunosrefugio@hotmail.com; r/studio US$45-50, 1-bedroom apt US$50-60, penthouse US$120; 🅿 🔀 🖭 🖳) Hands down, this is the best place to stay in town. Located on a quiet road across from Neptuno's Club Restaurant (opposite), rooms and apartments are spotless and nicely appointed. All have modern amenities and boast full kitchens and spacious balconies. A shady courtyard out the back is set alongside a well-maintained pool and service is five star. Rooms on the upper floors have great views of the Caribbean beyond.

Hotel Residencial El Candil (☎ 809-523-4252; res.candil@verizon.net.do; Juanico García at Av 20 de Diciembre; r US$30, studio US$35, 1-bedroom apt with aircon US$50-65, 2-bdrm apt with aircon US$80; 🔀 🅿 🖳) Comfortable and pleasant, the simple rooms and apartments are good value. All are clean, well-maintained and have cable TV and small but fully equipped kitchenettes. A welcoming pool with a small waterfall is a good place to while away an afternoon. Airport pickup and drop-off is available.

Hostal Zapata (☎ 809-523-4777; www.hotelzapata.com; Av Abraham Nuñez 27; s/d US$45/55, s/d studio US$65/75, 1-bedroom apt US$75/85, 2-bedroom apt US$100; 🔀 🅿) This is the only midrange hotel in town with beachfront property. Rooms are small but surprisingly comfortable and clean, and those facing the ocean have pleasant balconies. All have hot water and cable TV. The beach out front also can't be beat.

Aparta Hotel Madejra (☎ 809 523-4434; fax 809-523-4532; Calle Dominguez at Av Abraham Nuñez; s/d US$30/45, 1-bedroom apt US$50, aircon extra US$5; 🔀) Located on a quiet sandy road, the rooms here are ample, airy and clean. Some have balconies with excellent views of the Caribbean – at no extra cost, you might as well ask for one when you check in. An elevator is a major plus.

Coral Villas Club (☎ 809-523-5096; plasa@verizon.net.do; Av 20 de Diciembre at Av Juan Bautista Vicini; 1-bedroom apt US$45; 🔀 🖭) Each of the seven apartments in this small complex has cable TV, a full kitchen and a sitting area. Rooms on the first floor lack natural light, but are pleasant nonetheless. The tiny pool is reminiscent of a bird bath.

TOP END

Hotel Boutique Don Emilio (☎ 809-523-5270; Av Abraham Nuñez; s/d US$46/70, with ocean view s/d US$87/105; 🔀 🅿) Located in a powder-blue building that is reminiscent of a tug boat, the Hotel Boutique Don Emilio offers bright, clean rooms that boast modern amenities like cable TV, in-room telephone and a minifridge. A glorious stretch of beach is right out front and the hotel provides plenty of chairs for guests to lounge in.

Don Juan Beach Resort (☎ 809-523-4511; Av Abraham Nuñez 8; s/d US$160/270; 🔀 🅿 🖭 🖳) Located on the best stretch of beach in town, this all-inclusive resort has comfortable rooms in various multilevel structures. Though not as nice as the Hamaca Coral, it's still quite popular, particularly with French and Dominican tourists. Its facilities include a well-maintained swimming pool and a buffet restaurant with a menu that changes daily.

Hamaca Coral (☎ 809-523-4611; www.coralbyhilton.com; Calle Duarte nr Av Caracol; s/d US$110/156; 🔀 🅿 🖭 🖳) Situated on the eastern side of Boca Chica, the Hilton-owned Hamaca Coral offers 598 rooms on one of the only private beaches in the country. The beach is separated from the town by walls and is pleasant, though often crowded. Rooms are set in a lush garden and are comfortable and clean; renovated accommodations near the back of the property are considerably nicer. Food is offered in four restaurants and receives mixed reviews.

Eating

Restaurant Boca Marina (☎ 809-523-6702; Calle Duarte 12-A; mains US$10-24; ☼ breakfast, lunch & dinner) Certainly one of the most enjoyable places to eat in Boca Chica is this spot on the east side of town. The decor is chic and airy with gleaming stone floors leading to polished decks, all with tables facing the Caribbean. The specialty is seafood and the menu boasts such treats as shrimp in Thai sauce (US$21) and seafood risotto (US$24). If you don't feel like eating, there also is an open-air lounge that extends over the turquoise water; it has comfortable chaise lounges and even ornately-carved full-size beds for patrons to relax in. A well-maintained swimming area is also a welcome surprise.

Neptuno's Club Restaurant (☎ 809-523-4703; Calle Duarte 12; mains US$16-25; ☼ breakfast, lunch & dinner) Just west of the Boca Marina is the equally popular, similarly situated Neptunos, which also specializes in seafood. This restaurant offers a bit more shade than the Boca Marina and half of its tables are on decking that extends out toward the surf. There's always a festive atmosphere, and usually a seat at the bar if you have to wait for a table. The food here is well worth waiting for: delicious dishes include lobster lasagna (US$16), spaghetti marinara (US$21) and the house specialty, seafood casserole (US$25).

Da Nancy (☎ 809-523-4376; Av San Rafael 16; mains US$6-17; ☼ lunch & dinner) Hidden behind the Hamaca Coral resort, Da Nancy is a classy but laid-back restaurant serving delicious Italian specialties. Among favorites are the mouthwatering penne with lobster sauce (US$12.50) and the traditional linguine with clams (US$8). Live music on Friday nights is a nice touch.

Restaurant Buxceda II (☎ 809-527-5320; Av Duarte at Calle Hungria; mains US$7-10; ☼ breakfast, lunch & dinner) For a classic Dominican eating experience, head to the Buxceda. Here there are long white tables under spinning fans, at which diners can order almost any type of seafood and have it prepared almost any way they please. The menu is painted on the wall and simply reads: *mero al gusto* (grouper any style), *lambí al gusto* (conch any style), *pulpo al gusto* (octopus any style), *camarones al gusto* (shrimp any style)…you get the idea.

Café Restaurant Fernando (☎ 809-523-4939; Calle Pedro Mella nr Av Duarte; mains US$5-11; ☼ lunch & dinner Mon-Sat) This thatch-roofed eatery serves up a good variety of Dominican dishes as well as international standards like pastas and sandwiches. The food is reliable and the setting charming. Just half a block from the beach, it's convenient too.

Restaurant La Mama de Tarzan (☎ 809-523-6724; Calle Juan Bautista Vicini 12; mains US$5.50-12.50; ☼ lunch & dinner) This low-key restaurant offers reliable Italian dishes that won't blow your budget. Among the wide variety of pastas on the menu, the *tortellini ai funghi* (tortellini with mushrooms) is particularly good. It is located just north of Parque Central.

For a classic Dominican culinary experience, head to the **food stands** (Av San Rafael at Av Caracol; ☼ 10am-6pm Fri-Sun) that line the eastern end of Av Rafael. Here, on weekends only, Dominican beachgoers line up to order fried whole fish, *plátanos* (fried green plantains) and *casabe* (flat round bread made of cassava). A meal costs US$5.50 and is often big enough for two.

GROCERIES

Supermercado Boca Chica (Av Duarte at Juanico Garcia; ☼ 9am-8pm Mon-Sat, 9am-6pm Sun) This is the largest grocery store in town with a good – although expensive – selection of food and toiletries.

Drinking & Entertainment

Boca Chica's nightlife has a reputation for being seedy. While Boca Chica has its fair share of sketchy bars and dodgy areas (what city doesn't?), there are also a couple of fun, safe places to drink and dance, without the concern of being accosted by prostitutes, pickpocketed, or worse. One cool thing about Boca Chica is the city closes Av Duarte to cars from around 7pm, and restaurants and bars set tables up on the street, creating a sort of mini *Malecón*. Not exactly a raging party scene, but a good place for a beer or two all the same.

Dapathan (☎ 809-523-5476; Av Duarte 24; ☼ 8am-midnight) With picnic tables and umbrellas for shade, this German eatery makes a good place to cool off. The food is decent but the beer is better.

Hamaca Coral (☎ 809-523-4611; www.coralbyhilton .com; Calle Duarte & Av Caracol; cover US$16; ☒ 11pm-3am) The only decent place to get your groove on is at the Hilton's discothèque. While not exactly the hippest place, the music selection is varied and you're sure to meet other travelers.

Getting There & Away

Second class buses service from Boca Chica to Santo Domingo (*caliente/expreso* US$1/1.25, 30 minutes, *caliente* every 15 minutes, *expreso* every hour, 6:30am to 8:30pm). Buses stop on the north side of Parque Central and along Av San Rafael.

If you're heading east, *gua-guas* stop at the intersection of the highway and Av Caracol. Destinations include Juan Dolio (US$1.10, 15 minutes, every 30 minutes, from 6:30am to 10pm), San Pedro de Macorís (US$1.30, 30 minutes, every 30 minutes, from 6:30am to 10pm), La Romana (*caliente/expreso* US$1.75/2, 1½ hours, *caliente* every 20 minutes, *expreso* every hour, 6:30am to 7:30pm), and Higüey (*caliente/expreso* US$3.25/4, two hours, *caliente* every 20 minutes, *expreso* every hour, 6:30am to 7:30pm).

If you prefer taxis, you can often find one near the intersection of Av San Rafael and Av Caracol. Alternatively, you can get door-to-door service by calling the **Taxi Turístico Boca Chica** (☎ 809-523-4797). One-way fares include: Aeropuerto Internacional Las Américas (US$20), Santo Domingo (US$23), Juan Dolio (US$20), San Pedro de Macorís (US$50), Higüey (US$100) and La Romana (US$75).

Getting Around

Boca Chica is small and easily covered on foot. Still, if you don't feel like walking, *motoconchos* are often cruising the streets or waiting near the Parque Central and the Verizon office. Rides around town cost US$1.

JUAN DOLIO

Unlike Boca Chica, which has lost its buzz but not its fundamental appeal, Juan Dolio is a town that was once a Caribbean hotspot, but today is struggling to remain on the tourist radar. During the late 1980s, several developers eyed the beach here – which at that point remained completely undevel-

oped – and saw the next big multi-resort complex. But the global financial slump of 2001 hit Juan Dolio harder than other resort towns, primarily because it hadn't yet developed the name-recognition that Playa Dorada, Punta Cana or Sosúa had. Numerous hotels and resorts closed, and today the small community is littered with these decaying shells – forlorn monuments to a dream unrealized.

Most tourists here are guests in one of the several all-inclusive resorts on the east side of town, and just enough trickle down to the center of town to keep a handful of bars and restaurants in business. Juan Dolio also has a small but loyal following of both expats and Dominicans from the capital, but the beach and atmosphere here simply can't compete with the more attractive and lively beach areas in either direction down the coast.

Orientation

Juan Dolio consists of a long narrow sliver of land between Hwy 3 (aka Boulevard) and the beach. From Hwy 3, there's an access road called Entrada a los Conucos just east of a large Shell gas station. Take this one short block towards the beach to Carretera Local, the main street through town. The intersection of Entrada a los Conucos and Carretera local is the main area in town with a number of restaurants, bars, shops and services clustered nearby. The hotels are mostly east of there, with the exception of Hotel Fior di Loto, which is 500m west past the taxi stand.

Information

INTERNET ACCESS & TELEPHONE

Ilsa (☎ 809-526-2777; Plaza de la Luna, Carretera Local; ☒ 8am-11pm) Internet access (US$4 per hour) and international calls (to USA US$0.53 per minute, to Europe US$0.88 per minute). It is located nearby the Coral Hilton. **Verizon Centro de Comunicaciones** (☎ 809-526-2777; Blvd at Calle Entrada a los Conucos; ☒ 9am-7pm) Internet US$1.50 per hour. Calls to USA US$0.30 per minute, to Europe US$0.75 per minute.

LAUNDRY

Lavandería (Carretera Nueva; per load US$5.25; ☒ 8am-7pm) Inside Plaza Real Resort. Overnight service only.

MEDICAL SERVICES

Farmacia Boni (☎ 809-526-2561; across Blvd from Verizon; ☒ 8am-8pm Mon-Sat)

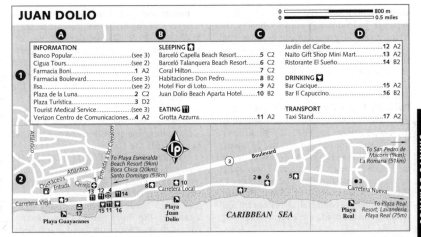

JUAN DOLIO

	0		800 m
	0		0.5 miles

INFORMATION
Banco Popular..........................(see 3)
Cigua Tours..............................(see 2)
Farmacia Boni............................1 A2
Farmacia Boulevard.................(see 3)
Ilsa.......................................(see 2)
Plaza de la Luna..........................2 C2
Plaza Turística...............................3 D2
Tourist Medical Service............(see 3)
Verizon Centro de Comunicaciones....4 A2

SLEEPING
Barceló Capella Beach Resort............5 C2
Barceló Talanquera Beach Resort......6 C2
Coral Hilton..................................7 C2
Habitaciones Don Pedro..................8 B2
Hotel Fior di Loto............................9 A2
Juan Dolio Beach Aparta Hotel........10 B2

EATING
Grotta Azzurra................................11 A2

Jardín del Caribe.............................12 A2
Naito Gift Shop Mini Mart...............13 A2
Ristorante El Sueño........................14 B2

DRINKING
Bar Cacique...................................15 A2
Bar Il Capuccino............................16 B2

TRANSPORT
Taxi Stand....................................17 A2

AROUND SAANTO DOMINGO

To Playa Esmeralda Beach Resort (9km); Boca Chica (20km); Santo Domingo (53km)

To San Pedro de Macoris (9km); La Romana (51km)

Boulevard

Carretera Nueva

To Plaza Real Resort; Lavandería Playa Real (75m)

Atlántico

Entrada a los Conucos

Crustáceos Entrada Canrejo

Carretera Vieja

Carretera Local

Playa Guayacanes

Playa Juan Dolio

CARIBBEAN SEA

Playa Real

Farmacia Boulevard (☎ 809-526-2041 ext 223; Plaza Turística, Carretera Nueva; ◷ 8am-8pm Mon-Fri, 8am-7pm Sat & Sun) Affiliated with, and next door to, the Tourist Medical Service.

Tourist Medical Service (☎ 809-526-2041; Plaza Turística, Carretera Nueva; ◷ 24hr) General and specialized medical services. English, German, and French spoken.

MONEY

The Shell gas station on the boulevard west of Entrada a los Conucos has a 24-hour Banco León ATM.

Banco Popular (Plaza Turística, Carretera Nueva; ◷ 9am-5pm Mon-Fri, 9am-1pm Sun) Located 400m east of the Barceló Capella. It has one ATM.

POST

There is no post office in town but hotels often send mail for guests upon request.

TRAVEL AGENCIES

Cigua Tours (☎ 809-526-2077; Plaza de la Luna, Carretera Local; ◷ 8am-11pm) This small travel agency can book domestic and international air tickets, reserve rental cars, and book hotels around the DR. It also organizes day trips to Santo Domingo (US$35 per person), Isla Saona (US$60 per person), Isla Catalina (US$60 per person), Parque Nacional Los Haïtises (US$60 per person) and whale watching (US$95 per person).

Sleeping
BUDGET

Hotel Fior di Loto (☎ 809-526-1146; www. fiordiloto hotel.com; Carretera Vieja; d US$10-20, tw US$30, apt with kitchen US$35-40) Located 500m west of En-

trada a los Conucos, it's a large rambling building with twenty-three rooms of varying sizes and decor tucked into its many nooks and crannies. Rooms are showing their age in the worn floors and bathroom fixtures, but are relatively clean and good value. The friendly Italian owner is an Indophile, evident in the tapestries in the rooms and artwork in the reception area. Some of the hotel proceeds go to supporting a girls education foundation in northwest India. Yoga and meditation courses are available in a huge sunny exercise area on the third floor (which is sometimes converted to a dorm area for backpackers). A mellow, affordable, gay-friendly place – it's too bad Juan Dolio doesn't warrant a longer stay.

Habitaciones Don Pedro (☎ 809-526-2147; Carretera Local; r with fan $24.50, with aircon US$35; ▣) Located 300m east of the main intersection, it has clean modern rooms at a fair price which make this a reliable choice. Rooms have firm beds, gleaming tile floors and attractive linens; some have a small sitting area with a sofa and coffee table, others have a kitchen. Guests can also make use of a common kitchen and dining area. The bar and sandwich shop across the street are run by the same family.

Juan Dolio Beach Aparta Hotel (☎ /fax 809-526-2612; Carretera Local; studio with shared kitchen US$30; 1-bedroom apt US$40; ▣) Accommodations at this apart-hotel are spacious and clean, most of which have balconies. They vary in size from studio units that share a kitchen with

AROUND SAANTO DOMINGO

their neighbor, to large apartments with a separate bedroom and another bed in the living area. The generator can be somewhat oppressive though; ask for a room facing the street for a quieter stay. Located within striking distance of a public beach.

MIDRANGE

Plaza Real Resort (☎ 809-526-1374; www.puntoreal .com; Carretera Nueva; studio US$35-40; 1-bedroom apt US$40-60, 2-bedroom apt US$70; ❋ P ⚑) Although showing some wear, the 51 apartments in this complex, just east of town, are decent enough. Rooms are clean, quiet and many have balconies. The pool is one of the best features with a small waterfall and swim-up bar. A good Italian restaurant and a laundromat on-site are added pluses.

TOP END

Barceló Capella Beach Resort (☎ 809-526-1080; www .barcelo.com; Carretera Nueva; s/d per person US$120/80; ❋ P ⚑ 🖳) Without a doubt, the Barceló Capella is the best of the three resorts in town. The grounds include lush vegetation, manicured lawns, reflecting pools with flamingos and peacocks and classic Caribbean architecture that is pleasing to the eye (think big gingerbread houses). Rooms are a bit hit or miss – the 4000 building has some of the best of the lot – but the food is generally acceptable. If you plan on swimming in the ocean, you'll appreciate having protection for your feet, as rocks and sea urchins dot the shallow areas in front of the hotel. There are neoprene booties made for the purpose (check in a surf or dive shop), but an old pair of tennis shoes works almost as well.

Coral Hilton (☎ 809-526-2244; www.coralbyhilton .com; Carretera Local; s/d US$150/240; ❋ P ⚑ 🖳) Set on lush grounds with two pools and three restaurants, overall the Coral Hilton makes a good impression. Rooms are spacious and comfortable, though somewhat dated in style. Three restaurants offer decent food, while five bars and a nightclub round out the social scene. The beach is set on a protected cove but unfortunately the swimming area is somewhat cramped for the number of guests that make use of it. Also, like the Capella, you'll probably want booties or other shoes to wear in the water to protect your feet from the rocky ocean floor.

Barceló Talanquera Beach Resort (☎ 809-526-1510; www.barcelo.com; Carretera Local; s/d per person US$89/59; ❋ P ⚑ 🖳) Popular with the college crowd, this resort has a definite party feel to it: pool volleyball, packed bars and scantily-clad guests are the norm. Rooms have seen better days; ask for one in the 400 and 500 series, which are the most recently renovated. The beach is small and jam packed with beach chairs, so if you're looking for some quiet time it's best to head east towards the Capella.

Playa Esmeralda Beach Resort (☎ 809-526-3434; www.hotel-playaesmeralda.com; Autopista de las Américas; r per person US$60; ❋ P ⚑ 🖳) About 9km west of Juan Dolio, you'll see the Playa Esmeralda, a small all-inclusive resort that's located in the dusty town of Guayacanes. Although the rooms are dated – soft beds, 1980s decor – the beach is pretty and the restaurant food decent enough. A good option if you're looking for an all-inclusive but your wallet is a little slim.

Eating

All of Juan Dolio's restaurants – there aren't many – are along the Carretera Local, within the vicinity of the main intersection.

Jardín del Caribe (☎ 809-526-2188; Carretera Local at Entrada a los Conucos; mains US$7-12; ✷ lunch & dinner, closed Thu) Set in an open-air dining room, meals at the Jardín del Caribe are excellent. The classic Italian menu includes a wide variety of pastas, pizzas and grilled meats. Meals often come with a complimentary appetizer and if you're the last customer to leave, you also might get a rose or a cigar for your patronage. Excellent service.

Ristorante El Sueño (☎ 809-526-3903; Carretera Local; meals US$4-12; ✷ dinner) Just east of Habitaciones Don Pedro, the dishes here are less expensive than at Jardín del Caribe, but not as good (neither is the service). The pizza is the best thing on the menu here, and the patio seating is pleasant on a clear night.

Grotta Azzurra (☎ 809-526-2031; Carretera Vieja; prices US$5-10; ✷ lunch & dinner, closed Tue) On the ocean side of the street right at the main intersection, this small but agreeable restaurant has good food and a pleasant view and sea breeze. Among the specialties are grilled beef fillet with green-pepper sauce, baked chicken and grilled fish fillet.

Naito Gift Shop Mini Mart (Carretera Local at Entrada a los Conucos; ✷ 8:15am-7pm) The largest market in the center of town, with canned food, produce, alcohol, snack foods, sunscreen and toiletries.

Drinking

Bar Cacique (Carretera Local; ☼ 9am-3am) Across from Jardín del Caribe this centrally located bar has a mostly German clientele, but anyone can stop in for a beer or a game of pool (US$0.35 per game).

Bar Il Capuccino (☎ 809-526-1245; Carretera Local; ☼ 24hr) A few doors down, this small bar and diner has a nice view of the ocean and a little of everything; from coffee to hard alcohol, from hot dogs to slot machines. The atmosphere can be a bit seedy, sometimes serving as a meeting place for older foreign men and young local women.

Getting There & Around

Gua-guas pass through Juan Dolio all day everyday, going westwards to Boca Chica (US$0.75) and Santo Domingo ($US1.40) and east to San Pedro de Macorís (US$0.75), La Romana (US$1.40) and Higüey (US$3.50). No buses originate here, so there is no fixed schedule, but they pass roughly every 15 minutes from 6am to 7pm – stand on Boulevard at the corner of Entrada a los Conucos and flag down any that passes. Be sure to tell the driver where you're going – not all buses make the whole loop, but the driver can drop you at the stop where you catch the connecting *gua-gua*.

Taxis (☎ 809-526-3507) can be found in front of any of the resorts in town, and at a taxi stand just west of Naito Mini Mart. Fares range from US$25 (to Boca Chica) to US$35 (to the airport) up to US$50 (to Santo Domingo); be sure to agree on the fare before you get in the car. You can also call **Juan Dolio Taxi** (☎ 809-526-2006) for door-to-door service.

You can easily walk to most locations in Juan Dolio.

SAN PEDRO DE MACORÍS

pop 300,000

Famous for producing more major league baseball players per capita than any other city – and for its prominent place in the popular song *Guavaberry* by Dominican merengue star Juan Luís Guerra – San Pedro de Macorís piques the interest of many travelers. Unfortunately, it simply doesn't follow through, and as a tourist destination, going to a baseball game is the one and only reason to come to this grimy semi-industrial city.

History

That wasn't always the case. Fifty years ago, San Pedro de Macorís was a sight to behold. Moving slowly through the fields of tall, dense sugarcane that ringed the city were 19th-century locomotives with wide, funnel-shaped stacks that belched steam in small thick clouds. Half the size of conventional locomotives, these engines puffed busily as machete-wielding workers piled long stalks of green cane onto railroad cars specially built for the task. From the fields, the locomotives carried millions of tons of cane to giant grinders that mashed the cane into pulp that was then refined into sugar. Not far away, Pan Am landed its American Clipper hydroplanes on the Río Iguamo for sugar hauls bound for the USA.

Today those wonderful locomotives and planes are gone, as are the stately mansions of the rich plantation owners. The same relentless humidity that converted the locomotives to heaps of rusting parts, transformed the elegant wooden homes into monuments of dry rot for termites to feast upon.

Sugar is still the basis of San Pedro's existence, the cane is still cut by use of machetes and the sweet substance continues to be loaded onto ships at San Pedro's port. But unlike other Dominican cities, this provincial capital, 65km east of Santo Domingo, has been repeatedly passed over for public improvements. The dictator Trujillo did little for the city, and Joaquín Balaguer, who was president during most of the years following the death of the dictator in 1961, never cared much for Macorís residents because of their repeated opposition to his regime.

It's hard to believe, as you drive past the harbor's crumbling balustrades, that San Pedro was once a cultural showplace of the Caribbean, with an opera hall where Jenny Lind (the 'Swedish nightingale') sang. This has become even more difficult to believe since Hurricane Georges paid its visit in 1998. The city was among those hardest hit by the storm, leaving more than a third of the city's residents homeless.

Sights & Activities

BASEBALL

The top attraction in San Pedro de Macorís is its baseball games, held in the city's most prominent building – Estadio Tetelo Vargas. The stadium appears on the north side of Hwy 3 if you're approaching from Santo Domingo, just beyond a large billboard that reads: 'Welcome to San Pedro de Macorís. The City Which Has Given the Most Major Leaguers to the World.'

And it's no exaggeration. During any given season, there are about 60 Dominicans in the majors, and upwards of 500 in the minor leagues. At least a third of those players grew up playing stickball in the streets of San Pedro, and most attended a major league training camp in, or near, San Pedro before signing on. Needless to say, the level of play at Estadio Tetelo Vargas – and just about any pickup game in the city – is very high.

Try to catch a game here if you're in the DR between mid-November and early February. Baseline seats cost around US$14, while bleacher seats go for less than US$2.

CATEDRAL SAN PEDRO APOSTOL

When approaching San Pedro de Macorís from the west, you can easily see the steeple of the **Catedral San Pedro Apostol** (8am-8pm; Calle Charro nr Av Independencia) from the bridge leading into town located at the east end of the city's seaside boulevard. Though it has plenty of stained glass, carved mahogany and marble floors, it is the church's stormy past that is most notable. A small church was built on this location in 1856, before nine years later a hurricane came along and blew it down. The church was rebuilt, this time using pine, and it stood for 20 years before it caught fire and burned to the ground. Two years after that, in 1887, Archbishop Meriño had the church built once again, and it has stood until the present day. It was elevated to the status of *parroquia catedral* (parish cathedral) in 1997.

BASKETBALL

With all the attention paid to baseball here, it's a wonder that any other sport has a following. But there are basketball games held almost every night at a court near San Pedro Apostol Cathedral on Calle Charro near Av Independencia. There are bleach-

ers for spectators, and the games and the crowds can get quite lively, especially when a tournament is being played.

Sleeping

Howard Johnson Hotel Macorís (809-529-2100; fax 809-529-9239; Calle Gastón F Deligne; r US$67; P) Near the *Malecón*, this is your best bet in town. Rooms are good-sized and comfortable and have the all modern amenities that you would expect: cable TV, security boxes and telephones. A pleasant pool, three restaurants and room service round out a restful stay. A taxi ride to the ballpark costs US$3.

There are a number of services nearby the Ho Jo, including food stands all along the *Malecón*, Internet access in the hotel and **Farmacia Miramar** (809-529-3161) for toiletries and medications.

WEST OF SANTO DOMINGO

West of Santo Domingo, Hwy 2 runs along the coast as far as Haina, where it cuts inland to the provincial capital of San Cristóbal. From there it continues south to the city of Baní, then further westwards. Hwy 41 branches off from Hwy 2 to the town of San José de Ocoa, in the foothills of the Cordillera Central.

SAN CRISTÓBAL

Rafael Trujillo, the strongman who dominated the Dominican Republic (DR) through fear and brutality from 1930 until his assassination in 1961, was born in this provincial capital located just 30km west of Santo Domingo. During Trujillo's rule, San Cristóbal became a sort of national shrine to the dictator; in fact its name was officially changed in 1934 to 'Meritorious City.' (It was changed back after Trujillo died.) An easy daytrip from Santo Domingo, San Cristóbal has tremendous potential for tourism. A huge palace built by Trujillo, currently unused, would be a perfect location for a much-needed national human rights museum with exhibits on Trujillo's life, rule and excesses, and about those who led resistance to the dictatorship, many of whom paid with their lives. San Cristóbal is also the nearest town to Reserva Antropológica El Pomier, a series of caves that contain the country's largest and most accessible collection of Taíno cave paintings. Unfortunately the caves have been carelessly over-developed and the Trujillo connection swept under the rug, and San Cristóbal remains unknown to most travelers. It's still an interesting stop, just not as much as it could be.

Orientation

The main road from the highway (Av Constitución) runs the west side of the central plaza, Parque Colón, and along the east side of the Plaza Pierda Viva, a few blocks further. A block to the east of Av Padre Ayala, is the main north-bound street and the one you take to get back to the highway. All of San Cristóbal's services are on those two streets, most within a few blocks of Parque Colón. If you arrive by bus, you'll be dropped off at Parque Colón.

Information

The **tourist office** (Av Constitución; ☯ 9am-3pm Mon-Fri) is in the municipal building a short distance north of Parque Colón. Most of the staff are enthusiastic about San Cristóbal's potential for tourism, but simply don't have institutional support to put their ideas into action. The **post office** (Av Constitución) is further up the street about 500 m.

Banco Popular (Av Constitución at Calle Mella, ☯ 8am-5pm Mon-Fri, 9am-1pm Sat) is at the southwest corner of Parque Colon and has a 24-hour ATM. A half block south, there's a **centro de llamadas** (call center ☎ 809-528-1314; ☯ 8am-10pm) where you can call the USA for US$0.25 per minute and Europe for US$0.75 per minute. Further south and around the corner, **A.D. Cibercom** (☎ 809-288-0952; ☯ 8am-10pm) has Internet access for US$1 per hour and often stays open until midnight.

Back on Av Constitución and another three blocks south, **Centro Médico Constitución** (CEMECO; ☎ 809-288-2121; Av Constitución at 19 de Marzo) is a private hospital with a 24 hour emergency room. The **Policia Nacional** (☯ 24hr) have a large station on the southwest corner of Parque Colón.

Sights

In addition to the below listings, one of San Cristóbal's most interesting attractions are the ancient cave paintings in the Reserva Antropológica El Pomier (p112) which is a short distance from town.

CASTILLO DEL CERRO

San Cristóbal's strangest sight is not technically open to the public, but the soldiers guarding the place are usually happy to take the padlock off the door and let you look around. Trujillo had the structure built for himself and his family in 1947 (at a cost of US$3 million) but he reportedly hated the finished product and never spent a single night there. The name means 'Castle on the Hill,' which is pretty accurate – overlooking the city, although the imposing concrete and glass structure looks like a medieval office building! But inside, huge dining rooms, ball rooms and numerous bedrooms and salons have fantastic ceilings and wall decorations made of plaster and painted in gaudy colors. The bathrooms – of which there must be twenty – have tile mosaics done in reds, blues and even gold leaf. There are six floors in all, and you can spend a half-hour or more just wandering through the abandoned structure. It is a monument to the material excesses of Trujillo, and is a curiously compelling stop despite the fact there are no signs or official tourist services.

Any taxi driver or *motoconchista* can take you there – it probably makes sense to ask the driver to come back in 30 to 60 minutes to pick you up, or to simply wait to hail another. If you've got a vehicle, from Parque Independencia take Calle María Trinidad Sánchez west 500m. Take a left onto Calle Luperón near the Isla gas station. Follow Calle Luperón 800m until you reach a fork in the road. There, Calle Luperón veers right and an unsigned street veers left and uphill. Take the unsigned street and proceed another 500m to the top. There are signs saying 'Do Not Enter,' but you can disregard those and pull right into the parking area facing the front doors. A soldier is always posted there.

Atop another hill on the other side of San Cristóbal is the house Trujillo and his family actually used. It is called **Casa de Caoba** (House of Mahogany) and was clearly once splendid, but has been completely gutted since. It is supposedly being restored, but is likely to remain closed for quite some time.

AROUND
SAANTO DOMINGO

MUSEO JAMAS EL OLVIDO SERÁ TU RECUERDO

Also interesting and slightly strange is the informal **museum and antique collection** (☎ 809-474-8767) in the home of local resident José Miguel Ventura Medina, known to some as 'el Hippi.' The museum's name translates literally to 'Forgetfulness will never be your remembrance,' or simply 'You will never be forgotten.' The 'you' in this case is none other than Generalísimo Trujillo, who, along with John F Kennedy, was Ventura's favorite world leader. Most will not agree with Ventura's assessment of Trujillo as a 'good dictator,' but the extensive collection of photos and other memorabilia – plus a slew of random antiques, from old corn and coffee grinders to early typewriters – is worth poking around. Ventura, who speaks Spanish and English, has plenty of stories to go along with them. The museum is free and open whenever Ventura is home; if he's not there, give him a call. It's located on Calle General Leger several blocks north of the park – look for a small white car perched on the rooftop.

PLAZA PIEDRA VIVA

Four blocks south of Parque Colón, this large plaza is built on the block where Trujillo's childhood home was located. On the plaza's south side is Iglesia Nuestra Señora de la Consolación, a highly decorated church built at the staggering cost of US$4 million in 1946. The church contains a mural by Spanish artist José Vela Zanetti, whose work also appears in the Palace of Justice in Santo Domingo and in the UN building in New York. Topping each of the church's two steeples is a pretty winged angel, and behind them is a dome crowned with a large white cross.

CASA DE LA CULTURA

On the south side of Parque Colón, the **Casa de Cultura** (☯ 9am-noon) has occasional photo and art exhibits, usually by local artists. It also hosts informal literary and art appreciation groups, but you're unlikely to be in town long enough to join.

MERCADO

San Cristóbal's main **market** (along Calle María Trinidad Sánchez) is housed in a big building two blocks west of Av Constitución. Here,

you'll find lots of images of Jesus, bottles of rum at bargain prices and inexpensive clothing and shoes (among a great many other things). If you've been wanting to buy a cassette tape featuring popular merengue artists, this is a good place to do it.

Sleeping & Eating

San Cristóbal isn't visited by many tourists, and has few accommodations.

Aparta-Hotel Ayala (☎ 809-528-3040; Av Padre Ayala 110, at Palo Hinchado; r US$21; ❄) Some rooms here are small and smell of cigarette smoke, but the majority are clean and surprisingly comfortable, and will definitely do in a pinch. All have cable TV, tile floors, minifridge and private bathrooms with coldwater only – while some of the rooms with just one bed have aircon.

Chichita (☎ 809-528-3012; Av Padre Ayala at Padre Borbón; mains US$3-8; ☯ 8:30am-midnight) The culinary claim to fame of San Cristóbal is the *pastelito en hoja*, literally 'pastry in paper.' It's an apt name, as it is basically a doughy empanada stuffed with cheese or meat that's served wrapped in a piece of butcher paper. They cost around US$0.50 a piece and Chichita is the eatery most people recommend. You can also get standard Dominican dishes here – fried chicken, grilled beef or pork served with rice, beans and fried bananas.

Getting There & Around

Buses for San Cristóbal leave from Santo Domingo from Parque Enriquillo. In San Cristóbal, *gua-guas* for the capital (US$1.40, 45 minutes) leave every 15 to 30 minutes from a stop at the southeast edge of the park. For towns west of San Cristóbal, you have to go out to the main highway – under the overpass is a popular place – and flag down a passing bus (to Baní US$1.40, 45 minutes, to Barahona (US$3.80, three hours).

There are taxis and *motoconchos* in the vicinity of Parque Independencia from sunrise until late at night.

RESERVA ANTROPOLÓGICA EL POMIER

Just 10km north of central San Cristóbal are limestone caves containing thousands of drawings and carvings that constitute the most extensive examples of prehistoric art yet discovered in the Caribbean; containing works by Igneri and Carib Indians as well as the Taínos. The drawings, painted with a mix of charcoal and the fat from manatees, depict birds, fish and other animals, as well as figures that may be deities. Relatively little is known about Hispaniola's earliest inhabitants, though the paintings here, believed to be as much as 2000 years old, provide some tantalizing clues.

In the area there are 57 **caves** (8am-5pm; admission US$3.50) that contain paintings, and five (containing almost 600 paintings) are open to the public. At the time of research (and for some time before then) the caves were closed for extensive renovation. Perhaps *too* extensive, including electric lighting and a wide cement pathway filling the entire floor of the main cave and tunnel system. The caves should be reopened by the time you read this.

The caves are almost literally inside a huge marble mining operation, which has and continues to threaten their preservation. The mine makes extensive use of explosives, and already a number of caves have been collapsed or weakened. (For safety, the caves are closed during blasting.) Even small cracks in the rock can alter the humidity content of the air inside the caves, and cause the paintings to fade. Some of the long-time guides at the caves tell fascinating stories of their fight to protect the site, including forming human barriers in front of miners armed with drills and dynamite. The amount of money invested in renovating the caves suggests there is at least some institutional support for their preservation, though the mines provide hundreds of jobs and hence wield tremendous influence. It's worth taking a look now, in case they aren't around (or accessible) in the future.

Getting There & Away

Getting to the caves is a challenge – there are almost no signs marking the road to the caves, and the entrance, also unmarked, is several hundred meters down a mine access road. The easiest way, of course, is to take a taxi or *motoconcho*. To take you there, wait for an hour and the return should cost around US$5 on a *motoconcho* or US$10 in a taxi. If you're driving, follow Av Constitución north to La Toma, a small community across the highway from San Cristóbal,

where there is one easy-to-spot sign. From there, it's another 2.5 km to a prominent but unmarked T-intersection, where you turn left and proceed up the hill for several more kilometers to the entrance. Ask as you go, as the turnoffs are easy to miss. Be alert for giant dump trucks coming down the road from the mine – there are a number of blind curves and the trucks are sometimes too loaded down to stop quickly.

SAN CRISTÓBAL TO BANÍ

A well-paved two-lane highway links San Cristóbal and Baní, and along the way you'll pass kilometer after kilometer of sugarcane fields. At certain times of the year, the tall sweet grass forms a wall at the highway's edge, broken up every so often by train tracks that seem to slice through the fields before inevitably being enveloped by them. In harvest season, it is common to see small diesel locomotives pulling huge contain-cars full of cane stalks like so many pick-up sticks.

BANÍ

A pleasant prosperous town, Baní has no sights to speak of but is the best place to stop for the night if you are driving between Santo Domingo and Barahona and can't make it all the way. Baní is best known as the birthplace of Generalísimo Máximo Gómez y Báez. As a young man Gómez served in the Spanish army in Santo Domingo. He later moved to Cuba and took up farming, an occupation that made him subject to Spanish taxation. During the 1860s, Gómez joined the insurgents opposed to Spanish rule, rose to the rank of general of the Cuban forces and, together with José Martí, led the revolution of 1868–78 that culminated in Cuba's independence from Spain.

Orientation

At Baní's heart is Parque Duarte, a spacious, clean and attractive park. To reach it coming from the east, turn right just after crossing the Río Baní and just in front of the oncoming one-way street that greets you almost at the foot of the bridge. Go two blocks and make a left onto Calle Máximo Gómez. Go six or seven blocks and make a left onto Calle Mella. After half a block you'll be at the intersection of Calle

Sánchez and Calle Mella, in front of the Iglesia Nuestra Señora de Regla (the city's main church).

To get to Parque Duarte from the west, turn right where Hwy 2 (also known as Sánchez Hwy) confronts an opposing one-way street. Turn left on Calle Sánchez – the first left you can make – and head six blocks to Parque Duarte. The hotels, restaurants and services are all within a block or two of Parque Duarte.

Information

Banco León (Hwy Sánchez at Calle Mella; 8:30am-5pm Mon-Fri, 9am-1pm Sat) and **Banco Popular** (809-522-3889; Gómez at Duarte; 8:15am-4pm Mon-Fri, 9am-1pm Sat) both have a 24-hour ATM.

Verizon Centro de Comunicaciones (8am-10pm; to USA per min US$0.30, to Europe per min US$0.85) is next door to Banco León. **Flash Point Cíber Café** (809-522-2436; 9am-11pm) is on Calle Mella a half-block south of the park and has Internet access for US$1.40 per hour.

Centro Médico Regional (809-522-3611; Presidente Billini at Restauración) is a recommended hospital four blocks east of Parque Duarte.
Farmacia Meniño (809-522-3344; Gómez btwn Duarte & Mella; 7:30am-9pm, 8am-noon Sun) is on the other side of the church from the park.

Sights

Baní's main tourist attraction is the **Casa de Máximo Gómez** (8am-5pm; admission free) which is essentially a small park built on what was the site of the leader's birthplace and childhood home. There's a marble bust of Gomez in the middle of the park, watched over by flags of Cuba and the DR and a mural of Gómez. The site is located two blocks east of the park on Calle Máximo Gómez, the main east bound street.

If you've got some time on your hands, check out the **Iglesia Nuestra Señora de Regla**, which hosts a patron saint festival every year on November 21. Also facing the park are several large **murals** of Máximo Gómez, and a nondescript **Museo Municipal** (City Museum; Calle Sánchez 1; admission free; 8am-noon Mon-Fri) on the ground floor of the Palacio del Ayuntamiento.

Sleeping & Eating

Hotel Caribani (522-3871; fax 522-3872; Calle Sánchez 12; r without/with aircon US$24.50/31.50;) Baní's best accommodations are definitely this

large hotel and restaurant, one block west of Parque Duarte. Rooms here are clean and comfortable, though some are a bit dim. All have hot water, cable TV and relatively new mattresses. Various services (bank, Internet, pharmacy etc) are all within a block or two.

Hotel Alba (809-380-0083; Mella; s/d with fan US$17.50/21, s/d with aircon US$24.50/35;) Half a block south of the park, this is a reliable if less comfortable option if the Caribani is full. Decent-sized rooms have hot water, cable TV and small fridge – the main drawback are the overly spongy beds.

Restaurant y Pizzería Yarey (809-522-3717; Calle Sánchez 10; mains US$4-10; breakfast, lunch & dinner) If you ask around town, this is the restaurant almost everyone mentions. Next door to the Hotel Caribani, tables are set up in a large open-air dining area and waiters in bow ties offer prompt service. The pizzas are cheap yet somewhat mediocre, but the seafood and beef dishes are pretty good, while the half-chicken plate with rice for US$3.50 is a bargain.

Getting There & Away

There are express *gua-guas* to Santo Domingo (US$1.75; 1¼ hours; every 15 minutes; 3:40am to 8pm) leaving from a terminal a half-block west of the main park. Regular *gua-guas* leave even more frequently – every five minutes – and cost US$0.30 less, but take a half-hour longer to get there.

Gua-guas to San José de Ocoa (US$1.10, 45 minutes, hourly, 7am to 8pm) leave from a terminal about a kilometer west of the park on Av Máximo Gómez. Buses to Barahona (US$3.50, two hours) pass by the same terminal roughly every 30 to 60 minutes – they're coming from Santo Domingo and don't have a fixed schedule for Baní. They don't linger long here, so be sure to be on the lookout.

SAN JOSÉ DE OCOA

The road to San José de Ocoa winds through mostly undeveloped countryside as it rises from 200m to nearly 2000m above sea level. Each ridgeline is followed by another, higher and higher, and from various points on the road you can see 10 or more sets of peaks simultaneously. It is a fine road for cyclists – particularly when coming down, with picturesque views of the hillsides and the Caribbean before you. (And it's a heck of a lot easier!)

Unlike most Dominican plazas, which have a few large shade trees around a gazebo and feel very urban despite any attempt to 'naturalize' the environment, the one in San José de Ocoa's central park has a jungle-like feel, with dozens of broadleaf trees and the sound of water running from four low-profile fountains. In several trees, the town has placed enormous birdhouses that each hold 20 pigeons or more.

As pretty as it is, there's not a whole lot to do in San José de Ocoa. It is most popular as a jumping-off point for the backroads route to Constanza. The area is rich with spring water and there are a few *balnearios* (swimming holes) and a large open-air restaurant which is popular with locals and weekend warriors.

Information

Banco Popular (☎ 8:15am-4pm Mon-Fri) is located at the southeast corner of the park, while **Banco Progreso** (☎ 8:30am-4pm Mon-Fri, 9am-1pm Sat) is at the southwest corner. Both have 24-hour ATMs.

You can make international calls at **Tele-Vimenca** (✆ 7:30am-10pm; Calle Duarte half-block from park; to USA per min US$0.25, to Europe per min US$0.50). There's an **Internet café** (Av San José a half-block from the park; US$1.75 per hr; ✆ 9am-12, 2-6pm Mon-Sat). The **post office** (☎ 809-906-0060; Calle Duarte btwn 16 de Agosto & Andrés Pimentel; ✆ 8am-5pm Mon-Fri, 8am-noon Sat) is across the street from the bus terminal.

Farmacia Quisqueya (Calle Duarte at Calle Manuel de Regla; ✆ 8am-noon, 2-6pm Mon-Sat) is one block from the park.

Sights & Activities

Rancho Francisco (☎ 809-558-4099; 1km south of town; admission US$1; ✆ 8am-11pm) The only *balneario* that was operating at the time of research, though there are several along this stretch. A large pool is fed by several smaller ones – the water bubbles up out of the ground just a few meters away, but is still filtered and chlorinated before being used in the pool. A huge dining area serves standard fish, chicken and meat dishes for around US$7 to $10. Not exactly an encounter with nature, but can be a pleasant way to cool off. It's quite busy on weekends, but is all but empty during the week.

Sleeping & Eating

Casa de Huéspedes San Francisco (☎ 809-558-2741; Calle Andrés Pimentel at Imbert; s/d/tw US$14/17.50/21; ⚡) Three blocks north of the park, this is the best option in town. Though not much to look at from the outside, the rooms here are simple but very clean and comfortable; all with cable TV and hot water. The friendly proprietors provide water and coffee for guests. There are several very basic rooms as well.

Hotel Marian (☎ 809-558-2086; Calle Andrés Pimentel at San José; s/tw with fan US$8.75/12.25, r with aircon US$12.25; ⚡) This hotel is on the southwest corner of the plaza and rooms are on the second floor overtop a bar and pool hall, so noise can sometimes be a problem. All rooms are relatively clean, but showing their age, especially in the bathroom. Some rooms have a door that opens onto a long common terrace – while letting in street noise it definitely brightens up the place. For less noise, ask for a room that's not directly above the bar.

Pollo Rey (Calle Duarte at Altagracia; mains US$3-7; ✆ 11am-1am) Right on the plaza, this fast food is the most reliable of a very limited choice of restaurants. Combo meals include greasy fried or roasted chicken, french fries or fried bananas, and a soda.

Cadena Colmado Detallista (☎ 809-558-2485; Calle Duarte; ✆ breakfast, lunch & dinner Mon-Sat, breakfast & lunch Sun) A decent-sized market next to the TeleVimenca call center between Altagracia and Calle Manuel de Regla, with canned food, soda and water, snacks etc.

Getting There & Away

The bus stop (Calle Duarte between 16 de Agosto and Andrés Pimentel) is a half-block west of the park, across the street from the post office. *Gua-guas* for Santo Domingo (US$2.80, 2 hours) leave every fifteen minutes from 4:15am to 5:30pm. If you're headed to Barahona, San Juan or other points west, take the Santo Domingo bus to the main highway (US$1.75) and flag a westbound *gua-gua* there.

For Constanza, pick-ups trucks make the tough, bumpy trip around three times per week. There is no fixed schedule or bus line, but either hotel can call around to see when the next truck is leaving. They typically leave very early – 5am or 6am – and charge from US$3 to $5 for the three to four hour trip.

The Southeast

The Dominican Republic's best beaches are in the southeast, with deep, white sand and spectacular turquoise water backed by thick stands of terrifically tall coconut trees. (Indeed, developers and marketers have dubbed the area *Costa de Coco*, or Coconut Coast, though it's not a term many Dominicans use.) With such beautiful beaches comes tourist development and nowhere more so than in the Dominican Republic (DR). All-inclusive resorts, close to a hundred at last count, dot the coast from just outside Santo Domingo clear around to Playa del Macao – some 200km not counting the innumerable inlets, coves and promontories that typify Hispaniola's perimeter. This is the vital heart of tourism in the Dominican Republic, drawing hundreds of thousands of beachgoers every year.

But the Southeast is more than all-inclusive resorts. Along its long coastline are a number of small enclaves and undeveloped beaches, where travelers looking for peace and isolation will find both in no short supply. There are two national parks, where you can snorkel on protected reefs or take a boat ride through mangroves to see ancient Taíno cave paintings. Speaking of reefs, the southeast has some of the country's best diving, with warm clear Caribbean water and brightly colored coral and tropical fish.

HIGHLIGHTS

- **Bávaro and Punta Cana** (p132) are home to the DR's most spectacular beaches and dozens of all-inclusive resorts.

- Take a boat ride throughout **Parque Nacional Los Haitises** (p146) to see mangrove forests and ancient Taíno cave paintings.

- Despite scores of tour groups passing through, one-road town **Bayahibe** (p122) still has a great public beach and laid-back atmosphere.

- **Parque Nacional del Este** (p127) has the best snorkeling and diving on the DR's southern coast.

- Escape the all-inclusives at **Playa Limón** (p142), a deserted beach paradise next to a protected lagoon.

THE SOUTHEAST

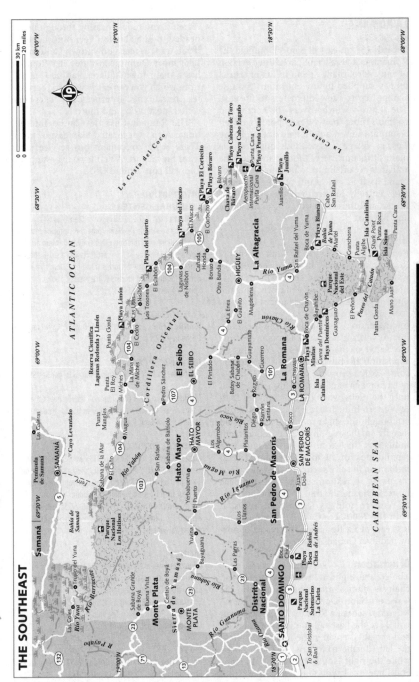

LA ROMANA

pop 208,437

Located 131km east of Santo Domingo, La Romana is a smaller but wealthier version of San Pedro, thanks to an influx of tourist money supplied by the enormous Casa de Campo resort a few kilometers to the east. The resort – which covers 7000 acres and contains more than a dozen pools, a dozen restaurants, even a polo field and an entire Tuscan village – is without question the main attraction here, though most of the activities are off-limits to nonguests. La Romana itself is a pleasant, prosperous place and centrally located between Santo Domingo and the resort areas of Punta Cana and Bávaro.

History

Beyond tourism, sugar is what drives La Romana's economy. It was a sleepy backwater until 1917, when an enormous sugar mill was built on the edge of town. The mill opened just as world sugar prices began to soar, sparking a demand for labor that drew many hundreds of families from the interior. As years passed, La Romana became the center of the country's sugar industry, a position it still holds today, employing some 20,000 people.

La Romana remained strictly a sugar town until the 1960s, when the US company Gulf & Western Industries arrived. Gulf & Western bought the sugar mill and also invested heavily in the region's cattle and cement industries. Its executives also decided to rebuild most of the town, spending US$20 million on the city's schools, churches, clinics, parks, recreation centers and employee houses. During the mid-1970s, before Gulf & Western sold its Dominican assets, it built the 7000-acre Casa de Campo resort just east of La Romana. The resort is now owned by a Cuban-American family.

Orientation

The coastal highway, which separates and changes names numerous times on the way from Santo Domingo, is named Hwy 3 when it reaches La Romana. Entering town, you'll see the baseball stadium on your left and shortly thereafter the highway splits – the left (northern) fork is Av Padre Abreu while the right (southern) fork is Av General Luperón. If you're driving, take Padre Abreu if you're just passing through or are headed to El Seibo, but veer onto Luperón if you want to reach downtown La Romana. Like most Dominican cities, La Romana has a main town square (Parque Central) from which you can easily walk to most hotels, restaurants, Internet cafés, telephone center, post office and more.

The Romana-Casa de Campo International Airport is located 8km east of town. There is no convenient bus service to or from the airport. A taxi is your best option and will cost around US$9.

Information

CULTURAL CENTERS

BoMana (☎ 809-556-2834; Calle Diego Avila 42; voluntary donation; 🕒 9am-7pm) This cultural center has an art gallery with rotating exhibits by Dominican artists, a permanent display of Taíno artifacts and a small theatre space where a troupe performs traditional Dominican dances for groups of tourists twice weekly. Shows are at 3pm on Tuesdays and Sundays.

EMERGENCY

Politur (Tourist Police; ☎ 809-550-7112; Calle Francisco Ducoudrey at Libertad; 🕒 24hr)

INTERNET ACCESS

Cybernet Café (Calle Eugenio A Miranda; per hr US$1.50; 🕒 8:30am-10pm)

Mundo Ciber@Net (Av Gregorio Luperón near Calle Francisco del Castillo Marquéz; per hr US$1; 🕒 8am-10pm Mon-Sat, 8am-6pm Sun)

MEDICAL SERVICES

Clínica Canela (☎ 809-556-3135 ext 228 or 299 for emergencies, ext 252 for pharmacy; Respaldo Av Libertad 44 at Restauranción) Recommended private clinic with 24-hour pharmacy and emergency room.

Farmacia Dinorah II (☎ 809-556-2225; Calle Ramón Berges; 🕒 7am-8pm Mon-Sat, 8am-noon Sun) Free delivery available.

MONEY

Banco León (Calle Duarte; 🕒 8:30am-5pm Mon-Fri, 9am-1pm Sat) Located at southeast corner of the main park, with a 24-hour ATM.

ScotiaBank (Av Gregorio Luperón at Av Santa Rosa; 🕒 8:30am-4:30pm Mon-Fri, 9am-1pm Sat) Near the Mercado municipal. One ATM.

POST

Post Office (Calle Farncisco del Castillo Marquéz near Av Gregorio Luperón; 🕒 9am-3pm Mon-Fri)

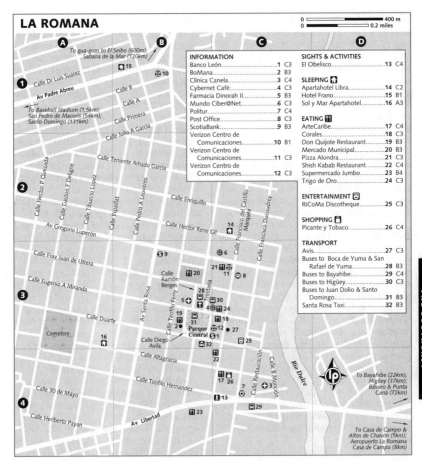

LA ROMANA

INFORMATION	
Banco León.................................1	C3
BoMana.......................................2	B3
Clínica Canela...........................3	C4
Cybernet Café...........................4	C3
Farmacia Dinorah II...................5	B3
Mundo Ciber@Net.....................6	C3
Politur..7	C4
Post Office..................................8	C3
ScotiaBank.................................9	B3
Verizon Centro de	
Comunicaciones..................10	B1
Verizon Centro de	
Comunicaciones..................11	C3
Verizon Centro de	
Comunicaciones..................12	C3

SIGHTS & ACTIVITIES	
El Obelisco..............................13	C4

SLEEPING	
Apartahotel Libra.....................14	C2
Hotel Frano..............................15	B1
Sol y Mar Apartahotel..............16	A3

EATING	
ArteCaribe...............................17	C4
Corales....................................18	C3
Don Quijote Restaurant............19	B3
Mercado Municipal...................20	B3
Pizza Alondra..........................21	C3
Shish Kabab Restaurant...........22	C4
Supermercado Jumbo...............23	B4
Trigo de Oro............................24	C3

ENTERTAINMENT	
RiCoMa Discotheque................25	C3

SHOPPING	
Picante y Tobaco.....................26	C4

TRANSPORT	
Avis...27	C3
Buses to Boca de Yuma & San	
Rafael de Yuma....................28	B3
Buses to Bayahibe...................29	C4
Buses to Higüey.......................30	B3
Buses to Juan Dolio & Santo	
Domingo..............................31	B3
Santa Rosa Taxi.......................32	B3

THE SOUTHEAST

TELEPHONE

The three Verizon offices in town provide the same service: international calls to the USA (US$0.32 per minute) and to Europe (US$0.75 per minute). All are open from 8am to 10pm daily.

Verizon Centro de Comunicaciones (Calle Diego Avila facing Parque Central)

Verizon Centro de Comunicaciones (Av Padre Abreu at Av Santa Rosa)

Verizon Centro de Comunicaciones (Av Gregorio Luperón at Calle Reales)

Sights & Activities

More a landmark than a sight, **El Obelisco** (The Obelisk; Av Libertad btwn Calles Márquez & Ducoudrey) is a replica of the George Washington monu-

ment in Washington, DC, though it is much smaller and painted on all four sides. There are similar monuments in other cities, Santo Domingo most notably, but La Romana's has the best paint job, including modern and realist depictions of Taíno culture and subjugation, and of contemporary Dominican life, from dancing and music to industrialization, agriculture and even a large cruise ship. The monument has been around for years, but in 2005 the city renovated the little pie-shaped corner it occupies, turning it into a nice little park with benches and shrubbery.

ALTOS DE CHAVÓN

On the grounds of nearby Casa de Campo (see p120) is **Altos de Chavón**, an artistic center that was constructed in the 1970s in the style of a 16th-century Mediterranean village. Cobblestone streets, stone carvings and Old World architecture convey the feeling that the place has existed for centuries. Within the village are several galleries, a handsome church and an impressive pre-Colombian museum that was being renovated when we passed through. There are also several restaurants, a number of gift shops and a 5000-seat amphitheater.

Unlike the rest of Casa de Campo, which is off-limits to nonguests, Altos de Chavón is open to the public. Because of this, however, bus-loads of tourists arrive every day jamming the streets, packing the shops and eateries, and all-in-all changing the atmosphere from a quiet village to an overflowing amusement park. Not a very pleasant way to spend a day. If you do choose to visit, try going in the mid to late afternoon; by that time, most of the buses have left and you and a handful of visitors may just have the place to yourselves.

Note that you must arrive by car, *motoconchos* (motorcycle taxis) are prohibited from entering the area. If you're driving from La Romana, take the main road past the gated entrance to Casa de Campo and continue on to a second entrance 5km up the road. The turn-off will appear on your left, marked with an 'Altos de Chavón' sign. Alternatively, you can take a cab from La Romana, which costs around US$8.75 one way, or US$17.50 roundtrip with an hour's wait.

GOLFING
Within the grounds of the Casa de Campo (right) are two Pete Dye-designed **golf courses**: 'The Teeth of the Dog' (greens fees US$200) and 'Links' (greens fees US$145). Both courses are open to guests and non-guests alike, but you should always call a day in advance. After 2:30pm both courses are US$93. Tee times can be reserved by email (t.times@ccampo.com.do) or fax (☎ 809-523-8800) only, phone reservations are not accepted.

Sleeping
Sol y Mar Apartahotel (☎ 809-556-3010; Calle Altagracia 55 btwn Espaillat & Pedro A Leuveres; r with fan/aircon US$15/19, tw with aircon US$27; ✕) A short walk from the center of town, the 18 rooms

at this newly renovated (and renamed) hotel all have aircon, cable TV and decent beds; some have a minifridge but none have hot water. The rooms are clean but smallish – ask for one upstairs where the extra light lends a feeling of more space. The hotel was also outfitting two studio apartments when we passed through, which should have nice furnishings but could use some windows.

Hotel Frano (☎ 809-550-4744; Av Padre Abreu 9; d/tw US$34/39; ✕ P) Popular with traveling businessmen, this hotel is a reliable, pleasant option, though it's rather removed from the center of town. Ample rooms have comfortable beds, patterned quilts, cable TV and large bathrooms with hot water and bathtubs. Ask for a room that's off the main street, but one that still has a window (some don't). The **restaurant** (mains US$4-6; ✕ 7am-9pm) here is also dependable, with friendly service and tasty Dominican dishes.

Apartahotel Libra (☎ 809-556-8820, fax 809-556-4833; Calle Hector Rene Gil 11; r US$21, tw US$28; ✕ P) Located within striking distance of the main plaza, rooms here all have kitchenettes, private hot water bathrooms, aircon and cable TV. Unfortunately, the rooms are showing serious signs of wear. Some rooms are better than others; ask to see a couple before you settle in. Acceptable for a night.

Casa de Campo (☎ 809-523-8698; www.casadecampo.com.do; Av Libertad; r US$224-353, all-inclusive per person US$260-353; ✕ ☇ P ☐) Several kilometers east of downtown, this is a sprawling, world-famous resort with 275 rooms and 150 villas that's best known for its two Pete Dye-designed golf courses: 'The Teeth of the Dog' and 'Links'. The resort is also known for its Sporting Clays Center, with 245 shooting positions, and Altos de Chavón (p119), a Tuscan-style village that's really a glorified mall but picturesque all the same. Rates include horseback riding, tennis, use of non-motorized water-sports equipment and gym access. Massage, facials, manicures and other pampering are available at additional cost. There are nine restaurants, more than a dozen swimming pools and a private airport.

Accommodations range from tropical-themed hotel rooms with mahogany furnishings and views of the Caribbean to luxurious villas complete with private gardens, a pool, a housekeeper and a cook. All come with top-notch amenities, including cable TV, Bose stereo systems and large closets with safety deposit boxes.

While the facilities are very appealing, the service is sometimes lacking, in part because the place is so big it takes a while for help (or an extra towel) to arrive. One persistent complaint is that the resort buses, which are supposed to pass by designated pickup points every 15 minutes, in reality take as much as 45 minutes. The resort rents golf carts, which are pricey at US$35 a day, but save you a great deal of time and aggravation.

The vast majority of the resort's guests arrive by air, either at the private landing strip or the airport that serves La Romana. If you are among the minority who arrive by car, a simple way to get here is to take Av Padre Abreu to the major fork in the road, turn right onto Av Santa Rosa, proceed 17 or 18 blocks to Av Libertad, turn left on Av Libertad and stay in the right lane. Av Libertad will lead you straight into Casa de Campo after several kilometers.

Eating

Don Quijote Restaurant (☎ 809-556-2827; Calle Diego Avila 44; mains US$7-18; ☽ lunch & dinner, closed Mon) Located on Parque Central, this pleasant restaurant offers some of the tastiest meals in town. Among the variety of main dishes, the most popular include fettuccine with shrimp, any of the beef filets and chicken breast sautéed in lobster sauce.

Pizza Alondra (☎ 809-550-4115; Calle Francisco del Castillo Márquez 88; mains $5-11; ☽ lunch & dinner Wed-Mon, dinner only Tue) This place makes pizzas just like mama did if you were lucky. Topping combinations are innumerable but include ham, pepperoni, mushroom, corn, pineapple and cherry – yes, cherry. All are served in a pleasant and shady courtyard with ironwork tables. If you prefer, pizzas can also be ordered to go.

Trigo de Oro (☎ 809-550-5650; Calle Eugenio A Miranda 9; mains US$1-4; ☽ breakfast, lunch & dinner Mon-Sat, breakfast Sun) As soon as you step through the front gate of this place, you're transported to a chi-chi French café/bakery with shade trees, a gurgling fountain and mosaic-tiled tables. The menu is simple but tempting with baguettes, sandwiches, croissants, pastries and all the coffee drinks you could want. If you're in the mood for a drink with a bigger kick, the menu also includes a full line of cocktails. An oasis of a place.

Shish Kabab Restaurant (☎ 809-556-2737; Calle Francisco del Castillo Marquéz 32; mains US$5-18; ☽ lunch & dinner, closed Mon) A local institution, this centrally-located restaurant serves Middle Eastern dishes like *baba ghanoush* (mashed eggplant mixed with parsley, sesame paste, garlic, lemon and olive oil), stuffed vine leaves and of course a variety of shish kebab, including grouper, garlic lobster and pepper steak.

Corales (☎ 809-556-9444; Calle Eugenio A Miranda 57; mains US$5-12; ☽ breakfast, lunch & dinner) A restaurant, café and bar all rolled into one, Corales gives you the choice of a classy indoor dining room or casual shady patio. Food service is the same in both and includes Creole and international dishes, especially seafood. At night, this is good place for drinks and something light.

ArteCaribe (☎ 809-556-3436; Calle Francisco del Castillo Márquez 15 at Calle Altagracia; mains US$1-8; ☽ lunch & dinner) This small cheery café serves great empanadas, including pepperoni, chicken or just cheese. A couple of those and a drink make a great snack on the go. If you're not in a rush, there are more complete meals, like grilled meats and *sancocho* (a filling vegetable and meat stew), and several small comfortable tables.

Mercado Municipal (Calle Teofilo Ferry at Calle Fray Juan de Utera; ☽ 6am-6pm Mon-Sat, 6am-noon Sun) This bustling market makes a good place to buy produce and snacks for the road. The aptly named **Supermercado Jumbo** (Av Libertad; ☽ 8am-9pm Mon-Sat, 9am-7pm Sun) has every sort of grocery item you could possibly want.

Shopping

Picante y Tobaco (☎ 809-556-3436; Calle Altagracia btwn Calles Reyes & Ducoudrey; ☽ 9am-9pm) An odd but oddly-fitting combination, this store sells hot sauce and cigars. The different hot sauces comes mostly from the US, but the owner has some local farmers attempting to grow habaneros, serranos and chilies. The cigars, of course, are 100% Dominican.

Drinking & Entertainment

There's not much in the way of nightlife in La Romana: it consists of one nightclub and a few restaurants and bars that are nice for a beer or two.

RiCoMa Discotheque (Calle Duarte btwn Calles Reales & Ducoudrey; admission usually free; ☽ 6:30pm-3am Wed-Sun) This block of Calle Duarte is

La Romana's party zone, such as it is. The large, two-story dance hall plays mostly Latin dance music and some house, rock and R&B. Live bands are occasionally featured, and a US$3 to US$5 cover may be charged.

Corales (☎ 809-556-9444; Calle Eugenio A Miranda 57; ☼ 8am-midnight) For a mellow night out, order a few beers and appetizers at this restaurant's pleasant open-air café area.

Getting There & Away
AIR
Aeropuerto La Romana Casa de Campo (☎ 809-813-9000) is 8km east of town. There are a few regularly scheduled flights, but most of the traffic here is chartered. Carriers include **American Airlines** (☎ 809-813-9080), **US Airways** (☎ 809-813-9364), **Caribair** (☎ 809-813-9070) and **IAS** (☎ 809-813-9114). Ground services giant **Swissport** (☎ 809-813-9364) handles ticketing for a number of carriers, including US Airways and USA3000.

A taxi to or from town costs about US$9.

BUS
La Romana is serviced by various *gua-guas* (small buses used for cheap local transport) that stop near or on the Parque Central.
Boca de Yuma US$2, 1 hour, every 20 minutes, 7am to 6pm
Higüey *caliente/expreso* US$1.75/2, 45 minutes, every 20 minutes, 5:30am to 10pm
Juan Dolio US$1.50, 1hour, every 10 minutes, 5am to 9pm
Santo Domingo *caliente/expreso* US$3/3.50, two hours, *caliente* every 10 minutes, *expreso* every 20 minutes, 5am to 9pm
San Rafael de Yuma US$1.75, 45 minutes, every 20 minutes, 7am to 6pm

Gua-guas to Bayahibe (US$1.10, 30 minutes, every 20 minutes, 6am to 7pm) depart from a stop on Av Libertad at Restauración.

To get to Samaná, take a *gua-gua* to El Seibo (US$1.75, 1¼ hours, every 20 minutes, 5:30am to 8pm) from a stop on Av Santa Rosa 600m north of Av Padre Abreu. From there you can connect to Hato Mayor, and then to Sabana de la Mar, where there are ferries across the bay. On each leg, tell the driver you are catching another *gua-gua* onward and he will likely drop you at the next terminal.

Getting Around
Motoconchos and taxis are typically found near the southeast corner of Parque Central. *Motoconcho* rides inside the city cost US$1 to US$3, taxis cost between US$3 and US$6. You can also call **Santa Rosa Taxi** (☎ 809-556-5313; Calle Duarte) for a pick-up.

To rent a car, try **Avis** (☎ 809-550-0600; Calle Francisco del Castillo Márquez at Calle Duarte; per day from US$75; ☼ 8am-6pm).

BAYAHIBE
pop 2000
Around 22km east of La Romana, Bayahibe is a study of contrasts. It is a sleepy seaside town with a couple of thousand residents and no paved roads. (And, happily, no *motoconchos* or scooters.) Nightlife consists of a congenial gathering of residents and visitors of all ages in the center of town, all sipping sodas and beers to a backdrop of loud *bachata* (Dominican 'country' music) and lively conversation. Yet every day, 25 or more tour buses rumble into town, carrying upwards of a thousand tourists from surrounding all-inclusive resorts. They are all headed to Isla Saona, a picturesque but overcrowded island in the nearby national park, where they spend the day snorkeling, sunbathing and enjoying seaside buffets and free drinks. In the short period that the tour groups are in town – in the morning and again in the afternoon – Bayahibe bustles with activity, as tourists are herded onto motorboats and townspeople cajole them into buying food, drinks, handicrafts or other small knick-knacks. At all other times, the other Bayahibe emerges, a quiet place with reliable hotels, fantastic snorkeling and diving, and a slow, friendly pace.

A short distance from Bayahibe is Dominicus Americanus, a relatively new upscale enclave of resorts, hotels and a few shops and services which are centered around a terrific public beach. Listings for Dominicus Americanus appear along with those for Bayahibe – be sure to double-check the address of the listings you're interested in.

Orientation
A single road not more than 2km long connects the coastal highway with the town of Bayahibe. It splits about 1km south at a

water tower – the right fork heads to the village of Bayahibe, the left towards Dominicus Americanus.

Headed towards Bayahibe, the road eventually becomes dirt. It feeds into a large parking lot next to the ocean before continuing east along a small beach. Within 100m the road loops around a restaurant and past a handful of hotels before heading north towards the highway. There also are several small and winding sand roads that open onto the main road; these lead to villagers' homes.

The road to Dominicus Americanus is well paved. The enclave itself contains only a handful of streets that are laid out in a grid, making it easy to negotiate. The Club Dominicus lies at the center of the complex; public access to the beach is at the far eastern end. The entrance to the Iberostar resort is found immediately south of the turn-off to Dominicus Americanus.

Information

Travelers' services are slowly emerging in Bayahibe. At the time of research, however, there was no bank, post office, hospital or tourist office. A few of the below listings are in Dominicus Americanus.

BOOKSTORE

El Mundo de la Hispaniola (Dominicus Americanus; ⏰ 8am-1pm & 2:30-8pm) Day-old editions of the *New York Times* and *Miami Herald* are sold at this large multipurpose store.

INTERNET ACCESS, TELEPHONE, & FAX

B@y@hibe Tele.com (east of the main parking lot; ⏰ 8:30am-7pm) Fast Internet connections (per hour US$4), international calls (to USA per minute US$0.32, to Europe per minute US$0.67) and fax, too (within the DR per page US$0.70, to USA per page US$1.75, to Europe per page US$2.65)

MONEY

Agencia de Cambio Sánchez (☎ 809-833-0201; next to the Hotel Llave del Mar; ⏰ 8am-10pm Mon-Sat, 8am-6pm Sun) The only place to get money in town is this exchange kiosk. Travelers checks, cash dollars and euros accepted.

Banco Popular (Dominicus Americanus; ⏰ 24hr) ATM located just outside the Viva Beach Hotel.

BanReservas (Next to Hotel Bayahibe) Though not open at the time of research, there should be an ATM and small branch office by the time you read this.

Sights & Activities

The main attraction in Bayahibe is to take a tour of some sort to one of the nearby islands. On the way to the islands, most tours stop to look at the mouth of a large cave and zip through the tangled mangrove forest. See the Parque Nacional del Este section (p127) for information on visiting the park on foot from Bayahibe, including a cave with Taíno pictograms.

BEACHES

Playa Bayahibe is the beach right in town and a pleasant if not spectacular stretch of shoreline. The sand is white, but somewhat thin and hard in places. There are a number of restaurants lining the beach (see Eating, p126) so you can eat overlooking the sand and sea. An all-inclusive resort has occupied much of the far end of Playa Bayahibe, but it's a long enough beach that you won't have any trouble finding a spot to lay out your towel. **Playa Dominicus** is a beautiful beach in Dominicus Americanus, with thick nearly-white sand and gorgeous rolling water. Plus there's an easy public access point – even a parking area in case you have a car – which means no cutting through hotels or restaurants to get to the beach. You can rent beach chairs for US$3, go parasailing for US$60, or eat at one of various food stands or restaurants. The beach can get busy, but not unpleasantly so.

ISLA SAONA

The largest **island** in the park is also the most visited. Photos of the island are truly stunning, with pristine white sand lapped by turquoise water and backed by dense palm forests. It is in many ways the prettiest spot in the country, which makes what has happened to it all the more upsetting. Visiting Isla Saona does not feel like visiting a national park and certainly not a deserted Caribbean island. Much of its beautiful beach has been filled with snack shacks and private seaside buffets operated by all-inclusives for use by their guests. Music blasts from competing sound systems and vendors ply the beach peddling hair-braids and other assorted knick-knacks. The coral has been seriously damaged by a combination of heavy boat traffic and inexperienced snorkelers kicking and stepping on the fragile formations.

Although the island has a charm and natural beauty that no amount of tourist silliness could ever outdo, it's still hard to recommend a trip there, at least as the main destination. (Although if you're interested they can be booked at any hotel for US$48 per person, including lunch.) The dive shops in Bayahibe offer rewarding trips that stop for lunch at Isla Saona, but only after visiting other spots for hiking, snorkeling or both (see below).

ISLA CATALINITA
This tiny uninhabited **island** on the eastern edge of the park is a common stop on snorkeling and diving tours. Arriving on the island's western (leeward) side, it's about a half-hour hike to the other side, where a lookout affords dramatic views of the powerful open-ocean waves crashing on shore. There is a coral reef in about 2m of water that makes for great snorkeling, and a good dive site called Shark Point, where sharks are often seen.

ISLA CATALINA
Located 18km west of the national park, **Isla Catalina** is actually much closer to La Romana and Casa de Campo than to Bayahibe. The island is ringed by fine coral reefs in 2m to 5m of water that are absolutely teeming with tropical fish (owing in no small part to their being fed by snorkelers from Casa de Campo and visiting cruise ships). There's a nice beach on the far side, and trips to Isla Catalina often include a couple of hours for lunch and relaxing on the sand. Trips there also typically include an hour's stop at Altos de Chavón (Chavón Heights, p119). True to its name, Altos de Chavón is at the top of a high bluff; there are some 250 steps from the pier which can be challenging for some travelers. Casa de Campo resort offers tours there for its guests, but everyone else typically visits from Bayahibe.

SNORKELING & DIVING
Bayahibe is arguably the best place in the country to dive or snorkel, featuring warm clear Caribbean water, healthy reefs and plenty of fish and other sea life. The diving tends to be 'easier' (and therefore ideal for beginners) than it is on the DR's north coast, where the underwater terrain is less flat, the

water cooler and the visibility somewhat diminished. There are about 20 open-water dive sites; some favorites include **Catalina Wall** and an impressive 85m ship in 41m to 44m of water known as **St Georges Wreck** after Hurricane Georges. Deep in the national park, **Padre Nuestro** is a weaving 290m tunnel flooded with freshwater that can be dived, but only by those with advanced cave diving training.

Tours
Two dive shops in Bayahibe offer a variety of diving and snorkeling tours at comparable prices. Both do a good job accommodating mixed groups (ie both snorkelers and divers) when necessary. Both also have multilingual guides and instructors, with Spanish, English, German, French and Italian spoken.

Casa Daniel (☎ 809-833-0050; www.casa-daniel.de; 100m from center across from Mare Nostrum; ⊙ 8am-6pm) This Swiss-run dive shop offers one-tank dives without or with equipment rental for US$33/39. Packages of six dives are US$182/210, ten-dive packages are US$292/325. Full-day snorkel/beach trips to Isla Catalinita and Isla Saona are US$68, including brief stops at El Peñon Cave and a swing through the mangrove forest. Isla Catalina trips with snorkeling, lunch on the beach and a stop at Altos de Chavón are US$59. PADI certification courses are available. Ask about accommodation packages as well.

Scubafun (☎ 809-763-3023; www.scubafun.info; ⊙ 7:30am-6pm) In operation for over nine years and located on the main strip in the middle of town, this PADI dive center offers two-tank dives in nearby reefs (US$65), excursions to Isla Catalina (US$100), and dive/day trips to Isla Saona (US$114) and Isla Catalinita (US$124). Full equipment rentals are an additional US$5. Beginner and advanced PADI courses are also offered. Accommodation/dive packages are available with Villa Iguana (opposite).

Sleeping
Bayahibe has a decent selection of hotels considering how small it is. Most are in the budget range and some quite basic; if it's in your budget, the midrange hotels are a significant step up. In Bayahibe proper, all the hotels are within easy walking distance

of each other and the center, making comparison shopping easy. That said, hotels here do fill up, so don't dally too much if it's busy.

BUDGET
All of these hotels are in Bayahibe proper.

Hotel Bayahibe (☎ 809-833-0159; hotelbayahibe@ hotmail.com; tw US$35; 🐾 P 🖥) Located at the end of the main street, Hotel Bayahibe is one of the nicer places in town. Rooms are spacious with big windows and have cable TV and telephone. About half have a nice balcony too. The hotel was about to undergo a major renovation when we passed through, so by the time you read this, the rooms should be even better.

Cabañas Maura (☎ 809-833-0053; r US$9-11; r with kitchen US$14) Very basic but very clean, the four cabañas offered by this friendly family are excellent value. Rooms have a fan, private bathroom and cold water only. It is located half a block east of Scubafun.

Cabañas Francisca (☎ 809-556-2742; r without/ with aircon US$18/25; 🐾 P) Located on the main street next to Hotel Bayahibe, Francisca offers basic and cleanish rooms that are in small stand-alone structures. All have private bathrooms with cold water, cable TV and a small fridge. Up to three can fit in a room.

Hotel Llave del Mar (☎ 809-883-0081; r without/with aircon US$25/28; tw with aircon US$32; 🐾 P) Unmistakable by its pink, green and blue paint job, this two-story hotel on the main street offers cramped – though clean – rooms. All have private bathrooms but only aircon rooms come with cable TV and mini-fridges. Some rooms also feature small balconies, which is a plus on breezy evenings.

Cabañas Trip Town (☎ 809-833-0082; fax 809-883-0088; cabins without/with aircon US$21/28; 🐾 P) Comparable to Cabañas Francisca in size and cleanliness. The main differences here are that there's hot water but only cable TV in rooms with aircon. Most also have small refrigerators. You'll find this place on the main street across from Hotel Bayahibe.

MIDRANGE
The first listing here is in Bayahibe proper and the rest are in Dominicus Americanus.

Villa Iguana (☎ 809-833-0203; www.villaiguana.de; 1 block south & 2 blocks east of Scubafun; r without/with air-con US$29/39, 1 bdrm apt US$49, ste US$69) Crowned with two thatch roofs, the Villa Iguana offers excellent accommodations at decent prices. Standard rooms are small but spotless, apartments are spacious and boast brand-new furnishings, and the ocean-view suite takes up the entire top floor and includes an outdoor living room, a solarium and a private pool (a treat if you can swing it!). The hotel also is affiliated with Scubafun (opposite) and offers good dive/ accommodation packages.

Hotel Bocayate (hbocayate@verizon.net.do; Av Eladia, Dominicus Americanus; r US$50) Facing the Viva Dominicus Palace, the Hotel Bocayate offers 14 pleasant rooms that are set on a shady courtyard. Rooms are spacious, have cleanish bathrooms and are fan-cooled. The beautiful Dominicus beach is just down the street and guests can often get discounted day passes to the Viva resort – both are major pluses.

Cabaña Elke (☎ 809-696-8249; www.viwi.it, in Italian; Av Eladia, Dominicus Americanus; r US$60, apt US$75, with 4 people US$90; P 🐾) In the Dominicus Americanus enclave, the Elke has nine rooms and nine apartments arranged in two long rows leading off the main lobby area. The rooms are large and comfortable but the split-level apartments are a better deal, with a master bedroom above and bathroom and living room (with sofa bed) downstairs, plus a small kitchen with an electric stove, small fridge and sink. The units are rather narrow, but have high A-frame roofs which lends more space. The red-tile bathrooms and polished wood paneling were once nice (and are still acceptable) but are definitely starting to show their age. The hotel has a nice little pool on site, and guests can get a day pass to the nearby Club Dominicus for just US$40 per person. Room prices are reduced by 25% in the low season.

Hotel Eden (☎ 809-688-1856; www.santodomingo village.com; Av La Laguna 10, Dominicus Americanus; r US$65; 🐾) The Hotel Eden offers 40 comfortable but charmless rooms that open onto a network of cement sidewalks. Not the prettiest of settings but with a fantastic beach just a few minutes' walk away, you probably won't be spending lots of time in the hotel anyway. Twenty-four hour electricity is included and cable TV costs US$5 extra.

TOP END

There are a string of all-inclusive resorts in Dominicus Americanus and along the road between there and Bayahibe.

Iberostar Hacienda Dominicus (☎ 809-688-3600; www.iberostar.com; Playa Dominicus; d per person US$180; ✿ Ⓟ ✇ 🖳) Running the length of a beautiful white-sand beach and set on lush grounds, this is one of the nicest all-inclusive resorts in the country. Rooms are spacious and tastefully decorated; all have modern amenities and boast comfortable terraces or balconies. There are three pools on site: an activities one; a large deep pool for scuba clinics; and the main one, which is separated by islands of vegetation, giving an impression of many small pools. A varied buffet and four specialty restaurants – Japanese, Mexican, French and steak – serve great cuisine. A full menu of activities (tennis, windsurfing, sailing, kayaking, volleyball, aerobics, dance classes, pool etc) keeps guests busy. An excellent choice.

Viva Dominicus Beach (☎ 809-686-5658; www.vivaresorts.com; Playa Dominicus; d per person US$110-130; ✿ Ⓟ ✇ 🖳) Five kilometers east of Bayahibe, the Club Dominicus also is a good choice. Rooms are comfortable, clean and feature balconies, many with spectacular ocean views. The beach is lined with thick white sand and calm turquoise waters, making it perfect for swimming or for kids at play. Facilities include four pools, several bars, a theater, a disco and several activities outlets. Four restaurants serve a variety of cuisines, though the food receives mixed reviews. A sister resort, the **Viva Dominicus Palace** (☎ 809-686-5658; www.vivaresorts.com; Playa Dominicus; d per person US$150-180; ✿ Ⓟ ✇ 🖳), is next door and as a five star is a bit fancier; some facilities are shared between the two.

Eating

The first four listings are in Bayahibe proper, while the last two are in Dominicus Americanus.

La Punta (☎ 809-833-0082; btwn the town beach & the main beach; mains US$10-25; ✇ lunch & dinner) This open-air eatery is considered one of the best seafood places in town. Fish and shellfish are often caught the same day and served up any way you like. Popular dishes include *camarones al ajillo* (shrimp sautéed in garlic) and *langosta a la parrilla* (grilled lobster). Bring your appetite.

Mare Nostrum (☎ 809-833-0055; mains US$13-25; ✇ lunch & dinner, closed Sun) Overlooking Bayahibe's town beach, the Mare Nostrum is a classy restaurant offering excellent Italian dishes. Pastas are all homemade and the chef offers delicious daily specials – cross your fingers that *risotto mare* (seafood risotto) is on the list when you stop in; the shellfish is super fresh and the risotto just melts in your mouth. A good selection of wines is also offered.

Café Restaurante Leidy (☎ 809-543-0052; Playa Bayahibe; mains US$5-15; ✇ breakfast, lunch & dinner) One of a string of more or less identical open-air eateries along the east side of Playa Bayahibe, the specialty here is seafood, including fish filets served *al coco* (in coconut sauce), *al ajillo* (in garlic sauce) and a half-dozen other ways. Pasta, chicken, pork and beef dishes are also available. Nice breeze and even nicer view.

Colmado Billy (✇ 7:30am-10pm Mon-Sat, 7:30am-7pm Sun) This tiny family run grocery one block west of Scubafun is the best of the handful in town. Some produce, lots of dairy and a variety of canned and dried goods are offered. It's the sort of place where you stand behind a counter and ask for items, so come prepared to speak Spanish or at the very least to point.

Río Marina Ristorante (☎ 809-688-5217; Dominicus Americanus; mains US$7-20; ✇ breakfast, lunch & dinner) Right in the middle of Dominicus Americanus, tables are scattered over a broad, covered patio open on two sides. Order a complete meal with fish or grilled meat, or something small like a baked potato (US$1.75) or grilled veggies (US$4). The daily special comes served with rice and beans and a main dish and is just US$3.50, amazing considering it's right in front of a high-end all-inclusive resort.

El Mundo de la Hispaniola (Dominicus Americanus; ✇ 8am-1pm, 2:30-8pm) Large store that is mostly filled with *artesanía* but also has beach necessities like sunscreen, film, water, snacks, plus a small grocery section with canned food, pasta, produce and (a little) more.

Getting There & Away

Gua-guas are the only means of public transportation to and from Bayahibe. *Gua-guas* leave from a set of trees in the center of town, a block north of the Hotel Bayahibe. Services run to La Romana (US$1.25, 25 minutes, every 20 minutes, 6am to 7pm) and Higüey (US$1.75, 40 minutes, irregular hours).

Bayahibe Taxi (☎ 809-833-0206) has a stand at the *gua-gua* stop. Rates include nearby hotels (US$10), La Romana (US$14), La Romana airport (US$20), Casa de Campo (US$30), Higüey (US$23), and the Punta Cana International Airport (US$70). Be sure to agree upon a price before you get in the car.

Impagnatiello Rent Car (☎ 809-906-8387; ⏰ 8am-noon, 1-6:45pm) is located in front of Hotel Llave del Mar; prices start at around US$50 per day.

Yaset Rent a Car (☎ 809-258-9340; Dominicus Americanus; ⏰ 9am-8pm) is across from the Viva Dominicus Beach resort in front of Hotel Llave del Mar. Compact cars start at US$60 per day.

Getting Around

Most everyone walks in Bayahibe, but there are a couple of *motoconchos* and at least one taxi stationed in town. The *motoconchos* mainly shuttle people to and from the coastal highway, where they then catch *guaguas* heading west toward La Romana or north toward Higüey.

PARQUE NACIONAL DEL ESTE

Designated a national park in 1975, the Parque Nacional del Este stretches over 310 sq km of territory. It is comprised mostly of semi-humid forest, though 110 sq km of the park includes the famous Isla Saona (p123), which is mostly covered in palms and white sand.

The park is also home to 539 species of flora, 55 of which are endemic. There is also a good variety of fauna: 112 species of birds, 250 types of insects and arachnids, and 120 species of fish. There also are occasional sightings of West Indian manatees and bottlenose dolphins; and if you happen to see a small bony animal with a long snout and tiny eyes – kind of like a rat – consider yourself fortunate. You've spotted a Haitian solenodon (p252), which is both endemic to the Hispaniola and quite rare.

Cueva del Puente

The park also has over 400 caves, many of which contain Taíno pictographs (cave paintings) and petroglyphs (rock carvings). Archaeologists have found several structures and artifacts inside and around the caves, including what appears to be the remains of a large Taíno city (perhaps the

---

THE LOST CITY

In his journals, Spanish missionary Bartolomé de las Casas described witnessing an incident that led to a Taíno massacre in 1503. According to de las Casas, Taínos were loading bread onto a Spanish galleon when a Spanish officer 'jokingly' suggested to another officer that he let his attack dog loose on the workers. Whether accidentally or not, the dog escaped from his handler and promptly disemboweled a Taíno, who also happened to be a minor chieftain.

The Taínos were infuriated and retaliated by killing several Spaniards. In response, the Spanish sent hundreds of heavily armed soldiers to an indigenous city where they killed approximately 7000 Taínos, cut off the hands of those they captured and ran several thousand more into the forest.

Archaeologists had never known where this Taíno city was located – indeed, most excavated villages had been home to no more than a couple of thousand people. However, in 1997 an American archaeological team dredging a sinkhole in Parque Nacional del Este uncovered an unusually large number of artifacts, including baskets, wooden war clubs, carved and decorated gourds and a variety of pottery. The sheer quantity suggested the area was once a major population center and, sure enough, the archaeologists discovered four large ceremonial sites nearby. It appears that the city held tens of thousands of people, making it the largest known city on the island.

But the archaeologists could not be sure it was the city where the massacre described by de las Casas took place, almost 500 years prior. Confirmation came in the form of a 5.5m pictogram that the Americans uncovered thanks to a tip from the director of the national park. The mural depicted a contract between the Taínos and the Spanish for the sale of bread. There were also drawings of Spanish galleons used to carry the Taíno bread, just as de las Casas had described.

largest) and the site of a notorious massacre of indigenous people by Spanish soldiers.

Only one of the caves that contain Taíno pictograms, **Cueva del Puente**, can be easily visited. Cueva del Puente is partially collapsed, but has a modest number of Taíno pictures, mostly depicting animals and humanlike figures that may represent people or deities. The cave also has some impressive stalagmites and stalactites.

For additional information you can also get in touch with the **park office** (☎ 809-833-0022; ☽ 8:30am-1pm) in Bayahibe, located at one end of the parking lot where all the tour buses park.

Getting There & Away

One entrance to Parque Nacional del Este is in the town of Boca de Yuma (p131), on the eastern side of the park. There is a ranger station there but no formal services. A road leads along the coast for several kilometers and has a number of nice vista points.

To visit Cueva del Puente, you must first drive to the national park entrance at Guaraguao, a well-marked ranger post about 5km past Dominicus Americanus. There you will pay the US$3.50 entrance fee and the guard will guide you to the cave, about a 40 minute walk. You'll need a flashlight and good shoes; a tip once you return is customary. There is another cave a short distance further, but it has been closed to visitors for several years. Still, it's worth asking the guard/guide if it can be visited, as it has many more pictograms than Cueva del Puente.

HIGÜEY

pop 123,787

Ringed by sugarcane fields as far as the eye can see, Higüey is most famous for its giant concrete basilica, which is said to contain a miracle-dispensing shrine (and also appears on the 50 peso bill). It is also an important transportation hub for the southeast, where buses from Sabana de la Mar, Bávaro, La Romana and Santo Domingo connect. Chances are you'll pass though it at least once on the way to or from one of these cities. The town is not really worth an overnight stay, but the church is interesting enough and there are a few good restaurants that might make this a convenient stop.

Orientation

Higüey has a number of twisting streets and odd intersections, which can make navigating the city on foot or car a bit challenging. (The church is a handy landmark, visible from many points in the city.) Some streets to keep in mind while in Higüey are southbound Av Hermanos Trejo, which becomes Hwy 4 headed toward La Romana; westbound Av La Altagracia, which becomes Hwy 4 toward El Seibo; and eastbound Av de la Libertad, which becomes the highway that connects Higüey and the Costa del Coco.

Information

INTERNET ACCESS

Tropical Internet Access Center (☎ 809-746-0164; Plaza El Naranjo, Av La Altagracia at Av Juan XXIII; per hr US$1; ☽ 8:30am-10:30pm) Popular with kids.

Spider Cíber Café (☎ 809-554-9903; Av La Altagracia; per hr US$1.40; ☽ 9am-noon & 2-10:30pm)

MEDICAL SERVICES

Farmacia Mello (☎ 809-554-2360; Av Hermanos Trejo at Gral Santana; ☽ 7am-11pm) Delivery available.

MONEY

Both of these banks are located near the Basilica and have one ATM apiece.

Banco Léon (Av Duarte at Av La Altagracia; ☽ 8:30am-5pm Mon-Fri, 9am-1pm Sat)

Banco Popular (Plaza El Naranjo, Av La Altagracia at Av Juan XXIII; ☽ 8:15am-4pm Mon-Fri, 9am-1pm Sat)

POST

Post Office (Calle Agustín Guerrero near Duverge; ☽ 8am-3pm Mon-Fri)

TELEPHONE

Centro de Llamadas Yenny (☎ 809-554-8019; Plaza El Naranjo; Av La Altagracia at Av Juan XXIII; to US per min US$0.30, to Europe per min US$0.75; ☽ 8am-10pm Mon-Sat, 10am-1pm & 4-8pm Sun)

Verizon Centro de Comunicaciones (Av Hermanos Trejo btwn Gral Santana & Cambronal; to US per min US$0.35, to Europe per min US$0.75, Internet per hr US$1.60; ☽ 8am-10pm)

Basílica de Nuestra Señora de la Altagracia

Completed in 1956, the ultra-modern **Basílica of the Virgin of Altagracia** (☽ 8am-6pm Mon-Sat, 8am-8pm Sun) is one of the most striking – and famous – cathedrals in the country. Designed by Frenchmen Pierre Dupré and

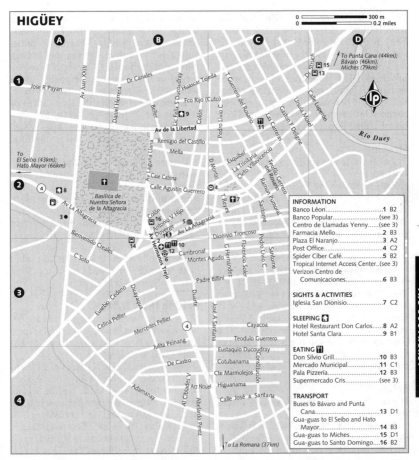

HIGÜEY

INFORMATION	
Banco Léon	1 B2
Banco Popular	(see 3)
Centro de Llamadas Yenny	(see 3)
Farmacia Mello	2 B3
Plaza El Naranjo	3 A2
Post Office	4 C2
Spider Ciber Café	5 B2
Tropical Internet Access Center	(see 3)
Verizon Centro de Comunicaciones	6 B3

SIGHTS & ACTIVITIES	
Iglesia San Dionisio	7 C2

SLEEPING	
Hotel Restaurant Don Carlos	8 A2
Hotel Santa Clara	9 B1

EATING	
Don Silvio Grill	10 B3
Mercado Municipal	11 C1
Pala Pizzería	12 B3
Supermercado Cris	(see 3)

TRANSPORT	
Buses to Bávaro and Punta Cana	13 D1
Gua-guas to El Seibo and Hato Mayor	14 B3
Gua-guas to Miches	15 D1
Gua-guas to Santo Domingo	16 B2

Dovnoyer de Segonzac, it is in the shape of the Latin cross and is topped with a set of centrally aligned arches that are intended to represent hands in prayer. Inside, the long walls consist mostly of bare concrete and approach each other as they rise, connecting at a rounded point directly over the center aisle. The entire wall opposite the front door consists of stained glass and is quite beautiful, especially in the late afternoon, when the sunshine casts honey-colored shadows across the floor.

But it isn't the architecture of the church that attracts Dominicans from across the country. Rather, it's a small, glass-encased image of the Virgin of Altagracia. According to the story, a sick child in Higüey was healed when an old man thought to be an Apostle asked for a meal and shelter at the city's original church, the **Iglesia San Dionisio** (Calle Agustín Guerrero at T Reyes; ☻ varies). On departing the following day, he left a small print of Our Lady of Grace in a modest frame. Since that day the 16th-century image has been venerated by countless devotees, upon whom the Virgin is said to have bestowed miraculous cures. Originally housed in the handsome Iglesia San Dionisio, the image of the Virgin has been venerated in the basilica since the mid-1950s.

Festivals & Events

Every January 21 thousands of people travel to the basilica to pay homage to the Virgin.

On this day the church is filled with the country's most devout, all dressed in their best. Bathed in colored light from the stained-glass window, the pilgrims file past the Virgin's image, seeking miracles and giving thanks. The outpouring of faith, when seen in this light, is moving even to the non-believer, and the church's many tuned bells, sounded by hammers controlled from a keyboard, chime throughout the day.

Sleeping

There are only two recommendable hotels in Higüey.

Hotel Santa Clara (☎ 809-554-2040; Lic Felix S Ducoudray 9; r without/with aircon US$17/23; ✷) Located on a quiet street near the basilica, this hotel offers spotless and pleasant rooms around a small interior courtyard. All rooms have private hot-water baths and cable TV. An on-site generator guarantees 24-hour electricity.

Hotel Don Carlos (☎ 809-554-2344; Calle Juan Ponce de León at Sánchez; d US$28-35, tw US$35-42; ✷ P) Rooms at this large, orange-painted hotel are clean and modern, though somewhat musty. All have tile floors, cable TV and extra details like quilts and headboards. The beds are aging but still pretty firm, and the restaurant is very good. Overall the hotel is a reliable if not awe-inspiring choice.

Eating

Higüey has several recommended eating options.

Don Silvio Grill (☎ 809-554-4309; Av La Altagracia at Duarte; mains US$5-10; ☟ lunch & dinner) This friendly bustling restaurant occupies a breezy patio with an open kitchen so you see and hear your food being prepared fresh. Grilled meats are the specialty here, especially the *conejo* (rabbit), pork chops, grouper filet and several cuts of beef. Food is served at tables with bamboo chairs and checkered tablecloths. A great choice.

Pala Pizzería (☎ 809-554-4949; Gral Santana near Av Hermanos Trejo; mains US$4-12 ☟ lunch & dinner) Classic take-out pizzería with plastic tables and chairs out front if you'd rather eat there. Pizzas and calzones are good but a little greasy. Delivery available.

Hotel Don Carlos (☎ 809-554-2344; Calle Juan Ponce de León at Sánchez; mains US$5-8; ☟ breakfast, lunch & dinner) This restaurant is surprisingly good, especially as hotel restaurants go. The decor is very plain, but the food tasty and the

service excellent, making it popular with local professionals and families. *Pollo guisado* (chicken baked in a gravy-like sauce) comes with a hefty plate of chicken and a large portion of rice for US$5.25. Fresh juices are served in tall glasses and a pitcher of ice water is complimentary with every meal.

Supermercado Cris (Plaza El Naranjo, Av La Altagracia at Av Juan XXIII; ☟ 7:30am-9pm Mon-Sat, 7:30am-1pm Sun) This good-sized grocery store is well stocked with the usual suspects: produce, meats and canned food.

Mercado Municipal (Av de la Libertad btwn Guerrero del Rosario & Las Carreras; ☟ 7am-3pm) Great for fresh fruits, vegetables, and just to get a feel for the hustle and bustle of everyday life in this commercial town.

There are also a number of snack shacks on the first several blocks of Av La Altagracia's leafy median, east of the Basílica. You can get sandwiches, empanadas and other light fare, plus beer, soda or juices. Most have a table or two to sit at.

Getting There & Away

Gua-guas to Santo Domingo (US$4.25, 2¾ hours, every 15 minutes, 4:30am to 7:30pm) leave from a large busy terminal on Av Laguna Llana at Colón.

For Samaná, take a *gua-gua* to Hato Mayor (US$4, 2½ hours, every hour, 4:40am to 8pm) and transfer to the bus for Sabana de la Mar, where there are ferries across the bay. If you just missed the Hato Mayor bus, you can also take an El Seibo bus (US$1.75, one hour, every 20 minutes, 4:30am to 8pm) and transfer there. Buses for Hato Mayor and El Seibo use the same stop on Av La Altagracia at Av Laguna Llana. Be sure to tell the driver that you are planning to connect to another bus, as they will often drop you right at the next terminal.

Gua-guas to Bávaro and Punta Cana (US$1.75, 1½ hours, every 15 minutes, 4:55am to 10pm; express aircon service US$2.10, 1¼ hours, every hour at the top of the hour) and Miches (US$2.75, 2½ hours, every 30 minutes, 5am to 6:20pm) leave from two side-by-side terminals on Av de la Libertad past Calle Luperón.

Getting Around

There are lots of taxis and *motoconchos* around during the day and well into the night.

SAN RAFAEL DEL YUMA

pop 5285

San Rafael del Yuma, just east of the two-lane highway linking Higüey to Boca de Yuma, is a fine rural Dominican town surrounded by fields in all directions, with dirt roads and nondescript houses varying little from one to the other. A pleasant enough place, the main reason to come is to visit the interesting Casa Ponce de León museum, in the former home of the infamous Spanish explorer.

Casa Ponce de León

Spanish explorer Juan Ponce de León had a second residence built in the countryside near San Rafael del Yuma during the time he governed Higüey for the Spanish Crown. Still standing nearly 500 years later, **Casa Ponce de León** (Ponce de León House; admission US$1.40; ☺ 7am-5pm) is now a museum to this notorious character of the Spanish conquest.

Born in 1460, Ponce de León accompanied Christopher Columbus on his second voyage to the New World in 1494. In 1508 he conquered Boriquén (present-day Puerto Rico) and served as governor there from 1510 to 1512. While there, he heard rumors of an island north of Cuba called Bimini which had a spring whose waters could reverse the aging process – the fabled fountain of youth.

Setting off from Puerto Rico in 1513, Ponce de León reached the eastern coast of present-day Florida on Easter day and named it Pascua Florida (literally 'Flowery Easter'). Believing the peninsula to be an island, he tried to sail around it, going south to what is now Key West, up the west coast of Florida, but then – seeing the coast was turning west instead of east – he returned to Puerto Rico. Eight years passed before he could resume the search. When he did return, Ponce de Leon landed on Florida's western coast, were he and his party were immediately attacked by Indians. Wounded by an arrow, Ponce de León withdrew to Cuba, where he died shortly after landing.

The residence-turned-museum contains many original items belonging to Ponce de León, including his armor and much of his furniture. Also original are the candelabra and his bed; his coat of arms is carved into the headboard. The guard will also serve as a guide; the tour and the signs are in Spanish only.

There are no signs to the museum, oddly enough. If you have a car and are entering from the north, you'll encounter a fork in the road right past the police station. Bear left and then turn left onto a dirt road just before the cemetery (it's surrounded by a tall white wall). After 1.2km you'll see a long access road with a boxy stone building at the end, which is the museum. If you arrive by bus, the terminal is a short distance from the cemetery and the turn-off to the museum, a long but very doable walk. There should be a *motoconcho* driver around who can take you as well.

Getting There & Away

Buses leave the bus depot, on the main road into town just beyond the cemetery, bound for La Romana (US$2.25, 40 minutes, every 30 minutes, 6am to 5pm) and Higüey (US$1.50, 25 minutes, every 20 minutes, 6am to 5pm).

There's only one really rustic hotel and a few lousy food stands in San Rafael del Yuma.

BOCA DE YUMA

pop 1991

South of San Rafael del Yuma where the river meets the ocean is Boca de Yuma, a forgettable little place were it not for a large cave with Taíno paintings and an entrance to Parque Nacional del Este just outside of town. Tour groups come here from nearby resorts, mostly to go on underwhelming paddles up the river and to have lunch at El 28. There are no services in Boca de Yuma, but it does have a surprisingly modern children's playground set on a rocky point overlooking the ocean in the middle of town – hands down the best view from a tube slide you'll ever come across.

Sights & Activities

Cueva de Berna (☺ 8am-2pm; guide US$0.50) is a large cave just west of town, on the way toward the entrance of the national park. It is now protected but the graffiti at its entrance is reminder that it wasn't always taken care of. The cave has a number of Taíno pictograms around the entrance – in and among the graffiti in fact – as well as deeper in. A guide is not required, but can help point out some of the harder-to-spot pictures. The visit takes about 20 minutes.

THE SOUTHEAST

The eastern entrance of **Parque Nacional del Este** (admission US$3.50) has even fewer facilities than the under-served western entrance, but there's a long easy-to-follow road that hugs the coast for many kilometers, making it a nice walk peppered by various nice views of the ocean from atop rugged bluffs. If you walk far enough, you can even spot Isla Saona. There is good bird-watching here if you're out early enough. The park ranger sleeps at the small cabin at the entrance, so you should find someone there at all hours.

Playa Blanca is a pretty, mostly deserted beach about 2km east of town, on the other side of the river. The easiest way to get there is by boat, and the boatmen congregated at the mouth of the river at the east side of town can take you there. Unfortunately for indy travelers, they are accustomed to taking package groups from the resorts and many are shameless gougers. The asking price to take you the beach and pick you up later is US$35; a reasonable fare would be about half that, but you may have to bargain very hard to get the boatmen to come down anywhere near that. You could also have them ferry you just to the other side of the river and walk to the beach. There's no path, though, and the rocks can be very sharp – only do this with sturdy, closed-toe shoes and give yourself plenty of time to get there and back. Driving is the hardest route of all, as the nearest bridge is well upriver and the access road in terrible condition.

Sleeping & Eating

There are just two hotels in Boca de Yuma, one grubby and the other overpriced.

El Viejo Pirata (☎ 809-282-3693; Calle Duarte 1; r US$18, mains US$4-12; ☽ breakfast, lunch & dinner) Very clean modern rooms with ceiling fan, hot water, satellite TV and minifridge, most opening onto a large breezy patio with a great view of the ocean. The pool is pretty but filled with saltwater. The nicest hotel around, but the price is way too high considering the town it's in.

Hotel Restaurant Club El 28 (☎ 809-355-3365; road to Cueva de Berna; r US$49) The three two-bedroom cabañas here have clean sheets but the rest is run down and of questionable cleanliness. Rooms have fan only, no TV and a private bath with hot water. The restaurant here is a popular stop with tour

groups, and serves basic reliable Dominican and international food, from pizza and pasta to grilled seafood and stewed meat.

El Arponero (☎ 809-292-9797; center of town; mains US$5-7; ☽ lunch & dinner) Perched on a bluff overlooking the ocean, the view here is as good as the pizza – and the pizza is great, made fresh with a variety of toppings, from pepperoni to lobster. Pasta and grilled fish and meat dishes are also available. The friendly Italian owner is a good source of information about the area, as well.

LA COSTA DEL COCO

The DR's southeastern coast has been dubbed *la Costa del Coco* – the Coconut Coast – undoubtedly for the impressively tall coconut trees that fringe the shoreline. Few Dominicans use the moniker (it was thought up by developers) but it's a catchy name for what many people consider the best beaches and finest resorts in the Dominican Republic. Bávaro and Punta Cana have scores of all-inclusive resorts, and are where the largest proportion of vacationers to the DR go. But while *la Costa del Coco* is synonymous with mega-resorts, it also contains the antithesis – long stretches of untouched beaches, pristine wetlands and coconut palm forests taller and denser than the ones at the resort areas. For that, you just have to head north along the coast to places like Playa Limón and Punta El Rey. Eventually the coast folds inland to form the bottom edge of the Bahia de Samaná, where Parque Nacional Los Haitses offers a chance to explore mangroves and see ancient Taíno cave paintings. All in all, it is an area of great natural and commercial diversity where travelers of all ilks can find something to enjoy.

BÁVARO & PUNTA CANA
pop 5000

If the southeast has the best beaches in the DR, then Bávaro and Punta Cana have the best beaches of the southeast. Punta Cana (Grey-Haired Point) is the easternmost tip of the region and country. And though it's the name many travelers recognize, there are just a few resorts and a beautiful seaside golf course here. Several kilometers north, Bávaro is significantly more developed,

BÁVARO & PUNTA CANA

INFORMATION	
Banco Popular	(see 4)
Banco Progreso	(see 5)
Banco Progreso	(see 35)
Bávaro Shopping Center	1 C1
Centro Médico Punta Cana	2 C1
Farmacia El Manglar	(see 8)
Hemisferio	(see 8)
Hospitén Bávaro	3 A3
Internet Café Tropical	(see 7)
Laundry Euro	(see 8)
Pharma Cana	(see 5)
Plaza Bávaro	4 C1
Plaza Bolera	5 B3
Plaza Las Brisas	6 C1
Plaza Punta Cana	7 C1
Plaza Riviera/Estrella	8 C1
Politur	9 C2
Politur	(see 5)
Punta Cana Lanes	(see 5)
Scotiabank	(see 6)
Tricom	10 D1

INFORMATION (continued)	
Verizon Centro de Comunicaciones	11 B2
Verizon Centro de Comunicaciones	(see 35)

SIGHTS & ACTIVITIES	
Catalonia Bávaro golf course	12 C2
Golden Power Gym	(see 6)
La Cana Golf Course	13 B4
Marinarium	14 B2
Parque Ecológico Punta Cana	15 B4
RH Tours and Excursions	16 D1
Tropical Racing	17 B2

SLEEPING	
Barceló Bávaro Beach	18 B2
Club Mediterranée Punta Cana	19 B4
El Cortecito Inn	20 D1
Hotel Bávaro Princess	21 C1
Hotel Cayacoa	22 C1
Hotel Grand Caribe	23 D1
Hotel Naragua	24 B2
Hotel Riu Taíno	25 A1
La Posada de Piedra	26 D1
Natura Park Eco-Resort & Spa	27 B2
Ocean Bávaro Spa & Beach Resort	28 D1
Punta Cana Resort & Club	29 B4
Residencial Guadalupe	30 B2
Sueño Resort and Wellness Center	31 D1
Villas Los Corales	32 D1

EATING	
Caribbean Coffee	(see 1)
Jalapeño	(see 6)
Langosta del Caribe	33 D1
Mamma Luisa	(see 5)
Restaurant Capitán Cook	34 D1
Restaurante El Delfín	(see 7)
Rincón de Pepe	(see 1)
Supermarket	35 D1
Supermarket	(see 8)

TRANSPORT	
Bus Terminal	36 C1
Europcar	37 C1
Gas Station	38 C1
Gas Station	39 A3
National/Alamo	40 B2

THE SOUTHEAST

with more than 30 resorts plus the area's best options for independent travelers.

Orientation

Most of Bávaro's services are located in the small one-road enclave of El Cortecito, or in one of several outdoor *plazas* (malls) just north of there. The area known as Plaza Bávaro is actually made up of three malls: Plaza Punta Cana is the first one you hit driving north from El Cortecito; across the street, Plaza Bávaro is the oldest and the least useful; and Bávaro Shopping Center is the newest and nicest, a hundred meters northwest of the first two and across from the Bávaro Princess Resort. West of Plaza Bávaro you'll come across two more small commercial centers – Plaza Las Brisas with a bank, gym and two good restaurants and Plaza Riviera/Estrella with the area's cheapest Internet and only per-load laundromat – before reaching an intersection with a gas station and the main bus terminal and police station.

Information

EMERGENCY

Politur (Tourist Police; ☎ 809-686-8227) There are 24-hour stations next to the bus terminal in Bávaro and at Plaza Bolera in Punta Cana.

INTERNET ACCESS

Hemisferio (☎ 809-552-0883; Plaza Riviera/Estrella, Bávaro; per hr US$1.75; ⏰ 8am-8pm Mon-Sun) The cheapest Internet around, in an airconditioned office on the 2nd floor. The area's only per-load laundry is nearby in case you're multitasking.

Internet Café Tropical (☎ 809-552-1229; Plaza Punta Cana, Bávaro; per hr US$5; ☒ 8am-11pm Mon-Sat, 9am-11pm Sun) Spacious café-restaurant where you can use the Internet, make phone calls and order sausages, sandwiches and other German fare.

Punta Cana Lanes (☎ 809-959-4444; Plaza Bolera, Punta Cana; per hr US$4.25; ☒ 4pm-midnight Mon-Thu, 4pm-2am Fri, 1pm-2am Sat, 1pm-midnight Sun) Popular bowling alley has Punta Cana's only public Internet café.

Tricom (El Cortecito; per hr US$3; ☒ 9am-11pm) The only public Internet connections in El Cortecito proper.

Verizon Centro de Comunicaciones (Cabeza de Toro; ☒ 8am-9pm Mon-Sat, 8am-4pm Sun) Still just a call center at the time of research, but should have Internet terminals by the time you read this.

LAUNDRY

Laundry Euro (☎ 809-552-1820; Plaza Riviera/Estrella, Bávaro; ☒ 8am-8pm Mon-Sat, 8am-5pm Sun) Charges by load – US$4.50 for up to 7kg – with same-day service if you drop it off in the morning. The shop can be a little hard to find – look for the *Lavandería* sign down a passageway at the back of Plaza Estrella.

MEDICAL SERVICES

Every all-inclusive hotel has a small on-site clinic and medical staff, which can provide first aid and basic care to guests and non-guests alike. (These services usually have an extra charge.) For serious cases, head to one of several good private hospitals in the area.

Centro Médico Punta Cana (☎ 809-552-1506; btwn Plaza Bávaro & the bus terminal, Bávaro) The name notwithstanding, this is the main private hospital in Bávaro, with a multilingual staff, 24-hour emergency room and in-house pharmacy.

Farmacia El Manglar (☎ 809-552-1533; Plaza Punta Cana, Bávaro; ☒ 8am-midnight) Convenient Bávaro pharmacy offers free delivery service to local hotels (until 10pm).

Hospitén Bávaro (☎ 809-686-1414; btwn airport & turn-off to Bávaro) This is the best private hospital in Punta Cana, with English-, French- and German-speaking doctors and a 24-hour emergency room. The hospital is located on the road to Punta Cana, a half-kilometer from the turn-off to Bávaro.

Pharma Cana (☎ 809-959-0025; Plaza Bolera, Punta Cana; ☒ 9am-10pm Mon-Sat, 8am-11pm Sun) Punta Cana's main pharmacy stocks sunscreen, toiletries, snacks and drinks in addition to prescription and non-prescription drugs.

MONEY

The following all change euros, US dollars and travelers checks. As usual, you'll need to show your passport and may be asked for receipts to change TCs. All of these listed banks have ATMs.

Banco Popular (Plaza Bávaro, Bávaro; ☒ 9am-4pm Mon-Fri)

Banco Progreso inside El Cortecito supermarket (☒ 9am-9pm Mon-Sat); Plaza Bolera, Bávaro (☒ 9am-4pm Mon-Fri)

Scotiabank (Plaza Las Brisas, Bávaro; ☒ 9am-5pm Mon-Fri, 9am-1pm Sat)

POST

Most all-inclusive hotels will post letters and postcards for guests, for a small premium of course.

TELEPHONE

Tricom (El Cortecito; to USA per min US$0.42, to Europe per min US$0.70; ☒ 9am-11pm)

Verizon Centro de Comunicaciones (inside El Cortecito supermarket; to USA per min US$0.35, to Europe per min US$0.77; ☒ 9am-5pm)

Verizon Centro de Comunicaciones (Cabeza de Toro; to USA per min US$0.30, to Europe per min US$0.85; ☒ 8am-9pm Mon-Sat, 8am-4pm Sun)

Sights
BEACHES

La Costa del Coco has the Dominican Republic's best beaches. Postcards don't do justice to their pure white sand and aquamarine water, with coconut palms reaching up into cloudless skies. Developers know a good thing when they see it, and have built all-inclusive resorts along most of the picturesque stretches of sand. That said, all beaches in the DR are public by law – and although hotels can and do restrict the use of their beach chairs and umbrellas to hotel guests, it is perfectly okay to walk along the water and set up your towel on the sand wherever you like.

Playa El Cortecito is open to all, and is quite nice, though a bit crowded at times with vendors and seaside food shacks. Many travelers use El Cortecito to get to the even better beaches in front of the nearby resorts, a short walk in either direction. This also is a good place to **parasail** (US$40 for 12 to 15 minutes) since you're guaranteed to find an operator here.

Playa Cabo Engaño is an isolated beach south of Cabeza de Toro where you'll find great shells and are all but guaranteed to have it to yourself. You'll need a car to get there, preferably a full-size or SUV. On the road to Cabeza de Toro, turn right on the first dirt road that's past the go-cart track. The beach is just a few kilometers down, but because the road is in bad condition it'll take you a good 20 minutes to get there.

Playa del Macao is a gorgeous stretch of beach some 12km north of Bávaro, also best reached by car. Unfortunately, it is also a favorite stop-off for a slew of ATV (All-Terrain Vehicle) tours popular at all-inclusive resorts. Hundreds of people on four-runners tear up and down the beach every day, their engines racing and the sand flying. The Secretary of Tourism was reportedly considering restricting or even prohibiting ATV use on Playa Macao, but the tour operators will surely put up a fight. Hyatt may also be building a mega-hotel here, which would get rid of the ATVs but may add a new set of limitations. Until then, you'll find less noise and intrusion at the far northern end of the beach. **Caribe Macao** (☾ 11am-9pm) is a good restaurant on a bluff on the beach's south side – it's sometimes crowded with ATV riders taking a pit-stop, but anyone can enjoy the tasty fish and seafood dishes and the fantastic view.

PUNTA CANA ECOLOGICAL PARK

Though development may eventually cover every inch of the Dominican coastline, for now there are still large areas of pristine coastal plains and mangrove forests, even along *la Costa del Coco*. A half-kilometer south of Punta Cana Resort and Club, the **Punta Cana Ecological Park** (☎ 809-959-8483; www .puntacana.org; ☾ 8am-4pm) covers almost 2000 acres of protected coastal and inland habitat and is home to some 80 bird species, 160 insect species and 500 plant species. Visitors can take very worthwhile **guided tours** (adult/child US$10/5; 1½hrs; English, French, German & Spanish spoken) through a lush 45-acre portion of the reserve known as Parque Ojos Indígenas (Indigenous Eyes Park), so named for its 11 freshwater lagoons all fed by an underground river that flows into the ocean. The tour also includes a visit to the park's botanical and fruit gardens, iguana farm (part of a breeding program) and a farm-animal petting zoo. The visitor center has a great collection of insects that was compiled by entomology students from Harvard, and interesting maps and photos of the area. At the time of research, the center's staff was preparing booklets which will allow visitors to take self-guided tours for the cost of the booklet only. **Horseback riding tours** (1hr US$20, 2hrs, US$30) through the park and along the coast can also be arranged with advance notice. The park is operated by the Punta Cana Ecological Foundation, a nonprofit foundation created in 1994 that works to protect the area's ecosystems – including 8km of coral

AVOIDING MOSQUITOES

Malaria is a tropical infection that is spread by mosquitoes that carry the disease and pass it when they bite humans. Mosquitoes are prevalent in lowland and coastal regions and they typically feed during sunset and sunrise. The Dominican Republic is one of the few Caribbean countries that has malaria year round. Few travelers contract it but, as with any disease, it's better to take precautions. Some suggestions include:

- Cover up! And especially during prime feeding hours or when traveling on the coast. Wear pants, socks, a long sleeve shirt and even a hat.
- Wear light colored clothing. Mosquitoes are attracted to dark colors.
- Avoid cologne, perfume, or any product with a strong scent. Mosquitoes gravitate towards these items.
- Wear plenty of insect repellent. Make sure that it has at least a 20% concentration of DEET and no more than 30% since higher levels can cause allergic reactions. Note – DEET can be toxic to children. If you're traveling with them, use Avon's Skin So Soft instead, which has insect repellent properties but is gentler.
- Make sure that screens in your hotel room are intact or, better yet, travel with a mosquito net.
- Light mosquito coils. They burn like incense but release a smoke that repels mosquitoes.

reef along the reserve's shoreline – and to promote sustainable tourism and hotel practices. Unfortunately, there is no hotel pick-up service; a cab here will cost around US$25 each way from Bávaro or El Cortecito.

Activities

BOWLING & POOL

A half-kilometer west of the Punta Cana airport, **Punta Cana Lanes** (☎ 809-959-4444; Plaza Bolera, Punta Cana; 4pm-midnight Mon-Thu, 4pm-2am Fri, 1pm-2am Sat, 1pm-midnight Sun) is the biggest building in this small shopping complex and the only one with huge bowling pins out front. Twenty lanes are US$8.75 per hour each, which includes two pairs of shoes (additional pairs US$1 each). The bowling alley also has video games, pool tables (per hour US$3) and even a high-tech full-swing virtual golf course, one of the only ones in the whole country (one to four players per hour US$28; Amex cardholders get 30 minutes free). You can order hotdogs, chicken burgers and other cheap eats at the snack bar, or tuck into an 18oz Sammy Sosa rib-eye at the alley's own **sports bar and grill** (mains US$10-25).

GO-CARTS

A short distance down the road to Cabeza de Toro, **Tropical Racing** (☎ 809-707-5164; 20min US$15-18; 10am-10pm) has a handful of nine-horsepower go-carts with top speeds of 75km/h and a winding 920m racetrack to drive them on. A 20-minute session during the daytime is about as long as you'll last before needing a break from the heat. Night-time is cooler, but also busier and a bit rowdier, especially once guests have made a few pit-stops at the track-side bar. That said, the owners do take safety seriously – helmets are required, first time drivers are limited to 45km/h, and people who have had too much to drink aren't allowed on the course – and there have been no serious injuries since opening in 1998. There's no minimum age, but children must be tall enough to reach the pedals; parents can also have the carts set to a given top speed. The track offers free hotel pick up if you make reservations ahead of time.

MARINARIUM

Of the many tours peddled to resort guests, the **Marinarium** (www.marinarium.com; adult US$72, child aged 2-12 US$36) tries harder than most to offer a family- and eco-friendly trip where you actually learn something. After a brief orientation at the pier in Cabeza de Toro, you board a custom pontoon boat (they call it a catamaran) for a short ride to a natural offshore pool where you go snorkeling for an hour. You'll see rays, nurse sharks, tropical fish and patches of coral, all relatively healthy thanks to the guides' constant reminders not to touch or kick anything. The boat has a large glass viewing chamber for those who prefer to stay dry. Yes, it's a pricey package tour with up to 80 guests at a time, but the snorkeling area is huge – 40,000 sq meters and 10ft deep – and they split everyone into three groups to keep things as personalized as possible. On the way back, there's a short coastal sightseeing tour and a quiz with a free tee-shirt up for grabs. Good for families. Drinks, snacks and snorkel gear are provided; reservations available via hotel concierge only. English, French and Spanish are spoken.

GOLF

La Cana Golf Course (☎ 809-959-2262; www.punta cana.com; Punta Cana Resort & Club, Punta Cana; 7:30am-6pm) is Punta Cana's top golf course and is located at the area's top resort, where service on and off the greens is impeccable. The 18-hole course, designed by PB Dye, has several long par-fives and challenging hill and sand features, not to mention the really big water hazard along the eastern side. Indeed, the stunning ocean views can make it had to concentrate on your swing. Green fees are US$144 for 18 holes or US$88 for nine, including a golf cart. Club rental is US$30 for 18 holes or US$17 for nine, and caddies (not obligatory) charge US$12 per round. Starting in late-2005, guests of the Punta Cana Resort can play for just US$10.

If you'd like to get in a round but La Cana is somewhat rich for your blood, the **Catalonia Bávaro Resort** (☎ 809-412-0000; Cabeza de Toro; 8:30am-5pm) has a decent nine-hole par-three course that costs US$45 for one round and US$60 for two. Carts are US$25 for 18 holes and US$20 for nine, and club rental just US$10.

GYM

Just in case walking between the pool and the buffet line isn't doing enough to preserve your pre-vacation physique, **Golden Power Gym** (☎ 809-552-1056; Plaza Las Brisas, Bávaro; day passes US$8.75, classes US$5.25; ☺ 6:45am-10pm Mon-Fri, 6:45am-noon Sat) has weight machines, free weights and exercise classes including aerobics, kickboxing, Tae-bo and yoga.

Tours

A handful of tour operators on El Cortecito beach offer **snorkel trips** (per person US$20-25, 2½hr) and **glass-bottom boat rides** (per person US$25-30, 2hr) to a nearby reef. Most also offer **deep sea fishing trips** (min 4 people, per person US$80-90) for marlin, tuna, wahoo and barracuda. Look for the kiosks near the north end of the beach, although enterprising employees are likely to find you first.

If you're looking to explore the region, **RH Tours and Excursions** (☎ 809-552-1425; www.rhtours .com; El Cortecito; ☺ 9am-7pm) is an established tour operator offering a number of decent day trips. Popular excursions include exploring Parque Nacional Los Haitises (US$79), boat trips to Isla Saona (US$79), and tours of Santo Domingo's Zona Colonial (US$49). Most trips include lunch and drinks. English, German and French are spoken.

Sleeping

Always book all-inclusive vacations online or through a travel agent, as they can offer discounts of up to 50% off rack rates. If you find a great deal, check up on the resort by logging onto hotel review sites – two good ones are www.tripadvisor.com and www .debbiesdominicantravel.com – bearing in mind that most resorts cater to a particular niche, whether it's families, honeymooners, golfers or the spring break crowd. The resorts listed below get consistently high marks, and are followed by some nonresort alternatives.

BÁVARO

Hotel Bávaro Princess (☎ 809-221-2311; www.princess hotelsandresorts.com; Playa Bávaro; d per person US$210; ☒ ℗ ☲) Located on a glorious stretch of white-sand beach, the Bávaro Princess offers 750 all-suite accommodations on immaculately tended grounds. Rooms are nicely appointed and come with a minibar that is replenished daily. Eight restaurants offer a variety of eating choices and themes; Bella Pasta and Chopin, both buffets, offer

particularly good dishes and excellent service. Be sure to reserve early for à la cart restaurants – even a day in advance – to guarantee a spot. If you want shade on the beach or by the pool, you'll meet with stiff competition from fellow guests; most of the prime spots are taken by 8am. A water sports center, four tennis courts, several bars and a discotheque round out this fine hotel. All in all a comfortable and pleasant place to vacation.

Natura Park Eco-Resort & Spa (☎ 809-221-2626; www.blau-hotels.com; Cabeza de Toro; d per person US$135; ☒ ℗ ☲) This resort has won numerous awards for its efforts to reduce its environmental impact, including bleach-free laundry, integrated waste-water systems, even reusable beach cups (instead of the plastic cups so ubiquitous elsewhere). Rooms are simple but comfortable, with unobtrusive decor, low beds and large glass doors opening onto balconies or terraces. The pool is a bit small, but the beach quite nice. Small lagoons on the grounds are home to egrets, flamingos and other water birds.

Ocean Bávaro Spa & Beach Resort (☎ 809-221-0714; www.oceanhotels.net; Playa Bávaro; d per person US$110-210; ☒ ℗ ☲) Set on tropical grounds with swaying palm trees, lagoons with flamingos, and a gorgeous stretch of beach, the Ocean Bávaro is a fine choice for any traveler. Rooms are attractive and spacious with wicker furnishings and balconies. Some of the older rooms suffer from mold, so be sure to ask for a different room if you get stuck with one of these. Better yet, request to be placed in either building five or seven, which seem to have the best rooms. Food is available 24 hours a day and, in general, is quite good. With five à la carte restaurants, one buffet and two snack bars, you're sure to find something that you like.

Barceló Bávaro Beach (☎ 809-686-5797; www.bar celo.com; Playa Bávaro; d per person US$110; ☒ ℗ ☲) This hotel is located inside a complex of five Barceló all-inclusive resorts, which combined have 1957 rooms, more than a dozen restaurants and grills, 18 bars, a casino and two dance clubs. Guests can use many of the facilities at the sister resorts, which is a major plus. The Barceló Bávaro Beach is one of the lower-end places in the complex. The grounds are beautiful – lush and dotted with tall coconut trees – but the rooms are just average – clean but a bit cramped. It's more

CHOOSING AN ALL-INCLUSIVE RESORT

The Dominican Republic is known as one of the most affordable places in the Caribbean to stay at an all-inclusive resort. With scores of resorts that seem to offer similar services, it can be a daunting task to narrow down your options to just one. Below are some helpful tips to keep in mind when choosing your next vacation spot.

■ Location: Consider what part of the country the resort is in. The southeast is known for its classic Caribbean beaches with powdery white sand and tranquil turquoise waters. Most sights are over an hour's trip away and all require at least two *gua-gua* rides. The North Coast's beaches are lined with tawny sand and often-rough teal waters. The north, however, has easily accessible sights and activities – towns to explore, isolated beaches to play on, great diving and lots of wind sports – and most just one *gua-gua* ride away.

■ The fine print: What does all-inclusive mean? Are all the restaurants included? How about alcoholic beverages? Motorized water sports? Excursions? Spa services? Golf? And what about tips?

■ Ocean front: Decide whether being on an oceanfront property is important to you. All resorts have beach clubs, but some shuttle their guests to the beach from inland properties.

■ Size of the resort: How far is the furthest hotel room from the restaurants? The beach? The main pool? Some resorts are so big that guests must rent golf carts to move around the complex. At US$35 per day, that adds up fast.

■ Variety of restaurants: How many buffets are there? À la carte restaurants? Snack bars? Remember that you're going to be eating all of your meals here; the larger the variety, the less likely that you'll get tired of the offerings.

■ Accommodations: When were the rooms last updated? Recent renovations mean better rooms and less likelihood of mold or bugs.

■ Children: Is this a kid-friendly resort? Is there a kids club? Babysitting service? Are there lifeguards at the pools and the beach? If your kids are taken care of and having fun, it'll mean you'll have more time to have fun yourself.

■ Pools: How many pools are there? Are there separate active, quiet and kiddie pools? The more pools there are, the more likely you'll be able to find a place that suits your mood.

■ Drinks: Is top shelf alcohol included? What about bottled beer? If kicking back on the beach with a Grey Goose cocktail or a Corona is one of the things you're looking forward to, definitely find out whether you'll be paying extra for it.

■ Entertainment: Are there nightly performances or live music venues? How about a discotheque? Some resorts are a lot more low key than others; figure out if you want to be out late or if turning in early is the pace you're looking for.

■ Nudity: How do you feel about toplessness and thongs? Whether it bothers you or you're looking forward to baring all, find out what the custom is at the resort. A good rule of thumb: if the resort is frequented by Europeans, you'll see a lot of flesh. If Americans and Canadians are the main clientele, covering up is more the style.

■ Internet research: Before you hand over your credit card, go online and see if there are any specials; rates vary widely among resorts and even from week to week at the same place. Once you've narrowed your options, see what people are saying about the contenders; *www .tripadvisor.com* and *www.debbiesdominicantravel.com* are both particularly useful websites.

of a party scene here, which is great if you're looking to spend your time at the swim-up bar or playing beach volleyball but not the best if you have young children. Good value, especially considering that you have the option to spend your days resort-hopping.

Hotel Riu Taíno (☎ 809-221-2290; www.riu.com; Punta Arena Gorda; d per person US$120-180; ✖ Ⓟ ☂) The 360 guest rooms here are housed in two-story bungalow complexes that are surrounded by possibly the highest ratio of coconut trees to guests in the country – even the swimming pool has an island of them. The tropical grounds are lush and maintained with pride, and the beach area is beautiful. Rooms are dated but comfortable and have fully-stocked (and re-stocked) minibars. Like the Barceló Bávaro Beach, the Riu Taíno is located within a complex of five resorts; here, however, guests only have access to three other resorts.

Hotel Sirenis Resort (☎ 809-688-6490; www.sirenis hotels.com; Uvero Alto; d per person US$100; ❇ P ❄) Located about 42km north of the Punta Cana airport, the Sirenis is set on a beautiful and isolated stretch of beach. The resort itself has lovely grounds and the rooms are good-sized and comfortable, though some are quite a hike from the ocean. The resort is particularly popular with families – there are lots of activities at the Kids Club and even a discotheque for pre-teens. There are eight eateries on site – all receive rave reviews.

PUNTA CANA

Though it's a more famous name, Punta Cana really just has two resorts – all the rest are in and around Bávaro. That said, both of Punta Cana's options are quite nice, and among the most upscale in the area.

Punta Cana Resort & Club (☎ 809-959-2262; www .puntacana.com; Punta Cana; d with breakfast & dinner only per person US$93-150; ❇ P ❄) This 400-room resort features spacious rooms in three-story buildings all along a white-sand beach. It's not a typical Dominican resort – lunch and drinks are not included, there are few daytime activities, and only two evening performances per week. Families and young couples may find this resort a little dull, but it's popular with travelers looking to unwind in a quiet, beautiful setting.

Club Mediterranée Punta Cana (☎ 809-687-2767; www.clubmed.com; Punta Cana; d per person US$125-240; ❇ P ❄) Geared towards families and travelers who enjoy an active vacation, this resort includes activities such as snorkeling, kayaking, windsurfing, waterskiing, tennis, water exercises, yoga, dance lessons…even trapezing (yes, like in the circus!). Children also can participate in the resort's kid's club, a summer camp–type program with organized activities, which leaves kids tired and happy by sunset. Rooms are set on acres of lush grounds and are comfortable but not luxurious; be sure to request one near the

reception area as many rooms are located up to a kilometer away. If you have small children and you end up in one of these outlying rooms, come prepared with a stroller; the little ones (and your back) will appreciate the wheels. Like most resorts in the area, Club Med also offers a variety of restaurants and bars. The food receives mixed reviews but is abundant and always available.

RESORT ALTERNATIVES

The Costa del Coco has some options, if not many, for budget travelers or those who simply don't care for the all-inclusive scene.

Budget

La Posada de Piedra (☎ 809-221-0754; www.laposada depiedra.com; El Cortecito; r with shared/private bath US$35/45) The only stone building in town, this guesthouse offers three rustic cabañas on the beach and two comfortable rooms with private bathrooms inside the owners' home. All guests have access to a laid-back, sand-floored lounge and those staying inside the main house share a balcony with an enviable view of the Caribbean. Excellent value, considering the location.

Hotel Cayacoa (☎ 809-552-0622; Bávaro; s/d US$25/32; ❇ P ❄) Just north of Plaza Punta Cana on the road toward the bus terminal, Hotel Cayacoa is one of just a few good, no-frills hotels in Bávaro. There's a nice pool and the clean, decent-sized rooms have cable TV. Some rooms can be a bit dim, so see a few before deciding. The location – on a busy road next to a dull shopping center – won't wow you, but there's at least one cheap restaurant nearby and the beach, laundry, Internet and bus terminal are all within easy reach by *gua-gua* or *motoconcho*.

Hotel Naragua (☎ 809-688-4060; Cabeza de Toro; d/tw US$35/42; ❇ P) The Naragua has nicer rooms and friendlier staff than the Cayacoa, but the location is less convenient and there's no pool. Rooms here are very clean, with large bathrooms. The upstairs rooms have high sloped ceilings and the ones on the ends get even better light than the rest. Some have small balconies, and the hotel has a good restaurant and two breezy lobby areas that lend a sense of openness to the place. If you have a car, this is a good quiet nonresort option. To get here, take the

Cabeza de Toro access road and bear left at the radio tower.

Residencial Guadalupe (☎ 809-688-5341; studios per wk US$210, 2-3 bdrm apt per wk US$350-490; 🅿 🅿) This complex of 30 fully-equipped villas is located in the Cabeza de Toro area of Bávaro. All are comfortable and well appointed with cable TV, kitchen, 24-hour electricity and spacious bedrooms and living areas. Designed for long-term and seasonal renters – about half the units are rented to people who work in Bávaro and Punta Cana – you may feel a little isolated here if you don't have a car. And while a decent beach is just steps away, it can be somewhat unappealing due to all the fishing and excursion boats docked nearby. Rental is by the week and does not include daily cleaning or other hotel-like services, though the Italian owners can help arrange excursions and day passes to area resorts.

Midrange

Hotel Gran Caribe (☎ 809-552-1039; www.grancaribe .it, in Spanish; Playa Bávaro; s/d US$45/62; 🅿 🅿 🅿 🅿) This quiet hotel offers 36 comfortable rooms surrounding an hourglass-shaped pool. Rooms are small but the attractive decor more than makes up for it. Although located 150m from the beach, hotel guests can use the facilities at a local beach club free of charge. A rooftop solarium also provides a good place to work on your tan. Breakfast is included in the rate.

El Cortecito Inn (☎ 809-552-0639; www.hotelcort ecitoinn.com; d/tw US$53/65; 🅿 🅿 🅿) Just steps away from the town beach, this hotel offers comfortable – if somewhat dated – rooms on well-tended grounds. Each room has a balcony or terrace and most overlook a welcoming pool dotted with palm trees. Unfortunately, maintenance is lacking and service is abysmal; make sure you have hot water, working aircon, and even towels before you move in. Otherwise, you'll be lucky to get a dismissive nod and a smile. Buffet breakfast is included in the rate.

Top End

Sueño Resort and Wellness Center (☎ 809-552-1690; Playa Bávaro; s/d US$80/140, with breakfast US$85/150, all-inclusive US$100/180; 🅿 🅿 🅿 🅿) Where Los Corales is best for long-term visits, Sueño is the place to go if you've got a minimal time to achieve maximum

relaxation and rejuvenation. (And if you've got time and money to stay longer, all the better!) Units are smallish but lovingly appointed, with pretty wood furniture, thick comfortable beds, and separate tiled rooms for toilet and bidet, washroom, and two-person whirlpool tub. For a bit more, VIP rooms feature four-poster king size beds. The hotel also has an excellent Italian restaurant and a small but well-equipped gym that's free for guests. The Orquidea Wellness Center, the hotel's intimate on-site spa, offers professional manicures, pedicures, facials, massages and specialty treatments, plus hair, nails and other salon services for US$10 to US$120.

Villas Los Corales (☎ 809-710-5791; Playa Bávaro; r US$115; 🅿 🅿 🅿) The 30 (and counting) apartments here are all comfortable and spacious, occupying attractive duplex villas scattered over a large leafy complex. Units range from studios to two-bedrooms, and all have fully-equipped kitchens, satellite TV and telephone. The complex – which feels more like a little community than a resort – has an Italian restaurant and a crêperie, small swimming pool and gym, even massage and hair salons. The grounds reach all the way to the hotel's beach club, with clean sand and a great beachside bar and restaurant. A variety of water toys, including kayaks, are available for guests. The Los Corales is popular with Italians, so be sure to call ahead for reservations. Weekly and monthly rates are available. Some property-owners in this area are trying to foment a village atmosphere (similar to the Bávaro Pueblo project further south) with a combination of restaurants, shops, services, hotels, long-term housing, and public spaces. It was still an idea at the time of research, but if realized would make this enclave all the more appealing.

Eating

With so many all-inclusive resorts, there are relatively few independent restaurants. But there are just enough condos, villas and resort guests sick of buffet food to keep a handful of eateries running. Two restaurants are in El Cortecito, while the rest are in the various shopping centers in the area, easily reached by *motoconcho* or taxi. Prices are relatively high, but that goes for most things around here.

Restaurant Capitán Cook (☎ 809-552-0645; El Cortecito; mains US$11-18; ☯ lunch & dinner). This well-established restaurant serves excellent seafood dishes that are prepared in a spotless outdoor kitchen. Large portions are the standard here although complimentary appetizers – crisp vegetables in a vinaigrette dressing, breaded crabmeat, hush puppies and homemade potato chips – almost make a meal on their own. Diners have a choice of eating under individual thatch-roofed tables on the beach or in a formal dining room overlooking the ocean. Always bustling, this place is particularly popular with locals on Sundays. Ask about the free lunchtime boat service to/from area resorts.

Langosta del Caribe (☎ 809-552-0774; El Cortecito; mains US$11-18; ☯ breakfast, lunch & dinner) This beachside restaurant offers good – if pricey – lunchtime specials (US$30 to US$50). Choices include grilled lobster, shrimp kabobs and a seafood platter and come with vegetable soup, fried yucca, homemade bread, dessert and drinks. If the specials seem like too much food to handle, à la carte items are also well prepared and more reasonably priced. At the time of research, a ride back to your hotel as well as a snorkel trip was included with any meal; ask if the latter is still available before you plan your day around it.

Rincón de Pepe (☎ 809-552-0603; Bávaro Shopping Center, Bávaro; mains US$8-15; ☯ lunch & dinner Mon-Sat) Located on the ground floor of the most pleasant of the three shopping centers in the Plaza Bávaro area, this classy but low-key restaurant serves quality Spanish food at sunny outdoor tables or inside an airy, Mexican-pink dining area. Tasty paella (US$23 for two) is prepared with seafood or Valencia-style with rabbit, beef and chicken.

Caribbean Coffee (Bávaro Shopping Center, Bávaro; mains US$9-14; ☯ breakfast, lunch & dinner) For lighter fare, go around the corner from Rincón de Pepe to this casual café and diner, where you can order wraps, crepes and nice green salads. The coffee here is fresh-brewed – if you really like it, you can order a bag to go.

Restaurante El Delfín (Plaza Punta Cana, Bávaro; mains US$5-10; ☯ breakfast, lunch & dinner) A basic friendly joint with a high thatch roof and loud, lively music, and one of the few places to get ordinary Dominican food at

relatively normal prices. Fish, chicken and meat dishes come with rice and beans and go down best with a tall cool *Presidente*. Tucked in the back of downscale Plaza Punta Cana, it's not exactly bursting with charm but should be a welcome option for budget travelers (who may well be staying at nearby Hotel Cayacoa).

Jalapeño (☎ 809-552-1033; Plaza Las Brisas, Bávaro; mains US$8-12; ☯ breakfast, lunch & dinner) The Tijuana tacos and Guadalajara chimichangas may bear only passing resemblance to food you'd actually find in those cities, but the names and flavors alone are enough to attract anyone craving Mexican food. Burritos, enchiladas and fajitas round out a Mexican and Tex-Mex menu, served in a colorful open-air dining area and accompanied by the crooning of Luis Miguel, Juan Gabriel and the like. There's a good, slightly pricier Italian restaurant a few doors down.

Mamma Luisa (☎ 809-959-2013; Plaza Bolera; mains US$8-15; ☯ lunch & dinner Mon-Sat) Wine glasses and checkerboard tablecloths lend a casual but classy air to this Italian trattoria and bar in Punta Cana's only commercial center, a half-kilometer west of the airport. Try the cream of carrot soup as an appetizer, then the Mediterranean fish filet, prepared with tomatoes and black olives and served with baked potatoes. Ironically, the pasta here is only so-so. There's also an interesting Portuguese restaurant nearby.

There are supermarkets located in **El Cortecito** (☯ 9am-9pm) and also in **Plaza Riviera/Estrella** (☯ 8am-10pm Mon-Sat, 9am-8pm Sun). Both are reasonably well-stocked, including produce and canned food, but the latter has slightly lower prices.

Getting There & Away
AIR

The Costa de Coco is served by the large, modern **Aeropuerto Internacional Punta Cana**, located on the road to Punta Cana about 9km east of the turn-off to Bávaro. The airport parking lot is an impressive sight, bristling with taxis, shuttles and full-length buses all waiting to whisk tourists to all-inclusive resorts.

American Airlines (☎ 809-959-2420), **Air France** (☎ 809-959-3002) and **LAN** (☎ 809-959-0144) all have offices at the airport. **Swissport** (☎ 809-959-3014) handles ticketing and other ground services of various airlines and charters

THE SOUTHEAST

serving Punta Cana airport, including US Airways, Air Canada, Northwest, Corsair, LTU, Iberworld and USA3000, and is the best place to call for ticketing matters on those carriers.

There is a **Banco Progreso ATM** located in the arrivals area, as well as a **Verizon Centro de Communications** (☎ 809-688-1153; Internet per hr US$1.50, telephone to USA per min US$0.30, to Europe per min US$0.75; ☺ 8am-6pm). There are no car rental booths, oddly enough.

Taxi fares between the airport and area resorts and hotels are surprisingly reasonable as airport taxis go, ranging from US$9 to US$30 depending on the destination.

BUS

Bávaro's main bus terminal is located 1.7km inland from El Cortecito.

Expreso Santo Domingo Bávaro Bávaro (☎ 809-552-0771); Santo Domingo (☎ 809-682-9670; Juan Sánchez Ruiz at Máximo Gómez) has direct first-class service between Bávaro and the capital, with a stop in La Romana. Departure times in both directions are 7am, 10am, 2pm and 4pm (US$3.75, four hours).

To all other destinations, take a local bus to Higüey and transfer there. (You can also get to/from Santo Domingo this way, but it's much slower than the direct bus.) *Caliente* buses to Higüey leave Bávaro's main terminal (US$1.75, 1½ hours, every 15 minutes, 6am to 9pm), as does the express service (US$2.15, 1¼ hours, every hour, 6am to 7pm).

Getting Around

Local buses start at the main bus terminal, passing all the outdoor malls (Plaza Riviera/ Estrella, Plaza Las Brisas, Plaza Bávaro etc) to El Cortecito, then turn down the coastal road past the large hotels to Cruce de Cocoloco, where they turn around and return the same way. Buses have the drivers' union acronym – Sitrabapu – printed in front and cost US$0.75. They are supposed to pass every 15 to 30 minutes, but can sometimes take up to an hour.

Renting a car for a day or two is a good way to see less-touristed areas along the coast. Prices are higher than elsewhere in the country – around US$75 per day including tax and insurance – but not prohibitive if you divide the cost among a few people. Since all the rental agencies here are

international chains, you may find better deals online. Be sure to ask if the insurance policy covers tires and glass – if not, definitely consider paying a little more for the extra coverage especially if you'll be driving north toward Macao and Miches. Some agencies allow you to drop off the car in Santo Domingo for no extra charge if you rent for three or more days – a good option if you have to get to the airport anyway. Rental agencies include **Europcar** (☎ 809-686-2861; near Plaza Punta Cana, Bávaro; ☺ 8am-6pm) and **National/Alamo** (☎ 809-688-5069; Cruce de Cocoloco; ☺ 8am-6pm Mon-Sat, 8am-5pm Sun).

Otherwise, there are numerous taxis in the area – look for stands at El Cortecito, Plaza Bávaro and at the entrance of most all-inclusives. You can also call a cab – try Siutratural taxi service on ☎ 809-552-0617 – or ask the receptionist at your hotel to do so. Fares vary depending on distance, but are typically US$5 to US$30. Water taxis also can be found on El Cortecito beach and cost between US$10 and US$50 per ride. *Motoconchos* are a cheaper option for short distances, but not recommended for longer trips or at night.

PLAYA LIMÓN

The scenic Hwy 104 takes travelers to one of the prettiest beaches in the country – Playa Limón. Located about 20km east of Miches and just outside of the hamlet of El Cedro, it's well worth a side trip. The highway is decent most of the way, but watch for potholes that seem to come out of nowhere.

Sights & Activities
PLAYA LIMÓN

A 3km stretch of isolated beach backed by a coconut forest makes Playa Limón one of the most beautiful beaches in the country. Tour groups descend upon it two hours a day to horseback ride but other than that it'll be yours to wander and enjoy. Watch for turtles, dolphins and the occasional manatee.

LAGUNA LIMÓN

One of two lagoons in a scientific reserve, Laguna Limón is a serene freshwater body of water surrounded by grassy wetlands and coastal mangroves. The lagoon feeds into the ocean on the eastern end of Playa Limón and is known for bird-watching.

Tours are organized by Rancho La Cueva (below) and involve boarding a flat-bottom boat at the beach, then following a channel through the mangroves and eventually crossing the lagoon, where buses are waiting to take travelers back to their cars or their hotels. Excursions include horseback riding on Playa Limón beforehand and a seafood buffet afterwards (per person US$45). The other lagoon – Laguna Redonda – is just 5km away but is more commonly visited from Punta El Rey (right).

Sleeping & Eating

Rancho La Cueva (☎ 809-470-0876; r US$30; Ⓟ)
Three kilometers down a dirt road at the western end of El Cedro, La Cueva is a great little hotel with eight clean, good-sized rooms with tile floors, gleaming fixtures and comfortable beds. Electricity runs 16 hours a day so prepare for still – and sometimes hot – nights. La Cueva also operates an excellent open-air restaurant. Breakfast and dinner are casual affairs where clients order whatever they're in the mood for (there's no menu) but lunch is a different story altogether; the dining room is jam packed with day-trippers and tour groups enjoying a seafood buffet complete with lobster, shrimp and grilled fish. English, Spanish and German are spoken.

Harley's Heaven (☎ 809-476-8682; lagunalimon@ gmx.net; studio US$35; ▣ Ⓟ) Sitting on a hill above La Cueva, Harley's Heaven offers 12 well-appointed and spotless studios, all with kitchenettes and satellite TV. Each studio also has a balcony with glorious views of Montaña Redonda and a nice breeze to match. High-speed Internet access is available in the main house. Plans for an RV park are in the works. Excellent value.

Getting There & Away

The easiest and most convenient way to get to Playa Limón and its hotels is to drive yourself. The road, though potholed, is empty and the ride is beautiful. From Higüey or Miches, take Hwy 104 until you reach El Cedral. From the western edge of town, head north on a dirt road (look for a dilapidated sign reading 'Club Playa Tortugas'); the beach is 5km from town, the hotels are only about 3.5 kilometers away.

Gua-guas running between Higüey (US$2, two hours) and Miches (US$1, 30

minutes) also stop in El Cedro every 30 minutes from 5:30am to 6pm. If arriving, be sure to let the driver know that you want to get off in El Cedro; it's easy to miss.

To get to the hotels (3.5km) or beach (5km) from town, you'll either have to walk down a dirt road near the western edge of town or take a *motoconcho* (US$1.50). If it's the latter, be sure to tell the driver to take it slow; it's a rough ride and presumably you'll be carrying luggage.

PUNTA EL REY

A beautiful virgin beach follows the curve of a large round bay just east of the Miches. A grassy point at the eastern end is Punta El Rey proper and the location of **Cabañas del Leo** (☎ 809-248-588; www.puntaelrey.com; r incl breakfast & dinner US$50, all meals US$60). Opened in 1991, the cabañas are run by an amusing Swiss fellow named Leo and have thatched roofs, mosquito nets over the beds, and shared baths. However, everything may have changed by the time you read this, as Leo was planning to move the whole operation down the beach and probably rebuild the cabañas in the process. The beach will be as charming as ever, though, and is the best reason for coming here in the first place.

At least one large tour group (60 to 80 people) from a nearby all-inclusive arrives every day, staying from usually 10:30am to 3:30pm. The day-trippers have buffet lunch at the Cabañas, use the beach, and go on boat tours to the nearby Laguna Redondo and on short snorkeling trips. Guests of the Cabaña can join the buffet (with the all-meals plan) and some of the boat trips, for free or for a small fee. Those who want to get away from the crowds simply spend the day at the other end of the beach.

To get here, look for a large sign in the town of La Mina de Miches, just east of Miches, pointing down a dirt road. Follow that for 9.5km, bearing right when you reach a fork in the road near the beach.

MICHES

pop 9273
The scruffy town of Miches on the southern shore of the Bahía de Samaná is mainly a transfer point between Sabana de la Mar and the southeastern coast. It's known mainly as a launching point for Dominicans trying to enter the USA illegally via

Puerto Rico. A number of Swiss people have settled in Miches and the surrounding area, and are responsible for what few sleeping options there are here.

Orientation

Miches is tucked into a small bayside basin surrounded by hills. From Higüey and El Limón, the highway descends to the basin floor where it crosses a short bridge. On the other side of the bridge is *la bomba* – literally 'the pump,' this is the local gas station and the terminal for *gua-guas* heading to and from Higüey. If you're driving, take the next right and an immediate left to get onto the main west-bound street. Banks and other services are on that street and the one up from it (Calle Mella, the main east-bound street); at the end is the terminal for *gua-guas* to and from Sabana de la Mar. Shortly after the *gua-gua* terminal is a turn-off headed up the hill to Hotel La Loma. Continuing straight will take you to Sabana de la Mar.

Information

There are very few services in Miches, including no hospital, no post office, and no Internet.

BanReservas (9:30am-3pm Mon, Wed & Fri) is in the center of town, one block south of Calle Mella. The bank was planning to open five days a week and to install an ATM by 2006. In the meantime, you can change US and European cash and Amex travelers checks. **Banco Agricola** (8:30am-4pm), two blocks north of Calle Mella, also changes cash and travelers checks. No ATM.

International calls can be made from **Verizon Centro de Comunicaciones** (Calle Mella; to USA per min US\$0.35, to Europe per min US\$1.25; 8am-7pm).

Sleeping & Eating

Hotel La Loma (809-553-5562; fax 809-553-5564; Miches; s/d US\$40/50;) High on a hill with a spectacular view of the city and bay, this is definitely the best hotel in town. Rooms are sparsely decorated, but stylishly so, with crisp linens, low firm beds, sunny colors, small potted plants and small balconies with amazing views. There's a small attractive pool, also with a view, and a just-okay restaurant. Perhaps the only drawback is the constant sometimes powerful wind that comes off the bay and buffets the hotel. Many areas, including the pool and restau-

rant, are protected by windscreens. A great option – too bad it's not in a town you'd actually want to stay at for a couple days.

Coco Loco Beach Club (/fax 809-553-5920; Playa Miches; s/d US\$25/35;) The Coco Loco offers 10 plywood cabins, all with tile floors, private cold water bathrooms and standing fans. Cabins are surprisingly clean and all have nice porches. A lounge area is located on the 2nd floor of a pleasantly rustic main building. It doubles as a **pizzeria** (mains US\$4-10; lunch & dinner) and makes a nice spot to kick back and relax. The beach in front is just OK but makes for good beachcombing. Look for the sign near the eastern entrance of town (before you cross the bridge into town) and follow the dirt road that runs alongside the Río Yaguada until the road becomes sand. You'll see the hotel about 100m away.

The Hotel La Loma **restaurant** (809-553-5562; Miches; mains US\$9-15; breakfast, lunch & dinner) is the best place in town to eat, though the view far outshines the food, which is okay at best. The breaded fish with tartar sauce and beef stroganoff are plain but reliable.

Getting There & Away

Gua-guas to Higüey (US\$3, 2½ hours, every 30 minutes, 5am to 5:30pm) leave from a terminal at the Isla gas station at the east end of town just before the bridge. The terminal for *gua-guas* going to and from Sabana de la Mar (US\$1.75, 1¼ hours, every 25 minutes, 6:55am to 6pm) is at the western edge of town.

If you are simply passing through town, whether from Sabana de la Mar to Higüey or vice versa, let the driver know you want to catch an onward bus and he will most likely drop you at the next terminal, saving you a *motoconcho* or taxi ride between the two.

SABANA DE LA MAR

pop 13,977

This small town has no real attractions itself, but is the gateway to Parque Nacional Los Haitises and is the departure point for the ferry across the bay to Samaná.

Orientation

The highway from Higüey descends from the hills straight into Sabana de la Mar, turning into Calle Duarte, the main street, and eventually bumping right into the pier where the

Samaná ferry leaves and arrives. The road from Miches intersects with the Higüey highway just outside (south) of town. *Guaguas* to Miches, Higüey and Santo Domingo all congregate at or near that intersection. The turn-off to Caño Hondo and Parque Nacional Los Haitises is a short distance north of the Miches intersection – look for a large sign pointing west.

Information

Sabana de la Mar is a small town with relatively few services.

BanReservas (Calle Duarte; 8am-5pm Mon-Fri, 9am-1pm Sat) is three blocks south of the ferry pier and has one ATM.

Verizon Centro de Comunicaciones (Calle Duarte; 8am-10pm) is two blocks south of the southernmost roundabout in town, and offers international telephone service (to the USA per minute US$0.32, to Europe per minute US$0.74).

Tours

Tourist Information Office (809-556-7815; Calle Duarte 37; 8am-6pm), despite it's name, is actually a tour operator that offers good area trips. Among those are boat and walking tours of **Parque Nacional Los Haitises** (p146), which typically last 3½ hours and include sailing around land formations and through mangroves, exploring Taíno caves and relaxing on the beach. The cost per person is US$35 for four or more people, or per person US$45 for smaller groups. **Whale watching** trips also are offered between January

15 and March 15 (p151). The trip lasts about six hours and includes lunch on Cayo Levantado (p149), a beautiful but touristy island across the Bahía de Samaná. The cost per person is US$60 for a group of four or more, and per person US$80 for smaller groups. English and French are spoken.

Paraíso Caño Hondo (809-248-5995; www.paraiso canohondo.com), a high end hotel 9km west of town, offers good tours inside Parque Los Haitises as well. Boat excursions range between US$15 and US$33 depending on the extent of the tour, and **hiking trips** (per guide US$18) through the park's Bosque Humedo (humid forest) also can be arranged. During the humpback season, Paraíso organizes whale-watching tours in the waters near Samaná (US$56 per person).

At the entrance to Los Haitises, town **boatmen** also offer to take visitors on tours of the park (US$17pp). While the excursions are similar to those offered by the tour operators, background information on the sights is often less detailed.

Sleeping & Eating

Paraíso Caño Hondo (809-248-5995; www.paraiso canohondo.com, in Spanish; s/d per person US$44/28) Located 1km from the entrance to Parque Los Haitises and offering several tours within it, Paraíso Caño Hondo is an excellent place to base yourself for exploring the park. It also is a perfect place to just sit back and relax. Rooms are rustic but well appointed, many with balconies that feature sweeping views of the beautiful countryside. Rambling

EL SEIBO & HATO MAYOR

During the early 19th century, French soldiers ruled Santo Domingo and most of the present-day Dominican Republic. However, a much larger Haitian force – led by a former slave and eager to unite the entire island under one flag – overran one city after another in central and eastern Hispaniola, in most instances slaughtering any French and Spanish colonists that were encountered.

After having attacked and burned Monte Plata, Cotuí and La Vega, the Haitians arrived in Moca, where they killed the entire population and burned the town to the ground. The same was done in Santiago, where more than 400 people were massacred. By 1806 only Santo Domingo, El Seibo, Bayaguana and Higüey remained standing. All the other towns in the region were deserted and remained so for many years.

At the time, El Seibo was a cattle-raising and agricultural center. Today, it remains so along with Hato Mayor, 24km to the west. Typical Dominican cities, each is the capital of a province where most workers still earn their living toiling in fields or tending to cattle. There's little for the tourist in either place, and their only hotels (which are on the road that bisects both cities) are unattractive.

stone paths lead guests to a series of 10 river-fed pools with waterfalls that make for a relaxing day (or days) swimming and soaking. Breakfast is included in the rate, though half-board and full-board plans are available. Weekends are often packed with student groups so best plan a visit midweek to have the place to yourself. Day passes for the hotel pools are also available (adults US$3.50, children US$1.75).

Acapulco Hotel (☎ 809-556-7815; s/d US$15/20; ✗) Worn but clean, this is the last resort if you get stuck in town. Expect dark rooms with peeling paint and saggy beds. Located two blocks east of the ferry pier, this place is good just for a night.

Getting There & Away

Gua-guas are the only means of public transportation out of town. They leave from the entrance of town, at the crossroads of Hwy 104 and Hwy 103. *Gua-guas* headed to Santo Domingo (US$4, 3½ hours, every 30 minutes, 6am to 4pm) stop along the way in Hato Mayor (US$1.40, one hour) and San Pedro de Macorís (US$2.50, two hours). *Gua-guas* also provide service to Miches (US$1.25, 1¼ hours, every 25 minutes, 6:45am to 6pm).

Transporte Maritimo (☎ 809-538-2556) provides a ferry service across the Bahía de Samana to Samaná (US$3.50, one hour, 9am, 11am, 3pm and 5pm). From there you can catch *gua-guas* to Las Galeras or puddle-jump to other destinations on the North Coast.

Getting Around

Sabana de la Mar is small enough to get around on foot. However, if you want to head to Parque Los Haitises or to Paraíso Caño Hondo, *motoconchos* are your best bet. A ride to the park or the hotel will cost around US$2.50. Of course if you have bags, a taxi is safer and more comfortable; unfortunately there are precious few cabs in this town. If you do find one – there is sometimes one meeting the ferry or the bus – a ride to the hotel will cost around US$5.

PARQUE NACIONAL LOS HAITISES

Eight kilometers west of Sabana de la Mar **Parque Nacional Los Haitises** (admission US$3.50; ⏰ 7am-8pm) is certainly the best reason to visit this small bayside town. Meaning 'land of the mountains,' this 1200-sq-km park at the southwestern end of the Bahía de Samaná contains scores of lush hills jutting some 30m to 50m from the water and coastal wetlands. The knolls were formed one to two million years ago, when tectonic drift buckled the thick limestone shelf that had formed underwater. The turn-off to the park is near the crossroads of Hwys 104 and 103, at the south end of town (near the bus stop). The road is paved and well marked, both by the park service and the owners of Paraíso Caño Hondo (p145), which is located just a kilometer past the main park entrance.

The area receives a tremendous amount of rainfall, creating perfect conditions for subtropical humid forest plants such as bamboo, ferns and bromeliads. In fact, Los Haitises contains over 700 species of flora, including four types of mangrove, making it one of the most highly bio-diverse regions in the Caribbean.

Los Haitises also is home to 78 species of birds, 13 of which are endemic to the island. Those seen most frequently include the brown pelican, the American frigate bird, the blue heron, the roseate tern and the northern jacana. If you're lucky, you may even spot the rare Hispaniolan Parakeet, notable for its light green and red feathers.

The park also contains a series of limestone caves, some of which contain intriguing Taíno pictographs. Drawn by the native inhabitants of Hispaniola using mangrove shoots, the pictures depict faces, hunting scenes, whales and other animals. Several petroglyphs (images carved into the stone) can also seen at the entrance of some caves and are thought to represent divine guardians.

Land and boat excursions inside the park leave from Sabana de la Mar and Samaná across the bay (see p149).

Península de Samaná

The Península de Samaná (Samaná Peninsula) is only a small sliver of land – just 40km long and 15km wide – but a major destination for independent-minded tourists. There are three main towns – Samaná which sits along the bay of the same name, and Las Terrenas and Las Galeras, both by the ocean on the northern side of the peninsula. Of the three, Samaná is the most well known – between mid-January and mid-March thousands of humpback whales arrive from the North Atlantic to mate, and Samaná is the place to go for great whale-watching trips. It is also a transportation hub with bus connections west to Puerto Plata and Santo Domingo, plus a ferry across the bay to head to the beaches and resorts of the southeast. Las Terrenas is the largest and busiest of the three, with several long pretty beaches lined with palm trees and hotels, plus a lively bar scene. Las Galeras is the most charming – a sleepy seaside town, it also happens to have three of the DR's most picturesque beaches, all the more appealing because they are reachable only by boat, hiking or rough dirt road. This is a place that is easy to get stuck in, and many people do. Though a tiny piece of land, Samaná looms large for many visitors to the Dominican Republic (DR).

PENÍNSULA DE SAMANÁ

HIGHLIGHTS

- See 30-ton humpbacks leap, splash and jostle about on a **whale-watching trip** (p149) from Samaná.

- **Playa Rincón** (p154) is one of the country's finest beaches, with mile after mile of tawny sand and gorgeous blue water.

- Go hiking around **Las Galeras** (p155) for stunning views and hidden beaches.

- The **Haitian Art Gallery** (p165) in Las Terrenas is hands-down the best place to buy quality Haitian art.

- Massive under-sea walls and vibrant sea life make **Cabo Cabrón** (p155) one of the DR's best dive sites.

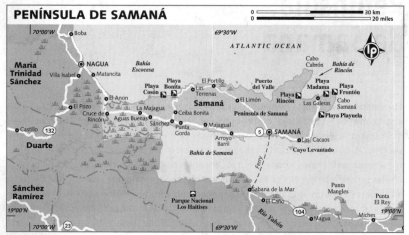

PENÍNSULA DE SAMANÁ

History

Bahía de Samaná (Samaná Bay) is a veritable graveyard of ships, some ripped apart by hurricanes, others plundered by pirates. On one occasion the pirate Roberto Cofresí sank his own ship near the throat of the bay when he found himself cornered by Spanish patrol boats. Cofresí and his crew escaped the advancing Spaniards by boarding small skiffs and rowing their way into the area's maze of marshes. Cofresí's ship went down off Punta Gorda laden with treasure, but to this day the vessel has never been found.

Two other famous sunken ships in Bahía de Samaná – the Spanish galleons *Nuestra Señora de Guadalupe* and *El Conde de Tolosa* – remained untouched for more than 250 years until they were discovered in 1976 and 1977, respectively. Both ships were en route to Mexico from Spain loaded with mercury when hurricane-whipped waves flung them into coral reefs, where they broke apart and sank within hours of each other (p101).

SAMANÁ

Samaná is a tranquil town built on a series of bluffs overlooking Bahía de Samaná. The houses are small and brightly painted and the streets quiet, with only the occasional tourist – for most of the year anyway. From mid-January to mid-March, Samaná is inundated with visitors – over 30,000 – who flock here to see the humpback whales that migrate from the North Atlantic to the

area's waters. Whale-watching season is a bustling time for Samaná – *motoconchos* (motorcycle taxis) tear up and down the main drag, tour buses line the streets and *gua-guas* (small local buses) are jammed with backpackers. And not without reason. The whale watching here is truly spectacular. At the height of the season, it's common to see groups of a dozen or more humpbacks jostling and breaching just meters away.

History

Samaná was founded as a Spanish outpost in 1756. It was first settled by émigrés from the Canary Islands but the political turmoil of Hispaniola – the sale of the island to the French, a Haitian revolution and two British invasions – kept the town's population growing and changing. In the early 1820s, approximately 2500 Black freemen and former slaves emigrated from the United States and settled in Samaná, adding yet another dimension to the local character. (Today, a community of their descendents still speak a form of English.)

After a failed attempt by the US to buy the Samaná peninsula in the 1860s for US$2 million – they wanted to establish a military base in the Caribbean but settled instead on Guantánamo, Cuba – Samaná faded from the world view. It remained an isolated fishing village until 1985, when the first whale-watching expedition set out, reinventing Samaná as a major tourist destination.

Orientation

Just about all of the town's services are within 200m of the ferry pier. The main street – Av la Marina – has most of the restaurants, a bank and the bus stations. The hotels are all reachable by foot, but a bit far if you're carrying bags. *Gua-guas* leave from the municipal market, about a kilometer down the road toward Sánchez.

Information

EMERGENCY

Politur (Tourist Police; ☎ 809-754-3066; Francisco de Rosario Sánchez; ⏱ 24hr) Near Av Circunvalación.

INTERNET ACCESS & TELEPHONE

CompuCentro Samaná (☎ 809-538-3146; Calle Labandier at Santa Barbara; per hr US$2.10; ⏱ 9am-12:30pm, 3-6pm Mon-Fri, 9am-4pm Sat) CD burning also available for US$3.

Verizon Centro de Comunicaciones (☎ 809-536-2133; Calle Santa Barbara; ⏱ 8am-1pm & 2-10pm Mon-Sat, 9am-1pm Sun) This dimly lit center, near Cristóbal Colón, offers reasonably fast Internet connections (per hr US$1.75) and international phone service (to USA per min US$0.32, to Europe per min US$0.74).

INTERNET RESOURCES

For information and listings on accommodations, activities and upcoming events in and around Samaná, get online and check out www.samanaonline.com or www.samana net.com.

LAUNDRY

Lavandería Santa Barbara (Calle Santa Barbara; ⏱ 8:30am-6pm) Same-day or overnight service available at US$1 per pound (450g). Some travelers have had items lost, so double check everything before leaving the shop.

MEDICAL SERVICES

Farmacia Giselle (☎ 809-538-2303; Calle Santa Barbara at Julio Labandier; ⏱ 8am-10pm Mon-Sat, 8am-noon Sun) This pharmacy offers a good selection of meds, toiletries and film.

Hospital Municipal (Calle San Juan; ⏱ 24hr) This is a very basic hospital; located near the Palacio de Justicia.

MONEY

Banco Popular (Av la Marina; ⏱ 8:15am-4pm Mon-Fri, 9am-1pm Sat) The branch of this bank is located on the Malecón across from the ferry dock.

BanReservas (Calle Santa Barbara; ⏱ 8am-5pm Mon-Fri, 9am-1pm Sat) BanReservas can be found one block north of the Malecón.

POST

Post Office (Calle Santa Barbara at 27 de Febrero; ⏱ 8:30am-5pm Mon-Fri)

TOURIST INFORMATION

Tourist Office (☎ 809-538-2332; Calle Santa Barbara; ⏱ 8:30am-3pm Mon-Fri) On the first floor of this dilapidated government office building, you'll find a dark office with a desk and perhaps a staffer who can offer basic information about the area. Good for regional maps. English, Italian and French are theoretically spoken but come armed with a Spanish dictionary.

Sights & Activities

CAYO LEVANTADO

Located seven kilometers from Samaná, Cayo Levantado is a lush island with a picture-perfect beach – think expansive white sand, turquoise waters and palm trees galore. Unfortunately, the idyllic setting is marred by hundreds of day-trippers shipped in from local resorts and scores of vendors hawking cheap handicrafts. If you choose to visit, try going in the mid- to late-afternoon when most of the activity is winding down. Boatmen at the pier make the trip for US$15 to US$20 per person each way.

WHALE WATCHING

Samaná is one of the top places in the world to observe humpback whales. The season begins around January 15 and continues to March 15. See the Traveling Giants boxed text (p151) for more about the whales, and the Tours section (p150) for information about how to see this amazing spectacle.

CASCADA EL LIMÓN

El Limon is a 50m **waterfall** a short distance from the town of El Limón. Travel agencies in Samaná offer trips there for around US$45, including transport, horses, guide and lunch. However, it's perfectly easy and much cheaper to do the trip yourself by taking a *gua-gua* to El Limón. See Las Terrenas (p160) for more details.

PARQUE NACIONAL LOS HAITISES

This national park, with its tiny, jungly islands and thick mangrove forests, makes for great exploring by boat. Victoria Marine and other outfits in town offer trips there for around US$45 per person, including a guide and transport to, and inside of, the park. For more information on the park see p146.

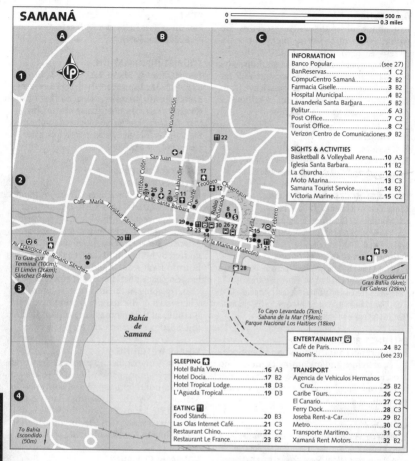

SAMANÁ

INFORMATION
Banco Popular....................................(see 27)	
BanReservas...**1** C2	
CompuCentro Samaná.............................**2** B2	
Farmacia Giselle...**3** B2	
Hospital Municipal....................................**4** B2	
Lavandería Santa Barbara.......................**5** B2	
Politur..**6** A3	
Post Office...**7** C2	
Tourist Office..**8** C2	
Verizon Centro de Comunicaciones.**9** B2	

SIGHTS & ACTIVITIES
Basketball & Volleyball Arena.......**10** A3	
Iglesia Santa Barbara...................**11** B2	
La Churcha...................................**12** C2	
Moto Marina.................................**13** C3	
Samana Tourist Service.................**14** B2	
Victoria Marine............................**15** C2	

SLEEPING
Hotel Bahía View........................**16** A3	
Hotel Docia................................**17** B2	
Hotel Tropical Lodge...................**18** D3	
L'Aguada Tropical.......................**19** D3	

EATING
Food Stands................................**20** B3	
Las Olas Internet Café.................**21** C3	
Restaurant Chino.........................**22** C2	
Restaurant Le France...................**23** B2	

ENTERTAINMENT
Café de Paris..............................**24** B2	
Naomi's......................................(see 23)	

TRANSPORT
Agencia de Vehiculos Hermanos	
Cruz...**25** B2	
Caribe Tours...............................**26** C2	
El Canario...................................**27** C2	
Ferry Dock..................................**28** C3	
Joseba Rent-a-Car.......................**29** B2	
Metro...**30** C2	
Transporte Maritimo....................**31** C3	
Xamaná Rent Motors....................**32** B2	

Tours

Victoria Marine (☎ 809-538-2494; www.whalesamana.com; Calle Mella at Av la Marina; adult US$48, ages 5-10 US$28, under 5 free; ☒ 9am-1:30pm, 3-6pm) is Samaná's most-recommended whale-watching outfit owned and operated by Canadian marine biologist Kim Beddall, who was the first person to recognize the scientific and economic importance of Samaná's whales back in 1985. Victoria Marine tours use a large two-deck boat with capacity for 60 people (though most tours have around 40). The skilled captains religiously observe the local boat-to-whale distance and other regulations – most of which Beddall helped create – while on-board guides offer interesting facts and information in

three languages over the boat's sound system. Sodas and water are provided free of charge. Tours leave at 9am and last three to four hours. There is also a 1:30pm trip when demand is high, and some tours include a stop at Cayo Levantado on the way back.

If Victoria Marine is booked solid or you just want to comparison shop, **Samaná Tourist Service** (☎ 809-538-2740; samana.tour@verizon.net.do; Av la Marina 6; ☒ 8:30am-12:30pm & 2:30-6pm Mon-Fri, 8:30am-12:30pm Sat) and **Moto Marina** (☎ 809-538-2302; Av la Marina; ☒ 8am-6pm) offer similar (and similarly priced) tours. These agencies also offer excursions to El Limón waterfalls and to Parque Nacional Los Haitises, both for about US$50 per person.

Sleeping

Accommodations options are slim in Samaná. Most people only stay long enough to take a whale-watching tour before moving on.

Hotel Bahía View (☎ 809-538-2186; Francisco de Rosario Sánchez 15 at Av Circunvalación; d/tw US$15.50/20, with balcony US$23.50, with aircon US$27; ❂) The best deal in town, though a bit removed from the center. Rooms here are basic and clean with hot water and a good restaurant (p152) downstairs. You probably won't need aircon, but the balcony rooms are worth the extra cost if you appreciate having more light and space (the balcony is big, with room for chairs and a table), though they're often taken.

Hotel Docia (☎ 809-538-2041; Teodoro Chasereaux at Duarte; r US$17.50) Sitting at the foot of a small hill, this no-frills hotel is a favorite among budget travelers. Rooms are clean and spartan with high ceilings, fan, hot water and great sea breezes. There's coffee in the morning and a kitchen with a fridge for guests to use. Call ahead to secure a room.

L'Aguada Tropical (☎ 809-249-8131; Av La Marina; d/tw US$21/28) Behind the Hotel Tropical Lodge and a five-minute walk from town, this small two-story hotel has large and relatively clean rooms, though some of the

---

TRAVELING GIANTS

Every winter more than 10,000 humpback whales – virtually the entire North Atlantic population – leave their feeding grounds around Greenland and Iceland and head south to the Caribbean. In mid-January they reach their destination, the waters around the Samaná Peninsula, where they remain for two months to court and breed. Most of the whales swim 3000km to 5000km to get here, though several individuals identified in Samaná were later spotted off the coast of Norway, a trip of some 7000km. It is one of the longest migrations of any mammal.

Before leaving, the whales gorge themselves on invertebrates and fish, consuming up to 1½ tons a day. It's not without reason – there is no food for the whales in the Caribbean and they depend on the fat they accumulate up north to survive their long journey south. In all, most of the whales go six months without a single meal and lose a fifth of their body weight.

That's not to say they aren't busy. Once in the Dominican Republic, the whales commence their famous antics – slapping their flippers, lifting their tails, leaping partially or entirely out of the water and returning with a tremendous splash. Scientists still don't know why the whales do it – perhaps as a form of communication or to simply break loose barnacles – but males, females and calves all join in.

Adult male humpbacks also sing long complicated songs that are made up of a variety of grunts, chirps and squeals. The music can be heard up to 20 miles away, and marine biologists believe that this is used to attract females. Curiously, the whales all sing the same basic song which evolves over time, so the following year it will be a new song altogether. Another way males attract females is through muscle and intimidation – males are known to bloody their heads as they ram and rake one another to win a female's attention.

After mating, a single calf is born 11 to 12 months later. A newborn humpback whale typically measures 3m to 4m and weighs up to 2 tons. Calves are nursed for nearly a year, drinking milk that's 50% fat and, as a result, gaining up to 45kg per day – that's close to 2kg every *hour*. A whale calf doubles its body length in its first year alone.

Whale-watching trips typically depart at 9am and sail for about 45 minutes before arriving in the area known as the sanctuary, a protected area covering more than 20,000 sq km. Once inside the breeding zone, the captain slows the boat and everyone is asked to look for the telltale spout, the spray a whale makes as it exhales near the surface. As soon as a whale is spotted, the captain directs the boat towards it and more often than not, observers are rewarded with breathtaking acrobatics. The larger boats have expert guides on board to explain whale behaviors and to answer any questions. Boats are only permitted to stay with a whale or a group of whales for 30 minutes. When that time is up, the boat turns away, the whales continue on their way and everyone aboard scans the water for another spout. Excursions typically last about three hours and sometimes include a stop on Cayo Levantado, a touristy but beautiful island a short distance from Samaná. Drinks and light snacks are often provided. For more details, see p149.

beds and furniture are showing their age. Rooms on the eastern side have small terraces which afford a little more light and fresh air, but you may want to keep the doors closed at dusk when the mosquitoes come out in force. The hotel kitchen is mainly used by management, but guests can gain access simply by asking. The L'Aguada is fan-cooled, has hot water and 24-hour electricity; there's a small common sitting area with lovely bay views.

Hotel Tropical Lodge (☎ 809-538-2840; www .samana-hotel.com; juan.felipe@verizon.net.do; Av La Marina; d/tw US$46/70; ☒ ☒) Samaná's nicest 'normal' hotel – there's an all-inclusive resort a few kilometers further on – is built on a hillside and is all about the view. A great pool and patio area look over the main building to the blue bay beyond, guests are served their breakfasts (included in the price) in a sunny dining room with the same view; and some (but not all) guestrooms have windows or glass doors facing the water. Rooms aren't exactly deluxe, but are large and perfectly comfortable. The five-minute walk to town can be a slight drag, especially at night. The on-site **restaurant** (mains US$6-15; ☒ lunch & dinner, closed Tue) serves reliable meals, including fish, pizza and crepes.

Occidental Gran Bahía (☎ 809-320-3988, in USA 800-858-2258; www.occidentalhotels.com; per person US$100; ☒ ☒ ☒) Located 6km east of Samaná, the all-inclusive Gran Bahía offers scores of rooms with truly glorious views of Bahía de Samaná (and between January and March, humpback whales too!). Rooms are spacious and clean but are showing their age a bit. Daily shuttles to Cayo Levantado also are included in the rate. The food is mediocre at best.

Eating & Drinking

Samaná's eating options are a bit better than its sleeping options, but the selection is still pretty limited. Most are right on the main drag.

Restaurant Le France (☎ 809-538-2781; Av la Marina; mains US$5-12; ☒ 10am-11pm, closed Mon) Also known as Chez Tony, the menu at this small open-air restaurant ranges from Dominican-style chicken and pork to French dishes like beef tartar and homemade paté. Low-key, friendly service with a few upscale flairs, like composing the tartar right at your table. A good choice.

Restaurant Chino (☎ 809-538-2215; Calle San Juan 1; mains US$4.50-12.50; ☒ 11am-11pm) Located on a hill with a fantastic view of the Bahía de Samaná, this aptly named restaurant serves up large portions of Chinese favorites – think won ton soup, spring rolls, chop suey and kung pao chicken. Dishes are tasty, if a bit greasy. Dominican dishes are also served.

Restaurante Rinconcito del View (☎ 809-538-2411; Hotel Bahía View; mains US$3-9; ☒ 8am-11pm Sat-Thu) While we don't usually include hotel restaurants, the breakfasts here are worth mentioning. Cheap and good, you can get a plate of fried eggs and *tostones* (fried banana slices) for US$3. The dining area is very clean and the service agreeable.

Las Olas Internet Café (☎ 809-538-2434; Av la Marina near Mella; mains US$3-8; ☒ 8am-8pm Mon-Sat, 8am-noon Sun) If you're looking for a good place to kick back, consider heading to this café which offers tempting pastries, coffee drinks, personal pizzas and beers. Add to that a good book exchange and a decent selection of board games and you'll probably find that you'll stay here a little longer than you thought you would. As the name suggests, Internet access also is available but at US$3.50 per hour, you're better off paying half that price a couple blocks away.

You can also get cheap eats and a taste of the local party scene at a series of food stands that line Av la Marina near Calle Maria Trinidad Sánchez. Beginning around 6pm and lasting until the early hours of the morning, fried chicken is served up with *Presidente* beers for Dominican and foreign customers alike. If you have trouble finding the party – which you probably won't – just listen for the *bachata* blasting from the west side of town.

Entertainment

At the time of research, a large sports facility was being built in the empty lot between the pier and the Hotel Bahía View. Designed for basketball and volleyball, it should be open by the time you read this and will be a great afternoon or nighttime option. Admission, if charged at all, will surely be minimal.

Café de Paris (Av La Marina; mains US$4-10; ☒ 8am-midnight, drinks only 10pm-midnight) This eclectic place next door to the Le France has a long drink list and there are plastic tables outside that are well suited to an afternoon beer.

Paris also serves up decent pizzas, including the house specialty made with chicken, onion, garlic, olives and egg. Crepes are served salty or sweet, and you can order a variety of salads.

Naomi's (Av la Marina; admission US$2; ☺ 9pm-4am Fri-Sun) Located above Restaurant Le France, a set of rickety stairs leads to the only discotheque in Samaná – a small, smoky place facing the bay. Naomi's gets going around midnight and features mostly merengue and *bachata* music. The crowd is decidedly local but foreigners are always welcome.

Getting There & Away
AIR
The nearest airport in regular operation is Aeropuerto Internacional El Portillo, just outside of Las Terrenas (p165).

BUS
Facing the pier, **Caribe Tours** (☎ 809-538-2229; Av la Marina) offers services to Santo Domingo at 7am, 8:30am, 10am, 1pm, 2:30pm and 4pm (US$7.50, 4½ hours, daily). The same bus stops along the way at Sánchez (US$2, 30 minutes), Nagua (US$2.15, one hour) and San Francisco de Macorís (US$3, 1½ hours). A block west, **Metro** (☎ 809-538-2851; Av la Marina at Rubio y Peñaranda) offers a similar service (US$8, 4½ hours, twice a day, 8am and 3:30pm). Like its competitor, it stops at Sánchez (US$2.30, 30 minutes), Nagua (US$2.30, one hour) and San Francisco de Macorís (US$3.50, 1½ hours).

The only direct service to Puerto Plata is with **El Canario** (☎ 809-291-5594; Av la Marina; US$7, 3½ to four hours). Buses leave at 10:15am beside the Banco Popular and at 1:45pm near Victoria Marina. Arrive 30 to 45 minutes early to reserve a seat.

For service to towns nearby, head to the **gua-gua terminal** (Av la Marina) at the mercado municipal, 90m west of the Politur station, near Angel Mesina. From here, trucks and mini-vans head to Las Galeras (US$1.75, 45 minutes, every 15 minutes, 6am to 6pm), El Limón (US$1.75, 30 minutes, every 15 minutes, 6am to 6pm), and Sánchez (US$1.75, 45 minutes, every 15 minutes, 6am to 4:30pm). You can also hail *gua-guas* on the main drag but more often than not they're packed with passengers, boxes and chickens so you'll either have to hang off the side or sit on one cheek to catch this ride.

FERRY
Transporte Marítimo (☎ 809-538-2556; Av la Marina) provides the only ferry service across the Bahía de Samaná to Sabana de la Mar (US$3.50, one hour, four daily at 7am, 9am, 11am and 3pm). From there, catch *gua-guas* to destinations throughout the southeast and to Santo Domingo. You used to be able to take the vehicle ferry, but it sunk not long before we came through. There was talk of an Italian company resuming service – call ahead for current information.

Getting Around
Samaná is easily covered on foot but if you've got luggage or are heading to the market from the eastern edge of town, you'll fare much better in a taxi or a *motoconcho* with a passenger cab (think motorized rickshaws). Both can be found near the ferry pier or hailed on the main drag (US$1 to US$3).

CAR
If you're in the market to rent a car, 4WD vehicles are your only option in this town. While definitely expensive, the roads in the peninsula are bad enough that you'll be happy you have the extra power. Rates run from US$70 to US$90 per day (tax and insurance included) and discounts of 10% to 15% are typically given for rentals of a week or longer. Agencies in town include:
Agencia de Vehículos Hermanos Cruz (☎ 809-751-5687; Calle Santa Barbara; ☺ 8am-noon & 2-6pm Mon-Sat) Between Cristóbal Colón & Julio Labandier.
Joseba Rent-a-Car (☎ 809-538-2124; Av la Marina; ☺ 8am-noon & 2-5pm Mon-Sat)
Xamaná Rent Motors (☎ 809-538-2380; Av la Marina; ☺ 8am-noon & 2-6pm)

LAS GALERAS
Before 1990, there were only two simple hotels in this rapidly changing fishing community 28km northeast of Samaná. Today there are more than a dozen hotels and bungalow options and almost as many restaurants. But the town still retains a peaceful, laid back quality that, along with some of the Dominican Republic's best beaches and outdoors options, make this a favorite stop for many travelers.

Orientation
The road coming from Samaná winds through lovely, often-forested countryside

before reaching the outskirts of Las Galeras. There's one main intersection in town (about 50m before the highway dead-ends at the beach) and most hotels, restaurants and services are walking distance from there.

Information

Most of Las Galeras' services are within a Frisbee throw of the main intersection.

Internet Las Galeras (Calle Principal at main intersection; per hr US$6.25; ⏰ 8:30am-8pm Mon-Sat, 9am-12:30pm & 2:30-8pm Sun) offers reliable – though pricey – Internet connections. Annoyingly, it charges US$2 to connect any USB device, whether a digital camera or a thumb drive, and US$1.50 if you need any assistance. Just steps away, **Gift Shop & Internet Habiby** (Plaza Lusitania, Calle Principal; per hr US$3.50; ⏰ 8:30am-1pm & 2-8pm Mon-Sat) was setting up shop when we passed through. Prices promised to be significantly more accessible than its competitor.

The Casa Marina Bay resort has a **small clinic** (☎ 809-538-0020; 1km east of town; ⏰ 24hr) that non-guests can use in emergencies. For more serious matters go to Samaná or Las Terrenas. **Farmacia Joven** (☎ 809-538-0103; Calle Principal; ⏰ 8am-9:30pm Mon-Sat), near the main crossroad, has basic meds.

There is no bank or ATM in Las Galeras but you can exchange cash dollars and euros at **Hermanos Cruz Agente de Cambio and Rent-A-Car** (☎ 809-341-4574; Calle Principal; ⏰ 8am-6pm Mon-Sat, 8am-noon Sun).

To call home, **Verizon Centro de Comunicaciones** (Plaza Lusitania, Calle Principal; to USA per min US$0.35, to Europe US$0.77; ⏰ 9am-noon & 1-6pm) offers the best long-distance rates in town. There is no post office, but Internet Las Galeras also sells express stamps for international destinations (US$1.60) and will post mail left in its drop box.

Sights

Las Galeras has a number of natural attractions that can be visited by boat, foot, car or horseback. All can be reached on your own, provided you're in decent shape or have a sturdy vehicle, but a guide will help you from getting lost and point out interesting things along the way.

PLAYA RINCÓN

Dubbed one of the top 10 beaches in the Caribbean by Conde Nast, Playa Rincón is indeed a beautiful and striking spot. Composed of several long softly curving beaches and stretching just over 3km, Rincón's sand is nearly white and its water gorgeously multi-hued. You can walk for hours along the shore with soft waves on one side and deep palm forest on the other. Seaweed and driftwood give the beach a rustic, deserted look and there's enough room for everyone to have their own piece of paradise. Several small restaurants serve mostly seafood dishes and rent beach chairs, making this a great place to spend the entire day. Most people arrive by boat – the standard option is to leave around 9am and return to pick you up at 4pm. If you join up with other beach-goers, it costs per person about US$12 to US$15. You can also drive there, though the last kilometer or so is too rough for small or midsize cars. The turnoff to Playa Rincón is 7km south of Las Galeras on the road to Samaná.

PLAYITA

Better than the beach in town, Playita (Little Beach) is easy to get to on foot or by *motoconcho*. It's a broad swatch of tannish sand, with mellow surf and backed by tall palm trees. There are several food shacks where you can get grilled fish or chicken, plus chilled water, soda or beer. On the main road just south of Las Galeras, look for signs for Hotel La Playita pointing down a dirt road headed west.

PLAYAS MADAMA AND FRONTÓN

The trail begins at the far east end of the Casa Marina Bay beach, about 200m past the resort's entrance, near a private house which most people know as 'La Casa de los Ingleses' (House of the English) after its original owners. Coming from town, the house and the trail will be on your right. In the first kilometer you'll pass a German beer garden and the turnoff to the Museo Taíno (actually the home and private collection of a quirky Frenchwoman named Ivette 'La Bruja' Durrieu) before reaching the first of two cut-offs to Playa Madama. If you turn left there (or at the next cut-off a kilometer later) you'll walk another 2km to a small pretty beach, tucked into a narrow bay and framed by high bluffs. If you continue on the main trail, you'll pass a second cut-off to Playa Madama and a few kilometers later the cut-off to Playa Frontón. From there it's four winding kilometers to the beach itself, which rivals Playa Rincón in rustic beauty. You can also talk a boat to either of these beaches for around US$17 per person roundtrip, with a pick-up in the afternoon.

BOCA DEL DIABLO
'Mouth of the Devil' is an impressive vent or blowhole, where waves rush up a natural channel and blast out of a hole in the rocks. Car or motorcycle is the best way to get there – look for an unmarked dirt road 7km south of town and about 100m beyond the well-marked turnoff to Playa Rincón. Follow the road eastward for about 8km, then walk the last 100m or so.

Activities
DIVING
Cabo Cabrón (Bastard Point) is one of the North Coast's best dive sites and an easy boat-ride from Las Galeras. Other popular sites in the area include Piedra Bonita, a 50m stone tower that's good for spotting jacks, barracudas and sea turtles; Cathedral, an enormous underwater cave opening to sunlight; and a sunken 55m-container ship haunted by big green morays. Several large coral patches, none deeper than 10m, are good for beginner divers.

Casa Marina Bay Dive Center (Dive Samaná; ☎ 809-538-2000; www.dive-samana.de; Casa Marina Bay resort; ☼ 7am-6pm) is located at the far end of Casa Marina Bay's beach – non-guests are welcome to dive here but if you don't have a car you'll have to take a *motoconcho* to the gate and walk in from there, about 700m all told. The shop may close if business is slow, so definitely call ahead before making the trip out. One-/two-tank dives are, including all equipment, US$60/114 (US$5 to US$12 less if you have your own). Four- and six-dive packages bring the per-dive rate down, including gear, to US$48 to US$52. Various PADI (Professional Association of Dive Instructors) certification courses can be arranged as well.

HIKING
Better known as El Punto, this spectacular vista point is a 5km walk from Bungalows Karin y Roland. To get there, simply continue past the turnoffs to Playas Madam and Frontón and keep climbing up, up and up. Budget at least an hour to get to the top.

HORSEBACK RIDING
The Belgian owners of Bungalows Karin y Ronald offer well-recommended **horseback riding tours** (half-/full-day $42/54) to various spots around Las Galeras, including Boca del Diablo, El Punto lookout and Playas Madama and Frontón. Casa Marina Bay resort offers similarly priced but somewhat less-personalized horseback tours as well.

MOUNTAIN BIKING
Not to be outdone by their countrymen, the Belgian owners of La Bella Aventura offer half- and full-day **mountain biking tours** (per person $US42) in the area. Tours include bikes and helmets and can be tailored to the length, difficulty and destination you prefer.

Tours
While you can visit many of the beaches and sights on your own – or hire a *motoconcho* driver to act as your chauffeur and guide – organized tours usually include reliable transport, a professional and knowledgeable guide and you'll certainly learn more than going solo.

Aventura Tropical (☎ 809-538-0249; Calle Principal; ☼ 8am-7pm Mon-Sat, 8am-1pm Sun) offers numerous day trips including whale watching in Bahía de Samaná (per person US$80), land and boat excursions through Parque Nacional Los Haitises (per person US$70), hikes to the area's isolated beaches (per person US$20), and village tours that include a cock fight and stops in a typical home and primary school (per person US$69). Overnight trips can also be arranged, including visits to the waterfalls in Jarabacoa, rafting in Río Yaque del Norte and climbing Pico Duarte, the highest peak in the Caribbean. English, French, German and Spanish are spoken.

Guariquén (☎ 809-248-5648 or 809-538-0201; guariquenlasgaleras@hotmail.com; ☼ 8am-6pm) is an Italian-run development foundation that offers area tours to help support its water, sanitation and other community projects. Different sites and attractions can be combined to make trips of varying length. You can visit any of the main beaches and sights, as well as an iguana farm, saltwater lagoon and the Museo Taíno. Guariquén also has a nascent volunteer program that may include free room and board – call or email well in advance for details. The main office is several kilometers south of town, but you can

PENÍNSULA DE SAMANÁ

contact the foundation and get additional information through Hotel Todo Blanco (opposite).

Casa Marina Bay Dive Center (Dive Samaná; ☎ 809-538-2000; www.dive-samana.de; Casa Marina Bay resort; ☾ 7am-6pm) also offers snorkeling trips (US$12), whale-watching tours (US$49), trips to Playa Rincón (US$10), and wind-surf and sailboat rental and instruction (US$10 to US$15 per hour), all available to guests and non-guests alike.

Courses

The Modern School Arizon (☎ 809-538-0046; Plaza Lusitania, Calle Principal; from per hr US$15) Is a newly-opened school which offers individualized Spanish programs for students of all levels; from beginners to advanced speakers looking to brush up their skills. Private and group classes are available and English, German and French instruction is also offered.

Sleeping

With the exception of a few, all of the hotels and bungalows in Las Galeras are within walking distance of the main intersection.

BUDGET

Bungalows Karin y Ronald (r US$30, bungalow US$54) Although quite removed from the center, 2½km east of town, the units are ideally located for exploring the less-visited beaches and sights east of Las Galeras. Two rooms and a bungalow, all cozy, are set in a lush garden and have tiled bathrooms, fans, fridges and shaded patios with tables and chairs. The bungalow sleeps up to four and has a small clean kitchen; guests in the rooms can use a common kitchen or request a meal plan. The friendly Belgian owners will personally take you on horseback rides (p155) or will also draw you a map if you prefer to explore the area on foot. Karin works several days a week with Victoria Marine, Samaná's top whale-watching outfit.

Casa Por Qué No? (☎ /fax 809-538-0066; s/d US$32/40) Offering two charming rooms just steps from the beach, Casa Por Que No?, 25m north of the main intersection, makes a fine choice. Rooms flank the owners' home but each has a separate entrance, a private bathroom and a small patio that opens onto a lush garden. It is open from November to the end of April and rates include breakfast.

Paradiso Bungalows (☎ 809-967-7295; ruby@playarincon.com; Calle Principal at the crossroads; r US$25) Less than 100m from the beach, Paradiso Bungalows has seven clean cabins with one double bed each and a ceiling fan. All rooms have cold-water bathrooms and screened windows. Porches with rocking chairs make a nice place to laze away an afternoon.

MIDRANGE

Apart Hotel La Isleta (☎ 809-538-0016; www.la-isleta.com; 1-bedroom apt US$65) Located near the end of the main drag, this hotel offers six charming apartments, each with a fully equipped kitchen, a sitting area that can double as a small bedroom and a loft with a queen size bed. All apartments also have porches with enviable views of the ocean. Perfect for a couple looking for some R&R or for a family with young children. Two hotel rooms were being built at the time of research and when finished should go for US$30. Rates drop considerably in the low season and for stays of a week or longer.

La Bella Aventura (labellaventura@hotmail.com; r US$42, house US$54) Three small split-level houses – one occupied by the owners – and a comfortable stand-alone room share a large grassy lot right where the east-west road bends toward the ocean. Located 250m west of the main intersection, all are constructed of poured cement that's been brightly painted (and keeps cool during the day) and have clean private baths, fans, firm beds, sleeper sofas and 24-hour solar/battery power as well as small kitchens (the rate for the room includes breakfast). There's hot water in the houses but not in the room; all use rainwater instead of the semi-salted groundwater used by most other hotels.

Apart-Hotel Plaza Lusitania (☎ 809-538-0093; www.plazalusitania.com; r US$40; 1-bedroom apt US$50-100; ⬛ Ⓟ) Located at the main intersection on the second floor of a small shopping center, rooms and apartments at the Lusitania are spacious, spotless, well appointed and all have balconies. A good Italian restaurant (opposite) on the first floor is a plus. The one-bedroom apartments vary considerably in size (and therefore price).

Juan y Lolo Bungalows (☎ 809-538-0208; www.juanylolo.com; bungalows US$35-120) West of the main intersection, this is another of Las Galeras' excellent bungalow options, with several well-appointed cabañas of various sizes, styles and prices. All have kitchens, fans, thatched roofs and outdoor patios, but they vary between cement or tile floors; one, two or three bedrooms; indoor or outdoor common areas; and with or without foldout beds. They differ in style and decor too – the best thing is to look at a few before deciding. Weekly rates are available, and are great value overall. The owners also run Xamaná Rent Moto and may be easier to find there.

Todo Blanco (☎ 809-538-0201; todoblanco@hotmail .com; tw/t US$80/90) This Italian-run hotel is adjacent to the Club Bonito Hotel on the beach, 75m east of the intersection. It features eight bright rooms with two or three double beds each, a ceiling fan and a sea-facing balcony, all housed in a wooden, two-story Caribbean-style structure (which is painted, as the name implies, all white). Rooms on the second floor have high sloped ceilings – numbers five and eight are at the ends and get the best light. The decor is a bit bubblegum, but the red-tile floors and wicker chairs on the balconies are a good touch. The grounds feature several fine sitting areas but no pool. Prices given here include breakfast and drop almost 50% in the low season.

TOP END

Club Bonito Hotel (☎ 809-538-0203; www.club-bonito .com; r without/with aircon US$80/90; r with aircon & ocean view US$120-140; ❑ P ❑) Located at the end of the main street, the Club Bonito features 21 tropical chic rooms in an attractive adobe building on the beach. Most rooms feature two double beds, cable TV and a phone; those with ocean views have huge balconies as well. A welcoming pool runs the length of the property and an open-air lounge makes a great place to admire the beautiful view. Full breakfast for two is included in the rate and is served at the hotel's beachside restaurant.

Casa Marina Bay (☎ 809-538-0020; www.amhsa marina.com; per person US$110-135; ❑ ❑ P) Las Galeras' only all-inclusive resort is 2km west of town in a wide cove all to itself. The beach is thin, but backed by a huge grassy area studded with palm trees – beach chairs are set up on the grass, which is a little odd but not unpleasant. Standard rooms are just that, with two queen beds and adequate, if bland, decor and furnishings. The villas are

better – stand alone A-frame cabins with exposed beams and red-tile floors, a separate living room, two-sink bathrooms and a walk-in closet. The master bed is comfortable though rather inelegantly placed in the corner; a loft with two single beds would be fun for kids. A bit expensive for what you get, but the many excursion possibilities are a big plus.

Villa Serena (☎ 809-538-0000; http://villaserena.com; 300m east of main intersection; r US$140; ❑ ❑ P) The most upscale hotel in town is a bit overpriced though admittedly quite pretty. Each of the 21 bright spacious rooms is decorated differently, but all have comfortable beds and a sea-facing balcony or terrace. It would be hard to say which is the best room – some have balconies large enough for a rocking chair and chaise lounge, others have four-poster beds and stunning ocean views. The large seafront garden and swimming pool are attractive and well-maintained, and guests can make free use of the hotel's bikes and kayaks. One of the bay's best snorkel spots is just off shore, an easy paddle from the hotel grounds. Breakfast included.

Eating

For a small town, the variety of restaurants is decent; you can stay for a few days and not eat at the same place twice. Although some outlying hotels have restaurants, those listed below are located on the main street.

Pizzeria (Calle Principal; mains US$6.50-8.50; ❑ 11am-3pm & 6pm-midnight, closed Tue) The best thin crust pizza this side of Santo Domingo can be found in this open-air joint; pizzas come crisp, loaded with toppings and are big enough for two. Look for the sign of the leaning tower of Pisa towards the entrance of town.

Plaza Lusitania Italian Restaurant (☎ 809-538-0093; mains US$6-12; ❑ breakfast, lunch & dinner; dinner only May-Oct, closed Wed) Located in the center of town, this Italian restaurant serves excellent pasta dishes at good prices. Service is in a high-ceiling dining area or, even better, at comfortable tables set along a wrap-around patio. A perfect spot to see the comings and goings of Las Galeras.

Chez Denise (☎ 809-538-0219; Calle Principal; mains US$4-14; ❑ 9am-10pm Mon-Sat) Specializing in crêpes – salty, sweet and just down-right good – this restaurant, located near the crossroads, serves some of the best French pancakes in town. Seating is in a pleasant open-air dining room with tables overlooking Calle Principal. Service can be exasperatingly slow but the wait is worth it.

El Pescador (☎ 809-538-0052; Calle Principal; mains US$7-15; ☻ dinner Tue-Sun) Located at the turnoff to Playita beach, this Spanish-owned restaurant is said to have the best seafood in town. El Pescador was closed for remodeling at the time of research, but local expats highly recommend it.

El Kiosko (Calle Principal; mains US$5-7; ☻ 7am-midnight) On the beach, this thatch-roofed restaurant serves tasty Dominican dishes at weathered picnic tables. *Lambí a la criolla* (creole conch, US$7) is a house specialtie. Popular among Dominicans.

Patisserie Boulangerie Français (Calle Principal; mains US$1-3.50; ☻ 7am-7pm Tue-Sun) Down a small footpath off Calle Principal, near the crossroads, a bright yellow clapboard house offers excellent French breads and tempting pastries. All are made with French ingredients, which lend the baked goods their authentic (and mouth watering) taste. Coffee drinks and continental breakfast combos are also available.

Supermercado £1 (Calle Principal; ☻ 7:30am-9:30pm) Of the two grocery stores in town, this one is the best. It has a good selection of produce and dairy products and sometimes has freshly baked bread too. A pool hall on the second floor makes it easy to spot on the main drag.

Entertainment

While the nightlife is pretty mellow in this town, two bars/discotheques – Chez Manuel and V.I.P. – are hopping on most weekends. Located on Calle Principal about 50m apart, you'll be hard pressed to miss either once the *bachata* or merengue starts playing. Things typically get started around 9pm and if one place seems a little empty, head to the other – you're sure to find the party there. Popular with locals and expats alike, travelers are always welcome. No cover.

Cine Triángulo (admission US$1) has just one screening per week (Friday night) for which it seems every local and expat turns out to see. Really popular movies are shown on Tuesdays as well. Look for a small sign on the west side of the road a few hundred meters south of town.

The open-air **pool hall** (Calle Principal; per game US$0.20; ☻ 10am-10pm) above Supermercado £1 is an all-male affair at night, but women should feel welcome during the day.

Getting There & Around

The only public transportation out of town are gua-guas that head to Samaná (US$1.75, 45 minutes, every 15 minutes, 7am to 5pm). They leave from the beach end of Calle Principal but also cruise slowly out of town picking up passengers.

You can pretty much walk everywhere in Las Galeras proper. For outlying areas, a *motoconcho* ride costs around US$0.50 to US$1 – consider arranging with the driver to pick you up if you know when you'll be returning.

Renting a car is an excellent way to explore the peninsula on your own. **RP Rent-A-Car** (☎ 809-538-0249; Calle Principal; ☻ 8am-7pm Mon-Sat, 8am-1pm Sun) and **Hermanos Cruz Agente de Cambio and Rent-A-Car** (☎ 809-341-4574; Calle Principal; ☻ 8am-6pm Mon-Sat, 8am-noon Sun) both rent 4WD vehicles for US$60 to US$90 per day. While definitely pricey, you'll be glad you have the extra power on the area's rough roads. **Xamaná Rent Moto** (☎ 809-538-0208; per day US$25; ☻ 9am-noon & 3-6pm Mon-Fri, 9am-noon Sat & Sun), 50m west of the intersection, rents motorcycles as well.

Mountain bike rentals are also available at **Piccola Italia** (☎ 809-325-4018; Calle Principal; per day US$12.50; ☻ 8am-noon & 3-7pm Mon-Sat), a shop near the entrance to town. Most bicycles are 21-speed and in good condition.

LAS TERRENAS

Although Las Terrenas has grown from a rustic fishing village into a bustling tourist destination it still exudes a small town quality. The main road is congested with *motoconchos* and ATVs (All Terrain Vehicle), but the sand road along the beach gets quieter the further you walk, with scattered hotels on the inland side and pretty beaches with tan-colored sand, high palm trees and calm aquamarine waters on the other. The nightlife is much livelier here than in Las Galeras or Samaná.

Orientation

The road from Samaná to Las Terrenas makes a sharp left when it hits town and turns into Av Duarte. The main drag in town, Av Duarte has banks, Internet, laundry and other services. Where the highway bends and turns into Av Duarte, a dirt road continues along the beach, eventually hitting a cluster of bars and restaurants known as Pueblo de los Pescadores (Fisherman's Village). The best beaches are beyond that, as well as a number of hotels and restaurants.

Information
BOOKSTORES
Newsstand (Av Duarte; 9am-8pm) This good-sized stand at the back of Plaza Taína sells a surprising variety of international newspapers and magazines. If you're willing to pay the premium price – about five times the regular newsstand rate – and don't mind that they are a day or two old, you'll find such goodies as the *New York Times,*

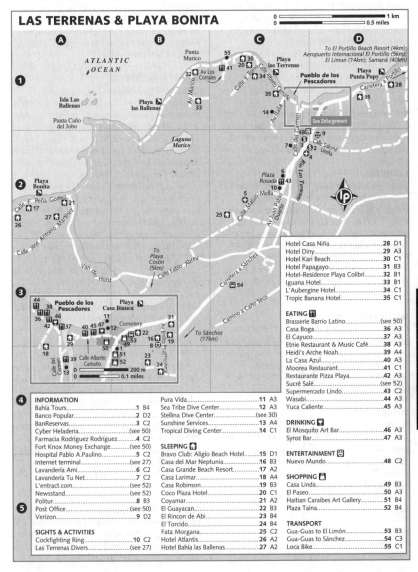

LAS TERRENAS & PLAYA BONITA

PENÍNSULA DE SAMANÁ

Le Monde, and *Le Figaro*. An excellent selection of dictionaries is also for sale.

EMERGENCY
Politur (Tourist Police; ☎ 809-754-2973; Av Emilio Prud'Homme; 🕒 24hr)

INTERNET ACCESS & FAX
Cyber Heladería (El Paseo shopping center, Calle Alberto Camaño; per hr US$6.35; 🕒 8am-9pm Mon-Sat, 8am-3pm Sun) This ice-cream parlor and Internet shop offers convenient but expensive connections.

L'entract.com (Plaza Taína, Av Duarte; 🕒 9am-1pm & 3:30-7:30pm Mon-Sat) Fast Internet connections (per hr US$4.25) and fax service (to USA per min US$0.35, to Europe per min US$1.40) are offered in this airconditioned Internet café.

Verizon Centro de Comunicaciones (Av Duarte; per hr US$1.75; 🕒 8am-10pm) Near the Plaza Taína, this call center offers the cheapest Internet in town but with only two computers available, there's often a queue.

LAUNDRY
Lavandería Ami (Av Duarte; 🕒 8am-6pm Mon-Sat) Located next to Plaza Rosada. Wash per load US$2.25, dry per cycle US$3.50; detergent and fabric softener each US$0.75; drop-off service extra US$1. Same day service if you drop off early; heavy clothes may require two dry cycles.

Lavandería Tu Net (Lavandería Pat y Memo; ☎ 809-848-1661; Calle del Carmen; wash & dry per lb US$2.50; 🕒 8:30am-noon, 4-6:30pm Mon-Fri, sometimes 8:30am-noon Sat) Wash and dry US$1.25 per lb, same day service not always available.

MEDICAL SERVICES
Farmacia Rodríguez Rodríguez (☎ 809-240-6084; Av Duarte; 🕒 8am-8pm Mon-Sat, 8am-6pm Sun) A door south of Banco Popular, this pharmacy offers a good selection of meds, toiletries and other personal items.

Hospital Pablo A. Paulino (☎ 809-274-6474, ext 24; Calle Matias Mella; 🕒 24hr emergency room)

MONEY
Banco Popular (Av Duarte; 🕒 9am-5pm Mon-Fri, 9am-1pm Sat) Located just east of the river. Has a 24-hour ATM.

BanReservas (Av Duarte; 🕒 9am-6pm Mon-Fri, 9am-1pm Sat) Across the street from Banco Popular, also has a 24-hour ATM.

Fort Knox Money Exchange (El Paseo shopping center, Calle Alberto Camaño; 🕒 8am-1pm & 4-8pm Mon-Sat, 10am-1pm Sun)

POST
Post Office (El Paseo shopping center, Calle Alberto Camaño; 🕒 9am-1pm, 3-5pm Mon-Fri)

TELEPHONE
Verizon Centro de Comunicaciones (Av Duarte; to USA per min US$0.32, to Europe per min US$0.74; 🕒 8am-10pm) Near the Plaza Taína, it offers the best phone rates around.

TRAVEL AGENCIES
Bahia Tours (☎ 809-240-6088; www.bahia-tours.com; Av Duarte 237; 🕒 9am-1pm & 3:30-7pm Mon-Fri, 9:30am-1pm & 4:30-6:30pm Sat) A recommended travel agency that can handle airline, hotel and car-rental reservations. Area excursions are also organized and English, French and Spanish are spoken.

Sights & Activities
CASCADA EL LIMÓN
A half-hour from Las Terrenas is the small town of El Limón, whose primary attraction is the **El Limón Waterfalls**, an impressive 52m waterfall with a beautiful swimming hole at the bottom. Just about everyone who visits does so on horseback, and a dozen or more *paradas* (horseback riding operations) in town and on the highway toward Samaná offer tours. (It is not recommended you hire someone off the street, as there's little savings and the service is consistently substandard.) All outfits offer essentially the same thing: a 30- to 60-minute ride up the hill to the waterfalls, 30 to 60 minutes to take a dip and enjoy the scene, and a 30- to 60-minute return trip, with lunch at the end. Your guide – who you should tip, by the way – will be walking, not riding, which can feel a little weird, but is the custom.

Spanish-owned **Santí** (☎ 809-452-9352; limonsanti@terra.es; per person without/with lunch US$15.50/24.50; 🕒 8am-7pm), at the main intersection in town, is the most popular of the *paradas* and also the most expensive. The lunch is excellent and the guides and staff (all adults) are better paid than elsewhere. Most other operators charge without/with lunch around US$7/14; try **Parada la Manzana** (☎ 809-360-9142; 🕒 8am-4pm) 5km east of El Limón towards Samaná, or **Parada María y Miguel** (☎ 809-282-7699; 🕒 7am-5pm) 2km east of El Limón towards Samaná. A *motoconcho* to either costs US$1 to US$2.

DIVING & SNORKELING
Las Terrenas has reasonably good diving and snorkeling and at least three shops in town to take you out. Favorite dive spots include a wreck in 28m of water and Isla Las Ballenas,

visible from shore, with a large underwater cave. Most shops also offer special trips to Cabo Cabrón (p155) near Las Galeras and Dudu cave near Río San Juan. Standard one-tank dives average US$40 with equipment, less if you have your own. Four-, 10- and 12-dive packages bring the per-dive costs to around US$26 to US$35 including equipment. Two-tank Cabo Cabrón and Dudu trips run from about US$80 to US$100, including gear, lunch and transport.

Snorkelers also go to Isla Las Ballenas, which has good shallow coral flats (one hour; per person US$20). A popular full-day snorkel trip is to Playa Jackson, several kilometers west of town, reached by boat with stops in two or three locations along the way (per person including lunch, minimum six people US$60). See the Tours section (below) for a list of places that run diving and snorkeling tours.

WATERSPORT EQUIPMENT RENTALS

Pura Vida (☎ 809-862-0485; www.puravidacaraibes .com; Calle Libertad 2; ⏰ 10am-5:30pm) across from El Paseo shopping center, is run by friendly French Dominicans and is a good place to rent windsurf boards, body boards, surf-boards, mountain bikes and kiteboarding equipment. You can also arrange lessons, including kiteboarding (US$70 for a two-hour beginner's lesson).

COCKFIGHTING

Two Italian dive instructors have rented and completely renovated Las Terrenas' old **gallera** (cockfighting ring; ⏰ 3-7pm), located on Av Duarte just past Plaza Rosada. There are around a dozen match-ups per night. While many *galleras* are rather seedy places, the idea here is to provide a safe, comfortable place for tourists and locals alike to experience this quintessential Dominican sport/pastime. The fights are certainly not watered-down – they are bloody, to-the-death affairs – and betting is still an integral part of the event. Volunteers help explain the rules, strategy and wagering to cock-fight neophytes.

Tours

Along with booking airline tickets, hotels and car rentals, the full-service travel agency **Bahia Tours** (☎ 809-240-6088; www.bahia -tours.com; Av Duarte 237; ⏰ 9am-1pm & 3:30-7pm Mon-Fri, 9:30am-1pm & 4:30-6:30pm Sat) organizes many area tours. Popular day trips include whale watching in Bahía de Samaná (per person US$66), excursions to Los Haitises National Park (per person US$60), jeep tours to El Rincón beach (per person US$70) and horse back riding to El Limón waterfalls (per person US$25). Overnight trips include rafting, canyoning and trekking in Jarabacoa (p226) as well as climbing Pico Duarte, the highest peak in the Caribbean. English, French and Spanish are spoken.

For organized tours and excursions in the area, call **Sunshine Services** (☎ 809 240-6164; www.sunshineservices.ch, Calle del Carmen at Calle Libertad; ⏰ 9am-12:30 & 4-9pm Mon-Fri, noon-4pm Sat).

For those interested only in aquatic pursuits, these places can get you where the action is:

Sea Tribe Diving Center (⏰ 8:30am-1pm, 3-6:30pm Mon-Sat, open Sun Nov-May) Across from El Paseo shopping center.

Tropical Diving Center (☎ 809-240-9619; www .tropicaldivingcenter.com; Av Italia; ⏰ 8:30am-6pm)

Stellina Dive Center (☎ 809-868-4415; www.stellina diving.com; at Kari Beach Hotel; ⏰ 9am-noon)

Las Terrenas Divers (☎ 809-889-2422; at Hotel Bahía las Ballenas, Playa Bonita; ⏰ 9am-noon)

Sleeping

Las Terrenas' accommodations are in two general areas – along the beach and on side streets off the highway east of town. The latter tend to be less expensive, as they're further from the beach and the main bar and restaurant scene.

BUDGET

El Torcido (☎ 809-240-6395; eltorcido.gitta@gmx.de; Av Emilio Prud'Homme; r US$15, r with kitchenette US$18, cabaña US$20) This hidden hotel offers three comfortable rooms each with gleaming tile floors, bright white walls and terraces. If you can swing it, the cabaña – a free standing house with a large kitchen and great porch – is worth the extra couple of dollars. Towards the end of a quiet road and just a block to the beach, this is the best value in town. German, Spanish and a little English are spoken.

Casa Robinson (☎ /fax 809-240-6496; Av Emilio Prud'Homme; r US$30, studio US$35, 1-bedroom apt US$45; **P**) Set in brightly colored wood-frame houses on well-landscaped grounds, this hotel offers 13 cozy rooms with balconies or terraces. All rooms have fans, private hot-water bathrooms and most have kitchenettes. Those on the second floor afford considerably more privacy and better views of the towering palm trees. Reluctant client service, unfortunately, mars an otherwise pleasant place to stay.

Casa del Mar Neptunia (☎ 809-240-6617; www .casas-del-mar-neptunia.com; Av Emilio Prud'Homme; s/d US$35/40; 1-bedroom apt US$70; 🕸 Ⓟ) Twelve charming rooms and a sprawling apartment make up this pleasant hotel. All have large bathrooms and boast balconies or terraces. The grounds are still very much in their infancy – trees and shrubs are tiny, flowers almost non-existent – but it's easy to see that in a few years, it'll be quite lush. A thatch-roofed lounge in the middle of the complex is especially welcoming. Breakfast is included in the rate and can be served on your balcony or terrace.

Hotel Papagayo (☎ 809-240-6131; fax 809-240-6070; Carr a Portillo; r US$28; Ⓟ) Located just steps from the beach, rooms here are nicely appointed and well-maintained. Four have spacious terraces with ocean views – a definite plus if you can snag one. All rooms come with fan, private hot-water bathroom and safe. A full breakfast is also included in the rate.

El Rincon de Abi (☎ 809-240-6639; elrincondeabi@ yahoo.fr; Av Emilio Prud'Homme; r US$28, 2-bedroom apt US$45) Just down the gravel road from El Torcido, this hotel offers six roundish rooms and a good-sized apartment. Accommodations are dark but clean and all have access to a well-equipped outdoor kitchen. A comfy thatch-roofed lounge makes a relaxing place to socialize or just to catch up on your postcards. A continental breakfast is included in the rate.

Hotel Diny (☎ 809-240-6113; r with shared bath US$12.50, r US$17.50-26, tw US$28) East of the Pueblo de los Pescadores, facing the beach, Hotel Diny offers bare-bones accommodations near the river. Rooms are worn but clean. Although popular with budget travelers, accommodations with shared bathroom open directly onto the street; which is somewhat disconcerting since ne'er-do-wells could just walk into the hotel day or night. Make sure your door is locked and your valuables secured. Better yet, stick with a room with a private bathroom.

El Guayacan (☎ 809-873-5918; Carretera a Portillo; r US$35-42) Located near the intersection of Av Duarte and the road to the airport, El Guayacan is the newest hotel in town. Its eight rooms are divided between two floors; the ones on the first floor are dark and unappealing, those on the second, are well-appointed and have ocean views (albeit from across the street, around an abandoned building and through several palm trees). Ironically, the nicer ones are cheaper – definitely stay in one of these. Note that the rooms towards the front of the hotel are especially affected by the street noise.

Fata Morgan (☎ 809-836-5541; www.samana.net/ fatamorgana; r US$15) A couple dogs, a cat and even a donkey greet you at this simple bungalow-style lodging, located 500m west of the hospital. Simple rooms have fans, clean tiled bathrooms, high sloped ceilings, brightly painted walls and a porch with a rocking chair. There's a kerosene lamp if the power goes out and a large grassy area in front. The owner also offers guided tours of the area. The only drawback here is the location; neither in town nor on the beach, you'll have to hoof it or take *motoconchos* whenever you want to get anywhere.

MIDRANGE
Casa Larimar (☎ 809-240-6539; Pueblo de los Pescadores; d US$40-45, t US$50-55; 🖳 🖳) Large rooms, a good pool, and convenient location near the beach and Pueblo los Pescadores make this hotel good value. Sparsely decorated rooms are hospital-clean, with fan, fridge, comfy beds and separate toilet and washroom; some have cable TV. Small windows don't let in much natural light, but you can get plenty of sun at the hotel's spectacular roof-top patio, complete with hot tub, lounge chairs and the best view in town. At 5pm it opens as a bar, with cool jazz and free tapas. Guests can check email on the hotel computer for free.

Iguana Hotel (☎ 809-240-5525; www.iguana-hotel .com; d/q bungalows US$70/100; 🖳) Down a quiet dirt road at the far end of the beach, the Iguana Hotel's location will be a disadvantage for some but a godsend for others. Eight free-standing bungalows occupy a leafy lawn and garden area; all have red-painted cement floors, blue-tiled bathrooms, A-frame ceilings, good fans and pleasant front patios. Guests with the right equipment can access the hotel's wireless Internet connection for free. A large and very well-equipped kitchen is available for guest use (though breakfast is included), and drinks are served at the small bar. French owner-manager Annette Liétard is a delight and speaks English, French and Spanish; her brother Pierre fills in part of the year. Car and bike rentals and excursions in the area can be arranged.

Coco Plaza Hotel (☎ 809-240-6172; jesuscampelo@ hotmail.com; Calle F Bono 2; r US$45, studio US$60-80, apt US$85-100;) This rambling four-story Mediterranean-style hotel is a short distance from the beach, restaurants and bars of Pueblo de los Pescadores. The 29 units vary in size and layout but all are clean and tastefully decorated rooms with fridge, hotwater bathrooms, tiled floors, fans, cable TV and a safe. Studios and apartments have small modern kitchens, some have a sitting room, terrace and/or ocean views – you really have to see a few before deciding, though it's hard to go wrong. A large complementary breakfast is served in an openair dining area downstairs. Big discounts in low season.

Hotel-Residence Playa Colibrí (☎ 809-240-6434; www.playacolibri.com; Fransisco Cāmaño Deño; apt US$75-130;) This spacious complex has 45 apartments in modern three-story buildings overlooking a swimming pool, spa bath and a pretty stretch of beach. Every apartment has a fully equipped kitchenette, balcony, in-room safe and satellite TV. Units range from two-person studios to split-level apartment with two bedrooms, two baths, separate living room and room for four adults and a child. Prices vary accordingly, and also depend on the season and the length of stay. Some may find the location a bit too removed, but this is a good deal for families or groups staying for more than a couple of days. There's a restaurant and a bar on the premises, and guests can use the office Internet for free.

Hotel Casa Niña (☎ 809-240-5490; casanina@verizon .net.do; Carretera a Portillo at Av España; r US$45, r with loft US$55;) In need of a coat of paint, rooms at the Casa Niña are showing their age but are still acceptable. The lush pool area has an inviting bar/lounge beside it, which is a major plus. Rooms with lofts are effectively standard rooms with a few planks of wood and a bed thrown on top. All rooms have fans, hot water and small refrigerators.

Hotel Kari Beach (☎ 809-240-6187; www.kari beach.com; Calle Alberto Camaño; s/d US$52/58;) A large somewhat gaudy hotel with 24 rooms, many facing the ocean. Rooms have cable TV and high A-frame ceilings with overhead vents to help keep the room cool (only three rooms have aircon). A reliable and well-located option, though not terribly memorable. One of the dive shops is based here and rates include breakfast.

TOP END

Tropic Banana Hotel (☎ 809-240-6110; www.tropic banana.com; Calle Alberto Camaño; d/t US$100/110, ste US$140;) One of the first hotels in Las Terrenas, the Tropical Banana manages to hide its age, featuring simple snug rooms, with terraces and yellow-painted walls. Suites are larger than the standard rooms, with cool cement floors and better bathrooms. Other features include a snooker table, library and even a hair salon. The Tropic Banana is decent value in the off-season, when prices drop by half. Breakfast is included and the restaurant (p164) here is one of the best in town.

Bravo Club: Aligío Beach Hotel (☎ 809-240-6255; www.bravoclub.it; Carretera a Portillo; s/d US$160/128;) This all-inclusive resort offers 80 smallish, though modern, rooms on a palm tree–studded property. Two handsome pools adorn the grounds and a restaurant serves acceptable meals. Beach facilities are available for guests although the beach immediately in front of the hotel is narrow and the main street runs alongside it.

El Portillo Beach Resort (☎ 809-240-6100; www .portillo-resort.com; d per person US$65-85;) Located 4km from Las Terrenas, the all-inclusive El Portillo offers 171 comfortable rooms on a spectacular stretch of beach. The water is tranquil and teal – excellent for snorkeling, especially in the late afternoon. Food service is limited to three meals and an afternoon snack, and is offered at two restaurants – one buffet, one à la carte. A free shuttle takes guests to and from Las Terrenas throughout the day.

Eating

The best restaurants in Las Terrenas are in Pueblo de los Pescadores, a cluster of fishermen's shacks-cum-waterfront restaurants just west of the river on what was the original site of the town. Virtually every restaurant has an entrance facing the road and an open-air dining or bar area out back, overlooking the ocean and narrow beach.

Etnie Restaurant & Music Café (☎ 809-852-4768; Pueblo de los Pescadores; mains US$9-18; ✆ dinner) Fresh gnocchi, vegetable ravioli, *tagliolini al limón* (ribbon pasta) are among the tasty fresh pastas served up in this hip restaurant and café, along with fresh grilled fish and meats. There's always lively world music playing, especially on Saturdays when it throws a party with a DJ and drink specials.

Wasabi (Pueblo de los Pescadores; mains US$8-25; ✆ late lunch & dinner) A small but classy Japanese restaurant serving quality sushi, sashimi and rolls – the sushi-sashimi combo is US$21 – and a variety of soups and noodle dishes. Service is at a little white-washing patio facing the beach.

Restaurante Pizza Playa (☎ 809-240-6399; Pueblo de los Pescadores; mains US$2-10; ✆ lunch & dinner) There are 37 different types of pizza at this cheerful, well-located eatery. Choose from a cheese and tomato pie to the house special with mozzarella, shrimp, clams, mussels, calamari and chunks of fish.

Casa Boga (☎ 809-240-6110; Pueblo de los Pescadores; mains US$12-25; ✆ lunch & dinner, closed Sun) This is a tiny but highly recommended Basque seafood restaurant. Dishes are divided according to the type of fish – surface, bottom and a category just for *róbalo*, a delicious whitefish that thrives where fresh water rivers and inlets run into the ocean. The beachfront open-air dining area is easy to miss – look for the sign and menu posted at the entrance of a little passageway between two restaurants.

El Cayuco (Pueblo de los Pescadores; mains US$5-12; ✆ noon-11pm) Paella is one of the specialties at this casual Spanish restaurant, served with seafood, veggies-only, or mixed seafood and chicken. Be sure to order a few tapas for starters too, like carpaccio, stuffed calamari or tomatoes with anchovies.

La Casa Azul (Calle Alberto Camaño; mains US$3-12; ✆ 9am-11pm) Once a beachside shack, this modern thatch-roofed eatery is known for its excellent seafood dishes. The mussels in garlic (US$10) are particularly good. Also a top place to watch the sunset.

Yuca Caliente (☎ 809-240-6634; Calle Alberto Camaño; mains US$10-23; ✆ lunch & dinner) Specializing in Spanish food, this oceanside restaurant serves excellent paellas and seafood dishes.

Tapas – small portions of mouth watering delights like bacalao, shrimp kabobs, and sautéed octopus – are also quite tempting. Service is gruff but the food is worth it.

Brasserie Barrio Latino (☎ 809-240-6367; El Paseo shopping center, Calle Alberto Camaño; mains US$2-10; ✆ breakfast, lunch & dinner Mon-Sat) This open-sided eatery offers a variety of European and American breakfasts, international favorites such as salads, sandwiches and burgers, and hearty dinner entrées including beef fillets imported from Argentina. A laid back place, there is truly something for everyone here.

Sucré Salé (☎ 809-860-0863; Plaza Taína, Calle Duarte; ✆ 7am-7pm) If you're craving something sweet, head to this upscale French bakery where an army of beautiful pastries are prepared everyday. Coffee drinks are also served and a street side terrace makes the perfect place to enjoy both.

Moorea Restaurant (☎ 809-240-6261; mains US$6-15; ✆ breakfast, lunch & dinner) This pleasant, open-sided restaurant at the western end of the beach, changed hands shortly before we came through, but the new owner said he intended to keep many of the same dishes that made the Moorea a favorite before, including shrimp and chicken salad and *dorado ceviche* (ceviche made with mahi-mahi). Look for some new additions as well, like an Indian sampler plate with portions of curry, fish and vegetable dishes.

Heidi's Arche Noah (☎ 809-240-6575; Calle del Carmen; meals US$3-10; ✆ noon-10pm Mon-Sat) This simple open-sided restaurant beside the Río Las Terrenas specializes in German cuisine, including sausage sandwiches and scalloped potatoes, but also has grilled fish, rice and beans, and other standard Dominican dishes. Three computers provide Internet access for US$4.25 per hour, after 8pm US$6.25 per hour.

Hotel Tropical Banana (☎ 809-240-6110; Calle Alberto Camaño; mains US$15-25; ✆ 8am-midnight) This restaurant is one of Las Terrenas' classiest, its hotel location notwithstanding. Tablecloths with wineglasses and gleaming silverware occupy a patio with rose-colored walls and open on two sides. Specialties include *chello al sal* (baked fish encrusted with coarse sea salt) and Japanese tartar served with a wasabi-mustard sauce. An excellent selection of French, Californian and Chilean wines rounds out the menu.

Supermercado Lindo (Plaza Rosado; ☻ 8am-9pm Mon-Sat, 8am-6pm Sun) This is a large supermarket with canned foods, pastas, produce, snacks, water and more.

Drinking & Entertainment

Pueblo de los Pescadores also has Las Terrenas' best drinking scene. There are a few hipster bars, and most of the restaurants stay open for drinks and music well after the kitchen has closed. Bar hopping could scarcely be easier, as it takes about forty-five seconds to walk (or stagger, as it were) from one end of Pueblo de los Pescadores to the other. There are a few notable spots outside of Pueblo de los Pescadores as well, including Las Terrenas' only night club.

El Mosquito Art Bar (☎ 809-857-4684; Pueblo de los Pescadores; ☻ 6pm-midnight, from 4pm Sat) A small, super cool bar with low sofas on its beachside patio instead of tables and chairs. The drink list goes on for pages, including Long Island Ice Tea, Whiskey Sour, several martinis and a dozen different whiskeys. Some full meals are served, but most people go for the tapas and other light fare. Great music.

Syroz Bar (☎ 809-866-5577; Calle Alberto Camaño; ☻ 6pm-4am, closed Sun) A hipster jazz bar and lounge that occasionally features live Brazilian jazz. Seating is outdoors on a pleasant deck overlooking the Caribbean or indoors in an Asian-themed bar area that is lit mostly by candles. Striking Dominican, Haitian and Thai art adorns the walls.

Nuevo Mundo (Av Duarte; ☻ 9pm-4am Wed-Sun) Located about 150m south of El Paseo shopping center, this discotheque features mostly merengue and *bachata* tunes. Popular with Dominicans, this is a good place to get a taste of the local nightlife.

Shopping

There are three shopping centers a stones throw away from one another on Av Duarte: Plaza Taína, Casa Linda, and El Paseo. Each has several high end boutiques, eateries and a smattering of the requisite kitsch shops. All are open from 9am to 8pm Monday to Saturday and from 9am to 3pm Sunday.

Haitian Caraibes Art Gallery (☎ /fax 809-240-6250; Av Duarte 159; ☻ 9am-1pm & 4-8pm Mon-Sat) Among the shell necklaces and batik sarongs, this gallery/boutique houses a phenomenal display of Haitian paintings. If you like what you see – and you likely will –

head towards the back of the shop where you'll find an outstanding selection of paintings from which to choose. Definitely worth a stop.

Getting There & Away

AIR

Aeropuerto Internacional El Portillo is a one-strip airport with no terminal, located a few kilometers east of Las Terrenas along the coastal road, in the hamlet of El Portillo. The occasional arrival of a charter flight from France or elsewhere in Europe gives it its international cred. As there's no terminal, there's no phone number. For information you're best off calling Aerodomca.

Aerodomca (☎ 809-240-6571; Santo Domingo ☎ 809-567-1195) operates propeller planes between El Portillo and Santo Domingo (US$65, 30 to 50 minutes), stopping first at Aeropuerto Las Américas and then jumping over to Aeropuerto de Herrera. At the time of research, flights left Portillo twice daily at 3pm and 4:45pm; a flight to Herrera was only leaving at 8:30am Monday to Saturday. Return flights depart from Herrera airport only (US$55, 30 minutes) and were scheduled for 10am and 4pm.

Aerodomca also offer an air taxi service – it costs the same and requires a minimum of just three people. Flights leave whenever the passengers choose – the most popular destinations are Las Américas airport (per person US$65), Herrera airport (per person US$55) and Punta Cana (per person US$85) but flights can be arranged to La Romana, Puerto Plata and El Cibao airport in Santiago. Regular or air-taxi tickets can be arranged through Bahía Tours (see p160).

BUS

Las Terrenas has two gua-gua stops at opposite ends of Av Duarte. *Gua-guas* headed to Sánchez (US$1.40, 30 minutes, every 25 minutes, 7am to 6pm) take on passengers at a stop 500m south of Calle Luperón. Those going to El Limón (US$1.75, 20 minutes, every 15 minutes, 7am to 5pm), leave from the corner of Av Duarte and the coastal road.

Getting Around

You can walk to and from most places in Las Terrenas, though getting from one end to the other can take a half-hour or more. Taxis charge US$10 each way to

PENÍNSULA DE SAMANÁ

Playa Bonita and El Portillo and US$15 to US$20 to Playa Cosón and El Limón. *Motoconchos* are cheaper – US$1.75 to Playa Bonita and US$7 to Playa Cosón – but are less secure. There are taxi and *motoconcho* stops in front of El Paseo shopping center and *motoconchos* are plentiful on Av Duarte and around Pueblo de los Pescadores. A bike can be handy for getting around town, and **Loca Bike** (☎ 809-889-3593; per day US$10.50; 8am-noon & 2-6pm) near Moorea Restaurant rents bikes.

PLAYA BONITA

A few kilometers west of Las Terrenas is Playa Bonita (Pretty Beach), a peaceful beach shaped like a half-moon and backed by a handful of hotels with good but pricey restaurants. While the beach itself isn't spectacular – it's narrow and much of it is strewn with seaweed – Playa Bonita is still an attractive and restful place to spend an afternoon, with fewer people and traffic than at Las Terrenas. The western end of the beach is broader and flatter, and the hotels there do a better job of keeping it clean.

There's a public **Internet terminal** (per hr US$6.25; 7am-11pm) at Hotel Bahía las Ballenas. **Las Terrenas Divers** (☎ 809-240-6066; 9:30am-noon, 3-5pm) is at the same hotel, offering dive trips and courses (one-tank US$34; 10 tanks US$280; open water certificate US$345) as well as snorkel trips to Isla Ballenas (US$15, one hour) and Playa Jackson (minimum three people, per person US$25 to US$30). You can also rent kayaks, body boards and surfboards by the hour or the day.

Sights & Activities

Just around the southwestern bend of Playa Bonita, you'll bump up against the 6km-long **Playa Cosón**. Here you'll find beautiful isolated beaches and thick palm tree forests – exactly how you'd picture an untouched tropical beach to look like. There are two small rivers that open onto the ocean as well. The easternmost, which runs through an abandoned resort, is said to be contaminated with agricultural run-off, the second is said to be safe. Better not to swim in (or near!) either.

Sleeping & Eating

Coyamar (☎ 809-240-5130; www.coyamar.com; Calle F Peña Gomez at Van de Horst; s/d US$45/60; P 🛏) Ten

ample rooms with balconies and terraces make up this pleasant hotel. Rooms are fan-cooled, tile-floored, and feature security boxes, radios and batik art. An excellent **restaurant** (mains US$7-14) is near the front of the property and serves a little of everything – sandwiches, pastas, seafood, grilled meats and a mean Thai chicken. It is especially popular with Germans.

Casa Grande Beach Resort (☎ 809-240-6349; www.casagrandebeachhotel.com, in French; Calle F Peña Gomez; r US$50-100) Most of the 13 rooms in this hotel are located inside a huge two-story house that faces the ocean. Each has a slightly overdone theme – Persia, Africa, India, Mexico – but the luxurious linens, gauzy curtains and gleaming bathrooms go a long way in making the rooms pleasant. Rates vary with the view. Two small basic rooms are located behind the main house but for US$50, you're better off with a higher-end room in Las Terrenas. Continental breakfast is included and served at the hotel restaurant.

Hotel Atlantis (☎ 809-240-6111; www.atlantis-beachhotel.com; Calle F Peña Gomez; s US$60, d US$70-100, aircon extra US$10; 🛏 P) This rambling place with 18 airy rooms feels more like a small European village than a Caribbean beach-side hotel. Charming rooms unexpectedly appear around bends and bottom of staircases, at the top of a mushroom-shaped building and halfway through walkways. They are each uniquely decorated and – like its setting – come in surprising sizes and shapes. Many rooms have enviable ocean-views and all are just seconds away from an alluring stretch of beach. A fine French restaurant boasting the former chef of President François Mitterand also is on the premises. Breakfast is included in the rate.

Hotel Bahía las Ballenas (☎ 809-240-6066; www.las-terrenas-hotels.com; Calle José Antonio Martínez; d US$95-110; 🛏 🛏) All 32 rooms at this large well-kept resort, near Van de Horst, are decorated in either Creole, Mexican or south of France style. Sounds gimmicky, but it comes off well here, thanks mainly to the outstanding quality of the rooms themselves. Spacious with high, thatched ceilings, all have thick comfortable beds, stylish furnishings, great tile floors and a toilet and shower area that is open at the top for a bit of outdoorsy charm. An open-air restaurant has colorful tables with cushioned chairs, and serves creative Dominican dishes like roast goat and fish in coconut or lime and almond sauce. There is an on-site dive shop and the rates listed include breakfast.

There's also a chi-chi French restaurant – **Al Paso** (☎ 809-299-5806; Playa Cosón coastal road; mains US$8-18; ☺ lunch) located about 2km down the beach.

Getting There & Away

By car, Playa Bonita is reachable by a single road that turns off from the Sánchez–Las Terrenas highway. It's possible to walk from Playa Bonita to Playa Cacao in Las Terrenas via a coastal dirt/mud trail that is fairly steep at one section. A taxi ride here is US$10, a *motoconcho* around US$1.75.

There are usually a few *motoconchos* there when you're ready to return.

SÁNCHEZ

Sánchez is a non-descript town that is notable mainly as a transportation hub. Buses to and from Santo Domingo and Puerto Plata stop here briefly, and pickups wait nearby to take passengers on the gorgeous, winding road over the coastal mountains to La Terrenas. There's also frequent *gua-gua* services to Samaná.

Caribe Tours (☎ 809-552-7434) has services to Santo Domingo from Sánchez every 90 minutes from 7:30am to 4:30pm. **Metro** (☎ 809-552-7332) has capital-bound buses at 8:30am and 4pm. The fare on both bus lines is US$7.50 and the trip takes four hours.

PENÍNSULA DE SAMANÁ

North Coast

The North Coast stretches from the salt flats and high coastal promontories of Monte Cristi near the Haitian border clear across to Río San Juan, situated beside a small lagoon with terrific snorkeling and scuba diving just off shore. Between those bookends are well-known destinations like Puerto Plata and Playa Dorada, both former Caribbean hot-spots and now struggling to keep up with resorts in the south and east. West of Puerto Plata is Luperón – a little-known but surprisingly pleasant hotel and resort enclave beside a pretty beach. To the east is Cabarete which was little-known not too long ago but has exploded onto the tourist scene after it was discovered to have some of the best conditions in the world for windsurfing and kiteboarding. At the same time, the North Coast holds a lasting place in history – it was here that Christopher Columbus established the first European settlements in the New World and where the first Catholic mass conducted in the Americas was held. In all, the North Coast has a plethora of vacation and adventure options, from glorious beaches to great snorkeling and diving, from quiet fishing villages to raucous bars and nightclubs. Best of all, most spots along the coast are easy to reach by *gua-gua* (minibuses used for local transport) or car, so travelers have no trouble sampling the full variety of options the area has to offer.

HIGHLIGHTS

- The **Museo del Ambar Dominicano** (p171) in Puerto Plata is the country's best amber museum

- Learn **kiteboarding** (p193) in Cabarete, one of the world's top spots for this new high-flying sport.

- Big waves crash onto an even bigger beach at the beautiful and aptly named **Playa Grande** (p200).

- The Haitian market in **Dajabón** (p212) draws hundreds of Haitian vendors and Dominican shoppers and hardly a single tourist.

- Swim-throughs, fresh water caverns and massive coral heads make snorkeling and diving around **Río San Juan** (p200) truly superb.

NORTH COAST

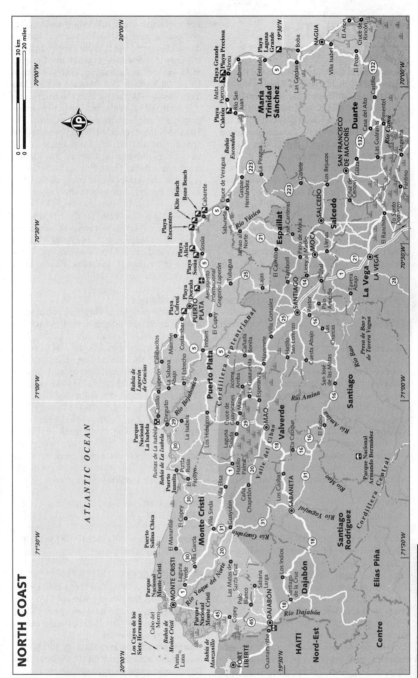

PUERTO PLATA

pop 119,897

Puerto Plata is a well-known name in the vacation and all-inclusive resort scene. It is the gateway to Playa Dorada, a huge complex of more than a dozen all-inclusive resorts that was once a premier jet-set destination in the Caribbean. But as Playa Dorada is eclipsed by resorts in Bávaro and Punta Cana, Puerto Plata is feeling the effects. Fewer tourists come this direction and the once vibrant city now has a large number of abandoned buildings and 'For Sale' signs.

Ironically, the success of the all-inclusives in the last decade or two also hurt Puerto Plata. Before then, tourists at nearby resorts came into town to eat, shop and go to nightclubs. But as the all-inclusives became more popular and prevalent, tourists no longer left the resort as everything they needed was provided there. A number of top restaurants have closed in recent years for lack of customers.

Puerto Plata is a nice enough place, with a shady park, two excellent amber museums and a fun cable-car ride to the top of a nearby bluff. It's also the largest city on the North Coast, with all the services you may need, including two well-recommended clinics. But the beach here is unpleasant, especially compared to those a short distance east or west, and the accommodations and eating options are not significantly better. Unless your time is unlimited, it doesn't make sense to linger here long. Indeed, many tourists bypass Puerto Plata for Sosúa and Cabarete to the east, or Luperón to the west.

History

On January 11, 1493, as Christopher Columbus approached what is now Puerto Plata Bay, the sunlight reflected off the water so brilliantly it resembled a sea of sparkling silver coins. Columbus named the bay Puerto Plata (Silver Port). Backing the bay is a 799m (2621ft) mountain, which he named Pico Isabel de Torres, in honor of the Spanish queen who sponsored his voyages.

An important port for the fertile North Coast, Puerto Plata was plagued by pirates. It eventually became more lucrative for colonists to trade with the pirates (who were supported by Spain's enemies, England and France) rather than risk losing their goods on Spanish galleons. Such trade was forbidden and enraged the Spanish crown. In 1605 the crown ordered the evacuation of Puerto Plata – as well as the trading centers of Monte Cristi, La Yaguana and Bayajá – rather than have its subjects trading with the enemy.

Puerto Plata remained virtually abandoned for more than a century, until the Spanish crown decided to repopulate the area to prevent settlers from other countries from moving in, namely the French from present-day Haiti. Puerto Plata slowly regained importance, suffering during the Trujillo period, but eventually reinvented itself as a tourist destination. The early 1990s were golden years for the city, and for the first time tourism revenues surpassed those of its three main industries – sugar, tobacco and cattle hides – combined. It remains to be seen if, and how, Puerto Plata will shake its current doldrums.

Orientation

The center of town is Parque Central (also known as Parque Independencia), which has shady benches and pretty flower gardens. Six blocks north of the park is the Malecón and beyond that the ocean. The Malecón (also known as Av General Luperón and Av Circunvalación Norte) runs along the ocean – Playa Long Beach, the main city beach, is located 2km east along the Malecón, but is unappealing and often closed because of contamination. The other main east–west street is Av Beller, which runs along the north side of the park and feeds onto Av Luis Ginebra. Take this road to go to the airport, Playa Dorada and beyond.

Information

EMERGENCY

Politur (Tourist Police; ☎ 809-320-0365; Hermanas Mirabal at the Malecón) Has a station at Long Beach with an officer on duty 24 hours a day.

INTERNET ACCESS

Dotcom (☎ 809-261-6165; Calle 12 de Julio 69; per hr US$2; ☻ 8:30am-8pm Mon-Fri, 8:30am-6pm Sat)

Internet Flash (Separación at Margarita; per hr US$1.25; ☻ 8am-9pm Mon-Sat, 10am-2pm Sun) Friendly service and a relatively fast connection.

Verizon Centro de Comunicaciones (☎ 809-586-4393; Beller at Padre Castellanos; per hr US$1.60; ☻ 8am-10pm) More expensive, but the office has longer hours and aircon.

LAUNDRY

Sofy's B&B (☎ 809-586-6411; www.popreport.com/ Sofybb.htm; Calle Las Rosas) Does laundry for US$5 per load up to 20lbs, the only place in town that doesn't charge per-piece. Not an official laundromat, the friendly owner has only one washer and drier, which are of course subject to the vagaries of the local power grid. But if you drop your clothes off early – it's a great place for breakfast – she tries hard to have them done that day. Call ahead if possible.

MEDICAL SERVICES

Centro Médico Dr. Bournigal (☎ 809-586-2342; Antera Mota) Between Doctor Zafra & Virginia Ortega, it is the hospital most recommended by local expats, with a multilingual staff, 24-hour emergency room and an on-site pharmacy.

Clínica Brugal (☎ 809-586-2519; José del Carmen Ariza) Also recommended, this smaller clinic also has 24-hour emergency services and a doctor who speaks English, German and Spanish. Located between 12 de Julio & Mella.

Farmacia Carmen (☎ 809-586-2525; Calle 12 de Julio; ☯ 8am-1pm, 2-7pm Mon-Fri, 8am-noon, 1-6pm Sat) Convenient to the center, near Calle José del Carmen Ariza, this pharmacy offers free delivery to your hotel.

Farmacia Centro (☎ 809-586-8821; Antera Mota; ☯ 8am-9pm Mon-Fri, 8am-4pm Sat) Well-stocked pharmacy attached to the Centro Médico Dr Bournigal, between Doctor Zafra & Virginia Ortega.

MONEY

Banco Mercantil (Separación; ☯ 8:30am-5pm Mon-Fri, 9am-1pm Sat) On Parque Central near Beller, it has an enclosed ATM.

Banco León (JF Kennedy; ☯ 8:30am-5pm Mon-Fri, 9am-1 Sat) Between San Felipe & 30 de Marzo, it changes cash & traveler's checks and has a reliable ATM in front.

Banco Popular (Av Circunvalación Sur; ☯ 9am-5pm Mon-Fri, 9am-1pm Sat) Near the stadium and Av Hermanas Mirabel. It has one ATM.

BanReservas (Duarte at Padre Castellanos; ☯ 8am-5pm Mon-Fri, 9am-1pm Sat) A block east of the center, has an ATM.

POST

Main post office (Calle 12 de Julio at Separación; ☯ 7am-5pm Mon-Fri, 7am-noon Sat) Is two blocks north of Parque Central.

TELEPHONE

Verizon Centro de Comunicaciones (☎ 809-586-4393; Beller at Padre Castellanos; to USA per min US$0.30, to Europe per min US$0.85; ☯ 8am-10pm)

TOURIST INFORMATION

Tourism Office (☎ 809-586-5059; Hermanas Mirabal at Malecón; ☯ 9am-6pm) On Long Beach on the second floor of the tourist police station. Moderately helpful, the staff have a number of free maps and brochures, and speak French and English in addition to Spanish.

TRAVEL AGENCIES

Cafemba Tours (☎ 809-586-2177; cafembatours@hotmail.com; Calle Separación 12; ☯ 8am-7pm Mon-Fri, 8am-1pm Sat) Half a block north of Parque Central, Cafemba is most handy for arranging air tickets, but also offers standard one- and two-day package tours to the surrounding area, including Samaná and Las Terrenas.

Sights & Activities
MUSEO DEL AMBAR DOMINICANO

The **Dominican Amber Museum** (☎ 809-586-3910; www.ambermuseum.com; Duarte 61; admission US$1.75; ☯ 9am-6pm Mon-Sat) presents an excellent exhibit on this prized resin. Guides walk visitors through the display, explaining the origins and history of amber and answering any questions. The collection is impressive and includes valuable pieces with such rare inclusions as a small lizard and a 30cm-long feather (the longest one found to date). Tours are offered in English and Spanish, although if you prefer walking through the museum on your own, the signage is equally as informative. A gift shop (p177) on the ground floor has a fine selection of amber jewelry.

GOOD GUIDES WEAR BABY BLUE

There are two kinds of guides that can be found around the country: those who wear baby blue dress shirts and carry tourism licenses, and those who don't. The blue guides are government-approved and have completed a demanding guiding course. They also have successfully passed an exam on Dominican history and attractions.

Although official guides have set rates for area sites, be sure you agree upon a fee before you begin your tour. Note that tours given in languages other than Spanish or English tend to be slightly more expensive. Also, if you're pleased with the service, remember to tip – 5% to 10% of the fee is typical and very appreciated. If you have any doubt about how much a tour should cost, stop by the local tourist office and ask what the rate should be.

PUERTO PLATA

A   **B**   **C**   **D**

INFORMATION
Banco León...1 E1
Banco Mercantil....................................2 E2
Banco Popular.......................................3 E6
BanReservas..4 E2
Cafemba Tours......................................5 E2
Centro Médico Dr Bournigal 6 C5
Clínica Brugal..7 E1
Decompression chamber (Hospital
   Dr. Ricardo Limbardo)...........8 E5
Dotcom...9 F2
Farmacia Carmen..............................10 E1
Farmacia Centro....................(see 6)
Internet Flash......................................11 F1
Laundry (Sofy's B&B) ....(see 37)
Politur.....................................(see 13)
Post Office..12 F1
Tourism Office.....................................13 F6
Verizon Centro de
   Comunicaciones...........................14 F2

SIGHTS & ACTIVITIES
Casa de Cultura...................................15 E2
Fuerte de San Felipe.........................16 B3
Galería de Ámbar................................17 E1

Iglesia San Felipe................................18 E2
Museo de Arte Taíno..........................19 E1
Museo del Ámbar Dominicano.20 E2

SLEEPING 🛏
Aparta-Hotel Lomar............................21 E5
Atlantic Guest House..........................22 E1
Hotel Ilra...23 F2
Hotel Montesilva.................................24 F5
Hotel Sarah...25 E2
Portofino Guest House.......................26 F6

EATING 🍴
Aguaceros Bar & Grill........................27 F1
El Provocón IV......................................28 E2
Heladería Mariposa............................29 E2
La Parrillada..30 F6
Mercado Municipal............................31 C5
Restaurant-Pizzería Portofino...32 F6
Restaurant-Pizzería Roma II...33 F2
Restaurante Barco's...........................34 E1
Restaurante Jardín Suizo.........35 D4
Sam's Bar & Grill.................................36 E1
Sofy's B&B...37 E5
Tam Tam Café.......................(see 42)

DRINKING 🍸
Casa Criolla...38 E1
La Terraza..39 E5

ENTERTAINMENT 🎭
Cine Teatro Roma...............................40 F2

SHOPPING 🛍
Canoa..41 E1
Cuevas y Hermanos Fabricantes de
   de Cigarros...................................42 E1
Museo del Ámbar Dominicano
   Gift Shop.......................(see 20)

TRANSPORT
Caribe Tours...43 B5
Europacar..44 F6
Gua-guas to Sosúa, Cabarete
   & Río San Juan..............................45 E2
Javilla Tours..46 B5
Lander Rent A Car..............................47 F1
Mambo 2 Rent A Car.........................48 C4
Metro..49 D4
Texaco Station.....................................50 B5
Texaco Station.....................................51 E6

Monumento á
General Gregorio
Luperón 🏛
16 🏛
Lighthouse 🗼

*Bahía de
Puerto Plata*

See Enlargement

To Teleférico (900m);
Costambar (2km);
Cofresí (5km);
Imbert (20km);
Luperón (54km);
Santiago (71km)

NORTH COAST

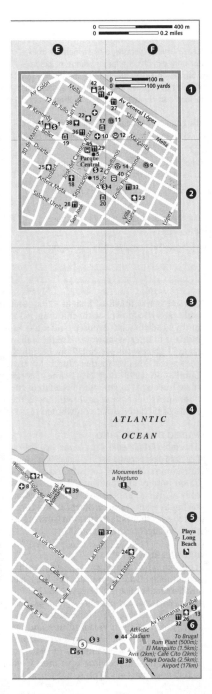

GALERÍA DE AMBAR

Equally as impressive as the Museo del Ambar, the **Amber Gallery** (☎ 809-586-6467; www.ambercollection.itgo.com; Calle 12 de Julio; admission US$1; ☷ 8:30am-6pm Mon-Fri, 9am-1pm Sat), near José del Carmen Ariza, would be almost non-distinguishable from its competitor were it not for its other exhibits. Once a guide leads you through the amber wing, a set of tinted doors opens onto one of the finest exhibits in the country on Dominican products. The exhibit is broken down into sections: rum, sugar, tobacco and coffee. Each station provides an excellent explanation of the history of the product and the steps it takes to make it. A rum tasting is offered and a cigar roller is always hard at work. There is also at least one staffer on hand to answer any questions that visitors may have. A small but good exhibit on Taíno artifacts is also presented. Signage is in English and Spanish and guides speak English, French, German and Spanish.

TELEFÉRICO

Pico Isabel de Torres, the peak Christopher Columbus named on January 11, 1493, is an enormous flat-topped mountain rising 799m (2621ft) just south of Puerto Plata. A **teleférico** (cable car; ☎ 809-586-2122; Camino a los Dominguez 1; round-trip US$10; ☷ 8am-5pm, closed Wed) takes visitors to the top where there's a statue of Christ the Redeemer that's similar but slightly smaller than the famous one in Río de Janeiro, and on clear days a spectacular view of the city and coastline. Board the *teleférico* at its base on the southern end of Camino a los Dominguez, 800m uphill from Av José Ginebra. From Parque Central, a *motoconcho* (motorcycle taxi) ride costs US$3.50 (one way) and a taxi ride costs US$5. The ride is notorious for opening late or closing early so cross your fingers before heading up there.

FUERTE DE SAN FELIPE

Located at the mouth of the Bahía de Puerto Plata, **San Felipe Fort** (eastern end of Av. Circunvalación; admission US$0.50; ☷ 9am-5pm) is the only remnant of Puerto Plata's early colonial days. Built in the mid-16th century to prevent pirates from seizing one of the only protected bays on the entire North Coast, the fort never saw any action. Instead, for much of its life, its massive walls and interior moat

NORTH COAST

AMBER: PREHISTORIC BEAUTY

Dominican amber – fossilized sap that was produced 25 million years ago by hymenaea trees – is widely regarded as the finest in the world. It not only exhibits the largest range of colors – from clear and pale lemon to warm oranges, gold, brown, and even green, blue and black – but it contains the greatest number of 'inclusions': insects, tiny reptiles and plant matter that was trapped in the resin before it fossilized. Such inclusions add character to a piece of amber and increase its value.

Amber can be bought in almost any town in the country. Plastic, honey-colored imitations, however, are sometimes sold as the real thing. To test the authenticity of a sample, try one of the following:

■ Examine the amber under a fluorescent lamp; if the glow changes, it's amber. If it doesn't, it's plastic. Most legitimate amber dealers have a fluorescent light on hand for this purpose.

■ Rub the piece against cotton and bring it close to your hair. If the hair moves, it's real. Amber acquires static electricity. Plastic doesn't.

■ Place unadorned amber in a glass of salt water. If it floats, it's amber. If it sinks, it's plastic. Remember this won't work if the piece is in a setting.

■ Ask the salesperson to hold a match to the amber. Heated amber gives off a natural resin, plastic smells like a chemical.

---

were used as a prison. Today, it is a brief stop on the tourist route. The views of the bay are impressive and the structure itself is fun to explore. A small museum also is on-site but its exhibits – a few rusty handcuffs, a handful of bayonets and a stack of cannonballs – are far from remarkable. A large grassy area in front of the fort has a nice view of the bay and makes for a restful stop.

Also at the fort is Puerto Plata's **lighthouse**, which first lit up on September 9, 1879, and nearly collapsed from disrepair before undergoing a major restoration starting in 2000. The white and yellow tower – 24.4m tall, 6.2m in diameter – is a melding of neo-classical style with industrial construction. Classically inspired columns, bracketed by prosaic I-beams, support an octagonal cast-iron cupola. The lighthouse originally used a novel revolving light-and-shadow system fueled by kerosene.

CASA DE LA CULTURA

In addition to dance and music workshops, this **cultural center** (☎ 809-261-2731; on Parque Central, Separación at Duarte; admission free; 🕑 9am-noon & 3-5pm Mon-Fri) often showcases work by Dominican artists in its first floor gallery.

IGLESIA SAN FELIPE

The twin-steepled **Iglesia San Felipe** (Parque Central, Calle Duarte; 🕑 8am-noon & 2-4pm Mon-Sat, 7am-

8pm Sun) is not much of a sight – its outer walls are run down, with chipping paint and a façade that has exposed cinder blocks. What is of interest, however, are the Italian stained-glass windows. Small but beautiful, they were donated to the church by area families in 1998 after Hurricane George blew through town and devastated the church. At the base of each window is the name of the family that contributed it.

MUSEO DE ARTE TAÍNO

The **Taíno Art Museum** (Plaza Arawak, Calle Beller at Calle San Felipe; admission free; 🕑 varies) is a small museum containing mostly replicas of Taíno pottery and figurines. The exhibit is only worth a stop if you're interested in seeing as many Taíno artifacts as you can – whether authentic or not – on your vacation. Signage in Spanish only.

BRUGAL RUM PLANT

You can smell the sugar cane fermenting from the highway as you pass this huge **rum distillery and bottling facility** (☎ 809-586-2531; Carretera a Playa Dorada; admission free; 🕑 8am-4pm Mon-Fri). Tours are free but none too exciting, consisting of a short video on rum and the Brugal company (the country's largest rum maker) and then a few minutes of watching the assembly-line bottling operation from a 2nd-floor gangway. You're not permitted into the distillery part, and the whole thing is over in about 15 minutes. There are complimentary daiquiris at the end and a gift shop where you can buy rum and Brugal-labeled hats and other souvenirs. Just out of town on the way to Playa Dorada, the tour is a major stop for package tours from the all-inclusive hotels and the place is often mobbed with tourists. All in all, it's pretty underwhelming.

Festivals & Events

The third week in June brings a weeklong **cultural festival**, which features merengue, blues, jazz and folk concerts at Fuerte de San Felipe. Troupes from Santo Domingo perform traditional dances that range from African spirituals to sexy salsa tunes. At the same time, the town hosts an arts-and-crafts fair for local artisans at the nearby Parque Central.

Puerto Plata hosts a popular **merengue festival** the first week of October. During the festival the entire length of the Malecón is closed to vehicular traffic, food stalls are set up on both sides of the oceanside boulevard and a stage is erected for merengue performances.

A **jazz festival** is also held in Puerto Plata during the entire month of October. International artists like Chuck Mangione, Ramsey Lewis and Bobby Sanabria come to perform in area nightclubs and hotels. Concerts are held Thursday through Saturday at 8pm. Admission is US$10 to US$15.

Sleeping

Puerto Plata's budget hotels are located near the center, and are all very basic. Places offering a bit more comfort are east of the center.

BUDGET

Hotel Ilra (☎ 809-586-2337; Calle Villa Nueva 25; r with fan & shared bath per person US$10) Housed in a Victorian-style home that's over a century old (and starting to show it), rooms here have white-washed wood walls and mosquito nets over the beds. All share a large but aging bathroom. For a couple to spend US$20 for a room with shared bath doesn't seem quite right; then again, the rooms here have better light and cross-ventilation than at the Atlantic Guest House. A small **restaurant** (mains US$3-7; ☯ breakfast, lunch & dinner Mon-Sat) downstairs occupies the cheeriest room in the house and is a pleasant place to start your day.

Atlantic Guest House (☎ 809-586-6108; Calle 12 de Julio 24; d/tw with fan US$10.50/14, tw with aircon & TV US$17.50; ☒) The beds here have seen better days, and having padlocks instead of door-knobs is always a red flag, but the Atlantic remains a reliable and popular budget hotel. There are just eight very basic rooms organized around a narrow interior courtyard; all have high ceilings and wood walls and tolerable private bathrooms. The one room with aircon and TV also has tile floors, a better bed, and is generally more modern and comfortable, but it takes a stroke of luck to show up and find it empty. Very friendly owner.

Hotel Sarah (☎ 809-586-4834; Calle Imbert 13; r US$7) Located in the heart of downtown Puerto Plata, this no-frills hotel is a tolerable option if you're on a tight budget. Rooms are cramped but basically clean and all have private bathrooms, fans and cable TV. Cold water only.

MIDRANGE

Hotel Montesilva (☎ 809-320-0205; Calle La Estancia; r/tw US$35/38; ☒ ☒ ⓟ) The most agreeable of the midrange options, the Montesilva has small but very clean and comfortable rooms, which all have fan, cable TV, good beds and private hot-water bathroom. Rooms numbers eight, nine, 10 and 11 have balconies and get great natural light. The friendly proprietors offer free coffee in the lobby.

Portofino Guest House (☎ 809-586-2858, fax 809-586-5050; Av Hermanas Mirabal 12; r/tw US$25/30; ☒ ☒ ⓟ) Just a block from the beach – albeit not a terrific one – this one-story hotel offers 20 clean rooms all with private hot-water bathroom, aircon and cable TV. A well-tended swimming pool under a flourishing mango tree is a plus. An excellent restaurant (p176) by the same name (but different owner) is next door.

Aparta-Hotel Lomar (☎ 809-320-8555; fax 809-586-5050; Av Circunvalación 8; r/tw US$28/30, 1-bedroom apt US$46-53; ☒ ⓟ) Rooms and apartments in this hotel are spacious and clean and feature cable TV and telephone. Kitchens in the apartments are small but adequate. Some also have balconies with ocean views. For the outlay, this place is excellent value.

Eating

BUDGET

As in much of the Dominican Republic (DR), good cheap food is somewhat hard to find.

Sofy's B&B (☎ 809-586-6411; www.popreport.com/sofybb.htm; Calle Las Rosas; dishes US$4-7; ☺ breakfast) Not just for guests, the breakfasts at this small B&B east of the center feature terrific omelets stuffed with tomatoes, ham, cheese, mushroom, onion or other goodies, accompanied by broccoli, potatoes or even a pork chop if you like. There's also French toast and pancakes, and the friendly owner-chef brews her coffee strong. With just three garden tables and one long table in the dining room, you'll be competing for space with a steady stream of expats who come here daily. In fact, it's the popularity of the breakfasts here that makes Sofy's less-than-ideal as a sleeping option – it gets noisy in the morning and you share your bathroom with breakfast-goers.

El Provocón IV (☎ 809-970-1200; Calle Separación 19; mains US$2-5; ☺ 24hr) As good as it is grubby, this popular indoor-outdoor diner specializes in cheap grilled chicken with all the fixings. A half-chicken is just US$3, to which you can add rice, beans, fried bananas, yucca, salad or other sides for US$1 apiece. Wash it down with a 40oz Presidente beer for US$1.75 and you're in business.

Restaurant Pizzería Portofino (☎ 809-261-2423; Hermanas Mirabal 12; mains US$7-11; ☺ breakfast, lunch & dinner) Near the eastern end of the Malecón, Portofino's is a thatch-roofed, open-sided restaurant that offers excellent pizza pies. Pasta dishes are also quite good. This is a reliable and tasty option.

Sam's Bar & Grill (☎ 809-586-7267; Calle José del Carmen Ariza 34; mains US$4-9; ☺ breakfast, lunch & dinner) With ragged flags flying over a clapboard façade, Sam's is the favored watering hole of the area's heavy-drinking resident gringos. If you're here long enough to earn VIP status, you can get two-for-one Bloody Marys or Tequila Sunrises with breakfast, among other food and drink discounts. The menu is verifiably international, including French toast, chicken Kiev, Mexican scramble, Philly cheese steak and Tijuana-style chili – all reliable. There's usually a game of some sort on the TV.

Heladería Mariposa (Calle Beller; mains US$1-4; ☺ 8am-11pm) Right on the park, this cheerful ice-cream shop serves simple but good sandwiches and homemade ice cream.

MIDRANGE

El Manguito (☎ 809-320-1025; mains US$4-15; ☺ lunch & dinner) On the highway to Playa Dorada, just east of the Iberostar resort, this hidden restaurant is the best seafood place around. Thatch-roofed but nice, El Manguito serves only the freshest seafood and prepares it Dominican-style – think goat or tripe stew, crab a la vinaigrette (similar to ceviche) and a variety of desserts. Service is excellent. Popular with locals, it gets especially busy around 8pm. There's a sign, but you can't see the restaurant from the road – many people mistake it for the building on the roadside which is often closed.

Café Cito (☎ 809-586-7923; mains US$7-15; ☺ lunch & dinner) A cozy place tucked alongside an Avis rental car agency 500m west of Playa Dorada, this café-restaurant is easy to miss despite being a Puerto Plata institution. Owned and managed by the Canadian honorary consul, Café Cito is a popular watering hole for expats, especially North Americans. The food here is tasty, including fillet mignon, tenderloin beef tips, jumbo pork chops and grilled chicken breast, though the prices are a bit high for what you get.

Restaurante Jardín Suizo (☎ 809-586-9564; Av Circunvalación 13-A; mains US$8-17; ☺ lunch & dinner Mon-Sat) With a nice view of the ocean, checkerboard tablecloths, and delicious Dominican and Swiss dishes, this is a very pleasant place to eat. Lunch is tops here – US$7 specials are offered daily and typically include a choice of soup or salad, a vegetable side and a main course like beef stroganoff, tuna salad or vegetarian pasta. If you like spicy food the chicken curry is extraordinary.

Aguaceros Bar & Grill (☎ 809-586-2796; Av Gral Luperón 32; prices US$7-12; ☺ lunch & dinner) This open-sided, thatch-roofed, fan-cooled bar and grill is pleasant for its casual-Caribbean, low-light ambience and its location on the Malecón. The clientele generally consists of locals, who gather around dark wooden tables and bamboo chairs each evening to discuss the day's events. Tex-Mex is the specialty here, including fajitas, burritos and a combo plate with nachos, quesadillas, soft tacos, chimichangas, flautas and more for under US$10.

Restaurant Barco's (☎ 809-320-0501; Av Gral Luperón 6; mains US$3-15; ✷ breakfast, lunch & dinner) On the Malecón, this restaurant has a breezy, open-sided dining room, but the mostly expat clientele prefers the sidewalk tables in front. The menu has a little of everything, from Dominican-style egg breakfasts to sandwiches and burgers to pasta and pizza. There are also seafood dishes of course, and daily specials that are a good deal off the regular prices. Main dishes come with choice of potatoes, fries or *mangú* (mashed plantains).

Tam Tam Café (☎ 809-970-0903; Av Gral Luperón; mains US$5-12; ✷ lunch & dinner) Next door to Barco's, Tam Tam offers much the same menu and ambiance. The *asapao* (tomato-and-rice stew) with shrimp or shellfish is very filling. The Tam Tam has a large-screen TV and shows major sporting events, from boxing to football (American and otherwise).

Groceries
For the best selection of produce and meats, head to the **Mercado Municipal** (Calle 2 at Calle Lopez; ✷ 7am-3pm Mon-Sat). At this local market, you'll not only find the freshest food around, but you'll also get a taste of the local lifestyle.

TOP END
La Parrillada (☎ 809-586-1401; Luís Ginebra at Cirunvalación Norte; mains US$6-15; ✷ lunch & dinner) On the eastern end of town, this popular meat-lovers restaurant serves quality grilled dishes in a classy, understated setting. Iron tables are covered with tablecloths and set with chargers, ceramic plates and wine glasses, either on a open-air patio or in the small, comfortable dining area. The *churrasco* is a house favorite, a sampler plate of steak cuts, sausage and chicken all grilled with a tasty Dominican sauce. There is also grilled fish prepared with garlic or Asian-style with ginger and *puerro* (leek) and several kinds of pasta.

Restaurant-Pizzería Roma II (☎ 809-261-6139; Calles Beller at Emilio Prud'homme 43; mains US$5-20; ✷ breakfast, lunch & dinner) The Roma II offers a variety of pastas, grilled meats and seafood dishes, all of which are tasty but somewhat overpriced. A better deal are the pizzas, which come in a dozen or more varieties, including one with octopus, another with tuna, and a sausage and onion pizza oddly

dubbed *cosa linda* (pretty thing). Wine glasses and red tablecloths are an apparent attempt to dress up the place, but the setting and service are still pretty low-key.

Drinking & Entertainment
La Terraza (Av Circunvalación at Calle A Brugal Montanez; ✷ 8:30am-1am) With pleasant outdoor seating under bright umbrellas, this sea-facing restaurant makes a good place to kick back and drink a couple of beers, though the food is forgettable.

Cine Teatro Roma (☎ 809-320-7010; www.cineteatroroma.tk; Beller; admission US$3.50) The only movie theatre convenient to the center, between Padre Castellanos & Emilio Prud'homme, shows mostly semi-recent Hollywood fare.

Casa Criolla (Calle 12 de Julio; ✷ 4pm-2am) Located across from Atlantic Guest House, the pool tables are raggedy but free with your beer at this downheel billiards/beer hall. Can be a bit seedy at night, but then it's rare to find a pool hall in Latin America that isn't.

Shopping
Museo del Ambar Dominicano Gift Shop (☎ 809-586-3910; www.ambermuseum.com; Duarte 61; ✷ 9am-6pm Mon-Sat) For a unique amber or larimar piece, this museum gift shop is your best bet in town. Here, you'll find exquisite figurines as well as fine jewelry in gold and silver. Take your time and ask questions; the staff is particularly knowledgeable about all items on sale. A room dedicated to the sale of cigars and rum is near the front of the shop.

Canoa (☎ 809-586-3604; Beller 18; ✷ 8am-6pm Mon-Sat, 10am-1pm Sun) From the outside, this rambling store appears to be just like every other gift shop in town: it has innumerable wood figures of peasants, acrylic paintings from Haiti, amber and larimar jewelry and lots of postcards. What you don't see at first glance, however, is the small but interesting amber exhibit, the jewelry workshop – where you can see a fine necklace or set of earrings being created, and a cigar room, where two men spend the day rolling *tabacos* for onlookers. Worth a stop, and you may just leave with a custom-made larimar necklace, a box full of Dominican cigars, or even just a T-shirt. Prices are negotiable.

Cuevas y Hermanos Fabricantes de Cigarros (☎ 809-970-0903; Av Gnrl López; ✷ 1-6pm, 9-midnight, Closed Mon) Come to this 2nd-floor shop, above

NORTH COAST

the Tam Tam Café, to buy high-quality Dominican cigars at distributor prices. All of the cigars sold here are made at Cuevas y Hermanos, a cigar factory located near Santiago, that makes cigars bearing various big-name labels. You can buy a La Perla Habana or Carlos Toraño – sold here under a different label but literally the same cigar made in the same plant – for about half the price of the name brand. The shop only carries quality cigars, and prices start at around US$4 per cigar, boxes of 25 are US$60 to US$100. US citizens are allowed to bring home up to 100 cigars duty free, while Canadians and Europeans are limited to 50. There are plans to open a sister shop at Café Cito.

Getting There & Away
AIR
Puerto Plata is served by **Aeropuerto Internacional Gregorio Luperón** (☎ 809-586-0107, 809-586-0219), 18km east of town along the coastal highway (past Playa Dorada). Numerous charter airlines use the airport, mostly in conjunction with the all-inclusive resorts. A taxi to or from the airport costs US$16.

Some of the airlines with international service here include:

Air Canada (☎ 809-541-5151)
American Airlines (toll free ☎ 809-200-5151)
Continental (toll free ☎ 809-200-1062)
LTU (☎ 809-586-4075)
Lufthansa (toll free ☎ 809-200-1133)
Martinair (toll free ☎ 809-200-1200)

BUS
Caribe Tours (☎ 809-586-4544; Camino Real at Eugenio Kunhardt; ⊗ hourly 6am-7pm) has a depot 1km south of Parque Central. The terminal provides service to Santo Domingo (US$7, four hours) and stops along the way at Santiago (US$2.50, 1¼ hours) and La Vega (US$3.15, two hours).

Metro (☎ 809-586-6061; Calle 16 de Agosto) is located eight blocks east of Parque Central, between Beller & JF Kennedy. The company serves Santo Domingo (US$7.50, 3½ hours) with a stop in Santiago (US$2.65, one hour). Buses depart daily at 11am, 2pm, 4pm and 6:30pm. Sundays have additional departures at 9:30am and 3pm.

Javilla Tours (☎ 809-970-2412; Camino Real at Av. Colón; ⊗ every 15 mins, 5am-7:30pm) provides a 2nd-class bus service to Santiago (US$2.50,

1½ hours) with stops along the way at Imbert (US$0.70, 20 minutes) and Navarrete (US$1.75, 40 minutes).

El Canario (☎ 809-291-5594; US$7) is a Spanish-operated bus that leaves daily to Samaná (3½ to four hours) at 5am from near the public hospital. This is your only option, as neither Metro nor Caribe tours has direct service there. Make two calls the day before – one to the bus line to reserve a spot and the other to a taxi line to arrange an early-morning pickup.

For points east and west of town, *gua-guas* are a cheap and reliable option. Eastbound *gua-guas* leave from a stop on the north side of Parque Central, passing by the entrance of Playa Dorada and through Sosúa (US$1, 30 minutes), Cabarete (US$1.75, one hour) and Río San Juan (US$3.50, two hours). From Río San Juan, you can catch another van to Nagua and then another to Samaná. You can flag them down – and be dropped off – anywhere along the way.

To get to Costambar and Cofresí, take any Santiago-bound Javilla Tours bus.

Getting Around
The center of Puerto Plata is very walkable. It's longer, but still do-able, to walk to and from the hotels, restaurants and other points of interest east of the center – just follow the Malecón.

CAR
There are enough public *gua-guas* so that a rental car isn't vital, but of course having one makes exploring the beaches and towns on the North Coast that much easier. Most local and international car rental agencies have offices along the Malecón and on the highway out of town (toward Playa Dorada). The larger ones have kiosks at the airport, too. Rates start at US$45 to US$55 per day, with taxes and insurance included. Discounts are available in low season (May to October) and if you rent for several days or weeks.

Avis (☎ 809-586-4426; ⊗ 8am-6pm) is located next to Café Cito restaurant, 500m west of Playa Dorada. It also has offices at the airport (☎ 809-586-7007; ⊗ 7am-10pm) and the Playa Dorada shopping center (☎ 809-320-4888; ⊗ 8am-6pm).
Europcar (☎ 809-586-7979; www.europcar.com; Av Hermanas Mirabal at Av Luis Ginebra; ⊗ 8am-6pm) is located near the state tourism office.

Lander Rent A Car (☎ 809-586-1486; José del Carmen Ariza at Sánchez; 🕑 9am-noon, 2-5:30pm) has the most convenient location in town, just a few blocks north of the main park. However, their insurance plan includes a whopping US$3000 deductible.
Mambo 2 Rent A Car (☎ 809-291-8238; Av Malecón 19; 🕑 8:30am-6pm) Somewhat older cars, but still reliable and for a lower price and lower deductible.

TAXI & MOTOCONCHO
Like much of the North Coast, there are two sets of taxi fares – one for locals and one for foreigners – and cabbies in Puerto Plata are especially notorious for gouging tourists. (Thanks mostly to the all-inclusives nearby.) Around town *should* be US$3, to/from the bus stations or the *teleférico* US$4, and to Playa Dorada or Cofresí US$7, but you may end up paying twice that, especially if you don't speak Spanish. You should definitely bargain and definitely agree on a price beforehand, but don't be surprised if you can't get the fare down. There is a **taxi stand** (☎ 809-320-7621) right at the main park or you can call to be picked up.

Motoconchos are cheaper – about US$1 for around town – but the drivers are also notorious, in this case for maniacal driving. Many expats won't take them. If you do, ask the driver to slow down if you feel unsafe.

AROUND PUERTO PLATA

Puerto Plata proper is the residential and commercial center of this part of the North Coast, but the area just outside of town has much better beaches, resorts and seaside accommodations. Most vacationers are headed to Playa Dorada, a group of a dozen or so all-inclusive resorts clustered on a pretty beach a few kilometers east of Puerto Plata. West of town, Costambar and Cofresí are small beach developments that cater to repeat visitors, with a large selection of condos and long-term rentals.

PLAYA DORADA
A few kilometers east of Puerto Plata along the coastal highway is Playa Dorada, which is both the name of an attractive beach and a gated complex with more than a dozen all-inclusive resorts. Guests have access to the beach, an 18-hole golf course, several dance clubs and casinos, and a shopping center

Beaches are technically public in the Dominican Republic, but the security here does everything it can to keep non-guests out. The best way to reach Playa Dorada if you are not a guest is to walk east along the beach from Puerto Plata. However, there have been assaults on this stretch so do not carry valuables and do not go alone or at night.

Information
All traveler services here are found inside of the **Playa Dorada Plaza**, an open-air shopping center with lots of kitschy gift shops and a food court. The Plaza is near the western entrance to the complex.

INTERNET ACCESS AND TELEPHONE
Tattoo Parlor (Internet per hour US$5, phone to USA per min US$0.50, to Europe per min US$0.95; 🕑 9am-10pm)

MEDICAL SERVICES
Playa Dorada Farmacia (☎ 809-320-6226 ext 2500; 🕑 9am-9pm Mon-Fri, 9am-7pm Sat & Sun)
Playa Dorada Medical Care (☎ 809-320-2222, after hr ☎ 809-586-6500; 🕑 8am-10pm)

MONEY
BanReservas (🕑 9am-6pm Mon-Fri, 9am-1pm Sat) One ATM.
Playa Dorada Money Exchange (🕑 8:30am-10pm)

POST
There is no post office in the complex, however, most hotels will post mail for guests.

TOILETS
There are public bathrooms near the atrium on the 1st floor.

Sights & Activities
Playa Dorada is made up of two long half-moon stretches of yellow sand facing attractive emerald water and backed by large resorts. It is a very appealing beach, though perhaps not the perfect-white sand and transparent turquoise water that has appeared in your dreams (and some hotel brochures). The beach is better in some places than others – wider, cleaner, less crowded – and we've noted that in our reviews. Though more all-inclusive guests hang out in the hotel chairs, it's nice to walk the length of the beach and see what the neighbors are up to.

All of the resorts offer area **excursions** including dive and snorkel trips, horseback

NORTH COAST

riding, deep-sea fishing, white-water rafting and day trips to Santo Domingo. For more information, stop by the guest services desk of your hotel.

GOLF

Playa Dorada Golf Club (☎ 809-320-3472; www.golf guide-do.com; ☺ 7am-7pm), designed by Robert Trent Jones, is an attractive 6218m (6800yd), par-72 course which is the centerpiece of the Playa Dorada hotel complex. The greens fee for nine holes US$53, 18 holes is US$76; caddies (US$7/14 for nine/18 holes) are obligatory, golf carts (US$18/24 for nine/18 holes) are not. Some resorts offer discounted rates for their guests – be sure to ask at your hotel before you reserve your tee time.

Sleeping & Eating

There are 14 all-inclusive resorts in Playa Dorada, many more than is practical to list here. Below are a sample of what's available in Playa Dorada, from modest to deluxe. The prices listed are rack rates and serve as only the roughest guide for comparing resorts. It is next to impossible to estimate prices as the resorts have frequent specials, and travel and online agencies also offer promotions. If you have decided to go to Playa Dorada, run a search on the Internet for promotions in the period you're looking for and begin comparing style and services from there.

Casa Colonial Beach & Spa (☎ 809-320-2111; www .vhhr.com; r US$350-550; 🞩 🅿 🕮) The Dominican Republic's first (and only) member of the Small Luxury Hotels of the World association, the Casa Colonial is the most chic hotel in Playa Dorada – and arguably the country. It offers 50 indulgent suites, each with marble floors, sparkling fixtures, canopied beds, ample balconies, a cedar lined closet, even plush bathrobes and slippers. The grounds are set in what looks like a sprawling mansion and boasts a tropical garden with orchids growing at seemingly every turn. An infinity pool with four Jacuzzis is located on the roof, providing a spectacular view of the blue ocean beyond. A high-end spa and two elegant restaurants are also on-site. Unlike its neighbors, the rates at the Casa Colonial are not all-inclusive.

Wyndham Viva (☎ 809-686-5658; www.vivaresorts .com; r per person US$82-140; 🞩 🅿 🕮) Completely renovated in 2005, the Wyndham offers spacious rooms with pleasant balconies, comfortable furnishings and modern amenities. The food is also good; an ever-changing buffet and two à la carte restaurants – serving Asian specialties and Mediterranean fare – keep guests happy. The beach is a five minute walk past a pretty lagoon and is well-tended, though somewhat cramped – by mid-morning it's hard to find a place to sit on the beach and what little shade there is, is taken. The good-sized pool with a waterfall provides a refreshing alternative.

Puerto Plata Village Caribbean Resort (☎ 809-320-4012; www.ppvillage.com; s/d per person US$126/94; 🞩 🅿 🕮) The 386 rooms in this resort are located in plantation-style houses and are clean, comfortable and nicely appointed. Five restaurants offer a variety of cuisines, though the Tex-Mex House gets the best reviews. The Puerto Plata Village fronts the golf course, which affords nice views but also means taking a shuttle to the beach. Fortunately, shuttles pass frequently and guests don't seem to mind the ride. Two pools, four clay tennis courts and a volleyball and basketball court are pluses, especially for kids.

Paradise Beach Club & Casino (☎ 809-320-3663; www.amhsamarina.com; per person US$110; 🞩 🅿 🕮) Straddling two wide beaches with a pleasant boardwalk between the two, the Paradise arguably has the best ocean front in Playa Dorada. The food, which is served at a buffet and two à la carte restaurants, is good and always has several options for vegetarians. The nightly entertainment also receives rave reviews. This resort would receive top marks if it weren't for the rooms – they're clean but the decor is dated and the furniture is shabby. If you can handle the accommodations, though, you're sure to have a pleasant stay.

Playa Naco Golf & Tennis Resort (☎ 809-320-3503; www.naco.com.do; per person US$110; 🞩 🅿 🕮) The Playa Naco's main attraction is its beautiful stretch of beach – lined with swaying palm trees, filled with plenty of lounge chairs and is kept free of debris. The grounds in the complex are just OK; they are well-maintained but the pool area is lined with gift shops and the restaurants are poorly lit. As with the Paradise, the rooms are clean but somewhat tired.

NORTH COAST

Occidental Caribbean Village Club on the Green
(☎ 809-320-1111; www.occidentalhotels.com; per person US$55-75; 🅿 Ⓟ 🌊) With rooms in 45 villa-style buildings on well-kept grounds, the Club on the Green offers a decent if not deluxe all-inclusive experience. Though somewhat musty, rooms are comfortable and clean, many with balconies overlooking the golf course. There is also a buffet restaurant that offers a good selection of dishes. A shuttle takes guests to the beach every 30 minutes, where there is a beach club with a bar and grill so you can spend the entire day on the beach without going hungry or thirsty.

Entertainment

Inside the Playa Dorada complex are four chi-chi dance clubs that are open to the public: Ambrosia in the Puerto Plata Village (opposite), Tops at Playa Naco (opposite), Crazy Moon in the Paradise Beach resort (opposite) and **Mangú** (☎ 809-320-3800; www .occidentalhotels.com) at the Occidental Allegro Jack Tar Village. All of the dance clubs play a mix of Latin beats and international pop music. They are generally open from 8pm to 2am, though no one usually shows up before 11pm. The cover charge is around US$5.

The complex also boasts three casinos that are located in the Jack Tar Village, Wyndham Viva and Paradise Beach Club. The casinos feature blackjack, craps, roulette, poker and slot machines. US dollars and Dominican pesos are accepted for all games except the slot machines, which accept US currency only. Each casino is open from 4pm to 4am.

Cinemar (☎ 809-320-1400; Playa Dorada Plaza; admission US$3.50) screens Hollywood's latest release movies with Spanish subtitles.

Getting There & Around

The easiest – and most convenient – way to get to Playa Dorada is to take a taxi. It's also possible to take a *gua-gua* to the front gate of the complex, but once you're there, you'll have to wait for a taxi to take you to your hotel. Taxis are also the best way to get around the complex – the distances are long and the fares not too steep.

Taxis can be found at any of the hotel entrances and also in front of Playa Dorada Plaza. Typical fares include rides to Gregorio Luperón Airport (US$25), Puerto Plata (US$12), Sosúa (US$25), Cabarete (US$30) and within the complex (US$5). Be sure to agree on the rate before you get in the cab.

COSTAMBAR

About 2km west of Puerto Plata is the turnoff for Costambar, a small community consisting mostly of townhouses, timeshare units and vacation homes, with a long tan beach shaded by almond trees. There are a couple of restaurants and a grocery store here, even Internet access, but no ATM and virtually no ordinary hotels.

Information

All of Costambar's main services are in the small village just past the gated entrance.

There was no ATM in Costambar at the time of research, and none apparently planned. **Inversiones Costambar Rent A Car** (☎ 809-970-7005; Calle Central; ☀ 8am-6pm Mon-Sat, 8am-10pm Sun) exchanges foreign cash and traveler's checks. There's no sign on the building, but it's across from Jenny's market and has a sandwich board with exchange rates out front.

There is no hospital in town, either – if you need medical service, go to Puerto Plata. **Farmacia de los Trópicos** (☎ 809-970-7607; Calle Central; ☀ 8:30am-7:30pm Mon-Sat) is a full-service pharmacy.

Tourist information, Internet access and international phone service are available at **Aqua Marina Tours** (Multi Servicio Costambar; ☎ 809-970-7615; www.dominican-holiday.com; Calle Central; Internet per hr US$1.75, phone to USA per min US$0.33, to Europe per min US$0.75; ☀ 9am-6pm Mon-Fri, 9am-4pm Sat), which also manages several rental properties and arranges area tours.

Sights & Activities

Costambar has the best beach in the Puerto Plata area. Pretty though not spectacular, it's as good as Playa Dorada and without all the big hotels blocking the way. Past the village, follow the winding main road down until you pass a large roadside parking area facing a sprawling swatch of sand. There's a small sign tied to an almond tree that reads 'Condo Lisa Club Playa,' and here you'll enjoy tan sand, plenty of shade and mild surf. It's very popular with an older European set, who play bocce, lay in beach chairs (which can be rented for US$1.75) and gab about the old country.

Sleeping & Eating

There are no standard hotels in Costambar, which is instead dominated by condos and timeshares.

Club Villas Jazmin (☎ 809-970-7010; www.villa jazmin.com; 1-/2-bedrooms US$80/100; ✱ ✱ ✱ ✱) A small timeshare club with an extremely loyal clientele, the Jazmin will rent apartments to independent travelers during the low season, roughly April to June and September to December. Like many timeshares, the units are large and comfortable if not exactly alluring, including full kitchens, cable TV, CD players and firm beds. You can order the all-inclusive plan for an additional US$160 per person per week. The club, which is a five to 10 minute walk from the best beach, has a small pool, tennis court and even a resident tennis pro. There's live music three nights a week in the small restaurant-bar area.

Aqua Marina Tours (Multi Servicio Costambar; ☎ 809-970-7615; www.dominican-holiday.com; Calle Central; ✪ 9am-6pm Mon-Fri, 9am-4pm Sat) This company manages a number of condos and vacation homes of various sizes and prices in Costambar. Contact them for information on renting.

Pizza Plus (☎ 809-970-7497; Calle Central; mains US$5-12; ✪ 24hr) As the name suggests, you can get pizzas here – there are a dozen different varieties, all reasonably priced – plus a slew of other Dominican and international dishes. There was a barbecue special going on when we passed through: hamburgers, cheeseburgers, chicken, pork, steak – you name it, you could have it with barbecue sauce. There's also a full bar, and karaoke on Sundays at 9pm.

El Rancho (☎ 809-970-7240; Calle Central; mains US$5-15; ✪ 24hr) There must be a lot of insomniacs in this town to justify *two* all-night eateries. Just down the street from Pizza Plus, about 50m from the town entrance, this restaurant serves standard grilled fare at expected prices.

Jenny's Market (Calle Central; ✪ 7:30am-10pm) is a medium-sized market that is often crammed with time-share renters stocking up for the week.

Getting there & around

Gua-guas (every 15 minutes, 6am to 6pm, sometimes later) between Puerto Plata and Santiago pass the Costambar turnoff, in both directions. Unfortunately, the village area is a good kilometer from the highway, and the beach and most condos are another kilometer past that. It's walkable, but budget your time accordingly. (Or you may be able to hail a *motoconcho* for all or part of the way.) A cab ride from Puerto Plata should cost US$5, but the cabbies will probably try to charge you US$10. *Motoconchos* also make the trip and are cheaper, but this entails high speeds on the highway with no helmet – your mom would not be pleased.

PLAYA COFRESÍ

Five kilometers west of Puerto Plata, this OK beach has two huge all-inclusive resorts on one end, and a marine park – with a huge gaudy sign – on the other. Besides the resorts, most people staying here have rented one of the many of stand-alone homes that fill the hillside above the beach. Though it has a number of long-time return visitors and the marine park is fun for kids, Cofresí's beach is only so-so and there's not much in the way of atmosphere – independent travelers will probably have a better time elsewhere.

Information

ATMs and exchange booths are located at the entrance of both all-inclusive resorts. Chris & Mady's were planning to install Internet terminals. Both all-inclusive resorts have pricey Internet cafés for guests.

Sun Village has a **medical center** (☎ 809-970-7518; ✪ 8am-1pm, 1:30-6pm, 24hr emergency service), clearly visible from the main road into town. **Tourist Medical Services** (☎ 809-586-1227, ext 40836; ✪ 24hr) is a medical clinic affiliated with the Hacienda resorts. There's a **pharmacy** (✪ 9am-noon, 1-6pm) next door. Both clinics have multilingual staff and serve guests and non-guests alike; for more serious cases, go to Puerto Plata.

Just outside the Hacienda Tropical Resort, **Columbus Plaza Shopping Center** (✪ 8am-12:40pm, 1:10-7:30pm) stocks sunscreen, film and a full selection of drinks and snacks.

Sights

With an enormous sign at the western end of the beach, it's impossible to miss this popular aquatic park, Cofresí's main attraction. **Ocean World** (☎ 809-291-1000; www.ocean-world.info; adults US$55, ages 4-12 US$40, under 4 free; ✪ 9am-6pm) features a 300-sq-m snorkeling tank filled with tropical fish and marine plants; an enclosed garden with tropical plants, parrots and other birds, a tiger 'grotto', daily sea-lion shows and shark- and stingray-feedings. For an additional cost, there are a number of programs that bring you into contact with the animals, including swimming with dolphins (US$125 per person), a dolphin encounter (US$100 per person), sea-lion encounter (US$80 per person) and a shark and manta ray encounter (US$55 per person). All programs last about 30 to 35 minutes and must be reserved ahead of time. Ocean World provides hotel pick-up and drop-off from as far away as Cabarete and Luperón and all prices include a buffet lunch.

Sleeping

Cofresí has two large all-inclusive resort complexes, though with a mediocre beach it's hard to get excited about either one. There are a few rooms for rent in town, and plenty of long-term rentals available.

Hacienda Resorts (☎ 809-586-1227; www.hacienda-resorts.com; s/d per person US$90-120/60-90;) This huge resort complex contains three hotels, though they share the same beach and a number of facilities. Hacienda Tropical is the primary one, a four star, while Hacienda Garden and Hacienda Suite are three stars. Large rooms have high ceilings, white-tile floors, wood furniture and misplaced autumnal decor. All have balconies, some have ocean views. Like the Sun Village, the resort is built on a bluff, with the pool and foyer above and the beach area below, with paths between the two. To get here turn right immediately after turning off the highway – strangely there's no sign.

Sun Village Beach Resort (☎ 809-970-3364; www.sunvillagebeachresort.com; s/d US$90/120;) An EMI resort, this resort is built on a hillside, with the lobby, bar-restaurant and main pool area perched well above the beach. Pathways lead down, past large units where bigish rooms have red-tile floors, aircon, and relatively comfortable beds; some have ocean views. At the beach are another two pools and a children's area. Beach chairs are on a broad sandy platform contained by a stone wall, as the beach itself can be a little hard. Most people here are on the all-inclusive plan, though Travelocity.com sells room-only packages. Turn off the highway, stay to your left and you'll pass right by the resort entrance.

Playa Villas Management Company (☎ 809-970-7821, in the US ☎ 800-390-1138; www.puerto-plata.com;) This enterprise manages around ten houses in Cofresí, ranging from two-bedroom cottages to seven-bedroom houses. Some have an ocean view and/or swimming pools. A housekeeper is assigned to each house and will help with cooking, cleaning, laundry and even shopping. Prices range from US$145 to US$400 per day in the high season (December 15 to April 30) and drop considerably in the off-season. With many repeat guests, the houses can get booked up months in advance – call or email for availability.

Capitán Cook (☎ 809-542-4533; Playa Cofresí; r US$35, with kitchen US$45) This beach-front restaurant has OK food, but also offers Cofresí's only ordinary hotel accommodations. Rooms are clean and relatively comfortable, all with private bathroom and view of the ocean. One has a kitchen.

Eating

Chris & Mady's (☎ 809-970-7502; chrismadys@yahoo.com; Playa Cofresí; mains US$6-18; 8am-11pm) This pleasant sea-facing restaurant run by a Canadian-Dominican couple is in many ways the hub of Cofresí, where long-time visitors congregate for good food and conversation, and newcomers stop for friendly information and directions or even help finding rental accommodations. Under an open-air thatch roof with tile floors and sturdy wooden tables, the restaurant serves some of the best seafood around, including fettuccine with shrimp, grilled catch of the day, *langostinos* (crayfish) and lobster, always at low prices. Sandwiches, burritos and beef and chicken dishes are also available, among other things. Important sporting events – and plenty of not-so-important ones – are shown on a huge 10ft by 12ft screen and there are pool tables and a small kids area free for clients.

Rancho Esmeralda (☎ 809-396-5087; mains US$6-10; breakfast, lunch & dinner) On a grassy bluff at the far east end of the beach – look for a signed set of stairs leading up the hillside – this Swiss-German restaurant serves simple hearty food in a low-key atmosphere. Pork chops and grilled sausages are favorites and go down well with a beer.

Le Pappilon (☎ 809-970-7640; mains US$12-25; ☽ dinner, closed Mon) This German-run restaurant, 50m east of Cofresí, serves excellent meals in a large palapa-roofed dining area with dark wood tables, a checkerboard floor and seafaring decor, including a tank of sea turtles. Favorites include leg of rabbit, smoked yellowtail or dorado, peppersteaks and vegetable curry. Daily specials are usually a good deal.

Restaurant Los Dos (☎ 809-970-7638; mains US$9-15; ☽ breakfast, lunch & dinner) Closer to the highway, on the same turnoff as Le Pappilon, this casual Austrian-owned bar and restaurant serves classic German and Austrian dishes like Weiner schnitzel and homemade apple strudel, plus a sampling of some other dishes from churrasco to Chinese sesame chicken. Seating is on bar stools at high wooden counters.

Getting There & Away

From Puerto Plata, take any Santiago-bound Javilla Tours bus and ask the driver to let you off at the Cofresí entrance (US$0.75, 15 minutes, departures every 15 minutes, 5am to 7:30pm). From there it's a steep downhill walk of about 700m to the main beach area. Buses return to Puerto Plata until about 7pm. If you're driving, simply follow the signs toward Santiago.

EAST OF PUERTO PLATA

Puerto Plata and Playa Dorada are the most well-known spots on the North Coast, but independently-minded travelers will almost certainly find more to like about the towns east of there. Sosúa has long been a good alternative to Puerto Plata, with many of the same services and conveniences, but with a better beach, tour options and nightlife. Cabarete has terrific surfing, kiteboarding and windsurfing, and a raucous bar scene, making it an indy travel Mecca. Further east, the small town of Río San Juan offers peace and quiet and some of the best diving and snorkeling on the North Coast.

SOSÚA

pop 44,938

Sosúa is situated at one end of a wide, boxy bay, with a long pretty beach and several sandy nooks. All the beaches here are covered with golden-yellow sand and the bay out front is calm and lends itself to snorkeling and scuba diving. Though Sosúa doesn't have the current cache of hot-shot Cabarete or small-town Río San Juan, it remains the most important city on the North Coast after Puerto Plata, by virtue of its size, history and proximity to the airport. And with a number of agreeable hotels and a large selection of shops and services, it can be a convenient base for exploring the North Coast.

History

Sosúa was where in 1940 around 350 Jewish families fleeing Germany and other parts of Europe were settled. Most left after just a few years, but not before building many fine homes and establishing what is to this day the DR's most recognizable cheese and dairy company. You can still see some of the homes built by the Jewish refugees along the western end of Calle Dr Alejo Martinez, though Sosúa has long since given itself over to condos and vacation homes.

Orientation

As it passes along the south edge of Sosúa, Hwy 5 becomes Carretera Gregorio Luperón. The main street into town off the highway is Calle Duarte, although Camino del Libre also works. Calle Pedro Clisante is Sosúa's main drag and is lined with shops, restaurants and bars.

The heart of the town is the intersection of Calles Duarte and Pedro Clisante. From there the beaches and most hotels, restaurants, bars and other services are a short walk away.

Information

BOOKSTORES

Call Center Sosúa (☎ 809-571-3464; Plaza Bohío Taíno; ☽ 8am-7pm Mon-Fri, 8am-6pm Sat-Sun) Besides phone service, this small shop has day-old copies of the *New York Times*, *Miami Herald* and other international newspapers.

Rocky's Rock & Blues Bar Hotel (☎ 809-571-2951; www.rockysbar.com; Calle Dr Rosen 22) Hosts a small English-language bookstore that's open Tuesday, Thursday and Saturday.

INTERNET ACCESS

Alf's Tours (☎ 809-571-1013; www.alftour.com; Calle Pedro Clisante 12; per hr US$2; ☽ 9am-6pm) This Internet café is run by the tour operator next door.

SOSÚA

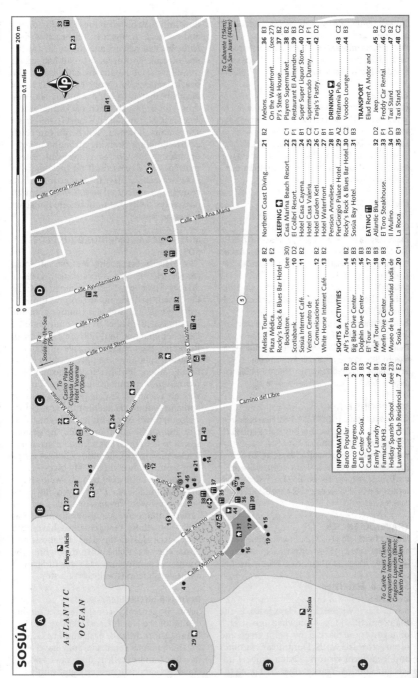

INFORMATION
Banco Popular.................................**1** B2		
Banco Progreso...............................**2** D2		
Call Center Sosúa...........................**3** B3		
Casa Goethe...................................**4** A2		
Family Laundry...............................**5** B1		
Farmacia KH3.................................**6** B2		
Holiday Spanish School..............(see 23)		
Lavandería Club Residencial.........**7** E2		

Melissa Tours..................................**8** B2		
Plaza Médica...................................**9** E2		
Rocky's Rock & Blues Bar Hotel		
Bookstore.................................(see 30)		
Scotiabank....................................**10** D2		
Sosúa Internet Café.....................**11** B2		
Verizon Centro de		
Comunicaciones.........................**12** B2		
White Horse Internet Café..........**13** B2		

SIGHTS & ACTIVITIES
Alf's Tours....................................**14** B2		
Big Blue Dive Center...................**15** B3		
Dolphin Dive Center....................**16** B3		
El' Tour...**17** B3		
Mel Tour......................................**18** B3		
Merlin Dive Center.......................**19** B3		
Museo de la Comunidad Judía de		
Sosúa...**20** C1		

Northern Coast Diving...................**21** B2		

SLEEPING 🛏
Casa Marina Beach Resort............**22** C1		
El Colibrí Resort............................**23** F1		
Hotel Casa Cayena........................**24** B1		
Hotel Casa Valeria.........................**25** C1		
Hotel Garden Keti..........................**26** C1		
Hotel Waterfront...........................**27** B1		
Pension Anneliese.........................**28** B1		
PierGiorgio Palace Hotel...............**29** A2		
Rocky's Rock & Blues Bar Hotel.....**30** C2		
Sosúa Bay Hotel............................**31** B3		

EATING 🍴
Atlantic Blue................................**32** D2		
El Toro Steakhouse.......................**33** F1		
Il Mulino......................................**34** D1		
La Roca.......................................**35** B3		

Melons...**36** B3		
On the Waterfront......................(see 27)		
PJ's Steak House..........................**37** B2		
Playero Supermarket....................**38** B2		
Restaurant El Almendro...............**39** B3		
Super Super Liquor Store..............**40** D2		
Supermercado Danny....................**41** F1		
Tanja's Pastry...............................**42** D2		

DRINKING 🍷
Britannia Pub...............................**43** C2		
Voodoo Lounge...........................**44** B3		

TRANSPORT
Eliud Rent A Motor and		
Jeep...**45** B2		
Freddy Car Rental.........................**46** C2		
Taxi Stand...................................**47** B2		
Taxi Stand...................................**48** C2		

Sosúa Internet Café (☎ 809-571-1050; Calle Duarte at the park; per hr US$2; ☺ 8am-11pm)
White Horse Internet Café (Calle Duarte at the park; per hr US$2; ☺ 8am-6pm) Computers are set up in old-time diner booths with cushiony bench seats.

LAUNDRY
Family Laundry (☎ 809-324-7922; Calle Dr Rosen at Calle Dr Alejo Martínez; per load US$5; ☺ 9am-5pm Mon-Sat)
Lavandería Club Residencial (per load US$4.25; ☺ 8:30am-6pm Mon-Fri, 8:30am-2pm Sat) Same day service US$1.75 extra. Located behind Plaza Médica, near Calle Pedro Clisante.

MEDICAL SERVICES
Farmacia K.H.3. (☎ 809-571-2350; Calle Pedro Clisante; ☺ 8am-9pm Mon-Fri, 8am-8pm Sat)
Plaza Médica (☎ 809-571-3007, emergency ☎ 809-854-1633; Calle Pedro Clisante 30; ☺ 24hr) Medical clinic staffed by a general practitioner. Spanish only spoken.

MONEY
All of the following have at least one 24-hour ATM.
Banco Popular (Calle Dr Alejo Martínez at the park; ☺ 8:15am-4pm Mon-Fri, 9am-1pm Sat)
Banco Progreso (Calle Pedro Clisante; ☺ 8:30am-4pm Mon-Fri, 9am-1pm Sat) Near Calle Ayuntamiento.
Scotiabank (Calle Pedro Clisante; ☺ 8:30am-4:30pm Mon-Fri, 9am-1pm Sat) Near Calle Ayuntamiento.

TELEPHONE & FAX
Call Center Sosúa (☎ 809-571-3464; Plaza Bohío Taíno; to USA per min US$0.30, to Europe per min US$0.70; ☺ 8am-7pm Mon-Fri, until 6pm Sat & Sun)
Verizon Centro de Comunicaciones (☎ 809-571-2001; Calle Duarte at Calle Dr Alejo Martínez; to USA per min US$0.32, to Europe per min US$0.75; ☺ 8am-10pm) Fax service is US$0.35 per page to USA and US$1.25 per page to Europe.

TRAVEL AGENCIES
Melissa Tours (☎ 809-571-2567; www.melissa-tours .com; Calle Duarte 2; ☺ 8am-5:30pm Mon-Fri, 8am-noon Sat) Handles domestic and international airline reservations.

Sights & Activities
BEACHES
Sosúa has two beaches. **Playa Sosúa** is the main beach, a long, somewhat thin stretch of tawny sand backed by palm trees and often crowded with Dominican families and long-term visitors staying in local hotels and condos. You get there by taking the

downhill road between the Voodoo Lounge and La Roca. A much better beach is **Playa Alicia**, located just around the corner at the end of Calle Dr Rosen. A broad half-moon of yellow sand lapped by blue water, the beach is virtually empty because the city hasn't bothered to build a public stairway down the rocky cliff that backs the beach. The Casa Marina Beach Resort (p189) has a set of stairs, however, which you can reach easily enough by walking through the hotel or through the On the Waterfront restaurant (p190). Expats do it all the time and insist travelers are free to do the same – sure enough, no one batted an eye when we tried both ways. Sadly, Dominicans are not given the same leeway.

MUSEO DE LA COMUNIDAD JUDÍA DE SOSÚA
The **Jewish Community Museum of Sosúa** (☎ 809-571-1386; Calle Dr Alejo Martínez; admission US$2.50; ☺ 9am-1pm, 2-4pm Mon-Fri), near Calle Dr Rosen, has exhibits describing the Jewish presence in, and contributions to, the Dominican Republic. At the multinational Evian conference in 1938 the Dominican Republic, then under the rule of dictator Rafael Trujillo, was the only country to officially accept Jewish refugees fleeing Nazi repression in Germany. Ironically, Trujillo was no friend of Jewish people – a racist and anti-Semite, he had just the year before welcomed two Nazi visitors with great fanfare and media attention – and the gesture seems to have been less a humanitarian one than a ploy by the dictator to deflect attention from the brutality of his own regime. Around 350 families of refugees were settled in and around Sosúa. Most stayed only a few years – few were farmers by trade and they suffered tremendous anti-Semitism here as well – but those that remained have been very successful in the dairy business, and Sosúa cheese is well-known throughout the country. The museum has signs in Spanish and English, and is well worth a stop.

DIVING & SNORKELING
Sosúa is generally considered the diving capital of the North Coast, though Río San Juan, a short distance east, and Las Galeras on the Samaná Peninsula both have quality shops and excellent dive sites, and the coral reefs and patches see significantly less

traffic than at Sosúa. But Sosúa remains a popular dive destination for its proximity to the airport, large selection of dive operators and variety of hotels, resorts, restaurants and other services.

There are little more than a dozen regularly dived spots around Sosúa – the exact number depends on who you ask – and many more less-common destinations for divers who want to do some exploring. Among the popular dives are Airport Wall, featuring a wall and tunnels in 12m to 35m of water; Zíngara Wreck, an upright 45m ship sunk in 1993 as an artificial reef in around 35m of water; and Coral Gardens and Coral Wall, both offering excellent coral formations in depths ranging from 14m to 53m.

Prices vary somewhat from shop to shop, but are generally US$30 to US$35 for a one-tank dive, plus US$5 to US$10 for rental equipment. Booking a dive package brings the price down considerably – with a 10-dive package, the per-dive price can be as low as US$25 if you have your own gear. All of Sosúa's shops offer certification courses and special trips, like to Río San Juan or Dudu cave. Snorkeling trips are available at all shops, and cost US$25 to US$40 per person, depending on the length and number of stops; equipment is always included.

One big difference among the shops is the predominant language among the staff, though English is spoken at all. Here are some of Sosúa's most established dive outfits:

Big Blue Dive Center (☎ 809-571-2916; ☽ 9am-5pm) End of road to Playa Sosúa.

Dolphin Dive Center (☎ 809-571-3589; www.dolphin divecenter.com; Playa Sosúa; ☽ 9am-5pm) This operation has its office at the Sosúa Bay Hotel.

Merlin Dive Center (☎ 809-571-4309; www.tauch schule-merlin.com; end of road to Playa Sosúa; ☽ 9am-5pm)

Northern Coast Diving (☎ 809-571-1028; www.north erncoastdiving.com, Calle Pedro Clisante 8; ☽ 8am-6pm)

Courses
There are two places in town you can learn Spanish.

Spanish classes by the week are offered at **Holiday Spanish School** (☎ 809-571-1847; www .holiday-spanish-school.com; El Colibri Resort, Calle Pedro Clisante 141) on El Colibrí Resort (p188). Lessons are offered to beginners and advanced students alike and are given in two hour increments; the first hour typically focuses on grammar and vocabulary, the second is centered around speaking. Prices vary according to the length of the course and the number of students. A private week-long course costs US$280, a group course is US$145. Housing packages are available.

The German-run **Casa Goethe** (☎ 809-571-3185; www.edase.com; Calle Morris Ling; ☽ 8am-5pm Mon-Fri) offers German and English classes to locals, and Spanish classes to foreigners. Private and group classes are available, both on the ordinary (four hours per day) and intensive (seven hours per day) schedules. Classes are held in the mornings and afternoons, and the school organizes outings and conversation exchanges. Long-term housing can be arranged either at the center itself or in area hotels, and usually include breakfast.

Tours
Tour operators in town offer a variety of excursions in the area and to as far away as Jarabacoa, Santo Domingo and Samaná. All the shops have brochures and photo albums describing their trips in detail (including prices) and it's worth speaking to a couple of different shops before signing up. Be sure to ask how long you will be at each destination (and how much time you are stuck in a bus), how many people will be on the tour, what exactly is and is not included (lunch, drinks, snorkel equipment etc) and if the guide speaks your language (or one you understand).

Among the many tour options include: tours on horseback or ATV (All-Terrain Vehicle); river rafting or canyoning around Jarabacoa; catamaran tours along the coast; whale-watching in Samaná (mid-January to mid-March only), deep-sea fishing; and Santo Domingo city tours. Of course all of these excursions can be done relatively easily on your own – using this book! – but organized tours save you all the planning and organizing, and can be a good option for families or those with limited time.

Tour operators in town include:

Alf's Tours (☎ 809-571-1013; www.alftour.com; Calle Pedro Clisante 12; ☽ 9am-6pm) Is run by a friendly operator with staff who speak Spanish, French, English and German.

El' Tour (☎ 809-571-4195; ☽ 9am-5pm Mon-Fri, 9am-1pm Sat) On the road to Playa Sosúa, El' Tour is a well-established agency which mostly caters to German and English-speaking travelers.

Melissa Tours (☎ 809-571-2567; www.melissa-tours .com; Calle Duarte 2; ☺ 8am-5:30pm Mon-Fri, 8am-noon Sat) A long-time locally owned agency.

Mel' Tour (☎ 809-571-4002; ☺ 9am-5pm Mon-Fri, 9am-1pm Sat) On the road to Playa Sosúa.

Sleeping
BUDGET

Rocky's Rock & Blues Bar Hotel (☎ 809-571-2951; www.rockysbar.com; Calle Dr Rosen 22; r US$18) Basic but comfortable, the five rooms at Rocky's are a great deal. All are spotless, breezy and have cable TV. A mellow lounge with couches and tables spills into the bar/restaurant area, where locals and travelers hang out most of the afternoon and evening. Wireless Internet runs throughout the place, so if you're traveling with a laptop, this is a goldmine. The Canadian owner is friendly and especially knowledgeable about the area.

El Colibrí Resort (☎ 809-571-1847; www.elcolibri. net; Calle Pedro Clisante 141; s/d with fan US$18/20; s/d with aircon US$30-35/33-40; ✗ ☎) With basic but clean rooms, this Dutch-owned hotel is a good option for travelers on a tight budget. Accommodations are located inside a long, slightly run down building in front of a pleasant pool and garden. Rooms with air-con face the pool and have nice terraces, the others have a fan and one window. A Spanish-language school also operates on-site (p187) and school/housing packages are available. English, German and Dutch are spoken.

Hotel Voramar (☎ 809-571-3910; www.voramar .ok4y.de; eastern end of Calle Dr Alejo Martínez; r US$30, studio US$30, 2-bedroom apt US$60, aircon extra US$5; ✗ P ☎) Outside of town, this 20-room hotel features two three-story buildings overlooking a pleasant swimming pool. The rooms and apartments in one building are fan-cooled, while those in the other have aircon. All accommodations have cable TV, telephone and tasteful decor. Although there is a restaurant on-site, you'll have to take a cab to check out other options in town.

Hotel Casa Valeria (☎ 809-571-3565; mayelaflores@ hotmail.com; Calle Dr Rosen 28; s/d US$25/30, s/d with kitchen US$30/35) All nine rooms at this cozy hotel are slightly different, whether in size, furnishings or decor. Three units have a kitchen, the others are hotel-like rooms with comfortable beds, brand-new furnishings and painted a great *rosa Mexicano* (Mexican pink). Rooms are set around a leafy courtyard with a clean pool in the middle; all have cable TV, fans and new ceramic-tiled bathrooms. Operated by a friendly German-Costa Rican couple who give discounts for longer stays. This is an excellent choice.

Hotel Garden Keti (☎ 809-571-1557; www.garden keti.com; Calle Dr Rosen 32; s/d US$35/40; s/d with aircon US$40/65; ✗ ☎) Right next door to Casa Valeria, this is a decent alternative if the Valeria is full. All 25 guest rooms have hot-water bathrooms, firm beds and balconies overlooking the pool. Twelve of the rooms have cable TV. The rooms are showing wear, but they are still decent value.

Pension Anneliese (☎ 809-571-2208; end of Calle Dr Rosen; s/d US$25/40; ☎ P) This small home has been renting rooms at affordable rates for a quarter of a century. Ten decent-sized rooms all have fans, private hot-water bathrooms, either one king- or two queen-size beds and nice ocean views from the front terrace. In addition to the pleasant little pool, Playa Alicia, the best beach in town, is just steps away.

MIDRANGE

Hotel Waterfront (☎ 809-571-2670; www.water frontdr.com; Calle Dr Rosen 1; s/d/t US$35/40/45, with aircon US$40/45/50; ✗ ☎ P) The Waterfront offers 27 plain but comfortable rooms – 10 in stand-alone bungalows, the rest in a two-story building. All have a terrace or balcony, overhead fan, clean hot-water bathrooms, fridge and up to three firm beds. All rooms are in a leafy garden tucked behind the inviting pool, with a great seaside restaurant and Sosúa's best beach right in front.

Hotel Casa Cayena (☎ 809-571-2651; www.casa cayena.com; Calle Dr Rosen 25; s/d US$53/63, w breakfast US$63/70, penthouse s/d US$70/87; ✗ ☎ P) This hotel contains 24 rooms on two floors, connected by broad breezy corridors. All rooms have red-tile floors, clean modern bathrooms with hot water and the upstairs units have great sea views. There's a pretty L-shaped pool, and Playa Alicia is just down the street. The hotel also has a spacious top-floor penthouse with a separate dining room and bedroom and a large fully equipped kitchen which is a good deal if you're staying for more than a couple of days and don't want to eat out every meal.

Sosúa-by-the-Sea (☎ 809-571-3222; www.sosua bythesea.com; Calle B Phillips at Calle David Stem; d per person US$70; ✗ ☎ P) The interior of this all-inclusive resort doesn't quite live up to its poetic name – the whole thing could use remodeling – but it does offer comfortable rooms in a friendly personalized atmosphere. The rooms and facilities are less modern and grand here than at the Casa Marina Beach next door, but the setting is more intimate, including a well-kept beach area.

PierGiorgio Palace Hotel (☎ 809-571-2626; www .piergiorgiohotel.com; Calle La Puntilla; r US$85; ☒ ☒) This three-story 51-room, neo Victorian-style hotel is built on a rocky cliff overlooking the ocean. Built in 1998, it is the realized dream of Italian fashion designer Piergiorgio, who can often be found in the open-air restaurant in front. Ironically, the decoration is the hotel's least appealing feature, with flowery linens and a child-like design. (Or maybe we're just out of touch with high fashion?) All rooms have cable TV and two telephones (including one in the bathroom) and 28 of them have wonderful sea views. Room prices include breakfast and there are even better views from the good Italian restaurant, plus handsome gardens.

TOP END
Both of the top-end hotels in Sosúa are all-inclusives.

Sosúa Bay Hotel (☎ 809-571-4000; www.starzresorts .com; end of Calle Pedro Clisante; r per person US$145-210; ☒ ☒ ☒) Part of the Starz Resorts chain, this is Sosúa finest hotel. It's built on a steep bluff giving a unique design and layout, though not much in the way of gardens or open space common at other resorts. The large welcoming lobby, main restaurant area and most of the rooms are at the top of the hill, affording great views of Bahía Sosúa. There are two pools, one built above the other and connected by a small waterfall. The hotel beach is tiny – instead lounge chairs are set up on a broad wooden platform running along the ocean's edge with a ladder leading into the water. There's a dive center on-site.

Casa Marina Beach Resort (☎ 809-571-3635, in USA ☎ 800-472-3985; www.amhsamarina.com; Calle Dr Alejo Martínez; r US$90-120; ☒ ☒ ☒) Where the Sosúa Bay Hotel has little in the way of grounds, the Casa Marina (an Amhsa Marina resort) is a huge leafy complex with three pools, five restaurants and almost 400 rooms arranged in three-story buildings. The rooms are classic all-inclusive: clean

and comfortable but not memorable in any way, with cable TV, a balcony and most looking onto the pool. The hotel has direct access to Playa Alicia and a more rustic beach about 150m to the east. In the rocky area between the two beaches are a series of platforms for lounge chairs, shaded by trees, and several hot tubs set right into the rocks on the water's edge, with waves crashing just beyond. There's a nightclub, games room and plenty of water-sports equipment.

Eating
BUDGET
Despite the heavy tourist and expat presence, Sosúa does have some inexpensive restaurants that serve good food.

Restaurant El Almendro (☎ 809-963-7620; mains US$3-7; ☒ breakfast, lunch & dinner) Situated on the road to Playa Sosúa, this modest restaurant has a tiny, odd-shaped dining room, no view, and is down a narrow, easy-to-miss path, but it's worth looking for if you are in mood for down-home Dominican food at great prices. Lunch plates come with rice, beans and a main dish – like roast chicken, grilled beef with onions, or fish fillet – all for under US$4. The *asapao de camarones* (tomato-based shrimp and rice stew) is also tasty.

Melons (☎ 809-571-3173; mains US$4-7; ☒ breakfast, lunch & dinner) On the road to Playa Sosúa, this German-run restaurant and bar could really use a different name, but the food here is good and cheap. One of the proprietors is a butcher, so the homemade sausages are excellent – already a bargain at US$1.50 to US$3, they are sometimes on special for a buck. Other options include baguette sandwiches, gyros and hefty breakfasts.

Il Mulino (☎ 809-571-3023; Calle Ayuntamiento; mains US$5-9; ☒ dinner) This thatch-roofed, open-air restaurant specializes in top notch pizzas. Here you can get specialty pies like the *Diavolo* (literally, the Devil) which has paprika, red chilies and Tabasco sauce in the mix or the *Banana*, which comes with ham and, well, banana. Favorites like veggie lovers, meat lovers and just plain ol' cheese lovers are also served up quick and hot.

Tanja's Pastry (☎ 809-571-3515; Calle Pedro Clisante at Calle David Stern; mains US$1.50-5; ☒ 8am-4pm Tue-Sat, 8am-1pm Sun) A delightful place to get a treat, Tanja's Pastry is in a cookie-cutter house that has been converted into a pastry and ice-cream shop. Inside are wicker chairs and tables where you can enjoy any number of homemade treats, coffee drinks and dozens of ice-cream flavors. If you prefer the breeze, the porch has tables and chairs too.

Groceries

Playero Supermarket (☎ 809-571-2554; Calle Pedro Clisante; ☼ 8am-10pm) near Calle Duarte is well stocked and inexpensive, which may explain the long lines.

Supermercado Danny (Calle Pedro Clisante; ☼ 8am-midnight Mon-Sat, 4pm-midnight Sun) This small grocery store near the Plaza Médica offers the basics – produce, dairy, canned goods and sometimes even fresh bread.

Super Super Liquor Store (Calle Pedro Clisante at Calle Ayuntamiento; ☼ 8am-8pm Mon-Sat) This shop offers a decent selection of liquors, wines and cigars. Not super – definitely not *super* super – but still good.

MIDRANGE

El Toro Steakhouse (☎ 809-571-3680; Calle Pedro Clisante; mains US$7-21; ☼ dinner) Recommended by locals, this steakhouse east of El Colibrí Resort serves up some of the best cuts of beef in town. Patrons order by the body part: hip, rump, rib etc. The ambience is pleasant – a thatch-roofed dining room with wood tables and chairs – and the service is good.

La Roca (☎ 809-571-3893; Calles Arzeno at Pedro Clisante; mains US$7-12; ☼ breakfast, lunch & dinner) This large restaurant and bar is popular with foreign visitors and has a few good specials like an all-you-can-eat barbeque on Fridays for US$10, and soups, desserts and cocktails for around US$3. Seating is in a large indoor dining area or under a large veranda on the wrap-around patio.

PJ's Steak House (☎ 809-571-2091; Calles Pedro Clisante at Duarte; mains US$7-20; ☼ 24hr) Right downtown, painted all in orange, and open 24/7, it's virtually impossible to miss this Sosúa institution. Daily specials (US$12) include salad, main dish, brownie and choice of wine or beer. Burgers and sandwiches, all served with fries, run to about US$6, while the all-you-can-eat barbeque special goes for US$20. A little edgier than the other restaurants nearby, PJ's turns into a popular drinking hole at night.

TOP END

On the Waterfront (☎ 809-571-3024; at Hotel Waterfront; Calle Dr Rosen 1; mains US$4-20; ☼ breakfast, lunch & dinner) This elegant but casual restaurant is on a bluff overlooking Sosúa's prettiest stretch of beach. Seafood options include almond-brandy grouper and fillet of sole in orange sauce. For meats, try the fillet mignon, which comes in standard or jumbo cut and smothered in pepper, or pork chops in Dijon sauce. The restaurant's position and the orientation on the bay make this a great spot for sunsets.

Atlantic Blue (☎ 809-571-4730; Calle Pedro Clisante 26; mains US$11-23; ☼ lunch & dinner) The Atlantic Blue is considered to be the best seafood place in town. It serves only the freshest of seafood in a classy open-air dining room. Portions are large and the service is excellent. If you're in the mood for fish, try the mouthwatering sea bass in coconut sauce (US$11). If lobster is more your thing, choose your own from the live tank at the entrance.

Drinking

Most of Sosúa's nightlife is found on its main commercial drag, Calle Pedro Clisante.

Voodoo Lounge (☎ 809-571-3559; www.voodoo loungeonline.com; Pedro Clisante at Calle Arzeno; ☼ 1pm-1am) Just outside the entrance to Sosúa Bay Hotel, this hip Canadian-owned bar has happy hour every day from 1pm to 8:30pm, live shows and music every Friday and karaoke on Sunday. The bar and tiny stage area are downstairs (where the party sometimes spills onto the sidewalks) and there's a mellow lounge area upstairs. A good alternative to Sosúa's other mostly seedy nightclubs.

Rocky's Rock & Blues Bar Hotel (☎ 809-571-2951; www.rockysbar.com; Calle Dr Rosen 22; ☼ 7am-4am) A laid-back sort of place with cold beers, strong drinks and killer ribs. This is the place to come to while away an afternoon. Travelers and locals alike mingle here and stay late into the night. The music – like the name suggests – is pure rock and blues.

For a beer, a bite and the companionship of hard-drinking long-time expats, head to **PJ's Steak House** (Calles Pedro Clisante at Duarte; ☼ 7:30am-midnight) or the **Britannia Pub** (☎ 809-571-1959; Pedro Clisante; ☼ 10am-midnight) between Duarte & Camino del Libre. There are a handful of bars and clubs further east at the corner of Pedro Clisante and Camino del Libre, but they're a bit rougher and some are frequented by prostitutes.

Entertainment

Casino Playa Chiquita (☎ 809-571-2591; eastern end of Calle Dr Alejo Martínez; ☒ 8pm-4am Mon-Thu, 4pm-4am Fri-Sun) If you're up for a little Texas hold 'em or just want to try your luck on the slot machines, then this casino is a decent place to spend an evening. Located about a kilometer from town, it's best to take a cab there and back. Free drinks for all players.

Getting There & Away

AIR

Sosúa is much closer to the **Aeropuerto Internacional Gregorio Luperón** (☎ 809-586-0107, 809-586-0219) than Puerto Plata, although it's commonly referred to as 'Puerto Plata airport.' We're guilty of the same bias – see the Puerto Plata section for complete airport info. A taxi from there to Sosúa is US$20.

BUS

Caribe Tours (☎ 809-571-3808; Carretera a Puerto Plata) has a bus depot on the highway at the edge of Las Charamicos neighborhood, 1km southwest of the city centre. It offers bus services from Sosúa to Santo Domingo (US$5.65, five hours, hourly, 5:20am to 6:20pm).

For destinations along the coast, go to Hwy 5 and flag down any passing *gua-gua*. They pass every 15 to 30 minutes, with services to Puerto Plata (US$1, 30 minutes), Cabarete (US$1, 30 minutes) and Río San Juan (US$2.50, 1½ hours).

Getting Around

You can walk just about everywhere in Sosúa, except the hotels east of the center, which are better reached by *motoconcho* or taxi. The former are easy to find around town, while taxis can be located at a **taxi stand** (☎ 809-571-3027) on the corner of Calle Pedro Clisante and Dr Rosen.

To rent a car, try **Freddy Car Rental** (☎ 809-571-3146; 50m off Calle Dr Alejo Martínez; per day from US$40; ☒ 8am-6pm) or **Eliud Rent A Motor and Jeep** (☎ 809-889-6272; Calle Duarte at the park; per day from US$40; ☒ 8am-7pm) which operates out of a tiny kiosk marked, logically, Sol Car Rental. Rates start at around US$40 per day.

CABARETE

pop 15,000

This is the center of the North Coast's adventure sport activity. One look at the beach will prove as much, the colorful windsurfing sails brightening the shore and dotting the aquamarine water. The activity is relatively new – a decade ago there were only a handful of hotels – and the crush of people, cars and *motoconchos* can be off-putting at first. But don't let the congestion prevent you from stopping – Cabarete's boisterous nightlife and ideal conditions for windsurfing, kiteboarding and other sports make it well worth sticking around.

Orientation

Cabarete is a one-road town, built up around the highway which runs right through the middle. Virtually all hotels, restaurants and shops are on the main drag, making it a congested, though easy-to-navigate place.

Information

BOOKSTORES

Bill's Books (☎ 809-753-5800; ☒ 2-5pm Mon, Wed, Fri) Small bookshop located in the far east end of town with plenty of beach trash and the occasional good find. Titles are available in English, French, German and Spanish; US$4.25 each or US$2 with acceptable trade-in.

Luis Anselmo Gift Shop (☎ 809-640-3299; ☒ 8:30am-7pm) The only place in town to get international magazines and newspapers. Prices are as much as five times the newsstand rate but it's worth it if you need a fix. A good selection of maps and dictionaries are also sold. Located at the east end of town.

EMERGENCY

Politur (Tourist Police; ☎ 809-571-0713; Carr a Gasper Hernandez; ☒ 24hr) At the eastern entrance to town.

INTERNET ACCESS

Internet Center (per hr US$3.50; ☒ 9am-9pm Mon-Sat) Quiet and cool, this is the only place in town with data ports to connect your laptop. At the west end of town, it is near the entrance to the only public parking lot in town.

Kaoba Internet (Hotel Kaoba; per hr US$1.75; ☒ 7am-11pm) Best rates and longest hours in town. Situated in the west end of town

INTERNET RESOURCES

Check out www.activecabarete.com for info on Cabarete's many outdoors and sports activities.

LAUNDRY

Lavandería Familiar Cabarete (☎ 809-751-4353; per lb US$0.70; ☒ 8am-7pm Mon-Sat) At the west end of town, it provides same day service if clothes are dropped off early. Delivery available.

CABARETE

NORTH COAST

To
Kite Beach (1km); Kite Club (2km);
Kitecite (2km); Playa Encuentro (4km);
Take Off (4km); Sosúa (24km)

ATLANTIC OCEAN

300 m
0.2 miles

INFORMATION
Banco Popular..................................1 B3
Biblioteca Frances.........................(see 14)
Bill's Books.......................................2 E2
Centro de Telecomunicaciones.........3 C3
Internet Center................................4 B3
Kaoba Internet.................................5 B3
Lavandería Familiar Cabarete...........6 B3
Luis Anselmo Gift Shop....................7 D3
Politur...8 F3
Scotiabank..9 D3
Servi-Med Medical Office................10 C3
Tele-Vimenca...................................11 C3

SIGHTS & ACTIVITIES
Club Mistral....................................12 E2
Club Nathalie Simon.......................13 B3
Dolphin Dive Center.......................14 E2
Fanatic Windsurf Center.................15 D3
Happy Surfpool...............................16 B3
Iguana Mama..................................17 D3
Laurel Eastman Kiteboarding..........18 A1
No Work Team................................19 C3

SLEEPING
Albatros Hotel & Condos................20 B3
Azzuro...21 B3
Hotel Alegría...................................22 E2
Hotel Kaoba....................................23 B3
Hotel Laguna Blu.............................24 C3
L'Agence...25 B3
Sans Souci Beach............................26 E2
Tropical Beach Club Hotel...............27 C3
Tropical Casa Laguna......................28 C3

Villa Taína Hotel.............................29 B3
Wind Chime Condos.......................30 E3
Windsurf Resort..............................31 E3

EATING
Beach Break Sandwicherie..............32 B3
Bon Ice Cream................................33 C3
Coco Rico..34 B3
Friends Bistro..................................35 C3
Hexenkessel....................................36 D3
Ho-La-La Café.................................37 C3
Janet's Supermarket........................38 F2
La Casa del Pescador......................39 D3
Miró's on the Beach........................40 D3
Panadería Repostería Dick...............41 C3
Paradise...42 B3
Restaurante China...........................43 C3

DRINKING
Bambú...44 C3
LAX..45 C3
Onno's...46 D3

ENTERTAINMENT
Las Brisas...47 E2

SHOPPING
Carib Bic Center..............................48 D3
Planet Arte......................................49 D3

TRANSPORT
Sandro's Rent A Car.........................50 E2

To Blue Moon Hotel
& Restaurant (17.5km);
Río San Juan (40km)

Callejón 2

Playa Cabarete

Av Principal

Bahía Cabarete

Laguna Cabarete

Bozo Beach

MEDICAL SERVICES

Servi-Med Medical Office (☎ 809-571-0964; 🕑 24hr) Four MDs, one dentist and a chiropractor staff this clinic in the center of town. They make house calls and speak English and German.

MONEY

Banco Popular (Carr a Sosúa; 🕑 9am-5pm Mon-Fri, 9am-1pm Sat) Located at the western entrance to town. One 24-hour ATM.

Exchange offices On the main drag and accept euros, US dollars and traveler's checks.

Scotiabank (🕑 8:30am-4:30pm Mon-Fri, 9am-1pm Sat) At the eastern end of town, it has one 24-hour ATM.

POST

There is no post office in Cabarete but hotels often post guest mail.

TELEPHONE

Centro de Telecomunicaciones (to USA per min US$0.32, to Europe per min US$0.74; 🕑 9am-9pm Mon-Sat) Located on a public walkway to the beach at the west end of town.

Tele-Vimenca (to USA per min US$0.32, to Europe per min US$0.74; 🕑 8am-10pm Mon-Fri, 10am-5pm Sat) Located on the walkway to Hotel Laguna Blu in the center of town.

TRAVEL AGENCIES

There were no travel agencies in Cabarete at the time of research. For plane tickets and other services, try Melissa Tours in Sosúa (p186).

Ozone Travel (in USA ☎ 888-824-6359; www.ozone travel.com) Florida-based travel agency specializes in customized kiteboarding vacations in Cabarete and around the world.

Sights

Cabarete's beaches are its main attractions, and not just for sun and sand. The beaches are each home to a different water sport, and they are great places to watch beginner and advanced athletes alike.

Playa Cabarete, the main beach in front of town, is the best place for watching windsurfing, though the very best windsurfers are well offshore at the reef line. Still, look for them performing huge high-speed jumps and even end-over-end flips.

Bozo Beach is the western downwind side of Playa Cabarete, and so named because of all the beginner windsurfers and kitesurfers who don't yet know how to tack

up wind and so wash up on Bozo's shore. There are more kiteboarders at Bozo and the surf here is better for boogie boarding. Both Cabarete and Bozo have nice sand and pretty palm trees.

Kite Beach, 2km west of town, is a sight to behold on windy days, when scores of kiters of all skill levels negotiate huge sails and 30m lines amid the waves and traffic. On those days, there's no swimming here, as you're liable to get run over.

Playa Encuentro, 4km west of town, is the place to go for surfing, though top windsurfers and kitesurfers sometimes go there to take advantage of the larger waves. The beach itself is OK, but the strong tide and rocky shallows make swimming here difficult.

Activities

More information on all of these activities can be found in the Outdoors chapter (p50).

DIVING

Dolphin Dive Center (☎ 809-571-3589; www.dolphin divecenter.com; 🕑 9am-1pm, 2-6pm Mon-Sat) is a Sosúa-based shop with an office in far east end of Cabarete where you can arrange fun dives, certification courses, and dive safaris to Dudu cave and elsewhere. Transportation can be arranged to Sosúa, where the majority of dive sites are located. One-tank dives run from US$31 to US$46, depending on if you have your own gear or not, or from US$25 to US$36 per dive with a 10-dive package. Snorkeling trips are also available (US$15 to US$18, one hour).

KITEBOARDING

Cabarete is one of the top places in the world to windsurf, and the sport is quickly eclipsing windsurfing as the town's sport du jour. Kite Beach, 2km west of town, has ideal conditions for the sport, which entails strapping yourself to a modified surfboard and a huge inflatable wind foil then skimming and soaring across the water. Bozo Beach at the west end of the city beach, is also a good spot and typically less crowded. A number of kiteboarding schools offer multi-day courses for those who want to learn – most people need at least six hours of instruction but nine or 12 is recommended. Costs average US$240 to US$275

NORTH COAST

for six hours, US$350 to US$400 for nine and from US$420 to US$450 for 12. Schools and instructors vary considerably in personality, so spend some time finding one where you feel comfortable. Kiteboarding is a potentially dangerous sport and it is extremely important that you feel free to ask questions and voice fears or concerns, and that you receive patient, ego-free answers in return. Some of the kiteboarding schools in town:

Club Mistral (☎ 809-571-9791; www.club-mistral.com) Based in Germany with shops all over the world, this is a professional and very well-known wind- and water-sports outfit. Combo windsurf and kiteboard packages available.

Kite Board Cabarete (☎ 809-856-9853; www.kite boardcabarete.com; per hr US$60, 3-day course US$440) One-man operation offering specialized training for advanced kiters only. Instructor Gaël Brunhes has helped train top kiters including Susi Mai and José Luis Ciriaco.

Kite Club (☎ 809-571-9748; www.kiteclubcabarete .com; 1-hr group beginner's lesson $25, 1-hr private lesson $70) At the top of the infamous 'Kite Beach' in Cabarete, is a well-run club with a pleasing *tranquilo* atmosphere fantastic to hang out and relax in between sessions. The tiny kitchen delivers delicious fresh ahi tuna salads and sandwiches.

Kitexcite (☎ 809-571-9509; www.kitexcite.com; Extreme Hotel at Kite Beach) Uses radio helmets and optional off-shore sessions – ergo less waiting and walking time – to maximize instruction.

Laurel Eastman Kiteboarding (☎ 809-571-0564; www.laureleastman.com; Hotel Caracol Beach Club) Friendly, safety-conscious shop located on Bozo Beach and run by one of the world's top kiteboarders.

Pura Vida (☎ 809-862-0485; 2 Calle Libertad; www .puravidacaraibes.com; 2-hr beginner's lesson $70, 1-day kite & board rental $60) Run by friendly French-Dominicans out of Las Terrenas, utilizes three excellent locations, ensuring awesome downwind opportunities for experienced riders and uncrowded lessons for beginners. The variety of lesson plans mean you can really indulge if you fall in love with the sport.

SURFING

Some of the best waves for surfing on the entire island – up to 4m – break over reefs 4km west of Cabarete on a meandering beach called Playa Encuentro. The waves break both right and left are known by names like El Canal, Encuentro, La Barca and Preciosa (Precious One). To find Playa Encuentro, take the first major road toward the sea west of Cabarete. Several outfits in town and on Playa Encuentro rent surfboards

and offer instruction. Surfboard rental for half a day is from US$10 to US$20; a three-hour course costs US$30 to US$40 per person, and five-day surf camps costs US$110 to US$175 per person. You can rent gear and arrange classes at the kiteboarding and windsurfing schools, which coordinate with the surf shops:

Take Off (☎ 809-963-7873; www.321takeoff.com; Playa Encuentro)

No Work Team (☎ 809-571-0820; www.noworkteam cabarete.com) In the center of town.

WINDSURFING

Although kiteboarding has grabbed much of the limelight, windsurfing is the sport that put Cabarete on the map and it is still extremely popular here. The combination of strong, steady winds, relatively shallow water and a rockless shore creates perfect conditions for the sport. Windsurfing generally needs stronger winds than kiteboarding – May to July is the best time, when average wind speeds exceed 25km/h.

The broad bay directly in front of town is used by beginner and expert windsurfers alike. The calm waters close to shore are ideal for learning to stand up and control the board and sail, while a coral reef about a half-kilometer from shore creates large swells and breakers which advanced windsurfers use to do flips and other athletic feats. Shops right on the beach offer rentals and courses. In general, windsurfing is harder to master than kiteboarding, but the lessons are less expensive and novices tend to suffer fewer faceplants (and other injuries to ego and body). Board and sail rentals average US$20 to US$25 per hour, US$50 to US$55 per day or US$230 to US$270 per week. For a bit more, shops offer 'non-consecutive rentals' so you get multiday prices but you don't have to go out every day. Renters are usually required to purchase damage insurance for an additional US$45 per week. Private lessons cost around US$40 for an hour, US$150 for a four-session course, with discounts for groups.

Club Nathalie Simon (CNS; ☎ 809-571-0848; www .cabaretewindsurf.com; ☻ 9am-6pm) Very professional operation, at the western end of the beach, that's popular with French visitors and offering high quality equipment for differing skill levels. Also rents sea kayaks, boogie boards and Hobie Cats.

Fanatic Windsurf Center (☎ 809-571-0861; www
.fanatic-cabarete.com; main beach) A short distance
east of the other two shops, Fanatic has somewhat older
equipment but notably lower prices and offers a free intro
to windsurfing – getting familiar with the equipment
and some basic concepts – on Mondays, Wednesdays and
Fridays at 10am.

Happy Surfpool (☎ 809-571-0784; www.happy
cabarete.com; Villa Taína Hotel; ☷ 9am-6pm) Next door
to Club Nathalie Simon, this friendly shop also carries quality windsurf and other water-sport equipment.

Tours

Iguana Mama (☎ 809-571-0908, in USA ☎ 800-849-
4720; www.iguanamama.com; ☷ 8am-5pm), located
at eastern end of town, is one of the most
highly regarded tour operators in the Dominican Republic and for good reason.
Founded by an American and currently
owned and operated by a friendly Basque
expat since November 2003, Iguana Mama
offers a variety of excursions and activities,
from canyoning and cascading (climbing,
rappelling, sliding and swimming through
a series of waterfalls and gorges) to more
mellow outings like sailing and horseback
riding. But the shop's specialty is mountain bike tours, which also range in length
and difficulty: the half-day downhill rides
through local villages is easy and fun, while
more serious bikers should consider the
challenging 12-day cross-country tours.
Iguana Mama also operates good three-day
Pico Duarte trips. Stop by and browse the
folder full of photos, prices and detailed
descriptions of every tour. If you don't see
what you're looking for the shop will happily create a customized excursion. Guides
are engaging and professional, safety is
taken very seriously, and all equipment is
reliable and up-to-date.

Festivals & Events

Master of the Ocean (☎ 809-963-7873; www.master
oftheocean.com), started in 2002 and usually
held the last week of February, is a popular event featuring individual windsurfing,
kiteboarding and surfing divisions, but the
real test is the namesake category: a triath-
lon of all three events. Preliminary rounds
are held at various beaches in and around
Cabarete, but the finals for all three events
usually take place at Playa Encuentro,
where the high wind and big waves make
for challenging conditions (and awesome

performances) in all three sports. As the
competition nears, look for posters around
town with specific event schedules and locations. The public is welcome to watch
from the shore, where loud music and a
party atmosphere always prevail.

For almost two decades, sand sculpture
enthusiasts have convened in Cabarete in
the first week of March to display and test
their skills in the **International Sand Castle
Competition** (www.castillosdearena.org). Also includes a Kids Day.

Held in Puerto Plata, Sosúa and Cabarete at the end of October, the **Dominican
Jazz Festival** (www.drjazzfestival.com) attracts top
musical talent from around the country and
even abroad.

Sleeping

Most of Cabarete's accommodations are
along the main drag. Hardcore kiters may
want to stay at one of the hotels right on
Kite Beach.

If you're looking to stay a week or longer,
a vacation rental can often prove more
affordable – and comfortable – than a hotel.
On the west side of town, **L'Agence** (☎ 809-
571-0999; www.Agencerd.com; ☷ 9:30am-12:30pm &
3:30-6:30pm Mon-Fri), can help you find a place
that suits your needs; it has a wide range of
properties from which to choose and lists
many of them on its website. English and
French spoken.

BUDGET

Hotel Laguna Blu (☎ 809-571-0802; r/tw US$25/35;
tw with kitchenette US$53; ☐P☐☒) Not much to
look at from the outside, the rooms in the
Laguna Blu, in the center of town, are surprisingly comfortable and clean. All have
ceiling fans, private hot-water bathrooms
and are sponge-painted in bright colors.
Sadly, the pool is often neglected; if you
want to swim, stick to the ocean.

Hotel Alegría (☎ 809-571-0455; www.hotel-alegria
.com; Callejón 2; r US$22, with ocean view US$30, studio
US$45) Hidden down one of Cabarete's few
side streets, the cheapest rooms are small
and somewhat dim, but very clean and perfectly adequate for travelers on a budget. For
a bit more, the ocean-view rooms are larger,
with 2nd-floor balconies and better light
and ventilation. Studios are on the ground
floor, with white-tile floors and a small terrace – the kitchens are a bit old, but this is

still a bargain considering what you save by not eating out every meal. There's also a simple food service, a pool table and a small common TV room. Friendly owners.

MIDRANGE

Albatros Hotel & Condos (☎ 809-571-0841; h.albatross@ verizon.net.do; r US$35, with kitchenette US$60, 1-bedroom apt US$75, 2-bedroom apt US$100; P ⊠) Set back from the road, at the west end of town, the Albatros offers clean and cheerful rooms amid a palm tree-laden garden. Standard rooms come with a sitting area, ceiling fan and a fridge. Studios and apartments come in various sizes; the smallest is a regular-sized room with a kitchenette, the largest a two-story condo. A welcoming pool is the centerpiece of the grounds. Ask for a room facing the lagoon, as the street-side generator can be loud. Discounts are often given for stays of a week or longer.

Wind Chime Condos (☎ 809-889-2203; studio US$60, 2-bedroom apt US$85; ⊠ ⊠ P) Although set on somewhat barren grounds, the studios and apartments in this complex, on the eastern side of town, are quite pleasant. Each is spacious, well appointed and gets lots of direct sunshine. All also have a private balcony or terrace. Discounts for stays of a week or longer.

Hotel Kaoba (☎ 809-571-0300; www.kaoba.com; r US$37-40, tw US$40-44, s/d studio per person US$42-47/46-50; ⊠ P ⊠ ⊑) The Kaoba has 25 charming bungalows set on lush grounds away from the main drag. Most rooms have kitchenettes but all have cable TV and minibars. The inviting pool welcomes guests as they enter the complex and a restaurant/bar at the front of the hotel is often hopping.

Agualina (☎ 809-571-0805; www.agualina.com; Kite Beach; r US$70, studio US$85, apt US$150; ⊠ P ⊑ ⊠) Opened in 2004, this may be the most comfortable lodging in Cabarete. Studios and apartments have stylish, well-equipped kitchens – stainless steel refrigerators are an especially nice touch – and large modern bathrooms with glass showers and gleaming fixtures. There's a large late-model TV and free Internet access in the lobby.

Kite Beach Hotel (☎ 809-571-0878; www.kitebeach hotel.com; Carr a Sosúa; s/d US$52/58; s/d ste US$85/92; 1-bedroom apt US$140-160; ⊠ P ⊠ ⊠) Completely renovated in 2005, this oceanfront hotel boasts well-appointed rooms with gleaming tile floors, good-sized bathrooms

and satellite TV. All suites and apartments have balconies that afford at least partial ocean views and wireless Internet makes checking your email especially easy if you're traveling with your laptop. The laid-back pool area makes a great place to watch the action in the sky and on the water. An extensive breakfast buffet is also included in the rate.

Extreme (☎ 809-571-0880; www.extremehotels.com; Carr a Sosúa; s/d US$45/60) Other than being painted extremely gray, there's not much that's over the edge at this place. Yeah, there's a skateboarding ramp but it costs extra to use it, yoga is offered but only once a week, and there's a kiteboarding school but then again every hotel on this beach has one. If you can see past the obvious marketing ploy though, the rooms here are quite nice; sleek in a low-key way, tile-floored and with balconies, it makes a comfortable place to crash for a few days or more. Breakfast included in the rate.

Sans Souci Beach (☎ 809-571-0755; sanssouci@ verizon.net.do; 1- or 2-bedroom apt per person US$20; ⊠) As soon as you drive into town, you'll see huge signs for the San Souci every 20m or so. That's because this German-owned hotel is a chain that operates seven aparta-hotels in Cabarete alone. At the eastern end of town, the Sans Souci Beach is the nicest of the lot with ocean-front property. Though showing some wear, rooms are clean and have cable TV. Most also have a sea-facing balcony. If this place is full, ask about availability in its six sister hotels down the strip. Prices start at US$12 per person based on double occupancy.

TOP END

Villa Taína Hotel (☎ 5809-571-0722; www.villataina .com; d garden/ocean view US$75/95; tw garden/ocean view US$95/120; ⊠ ⊑ ⊠) This appealing boutique-y hotel at the western end of town, has 55 tastefully decorated rooms, each with balcony or terrace, aircon, comfortable beds, in-room data ports and modern bathrooms. There is a small clean pool and a nice beach area fringed by palm trees. Guests can use the hotel kayaks and body boards for free and are given a complimentary 90 minute windsurf lesson and an hours board rental at Happy Surfpool, right in front. Breakfast is included in these prices listed and a half-board plan is available for an extra US$15; suites and deluxe suites are also available.

Tropical Beach Club Hotel (☎ 809-571-0725; www.tropicalclubs.com; on the beach, s/d US$85/130; ❌ Ⓟ ⓢ) Situated on the western side of town, this hotel features 46 beachfront rooms on a nice stretch of sand. All are decorated in a colonial style and half have ocean views. Two swimming pools with whirlpools, a bar and a good restaurant are also on the premises. Prices drop considerably in the low season. All-inclusive plans available for US$24 extra per person.

Tropical Casa Laguna (☎ 809-571-0725; www.tropicalclubs.com; d per person US$94; ❌ Ⓟ ⓢ) An all-inclusive resort in a town filled with independent travelers is an anomaly but nevertheless, the Tropical Casa Laguna is a busy place. Located in the center of town, and renovated in 2003, rooms are comfortable and have modern amenities. The grounds, however, are somewhat lacking – the vegetation is sad looking, the pool is neglected and there is only one restaurant to eat at. Considering how much food costs in this town though, it's not a bad deal. Guests can also use the beach facilities at the affiliated Tropical Beach Club just down the street.

Windsurf Resort (☎ 809-571-0718; www.windsurf cabarete.com; r US$60, 1-bedroom apt US$85, 2-bedroom apt US$149; ❌ Ⓟ ⓢ 🖥) This condominium complex in the eastern end of town boasts 60 comfortable apartments with fully equipped kitchens and balconies. The well-tended grounds also hold two bars (including one swim-up), an international restaurant and a travel office.

Azzuro (☎ 809-571-0808; www.azzurroclubs.com; d per person US$85-90) Rooms in the new wing of this recently renovated all-inclusive resort, in the west end of town, have slate floors, a terrace, a minifridge, up-to-date furnishing, and are definitely worth the few extra dollars over those in the old wing. The pool area has a desert oasis theme going on, with artificial sandstone formations that manage not to be too tacky. The sloping beach is bit dune-like, though nicely shaded by almond trees. Building numbers one, six and seven have ocean views.

Eating

Cabarete's beach is lined with restaurant after restaurant, all boasting open-air dining areas facing the water. The view and breeze

are terrific, but you definitely pay a premium for it. A few of the beach-side restaurants are worth the splurge, but in general you'll find much better value off the beach.

BUDGET

Hexenkessel (☎ 809-571-0493; mains US$3.50-11; ⏱ 24hr) Reminiscent of a German beer garden, this eatery on the eastern side of town makes a great place to sit back, have a burger and drink a couple of beers. Clients sit side by side at picnic tables and can order such house specialties as potato pancakes with ground beef (US$6.50), fried Bavarian bratwurst (US$4) and, if you order a day in advance, whole roasted pork knuckle with sauerkraut (US$20). Fried fish, pizza and pastas are also available for those who are trying to lay off animal joints.

Coco Rico (☎ 809-847-1094; mains US$6-12; ⏱ dinner) Easy to miss at the end of a commercial walkway, this low-key French-run eatery, in the western end of town, is worth looking for. The only place in town to have real rotisserie chicken, served in huge half- or whole-bird portions with boiled veggies and fries. Look for daily seafood specials too, from fish lasagna to grilled mahi mahi. Red checkerboard tablecloths and simple wood tables complete an appealing provincial look.

Beach Break Sandwicherie (mains US$3.50-6; ⏱ lunch & dinner) This tiny eatery in the west side of town serves up French-inspired goodies like crêpes, quiche, and make-your-own baguettes. Portions are large and service is quick. Great for taking to the beach.

Panadería Repostería Dick (☎ 809-571-0612; mains under US$3-6; ⏱ 7am-6pm, closed Wed) Locally famous for its fresh baked bread and large international breakfasts – the German has ham and boiled eggs, the English has scrambled eggs, sausage, ham and potatoes, the Dominican has scrambled eggs with salami and cheese etc, all for under US$4. Breakfast is served until 1pm, then good sandwiches and pie are on offer. Located on the western side of town.

Restaurante China (☎ 809-571-0385; mains US$4-11; ⏱ lunch & dinner) Although the dingy setting is less than appealing, the continually packed dining room is testament to the quality of the food. More than 100 dishes make up the menu and regardless of what you order, food comes almost immediately and is always piping hot. On the west side of town.

NORTH COAST

Bon Ice Cream (cones from US$1.50; ☺ 11:30am-11pm) If you want a cool treat, Bon offers over 30 flavors of ice cream and frozen yogurt in its airconditioned shop in the center of town.

Groceries

There are three supermarkets in Cabarete, one in the center and the remaining two at the opposite ends of town. Of these, **Janet's Supermarket** (Carr a Gasper Hernandez; ☺ 8am-8pm Mon-Sat, 8am-1pm Sun) on the eastern end of town is the biggest and has the best selection of canned food, produce, baked goods and toiletries.

MIDRANGE

Paradise (☎ 809-979-4863; mains US$7-12; ☺ 8am-11pm) Tucked in between a sandwich shop and an uninspired miniature golf course on the west end of town, this open-air eatery offers excellent Italian, French and fusion specialties. Dishes are nicely presented and service is excellent. For a change of pace, try the chicken curry pasta (US$8); if you like spicy food, you'll love this dish. Delivery is available.

La Casa del Pescador (☎ 809-571-0760; on the beach; mains US$7-16) This seaside seafood restaurant in the center of town, with its little wooden tables and so-so decor, is none too fancy but the food is very good. Among the more popular items are the fish of the day, seafood spaghetti and lobster. For dessert, try the banana flambé.

Ho-La-La Café (809-571-0806; mains US$10-20; ☺ 10am-midnight) Fancy seaside restaurant in the middle of town serving high-quality French cuisine in a cool classy dining area that opens onto the beach. Shrimp with passion fruit sauce is a favorite, as well as surf-and-turf with very recently deceased lobster (from a tank) and perfectly grilled meat.

Miró's on the Beach (☎ 809-571-0888; mains US$12-17; ☺ 3pm-midnight) What started out as a pizzeria in 1986 is now Cabarete's longest-operating restaurant and arguably its finest. The pizzas are long gone, replaced by high quality Moroccan food (and other select international fare) served in a classy, slightly bohemian setting located in the middle of town. Specialties include duck tagine with couscous, 'Calypso curry' made of seafood slow-simmered in coconut milk and curry masala, Asian-seared tuna served

with wasabi and the list goes on and on. Great ocean views, rotating art exhibits and Saturday night live jazz round out an altogether excellent dining experience.

Blue Moon Hotel & Restaurant (☎ 809-223-0614, 809-883-1675; Los Brazos; mains US$15; ☺ dinner, by reservation only) On 38 acres of rolling hills a short drive from Cabarete, this bungalow-style hotel and restaurant hosts family-style Indian dinners that are popular with kiteboarding and windsurfing schools. The Blue Moon requires a minimum of eight people for its dinners, but independent travelers can often tag along when there's a larger group scheduled. Dinner is served in a round thatched kiosk, with cushions arranged in a large circle on the floor. Food is served on banana leaves and is always quality South Asian fare, including two different veggie dishes, a main course like Tandoori or curried chicken or fish, rice, salad, coffee, tea and dessert. The **bungalows** (US$50) include breakfast in the price, are cool and comfortable with inventive Indian-style decor and a sitting area and library in each one. To get there from Cabarete, head east on the highway to Sabaneta and turn right on the road to Jamao al Norte. Proceed a few kilometers and you'll pass a bridge in the town of Los Brazos where you should begin looking for a sign to your left as you climb the hill.

Drinking & Entertainment

The drinking and party scene in Cabarete is fun and predictably raucous, with bars open to the wee hours almost every night of the week. It's also extremely easy to follow – like surf and ski towns elsewhere, everyone goes to the same spots with the same people and exchanges the same stories, most of which begin with 'No shit, there I was…'

In Cabarete, everyone starts the night at **LAX** (☺ 9am-1am) a mellow bar – the name comes from 'relax' not the airport in LA – with drink specials and house music, and pizzas until 10:30pm in case you get hungry.

Around 11pm or midnight everyone migrates down the beach to either **Onno's** (☎ 809-571-0461; ☺ 9am-5am) or **Bambú** (☺ 6pm-6am), adjacent bars where the party starts in earnest, with video screens, crazy drink specials – three-for-one cocktails, half-price *pitchers* of Cuba libre etc – and hours of dancing. Somewhere around 4am, people begin making their way home – good thing the wind doesn't pick up until the afternoon. (Pity the surfers though – the best waves are at 6am.)

Las Brisas (☎ 809-571-0614; ☘ 8am-5am) is a short distance away and the only place that plays primarily Latin dance music, especially merengue and salsa. The scene is a little seedy though, notwithstanding the huge signs reading 'No one under 18, no firearms, no drugs.'

Shopping

Plagued by row upon row of kitschy souvenir shops, this town thankfully has a couple of shops that break the mold.

Carib Bic Center (☎ 809-571-0640; ☘ 9am-7pm) Located at the east end of town, this is the best of the smattering of shops catering to water-sports enthusiasts. Here you'll find a good variety of sporting equipment and accessories. A fine selection of hipster clothing is also on hand.

Planet Arte (☎ 809-571-3686; ☘ 8am-10pm) Unless you enjoy the hunt, this boutique is the best place in town to find high quality and unique handicrafts. Items sold include handmade paper, amber and larimar jewelry, polished coconut objects and clothing you could actually wear back home. Situated in the center of town.

Getting There & Around

Minibuses heading east to Río San Juan (US$1.75, one hour) and west to Sosúa (US$1, 30 minutes) and Puerto Plata (US$1.75, one hour) trundle through town every 15 to 30 minutes picking up passengers anywhere along the way. **Taxis** (☎ 809-571-0767;) are good for getting to Kite Beach (US$3), Playa Encuentro (US$10/18 one way/return). *Motoconchos* cover the same ground for significantly less but there have been a number of accidents so take care to pick a driver who's not overly aggressive. You can rent cars at any number of agencies with booths along the main drag. At the east end of town, try **Sandro's Rent A Car** (☎ 809-571-9716; www.sandroreantacar.com; per day from US$40; ☘ 8am-6pm).

RÍO SAN JUAN
pop 8983

A world away from the hustle and bustle of Sosúa and Cabarete, Río San Juan is a sleepy seaside town that's near two of the

North Coast's best beaches, and has excellent snorkeling and diving nearby. There are only a couple of hotels – fortunately one is quite good and surprisingly affordable – and not much in the way of nightlife. You'll find all the basic services here, including bank, Internet and pharmacy, and Cabarete is an easy drive or *gua-gua* ride away. The best reason to come here (besides the diving and the beaches) is to enjoy some small town tranquility, which isn't always easy to find on this coast.

Information
EMERGENCY
Politur (Tourist Police; ☎ 809-754-3241; ☘ 24hr) Located on the highway, 600m west of Calle Duarte.

INTERNET ACCESS
J&R.net (☎ 809-589-2325; Calle 30 de Marzo; per hr US$2.10; ☘ 8am-8:30pm Mon-Sat, 8am-noon Sun) Between Duarte & Capotillo.

Solan@.com (☎ 809-549-2498; Calle Capotillo; per hr US$2.10; ☘ 8am-noon, 2-8pm Mon-Sat) Between 30 de Marzo & Padre Billini.

MEDICAL SERVICES
Farmacia Reyes (☎ 809-589-2234; Calle Duarte at Calle Luperón; ☘ 8am-noon, 2-6pm Mon-Fri, 8am-noon Sat)

MONEY
Banco Progreso (Calle Duarte at Generoso Alvarado; ☘ 8:30am-4pm Mon-Fri, 9am-1pm Sat) One 24-hr ATM.

POST
Post Office (Calle Duarte; ☘ 8am-5pm Mon-Fri, 8am-noon Sat) Between Calles Mella and Rufino Bulbuena.

TELEPHONE
Verizon Centro de Comunicaciones (☎ 809-589-2736; Calle Duarte at Calle Mella; to USA per min US$0.30, to Europe per min US$0.75; ☘ 8am-10pm)

TOURIST INFORMATION
Tourist Office (☎ 809-589-2831; Calle Mella at Calle 16 de Agosto; ☘ 8am-4pm Mon-Fri) Staffers offer little information but there are plenty of maps and brochures on hand.

Sights & Activities
LAGUNA GRI-GRI
This lagoon at the northern end of Calle Duarte was once Río San Juan's claim to fame, drawing tourists from near and far for boat rides through it's tangled mangrove

channels. Unfortunately, overuse and the growth of Río San Juan have left the lagoon quite polluted – swimming is no longer recommended – and the water and mangroves are less picturesque than they once were. That doesn't prevent a dozen or more boatmen from offering tours of the lagoon, which typically cost US$30 for up to seven people and last around an hour, with visits to the mangrove forests, some interesting rock formations and a cave populated by hundreds of swallows. You'll get pretty much the same tour if you book a snorkeling trip with Gri-Gri Divers (see Diving & Snorkeling), plus you get to go snorkeling. You can also visit the lagoon on foot – there's a path from the Hotel Bahía Blanca to the water's edge, where you turn right to head into the mangroves.

PLAYA CALETÓN

Located about 1km east of town, this small bay is a peaceful and beautiful place to spend an afternoon. The tawny sand is lapped by teal waters, and almond trees interspersed with towering palms which provide plenty of shade. Food stands are near the entrance. The easiest way to get here is to take a *gua-gua* (US$0.35) or *motoconcho* (US$1) to the turnoff, from which it's a 200m walk down a rocky access road past a goat farm to the beach. If you have a car, you can make it all the way to the beach, but take it slow on the rough parts.

PLAYA GRANDE

Just 15km east of Río San Juan is Playa Grande, one of the most beautiful beaches in the Dominican Republic. Here, the long, broad tawny beach has aquamarine water on one side and a thick fringe of palm trees on the other, with stark white cliffs jutting out into the ocean in the distance. It's a picture postcard everywhere you look. There are a number of facilities at the entrance – food stands selling snacks and beer, vendors renting beach chairs (US$1.75 per day), umbrellas (US$5 per day), snorkel equipment (half/full day US$10/15), body boards (hour/half-day/full-day US$5/10/20) and surfboards (hour/half-day/full-day US$10/20/25) plus a smattering of gift shops selling shell necklaces, bikinis and sunscreen. If you're interested in a quieter stretch of beach, start walking east along the

sand (an all-inclusive resort has claimed the far western end for its guests). The beach goes on for ages and you're sure to find plenty of secluded spots.

A word about safety: Playa Grande has heavy surf and a deceptively strong undertow. Riptides – powerful currents of water flowing out to sea – do form occasionally and tourists have drowned here in the past. Be conservative when swimming at Playa Grande, and children and less-experienced swimmers should probably not go in at all unless the surf is very low. If you do get caught in a riptide, swim parallel to the shore until you get out of the current and then swim in.

The area all around Playa Grande has been bought by hotel developers, who have put a gate across the road to the beach although it remains open to the public. If you take a *gua-gua* from town, most drivers will drive you right to the beach if you ask – it's not a detour for them as the beach road reconnects with the highway a couple of kilometers past the beach. Sometimes the gate is closed, however, in which case it's an easy 2km walk from the highway. You can also hire a *motoconcho* (US$2.50) or cab (US$10) to bring you directly to the beach.

PLAYA PRECIOSA

Off the same access road to Playa Grande but 500m east of it, is a steep path leading to a narrow and solitary beach known as Playa Preciosa (literally, beautiful beach). This spectacular stretch of sand is pounded by serious waves and few attempt to play in the surf. Those who do – typically surfers at dawn – do so for the thrill. A great place to relax and take in the sun, as long as you don't mind staying dry.

DIVING & SNORKELING

Opened in 1994 by a friendly American-British couple, Río San Juan's most established dive shop **Gri-Gri Divers** (☎ 809-589-2671; www.grigridivers.com; Calle Gastón F Deligne; ☑ 8am-5pm Mon-Sat) caters largely to divers staying at the nearby all-inclusives, but independent travelers will feel perfectly welcome on all dives. Río San Juan has a great variety of nearby dive sites, including **Seven Hills**, a collection of huge coral heads descending from 6m to 50m, and **Crab Canyon**, with a series of natural arches and swim-throughs.

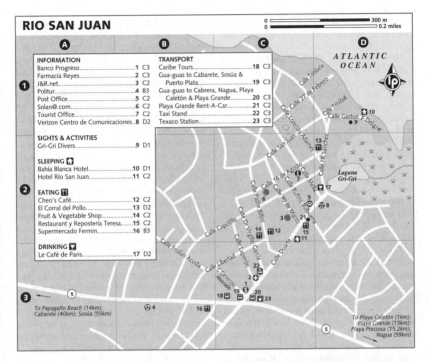

RIO SAN JUAN

INFORMATION	**TRANSPORT**
Banco Progreso..........................1 C3	Caribe Tours................................18 C3
Farmacia Reyes...........................2 C3	Gua-guas to Cabarete, Sosúa &
J&R.net......................................3 C2	Puerto Plata............................19 C3
Politur.......................................4 B3	Gua-guas to Cabrera, Nagua, Playa
Post Office..................................5 C2	Caletón & Playa Grande...........20 C3
Solan@.com................................6 C2	Gua-guas to Cabrera, Nagua, Playa
Tourist Office..............................7 C2	Taxi Stand..................................22 C3
Verizon Centro de Comunicaciones..8 D2	Texaco Station.............................23 C3
SIGHTS & ACTIVITIES	
Gri-Gri Divers..............................9 D1	
SLEEPING	
Bahía Blanca Hotel.......................10 D1	
Hotel Río San Juan......................11 C2	
EATING	
Cheo's Café................................12 C2	
El Corral del Pollo........................13 D2	
Fruit & Vegetable Shop.................14 C2	
Restaurant y Repostería Teresa......15 C2	
Supermercado Fermín...................16 B3	
DRINKING	
Le Café de Paris..........................17 D2	

Inland is **Dudu Cave**, one of the best freshwater cavern dives in the Caribbean. The waters here are rich with animal life, including octopuses, scorpionfish, barracuda, lobsters, sponges, yellow stingrays and even sea turtles. During whale season, you can hear humpback whale songs, which range from low growls to high-pitch squeals. On some dives, there are opportunities to snorkel on shallow wrecks during your surface interval. Prices start at US$40 per tank (US$45 with equipment rental) and go down according to the number of dives you book – a 10-dive package works out to US$28 per dive if you have your own gear, US$30 if not. Snorkel trips (US$30 per person, two hours) include snorkeling in two spots, plus a tour of Gri-Gri lagoon and a stop at Playa Caletón. Certification courses are available.

GOLF

Playa Grande Golf Course (☎ 809-582-0860; Carretera a Nagua; nine/18 holes US$65/120; ⏰ 7am-4:30pm) is a par-72 course built on a verdant cliff above Playa Grande. It is a well-tended course that boasts a spectacular ocean view from almost every hole. Caddies and carts are obligatory but not included in the rate (US$15 extra for 18 holes). Multigame discounts also are available.

Sleeping

There are two acceptable hotels in town – one much better than the other – and three outside of town. The accommodations outside of town are all very different – one's a large all-inclusive resort, another's a boutique hotel, and the third has rustic beach-side cabañas – but each can be well-recommended within its category.

Bahía Blanca Hotel (☎ 809-589-2563; Calle Gaston F Deligne; bahia.blanca.dr@verizon.net.do; r US$15-35) Jutting out over teal blue waters, the Bahía Blanca has one of the best ocean views on the North Coast. Rooms are decent – clean, tile-floored and with private bathrooms – but are showing their age. All but two have at least partial ocean views but wide balconies on each of the three floors provide plenty of opportunities to enjoy the beauty. Rooms on the third floor are the most spacious

NORTH COAST

and have small private balconies. The hotel is also flanked by two calm bays, which are great for swimming.

Hotel Río San Juan (☎ 809-589-2402; Calle Duarte; r US$20-25) If you ever wondered what your high school would look like if it were converted into a hotel, wonder no more. The Hotel Río San Juan, near Calle 30 de Marzo, offers painted cinderblock rooms, industrial carpeting and overhead fluorescent lights. Frankly, the only things missing are chalkboards and lunch ladies. That said, if you're in a pinch, this hotel will do; beds are a little saggy and the rooms could be a little cleaner but they're tolerable for a night.

Occidental Allegro Playa Grande (☎ 809-320-3988; www.occidentalhotels.com; s/d per person US$118/98; 🍴 P 🐾 🖳) Located on a cliff above Playa Grande, the all-inclusive Occidental Allegro is set on pleasant grounds that are surrounded by a private golf course. Rooms are clean and comfortable, though the bathroom doors are made of partially frosted glass so be aware that your roommate will be able to see you showering and, er, going about your business. Food is offered at a buffet restaurant, two à la carte places and a snack bar, and receives excellent reviews. The biggest selling point here, however, is its direct access to glorious Playa Grande; the resort even has a snack bar on the beach for guests. Reduced rates to the golf course are also offered.

Hotel La Catalina (☎ 809-589-7700; www.lacatalina.com; Cabrera; s/d US$71/98, s/d 1-bedroom apt US$89/138, 2-bedroom apt US$178; 🍴 P 🐾) Perched on a lush hill several kilometers east of Río San Juan proper, La Catalina offers charming and airy rooms with modern amenities like cable TV, in-room telephones and mini-fridges. All rooms and most common areas have spectacular views of the Atlantic Ocean and the palm-studded countryside. A full breakfast is included in the rate and is served in a classy, upscale restaurant. Free shuttles takes guests to and from Playa Grande but rental cars make exploring the area that much easier.

Papagallo Beach (☎ 809-844-3452; www.papagallobeach.com; Playa Magante; r US$50) Five simple beachside bungalows built of wood with thatched roofs, somewhat grubby bathrooms, plywood porches with hammocks and mosquito nets over the beds. Some are definitely better than others so look at a few. The broad unkempt beach is strewn with shells and driftwood and has a rustic charm. The draw here is definitely the isolation – it's a good 3km from the highway, 14km west of Río San Juan. Scuba dives can sometimes be arranged and breakfast is included.

Eating & Drinking

Restaurant y Repostería Teresa (Calle Duarte; mains US$3.50-9; 🕑 breakfast & lunch) Inside a yellow clapboard house, near Calle 30 de Marzo,

---

SALVAGING SUNKEN GALLEONS

During the colonization of the New World, galleons left Europe carrying supplies to the colonies and returned loaded with exports like gold, silver, tropical woods, tobacco and sugar. Thousands of these ships sank in the turquoise waters of the Caribbean Sea, overcome by looting pirates or devastating hurricanes. Both resulted in a tremendous loss of lives and cargo.

The frequency of shipwrecks spurred the Spanish to organize operations to recover sunken cargo. By the 17th century, Spain maintained salvage flotillas in the ports of Portobelo (Panama), Havana (Cuba) and Veracruz (Mexico). These fleets awaited news of shipwrecks and then proceeded immediately to the wreck sites, where Caribbean and Bahamian divers – and later African slaves – were employed to scour sunken vessels and the sea floor around them.

As early as the 1620s, salvagers used bronze diving bells to increase the time they could spend underwater. The bells were submerged vertically from a ship so that air pockets were formed in the upper ends. Divers would enter the bell to breathe and rest. Over time, divers became very skilled and the salvaging business became quite lucrative. So much so that the English, who were established in Bermuda and the Bahamas, entered the Caribbean salvage business as well.

Today, advances in diving and underwater-recovery equipment have led to a boom in Caribbean salvaging efforts. In most cases, salvagers are allowed to keep a portion of the treasure they recover, but the larger share is turned over to the government in whose waters the recovery takes place.

you'll find this charming eatery with a handful of tables. Patrons are treated to excellent Dominican fare, good-sized portions and friendly service. Travelers will happily discover that locals eat here too.

El Corral del Pollo (☎ 809-251-2192; Calle 16 de Agosto at Sánchez; mains US$7-16; ❍ breakfast, lunch & dinner) Specializing in Spanish food – paella, Spanish tortillas and gazpacho – this was the newest eatery in town when we passed through. A pleasant restaurant with bamboo walls, picnic tables and a gravel floor, this is a popular dining spot with tourists after a boat ride on the lagoon. Lunch specials include a salad, choice of entrée, drink and dessert for US$8.

Le Café de Paris (☎ 809-844-4899; Sánchez; mains US$5-16; ❍ breakfast, lunch & dinner) Directly in front of the lagoon, near Calle Duarte, this French-owned café is a good spot to have a drink and watch boats launch from the pier. The food is varied – a little Italian, lots of French and some seafood – but forgettable. Stick with the beer and catch up on your postcards.

Cheo's Café (☎ 809-589-2290; Calle Padre Billini; mains US$7-15; ❍ lunch & dinner) This friendly little café is off the main drag between Calles Libertad & Capotillo, and has a palapa roof, wooden floor and walls, and plastic tables covered with tablecloths. The menu includes *conejo al coco* (rabbit in coconut sauce) and *parrillada de marisco* (large platter of grilled seafood, usually served for two people), in addition to familiar beef, chicken and pasta dishes. Popular with locals and travelers alike.

Supermercado Fermin (Hwy 5; ❍ 8am-noon & 2-8pm) Located just west of Calle Duarte, this supermarket has a good selection of canned goods, produce and dairy. There's also a small **fruit and vegetable shop** (❍ 6am-7pm) at the corner of Calles Libertad and Padre Billini.

Getting There & Around

Caribe Tours (☎ 809-589-2644; Hwy 5), just west of Calle Duarte, provides a bus service between Río San Juan and Santo Domingo (US$7, 4½ hours) and stops along the way at Nagua (US$1.75, 45 minutes) and San Francisco de Macorís (US$2.80, 2½ hours). Buses depart at 6:30am, 7:45am, 9:30am, 2pm and 3:30pm.

Gua-guas come and go from the intersection of Calle Duarte and Hwy 5, known around town as simply *la parada* (the stop). West-bound *gua-guas* line up at the northwest corner of the intersection, departing every 15 minutes from 6am to 5pm for Cabarete (US$1.75, one hour), Sosúa (US$2.50, 1½ hours) and Puerto Plata (US$3.50, two hours).

Eastbound *gua-guas* line up on the northeast corner of the same intersection and leave every 10 minutes from 6:30am to 6pm for Playa Caletón (US$0.35, five minutes), Playa Grande (US$0.50, 15 minutes) and Nagua (US$1.75, 1¼ hours). From Nagua you can catch *gua-guas* to Samaná or 1st-class buses to Santo Domingo; see Nagua for details (below). If your bags take up more space than your lap, you may be charged double fare.

There's a **taxi stand** (☎ 809-589-2501) on Calle Duarte between Calles Luperón and Dr Virgilio García. The fare to Playa Caletón is US$10 and to Playa Grande is US$15. If you prefer to take a *motoconcho*, a fleet can be found at the main intersection throughout most of the day. Rides to Playa Caletón cost around US$1 and about US$2.50 to Playa Grande.

Playa Grande Rent-a-Car (☎ 809-589-2391; Calle Duarte 15 at Calle Rufino Balbuena; ❍ 8am-6pm) rents cars starting at around US$42 per day, taxes and insurance included.

NAGUA

pop 33,862

On the coastal highway 36km northwest of Sánchez and 54km southeast of Río San Juan, Nagua is a hot, dusty town whose interest to tourists is strictly as a transportation hub. It is the main transfer point for *gua-guas* heading in either direction along the coastal highway. The inland road to San Francisco de Macorís, Moca and Santiago begins here as well, meaning you can catch a *gua-gua* to just about anywhere from here.

To catch a coastal bus, simply walk to the coastal highway and wave down a *gua-gua* going the direction you want. To catch an inland-bound bus, you must go to the intersection of the two highways and hail a bus that is turning off of the coastal highway onto the inland highway. There are usually a few people waiting for the same bus there and are usually happy to point you to the right bus. *Gua-guas* on the coastal road pass every 15 minutes, while inland buses can take up to an hour.

NORTH COAST

Caribe Tours (☎ 809-584-4505; Calle Mella at Emilio Conde) has services to Santo Domingo at 7:30am, 8am, 8:50am, 9:30am, 10:30am, 11am, 2pm, 3pm, 3:30pm, 4:30pm and 5pm. **Metro** (☎ 809-584-3159; Calle Sánchez 71) has identical service at 7am, 9:15am and 4:15pm, with an extra departure at 2:15pm Friday to Sunday. On both bus lines, the fare is US$6 and the trip takes 3½ hours.

WEST OF PUERTO PLATA

The coastal areas west of Puerto Plata see fewer foreign visitors than any other part of the North Coast. Those tourists who do visit typically come on organized tours from all-inclusive resorts and stay just for the day – Punta Rusia and the Imbert waterfalls are especially popular. To be sure, travelers with limited time are unlikely to head this direction – there is just too much to see and do elsewhere. But if you have time, the area can make for a rewarding several days. The town of Luperón has a great beach and a variety of good eating and sleeping options. Parque Nacional La Isabela marks the first organized European settlement in the New World. The town of Monte Cristi has excellent snorkeling and diving (if you can find someone to take you out) and a notoriously rowdy Carnival celebration. It is also the gateway to the border town of Dajabón, where a fascinating Haitian market is held twice weekly.

IMBERT
pop 8024
About 22km southwest of Puerto Plata, connected by a well-maintained two-lane stretch of Hwy 5 that winds through sugarcane fields and rolling farm and cattle country, is the small roadside community of Imbert.

The one and only reason to come here is to visit a set of **waterfalls** on the Río Damajagua. Twenty-something falls crash down the steep, rocky hillside – an impressive sight diminished only by the large tour groups that often stop here.

To get to the falls, go south from Imbert on the highway for 3.3km (and crossing two bridges) until you see a sign on your left with pictures of a waterfall. From there it's a five minute drive down a dirt road through cane fields (there's one fork, where you

should turn right) to the river and a large parking area. Ford the river on foot – it's shallow – and follow a wide muddy path to the falls. There is no admission fee, but guides hanging around will insist you hire their services. It's hardly necessary with all the tour group traffic; then again, it should be less than US$10 and it is a good way to support the local economy.

The big Texaco station at Imbert serves as a crossroad for the entire area. There is a frequent *gua-gua* service to Santiago (US$2.25, 1¼ hours), Luperón (US$1.50, 40 minutes) and Puerto Plata (US$1, 30 minutes).

LUPERÓN
pop 4393
Luperón is a quiet town with a large contingent of expats. Located 54km west of Puerto Plata by road, it has a big beautiful beach (appropriately called Playa Grande) and has a pleasant friendly atmosphere not always in high supply in expat-heavy towns. The lodging and food is also less expensive here than many coastal towns.

Orientation
The road from Imbert enters Luperón from the south. Staying to your left, the highway becomes Calle Duarte and eventually intersects with Calle 27 de Febrero, Luperón's main east-west drag. That intersection is the commercial center of town. The town park is a few blocks east of there, while Playa Grande and Marina Puerto Blanco are a kilometer west and Parque Nacional La Isabela beyond that.

Information
Verizon Centro de Comunicaciones (Calle Duarte at 27 de Febrero; to USA per min US$0.30, to Europe per min US$0.75; ☼ 8am-10pm Mon-Sat, 8am-6pm Sun) is a half-block north of the main intersection and has international phone service and Internet access (per hr US$1.40). The **post office** (Calle Luperón; ☼ 8am-noon, 2-5pm Mon-Fri, 8am-noon Sat) is on the east side of the park.

BanReservas (☼ 8am-5pm Mon-Fri, 9am-1pm Sat) and **Politur** (☎ 809-581-8045; ☼ 24hr) are across the street from each other on Calle Duarte at 16 de Agosto, four blocks south of town, near the *gua-gua* stop.

Farmacia Danessa (☎ 809-571-8201; Calle Independencia; ☼ 7:30am-10pm) is on the west side of the park.

Sights & Activities

Luperón doesn't have much in the way of sights and activities, but it is the nearest town to Parque Nacional La Isabela (p206), which is worth a visit and has a pretty beach nearby.

Luperón has one of the best beaches west of Puerto Plata in **Playa Grande**, a long broad swath of thick yellow sand lapped by pretty blue water. Though fronted by large all-inclusive resorts, there is easy public access and plenty of room for resort guests and non-guests alike. The main drawback are the sea urchins, which live in the large underwater patches of rock just offshore. Covered in spines, they are no fun to step on. Fortunately the water is clear enough that you can easily stick to the sandy areas while going in and out of the water. There are two entrances to the beach – one is a path running beside the Luperón Beach Resort and the other at the end of a well-marked dirt road off the highway another 700m further west. A *motoconcho* ride costs about US$1.50.

Sailing is on offer west of town in the Marina Puerto Blanco, where large yachts and catamarans of all sizes are moored and their owners hang out at the pier bar and restaurant. There are no official tours, but visitors often ask around at the pier and find someone to take them sailing. Prices vary widely depending on the captain, but expect to pay US$30 to US$50 for a half-day trip, or US$60 to US$100 for a full day.

Sleeping

The Hotel Dally is the only lodging in town; the rest are west of the center.

Hotel Dally (☎ 809-571-8682; Calle 27 de Febrero at Calle Duarte; r US$17.50; apt s/d US$20/36) Right in the middle of town, the Dally's large rooms have high-ceilings, one queen-size bed and a small sofa or set of chairs. Bathrooms are aging but adequate and have hot water. There's a huge apartment, with separate living room and bedroom and a giant bathroom (and for the same price!), but it's reserved for families or larger groups. Enter through Restaurant Letty's on the corner.

La Casa del Sol (☎ 809-571-8403; www.casadelsol .de.ms; Calle 27 de Febrero; r US$20, with aircon & hot water US$25; 🖳) This German-run hotel, set on a leafy lot about 100m west of La Yola Bar Restaurant, features five comfortable rooms

each with large firm beds and high ceilings and some with sofas or chairs and table. The hotel is a 1.5km walk from town and 1.5km from the beach, and rents bikes and scooters to guests for rock-bottom prices. There's a recommended restaurant on-site – breakfast for guests only, but everyone's welcome from 3pm.

Pequeño Mundo (☎ 809-264-3511; extension of Calle 27 de Febrero; d/q US$24.50/31.50; 🖳 🖳) A friendly German-Dominican couple runs this small hotel 2km west of town. All five rooms are spacious with a small fridge, cold-water bathrooms, high ceilings and a small table and chairs, but only two rooms have aircon. The furthest of the hotels from town, but the only one with a swimming pool.

Tropical Luperón Beach (☎ 809-571-8303; www .besthotels.es; Carretera de las Américas; per person US$110-150; 🖳) and **Luperón Beach Resort** (per person US$90-125; 🖳) are sister hotels facing Playa Grande and sharing a number of the same facilities. The grounds are tidy though a bit plain, but the pool is very nice and the beach even better. Like most all-inclusives, the rooms and food service are ok but not terrific. All rooms have balconies either facing the ocean or the grounds. Windsurfing, sailing, horseback riding and scuba clinics in the pool are available.

Hotel Iberostar Costa Dorada (☎ 809-320-1000; www.iberostar.com; Carretera Luperón Km 2.5; d per person US$125-200; 🖳) Just 15km from the airport, the Iberostar Costa Dorada offers 516 rooms on beautifully manicured grounds right on the ocean. Accommodations aren't fancy but they're adequate, clean and comfortable. The pool is immense and is curved in such a way to create pod-like sections, which lend a private feel to them. The beach is shaded with more almond trees than palm trees but is beautiful nonetheless. The food here also receives praise. Overall, a fine choice.

Eating & Drinking

La Yola Bar Restaurant (☎ 809-571-8511; Calle 27 de Febrero; mains US$4-15; 🕑 late breakfast, lunch & dinner) This pleasant, open-sided, thatch-roofed restaurant 500m west of the center isn't on the water yet always seems to catch a refreshing sea breeze. The most popular items here are seafood, but the goat, chicken and pork dishes are also good. Pizzas and pasta start at just US$4.

Gina's (Calle Duarte at 27 de Febrero; mains US$3-8; ⏲ lunch & dinner Mon-Sat, dinner only Sun, closed Fri) With great homey food, a friendly ambience and always hopping with one thing or another – dice games, pool tourney etc – Gina's is definitely Luperón's most appealing eatery (and the best bar). Cheeseburgers with fries may be the most popular item, but the menu also includes sandwiches, wraps, shish-kabobs and huge nacho plates. The small open-air dining area is on the 2nd floor and gets great breezes, and food is made fresh in front of your eyes at small burners behind the bar. Half a block north of the main intersection.

Entertainment

Cinema Café (Calle Duarte; admission US$2.10) A bakery by day and movie theatre by night, come here to see recent Hollywood movies shown on a 9ft screen with a digital projector in full-surround sound. Shows are on Tuesday, Thursday, Saturday and Sunday, with an extra Spanish-language Sunday matinee for local kids. The popcorn, hotdogs and soda on sale will make you feel right at home. The bakery, open 8am to 2pm daily except Sunday, has tasty sweets and pastries. Movie times vary, stop by for the latest. One block north of main intersection.

Mi Sueño (Calle 27 de Febrero at park; admission free; ⏲ 9pm-2am Thu-Sun) Luperón's only nightclub starts getting lively around 11pm, with a mix of Latin, rock and house music.

Getting There & Away

Gua-guas to Imbert (US$1, 40 minutes, every 15 minutes, 5am to 6:40pm) leave from a stop on Calle Duarte at 16 de Agosto, four blocks south of Calle 27 de Febrero. From Imbert you can pick up *guaguas* headed south to Santiago or north to Puerto Plata.

PARQUE NACIONAL LA ISABELA

La Isabela National Park (admission US$1.75; ⏲ 8am-6pm) contains the remains of the first European settlement on Hispaniola. Or maybe the second – it depends on who you ask and what you mean by 'settlement.'

On his first voyage, Columbus swung by present-day Bahamas and Cuba before coming to Hispaniola, where he came ashore near Cap-Haïtien, Haiti, around December 25, 1492. He set up a camp which he named Villa de Navidad – Christmas Village – in honor of his yuletide landing. The camp (or was it a settlement?) consisted of a fort and several houses. Columbus returned to Spain soon after, leaving 39 men to watch over La Navidad. But when he returned a year later, Columbus found everyone in Villa La Navidad dead and the camp burned to the ground. (It turned out the settlers had taken to kidnapping and raping native women, until a local chief had them all killed.) Columbus founded a new settlement 110km to the east, which he called La Isabela in honor of the Spanish queen (and which is now a national park).

Rangers at the park defend the large sign reading 'First European Settlement in the New World' by pointing out that La Isabela, unlike La Navidad, had a church, a cemetery, a storage facility and numerous permanent houses, including one for Columbus. Perhaps most importantly, La Isabela was the site of the first Catholic mass in the New World, held in its little church on January 6, 1494. La Isabela also lasted more than a year, though not by much – it was abandoned within five years in favor of present-day Santo Domingo.

The park was founded in 1998, although some celebrations of the 500th anniversary of Columbus' arrival and the first mass had been held there earlier. Though a worthwhile stop if only for its historical value, there's little left to see, save the stone foundations of the storage facility and Columbus' house, and a few protective walls. There used to be quite a lot more, but when a local official was ordered by dictator Rafael Trujillo to clean up the site, he had everything bulldozed into the bay. Some rubble has been recovered, but the effect was irreparably lost. (Trujillo apparently only wanted some trees cut back so visiting dignitaries could appreciate the ruins; he had the local official killed.)

There's a skeleton on display – a settler who probably died of malaria – and an interesting museum containing artifacts uncovered in and around the site, including rings and tools. There are also coins dating from 1474 and artists' renditions of what La Isabela looked like. The admission price covers entrance to the park, the museum and a personal guide, though it is customary to tip guides after your visit.

Across the road from the park is the mildly impressive **Templo de las Américas** (☼ 7am-6pm; admission free). It's a loose replica – though much larger – of La Isabela's original church and was built as part of the 500th anniversary celebrations. Mass was held here on January 6, 1994, to commemorate the one held in La Isabela.

Also nearby is **Playa Punta Deborah**, a broad outward curving beach with coarse sand and beautiful, ultra-calm water. There are a couple of small beach restaurants and usually at least one knick-knack stand that rents snorkel gear (US$3.50) – ask the vendor to point you in the direction of the best coral patches. When swimming or wading, be alert for sea urchins lurking in the rock patches in the shallows.

Hosteleria Rancho del Sol (☎ 809-696-0325; Carretera de las Américas; s/d with fan US$35/50, r with aircon US$60; ⏾ ⏾) located just outside the entrance to the national park, is an agreeable little hotel set on a large ocean-front plot. All eight rooms have a terrace with rocking chairs and ocean view, tile floors, hot water and are big enough for a queen-size bed, twin bed, plus a coffee table and chairs. The decor is a bit dated, but the rooms are very clean and comfortable and there's a swimming pool and kayaks for guest use. breakfast is included in rates and you can also ask here about boat trips to Cayo Arena, near Punta Rusia.

Getting There & Away

By far the easiest way to get to the national park is from Luperón, by car if you have one, or *motoconcho* or taxi if you don't. *Motoconchos* charge around US$3 one way, and US$8 for the round-trip with a one-hour wait. The same trip runs to about US$25 in a taxi.

It's possible, but somewhat harder, to get to La Isabela from the main highway between Santiago and Monte Cristi. Turn off at Laguna Salada and head north 25km to Villa Isabella, passing through Los Hidalgos on the way. (The signs can be a little confusing, so ask for 'El Castillo' – the town where the park is located – as you go.) The park is 7km from Villa Isabela, but the road is dirt and you have to cross two broad rivers – ask at a *motoconcho* stand in Villa Isabella how high the water is and if the car you're driving will make it across. After crossing the second river, turn right on the main road and you'll drive past the park – look for Templo de Las Américas on your right.

PUNTA RUSIA
pop 200

Punta Rusia is a laid-back fishing village at the end of several kilometers of muddy rutted road – and also an extremely popular destination for package tours from all-inclusive resorts. At one moment the town is quiet and peaceful, the next it's brimming with tourists in bikinis and floppy hats. Fortunately for independent travelers – most of whom come here seeking isolation, after all – the tour groups come and go like clockwork, and it's fairly easy to arrange your visit to avoid the crowds and enjoy the small town atmosphere. Punta Rusia is also well-known for its wild orchids, which grow on the branches of decaying trees. The trees are inland, beginning a couple of kilometers from the beach and 5km west of town.

Punta Rusia has no services to speak of, and virtually no stores, so you should stock up before going there. For excursions, try **El Paraíso Tours** (☎ 809-612-8499; wwwcayoparaíso.com) or **Cayo Arena Tours** (☎ 809-656-0020; www.cayoarenatours.com) located next to each other, just left (west) of where the road into town hits the beach road. Both agencies also rent rooms and have a restaurant service, and give discounts on tours to people staying with them (see p208).

Sights & Activities
CAYO ARENA

This is the place all the tour groups are headed, a picturesque sandbar island about 10km northwest of Punta Rusia which grows and shrinks according to the season and currents. Tour groups are shuttled there by speed boat to spend a couple of hours relaxing in the sun and snorkeling offshore, before returning to Punta Rusia, via coastal mangrove canals, for a buffet lunch. (There are small food shacks on the island as well.) The tour operators in Punta Rusia try to coordinate with each other so no more than 100 people are on the Caye at any one time, but even that's a fair crowd on an island that rarely grows bigger than 150m x 50m.

Both El Paraíso Tour and Cayo Arena Tours run daily trips to Cayo Arena, which independent travelers can join for around

US$30 per person, including unlimited drinks on the island and a buffet lunch afterward. Most trips leave at around 9:45am and return between 12:30pm and 1pm, but you can beat them to it by going to the island with the service and supply boat, which leaves Punta Rusia daily around 8:15am. You'll have the island to yourself for more than an hour. Otherwise, go on an afternoon boat, when there are fewer people. Assuming you're staying the night in Punta Rusia, you can come back as early or late as you like.

SAILING

Cayo Arena Tours offers all-day catamaran trips that include visiting La Isabela, coastal mangrove forests and a stop at Cayo Arena for just US$40 per person, including buffet lunch. They were also planning to offer a second similarly priced catamaran trip that instead of stopping at Cayo Arena would spend more time touring the coast, and would include two stops for snorkeling.

El Paraíso Tours offers independent travelers a good deal on a 'VIP' yacht tour that's a popular alternative to standard Cayo Arena tours. With just 30 passengers taken aboard a deluxe sailing yacht, the tour includes a visit to La Isabela, La Ensenada (a pretty bay), a champagne and oyster snack on-board, a lobster lunch back at Punta Rusia and the afternoon at Cayo Arena, including snorkeling and a return trip through the mangroves. The tour is normally US$145 per person, but those staying at Punta Rusia go for US$80.

DIVING

Ask at Cayo Arena Tours about diving trips around Punta Rusia. The diving is something of a one-man operation, so it's worth calling ahead to be sure he's available and has whatever rental equipment you need.

Sleeping & Eating

El Paraíso Tours (r US$30) and Cayo Arena tours (r US$30) also have rooms for rent. Both let rooms in the same large apartment complex across the street from their offices. The rooms are basically the same, with private cold-water bath, two large beds and a small terrace. They are far from deluxe, but about what you'd expect in this neck of the woods.

Hotel Restaurant Punta Rusia Sol (r US$42) has rooms which are nicer than the others, with firm beds, tile floors and hot water. They are a bit small, however, and the low ceilings and small windows don't help much on that score. Still, these are the best accommodations in town.

For food, you can join one of the tour group buffets for US$11, including drinks. There are also a number of **modest restaurants** (mains US$3-7) and beach-side fish stands that serve basic, cheap meals.

Getting There and Away

There is no regular bus service to Punta Rusia. If you have a car, there are two routes – one a 25km dirt road from Villa Isabel, which can be reached by paved roads from either Imbert or Highway 1 (turn off at Laguna Salada). You have to ford two rivers on this route, so ask in Villa Isabel about conditions. The other, and easier, route is from Villa Elisa, 20km west of Laguna Salada on Hwy 1. From there, the road north is paved for 8km and deteriorates steadily for the next 12km, but does not require you cross any rivers.

MONTE CRISTI
pop 17,000

In the northwest corner of the Dominican Republic is the city of Monte Cristi, the capital of the sparsely populated province of the same name. The majority of the town's residents make their living fishing and tending cattle and goats, just as they have done for generations. Another major source of revenue is salt, which is harvested from evaporation ponds north of town and sold in the USA by Morton Salt.

Monte Cristi's main attraction is Parque Nacional Monte Cristi, a little-visited national park that includes a huge flat-topped mountain, a pretty beach and the country's most pristine coral reefs. In town, the park clock tower and several restored Victorian-style houses are worth a passing look. Most tourists who spend a night here do so on their way to or from Haiti. The main northern border crossing is at Dajabón, 35km south of Monte Cristi.

History

One could say Monte Cristi was founded twice – during the 16th century and again in the 18th century. Like many of the towns that were settled in the northwest, its residents traded cattle hides for manufactured goods, with most commerce conducted by sea. When a surge in pirates scared off Spanish galleons at the end of the 16th century, residents began trading with Spain's enemies. In 1605 the king of Spain, furious with what he viewed as treasonous behavior by the Spanish colonists, ordered Monte Cristi to be abandoned and its people relocated to the Santo Domingo area.

For nearly 150 years, hot, dusty Monte Cristi remained a ghost town. Then French colonists began settling abandoned areas. Not wanting to lose control of the area, the Spanish Crown ordered that all of the depopulated towns in the northwest be repopulated. So in 1751 Monte Cristi was refounded with 100 families from the Spanish-ruled Canary Islands, who survived by raising cattle and goats. As time passed, Monte Cristi's natural harbor became an important port for export timber felled inland and floated down the Río Yaque del Norte. Many Europeans, attracted by the timber industry, settled here through the 18th century.

In the 1860s most of the city was destroyed during the four-year Restoration War, in which Dominicans fought Spanish troops to regain their independence. During the next three decades, Monte Cristi's European citizens built many Victorian-style homes, some of which are still standing.

Orientation

Highway 1 enters Monte Cristi from the east, where it turns into Calle Duarte and becomes the main east-west road through town. Main intersections include the ones with Mella (which turns into Hwy 45 south to Dajabón), Benito Monción (with a hotel,

call center and several restaurants) and San Fernando (which runs along the far side of the park and leads to the beaches and El Morro and Parque Nacional Monte Cristi. The main beach is called Playa Juan de Bolaños, though Playa Detras del Morro (literally 'Beach behind el Morro') is much nicer and from there you can take a short but rewarding hike to the top of a bluff for an incredible view.

Information

Just about everything you'll need is on or within a block or two of Calle Duarte.

Politur (☎ 809-754-2978; ☒ 24hr) has an office on Playa Juan de Bolaños. The **Policía Nacional** (☎ 809-579-2511; ☒ 24hr) has a station on Calle Duarte at the eastern end of town.

There's a **Verizon Centro de Llamadas** (call center; to USA per min US$0.30, to Europe per min US$0.75; ☒ 8am-midnight) inside an ice-cream shop on Av Benito Monción near Calle Duarte. The **post office** (☒ 8am-5pm Mon-Fri) is on Calle Duarte near Av Juan de la Cruz Álvarez. There is no public Internet in town.

Hospital Padre Fantino (☎ 809-579-2401; Av 27 de Febrero), located two blocks north of Calle Duarte, is a modest hospital with a 24-hour emergency room. **Farmacia Marcony** (☒ 8am-8pm Mon-Sat) is on Av San Fernando two and a half blocks north of Calle Duarte.

BanReservas (Calle Duarte; ☒ 8am-5pm Mon-Fri, 9am-1pm Sat), between Colón & Santiago Rodríguez, has a 24hr ATM.

Sights & Activities
PARQUE NACIONAL MONTE CRISTI

This 1100-sq-km national park surrounds Monte Cristi on three sides and consists of subtropical dry forest, numerous coastal lagoons, a cluster of small islands and a massive flat-topped hill called El Morro – at 239m above sea level, it is the highest coastal

---

WHAT A RIOT!

Monte Cristi is known around the country for its particularly savage Carnival celebration. Here, townspeople divide into two groups – the *toros* (bulls) who dress in bull masks and wear colorful costumes, and the *civiles* (civilians), without costumes. Both sides carry bull whips – the police measure them so they aren't too long – and spend every Sunday in February attacking each other in the street with great vigor. Participants all wear several layers of clothes, and are not supposed to hit anyone on the face, but bruises and bloody cuts are common and some people have even lost an eye. Observers are supposed to be free from attack, but you'd be wise to stay well off the street, or watch from a hotel or restaurant balcony.

promontory in the country. The park is home to 165 species of birds including great egrets, brown pelicans and yellow-crowned night herons. It also has one of the DR's few known manatee populations as well as solenodons, endangered possum-like creatures. Both are extremely hard to spot, however.

The park's chief ranger station is 5km northeast of Monte Cristi – follow Av San Fernando north of town to the beach and continue to your right past the Politur office until the road dead-ends. Opposite the ranger station, a long set of wooden stairs – 585 in all – lead to the top of El Morro. Unfortunately the stairs are in disrepair and have been closed since 2002; there are plans to restore them, but don't hold your breath. However, on the other side of the road, just before reaching the station, a dirt road (which quickly becomes a path) leads to the top of a secondary bluff that, although not nearly as big as El Morro, still affords an awesome view of the surrounding coastline. Playa Detras del Morro is reached via a short downhill path from the parking area by the ranger station.

BEACHES
The main public beach in Monte Cristi is **Playa Juan de Boloños**, a kilometer north of town where Av San Fernando hits the water. There are a few hotels, beach restaurants and a Politur office there. Several hundred meters off shore is **Isla Cabra**, which has a pretty beach you are almost guaranteed to have to yourself. Boatmen at the main beach can drop you off and pick you up later for US$25 (one to four people). **Playa Detras del Morro** is, sure enough, tucked behind the mountain in the national park. This is the prettiest beach in the area, a long slow curve of tan sand backed by a towering precipice. To get there, follow the main road past the Politur office almost 4km – just the first 100m or so is dirt road, the rest is well-paved – until dead-ending at the national park. There is no admission fee, and plenty of parking. A *motoconcho* ride here is around US$3; be sure to arrange a pick-up if you don't fancy walking all the way back.

SNORKELING & DIVING
The coastal waters around Monte Cristi contain the Dominican Republic's best-preserved coral reefs, which make for excellent snorkeling. Ask the officer in the Politur office on Playa Juan de Bolaños to set you up with a reliable boatman. The cost varies considerably and you'll have to bargain over the length and extent of your trip to get the price you're willing to pay.

There was no established dive center in Monte Cristi at the time of research, though there are some great dives in the area, including to the wreckage of a colonial-era Spanish Galleon in 60m of water. The Hostal San Fernando had plans to open a dive center – call ahead to see if they did.

PARQUE CENTRAL
Monte Christi's **city park** (Calle Duarte at San Fernando) is notable for the 50m clock tower at its center. The tower was designed by French engineer Alexandre Gustave Eiffel and looks like a miniature version of the same engineer's more famous tower in Paris. It was imported from France in March 1895, reassembled and inaugurated by Monte Cristi's mayor three months later. The clock tower was allowed to deteriorate, but in 1997 the Leon Jimenez family, of Aurora cigar and Presidente beer fortune, financed the tower's restoration.

In the immediate vicinity of the park are several dilapidated Victorian homes. Some have been partially restored, in some cases enough to appreciate their one-time glory.

Tours
Rather than haggling with local fishermen, it may be easier and more enjoyable to take an organized tour. Two local hotel-restaurants offer trips to the various sights around Monte Cristi.

Restaurante El Bistrot (☎ 809-579-2091; www .elbistrot.com; Calle San Fernando 26) and its sister hotel Los Jardines organize tours of **Los Cayos de los Siete Hermanos** (Cayes of the Seven Brothers), a collection of seven uninhabited islands in the national park, as well as tours of the area mangroves and wetlands. They also rent windsurfing equipment, do deep-sea fishing trips and conduct excursions to the Haitian market in Dajabón on Mondays and Fridays. Also available are interesting tours of Fort Liberté, King Christopher's Citadel and the Sans Souci Palace in Haiti. Tours around Monte Cristi start at around US$40 for a small group; trips to Haiti vary considerably in price according to the length of trip, number of people and conditions and availability in Haiti. Call in advance for reservations and up-to-date rates. Rooms in Hotel Los Jardines, located just west of Playa Juan de Boloños, are US$30 to US$40 with fan or aircon.

Hostal San Fernando (☎ 809-964-0248; road to El Morro) organizes group excursions, open to guests and non-guests alike. The most popular is a four- to five-hour tour of Los Cayos de los Siete Hermanos. The tour visits all seven islands, with a chance to swim and snorkel at two of them. There's also a 2½-hour tour through the coastal mangroves with a stop at Isla Cabra. Tours aren't cheap – US$315 and US$175 respectively for a group, and can accommodate up to 12 people. Assuming the other members of the jury stayed home, call ahead to see if you can join another group – you'll have the most luck on weekends. You can also try asking at the Politur office on Playa Juan de Bolaños about hiring a local boatman to take you on either route.

Sleeping

The hotels in town leave a great deal to be desired, but will do if you're on a tight budget. If you have a car, the hotels on the beach (1km north of town) are better value.

Chic Hotel (☎ 809-579-2316; Benito Monción; r with fan US$14, d/tw with aircon US$23/26; ☒) Rooms here are a bit grubby but have cable TV, small tables and decent beds. In the center of town, beside a cluster of busy eateries between Duarte & Rodríguez Carmargo, the hotel is convenient for the bus, restaurants and other services, but can get noisy in the evenings.

Hotel Don Gaspar (☎ 809-579-2477; Pte Jiménez at Calle Rodríguez Carmargo; r 1-/2-bedroom US$14/17) The 15 rooms in this older hotel are located in two floors above a restaurant and a disco that sees few patrons, but leaves the music blasting until the wee hours just in case. Rooms have ceiling fans, cold-water bathrooms and worn beds, some have cable TV. Between the two, the Chic is a better choice.

Hotel Montechico (☎ 809-579-2565; Playa Juan de Bolaños; d/tw with fan US$19/26, with aircon US$26/33; ☒ P) The best midrange option is impossible to miss – it's the huge hotel right

where Calle San Fernando hits the ocean. Clean modern rooms have good beds, high ceilings and some with pleasant wood-panel decor. All rooms have a balcony – definitely ask for one facing the ocean, as the view and sea breeze are terrific. Service can be a bit lacking here, however.

Aparta-Hotel Cayo Arena (☎ 809-579-3145; Playa Juan de Bolaños; Mon-Thu d/t/q US$53/70/88, Fri & Sat r US$88; ☒ ☒ P) The Cayo Arena is 100m west of the Hotel Montechico on a dirt road along the water. Eight very appealing two-bedroom apartments feature fully equipped kitchens, a spacious living room with attractive wicker furniture, one queen-size bed and two twin beds, cable TV and hot water in the bathrooms. Bicycles and kayaks are free for guest use – the sea here is incredibly calm, making for safe, easy paddling. Great if you're in a group and staying a while.

Hostal San Fernando (☎ 809-964-0248; s/d/tw US$42/48/51; ☒ ☒) Renovated, renamed and reopened in August 2003, this is definitely the nicest lodging available in Monte Cristi. On the road to El Morro, large rooms are in bungalow-like units with high, sloped ceilings, white-washed walls, firm beds and clean bathrooms and tile floors. All rooms have a small deck in front. A decent beach is right in front, and the national park is a 15 minute walk away.

Eating & Drinking

The **restaurant** (☎ 809-964-0248; mains US$7-15 ☒ breakfast, lunch and dinner) at Hostal San Fernando, on the road to El Morro, is also the best in town, with an open-air dining room on a raised platform so the ocean is visible through the trees. Full breakfasts start at US$4.50, and lunch and dinner plates include grilled chicken, and fillet of fish served in a half-dozen different ways, also at very reasonable prices.

Ocean (☎ 809-579-3643; Calle Benito Monción 1; mains US$5-15; ☒ 9am-midnight) Four blocks south of Calle Duarte – look for the prominent green stairway – this restaurant and discotheque offers the diner loads of choices, from chicken dishes to lobster. The open-sided, fan-cooled dining area is situated under a large thatch roof, while the adjacent disco is a concrete structure that's packed with Dominicans on Friday and Saturday nights (free admission).

NORTH COAST

There are several **no-name eateries** (mains US$2-7; 🕐 breakfast, lunch and dinner) next to the Hotel Chic on Calle Benito Monción just off Calle Duarte. Come here for sandwiches, empanadas and other fast-food. Order at the counter and eat at small plastic tables on the sidewalk or take it to go.

Super Fria Nina (Calle Duarte at Colón) and **Terraza Fedora** (Calle San Fernando), five blocks north of Duarte, are large beer gardens that get incredibly packed almost every evening, but especially on weekends. People of all ages share tall Presidentes at plastic tables, and when there's no room, spill onto the sidewalk and street.

Getting There & Away

Caribe Tours (☎ 809-579-2129; Calle Mella at Calle Rodríguez Carmargo) has a depot a block north of Calle Duarte. Buses to Santo Domingo (US$7.50, four hours) leave at 7am, 9am, 10:45am, 1:45pm, 2:45pm and 4pm, with a stop in Santiago (US$3.50, two hours).

Monte Cristi's gua-gua terminal is on Calle Duarte between 27 de Febrero and Benito Monción. *Gua-guas* to Dajabón (US$1.25; 40 minutes, every 20 minutes, 7:35am to 10pm) leave from here. *Gua-guas* to Santiago (US$3.50; 1¾ hours, every 20 minutes, 6:15am to 6pm) originate in Dajabón but pass in front of the terminal in Monte Cristi .

If you're driving, it's hard to get lost – Calle Duarte becomes Hwy 1 (Autopista Duarte) to Santiago, while Av Mella becomes Hwy 45 to Dajabón. Avoid driving the Monte Cristi–Dajabón road at night, as assaults on cars have occurred in the past.

Getting Around

Most of Monte Cristi is navigable by foot. The exception is el Morro and Parque Nacional Monte Cristi – for those a cab or *motoconcho* is best.

DAJABÓN

pop 16,398

Like so many other northern towns, Dajabón was depopulated during the early 17th century because its Spanish colonists had taken to trading with people from other nations against the king's wishes. It was resettled at the insistence of the Spanish Crown more than 100 years later, when the king realized that French settlers were moving into unoccupied Spanish territory. Today, just as it was hundreds of years ago, trade between the Dajabón residents and people of another nation is the major local business activity.

Most foreigners here are on their way to or from Haiti. Reaching the border is simple; coming from Monte Cristi on Hwy 45, as most people do, you'll come to a huge arch (the formal entrance to town) and a short distance further from the Parque Central on the east side of the street. Just past the park is Calle Presidente Henriquez; turn right (west) and the border is six blocks ahead. If you're arriving by Caribe Tours bus, the bus station is on Calle Presidente Henriquez. Just walk west from the bus station five blocks to get to the border.

Sights

HAITIAN MARKET

Every Monday and Friday, Haitian vendors come by car, bus, foot and even *burro* (donkey) to Dajabón for an intriguing **Haitian market**. By 7am the vendors will have already begun to fill the available space with merchandise, primary T-shirts, shoes and all sorts of household items, from pots and pans to sheets and pillowcases. Dominicans come in equal or greater numbers to take advantage of cut-rate prices. There isn't much in the way of artesanía or souvenirs, but the scene – Haitian women in bright shirts and headwraps, high stacks of merchandise

---

GOING TO HAITI

The Dominican immigration office opens at 8am daily and closes around 5pm, though the Haitian side doesn't usually open until 9am. You'll pay US$20 to leave the Dominican Republic and US$10 to enter Haiti. Returning to the DR, you theoretically do not have to pay either a departure fee in Haiti or an entrance fee in the Dominican Republic, but officials at both points sometimes levy a US$10 'fee' on tourists.

On both sides of the border, there are buses to whisk you away from it. Most west-bound travelers head straight for Cap-Haïtien after crossing the border. If it's late and you want to remain in Ouanaminthe, you will find two budget hotels there.

and a multilingual cacophony – is fascinating in itself.

Sleeping

Hotel Juan Calvo (☎ 809-579-8285; Calle Presidente Henríquez 48; d/tw with fan US$10/13, with aircon US$13/16.50; ✷) Next to Parque Central, the Juan Calvo is the best place in town, with 44 clean and comfortable rooms and just six blocks from the border.

Getting There & Around

In Dajabón, **Caribe Tours** (☎ 809-579-8554; Calle Marcelo Carrasco at Presidente Henríquez) has a depot five blocks from the border. Buses to Santo Domingo (US$7.50, five hours), with stops in Monte Cristi and Santiago, leave at 6:45am, 8:30am, 10:15am, 1pm, 2:25pm and 3:15pm

Gua-guas will also take you to Monte Cristi (US$1.25; 40 minutes). The terminal is just beyond the arch at the entrance to town on the east side of the road. The *guagua* station is just beyond it, also on the eastern side of the road.

There are taxis and *motoconchos* near the crossing point every day until the time the border closes. After that, taxis and *motoconchos* may still be found on the main road.

The Interior

The backbone of the Dominican Republic (DR) is the Cordillera Central, which runs north-west–southeast from the Haitian border to the outskirts of Baní and San Cristóbal, nearly to Santo Domingo. The mountains are protected by two huge adjoining national parks, which provide excellent opportunities for outdoor activities, including river rafting, mountain bike riding, horseback riding and a sport called 'canyoning,' which involves jumping, rappelling and sliding down a rushing river gorge. But the granddaddy of eco-adventures is climbing the 3175m Pico Duarte, the highest mountain in the Caribbean. Though not a technical climb, it is still a challenging multi-day trek that attracts mountaineers from all over the world. Even if you don't climb the peak, there are a number of beautiful and rewarding one- and multi-day hikes you can undertake, including two stunning alpine valleys, Valle del Tétero and Valle de Bao.

Nestled in the mountains are small cities that serve as staging grounds for the various eco-activities, as well as cool getaways for Dominicans living in the hot lowlands. Jarabacoa and Constanza are the main towns, followed by San José de las Matas and the trailhead communities of Mata Grande and La Ciénaga. At the foot of the mountains is Santiago, the Dominican Republic's second-largest city. An interesting city in itself – it has the country's best museum and a fantastic tradition of Carnival celebrations – Santiago is a logical base for the various routes into the mountains and up the peaks, and a gateway to the North Coast.

HIGHLIGHTS

- Visit Santiago's **Centro León** (p218), the best museum in the country

- Head to little La Vega in February when it throws one of the country's best **Carnival celebrations** (p236)

- Catch sunrise from atop **Pico Duarte** (p230), the Caribbean's highest peak with views of the Atlantic and the Caribbean

- Enjoy myriad **eco-adventures in Jarabacoa** (p226), from whitewater rafting to 'canyoning'

- See the **tobacco fields** (p237) of central Dominican Republic, where some of the world's best cigars are born

THE INTERIOR

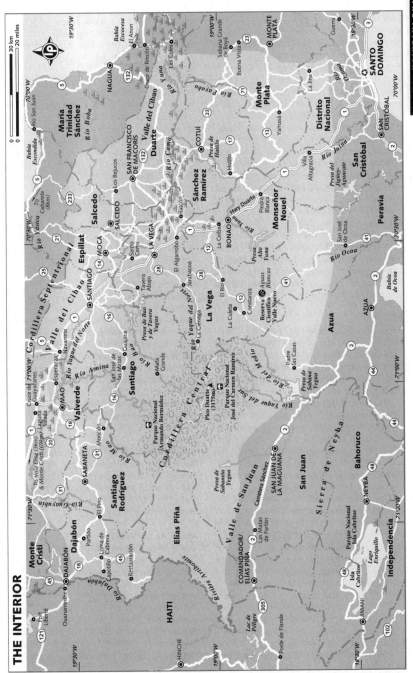

SANTIAGO

pop 555,904

The breadbasket of the nation, Santiago de los Caballeros (more commonly just Santiago) is the Dominican Republic's second-largest city and the commercial hub of the Valle del Cibao. The valley yields sugarcane and tobacco, which the city converts into rum, cigarettes and cigars.

As a tourist destination, Santiago doesn't have the historical richness of Santo Domingo nor the small town air or outdoor options of other cities of the interior. For that reason, most people stay only long enough to make bus connections. That said, Santiago does have a decent bar scene and a handful of interesting sights that make a day or two here worthwhile. It's also a great place to go for Carnival; the city offers its own festival, with rich traditions (including incredibly beautiful handmade masks), and also serves as a base for La Vega, which hosts one of the more famous Carnival celebrations in the country.

History

Santiago was founded in 1495 by Christopher Columbus's elder brother, Bartholomew. However, the earthquake of 1562 caused so much damage to the city that it was rebuilt on its present site beside the Río Yaque del Norte. It was attacked and destroyed several times by invading French troops, as part of long-simmering tension between Spain and France over control of the island of Hispaniola. Santiago also suffered terribly during the DR's 1912 civil war. The city's jails were filled with political prisoners, and governmental executions were carried out by the dozens.

The years immediately following the civil war were some of the city's best. WWI caused worldwide shortages of raw tropical materials, so prices soared for products such as sugar, tobacco, cacao and coffee – all of which were being grown around Santiago. From 1914 through the end of the war and into the 1920s, Santiago's economy boomed. Lovely homes and impressive stores, electric lighting and paved streets appeared throughout town. In May 1922, Hwy Duarte opened, linking Santiago with Bonao, La Vega and Santo Domingo.

Today, Santiago still relies on agriculture as its chief source of revenue. The prices of sugar and tobacco have fallen, which has had the effect of tempering traffic and other activity on the sometimes narrow streets.

Orientation

The center of town is Parque Duarte, a busy, leafy park with the cathedral on its south side and Palacio Consistorial on its west side. The park is at the corner of Av 30 de Marzo and Calle del Sol, both large commercial avenues with ATMs, hotels and assorted shops nearby. The former runs south to the Río Yaque del Norte and north to Av Las Carreras and Av 27 de Febrero, the main roads in and out of town.

Calle del Sol runs east to the Monumento a los Héroes de la Restauración de la República and the bar scene nearby – you can also take Av Restauración, two blocks north.

Information

INTERNET ACCESS

Camber.Net (☎ 809-734-2232; España 41 near Av Restauración; per hr US$0.70; ⏰ 8am-10pm Mon-Sat) Professional staff, new-ish computers and a fast connection.

Centro de Internet Yudith (☎ 809-581-4882; Calle 16 de Agosto near Mella; per hr US$0.60; ⏰ 8:30am-8:30pm Mon-Fri, 8:30am-5pm Sat) A block south of the Hotel Aloha Sol, Internet access here costs incredibly little.

Centro Internet (Av Cucurullo, btwn 30 de Marzo & España; per hr US$0.70; ⏰ 8am-9:30pm Mon-Sat, 8am-5pm Sun) Next to the Hotel Colonial, this small shop has three computers with a reasonably fast connection.

LAUNDRY

Joseph Cleaners (☎ 809-583-4880; Las Carreras btwn Juan Pablo Duarte & Tolentino; ⏰ 7am-7:30pm Mon-Fri, 7am-1pm Sat) The only place in town that charges by the load – the rest are per piece and quite pricey. It's US$1.40 per load (up to 18lbs) and per minute US$0.10 for drying. Same day service if you drop off early.

MEDICAL SERVICES

Centro Médico Semma (☎ 809-226-1053; Pedro Francisco Bonó btwn Sánchez & Cuba) Free for local teachers and their families, this well-regarded hospital treats all other patients at reasonable rates and has a 24hr emergency room.

Farmacia Jorge (☎ 809-582 2887; España at Av Máximo Gómez; ⏰ 8am-6:30pm Mon-Sat)

Farmacia Virginia (☎ 809-582-4142; Av 30 de Marzo btwn Cucurullo & Independencia; ⏰ 8am-8pm Mon-Sat) Will deliver to your hotel at no extra charge, though a tip is customary.

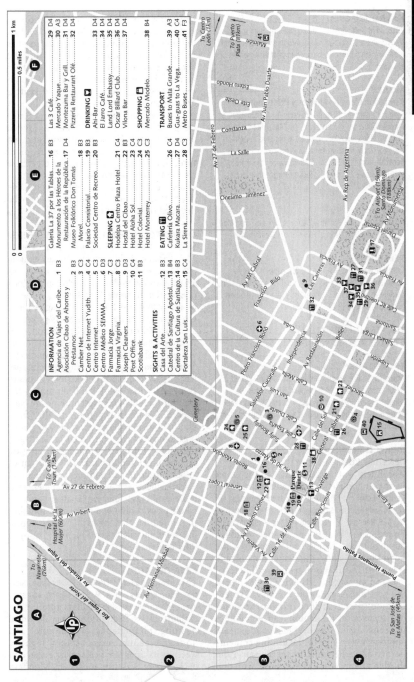

SANTIAGO

INFORMATION
Agencia de Viajes del Caribe......1 B3
Asociación de Cibao de Ahorros y
  Préstamos......2 B3
Camber Net......3 C3
Centro de Internet Yudith......4 C4
Centro Internet......5 C3
Centro Médico SEMMA......6 D3
Farmacia Jorge......7 C3
Farmacia Virginia......8 C3
Joseph Cleaners......9 D3
Post Office......10 C4
Scotiabank......11 B3

SIGHTS & ACTIVITIES
Casa del Arte......12 B3
Catedral de Santiago Apóstol......13 B4
Centro de la Cultura de Santiago..14 B3
Fortaleza San Luis......15 C4

Galería La 37 por las Tablas......16 B3
Monumento a los Héroes de la
  Restauración......17 D4
Museo Folklórico Don Tomás
  Morel......18 B3
Palacio Consistorial......19 B3
Sociedad Centro de Recreo......20 B3

SLEEPING
Hodelpa Centro Plaza Hotel......21 C4
Hostal del Cibao......22 B3
Hotel Aloha Sol......23 C4
Hotel Colonial......24 C3
Hotel Monterrey......25 C3

EATING
Cafetería Olivo......26 C4
Kukara Macara......27 D4
La Sirena......28 C4

Las 3 Café......29 D4
Mercado Yaque......30 A3
Montezuma Bar y Grill......31 D4
Pizzería Restaurant Olé......32 D4

DRINKING
Ahí-Bar......33 D4
El Jarro Café......34 D4
Land Lord Embassy......35 D4
Oscar Billiard Club......36 D4
Vilona Bar......37 D4

SHOPPING
Mercado Modelo......38 B4

TRANSPORT
Buses to Mata Grande......39 A3
Gua-guas to La Vega......40 C4
Metro Buses......41 F3

Hospital de la Mujer (☎ 809-575-8963, 809-576-3838; Av Imbert opposite Estadio Cibao) Though specializing in women's care, this large hospital has doctors and a 24hr emergency room equipped to treat emergencies of any kind.

MONEY
Asociación Cibao de Ahorros y Préstamos (Cibao Saving & Loans; Av 30 de Marzo btwn Avs Restauración & Máximo Gómez; ☼ 8am-5pm) The 24hr ATM here is in a well-lit cabin with a locking door, as opposed to right on the street as at most other banks in the center.
Scotiabank (Calle del Sol at 30 de Marzo; ☼ 8am-5pm Mon-Fri, 8am-12:30pm Sat) Just off Parque Duarte, this bank has one ATM.

POST
Post office (Calle del Sol at San Luis; ☼ 8am-5pm Mon-Fri, 9am-1pm Sat) Three blocks east of Parque Duarte.

TELEPHONE
Camber.Net (☎ 809-734-2232; España 41 near Av Restauración; ☼ 8am-10pm Mon-Sat) This Internet café doubles as a call center; calls to the USA are US$0.30 per minute, to Europe US$0.75 to US$1.

TOURIST INFORMATION
There is no tourism office in town.

TRAVEL AGENCIES
Agencia de Viajes del Caribe (☎ 809-241-1368; Av Restauración 123; ☼ 8am-noon, 2-6pm Mon-Fri, 8am-noon Sat) Small, conveniently located agency that issues domestic and international air tickets and can book package tours in the area.

Sights & Activities
CENTRO LEÓN
Absolutely not to be missed is the state-of-the-art museum and cultural center, **Centro León** (☎ 809-582-2315; www.centroleon.org.do; Av 27 de Febrero 146, Colonia Villa Proegreso; admission US$1.75, free Tue; ☼ 9am-6pm Thu-Tue, 9am-8pm Wed). Founded in 2003 by one of the wealthiest families in the Dominican Republic – the León Jimenes clan – this center not only offers artistic workshops, seminars, film festivals and music concerts, but also has one of the best museums in the country. The exhibition space is divided into four sections: one focuses on the Dominican Republic – its ecosystems, history and population; another houses one of the leading contemporary art collections in the country; the third is a temporary exhibit room, with dis-

plays that change every couple of months; and the final is a stand-alone building that explains the family history, its beginnings in the tobacco industry, its break into the beer market, and its success in the banking world. This final exhibit space also has an interesting cigar workshop where visitors can watch cigars being rolled throughout the day. Guided tours are available in Spanish (US$3.50 per person), English, French and German (US$5.50 per person) and last about 1½ hours. Reservations are required three days in advance for tours. To get here via public transportation, pick up a Ruta A *público* (shared taxi or minivan) on Calle del Sol on Parque Duarte and ask to be dropped off in front of the center.

MUSEO FOLKLÓRICO DON TOMÁS MOREL
Renowned poet and cultural critic Tomás Morel founded this eclectic **folk art museum** (☎ 809-582-6787; Av Restauración 174; admission free; ☼ 9am-noon, 3:30-6pm Mon-Fri) in 1962, and helped operate it until his death in 1992. Considered by many to be the father of Santiago's modern Carnival, Morel was a tireless promoter and chronicler of the yearly celebration, even writing a book-length poem about it. He was especially fond of the distinctive *caretas* (masks) and since its founding, the museum has displayed the best masks for visitors to enjoy. And that's just the beginning – the walls of this small converted home are jam-packed with Carnival memorabilia, from photos and newspaper clippings to paintings and dolls depicting each of Santiago's traditional Carnival characters. There are also innumerable knick-knacks and curios knocking about – an antique typewriter and Taíno artifacts, among others. The effect is more exuberant than explanatory (and the whole place could use a serious dusting) but the museum makes for an interesting stop all the same, and the docents there are happy to offer explanations.

CASA DEL ARTE
This small **gallery** (☎ 809-583-5346; Benito Monción btwn Restauración & Máximo Gómez; admission free; ☼ 9am-7pm Mon-Sat) displays rotating art exhibits in its front rooms (usually local painting, photography or sculpture) and hosts free cultural events several nights a week in its open-air performance space in back. There was live music on Mondays

and art films on Tuesdays when we passed through, but you should swing by to get the latest schedule.

GALERÍA LA 37 POR LAS TABLAS

Across the street from the Casa del Arte, **La 37** (☎ 809-587-3033; Benito Monción 37 btwn Avs Restauración & Máximo Gómez; admission varies; ✆ 9am-7pm Mon-Sat) also hosts local art shows in its foyer, and has an outdoor stage for live music, dance and theater performances, both amateur and professional. La 37 also has ballet classes, yoga instruction, and hosts interesting *charlas* (talks) about current social and cultural issues. During Carnival, for example, the gallery invites families to a discussion of the history and traditions of Carnival, complete with child-size masks and costumes to introduce kids to the characters without scaring them, as some costumes can be quite fearsome.

CENTRO DE LA CULTURA DE SANTIAGO

Though not much to look at from the outside, the **Centro de la Cultura de Santiago** (Santiago Cultural Center; ☎ 809-226-5222; Calle del Sol; ✆ 9am-6pm daily), a half-block from Parque Duarte, offers a regular program of musical and theatrical performances, including plays, choral singing, children's theatre and holiday concerts. They also offer courses in guitar, painting, dance and more, if you are in Santiago for more than just a day or two. Check the bulletin board inside the main doors for the month's programming.

CATEDRAL DE SANTIAGO APÓSTOL

Santiago's **cathedral** (Calles 16 de Agosto at Benito Monción; ✆ 7-9am Mon-Sat, 7am-8pm Sun), opposite the south side of Parque Duarte, was built between 1868 and 1895 and is a combination of Gothic and neoclassical styles. The cathedral contains the marble tomb of the late-19th-century dictator Ulises Heureaux, an elaborately carved mahogany altar and impressive stained-glass windows by contemporary Dominican artist Dincón Mora.

PALACIO CONSISTORIAL

Next door to the Sociedad Centro de Recreo is the former town hall, which now includes a small **museum** (Parque Duarte on Calles del Sol at Benito Monción; admission free; ✆ 9am-6pm Mon-Fri, 9am-2pm Sat, may vary) devoted to the city's colorful history. If you're here during Carnival, don't miss the huge and stunning display of masks and *fichas* (posters), part of a yearly competition that draws entries from the top artists and mask-makers in Santiago and the country.

MONUMENTO A LOS HÉROES DE LA RESTAURACIÓN DE LA REPÚBLICA

On a hill at the east end of the downtown area is Santiago's most visible and recognizable sight, the **Monumento a los Héroes de la Restauración de la República** (Monument to the Heroes of the Restoration of the Republic; Av Monumental; admission free; ✆ 8am-5pm Mon-Sat). The eight-story pedestal and tower was originally commissioned by Trujillo as a tribute to himself, but was rededicated after his assassination, along with many other such monuments, to those who died in the War of Restoration (1863–65). Local residents come here in the late afternoon to take in the view of the city and surrounding mountains, sip a beer or soda sold by collar-toting vendors, and to fly kites in the evening breeze with their kids. The view from the top of the monument is even more impressive; unfortunately the elevator broke down in 1991 and is yet to be fixed. There is a dusty little museum one floor up from the spacious marble rotunda, but you can only go up with a guide, who won't just take you up, but charge US$10 per person for a full city tour of museums and sights that you could easily see on your own. In any case, just hanging out at the monument is much more interesting than squinting at cases of fading photos.

SOCIEDAD CENTRO DE RECREO

Opened in 1894, this private **social club** (Parque Duarte, Benito Monción at 16 de Agosto) is the oldest in the country. Owned by Bermudez Rum, the club is a throwback to Santiago's boom days. Inside there is a ballroom, a pool hall, and a library that contains a custom-made chair Trujillo used when he had his shoes shined. Open to members only.

FORTALEZA SAN LUIS

Built in the late 17th century, the **Fortaleza San Luis** (San Luis Fort; Boy Scouts at San Luis) operated as a military stronghold until the 1970s, when it was converted into a prison. Today, it is being transformed again; this time into a cultural center and art museum, due to open in early 2006.

Festivals & Events

Carnival (held in February) is big all over the country, but it is especially big in Santiago. The city is famous for its incredibly artistic and fantastical *caretas* (masks) and hosts an annual international *careta* competition leading up to Carnival. Santiago is also a convenient base from which to visit La Vega, which has one of the country's largest and most boisterous celebrations. In short, you could do much worse than parking yourself in Santiago for a good part of Carnival. Just be sure to make reservations – the hotel rooms here fill up fast at this time of year.

Sleeping

Santiago's accommodations are disappointingly slim, especially considering it's the second-largest city in the country. Hotels can fill up even in the low season, so call ahead whenever possible.

Hotel Colonial (☎ 809-247-3122; Salvador Cucurullo 115; r/tw US$12.50/13) Rooms here are almost identical to most of those found in the neighboring Hotel Monterrey: basic, clean and with cable TV. The difference here is the service; the proprietors rank among the friendliest in the country. There is also a restaurant on-site, which is good for breakfast.

Hotel Monterrey (☎ 809-582-4558; Salvador Cucurullo 92; r/tw US$12.50/13, r with aircon US$16; 🌀) This basic hotel offers 35 clean rooms with private hot water bath and cable TV. While most rooms are bare bones (think one bed, one sheet, one light bulb), the Hotel Monterrey has remodeled two rooms – 22 and 26 – into very pleasant and well-decorated accommodations. These rooms are larger than the rest, have a small sitting area, tile bathrooms, aircon and brand new furnishings. Frankly, this is the best deal in town.

Hostal del Cibao (☎ 809-581-7775; Calle Benito Monción 40; hostal_del_cibao@hotmail.com; r with cold water US$9, r/tw with hot water US$12.50/16) Located on a quiet street a couple of blocks from Parque Duarte, this hotel has 14 spacious rooms, all with fan, cable TV and private bath. A pleasant balcony with rocking chairs makes a nice place to spend an early evening. Popular with budget travelers.

CARNIVAL

Carnival is the most popular festival in the Dominican Republic; it is celebrated with great vigor every Sunday in February and culminates in a huge pre-Lent bash in Santo Domingo. Celebrations revolve around parades – some more organized than others – where people display costumes that they have been creating all year. The costumes and customs vary from city to city but all are invariably colorful and fun to watch. Some of the most popular Carnival celebrations take place in the following locations.

■ La Vega: this city hosts the largest and most organized of the carnivals in the country. Here, thousands of participants dress up in intricate devil's costumes and swing thick rubber balloons, hitting onlookers in the behind as they march by. If you don't want to get spanked, sit in the bleachers and never leave your backside exposed.

■ Santiago: the parade in this town is made up of rival neighborhoods – La Joya and Los Pepines. Onlookers watch from overpasses, apartment buildings, even the tops of lampposts. Costumes focus on two images: the *lechón* (piglet), which represents the devil, and the *pepín*, a fantastical animal that appears to be a cross between a cow and a duck. The most obvious difference between the two is that *lechón* masks have two smooth horns and those of the *pepines* have horns with dozens of tiny papier-mâché spikes. All participants swing *vejigas* (inflated cow bladders) and hit each other and onlookers from behind. Prepare to run or brace yourself for a wallop; the parade-goers in this town have little mercy.

■ Monte Cristi: considered the most brutal Carnival in the country. The characters in Monte Cristi's parade are the *toros* (bulls) and the *civiles* (shepherds). Participants wield bullwhips and crack each other as they walk through the streets. Onlookers are sometimes hit, though more often than not it's unintentional. Wear thick clothes and protect your eyes if you choose to attend; better yet, look for a rooftop or a balcony where you can enjoy the colorful (and sometimes painful!) display from a distance.

Hotel Aloha Sol (☎ 809-583-0090; www.alohasol
.com; Calle del Sol 50; s/d US$54/64, tw s/d US$60/70,
ste US$112; 🗱 🅿 🖵) Although somewhat
cramped, rooms at the Aloha Sol are the
best in downtown Santiago. They have
modern furnishings and amenities, pleasant decor and are spotlessly clean. Many
don't have outward facing windows, which
makes for a quieter stay but also a darker
one. Breakfast is included in the rate.

Hodelpa Centro Plaza Hotel (☎ 809-581-7000;
www.hodelpa.com; Calle Mella 54; s/d US$70/75, ste US$91-
131; 🗱 🅿 🖵) Next door to the Aloha Sol,
the Hodelpa offers 85 rooms, which could
all use some sprucing up; beds are soft, the
bathrooms need attention, and the decor is
reminiscent of a 1970s rec room. An on-site
discotheque opens on weekends and can be
heard in most guest rooms – bring earplugs.
If the Aloha Sol is full but you like having
modern amenities, this is the only choice
downtown. Buffet breakfast is included.

Eating

Pizzería Restaurant Olé (☎ 809-582-0866; Av Duarte
at Independencia; mains US$3-8; 🕑 breakfast, lunch & din-
ner) Facing a shady park, this large open-air
restaurant serves good pizzas, sandwiches
and snacks. A medium pizza – just US$5 –
is big enough for two. Good for a pit stop
between downtown Santiago and the Monumento a la Restauración.

Cafetería Olivo (☎ 809-724-5135; 16 de Agosto
89; mains US$2-5; 🕑 breakfast, lunch & dinner Mon-Sat)
Popular with students, this cafeteria-style
eatery offers good sandwiches and friendly
service. The daily lunch special comes with
rice, beans, salad and a meat main.

Las 3 Café (☎ 809-276-5909; Tolentino 38; mains
US$6-11; 🕑 dinner) Located in the middle of
the bar scene, this charming restaurant
offers high-end Dominican fare in a converted wood-plank house. Windows face
onto the main drag, which makes for excellent people-watching. If you're only in the
mood for a drink and something light, try
the Picaderas Las 3 Café – the house appe-
tizer special, which comes with a sampling
of meats, cheeses and veggies.

Montezuma Bar y Grill (☎ 809-581-1111; Av Francia at Beller; mains US$7-12; 🕑 11am-2am) Facing the
Monumento a la Restauración, this popu-
lar restaurant specializes in Mexican dishes,
from tacos and burritos to filet of grouper
grilled with chili and garlic. Prices are a bit

high for the main dishes, but the smaller orders are reasonable and the restaurant itself –
spread over three levels with patio seating,
long bar tables and rusted steel stools – is
worth a look. There's live mariachi music
every Friday starting at 10pm.

Kukara Macara (☎ 809-241-3143; www.kukara
macara.com; Av Francia 7; mains US$5-13; 🕑 breakfast,
lunch & dinner) Next door to Montezuma is
this Old American West theme restaurant,
replete with hay stacks, posters of outlaws,
and waiters in chaps and cowboy hats. The
menu is varied but focuses on steak and
Tex-Mex dishes. The veggie burrito (US$4)
and the salads (US$5 to US$7) are the only
options for vegetarians.

Mercado Yaque (Mercado Hospedaje; 16 de Agosto
btwn Hungria & Captillo; 🕑 6am-6pm) Sprawling
over several city blocks west of Parque Duarte, Mercado Yaque is primarily a fruit and
vegetable market, evidenced by the huge
piles of bagged onions, wooden carts full
of watermelons, eggplants and carrots, and
lettuce and cabbage leaves plastering the
streets. The indoor area is easy to miss –
look for entrances on the south side of 16
de Agosto – with passages dim and narrow enough to give pause to even the most
gung-ho market-goer. Inside is a fascinating array of flowers, meats, herbs, religious
and ceremonial icons, and virtually no
tourists. Chaotic but generally safe, this is
still a place you ought to be extra cautious
of pickpocketing and is not a good place to
hang out at night.

La Sirena (Calle España btwn Máximo Gómez & Calle
del Sol; 🕑 8:30am-8pm Mon-Sat, 8:30am-3pm Sun) This
huge all-purpose supermarket is sure to
have what you're looking for. Here, you'll
be able to find anything from fresh bread
to flip-flops.

Drinking

Clustered around the Monumento a la Restauración are about a dozen bars, restaurants and late-night eateries (and one pool
hall), making this Santiago's best place for
bar-hopping, people-meeting and general
revelry. The immediate surrounding area
has enough foot traffic to make it quite safe,
but the several blocks between there and the
Zona Colonial can be a bit dodgy, especially
if it's late and your faculties are, shall we say,
impaired. Play it safe and take a cab – it'll cost
the same as one of those tall Presidentes.

Ahi-Bar (☎ 809-581-6779; Calle Tolentino at Av Restauración; ✆ 4pm-3am) This is the biggest of a string of bars on Calle Tolentino, with a large patio set above street level featuring high bar tables and stools. Most people come to drink, but in case you missed dinner the food here is actually pretty good – try the chicken fajitas, chorizo plate, or even a steak, served ten different ways. The crowd is a bit more upper-crust than other bars here, but it's still a lively place.

El Jarro Café (☎ 809-971-4942; Calle Tolentino btwn Avs Beller & Restauración; ✆ 4pm-3am) This is smaller and a bit edgier than Ahi-Bar, with wooden tables set under a low open-air awning. The clientele is younger and you'll hear less pop music and more alternative rock, rock en español, and a good selection of Latin and merengue music. The sign out front is a rip-off of the Hard Rock Café; the name is too, if you're familiar with the Dominican accent in English.

Other bars on this stretch of Calle Tolentino include Vilona Bar and Land Lord Embassy. The Kukara Macara (p221) and Montezuma Bar y Grill (p221) restaurants are around the corner and are also good spots for a drink or two.

Oscar Billiard Club (☎ 809-241-4730; Beller btwn Calle Tolentino & Av Francia; tables per hr US$2; ✆ 2pm-4am) This club has 18 pool tables scattered through a large room with a bar fronting onto the street. Like most pool halls in the Latin American region, the atmosphere can be rowdy and you can cut the testosterone with a knife.

Shopping

Mercado Modelo (Calle del Sol at España; ✆ 9am-5pm Mon-Sat) Two blocks east of Parque Duarte, this gymnasium-sized market sells Dominican handicrafts, kitschy souvenirs, and lots of T-shirts. You'll have to dig hard to find anything of high quality but if you look long enough, you'll most likely be surprised – prepare to bargain for it.

Getting There & Away
AIR
Santiago's **international airport** (☎ 809-233-8000; Avs Bartolomé Colón & Metropolitana) is a 20-minute drive from the center. It is serviced by the following airlines:

American (☎ 809-233-8401 or toll-free reservations ☎ 1-200-5151)

American Eagle (☎ 809-233-8401 or toll-free reservations ☎ 1-200-5151)
CaribAir (☎ 809-233-8270)
Continental (☎ 809-233-8161 or toll free reservations ☎ 1 200 1062)
Jet Blue (☎ 809-233-8116)

Delta was due to begin service in 2005, but did not have a local telephone number at the time of research. There are no buses or *públicos* (private van or truck used for local transport) convenient to the airport, so taxis are your only option (US$16 one way).

BUS
Metro Buses (☎ 809-587-3837, 809-582-9111; Av Juan Pablo Duarte at Maimón) is located east of the center. Buses to Santo Domingo (US$7, two hours, hourly, 6am to 7:45pm), leave from here with a reduced schedule on Sundays. Buses to Puerto Plata (US$2.50, 1¼ hours) leave at 9am, 11am, 1pm, 4pm, 6pm and 9pm.

Caribe Tours (☎ 809-576-0790; www.caribetours .com.do) has two terminals in Santiago – you want the Las Colinas terminal at the corner of Avs 27 de Febrero and Las Américas, about 3km north of the center. Destinations include Santo Domingo (US$5.25, 2½ hours, 26 times daily, 6am to 8:15pm); Puerto Plata (US$2.50, 1¼ hours, hourly 8:30am to 9:30pm); and Monte Cristi (US$3.50, 1¾ hours, six departures from 9am to 6:15pm); La Vega (US$1.75, 45 minutes, take Santo Domingo bus); Dajabón (US$3.75, 2½ hours, take Monte Cristi bus); and Sosúa (US$2.75, two hours, take Puerto Plata bus). To get to the terminal, you can catch a Ruta A *público* (US$0.25) on Calle España at Cucurullo – some drivers won't take you if you've got luggage or will charge you double fare (which is fair enough). Taxis are faster and have more room, charging around US$3.

Getting Around
You can walk to most of the sights in Santiago, including the Monumento a la Restauración. If you are leaving the bars around the monument late, consider taking a cab back as the area has some dark corners and unsavory characters. Other sights (and both main bus terminals) are reachable by *públicos* – beat-up private cars that follow set routes around town and charge just US$0.25. Drivers cram as

SANTIAGO TO MONTE CRISTI

The stretch of Hwy 1 between Santiago and Monte Cristi, also called Hwy Duarte, runs almost perfectly straight along the northern side of a large valley that is flanked by the Cordillera Septentrional to the north and the much bigger Cordillera Central to the south.

The Río Yaque del Norte, the most significant river in the country, winds east to west through the same valley. It descends from near Pico Duarte at an altitude of 2580m and runs almost 300km before splintering into a delta and emptying into the Bahía de Monte Cristi. The delta forms an important wetland ecosystem and is protected as part of the Parque Nacional Monte Cristi.

There are numerous small towns along the way (most with multiple speed bumps through town) so the driving time on this stretch is longer than the distance would suggest. Navarrete is the largest town between Santiago and Monte Cristi and has plenty of services right along the highway through town, including a Verizon call center, Internet cafés, gas stations, restaurants and shops. Three smaller towns are of greater interest to travelers: José Bisonó is the turnoff for Hwy 5, leading to Imbert, Luperón and Puerto Plata; Cruce de Guayacanes is a roadside village built up around the intersection with Hwy 29, which leads to Los Hidalgos and Parque Nacional La Isabela (though the park is much easier to reach via Luperón); and Villa Elisa, the most direct road to Punta Rusia. (There is a sign to Punta Rusia in Laguna Salada, but the Villa Elisa route is better.)

If you're driving, you'll encounter a number of military checkpoints, at which you are almost never stopped. If a soldier does flag you down, it is most likely to ask you for a lift to Monte Cristi or Santiago, depending on the direction you're headed. Though they tend to be friendly young guys, you are not at all required to pick them up or even stop when they wave at you – most people don't. (Of course if they appear to be searching cars or questioning drivers, you should stop.)

many as eight people into a single car; if you have bags you may have to wait for an empty(ish) car and may be asked to pay double – still a bargain. Taxis charge from US$2.50 to US$3.50 for most destinations around town, including the bus stations. *Motoconchos* (motorcycle taxis) are cheaper but not for the faint of heart.

SAN JOSÉ DE LAS MATAS
pop 9853

This attractive mountain city is 38km southwest of Santiago, and it is a jumping-off point for one of the major hiking trails in the Parque National Armando Bermúdez (from Mata Grande, p232). Although there's little reason to come here other than accessing the national park, most travelers find the town pleasant and friendly – a good place to linger the day before or after a long hike.

The people of San José de las Matas have been practising subsistence agriculture since the 18th century, and continue to do so today, though more and more people commute to Santiago for jobs there.

The town is a tangle of curving one-way streets, which is confusing at first but adds to the appeal of exploring it. If you're driving it's easy to get turned around (though hard to get really lost, as most streets lead back to the main square).

The road to San José de las Matas from Santiago is well paved and winds through lush, hilly terrain. Several kilometers before San José is a well-marked turnoff to the village of Pedregal and, following another turnoff, the road to Mata Grande and the national park. If you don't make the second turnoff, the road eventually reconnects with the highway about 200m from the entrance to San José.

Information

BanInter (Padre Espinosa at Felix Zazuela; 🕑 8:30am-5pm Mon-Fri) Has a 24hr ATM.

Policia Nacional (☎ 809-578-8278; Calle San José; 🕑 24hrs) One block from the park.

Post office (30 de Marzo; 🕑 8am-noon, 2-4pm Mon-Fri, 8am-noon Sat) A few doors beyond the park.

Super Farmacia Bisono (☎ 809-578-8206; 30 de Marzo at Padres Moscoso; 🕑 7:30am-9pm Mon-Sat, 8am-6pm Sun) Two blocks from the park, next door to Verizon.

Verizon (30 de Marzo; to USA per min US$0.30, to Europe per min US$0.75) Two blocks from the park.

Pico Duarte

San José de las Matas is the jumping-off point for an ascent of Pico Duarte. Longer, less-trafficked, and more challenging than the route from Jarabacoa, this hike begins from Mata Grande, a small town about 20km by winding dirt road from San José de las Matas. (Actually, the trailhead is in an even smaller town called Atonsape Bueno, 3km past Mata Grande, but all the signs are to Mata Grande.) The hike is 45km in each direction and involves approximately 3800m of vertical ascent, including going over La Pelona, a peak only slightly lower than Pico Duarte itself. Most people make the trip in five days, spending the first night at Río La Guácara and the second in pretty Valle de Bao. You summit Pico Duarte on the third day, returning to Valle de Bao that same afternoon. It's possible to get all the way to Mata Grande the following day, but it's a long, hard haul and most people spread it over two days, overnighting once again at La Guácara.

Few tour operators go this direction – Iguana Mama (p228) is the most likely to be willing to organize a trip on this route. You can hire a guide and mules in Mata Grande, although since there is relatively little traffic from this side you may have to go there a couple days before your actual hike to organize the trip. Costs are typically US$10 per guide per day, and US$10 per mule per day. With small groups the mule-tender may be able to function as the guide; for large groups, consider hiring a *cocinero* (cook), also for US$10 per day. You are responsible for bringing food and water (though the mule carries it), and any additional supplies. There are small stores in Mata Grande; otherwise buy everything in Santiago or San José de las Matas. Definitely discuss these matters with your guide beforehand. There is a US$3.50 per person park entrance fee as well.

Buses from Santiago to Mata Grande (US$2.75, two hours, 9am, 12:30pm and 3pm) leave from the stop at the corner of Av Velario and Calle Boy Scouts. However, even taking the first bus puts you in Mata Grande a little late to start the first day – it may make more sense to camp a night in Mata Grande (or ask your guide about lodging, as there are no official campsites) and set out early the following day. You'll have to do the same on the return, as the buses from Mata Grande leave in the morning.

Alternatively, call **Rodriguez Tours** (☎ 809-642-3615) which operates the public bus, but can also provide private transportation.

Sleeping & Eating

Hotel y Restaurant San José (☎ 809-578-8566; Calle 30 de Marzo; r US$10.50-12.50) Rooms have green-tiled floors and chipping green paint, but they are clean and the location is convenient. There are no rooms with two beds and the rooms vary from small to less-small, but are comfortable enough. At the time of writing, the owners were planning to build a sister hotel on the other side of the park, which would have larger rooms with aircon – worth asking about.

Hotel Restaurant Los Samanes (☎ 809-578-8316; Av Santiago 16; d/tw US$8.75/10.50) On the right as you enter town, before the Texaco station, this friendly hotel has 10 boxy, slightly grubby rooms with fan and cold-water bathrooms. Rooms with windows are more agreeable and a few have TVs. Though not right in the center, you're a few minutes' walk from there, and just steps from the *gua-gua* (minibuses used for local public transport) terminal.

Both hotels have restaurants – the one at **Los Samanes** (☒ 7:30am-10:30pm) has a small outdoor patio and serves a variety of sandwiches (most under US$3), chicken and rice (US$3.50), several seafood and beef dishes (both around US$6). The fare is much the same at **Hotel San José** (mains US$5-12; ☒ 9am-11pm) with a few additional dishes like sweet-and-sour chicken and your choice of either the sunny front area or air-cooled dining room.

Getting There & Away

San José's *gua-gua* stop is opposite the Texaco station at the entrance of town. *Gua-guas* for Santiago (US$1.75, 45 minutes, 6:15am to 7pm) leave whenever they fill up. Buses leave roughly every 15 minutes in the mornings, but you may have to wait an hour or more in the middle of the day. There are also a number of taxi stands around town, include **Taxis Las Matas** (☎ 809-574-6415).

NORTHERN FOOTHILLS

The road to San José de las Matas (variously Hwy 31 and Hwy 16) continues west running through the foothills of the Cordillera Central, eventually reaching the town of Dajabón on the border with Haiti (p212). While this route may look shorter on the map – and is in fact fewer total kilometers – it is actually much faster and easier to take Hwy 1 (Autopista Duarte) to Monte Cristi and cut down to Dajabón from there. It's also safer, as you can go longer distances on the other route without seeing another car.

That said, the Santiago–Dajabón road is passable and cuts through rolling arid country and past small farming and ranching communities, including Monción, Sabaneta and Partido.

Monción
pop 6625

Monción is the next community west of San José de las Matas that has any services. There are two gas stations (one with a mechanic), many homes made of clapboard or cinder block, a few paved roads, a central park, a couple of simple restaurants and no accommodations.

Sabaneta
pop 16,380

Sabaneta is a hot, dry farming town that developed along both sides of the Santiago-Dajabón road. There are several struggling hotels along the road. **Hotel Don Chucho** (☎ 809-580-2431; Carretera Santiago-Dajabón; s/d/t US$10.50/14/17.50; ✷) is the best of the lot. It has 11 rooms with TV, telephone and private cold-water bathroom. When the electricity goes, the hotel's generator fires up but only supplies electricity to the hotel's ceiling fans, not to its air conditioners.

Partido
pop 2170

Partido is the last town before Dajabón that has any public services. These are limited to a couple of eating places and a gas station with a mechanic on duty during the day.

JARABACOA
pop 29,983

At 800m above sea level, Jarabacoa is sometimes described as 'Switzerland in the tropics.' While not exactly the Alps, the mountain setting and cool, crisp climate here can be a welcome change from the muggy lowlands and coastal areas. Many wealthy Dominicans maintain weekend homes in

and around town and this also is a favorite getaway for *capitalinos* (Santo Domingo residents) of all walks. (Perhaps the main drawback here is the air and noise pollution caused by seemingly hundreds of scooters and motorcycles plying the streets.)

Beyond its pleasant climate, Jarabacoa has the country's best outdoor options, chief among them climbing Pico Duarte, the Caribbean's highest peak. Many day trips can also be arranged, including visiting three impressive waterfalls, rafting the Dominican Republic's only white-water river, taking a 'canyoning' trip, in which you descend a river gorge by rappelling down cliffs, jumping into pools and sliding down rocks, all with the river roaring beside you. Add to that horseback riding, mountain bike riding and ATV (all-terrain vehicle) excursions, and there is really an outdoor excursion for everyone here.

Orientation

Av Independencia and Calle María N Galán, one block over, are Jarabacoa's main north-south streets – Parque Central (the central plaza) is at one end of Av Independencia and the Caribe Tours bus terminal at the other. The city's major east-west street is Calle del Carmen, which borders Parque Central and is the road you take from Jarabacoa to get to Rancho Baiguate and Constanza.

Information
EMERGENCY
Politur (Tourist Police; ☎ 809-754-3216; José Duran at Mario N Galán; ✷ 24hrs) Located behind the Caribe Tours terminal; always available to assist travelers.

INTERNET ACCESS
Centro de Copiado y Papelería (☎ 809-574-2902; Duarte at Av Independencia; per hr US$1; ✷ 8am-noon & 2-8pm Mon-Fri, 8am-noon & 2-7pm Sat) This busy copy shop also doubles as an Internet center.
Net Café (Parque Central, 1st fl; per hr US$0.70; ✷ 9am-1am) Reliable but often packed with kids playing on-line games.

MEDICAL SERVICES
The town has two private clinics that offer 24-hour medical services and a pharmacy.
Clínica Dr Terrero (☎ 809-574-4597; Av Independencia 40)
Centro Medico Dr. Abad (☎ 809-574-2431; Calle del Carmen near Gaston Fernando Deligne)

THE INTERIOR

Farmacia Miguelito (☎ 809-574-2755; Mario N Galán 70; ⊗ 7:30am-9:30pm Mon-Sat, 7:30am-4pm Sun) A well-stocked pharmacy that offers delivery service.

MONEY

There are no shortages of banks in this town; all exchange dollars and euros and have 24-hour ATMs.

Banco Léon (Duarte at Mario N Galán; ⊗ 8:30am-5pm Mon-Fri, 9am-1pm Sat) Near the main plaza.

Banco Popular (Av Independencia near Prof Pelegrina Herrera; ⊗ 8:15am-4:30pm Mon-Fri, 9am-1pm Sat) Just south of the Caribe Tours terminal.

Banco Progreso (Calle Luis F Gomez Uribe, near Av Independencia; ⊗ 8:30am-4pm Mon-Fri, 9am-1pm Sat) Also just south of the Caribe Tours terminal.

BanReservas (Sánchez at Mario N Galán; ⊗ 8am-5pm Mon-Fri, 9am-1pm Sat) Near the main plaza.

POST

Post office (Av Independencia; ⊗ 8am-noon & 2-4pm Mon-Fri) Located on the northern edge of town.

TELEPHONE

A&G Servicios Multiples (☎ 809-574-4044; Av Independencia 43; calls to USA per min US$0.32, to Europe per min US$0.74; ⊗ 8am-10pm) This travel agency doubles as telephone center.

TOURIST INFORMATION

Tourist office (☎ 809-574-7287; Plaza Ramírez, 2nd flr; ⊗ 9am-1pm, 2-6pm Mon-Fri) On the west side of the central plaza, a small tourism office (Spanish only) shares basic information about the area's activities; if you're lucky, you also may be able to get a map or two.

Activities

You can easily visit Jarabacoa's waterfalls independently, but most other activities are only available with organized excursions. All of the following activities are offered by the tour operators listed following this section. Advance reservations are always a good idea, and are required for certain excursions.

WATERFALLS

There are three waterfalls in the vicinity of Jarabacoa that can be visited in day. Any of the *motoconcho* drivers around town can take you to one, two or all three of the falls for around US$12 to $17 per person. Hiring a taxi or pickup costs around US$50 to US$75, a good option if you're in a group or not keen on *motoconchos*. No matter how you go, be sure clarify with your driver how long you'll stay at each place – some try to rush you through.

Salto de Jimenoa Uno is definitely the prettiest, a 60m waterfall that pours from a gaping hole in an otherwise solid rock cliff. (A lake feeds the waterfall via a subsurface drain.) There's a nice swimming hole, but the water is icy cold. The trail to the waterfall is 7.1km from the Shell station in Jarabacoa along Calle del Carmen, the road to Constanza. The road is paved and flat at first, then turns into a winding, hilly dirt road. Look for the access trail on your left opposite a small restaurant – it leads from the road down a steep canyon wall to the falls.

Salto de Jimenoa Dos is a 40m cascade with an appealing bathing pool. The turnoff to the falls is 4km northwest of Jarabacoa on the road to Hwy Duarte. Coming from town, you'll reach a major fork in the road with a large bank of signs, one of which points to the right toward the falls. From there, a paved road leads 6km past the golf course to a parking lot. The waterfall is a 500m walk from there, over a series of narrow suspension bridges and trails flanked by densely forested canyon walls.

Salto de Baiguate is also in a lush canyon but isn't nearly as impressive as the others, nor is the pool as inviting. To get there, take Calle del Carmen east out of Jarabacoa for 3km until you see a sign for the waterfalls on the right-hand side of the road. From there, a badly rutted dirt road, which at one point is crossed by a shallow creek, leads 3km to a parking lot. From there, a lovely 300m trail cut out of the canyon wall leads to the Salto.

WHITE-WATER RAFTING

The Río Yaque del Norte is the longest river in the country, and rafting a portion of it can be a fun day-trip. A typical rafting excursion begins with breakfast, followed by truck-ride upriver to the put-in. You'll be given a life vest, helmet and wetsuit (the water is frigid) plus instructions on paddling, safety and some of the ecology of the area. Then everyone clambers into the rafts and sets off downriver. You are usually asked to paddle a fair amount of the time, both in the rapids to keep the boat on its proper line, and in the flatwater areas to stay on pace. You'll stop for lunch about two-thirds of the way downriver.

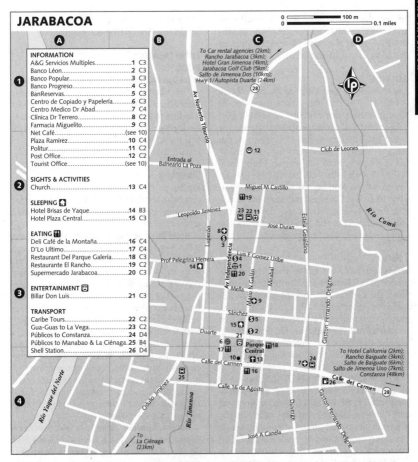

JARABACOA

INFORMATION	
A&G Servicios Multiples	**1** C3
Banco Léon	**2** C3
Banco Popular	**3** C3
Banco Progreso	**4** C3
BanReservas	**5** C3
Centro de Copiado y Papelería	**6** C3
Centro Medico Dr Abad	**7** C4
Clínica Dr Terrero	**8** C2
Farmacia Miguelito	**9** C3
Net Café	(see 10)
Plaza Ramírez	**10** C3
Politur	**11** C2
Post Office	**12** C2
Tourist Office	(see 10)

SIGHTS & ACTIVITIES	
Church	**13** C4

SLEEPING	
Hotel Brisas de Yaque	**14** B3
Hotel Plaza Central	**15** C3

EATING	
Deli Café de la Montaña	**16** C4
D'Lo Ultimo	**17** C4
Restaurant Del Parque Galería	**18** C3
Restaurante El Rancho	**19** C2
Supermercado Jarabacoa	**20** C3

ENTERTAINMENT	
Billar Don Luis	**21** C3

TRANSPORT	
Caribe Tours	**22** C2
Gua-Guas to La Vega	**23** C2
Públicos to Constanza	**24** D4
Públicos to Manabao & La Ciénaga	**25** B4
Shell Station	**26** D4

The Río Yaque del Norte is no Zambezi but has enough rolls and holes to keep things interesting. The landscape is beautiful at times and sadly deforested in others. There is some litter as well, though much less here than elsewhere as the guides regularly remove trash from the river. The forest, the river, the litter, the tourists, the local residents – all play a role in the complicated task of doing right by people and right by the environment. The guides often have interesting insight, and it at least makes for an interesting discussion over lunch.

CANYONING

This is definitely not an activity for people who fear heights. A typical trip involves hiking down into a deep canyon just below Salto de Jimenoa Uno, leaping from the top of an enormous boulder into the chilly Río Jimenoa below, swimming down part of the river, then rappelling twice down rocky cliff faces to solid-rock landings. There are two levels – one for beginners and another for more experienced climbers. Tour operators provide all the equipment you will need, but you should wear sturdy shoes and leave your nerves at the hotel. (Leave your camera too – unless you have a strong waterproof case, it'll only get wet.)

HIKING

In addition to its waterfalls, Jarabacoa is a good base for hikes in the nearby mountains and national park, primarily the multi-day ascent of Pico Duarte. For details on climbing Pico Duarte as well as shorter hikes in the area, see p230 and p224.

GOLFING

Just outside of town, the **Jarabacoa Golf Club** (☎ 809-441-1940; ☺ 7:30am-7:30pm) has a decent though rather nondescript nine-hole golf course that will do for anyone desperate for a golf fix. The course has two par-fives, the longest being 433m. Green fees are US$27 for two laps around the course. Club rental is US$11 with balls – oddly, rental is for one round only, so you have to pay it twice if you play 18 holes. Caddies and carts are available for hire. To get there, take the turnoff to Salto de Jimenoa and look for signs for the *Campo de Golf*, about 3km down.

Tours

Jarabacoa has two main tour operators, whose main clientele are Dominican groups from the capital and foreign guests of all-inclusive resorts near Puerto Plata. However, independent travelers are always free to join any of the trips, usually by just calling the day before. Canyoning and longer hiking trips (including Pico Duarte) should be arranged several days in advance.

Rancho Baiguate (☎ 809-574-6890; www.rancho baiguate.com.do; Carretera a Constanza) and **Rancho Jarabacoa** (☎ 809-248-7909; ranchojarabacoa@hotmail .com; Carretera a Salto de Jimenoa Dos) offer all the activities described above at similar prices: 1½-hour tour of one or two waterfalls on horseback (per person without/with lunch US$10/16), jeep (per person without/with lunch US$10/16), ATV (from US$30) or mountain bike (US$20 per person). Canyoning trips last 3½ hours and cost US$56. Pico Duarte trips can be three, four or five days, and vary in price depending on the number of people in the group. For two people, expect to pay US$310/437/540 per person for a three-/four-/five-day outing. With five people, the rates fall to US$210/270/340 per person. Note: a three-night tour may include two nights in a hotel.

Iguana Mama (☎ 809-571-0908, in US ☎ 800-849-4720; www.iguanamama.com; Cabarete; ☺ 8am-5pm) is a highly recommended tour operator based in Cabarete that does tours around Jarabacoa, including mountain biking and climbing Pico Duarte. Trips typically leave from

Cabarete, but you can pick up the tour in Jarabacoa. See (p195) for details.

Entertainment

POOL

Billar Don Luis (Mario N Galán at Duarte; per hr US$0.90; ☺ 3pm-midnight) If you have some downtime between waterfalls and rafting, consider heading to this eight-table pool hall. A laid-back place with cheap beers and a view of the park, both women and men will feel comfortable shooting pool here.

Sleeping

Jarabacoa has two acceptable hotels – one much better than the other – and a number of more upscale options in the wooded areas around town.

Hotel Brisas de Yaque (☎ 809-574-4490; Luperón at Prof Pelegrina Herrera; r US$25; ☒) The best option in town, this hotel offers cozy rooms with exposed brick walls, wood trim and nice balconies. Be sure to ask for one facing west – the view of the surrounding mountains is excellent.

Hotel Plaza Central (☎ 809-524-7768; Mario N Galan near Sánchez; r/tw US$10.50/17.50; ℗) Half a block from the Parque Central, this hotel offers 15 no-frills rooms with fans and cleanish bathrooms. The large windows let in lots of light and a good breeze. On weekends, the discotheque on the first floor will keep you up until sunrise – bring earplugs or just join the party.

Rancho Baiguate (☎ 809-574-6890; www.rancho baiguate.com.do; Carretera a Constanza; s/d US$35/50; ☒ ℗) Rancho Baiguate offers plain but comfortable accommodations on its 72-sq-km complex, about 5km east of town. Several two-story units contain boxy guest rooms with private hot-water bath, screened windows, ceiling fan and heater. Full meal plans are available and the rates listed here include breakfast. Most have two beds (either single or queens) and shiny enamel paint to dress up the cinder-block construction. Also on the grounds are volleyball and basketball courts, a soccer field and a gift shop. This is a good place if you have kids and/or plan on joining some of the many tours offered here. Electricity turns off at around midnight – ask for candles or a flashlight when you check in.

Hotel California (☎ 809-574-6255; Carretera a Constanza; r without/with breakfast US$28.50/35) Two kilometers east of town, this friendly hotel has 10 OK rooms, all with cement floors, clean bathrooms, and ceiling fans. The beds are saggy in some, and the lighting could be better, but all face a grassy courtyard that has tables and chairs and is reasonably pleasant. Breakfast is served in a small open-air dining area near the entrance, and includes eggs, fruit, bread, juice and coffee. More convenient if you have your own car, though *motoconchos* do pass by and you can call for a taxi.

Hotel Gran Jimenoa (☎ 809-574-6304; Av La Confluencia; www.granjimenoa.com; d/tw US$47/67; 🐃 🔀 P) Several kilometers from town, this is Jarabacoa's best hotel and good value if it's in your price range. All 28 rooms are spotless, spacious and were freshly-painted when we visited. Each has comfortable beds, tiled floors and a large terrace looking onto the attractive swimming pool – numbers 206 and 306 are corner rooms with even more space and a small sofa. The restaurant (right) may be the hotel's best feature though, with an open-sided deck perched right on the banks of the surging Jimenoa river, an undeniably dramatic location. Breakfast is included in the room rates. A small bridge leads across the river to a multi-purpose space, often for dance classes or group events. The hotel also has a sauna, ping-pong table and books tours with Rancho Baiguate (opposite).

Eating

Deli Café de la Montaña (☎ 809-574-7799; Calle del Carmen at Mario N Galan; mains US$2.25-5; 🕑 lunch & dinner, closed Mon) Great for vegetarians but good for anyone looking for a light meal, this eatery offers excellent sandwiches and wraps, hearty salads and good pita pizzas. The *tortilla Dominicana* (a flour tortilla filled with yucca and white onions, US$2) and the veggie sandwich (eggplant, green peppers, mozzarella, basil and onions packed between two slices of wheat bread, US$4.70) are especially good.

Restaurante El Rancho (☎ 809-574-4557; Av Independencia 1; mains US$4-10; 🕑 breakfast, lunch & dinner) On the northern edge of town, El Rancho offers a varied menu of chicken and beef dishes, crêpes, pastas and seafood. The walls of this semi-dressy, open-sided restaurant are graced with handsome local paintings although the *motoconcho* traffic outside detracts somewhat from the setting.

This place is highly recommended by locals and travelers alike.

Restaurant Del Parque Galería (☎ 809-574-6749; Duarte at Mirabal; mains US$3.50-10.50; 🕑 breakfast, lunch & dinner) Overlooking the Parque Central, this open-air restaurant/bar serves up traditional Dominican meals as well as international favorites. If you're in the mood to try something a little different, the *conejo criollo* (rabbit prepared Creole-style, US$10) and *cabrito al vino* (goat in wine sauce, US$8.50) are both excellent choices. A great place to people watch, you can also feel free to just order a drink and check out the goings-on in the park.

D'Lo Ultimo (☎ 809-574-7591; Av Independencia near Sánchez; mains US$3.50-10.50; 🕑 breakfast, lunch & dinner, closed Thu) This modest Dominican eatery offers reliable and tasty meals. Be sure to ask about the daily special; you can often get a salad, a meat-based entrée with a side of rice, and a dessert for US$5 to US$6.

Hotel Gran Jimenoa (☎ 809-574-6304; Av La Confluencia; www.granjimenoa.com; mains US$8-15; 🕑 7am-11pm) Jarabacoa's best hotel also offers one of the town's most unique dining experiences. The restaurant here occupies an open-air deck, shaded by low trees and perched right alongside the roaring Río Jimenoa. Tables along the edge have the best view – so close you may even feel some errant spray and have to speak loudly to be heard over the river's din. Dishes are fairly standard, though well-prepared, including parmesan chicken, rice with shrimp, or fish with the hotel's own special vegetable sauce.

Supermercado Jarabacoa (☎ 809-574-2780; Av Independencia; 🕑 8am-10pm Mon-Sat, 9am-1pm Sun) A good-sized supermarket, this place has the best selection of canned food, produce and dry goods in town.

Getting There & Away

Caribe Tours (☎ 809-574-4796; Calle José Duran near Av Independencia) offers the only bus service to and from Jarabacoa. Four daily departures to Santo Domingo (US$5.25, 2½ hours, 7:30am, 10am, 1:30pm and 4:30pm) include a stop in La Vega (US$1.75, 30 minutes).

Next door, a **gua-gua terminal** (Av Independencia at José Duran) provides frequent service to La Vega (US$1.40, 45 minutes, every 10 to 30 minutes, 5:30am to 6:30pm). If you prefer to hire a cab to La Vega (see p230), the ride costs around US$14.

Públicos to Constanza (in front of the Shell gasoline station, Gaston Fernando Deligne at Calle del Carmen) leave at 9am and 1pm daily (US$2.80, two hours). It's a scenic but rough ride in the back of a pickup truck; the first 29km are on a badly rutted road that winds around denuded mountains but once you hit El Río, the remaining 19km are on a paved road that passes through a lush valley. Worth a go if you're feeling adventurous.

Públicos to La Ciénaga (US$2.25, 1½ hours) leave roughly every two hours from Calle Odulio Jiménez near Calle 16 de Agosto. It's 42km long, of which the first 33km are paved. Returning can be more of a challenge, especially if you return from your hike in the afternoon. There are *públicos* (normal cars used for public transport), but don't hesitate to hail down any truck heading toward Jarabacoa. Chances are the driver will allow you to hop aboard. It's customary to tip the driver a couple of dollars.

Getting Around

The town of Jarabacoa is easily managed on foot but to get to outlying hotels and sights you can easily flag down a *motoconcho* on any street corner during the day. During the evening and if you prefer a bit more comfort (and safety), call **Taxi Jarabacoa** (☎ 809-574-7474) or just catch a cab at the corner of José Duran and Av Independencia.

CAR RENTAL

For such a small town, Jarabacoa has a surprising number of car rental agencies. Most rent small SUVs – known amusingly as *jeepetas* – which are better suited than cars for the sometimes-rough roads here. Rates average US$40 to US$45 per day, less if you rent for a week or more. Among many others, **Francis Rent A Car** (☎ 809-574-2981; Carretera a Salto Jimenoa Dos Km. 2; ☽ 8am-noon, 2-6pm Mon-Fri, to 7pm Sat, to 5pm Sun) is well-regarded for service and quality. On the same road closer to town, **Chachi Rent A Car** (☎ 809-574-2533; ☽ 8am-noon, 2-6pm Mon-Sat) offers slightly lower prices.

PARQUES NACIONALES BERMÚDEZ & RAMÍREZ

In 1956 the Dominican government established Parque Nacional Armando Bermúdez with the hope of preventing the kind of reckless deforestation occurring in Haiti. The park encompasses 766 sq km of tree-flanked mountains and pristine valleys. Two years later, an adjoining area of 764 sq km was designated Parque Nacional José del Carmen Ramírez. Between them, the parks contain three of the highest peaks in the Caribbean and the headwaters of 12 major rivers, including the Río Yaque del Norte, the country's only white-water and most important river.

Flora & Fauna

The most visible and impressive animals in the park are its birds. Among the more characteristic species you may see are the Hispaniolan parrot, the Hispaniolan woodpecker, the white-necked crow, the Hispaniolan trogon, the ruddy quail dove, the red-tailed hawk and the Dominican Republic's national bird, the palm chat. There are 47 known amphibians in the parks and several mammal species, most notably the wild boar, which was introduced. They reside chiefly in areas that are very difficult to access on foot.

Up to about 1200m above sea level, the parks' flora is mostly West Indian cedar, petitia, mountain wild olive, palo amargo and, close to the rivers, West Indian walnut and wild cane. From 1200m to 1500m, the flora shifts to mainly pasture fiddlewood, West Indian laurel cherry, sierra palm, copey oak and lirio, and shifts again between 1500m and 2000m to Krug wild avocado, tree ferns, cyrilla, wild braziletto and sumac. Above 2000m, the forest is ruled by Creole pine and a variety of bushes, such as *Garrya fadyenii* and *Baccharis myrsinites*.

Climbing Pico Duarte

Astonishingly, Pico Duarte – the Caribbean's tallest peak – was not climbed until 1944, as part of a celebration commemorating the 100th anniversary of Dominican independence. During the late 1980s, the government began cutting trails in the parks and erecting cabins, hoping to increase tourism to the country by increasing the accessibility of its peaks. Today, 3000 people a year ascend Pico Duarte, and a fair number of visitors summit the second- and third-highest peaks.

ORIENTATION & INFORMATION

There are ranger stations near the start of the major trails into the parks – at La Ciénaga, Sabaneta, Mata Grande, Las Lagunas and

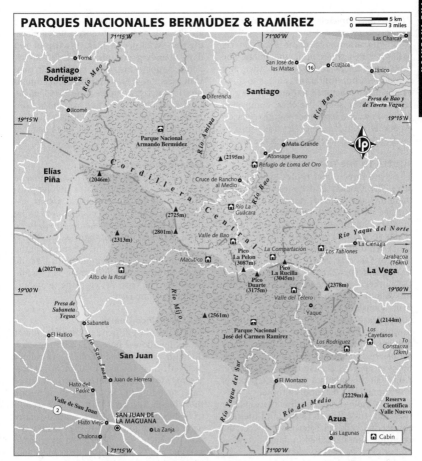

PARQUES NACIONALES BERMÚDEZ & RAMÍREZ

Constanza. Stations are officially open from 8am to 5pm daily, though the guards typically sleep in the station and so are there around the clock. There is usually a large map of the parks showing trails as well as the location of the free hikers' cabins at the ranger station, but unfortunately pocket-size trail maps are generally unavailable. The park entrance fee is US$3.50. As a safety precaution, everyone entering the park, even for a short hike, must be accompanied by a guide.

WHAT TO BRING
Cold-weather and rain clothing are musts for anyone intending to spend a night in either park. While the average temperature

ranges between 12°C and 20°C most of the year, lows of -5°C are not uncommon, especially in December and January. The Parque Nacional Armando Bermúdez receives between 2000mm and 4000mm of rain annually, which usually arrives in drenching downpours. Parque Nacional José del Carmen Ramírez, on the southern side of the range, generally receives about one-third as much rain, but still enough that you need to be prepared.

Stand-alone portable toilets are near most of the cabins, but they are usually in dire need of cleaning. Many campers generally prefer to slip behind a tree and hope to go unnoticed. Bring something you can dig a hole with, as well as extra toilet paper.

Be sure to completely bury your waste and paper.

Do not attempt to climb Pico Duarte without sturdy shoes, preferably boots. The trails are generally kept free of boulders and falling trees, but little effort is made to fill in deep ruts or otherwise smooth out choppy sections. Over some stretches, compacted dirt gives way to loose rock; in other places, especially after rain, the dirt trails turn to mud and shallow creeks form in the tracks.

ROUTES TO THE TOP

There are three direct routes up Pico Duarte. The shortest and easiest route (and therefore most utilized) is from La Ciénaga, reached via Jarabacoa. Another route starts in Mata Grande, south of San José de las Matas (p224) and Santiago. The third and least used route is from the south, from the town of Sabanete, reached via San Juan de la Maguana (p242).

Another way to the top is via the beautiful Valle del Tétero, which you can reach from Constanza (p234) or from Las Lagunas, reachable via Padre las Casas in the southwest. From Valle del Tétero, a trail links up with the Pico Duarte trails. Many people visit Valle del Tétero as a detour on the way up Pico Duarte from La Ciénaga. Although this involves some backtracking, it is a much less demanding route.

All six trails – the three direct ascents, the two trails to Valle del Tétero, and the trail connecting Valle del Tétero to the Pico Duarte trail – are described in detail below.

La Ciénaga–Pico Duarte

This is by far the most popular route. It is 23km in each direction and involves approximately 2275m of vertical ascent en route to the peak; included in this figure are the hills and valleys encountered along the way. Most people make the trip in two days, spending one night at La Compartición campground. They begin their final 5km ascent at 4:30am, giving them enough time to watch the sunrise from Pico Duarte. La Ciénaga may be reached by *público* from Jarabacoa. The road between the two communities is mostly paved (for more detailed directions, see p229).

Mata Grande–Pico Duarte

The second-most difficult route, this is 45km in each direction and involves approximately 3802m of vertical ascent, including hills and valleys encountered along the way. Most people make the trip in three days, spending the first night at the Río La Guácara campground and the second at the Valle de Bao campground. Mata Grande may be reached by *público* from San José de la Matas. The road between the two communities is unpaved.

Sabaneta–Pico Duarte

This is the most difficult of the three direct routes mentioned here. It is 48km in each direction and, with all the hills and valleys factored in, it involves 3802m of vertical ascent. Most people make the trip in three days, spending the first night in or beside the cabin at Alto de la Rosa and the second in or beside the cabin at Macutico (many people choose to erect a tent near the cabins). Sabaneta may be reached by *público* and *gua-gua* from San Juan de la Maguana. The road between the two communities is paved. Note that there is another Sabaneta north of the parks, on the road to Dajabón, so don't confuse the two.

RAT INVASION!

Although the Parques Nacional Bermúdez and Ramírez offer a number of well-built cabins, most visitors choose to sleep outdoors. The reason? Rats – big ones – that launch nightly raids on cabins in search for food.

If you end up sleeping inside, expect to have rats scurrying over and around you. Even if you pitch a tent inside a cabin to take advantage of the level floor, you'll have rats pestering you; they'll climb on your tent and gnaw through it to get to your rations or anything that smells like food.

For your well-being – and to get some rest – take a tent, pitch it away from the cabin, and zip yourself in for the night. Be sure to wrap your food in plastic and string it up and away from the ground. The best place, ironically, is from the rafters of the cabins.

Las Lagunas-Valle del Tétero

This route is 36km in each direction and involves approximately 2000m of vertical ascent. Most people make the trip in three days, spending the first night at the campground near the small town of Las Cañitas and the second at the Valle del Tétero campground. Las Lagunas may be reached by *público* from Padre las Casas. The road between the two communities is unpaved.

Constanza–Valle del Tétero

This route passes through lots of farmland before the scenery becomes pristine (encroachment on the parks is a big problem). It is 43km in each direction and involves about 1590m of vertical ascent. Most people make the trip in three days, spending the first night at Los Rodríguez campground and the second at the Valle del Tétero campground. Constanza may be reached by *gua-gua* from La Vega, Bonao and the turnoff at Hwy Duarte (Hwy 1).

Valle del Tétero–Pico Duarte

After a fairly arduous 8km trek, this 20km route connects with the La Ciénaga-Pico Duarte route at a fork in the trail called Agüita Fría. From Agüita Fría to the campground at La Compartición, it's another 3km. Most hikers spend the night at the campground and get a 4:30am start on the 5km ascent to the summit. Their intent: to watch the sunrise from the highest point on the island. On a clear day, you can see both the Caribbean and the Atlantic from the heap of boulders that forms the very top of the Cordillera Central.

GUIDES

The easiest and most worry-free way of climbing Pico Duarte is with an organized trip. If your time is short, or you don't have much experience on multi-day hikes, it makes sense to go with a professional. All three of the tour operators listed in the Tours section (p228) can arrange trips – usually from La Ciénaga but you should definitely ask about other routes if you're interested – and this is the way most people go.

If you've done hikes of this sort before – and your Spanish is decent – it's not terribly difficult to organize a trip yourself. You must hire a guide (per day US$20) who will insist you hire a pack mule (per day

US$10) and possibly an extra mule and/or a cook depending on the size of your group. Purists scoff at hiring mules, but for most people the mule is a practical and remarkably cheap way to bring all the equipment, provisions and water you need without worrying about weight – they even carry your personal gear. The mule is also useful if someone gets hurt (which is the main reason the guides want them along) and some people even ride them up instead of hiking. Discuss with the guide how long you have and any side trips you'd like – Valle del Tétero, for example – and together you can plan your trip. Guides typically bring along tools like a hatchet for cutting firewood, but it's important to double check who is bringing what. You are expected to bring food for yourself and your guide – basic provisions usually suffice. Guides and mules are easy to hire in La Ciénaga, owing to the steady traffic here. They are harder to arrange at the other trailheads, and you will likely need an extra day or two to make all the arrangements.

You can also hire independent guides in Jarabacoa – expect to pay around US$275 per person (minimum two) for a two-night/three-day trip that includes transportation to/from Jarabacoa, food, all equipment, pack mules and guide services. The best way to locate an independent guide is to ask at your hotel for a recommendation.

Sleeping & Eating

There are approximately 14 campgrounds in the parks, each with a first-come first-served cabin that hikers can use free of charge. Each cabin can hold 20 or more people and consists of wood floors, wood walls and a wood ceiling, but no beds, cots, mats, or lockers of any kind. That wouldn't be so bad except that the most-frequented cabins have developed a somewhat unnerving rat problem (see the boxed text on opposite); if you have a tent, consider bringing it along so you can avoid using the cabins altogether.

Most of the cabins also have a stand-alone 'kitchen': an open-sided structure with two or three concrete wood-burning stoves. Fallen, dead wood is usually abundant near the campsites – be sure you or your guide bring matches and some paper to get the fire started.

The only water in the parks is in the creeks. Bring along plenty of bottled water, but also bring a filter, purification tablets, or be prepared to boil your water (at least three minutes at a full boil).

CONSTANZA
pop 29,480

At 1300m, Constanza is even higher than Jarabacoa although its location in a broad valley filled with farmland and surrounded by mountains gives it a more bucolic than alpine feel. It is a popular getaway for city-slickers from the capital, and there are a number of large vacation estates owned by wealthy *capitalinos*. The chief crops here are potatoes, strawberries, apples, lettuce and especially garlic – in certain times of the year, the air is filled with the pungent aroma of fresh garlic.

Constanza isn't on the way anywhere and there's not a whole lot to do, especially if you don't have a car – the main reason people come is seeking some peace and quiet (and a respite from the lowland heat). Unfortunately, like Jarabacoa, the small-town atmosphere is somewhat spoiled by the profusion of motorcycles and scooters, which raise a constant and sometimes oppressive din on Constanza's main streets through much of the day. Constanza still has its appealing side – evening baseball games and nice views – but the town's growth is definitely threatening that.

Also calling Constanza home are a couple of hundred Japanese farmers who arrived during the 1950s at dictator Rafael Trujillo's invitation. In return for providing superior farmland at dirt-cheap prices to 50 Japanese families, Trujillo hoped the Japanese would convert the fertile valley into a thriving agricultural center, which they did.

Orientation

The main street is one-way Calle Luperón, which runs from east to west and has a prominent Isla gas station – also known as *la parada* (the stop) and *la bomba* (the pump) – at its eastern end. Most of Constanza's hotels and restaurants are on or near Calle Luperón. The exception is the Alto Cerro, which is 2km from town off the road toward Hwy Duarte and Bonao. Constanza has a tall radio tower poking up in the middle of town – it's right next to

the tourist office and is a useful landmark if you ever get turned around. The *mercado municipal* (municipal market) is at the far western end of town, a few blocks north of Calle Luperón.

Unlike most Dominican cities, Constanza's Parque Central is not a popular hangout. However, it represents the center of town and may be reached by proceeding eight or nine blocks down Calle Luperón from the Isla station and turning left. The adjacent church, which was erected in 1990 and is nothing special, can be seen after you turn left and go two blocks farther.

Information

INTERNET ACCESS
Ciber Bibilotec@ Emy (across from the baseball diamond; per hr US$2.10; �9am-8pm Mon-Sat)

MEDICAL SERVICES
There is no hospital or health clinic in town. The closest healthcare options are in Santiago.

Farmacia Constanza (☎ 809-539-2880; Luperón at Libertad; �8am-11pm Mon-Sat, until 9pm Sun) At the far west end of town.

Farmacia Yazdana (☎ 809-539-1142; Luperón near Duarte; �8am-noon & 2-9pm Mon-Sat, 8am-noon Sun) Two blocks east of the Isla gas station, this pharmacy offers free delivery.

MONEY
Banco Léon (Luperón at Miguel Andrés Abreu; �8:30am-5pm Mon-Fri, 9am-1pm Sat) Hard to miss on the main drag, this bank exchanges travelers checks and has one ATM.

BanReservas (Miguel Andrés Abreu btwn Luperón & Viñas; �8am-5pm Mon-Fri, 9am-1pm Sat) Around the corner and also has an ATM.

TELEPHONE
Mi Plazita (☎ 809-539-3239; Luperón at Libertad; calls to USA per minute US$0.32, to Europe per minute US$0.52; �8am-10pm) At the west end of town.

Tricom (☎ 809-539-1015; Luperón 42; calls to USA per minute US$0.32, to Europe per minute US$0.75; �8am-9:45pm) On the main drag.

TOURIST INFORMATION
Tourism office (☎ 809-539-2900; Calle Matilde Viña near Miguel Andrés Abreu; �9am-1pm & 2-6pm Mon-Fri) Next to a radio station, this office offers lots of helpful information and a friendly staff. Spanish only. Look for the radio tower three blocks west of the Isla gas station.

Sights & Activities

Though Constanza is surrounded by mountains, there aren't many established hikes or excursions in the area. The main sights are all quite distant, and require a 4WD drive to get there.

AGUAS BLANCAS

These impressive **waterfalls** are a beautiful but difficult 15km drive from Constanza. The falls – actually one cascade in three different sections – crash some 135m down a sheer cliff into a pretty pool. You'll need a 4WD to get there – turn north at the Isla gas station and continue past the Colonia Japonesa. A *motoconcho* ride out there runs about US$12.

LA PIEDRA LETRADA

Meaning 'Inscribed Stone,' **Piedra Letrada** is a shallow cave containing scores of Taíno petroglyphs and pictograms, mostly depicting animals and simplistic human-like figures. The site is a good 30km from Constanza via the town of La Culeta. The road to La Culeta is paved, but it deteriorates quickly after that. Ask for directions in La Culeta, as the road is easy to miss. A *motoconcho* ride there will cost about US$20.

SOFTBALL GAMES

One of the most enjoyable things to do in Constanza is to attend one of the friendly **softball games** held almost every night all year long at the local baseball diamond. Games begin at 7pm; there is no admission fee and you can usually find someone selling beer, soda and odd snacks from a cooler in the stands. The stadium is located several blocks west of the Parque Central.

Sleeping

Alto Cerro (☎ 809-539-1553; www.altocerro.com; 2km east of town on highway to Bonao; r US$19.50, ste with kitchen US$32, villa with kitchen US$43) Easily the best accommodation in Constanza, this large complex is several hundred meters off the highway into town. Perched partway up a high bluff, the rooms have terrific views of the whole valley, the bright green fields of carrots and strawberries spread out like a patchwork quilt below. Rooms have high ceilings and comfortable beds; the suites and villas are larger and convenient for their kitchens. Other than the restaurant

at the hotel, there are no other places to eat without going into town, but the hotel has a small market, where you can buy pasta and other basics for a simple meal. There was talk that the Alto Cerro would be completely rented for up to three years by a Brazilian company building a nearby dam – if so, here's hoping they leave a room or two available for independent travelers, as no other place in town compares.

Hotel Aguas Blancas (☎ 809-539-1561; Antonio M García near 14 de Julio; r weekdays/weekends US$10.50/14; Ⓟ) Near the *mercado municipal*, this small hotel offers eight spotless rooms with tiled floors, fans and private hot-water baths. Cable TV is offered in three rooms for an additional US$3.50.

Hotel Restaurant Mi Casa (☎ 809-539-2764; Luperón at Sánchez; r/tw US$15/26) A block west from the Isla gas station, rooms here are basic and clean. All have private baths but only some are tiled. Some rooms lack good ventilation; request one with an outward-facing window for a breeze. An on-site restaurant is decent for breakfast.

Eating

Restaurant Aguas Blancas (☎ 809-539-1561; Rufino Espinosa 54; mains US$3.50-7; Ⓨ lunch & dinner) With a pleasant dining room and excellent food, this is the best place to eat in town. Lunch specials are especially good value: for US$3.50, diners receive a plate of rice and beans, salad and a choice of a meat-based main.

Lorenzo's Restaurant Pizzería (☎ 809-539-2008; Luperón 83; mains US$4-11; Ⓨ breakfast, lunch & dinner) Towards the western edge of town, Lorenzo's is a homey eatery with a huge mountainscape mural and tinted windows. The service here is good and the food is classic Dominican fare – *chivo guisado* (sautéed goat, US$6) and *conejo al vino* (wild rabbit in wine sauce, US$6.50) – mixed with decent pizzas and sandwiches.

Super El Económico (☎ 809-539-2323; Luperón across from Isla gas station; Ⓨ 7:45am-noon, 1:45-8pm Mon-Sat, 9am-noon Sun) Medium-sized grocery store with canned food, snacks, water, produce and more.

Mercado Municipal (Gratereaux at 14 de Julio; Ⓨ 7am-6pm Mon-Sat, 7am-noon Sun) A good-sized market near the north end of town, here you'll find a wide variety of locally grown produce.

Getting There & Away

Buses depart daily from Constanza. **Transporte Cobra** (☎ 809-539-2004) goes to Santo Domingo (US$5.30, three hours, 5:30am and 12:30pm); **Linea Junior** (☎ 809-539-2177) heads to Santiago (US$5.30, three hours, 5:30am); and **Transporte La Princesa** (☎ 809-539-2415) serves La Vega (US$2.75, two hours, 5am). All three leave from La Parada but pickup can be arranged by calling a day in advance for a nominal surcharge.

Gua-guas also leave from La Parada. Destinations include Jarabacoa (US$2.80, two hours, no fixed schedule) and El Abanico (US$2.80, one hour, hourly from 6am–4pm), the intersection of Highway Duarte and the road to Constanza. From there, you can puddle-jump your way to Santo Domingo (via Bonao) and Santiago (via La Vega). Note that *gua-guas* in this part of the country are mostly pickup trucks so if you prefer to sit inside the cabin, be sure to be one of the first passengers on the truck.

Around Constanza itself, walking is easy enough; it's a small town and there's not much traffic. For area sights, *motoconchos* and taxis always can be found at or near La Parada. Be sure to agree on a price before you accept the ride.

LA VEGA

pop 102,426

Situated beside Hwy Duarte, 125km north of Santo Domingo, is the bustling provincial city of La Vega, which serves the farming interests of the lower Valle del Cibao. Today La Vega is big, busy, noisy and crowded, with little or nothing of interest to the tourist, save its Carnival celebration, which many consider to be the best in the country.

Famous nationwide, more than 70,000 people visit La Vega over the course of Carnival every year. Townspeople belong to one of numerous 'grupos de Carnaval' (Carnival groups), which range from ten to two hundred members and have unique names and costumes. The costumes (which can cost up to US$1000) are the best part of Carnival here – a colorful baggy outfit (it looks like a clown, but is supposed to represent a prince), a cape and a fantastic diabolic mask with bulging eyes and gruesome pointed teeth.

Groups march along a long loop through town, and spectators either watch from bleachers set up alongside or march right along with them. The latter do so at their own risk – the costume also includes a small whip with an inflated rubber bladder at the end, used to whack passersby on the backside. Carnival Vegano, as the celebration here is called, has been criticized lately for being overly commercialized. Indeed, you'll see booths and VIP viewing areas hosted by Orange, Presidente and other companies, and some Carnival groups stitch the name of sponsors onto their costumes (which are themselves typically bought, as opposed to handmade as in Santiago and elsewhere.) But for now, the celebration is still more personal than corporate, and the high level of organization and security are certainly a plus.

La Vega dates to the late 1490s, when Christopher Columbus ordered that a fort be built to store gold mined in the area. During the next 50 years, the first mint in the New World was established here; the nation's first commercial sugar crop was harvested in the vicinity; and the first royally sanctioned brothel in the Western hemisphere opened its doors for business.

But this prosperity came to an abrupt end in 1562, when an earthquake leveled the city. So severe was the damage that the city was moved several kilometers to its present site on the banks of the Río Camú. You can visit what remains of the old city near the town of Santo Cerro (opposite).

The main street is Av Antonio Guzman, which runs north-south and intersects Hwy Duarte on the north side of town. On the northern end of the avenue, there are two hotels and a Santiago-bound *gua-gua* stop; near the central part, you'll find the main plaza, the Cathedral, food stands and a bank.

Information

BanReservas (Padre Adolfo near Av Antonio Guzman; ✍ 9am-5pm Mon-Fri, 9am-1pm Sat) A half-block from the Cathedral, this bank exchanges travelers checks and has one ATM. It also has a stand-alone ATM in the auto repair shop next to Hotel El Rey.

Red Cross (☎ 809-277-8181; ✍ 24hr) This is your best bet in the event of a medical emergency.

Sights & Activities

Other than during Carnival, there's no real reason to stop or make a special trip to La Vega. If you are there, however, there are a few things worth checking out.

VALLE DEL CIBAO

The Valle del Cibao doesn't make it onto many travelers' itineraries – nor should it, for there is precious little for tourists to see or do there. But the towns there, and the extremely fertile land they occupy, played an important role in the development of Hispaniola and the Dominican Republic. Two of the more important towns in the area are San Francisco de Macorís and Moca.

San Francisco de Macorís is a bustling, prosperous place in the heart of the Valle del Cibao. It draws much of its prosperity from the fields of cocoa and rice that grow around it in all directions. (It may also derive some trickle-down effect from the wealthy drug lords who reputedly own some of the huge barricaded mansions visible around town.) There are a number of colonial buildings around town and a large, pretty plaza. San Francisco is also home of one of the Dominican Republic's six baseball teams, the Gigantes (Giants), so going to a baseball game may be the best reason to pay a visit.

The country town of **Moca** has prospered in recent decades as a result of its production of coffee, cocoa and tobacco. The tallest building in town is also its only tourist attraction, the **Iglesia Corazón de Jesus**, with a panel of beautiful stained glass imported from Turin, Italy. During the 19th century, Moca was one of the Spanish colony's chief cattle centers. Unfortunately for the people of Moca, its distance from Santo Domingo made it a natural target of forces seeking to wrest control of eastern Hispaniola from Spain. In 1805, a Haitian force led by Henri Christophe that was trying to place the entire island under the Haitian flag entered Moca, killed virtually the entire population and burned the town to the ground. Moca struggled back, and in the 1840s began to raise tobacco as a commercial crop; now, some of the world's finest cigars contain tobacco grown on the hillsides around the town.

CATEDRAL DE LA CONCEPCIÓN

La Vega's infamous **Cathedral** (Av Antonio Guzman at Padre Adolfo; ☺ varies), a fascinating eye-sore that looks more like a set of smokestacks than a place of worship. It is an odd mixture of Gothic and neo-industrial style constructed of concrete and decorated with sculpted metal bars and pipes alongside random ornamental windows. It faces the main park and is impossible to miss.

SANTO CERRO

Just north of La Vega, and several kilometers east of Hwy Duarte along a well signed road, is Santo Cerro (Holy Hill). Santo Cerro acquired its godly name the old-fashioned way – through a miracle. Legend has it that Columbus placed a cross he received as a bon voyage gift from Queen Isabela atop the hill, which commands a sweeping view of the Valle del Cibao. During a battle between Spaniards and Taínos, the Indians tried to burn the cross but it wouldn't catch fire. And then, with Taíno warriors looking on, the Virgen de las Mercedes appeared on one of its arms. The Indians are said to have fled in terror, and the Spaniards scored another victory for colonization.

Today the cross is gone – supposedly it's in private hands, but it is unclear whose – but you can still see the Santo Hoyo (Holy Hole) in which the cross was allegedly planted. The hole is inside the **Iglesia Las Mercedes** (☺ 7am-noon, 2-6pm) and covered with a small wire grill and tended by nuns and Jesuit priests. The beige-and-white church with its red-tile roof is a major pilgrimage site, drawing thousands of believers every September 24 to celebrate the patron saint day of Nuestra Señora de las Mercedes (Our Lady of the Mercies). Be sure to look for a fenced-off tree near the steps leading to the church – it is said to have been planted in 1495.

LA VEGA VIEJA

If you continue a few kilometers on the same road that brought you to Santo Cerro, you'll come to **La Vega Vieja** (admission US$1; ☺ 9am-noon, 2-5pm) the original site of the city. All that's left are the ruins of the fort Columbus ordered built as well as a church. Little of either actually survived the great earthquake of 1562 and most of what remained of the structures was taken to the latter-day La Vega, where it was used in construction.

Sleeping & Eating

Unless you are in La Vega for Carnival, there is no real reason to stay the night. If you do end up needing a place to crash, the pickings are pretty slim.

Hotel El Rey (☎ 809-573-9797; Av Antonio Guzman 4; r/tw US$32/42; ⛱ Ⓟ) This is a modern hotel with clean though somewhat dated rooms. Each has cable TV. Ask for a room towards the back since those facing the road can get loud. There's a restaurant on-site that serves decent Dominican fare.

Hotel Nueva Imagen (☎ 809-573-7351; Av. Antonio Guzman 3; r/tw US$11/14) Across the street from Hotel El Rey, this place could certainly use a facelift. Most rooms are run-down and marginally clean although some are significantly better than others. Ask to see a few before you settle in for the night.

Food stands serving fried chicken and *pastelitos* (flaky fried dough stuffed with meat, cheese or veggies) can be found in front of the Cathedral, just eight blocks south of the hotels.

Getting There and Away

La Vega is a regular stop on the well-covered Santo Domingo-Santiago route, so you'll have no trouble getting a bus or *gua-gua*. **Caribe Tours** (☎ 809-573-2488; Av Pedro A Rivera) has its terminal on the main highway 1.5km from the center of La Vega. From there, buses depart for Santo Domingo (US$3.75, 1½ hours, every 30 to 60 minutes, 6:30am to 9pm) and north to Sosua (US$3.50, 2½ hours, hourly, 7:30am to 8:30pm) with stops at Santiago (US$1.75, 40 minutes) and Puerto Plata (US$3, two hours). There are even more Santiago-only buses, plus *gua-guas* (US$1.50, 50 minutes) that leave from a terminal on the main road into town about five blocks from the Parque Central.

For Jarabacoa, the Caribe Tours bus from Santo Domingo passes La Vega terminal at roughly 8:30am, 11:30am, 3pm and 6pm (US$1.75, one hour). Alternatively, *gua-guas* and pickups leave whenever they're full from a stop called Quinto Patio (about a kilometer from the center, US$2 in a taxi) from 7am to 6pm.

For Constanza, there are two direct buses (US$3.50, two to three hours) leaving from La Vega's *mercado público* (public market) at around 8am and 2pm, though the actual departure times can vary by as much as an hour. Otherwise, you can catch a Bonao-bound *gua-gua* on Av Gregorio Riva south to the turn off to Constanza, known as El Abanico (US$1.50, 45 minutes). From there pickups leave whenever full until about 5pm (US$1.50, 1½ hours) – be aware that this leg goes over the mountains and can be quite chilly if you're in the back.

A taxi around town, including any of the bus or *gua-gua* terminals, costs US$2. In a pinch, you can also take a cab to El Abanico (US$11) or all the way to Jarabacoa (US$18).

BONAO
pop 73,269

Bonao, a commercial city along Hwy Duarte, is a struggling, unappealing mining town at the center of rich deposits of nickel, bauxite and silver. The town has very little to offer tourists and residents here, many of whom are connected in one way or the other to the hard-knuckled mining business, are largely unaccustomed to seeing foreign tourists (or national ones, for that matter). The town serves mainly as a place to stop for the night between Santiago and Santo Domingo, and has a comfortable roadside hotel and rest area north of town that's perfect for that use.

If you do need a place to crash, **Hotel Jacaranda** (☎ 809-525-5590; Hwy Duarte, 4km north of the Bonao exits; d/tw US$28/35), a classy hotel with 22 guest rooms that have all the creature comforts, including hot water, thick comfortable beds and clean modern baths. Service is very friendly – if you're staying here it's probably because you didn't get as far as you had hoped, which makes staying at a comfortable, reliable place all the more welcome.

If you just need a pit-stop, the hotel is part of the Plaza Jacaranda, a small shopping complex that contains a sit-down restaurant, several fast-food restaurants, a **Verizon call center** (to USA per min US$0.30, to Europe per min US$0.75; ✆ 7am-10:30pm), and an ATM. There's even a music store, a candy store and a shop selling suntan lotion, film and other useful items.

The Southwest

The southwestern region of the Dominican Republic (DR) is the most ecologically diverse in the country, a vast area that includes deserts and wetlands, mountains and valleys, oceans and lakes. The two largest cities, Barahona and San Juan de la Maguana, both have over 100,000 residents, but the vast majority of people here live in small communities and depend on either fishing or farming, especially sugarcane, bananas, corn, rice and cassava.

The southwest receives few tourists, and past efforts to attract large-scale tourism have met with little success. Most of the beaches are covered in smooth white stones – intriguing and beautiful, but not what most beach-hounds are looking for – and it can also get extremely hot (40°C plus is not uncommon). That said, the area has plenty of eco-tourism potential, including three national parks. One encompasses a massive saltwater lake that's home to crocodiles and innumerable iguanas; another has a freshwater lagoon with good bird-watching, including a permanent flamingo colony; and the third covers the Sierra de Bahoruco, which rises from scrubland to mountain pine forests.

The southwest doesn't outrank the beaches, adventure sports and eco-activities elsewhere in the DR, but it's definitely off the beaten path and can be a rewarding addition if you've got the time. There's an extensive network of *gua-guas* (minibuses used for local public transport), but you'll enjoy the southwest a lot more if you have a car. One of the highlights of the southwest is its scenic drives, whether along the dramatic coastline south of Barahona or through the interior's broad, roasting desert. Also many of the stops are short – likely to include visiting a Haitian market on the border or Taíno petroglyphs by the side of the road – and much more convenient if you don't have to wait around for buses.

HIGHLIGHTS

- Gorgeous drive along **Highway 44** (p249) passing white-stone beaches and cliff-top vista points

- The saltwater lake, **Lago Enriquillo** (p253) – the lowest point in the Caribbean – is teeming with crocodiles and beefy iguanas

- Take a boat through this freshwater lagoon, **Laguna de Oviedo** (p251) see flamingos, spoonbills and other aquatic birds

- With 8km of deserted shoreline reachable only by boat, **Bahía de las Águilas** (p252) is the most remote beach in the country.

- Vendors arrive on foot and on *burros* (donkeys) to sell produce and household goods at this intriguing **Haitian market** in Comendador/Elías Piña (p245)

THE SOUTHWEST

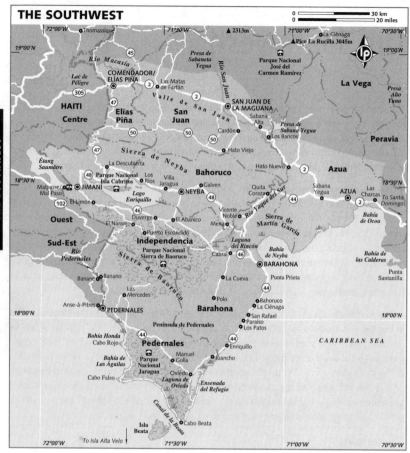

THE SOUTHWEST

INLAND

Just west of the Bahía de Ocoa, Hwy 2 heads inland to Azua and then north through the Valle de San Juan to Elías Piña and the Haitian border.

AZUA

pop 59,139

Azua is the first and largest town you'll encounter as you approach the southwest from the east, but it is little more than a pit stop for most travelers. There are hotels and basic services here, though nearby Baní is a much more pleasant place to spend the night.

History

Though none too appealing now, Azua does possess a very interesting history, having hosted three of the most notorious figures of the exploration and conquest of the New World. The city was founded in 1504 by Diego Velázquez, who reached Hispaniola 1493 as a member of Columbus's second voyage, and who is remembered for his later brutal subjugation of the indigenous people of Cuba. In 1494, Hernán Cortés came to town – Cortés fought under Velasquez in Cuba and would later lead the conquest of the Aztecs in present-day Mexico, but not before he had worked in Azua as a notary public. And Juan Ponce de León lived in Azua for a brief period as well – he was later to become the first European to reach present-day Florida while on his famously futile search for the fountain of youth.

But today, there are no memorials to commemorate Azua's three most (in)famous residents. In fact, Azua was originally about 12 km northwest of its present location, but was moved in 1751 after being leveled by an earthquake.

Orientation

Like many towns in the region, Azua is built up along the main highway, which splits into two one-way streets through town; here the west-bound street is Calle Emilio Prud'homme and the east-bound is Calle Duarte. If you are coming from Santo Domingo, the highway abruptly becomes Calle Duarte (headed in the wrong direction) and has just one small sign to warn you. To avoid ending up head-to-head with oncoming traffic, turn right at the first large intersection coming into town – look for a monument in the middle – and cut up a block to Calle Emilio Prud'homme, which heads west through town.

All of Azua's main shops and services are on one of its two main streets, or a side-street between them. Parque Central is on Calle Duarte between Calles Colón and Miguel Ángel Garrido. It is traditionally the city hub, and the best place to pick up *guaguas* heading in either direction. However it was closed for renovation at the time of research, and *gua-guas* were simply cruising down the main streets. It's possible they'll keep that system even after the park reopens, so definitely ask around.

Information

Banco Progreso (☎ 809-521-2592; Av Duarte at 19 de Marzo; ☟ 8:30am-1pm Mon-Fri, 9am-1pm Sat) has a 24hr ATM. **Farmacia Ramírez** (☎ 809-521-2973; Calle Emilio Prud'homme btwn Miguel Ángel Garido & Dr Aybar; ☟ 8am-10pm) is a small but complete pharmacy.

The **post office** (Vicente Noble at Calle Emilio Prud'homme; ☟ 8am-5pm Mon-Fri, 8am-noon Sat) is in a small blue building. Check email and make phone calls at **KMEL Comunicaciones** (☎ 809-521-3929; Colón; Internet per hr US$1.40, calls to USA per min US$0.35, to Europe per min US$0.70; ☟ 8am-10pm), between Calle Emilio Prud'homme and Calle Duarte.

Sights

Azua doesn't have much in the way of good beaches, although that doesn't stop both local residents and visitors from the capital from crowding along the coast on weekends. **Playa Río Monte** is the first and most popular of the beaches, with a number of food shacks along a gravel-littered shore. A better option is **Playa Blanca**, a rustic curve of almost-white sand about a kilometer west of Playa Río Monte along the dirt road that runs along the coast. It's unmarked and not visible from the road. To get there, after taking a right-hand curve about halfway up the first long uphill look for a small road/path on your left. Park there and follow the path, which leads about 500m around the corner and down the bluff to the beach. Bring insect repellent, as sand flies are irksome here.

The road also offers a few nice vantage points, before and beyond Playa Blanca. Keep your eye out for dolphins which frequent the bay usually around midday, and manta rays, which cruise for food along the surface and can sometimes be spotted from above.

The beaches are 6km from the highway, down a well-marked road a few hundred meters before entering the town from the east. If you don't have a car, *motoconchos* (motorcycle taxis) and taxis hang out near Parque Central and can take you to it. Expect to pay US$8 roundtrip on a *motoconcho*, and more for a cab.

Sleeping & Eating

Azua is not a great place to stop for the night – if possible head to Baní.

Hotel El Familiar (☎ 809-521-2272; Calle Emilio Prud'homme at Calle 19 de Marzo; r US$4.50, r with TV US$7, tw US$10.50) Very basic rooms have fan only and shed-like doors with padlocks, but are reasonably clean and will do in a pinch. The proprietors and their family live on-site, so there's no issues with noise or prostitution, as is common at other hotels in this range.

Kevin Sandwich (Calle Duarte btwn Miguel Ángel Garrido & Dr Aybar; mains US$1.50-5; ☟ 8am-1pm, 4pm-midnight) A bright light in an otherwise dreary dining scene, this small café has a bank of yellow and white doors, clean tile floors and tables and friendly service. Ham and cheese, chicken or *pierna* (literally 'leg', in this case of pork) sandwiches are a few of the many options, plus hamburgers and cheeseburgers, all prepared fresh.

Getting There & Away

Gua-guas to Santo Domingo (US$3.25, 1¾ hours) leave from a terminal at Calle Duarte and Miguel Ángel Garrido, on the corner opposite the park. They depart every 15 minutes from 5am to 6:30pm, and until 7pm on Sunday and Monday. If possible, take the *expreso* bus, which reaches Santo Domingo about 20 minutes faster. Westbound buses come from Santo Domingo so don't have a fixed schedule, but also pass about every 15 minutes, to both San Juan ($2.50) and to Barahona (US$2).

Caribe Tours buses running between Santo Domingo and Barahona stop in Azua – arriving and departing from the Parque Central. If you're already in Azua and headed to Santo Domingo, the bus departs at 7:15am, 7:30am, 10:45am, 11:15am, 2:30pm, 2:45pm and 6:15pm.

CARRETERA SÁNCHEZ (HWY 2)

Fifteen kilometers west of Azua is the turnoff to San Juan, the largest city in the southwest, and Comendador (better known as Elías Piña) on the Haitian border. The turn-off road to San Juan keeps the name (Hwy 2 or Carretera Sánchez), while the road that continues to Barahona becomes Hwy 44. The road is paved and in good condition, and is flanked most of the way by small farms and ranches and a dozen or so hamlets. There isn't a whole lot to do or see in this area, but the drive is enjoyable as are the local markets and festivals.

Being close to Haiti, the region endured considerable fighting between Haitian and Spanish troops during the 1840s, and a number of communities were destroyed. Some didn't fully recover until the late 1960s, when President Balaguer initiated a country-wide modernization effort to prepare the DR for the millions of tourists he hoped the republic would attract. Also, various international development agencies were pouring money into the country at the time, and they required the government to build ports, highways, aqueducts, streets and energy plants, which benefited the region well.

SAN JUAN DE LA MAGUANA

pop 72,950

San Juan de la Maguana is an old city, dating to the 16th century. The town takes its name from the combination of San Juan El Bautista (St John the Baptist) and the Maguana Indians, who were one of the Taíno tribes that inhabited Hispaniola at the time of Columbus's arrival. The city is often referred to as simply San Juan.

Though agreeable enough, San Juan isn't really a tourist destination. The main drawcard are its large festivals and El Corral de los Indios, a very modest archaeological site north of town. San Juan is also relatively close to the border town of Comendador/ Elías Piña, which has an interesting Haitian market every Monday and Friday and is one of the main entry points to Haiti itself.

Orientation

When Carretera Sánchez (Hwy 2) hits the town, it splits into two one-way streets – the westbound street is Calle Independencia, and the eastbound is Calle 16 de Agosto. All of the city's hotels, restaurants and services are on those two streets. A large white arch modeled on the Arc de Tríomphe stands dramatically at the eastern entrance of the city. At the western end of town is San Juan's large plaza, with a pretty cream-colored church on one side and a school of fine arts on the other.

Information

EMERGENCY

Policía Nacional (☎ 809-557-2380; Calle Independencia at Dr Cabral; ☽ 24hr) Located one block west of the large white arch at the east entrance of town.

INTERNET ACCESS

Cetecom (☎ 809-557-4353; Calle 16 de Agosto 49A btwn Mella & Colón; per hr US$0.90; ☽ 8am-7pm Mon-Sat)

MONEY

For a relatively small city, San Juan has an amazing profusion of banks. Most, including the two listed below, have 24-hour ATMs.

Banco León (Calle Independencia at Mariano Rodríguez; ☽ 8:30am-5pm Mon-Fri, 9am-1pm Sat) Two blocks west of the arch, across from a gas station.

BanReservas (☎ 809-557-2613; Calle Independencia at 27 de Febrero; ☽ 8am-5pm Mon-Fri, 9am-1pm Sat)

MEDICAL SERVICES

Farmacia Inmaculada (☎ 809-527-2801; Calle Independencia at 27 de Febrero; ☽ 8am-10pm Mon-Sat, 9am-3pm Sun)

THE SOUTHWEST

TELEPHONE

Codetel (☎ 809-557-4062; Calle 16 de Agosto btwn Anacaona & 27 de February; ☾ 8am-10pm) Across the street from a new Verizon office. The former, still open at the time of research, will eventually close and all operations will move to the Verizon office. They are across the street from each other and service should remain the same.

TRAVEL AGENCY

Viajes Vimenca (☎ 809-557-2100; Calle 16 de Agosto at 27 de Febrero; ☾ 8am-4pm Mon-Sat, 8am-noon Sat) Inside a money exchange office.

Sights

EL CORAL DE LOS INDIOS

Seven kilometers north of town on the road to Juan Herrera, this Taíno site consists solely of a circle of stones defining a 300m area. It is presumed that the Corral was a meeting place of the Taínos and was used in rituals or as a game field. To get to El Coral, take San Juan's main westbound road, Calle Independencia, to Av Anacaona and turn northward toward Juan Herrera.

Festivals & Events

DÍA DE SAN JUAN

June 24 is San Juan's patron saint day and the city marks the occasion with almost two weeks of street festivities: including food stands, kid's activities, and plenty of music, dancing and drinking. The celebration starts around June 12 and steadily grows more and more festive leading up to the actual saint day. Live bands play on a stage set up near the white arch at the east entrance to town, and the crowds spill out into the surrounding traffic circle and streets.

ESPÍRITU SANTO

Sometime in May – the date varies according to the date Easter falls – San Juan's faithful mount a unique procession that showcases, among other things, the strong

THE SOUTHWEST

A VILLAGE SWALLOWED

Images of the December 2004 tsunami in southeast Asia must have reminded many Dominicans of a smaller, though no less shocking, tragedy that occurred in the southwestern part of the country less a decade prior. Instead of a tsunami, however, the culprit was flooding caused by Hurricane Georges in 1998.

The victims were the 1000 villagers of Mesopotamia, a tiny town that was located just above the confluence of the Ríos San Juan and Yaque del Sur in the southern foothills of the Cordillera Central. On September 23, 1998 at approximately 3:05am, the whole town was washed away – every building, every street, every resident. Quite literally it was gone in less than a minute.

Ten hours earlier, Red Cross officials had urged the people of Mesopotamia to evacuate. 'A hurricane is coming,' they yelled over loud speakers. 'Your village could be flooded.' No one listened. Church leaders repeated the message, soldiers ordered people to leave their homes. But because it was not raining, their pleas and demands were ignored.

What the villagers didn't know was that Hurricane Georges was swirling in the mountain range just north of Mesopotamia. Torrential rains had caused the area's waterways to overflow; brooks became creeks, creeks became rivers and rivers became white-water torrents. But still there was no rain in Mesopotamia, and feeling safe, the villagers went to sleep.

Meanwhile, four kilometers up the Río Yaque del Sur, a man controlling a large dam there was faced with an impossible dilemma. Open the flood gates immediately to release pressure on the dam, or let the water continue rising and hope the dam doesn't collapse and release an even larger deluge later. It's possible the village was doomed either way – we will never know. But the dam tender had to make a decision and he chose to open the gates. In doing so, he released a catastrophic volume of water into a river already poised to burst its banks.

It's unlikely the people of Mesopotamia knew what hit them. One minute they were asleep in their beds, and the next, a wall of water 4m high and traveling at 30km/h swept through town, obliterating everything in its path. There was no time to think and no chance of escape.

Just before daylight, the river receded, revealing a landscape covered in mud where a church, businesses and homes had stood hours earlier. Gardens and chicken coops, parked cars and farming equipment were all gone. A day later, corpses and debris began appearing in the Bahía de Neyba, 50km downstream.

Haitian influence in this region. Beginning in the small town of El Batey, a procession carries a small religious figurine to San Juan, some 15km away. The procession includes drumming and chanting, and it's not uncommon for marchers to become possessed by either the Holy Spirit or Taíno ghosts, and to suddenly begin dancing around or speaking in tongues or to collapse on the ground. The festival continues for another day or so in San Juan, mostly in the plaza around the church.

Sleeping & Eating

The hotels in San Juan are all surprisingly good value.

Hotel Maguana (☎ 809-557-2244; Calle Independencia 72; d/tw US$18/26.50; 🍴 🅿) The Maguana was built in 1947 and has maintained a certain air of grandeur. This three-story hotel on the east end of town has 27 spacious rooms with high ceilings, firm mattresses and large private bathrooms with hot-water. The rooms are arranged around a breezy, tiled courtyard, and there is a good restaurant on-site.

Hotel y Supermercado El Detallista (☎ 809-557-1200; Calle Trinitaria at Eusebio Puello; d/tw with fan US$13.75/15.75, with aircon US$17.50/23.50; 🍴) This hotel and supermarket is one street up from Independencia and thought it is three blocks east of town, it is excellent value otherwise. Rooms are on the third and fourth floors, surrounding a large common area with couches and tables, and where guests can get coffee or tea in the morning and free ice water at anytime. Rooms are a little small, but comfortable and very clean. The supermarket downstairs has a payphone, ATM, plus all the produce, snacks and other foods you may need.

Hotel D'Angel (☎ 809-557-3484; fax ☎ 809-557-9263; Calle 19 de Marzo 3 btwn Independencia & Trinitaria; d/tw with fan US$15.75/18.50, with aircon US$17.50/24.50; 🍴 🅿) Built in 1998 the D'Angel has 32 rooms, all with good beds, high ceilings, white tile floors and nice touches like a bedside bureau and table lamp. Ask for a room in the new building as the rooms are fresher and better appointed. Less charming than the other hotels, but is better located and a bargain considering breakfast is included.

Rincón Mexicano (☎ 809-557-3713; Calle 27 de Febrero at Capotillo; mains US$2-8; 🕑 dinner, open late on weekends) It's hard to find good Mexican food outside of Mexico and the western US,

so this place comes as a big – and pleasant – surprise. With Mexican table cloths and a stereo playing mariachi and ranchero music, you'll find a wide selection of tacos, burritos, enchiladas and other typical Mexican fare, all served with authentic salsa. Portions are large – two or three tacos are enough for most people, and are just US$1.25 each.

Pica Pollo Central (Calle 16 de Agosto at Anacaona; mains US$3-5; 🕑 breakfast, lunch & dinner) Pica Pollo is the name used in the DR for any quick meal of fried or roast chicken and a side dish, usually fried bananas or french fries. And that's exactly what this small casual eatery serves, cafeteria style and at very reasonable prices.

The **sandwich shop** (☎ 809-557-2810; Calle 19 de Marzo btwn Independencia & Trinitaria; mains US$3-5; 🕑 breakfast, lunch & dinner) on the top-floor of Hotel El Líbano serves great, fresh-made grilled sandwiches in a huge sunny ballroom. Though most useful as a place to go for good food, the pool tables and domino sets make it a nice place to hang out for a while as well.

Getting There & Around

Caribe Tours (☎ 809-557-4520) has a terminal 75m west of the Hotel Maguana in the town's Caribe Tours depot. Buses to Santo Domingo (US$5.25, 2½ hours) depart at 6:30am, 10:15am, 1:45pm and 5:30pm.

Gua-guas for Santo Domingo (US$4.25; three hours, every 20 minutes, 4am to 6:30pm) leave from a terminal three blocks east of the arch, across from the baseball field. There are three express buses (US$4.25; 6:30am, 9:30am and 3pm) which make the trip a half-hour faster because they don't make a food-stop along the way.

If you are going to Barahona, you can take any of the four Caribe Tours buses to Azua (US$2.25; one hour) and catch a Barahona-bound bus there. Alternatively, take a Santo Domingo *gua-gua* and get off at Cruce del Quince, the main highway intersection, and catch another *gua-gua* from there.

For Comendador/Elías Piña (US$2.25, one hour, every 20 minutes, 7am to 6pm), the *gua-gua* terminal is at the far western end of Calle Independencia, past the Texaco gas station. If you are going to the Haitian border, ask if the driver will drop you at the immigration office or, better yet, wait for you to clear Dominican immigration and drop you at Haitian immigration. You'll probably have to pay an extra couple of dollars, but it's certainly convenient.

Taxis and *motoconchos* may be found near the Parque Central. You can also call a **taxi** (☎ 809-557-6400).

COMENDADOR DEL REY/ELÍAS PIÑA
pop 12,070

Comendador del Rey, or Comendador for short, is the official name of the border town west of San Juan. However almost everyone who doesn't live there calls it Elías Piña, which is the name of the state, and you'll have more luck using that name anywhere but in town. (The town has also been previously called San Rafael and Estrelleta, but who's counting?) Comendador is best known for the Haitian market held there every Monday and Friday, when hundreds of Haitians arrive on *burros* (donkeys) and on foot to sell their wares, and as many or more Dominicans come from as far away as Azua, Baní and San Cristóbal to take advantage of rock-bottom prices on many household items.

Comendador also has a major military base and a police headquarters, and every once in a blue moon they decide to stop travelers and search their cars. Assuming you don't have anything to hide, it's a quick and routine affair and the officers (many very young) are usually friendly and polite.

Orientation

As is common, the highway splits into two one-way streets when it enters town. The westbound street is Calle Santa Teresa and the east-bound is Calle 27 de Febrero. Almost everything you need is on or near those two streets. The park is on the east end of town, between Calles Las Carreras and Las Mercedes. There's a large roundabout at the west end of town, at which point the roads merge again and lead to the Haiti–DR border.

Information

For emergencies, contact the **Policía Nacional** (☎ 809-527-0290; Calle 27 de Febrero at Las Mercedes, 1 block west of the main park; ☽ 24hr). There is no tourist police office here.

BanReservas (☎ 809-527-0907; ☽ 8am-5pm Mon-Fri, 9am-1pm Sat) has a 24-hour ATM at its branch office located at a traffic circle near the market on the west end of town.

Make phone calls at **Verizon Centro de Comunicaciones** (☎ 809-527-9439; Calle Las Mercedes at Av Santa Teresa; to USA per min US$0.30, to Europe per min US$0.75; ☽ 8am-9:30pm) near the northwest corner of the main park.

Centro Médico Dra. Cabrera (☎ 809-527-0536; ☽ 24hrs) is near the eastern entrance of the town, set 30m off the south side of the street, across from the military base. Inside there's a **pharmacy** that's also open 24 hours.

Sights

The **Haitian market** is impossible to miss; just stay on the main road through town until you run into it. Vendors lay their goods out on the ground, shaded by large plastic tarps suspended from every available tree, road sign and telephone pole. Cooking utensils, clothing, shoes, fruits and vegetables are the primary items, sold for as little as 50% of the normal price. There's not much in the way of handicrafts, since few tourists attend the market, but just wandering around and taking in the scene is worthwhile. (And who knows, maybe you'll see a colander you like.)

The vast majority of vendors are women. Haitian women traditionally wear colorful head scarves, cotton blouses and long wrap-around skirts, though T-shirts, jeans and light dresses are more and more common.

Sleeping & Eating

There's not much reason to stay in Comendador, as the sleeping options are much

---

CROSSING INTO HAITI FROM ELÍAS PIÑA

The border crossing here is relatively simple. The border 1.5km west of the town – take the main road straight out to a large staging area, where the **Dominican immigration office** (☽ 8am-6pm Mon-Sat, sometimes closes early Sat) is in a blue building on the north side. There you'll get your passport stamped and pay a US$20 departure tax. From there, taxis or *gua-guas* take you another 2.5km to the **Haitian immigration office** (☽ 9am-6pm) where you pay a US$10 entrance fee. Buses to Port-au-Prince and other points in Haiti wait just across the border. Returning, there is no departure tax from Haiti and the Dominican officials often do not charge for the tourist card (it's US$10 at the airport and other border crossings).

THE SOUTHWEST

better in San Juan and there's a frequent bus service between the two towns. But there is one decent hotel and one pleasant restaurant, in case you see it differently.

Hotel Casa Teo (☎ 809-527-0392; Calle Santa Teresa at Las Mercedes; d/tw US$8.75/14) Facing the park and above a hardware store, rooms here are large, basic and a bit grubby, though the sheets and towels are clean. Bathrooms are also big though somewhat rundown and have cold water only. TVs have local channels only.

Restaurant La Fuente (☎ 809-527-0297; Calle Colón btwn Calles Santa Teresa & 27 de Febrero; mains US$6-10; ⏰ 8am-9pm) A surprisingly refined place for such a nondescript border town. The large dining room is downright pleasant with tablecloths, fake flowers and plenty of light from the large double doors at the front. Popular Dominican dishes, like grilled chicken or stewed *chivo* (goat), are well-prepared and reasonably priced.

Getting There & Away

The main *gua-gua* terminal is on Av 27 de Febrero, at the east end of the main park. Buses for Santo Domingo (US$6.25, four hours, every 30 minutes, 2am to 6pm). If you're just going to San Juan (US$2.25; one hour), take one of the *gua-guas* parked just outside the terminal, as the Santo Domingo bus doesn't officially stop in San Juan. For Barahona, take a Santo Domingo bus to Cruse del Quince from the main highway intersection; (US$3.50, two hours) and then catch a west-bound bus there. Or use Caribe Tours – see (p244) for details.

PENÍNSULA DE PEDERNALES

The huge pie-shaped peninsula jutting out from Hispaniola's southern shore has three unique national parks and hundreds of kilometers of Caribbean coast, making it seem at first glance like a can't-miss destination. Yet very few tourists go there. The beaches are not the ones of typical Caribbean daydreams – instead of sand, most are covered in smooth white stones or pebbles. While the parks are interesting, the infrastructure for travelers is lacking. And it's *hot* here – especially in the interior around Lago Enriquillo, the lowest point in the Caribbean

at some 40m below sea level. All of which doesn't mean it's not worth visiting, you just have to change your expectations. It is a place to admire the rugged shoreline as opposed to sunbathing on it, or to be awed by the desolate and unforgiving landscape, but mainly from a car and preferably one with aircon.

BARAHONA
pop 77,160

Barahona has a variety of sleeping and eating options, which, along with essential services and a central location, make it a logical base for exploring the Peninsula de Pedernales. The city, built on a calm bay, is pleasant enough but marred by a huge mining operation built incomprehensibly right in the middle of what could be a very nice waterfront avenue and promenade. Another giant facility belches smoke a few kilometers north of town. That said, Barahona is growing more and more popular with weekenders from Santo Domingo, most of whom go to the all-inclusive hotel at the south end of town.

By Dominican standards, Barahona is a young city, founded in 1802 by Haitian general, François Dominique Toussaint L'Ouverture. For over a century, residents mostly made their living taking what they could from the Caribbean sea, but today fishing accounts for only a small part of Barahona's economy. The dictator Rafael Trujillo changed everything when he ordered many square kilometers of desert north of town converted into sugarcane fields for his family's financial benefit. More than three decades after his assassination, the thousands of hectares of sugarcane continue to be tended, only now they are locally owned and benefit the community.

Orientation

The highway enters town from the west; after a large roundabout with a prominent square arch, it becomes Av Luís E Delmonte and Barahona's main drag. Av Delmonte continues straight as a sugarcane stalk downhill to the sea, or more exactly, to the seaside mining operation. From here, you can turn right or left onto Av Enriquillo. Left leads to an industrial area; right is the continuation of Hwy 44, leading another 75km down the east coast of the peninsula.

Information

INTERNET ACCESS

Verizon (Av Nuestra Santa del Rosario; per hr US$1.60; 8am-10pm) Conveniently located facing Parque Central, but has only one computer.

Cybernet (Av Uruguay; per hr US$1.25; 8am-9pm) Several blocks from center between Cabral and Messon.

MEDICAL SERVICES

Centro Médico Regional Magnolia (☎ 809-524-2470; Av Uruguay at Francisco Vásquez; 24hr emergency room)

Farmacia Dotel (☎ 809-524-2394; Av Luis E Delmonte at Duverge; 7:30am-10pm Mon-Sat, 7:30am-8pm Sun)

MONEY

Banco Popular (☎ 809-521-2102; Jaime Mota at Padre Billini; 9am-3pm Mon-Fri) Right at Parque Central & has a 24-hour ATM.

BanReservas (☎ 809-524-4006; Av Uruguay at Padre Billini; 8am-5pm Mon-Fri, 9am-1pm Sat) Around the corner, also has a 24-hour ATM

TELEPHONE

Verizon (Av Nuestra Santa del Rosario; to USA per min US$0.30; to Europe per min US$0.75; 8am-10pm) Facing Parque Central.

Sleeping

BUDGET

Inexpensive hotel rooms can be tough to come by in Barahona on weekends, when scores of *capitalinos* come for respite from the hectic capital city.

THE SOUTHWEST

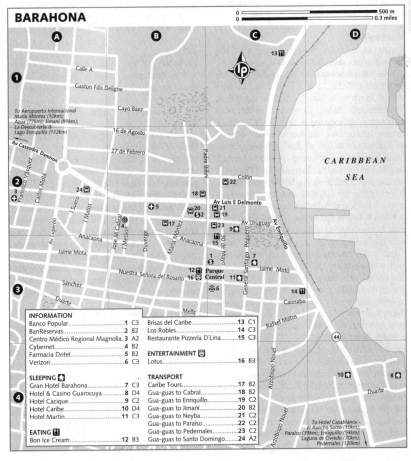

BARAHONA

Hotel Cacique (☎ 809-524-4620; Av Uruguay 2; d/tw with fan US$8.75/14, r with aircon US$24.50; ✷) One block and a half up from Av Enriquillo, this is the best of the budget options, with 16 clean rooms with okay mattresses, cable TV and private hot-water bathrooms. Fan rooms are decent value, but there are better aircon rooms for the same price elsewhere. Some of the upstairs rooms get better light.

Hotel Martín (☎ 809-768-3783; Gen Santiago Peguero at Calle Nuestra Señora del Rosario; d/tw US$8.75/10.50) Grubby and unappealing, this should be your last option if everything else is either full or out of your price range. Downstairs rooms have shared bathrooms, whereas the ones upstairs have in-room bathrooms (but that's not necessarily a good thing). Either way, there's no hot-water. Fan only.

MIDRANGE

If you can afford a bit more, these are a big step up from the budget options.

Gran Hotel Barahona (☎ 809-524-3445; Calle Jaime Mota 5; r from US$22; ✷ P) Probably the best overall option in town, considering price, location and quality. Rooms are clean, with hot-water bathrooms and cable TV. Some of the mattresses are better than others, so ask to see a few if that's an important issue. The higher-priced rooms aren't much larger, but have nicer furnishings. The ones on the top floor have high, sloped ceilings. It's near Parque Central and several restaurants, banks and Internet cafés.

Hotel & Casino Guarocuya (☎ 809-524-4121; Av Enriquillo near Duarte; d/tw US$28/35) On the ocean-side of Av Enriquillo across from the Hotel Caribe. All rooms have clean bathrooms and a small table and chairs. The ones on the ocean side have terraces and the light and breeze make them much more pleasant; unfortunately only one of these is a double, the rest are twins or triples. There's a restaurant and fairly low-key casino on-site.

Hotel Caribe (☎ 809-524-4111; Av Enriquillo at Duarte; d/tw US$31.50/33; ✷) Not quite as nice or well-located as the Gran Hotel Barahona and without the ocean views of the Guarocuya make Hotel Caribe the third choice in this range. It's also more expensive, although the price includes breakfast from Tuesday to Friday. Blue-painted rooms are clean and have old but firm beds. Rooms have ceiling fans and private hot-water bathrooms.

Hotel Casablanca – El Suizo (☎ 809-471-1230; susannaknapp@yahoo.de; d/tr US$28/35) About 10km south of town in the village of El Quemaíto, this hotel is a great option if you're looking for some isolation but still like having easy access to restaurants and other city services. Six simple but comfortable rooms are set on a well-tended garden. All rooms have a fan, clean bathrooms and either a king-size bed or a queen and twin. Fifty meters away, a beautiful curving cliff provides a dramatic view of the Caribbean, and stairs down one side lead to a narrow beach that's mostly rocky but has some nice sandy spots. There's a larger beach a five-minute walk away. Meals (not included) are served in the *table d'hôte* tradition, where guests discuss over breakfast what they'd like for dinner, which is served family style. The Swiss owner is a fine cook and delightful person to boot.

Eating

Los Robles (☎ 809-524-1629; Nuestra Santa del Rosario at Av Enriquillo; mains US$1.50-8; ☾ breakfast, lunch & dinner) Among the best value in town for size, taste and price; you can have sit-down service at picnic tables on a pleasant outdoor patio, or order hefty grilled sandwiches from a stand-alone to-go shack. There's a little of something for everyone – including pizzas (US$6 to $11), grilled beef and chicken plates (US$7 to $9) and of course plenty of seafood (US$8 to $15).

Restaurant Pizzería D'Lina (☎ 809-524-3681; Av 30 de Mayo at Calle Anacaona; mains US$1-10; ☾ breakfast, lunch & dinner) Even with the chain pizza and chicken places down the street, this Barahona institution has a loyal clientele who come for good pies and friendly family service. Large pizzas start at around US$8; there are also sandwiches and various meat, chicken and seafood dishes. Filling egg breakfasts go for around US$4. Convenient location.

Brisas del Caribe (☎ 524-2794; Av Enriquillo 1; most dishes around US$8; ☾ breakfast, lunch & dinner) Long a favorite of Barahona's upper class, Brisas specializes in seafood, with lobster dishes going for US$13 and shrimp dishes for half that. On a small rise about 500m north of Av Luis E Delmonte, the open-sided restaurant catches a cool breeze and most of the tables have a view of the green-blue Caribbean (and smoke stacks from nearby processing plants, unfortunately). Also available are sea bass and red snapper prepared several ways, as well as *carite* (kingfish) served in a coconut milk sauté.

Bon Ice Cream (Calles Jaime Mota at Padre Billini; breakfast, lunch & dinner) Right on Parque Central, this is the place to go if you're craving ice cream.

Drinking & Entertainment

Los Robles (809-524-1629; Nuestra Santa del Rosario at Av Enriquillo; 9am-2am) and other nearby open-air restaurants are popular spots for a beer. For a bit more action, **Lotus** (Calle Padre Billini at Nuestra Sra. del Rosario; 7:30pm-2am Wed-Sun) is a popular and long-running dance club right on Parque Central. Friday and Saturday are the busiest nights, and there's usually a US$1 cover. The scene is pretty wholesome as clubs go, with a lot of couples and not much in the way of prostitution.

Getting There & Away
AIR
Aeropuerto Internacional María Móntez (809-524-4144; Hwy 44) was imagined as a gateway for the droves of tourists expected to come to this 'new' Caribbean getaway in the southwest. That didn't pan out, and the airport is now all but closed. Located 10 km north on Hwy 44 charter flights arrive occasionally, operated by **Caribair** (in Santo Domingo 809-567-7050), **Aerodomca** (in Santo Domingo 809-567-1984) and **Servicios Aeros Profesionales** (in Santo Domingo 809-547-3554).

BUS
Gua-guas serve all points along the coast south of Barahona and inland as far as the Haitian border. However, because of union agreements, *gua-guas* headed down the coast do not stop at every town along the way, even though they pass right through them. Instead, each of the major towns has its own *gua-gua* service, with exclusive rights to stop in that town. (Smaller towns are served by all lines) The result is you should be careful to get on the right bus, or else you'll be let off outside of town and you'll have to walk or catch another ride in.

Unless otherwise indicated, *gua-guas* leave every 15 to 30 minutes from roughly 7am to 6pm. Main routes and their designated *paradas* (stops):
Santo Domingo (US$4.25; 3½hrs; Av Luis E Delmonte btwn Matos & Suero; every 15 min starting at 4am, express at 6:30am, 7:30, then hourly 9am to 6pm)

Paraíso (US$1.40; 40min; Calle 30 de Mayo at Colón; first departure 8:30am)
Enriquillo (US$2.10; 1½hrs; Calle 30 de Mayo btwn Avs Luis E Delmonte & Uruguay)
Pedernales (US$4.25; 2 hrs; Av Uruguay btwn Padre Billini & 30 de Mayo hourly; 7am to 3pm)
Cabral (US$1; 25 min; Padre Billini at Av Luis E Delmonte)
Jimaní (US$3.50; 2½hrs; Calle María Móntez btwn Avs Luis E Delmonte & Uruguay; every 45 min; until 3pm)
Duverge (US$2.50; 1hr; take any Jimaní bus)
Neyba (US$2.10; 1¾hrs; Av Luis E Delmonte btwn Padre Billini & 30 de Mayo)
La Descubierta & Lago Enriquillo park (US$2.50; 2½hrs; take any bus to Neyba & transfer there).

For San Juan de la Maguana and San José de Ocoa, take any Santo Domingo-bound *gua-gua* and get off at the respective intersection to catch a connecting bus.

Caribe Tours (809-524-4952; Av Uruguay btwn María Móntez & Duverge) has first class service to Azua (US$1.75, 45 minutes) and Santo Domingo (US$5.25, three hours) departing at 6:15am, 9:45am, 1:45pm and 5:15pm. Buses coming the other direction leave Santo Domingo at the exact same times. To get to San Juan, take the bus to Azua and switch there.

Getting Around
Barahona is somewhat spread out, though the area around the center is mostly navigable by foot. For points further afield, taxis and *motoconchos* can be found beside the Parque Central and along Av Luis E Delmonte.

BAHORUCO & LA CIÉNAGA
pop 7715
The adjoining seaside villages of Bahoruco and La Ciénaga are 17km south of Barahona, and are typical of the small communities along the east edge of the Península de Pedernales, with friendly local residents and a gravelly beach used more for mooring boats than bathing. Neither town have any services to speak of, but do has a few nice accommodations options.

Set on a hill overlooking the north end of Bahoruco, **Casa Bonita** (809-445-8610; north side of town; per person US$56;) is one of the area's best hotels. Twelve thatch-and-concrete cabins each have red-tile floors, linen bedspreads, high-sloped ceilings and a bank of shuttered windows with full or partial views of the ocean. There's a dining room and a bar beside a spacious sitting area. Breakfast and dinner are included in prices.

Coral Sol Resort (☎ 809-233-4882; www.coralsol resort.com; south end of La Ciénaga; per person US$45; 🏊) is on the other end of the two towns, this small resort has ten attractive and spacious cabanas, each with two double beds and two bathrooms, set on a tree-filled hillside sloping down to a pebbly beach protected from the pounding sea by a rocky strip. Breakfast and dinner are included in the price. To get here, continue south on the highway until you're nearly past the town where you'll see an access road with a sign for the hotel.

Brisas de Bahoruco (coastal road at border of Baho-ruco & La Ciénaga) used to be a Barceló resort and was the best all-inclusive on this coast. However, the relationship ended and the hotel was closed when we came through. There were plans to reopen, though, and the hotel's breezy elegant lobby, welcoming pool and small beach area, protected by a natural rock barrier, are worth checking out.

Restaurante Luz (☎ 809-630-9861; coastal Rd middle of town; mains US$4-8; 🍴 breakfast, lunch & dinner) is the best restaurant in town, with a tidy second-floor dining room overlooking the shore and a nice ocean breeze. Seafood is the main option here, including grilled fish and *lambí* (conch). All dishes come with rice and beans.

SAN RAFAEL
pop 5285

Three kilometers south of Bahoruco and La Ciénaga is the small town of San Rafael, notable mainly for several awesome highway **vista points** on either side of town, and a river with natural and artificial **swimming holes** that are popular with local kids and families. You'll see one set of pools right alongside the highway – a 100m north (downhill) from there is an unmarked dirt road leading to a second set of pools nearer the ocean. Fifty meters in the other direction, a steep paved road leads to **Villa Miriam** (🕗 8am-6pm; admission US$1.75), another swimming area that has several natural pools (with some help from sandbags) and a regular swimming pool. Whereas the free pools can get crowded and loud, these are almost always empty.

PARAÍSO & LOS PATOS
Paraíso
pop 6490

Another 10 km south is the small agreeable town of Paraíso, which has a decent hotel and a pretty beach (if you get away from the littered part). Paraíso also has what may be the most spectacular basketball courts on the planet; framed by tall coconut trees with the brilliant aquamarine ocean shining through the bleachers.

There are no services, however, save the **Clínica Hospital Amor el Prójimo** (☎ 809-243-1212; Calle Arzobispo Noel) with a doctor and nurse on call 24 hours per day.

The **beach** in front of town has a fair amount of litter and numerous boats moored there. There are much better spots several hundred meters outside of town – follow the shady coastal road (Av Gregorio Luperón) south past the Hotel Paraíso and look for small paths through the brush. As elsewhere, much of the beach is covered in white stones, but there are several patches of fine sand where you can lay out a towel.

At the south end of town and an easy walk to the area's best beaches, rooms at **Hotel Paraíso** (☎ 809-243-1080; Av Gregorio Luperón & Call Doña Chin; r with fan/air-con US$12.25/24; 🍴 🅿) are clean and very spacious, though somewhat unremarkable in their decor. Those on the top floor have peaked ceilings. Though tourists are relatively rare in Paraíso, Habitat for Humanity has an office here and the hotel is occasionally completely booked out with volunteers – as this is the only hotel in town, try calling ahead.

The *gua-gua* stop is on the highway at Calle Enriquillo, a few streets north of the main intersection. From here you can get buses to Barahona (US$1.40, 40 minutes, every 25 minutes), and southbound *guaguas* to Enriquillo (US$0.90, 15 minutes), Laguna Oviedo (US$1.40, 45 minutes) and Pedernales (US$3, 1½ hours) pass by roughly every 15 minutes.

Los Patos

Several kilometers south of Paraíso is the hamlet of Los Patos, which is notable mostly for **Playa Los Patos**, a pretty white-stone beach, and for the adjacent **balneario** (freshwater swimming area). Larger and more attractive than the Balneario San Rafael, the water here flows clear and cool out of the mountainside, forming a shallow lagoon before running into the ocean. Small shacks serve good, reasonably-priced food making this a nice place to spend a couple of hours. It's crowded on weekends with Dominican families, but much less busy midweek. There is a cave on the other side of the highway with what are supposedly Taíno petroglyphs, but we have our doubts.

ENRIQUILLO
pop 5423

Fifteen kilometers south of Paraíso (and 54km south of Barahona) is this typical Dominican town, which is notable for having the last two hotels and gas station until Pedernales, some 82km away.

Information

There is no ATM in Enriquillo. At the south end of town, you can exchange euros and US dollars at **Vimenca/Verizon** (☎ 809-524-8121; Calle Hermanas Mirabal at Monseñor Panal; ⏱ 8am-noon, 2-9pm Mon-Sat, 2-6pm Sun) provided they have sufficient Dominican pesos on hand. You can also make phone calls here for US$0.30 per minute to the USA and US$0.75 per minute to Europe. There was no Internet access at the time of research, but the Vimenca/Verizon office had vague plans to install a terminal at some point.

Farmacia Brujín (⏱ 8am-noon, 2-6pm) is on the main street through town.

Sleeping & Eating

There's really no reason to stay here considering there are much better options in Barahona and elsewhere on the coast. There is one nice restaurant, however.

Hotel Juan José (☎ 809-524-8323; s/d/tw US$5.25/8.75/12.25), The only recommendable hotel in town, and then only barely. The outside and entrance area are promising enough, but the rooms are cement cubes painted an unfortunate teal, with saggy beds and a low wall dividing the toilet and shower from the rest of the room. Each has a fan and cold water only. Coming from Barahona, look for the sign on your right just as you enter town.

Comedor D'Maira (Calle Hermanas Mirabal at Monseñor Panal; mains US$3-8; ⏱ 7am-11pm) This eatery has two locations in town, but the more pleasant one is near the south end of town, just down the street from the Vimenca/

Verizon office. You have to cut through the family's living room and go up the back stairs to the second floor, where several wooden tables are arranged on a bright open-air terrace. Good, solid Dominican fare includes large portions of rice and beans, plus a main dish such as roast chicken, grilled beef or pork, or fried or baked fish filet. There is a minimart below.

PARQUE NACIONAL JARAGUA

The **Parque Nacional Jaragua** (admission US$1.75; ⏱ 8am-5pm) is the largest protected area in the country. Its 1400 sq km include vast ranges of thorn forest and subtropical dry forest and an extensive marine area that contains the islands of Beata and Alto Velo.

This huge nature reserve was created, in part, to protect the country's largest group of flamingos, which spend much of the year on the shore of Laguna de Oviedo (however they are most numerous around mid-August). The lake also attracts impressive numbers of American frigate birds, black-crowned tanagers, roseate spoonbills, great egrets and various songbirds.

Named after a famous Taíno chief, the park has an average temperature of 27°C and receives 500mm to 700mm of rain each year. Not surprisingly, the predominant vegetation is cacti and other slow-growing desert plants. One hundred and thirty bird species, or about 60% of the nation's total, have been identified in the park. Among the terrestrial creatures that inhabit the park are the Ricord iguana and the rhinoceros iguana, both of which are endemic to Hispaniola.

There's a well-marked entrance to the park and lagoon off Hwy 44 about three kilometers north of the town of Oviedo. You'll be greeted by guides who can take you on a two to three-hour tour of the lagoon, including visits to the flamingo colony, three islands where birds nest (one has an observation tower) and a shallow cave with Taíno petroglyphs and pictograms. The official cost is US$65 for a group of up to eight people, but this ought to be negotiable if there's just one or two of you or if you only take the boat only (no guide). Arrive early – not only because the bird watching is better, but because there are usually one or two other independent travelers or small groups that you may be able to join with. Bring a hat and plenty of sunscreen.

THE SOUTHWEST

THE SOUTHWEST

SOLENODONS: HISPANIOLA'S CREATURES

Haitian solenodons – rat-like creatures with tiny eyes and ears, strong claws and a long snout found only on Hispaniola – have been around for over 30 million years. And it's a miracle that they have survived this long. Only 30cm in length and weighing about 1kg, these nocturnal creatures have a reputation for being slow, clumsy and easily trapped. They run in a zig zag line and if excited will often trip, tumbling head-over-heels. If threatened, however, solenodons will often stand motionless and hide their heads. They do have one line of defense – they are one of very few mammals that have poisonous saliva, and their bite can kill would be attackers. Unfortunately they aren't immune to their own poison, and a bite from another solenodon – which occasionally happens when two males fight – can be fatal.

Solenodons also have very low reproduction rates, producing just one to two litters per year. Of those, only two offspring typically survive due in large part to the fact that females have just two teats, both located uncomfortably close to her anus. Only a couple of young can feed (or perhaps, *want* to feed) and the rest die of starvation.

Today, Haitian solenodons are close to extinction. (A related species found on Cuba may already be extinct.) For millions of years solenodons had few natural predators, but in modern times they have been decimated by the introduction of dogs and cats. Today they are found only in the Dominican Republic's Parque Nacional Jaragua (p251), Parque del Este (p127) and in southern Haiti. If you happen to see one, you'll be one of a fortunate few.

Oviedo and Pedernales buses can drop you at the park entrance. The last bus back to Barahona passes by around 4pm, but try not to cut it that close.

BAHÍA DE LAS ÁGUILAS

Bahía de las Águilas is a pristine and extremely remote beach in the far southwestern corner of the Dominican Republic. It's not on the way to anything else, and getting there is something of an adventure, but those who do make it are rewarded with 10km of nearly deserted beach forming a slow arc between two prominent capes.

To get there, take a dirt road marked Cabo Rojo, about 12km east of Pedernales. The Aluminum Company of America (Alcoa) mines bauxite here (a key ingredient for aluminum), and you'll pass huge mountains of bauxite ore along the way. Drive carefully, as the road is used mainly by huge, fast-moving dump trucks.

You'll reach the town of Cabo Rojo after six kilometers, and a tiny fishing community called Las Cuevas three kilometers after that. From there, it's a 20 minute boat ride to Bahía de Las Águilas; fisherman will take you and pick you up later for around US$42 for up to six people. Be sure to be clear on where and when you want to be picked up – there are absolutely no facilities there (although there are rumors of an all-inclusive resort being planned).

PEDERNALES

pop 11,072

At the western end of Hwy 44, after a long journey through the thorn forest, is the hot and dusty frontier city of Pedernales, which has little tourist facilities aside from a grubby hotel that comes in handy if you get stuck here. Pedernales is on the Haitian border, but there is no official immigration post so foreigners are prohibited from passing here (and should not attempt it).

Hotel Rossy (Carretera Pedernales 3; d/tw US$6/12) offers rooms with private cold-water bathrooms and fans. If you must spend the night in Pedernales, look no farther than the Rossy, next to the Shell gas station at the eastern entrance to town. The Rossy is very basic, with 15 cubicles with screenless windows. It's a no-frills place, as is everything in Pedernales.

Gua-guas go back and forth between Pedernales and Barahona (US$4.25, two hours, hourly, 7am to 3pm).

PARQUE NACIONAL SIERRA DE BAHORUCO

This **national park** (admission US$4; ☺ 8am-5pm) directly west of Barahona covers 800 sq km of mostly mountainous terrain and is notable for the rich variety of vegetation that thrives in its many different climates, from desert dry to mountain humid. Valleys are home to vast areas of broad-leafed plants, which give way to healthy pine forests at higher elevations. In the mountains the average temperature is 18°C, and annual rainfall is between 1000mm and 2500mm.

Within the national park there are 166 orchid species, representing 52% of the country's total. Thirty-two percent of those species are endemic to the park. Flitting about among the park's pine, cherry and mahogany trees are 49 species of bird. These include the white-necked crow, which can only be seen on Hispaniola. The most common birds in the mountains are La Selle's thrush, white-winged warblers, Hispaniolan trogons and narrow-billed todies. At lower elevations, look for white-crowned pigeons, white-winged doves, Hispaniolan parakeets, Hispaniolan lizard cuckoos and Hispaniolan parrots.

Nearly 500 years ago, somewhere in the mountains within the park, the great Taíno chief Enriquillo and his people chose to fight the conquistadors rather than submit to slavery. Their battles raged off and on for 14 years – from 1519 to 1533 – during which time the Spaniards came to respect the *cacique* and finally made peace with him. The chief declared a small free republic in the highest reaches of the Sierra de Bahoruco, and for his defiance he is considered something of a national hero today.

Visitors to the park will find no trace of the republic-within-a-republic, or even a cabin in which to spend a night (camping is possible but not recommended). In fact, unless you have rented a 4WD or a motorcycle, the park is, for all practical purposes, off-limits. The roads through the park are too rugged for anything else. However, if you're traveling by Jeep or motorcycle, the remote and rarely visited Parque Nacional Sierra de Bahoruco makes a delightful full day's exploration.

To get to the park from Barahona, head to the town of Duverge along the southern side of Lago Enriquillo. In town, look for a sign pointing south to Puerto Escondido, a village 11km by bad road from Duverge. In Puerto Escondido, take your first right to the ranger station (no phone), where you must buy a permit to enter the park (US$3.50). After passing the ranger station, take the first road on the left, which leads to the pine forest of Loma de los Pinos and eventually to the lookout point El Acetillar. If you're

feeling invincible and want to take the road truly less traveled, you can keep following this route south all the way to Pedernales. There are no official guide or visitor services, but the ranger may be able to help you locate someone to show you around.

LAGO ENRIQUILLO LOOP ROAD

Taxi drivers in Barahona and other towns pitch a tour around the lake as a day trip, but the lake is obscured by low scrub brush virtually the entire way, so it's really just a tour of the non-descript towns along the way. Driving it on your own is somewhat more enjoyable as you can stop and linger wherever you like. The road is surprisingly well-paved, making it a decent route for sturdy bicycles as well. There are no steep sections, though the stretch east of Jimaní and south of the lake passes through rolling foothills that top 300m in places, and the heat can get intense.

Besides the national park, there are no other tourist attractions. Cabral is known for its pre-Lenten Carnival celebration, which includes elaborate masks and colorful dances. Cement giant Cemex Dominicana has an iguanarium at its facility on the far side of the tiny town of Las Salinas. It was closed at the time of research, but the cement and chain-link enclosures were none too promising.

If you're driving, soldiers standing beside the speed bumps or at military checkpoints will often signal you to stop so they can get a ride to the military posts near Jimaní or elsewhere. Though the soldiers are usually friendly young guys, you are not at all required to pick them up or even stop (most people don't, in fact).

PARQUE NACIONAL ISLA CABRITOS

This **national park** (admission US$1.75; ☼ 7am-5pm) is named after the 12km-long desert island in the center of Lago Enriquillo, an enormous saltwater lake that's below sea level. The lake is the remains of an ancient channel that once united the Bahía de Neyba to the southeast (near Barahona) with Port-au-Prince to the west. The accumulation of sediments deposited by the Río Yaque del Sur at the river's mouth on the Bahía de Neyba, combined with an upward thrust of a continental plate, gradually isolated the lake. Today is basically a 200-sq-km inland sea.

THE SOUTHWEST

The park includes the island, the lake and all of the shoreline. The highlights are the lake's creatures, including an estimated 500 American crocodiles that can be seen in and at the edge of the lake. They don't care much for the salt water and, therefore, tend to hang out at the mouths of the freshwater rivers that drain into the lake from the Sierra de Neyba and the Sierra de Bahoruco, which flank the lake to the north and south, respectively.

The island, which varies in elevation from 4m to 40m below sea level (receiving a scant 600mm of rain each year and an average temperature of 28°C) is a virtual desert, supporting a variety of cacti and other desert flora. It is home to Ricord iguanas and rhinoceros iguanas, some more than 20 years old and considerably beefier than most house cats, and can often be seen resting in the shade of the vegetation. At night they return to dens they've dug a meter or so deep. Some of the iguanas have become so accustomed to people that they'll let you pet them. The island also has lots of scorpions, so wear covered shoes if possible.

The park entrance is three kilometers east of the town of La Descubierta. It's unmarked, strangely enough, but it's the only large turnoff in the vicinity and has a small cabin and kiosk visible from the road. Tours of the park cost US$28 for up to 10 people, and include visiting the mouth of the Río de la Descubierta – where the most crocodiles and flamingos are visible – and Isla Cabritos. The tour usually lasts one to two hours. Bring a hat and plenty of water – the heat can be intense on the water and the island.

If you just want to see the lake and some iguanas and continue on, there is a small **lakeside park** (admission US$0.40) with a path leading down to the lake's edge. Along the way you'll see huge iguanas sunning themselves. The guards sometimes feed them bits of crackers, which brings the meaty fellows running from all directions – quite a scene. There is also a small river-fed *balneario* (swimming hole) which makes for a nice swim on a hot day.

A short distance east of the park entrance, look for **Las Caritas** (The Little Faces) – a set of Taíno petroglyphs on a rock outcropping on the north side of the highway. A short but somewhat tricky climb up the hillside – you'll need decent shoes or sandals – affords a close look at the pictures and a fine view of the lake. Very little is known about the meaning of the figures depicted in these (or other Taíno petroglyphs, but they are thought to represent deities, possibly serving as protection for important ceremonial sites. Las Caritas is unmaintained and poorly-marked, but the faces are visible from the road if you're looking for them. Note that much of the rock here is actually petrified coral, remnants of the time the entire area was under the sea.

Sleeping & Eating

The park is a short distance from the small town of La Descubierta, which is popular for its large swimming hole right in the middle of town.

Hotel Iguana (☎ 809-301-4815; main road west of park; d/tw US$10.50/14; ❄) Rooms are small and simple, but also clean and quiet, making this the best sleeping option in town. Three rooms have aircon, but are stuffier than the fan-cooled ones, which have private bathrooms and surprisingly comfortable beds.

The Iguana's friendly proprietor prepares excellent home-cooked meals, but she needs a day's notice. Call the night before you drive out to Lago Enriquillo, and she can have lunch for you when you're finished with the tour. Otherwise there are food shacks in town, near the park and swimming hole.

Getting There & Away

To get to here by *gua-gua*, take a *gua-gua* from Barahona to the town of Neyba, and from there take any westbound *gua-gua* to the ranger station. Be sure to tell the driver that that's where you want to go, or he'll drive right past it.

JIMANÍ
pop 6567

This dusty border town is on the most direct route between Santo Domingo to Port-au-Prince, and is therefore the most trafficked of the three official border crossings. Aside from crossing the border, though, there's no reason to visit Jimaní. Fortunately, the loop road running around Lago Enriquillo was completed in 1990, so the drive to and from the town isn't the hellish journey it once was. It can get oppressively hot – so be sure to carry extra water if you're driving here.

CROSSING IN TO HAITI FROM JIMANÍ

The border is 2.5km west of Jimaní and Haitian immigration and customs is another 5km past that. You'll have to take a taxi from town – it's about US$10 to US$12 to have the driver take you to the border, wait while you pass Dominican immigration and customs, and then get them to drive you the remaining few kilometers to the Haitian immigration and customs post. Leaving the DR, you must pay US$5 to immigration and US$20 to customs for departure tax. The Dominican immigration and customs offices are open 8am to 7pm, but the Haitian equivalents from 9am to 6pm only. Once in Haiti, there are brightly colored *taptaps* (the Haitian equivalent of a *gua-gua*) waiting to take passengers to Port-au-Prince.

Information

BanReservas (☎ 809-248-3373; ⊙ 8am-5pm Mon-Fri, 9am-1pm Sat) has a 24-hour ATM and is at the west end of Calle 19 de Marzo, the main road from Neyba just before it leaves town for the Haitian border.

Verizon (to USA per min US$0.30, to Europe per min US$0.75; ⊙ 8am-10pm) and **Farmacia Marian** (☎ 809-248-3304; ⊙ 8am-10pm) are across the street from one another, on the uphill road to/from Duverge.

Sleeping & Eating

Hotel Jimaní (☎ 809-248-3139; Calle 19 de Marzo 2; r US$17.50; ❄ ❄) On the right side of the road as you enter town from La Descubierta, Jimaní's best hotel looks a little like a small high school, but is surprisingly comfortable. Each of the 10 rooms has both a twin and queen-size bed – nice and firm – plus cable TV and a private cold-water bathroom. The hotel is showing its age and the bathrooms could stand to be remodeled, but this is much better than you expect for a border town.

The hotel has a somewhat popular **restaurant** (⊙ breakfast, lunch & dinner). Otherwise, the eating options are slim, limited to several small, forgettable eateries along the road to Duverge.

Getting There & Away

Jimaní is served by *gua-guas* from Santo Domingo, passing La Descubierta, Neyba and Baní along the way; and from Barahona via Duverge and the south side of Lago Enriquillo. Both bus stops are on the dusty sloping road that enters town from the Duverge side. The Santo Domingo route has a proper terminal near the bottom of the hill (US$7.50, five hours, every 30 to 45 minutes, 1am to 5pm). For La Descubierta, it's US$1 and takes 30 minutes. *Gua-guas* to Barahona leave from a shady corner about 200m up the hill, across from a small supermarket (US$3.50, two hours, every 45 minutes, 4am to 3pm). Caribe Tours has direct service from Santo Domingo to Port-au-Prince, with a stop in Jimaní (see p95).

THE SOUTHWEST

Directory

CONTENTS

ACCOMMODATIONS

Lodging in the Dominican Republic (DR) is more expensive than many travelers expect. A basic reliable room with private bath averages US$25 to $35 per night in most areas – for the purposes of this book, budget is any room that's US$40 and under. Most hotels at this level offer hot water and 24-hour electricity (though you may have to contend with generator noise). Cable TV and airconditioning are somewhat less common, and the latter may not function when the hotel is using its generator or inverter. There are a few towns where comparable rooms can be had for under US$15, but these are not

the norm. Dormitory or shared-bath options (which keep lodging prices down in other countries) are all but non-existent in the DR. The prevalence of prostitution is part of the problem – what few budget hotels there are, are often either unpleasant or unsafe to stay in. Camping is almost unheard of, except along several routes up Pico Duarte, and even that is viewed rather askance by most Dominicans.

Midrange hotels average US$35 to US$60 per night and almost always include cable TV, airconditioning and sometimes breakfast or off-street parking. You can expect the beds to be comfortable and the bathroom and linens clean, if not always brand new. This range makes up the majority of hotels in the Dominican Republic and, accordingly, in this book.

All-inclusive resorts generally fall into the top-end range, but considering what you'd pay per day staying at a hotel and eating at restaurants, most all-inclusive resorts qualify as solidly midrange. In fact, the Dominican Republic is famous for its affordable all-inclusive resorts. Internet specials bring the price even lower or, more accurately, give you more bang for the same number of bucks. Cable TV, hot water, 24-hour electricity are standard – aircon as well, though some older resorts have rather weak central air systems. More expensive resorts have somewhat better buffets and one or more à la carte restaurants, but it would be hard to say that the food at a top-end resort is categorically better than at a cheaper one.

What does differ is the quality of the pool area and especially the beach. Some of the best deals are at all-inclusives that don't have direct beach access, but offer regular shuttle service to the nearby beach club, which always have food and drink service. For more information choosing the right all-inclusive resort for you see our guide on p138.

Top-end hotels are relatively rare in the Dominican Republic, and are made up primarily of deluxe all-inclusives and a few upscale hotels in Santo Domingo. At these, expect modern classy furnishings, excellent restaurants and top facilities and service, from full spas and exercise rooms, to super-comfy beach chairs and poolside drink service. Prices at these hotels typically start at US$80 per night.

The Dominican Republic has two main high seasons – December to March, when Canadians and Americans do most of their traveling, and July to August, when many Europeans and Dominicans are on holiday. Semana Santa (Holy Week, ie the week before Easter) is also an extremely busy time, as all local schools, universities, government offices and many businesses are closed and Dominicans flock to beaches and riverside areas. Carnival is celebrated every weekend in February, and hotels can fill up in the most popular areas, like La Vega, Santiago and Santo Domingo. During all these times, expect prices to rise by about third, though some resorts, tour operators and car rental agencies hike prices even more. Reservations are recommended during those times, especially at beach areas, and you may have less luck bargaining for a reduced rate (though you should always try). If you know where you'll be during busy periods, try calling ahead to lock in a better rate – this is especially true for car rentals. No matter what season, weekend and weekday rates are generally uniform, but definitely ask for a discount if you'll be staying more than a couple of days.

Camping

Other than the none-too-appealing free cabins en route to Pico Duarte, there are no formal campgrounds and the whole idea of camping is very peculiar to a majority of Dominicans. It simply isn't done, either inland or on the beach. If you are dead-set on sleeping in a tent, you'll have the most luck in rural mountain areas or along deserted beaches – inland, you should ask the owner of the plot of land you are on before pitching a tent, and on the beach ask the Politur or local police if it is allowed and safe.

Hostels

The Dominican Republic has no proper hostels, and very little backpacker culture of the sort found in the rest of Latin America, Europe and elsewhere. In fact, it is the cost of accommodations that prevents the Dominican Republic from being a genuine budget travel destination.

Hotels

Most travelers will spend the majority of their nights in hotels, which of course can be found in virtually every town in the republic. A few questions to ask before booking a room include: Is there hot water? Is there 24-hour electricity? Is there cable TV? Will the airconditioner run all night or only until a certain hour? Is breakfast included? What time is check out? Those are some of the key pieces of information you'll find in most of the listings in this book, but it is a good idea to double check in case there have been any changes. You should also feel free to look at a room or two before checking in, and if they are not to your liking, feel free to leave. When you do choose a place to stay, most hotels ask you to fill in a form that includes your name, address, nationality and sometimes your passport number. You may be asked to pay ahead of time,

---

PRACTICALITIES

- *El Listín Diario, Hoy, Ultima Hora, El Siglo* and *El Nacional,* plus *International Herald Tribune,* the *New York Times* and the *Miami Herald* can be found in many tourist areas.

- There are about 150 radio stations, most playing merengue and *bachata*; and seven local TV networks, though cable and satellite programming is very popular for baseball, movies and American soap operas.

- The Dominican Republic uses the same electrical system as the USA and Canada (110 to 125 volts AC, 60 Hz, flat-pronged plugs). Power outages are common but many hotels and shops have backup generators.

- The Dominican Republic uses the metric system for everything except gasoline, which is in gallons, and at laundromats, where pounds are used.

though there is no standard practice on that score. If you stay a few days, you will most likely be asked/expected to leave your room key at the front desk, mainly so the cleaning staff can get into your room. (Of course they have a master key in case you forget.) Likewise, it is customary to leave a tip for the cleaning staff – US$1 to US$2 per night is a good guide.

Rental Accommodations

If you'll be in the Dominican Republic for long – even a couple weeks – renting an apartment can be a convenient and cost-effective way to enjoy the country. There are a number of homes that can be rented by the week or month; alternatively, look for 'apartahotels' which have studio, one-bedroom, and two-bedroom apartments, usually with fully equipped kitchens. The advantage to these places is that you don't have to eat out every night or pack and unpack your bag every couple of days. The disadvantage, of course, is that you spend all your time in one place and don't see much of the rest of the country. The trick to rental units is not being afraid to leave it for a day or two to make a short trip somewhere else. Even if you aren't there for a couple of nights, you are still seeing a savings over the course of your stay. This book lists a number of apartahotels, and in areas where long-term units are popular – such as Cabarete (p191) – provides information on how to rent one. A number of hotels have a small number of units with kitchens – such cases are also indicated in the listings.

Resorts

By far the most popular lodging option in the DR is the all-inclusive resort. The largest concentrations of all-inclusives are at Bávaro/Punta Cana and Playa Dorada, though there are excellent resorts in the Bayahibe, Río San Juan, Sosúa and Luperón areas as well. The appeal of all-inclusives is the worry-free vacation – everything you need, including your room, meals, drinks and entertainment, plus the beach and pool, are all in a single contained location. Resorts offer a variety of tours to the surrounding area, whether snorkeling, ATV (All-Terrain Vehicle) riding or city tours, but the vast majority of people spend their time on the beach or by the pool, leaving only to eat or to participate in one of the frequent activities or shows put on by the resort staff. You won't learn much about the country or its people, but it is without a doubt an extremely relaxing way to spend a week. The one thing that can spoil an all-inclusive vacation is poor service or disappointing facilities. That's where websites like www.tripadvisor.com and www.debbiesdominicantravel.com can be useful: posting detailed, first-person reviews from travelers who have stayed at various resorts. Of course no resort gets perfect marks, but you can get a pretty good idea of the strengths and weaknesses of different places and, armed with that knowledge, pick the resort that's best for you.

ACTIVITIES

Lounging on the beach may be Activity Number One for many people who visit the Dominican Republic – and who can blame them? But there is a surprisingly wide range of sports and eco-activities for those travelers looking for a little more action. You'll find the most sporting and outdoors options along the North Coast and the mountain region of the interior, though a few activities – notably diving and bird watching – are also quite good in the southeast and southwest, respectively. Many of the sports and activities listed below are covered in more detail in the Outdoors chapter (p50).

Diving & Snorkeling

The Dominican Republic has excellent and varied options for diving and snorkeling. Because it has the Caribbean to the south and the Atlantic to the north and east, the Dominican Republic offers divers and snorkelers a number of distinct underwater environments and conditions. At the same time, the country is small enough that dedicated divers can sample most or all the different areas over the course of a single trip. The southern coast faces the Caribbean and the water is typically warmer and clearer here than anywhere else. It is best reached using dive shops in Boca Chica and Bayahibe. The North Coast has cooler Atlantic waters with somewhat less visibility, but makes up for that with more varied underwater formations. You can explore this area from Las Galeras, Las Terrenas, Río San Juan and

Sosúa, all of which have recommended dive shops. A bit off the beaten path are the diving and snorkeling opportunities in the northwest, specifically Monte Cristi – the national park of the same name there has the DR's most pristine coral formations – and the small fishing village of Punta Rusia. The DR also has two cave dives – one near Río San Juan can be done by skilled divers with just Open Water certification while the second, deep inside Parque Nacional del Este, is for advanced cave divers only.

Golf

The Dominican Republic has some superb golfing, with some two dozen courses to choose from. Most are affiliated with (or located nearby) the top all-inclusive resorts, but they are open to guests and non-guests alike. There are three courses designed by Pete Dye, including La Cana Golf Course in Punta Cana and Teeth of the Dog at the Casa de Campo resort near La Romana, which many consider to be the finest course in the country. These and other courses take full advantage of their Caribbean setting, with fairways and greens overlooking the ocean and views that are impressive almost to the point of distraction!

Green fees range from under US$30 to over US$200, plus caddie and/or cart fees. Reservations are essential in high season at the top courses, though in low season you may have some courses practically to yourself. Many hotels and resorts have arrangements with area courses for guests to receive reduced green fees – be sure to ask at the concierge desk. A few resorts even offer golf packages that typically include green fees, lodging, cart rental and other amenities.

Hiking

The Caribbean isn't a place many people go for hiking, but the Dominican Republic is one of the few islands that affords a variety of hiking options, from pretty coastal hikes to challenging mountain ascents. If your flip-flops are giving you blisters between your toes, strap on your boots and enjoy some of the DR's trekking options.

The most notable (and challenging) hike in the DR is the ascent of Pico Duarte, at 3175m, the tallest peak in the Caribbean. It's not a technical climb, but it does take a couple days of tough climbing to reach the top. Most people start from the highland town of Jarabacoa, and some add a loop through the pretty Valle de Tétero to the excursion.

If you're not up for the summit, Jarabacoa has less ambitious, but still rewarding, hikes to area waterfalls and other sights. And for those who want to stretch their legs but still want to work on their tans, there are several pleasant hikes from Las Terrenas and Las Galeras, both in the Samaná Peninsula, which end at beautiful isolated beaches.

Mountain Biking

While road cyclists in the DR face heavy traffic and pot hole–laden highways, mountain bikers revel in hundreds of miles of back roads, dirt paths and one-track corridors. A few adventurous souls with good maps and good Spanish skills head out on their own, whether through the central highlands, or along the coast in the north or southwest, but most folks sign up for an organized tour. Several tour operators offer trips, but an outfit called Iguana Mama in Cabarete (p195) specializes in biking tours and is without question your best bet. There's something for everyone, from half-day downhill rides to two-week cross-country tours and, with advance notice, trips can be customized for just about any length or skill-level. There are good tours and plenty of bike rentals in Las Galeras and Las Terrenas in the Samaná Peninsula as well.

River Rafting

Jarabacoa is also the jumping-off point for trips down the Dominican Republic's longest river, the Río Yaque del Norte. While relatively mild as white-water adventures go, this portion of the river does have some nice rolls and rapids as it winds through an attractive gorge, making it a fun and worthwhile half-day excursion.

Surfing

Cabarete, better known as a place to go windsurfing and kiteboarding, is also one of the country's best places for surfing. In fact, there are great breaks to be found all along the North Coast. In addition to Cabarete, there are some good spots west of Sosúa and east of Río San Juan, near Playas Caletón and Playa Grande.

Whale Watching

Every year, around 10,000 humpback whales (about three quarters of the entire North Atlantic humpback whale population) migrate to the DR's Bahía de Samaná and surrounding waters to mate. They come in such high numbers and with such regularity that the DR is considered one of the best places in the world to observe humpbacks. The season is short – mid-January to mid-March – but the whale-watching spectacular is a must-see if you are in the DR during that time. Most tours depart from the town of Samaná, and guests are treated to numerous sightings, sometimes at very close range, of whales jostling, lifting their fins and tails and breaching. Reservations are a good idea – the tours are very popular and the season overlaps with Carnival and Independence Day.

Wind Sports

The DR is one of the top places in the world for windsurfing and kiteboarding, and the wind blows hardest in Cabarete, a town on the North Coast given over almost wholly to the two sports. Cabarete hosts major annual competitions in both sports and has numerous schools for those who want to learn. It is also an excellent place for sailing.

BUSINESS HOURS

Traditional business hours are 8:30am to noon and 2pm to 6:30pm Monday to Friday, but the midday siesta is becoming less and less common, especially for businesses serving the tourist industry. Restaurants keep the longest hours, typically staying open from 8am to 10pm or later every day, or at least Monday through Saturday. Expect Internet cafés and call centers to be open from 9am to 6pm Monday to Saturday and half-days on Sunday. Dominican banks are generally open from 8am to 4pm Monday to Friday and 9am to 1pm on Saturday, but almost all offer 24-hour ATM access. Most tourist attractions, tour operators and car rental agencies are open from 9am to 6pm (or later) daily, although museums, galleries and some historical monuments may close one weekday, usually Monday.

CHILDREN

All-inclusive resorts can be a convenient way for families to travel, as they provide easy answers to the most vexing of travel questions: When is dinner? Where are we going to eat? What are we going to do? Where's the bathroom? Can I have another Coke? Dominican resorts are affordable enough to make a Caribbean vacation do-able for families of all means. For independent-minded families the Dominican Republic is no better or worse than most countries – its small size means no long bus or plane rides and the beaches and outdoor activities are fun for everyone. At the same time, there are few kid-specific parks of attractions and navigating the cities can be challenging for parents and exhausting for children.

The good news is that major grocery stores sell many of the same brands of baby food and diapers (nappies) as in the US. For advice on eating out with your kids, see p61 and for excellent general advice on traveling with children, check out Lonely Planet's *Travel with Children*.

Practicalities

Not surprisingly, all-inclusive resorts have the best child-specific facilities and services, from high chairs in the restaurants to child-care and children's programming. That said, not all resorts cater to families with young children, so be sure to choose a place that does. Independent travelers will have a harder time finding facilities designed for children but that's not to say the staff at hotels and restaurants won't be quick to help. Few smaller restaurants will have high-chairs, but many may have a stack of phone books that works almost as well.

Child safety seats are not common, even in private cars, and are almost unheard of in taxis or buses. Seatbelts are required by law, however, so if you bring your own car seat – and it is one that can adapt to a number of different cars – you may be able to use it at least some of the time.

Breast feeding of babies in public is not totally taboo, but nor is it very common. It is definitely not done in restaurants, as in the US and other countries. If necessary, nursing mothers should find a private park bench and use a shawl or other covering.

Sights & Activities

Some places in the Dominican Republic are better suited for kids than others. If you do any traveling around the country, you'll almost certainly pass through Santo

Domingo, which while big and busy, does have a number of sights kids will like (p81). These include a terrific children's museum, an interesting colonial-era fort, a huge botanical garden and a decent zoo. The nearby town of Boca Chica (p102) has a great beach for kids, with a broad sandy area and very mellow surf.

The central highland town of Jarabacoa (p225) has a plethora of outdoors activities suitable for hardy children, including hiking, horseback riding and river-rafting.

Cabarete (p191) on the North Coast is a Mecca for windsurfing and kiteboarding, and although these sports are mostly practiced by adults, a number of schools in Cabarete give lessons to kids. At the same time, advances in children's and beginner's equipment – including larger and more stable boards, smaller sails and kites, and better safety features – have opened both sports to people of all ages, sizes and fitness levels. Cabarete also has some good tour operators with a number of fun, outdoorsy options for children.

Samaná (p148) offers its fantastic whale-watching tours from mid-January to mid-March which will surely delight kids who are into animals and nature.

And of course the all-inclusive resorts at Bávaro and Punta Cana (p132) are excellent for children and families, with myriad activities and programs for young people of all ages and the convenience of your meals, room, beach and pool all in the same spot. Club Med in Punta Cana receives especially high marks from parents and families. Outside of Bávaro and Punta Cana, the resorts in Playa Dorada (p179) and Luperón (p204) have large beaches and mild surf (though neither are as picturesque as in the southeast), an easy-to-reach marine park, and good outdoor excursions in the nearby mountains.

CLIMATE CHARTS

Looking at the accompanying charts, it's not hard to see why the Dominican Republic is sometimes said to have an 'eternal summer.' Month to month, region to region, temperatures remain fairly steady. Rainfall varies much more and travelers should note that although it's a small country, the rainy season peaks in different months in different parts of the country. In Santo Domingo, summer is the rainy

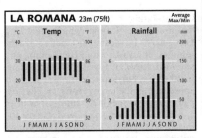

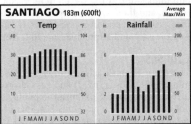

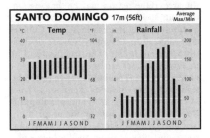

season, with strong daily rains from May to October. The North Coast's rains generally come later, beginning around October and sometimes lasting until March. Samaná is the wettest region, with on and off rain most of the year (February and March are the driest months). The southeast is much drier, and the southwest even drier still – in both areas the months from May to October have the most rain. But like many places in the tropics, rain storms in the DR tend to be short and sweet – that is, very heavy but lasting only an hour or so. With a little planning, the rains need not disrupt your plans much at all.

Hurricane season – August to October – can bring intense rain storms and the occasional hurricane, which typically affect the eastern part of the country. The big ones don't hit every year – the average is more like once or twice a decade. Of course it doesn't take a Category 5 hurricane – the highest rating – to spoil your vacation. Tropical Storm Jeanne, which grew to a Category 1 hurricane just before reaching the DR, caused extensive flooding and stranded scores of tourists in Punta Cana in 2004. If a hurricane or tropical storm is approaching, the large resorts are the best place to go, as they have sturdy structures and extensive emergency services (see the boxed text, p43). Of course sunny days outnumber stormy ones, even in hurricane season, and there are great deals to be had then – as long as a storm doesn't hit, it can be a pleasant and affordable time to travel.

COURSES

There are Spanish schools in Santo Domingo (p81), Sosúa (p187) and Las Galeras (p156), though the Dominican Republic is not as well-known a place to study Spanish as Guatemala, Mexico or other countries in the area. (One reason may be that the Dominican accent is quite pronounced – it's akin to learning English in Texas.) Courses cost US$250 to US$500 per week, including 20 to 30 hours of instruction and all materials. Classes can be one-on-one or in a group, and many schools arrange conversation exchanges, outdoor excursions, dancing and cooking lessons, and social events for their students, usually for no or minimal charge. Most schools can also arrange room and board, either in the home of a local family (which gives you lots of opportunities to practice) or in guesthouses or apart-hotels.

An excellent online resource for Spanish schools in the Dominican Republic and elsewhere is www.spanishcourses.info. It contains comprehensive listings and information about Spanish schools in Spain and Latin America (including photos, curricula, accommodations, fees and contact information) as well as general information of the countries and cities where the schools are located. You can even get a head start on your classes with the site's page of verbs and conjugations

The Dominican Republic is a great place to learn to kiteboard, windsurf and/or surf. Cabarete (p193) has numerous schools for each of the sports, and in some cases all three. Kiteboarding is definitely the 'in' sport in Cabarete, though it was first made famous as a place to windsurf. Most people need a minimum of six hours of instruction to pick up kiteboarding, but nine or 12 hours is recommended. A six hour course (usually spread over two to three days) runs from about US$240 to US$275, or US$350 to US$400 for nine hours and US$420 to US$450 for 12 hours.

Windsurfing lessons cost around US$40 per hour, US$150 for a four-session course, with discounts of groups of two or more. Most people can pick up the basics of windsurfing in a few hours, though it is a sport that takes months or years to really master.

Surf schools – many of which are affiliated with kiteboarding schools – charge around US$30 to US$40 per person for a three hour introductory course, or US$100 to US$175 per person for a full-on five-day surf camp (p54).

CUSTOMS

Customs regulations are similar to most countries, with restrictions on the import of live animals, fresh fruit or vegetables, weapons, drugs and the export of ancient artifacts and endangered plants or animals.

Along with personal items like clothing and toiletries, foreigners arriving in the Dominican Republic are permitted to bring in the following: one camera, one video camera, twelve rolls of film or video cassettes, one set of binoculars, one cellular phone, one laptop computer, five DVDs, 20 CDs, 200g of tobacco, 20 boxes of cigarettes or 25 cigars, up to 3L of beer, wine or liquor, medications (you must carry a prescription if it's a psychotropic drug), one tent and equipment for camping, personal sporting goods and no more than US$500 in gifts.

It is illegal to take anything out of the DR that is over 100 years old – including paintings, household items and prehistoric artifacts – without special export certificates. Mahogany trees are endangered and products made from mahogany wood may be confiscated upon departure. Black coral is widely available and though Dominican law does not forbid its sale, international environment agreements do – avoid purchasing it. The same goes for products made from turtle shells and butterfly wings – these animals are facing extinction. It is illegal to export raw unpolished amber from the DR, though amber jewelry is common and highly prized.

Where most travelers run into problems is with cigars, and it is not with Dominican customs as much as their own. The United States allows its citizens to bring up to 100 cigars duty-free. Canada and most European countries only allow 50 cigars before duty taxes kick in.

DANGERS & ANNOYANCES

The Dominican Republic is not a particularly dangerous place to visit, although, as anywhere, bad decisions greatly increase your chances of having problems. Street crime is rare in most tourist areas, especially during the day, but you should always be alert for pickpockets and camera-snatchers. Avoid walking on beaches at night, and consider taking a cab if you're returning home late from clubs and bars. Prostitution is dangerous mainly to those participating in it, though solo men may get annoyed by persistent propositioning and some readers have reported being pick-pocketed by prostitutes.

Scams

The Dominican Republic doesn't have the myriad scams and rip-offs found elsewhere. Perhaps the number one scam – if you can even call it that – is not giving the proper change after a purchase. In many cases it is a legitimate error in math. And it is also customary for merchants to round off a peso or two if the merchant doesn't have change – *Se lo debo* (literally, I owe it to you) is the usual euphemism and it's considered somewhat uncouth to argue the point. (Naturally the rounding rarely goes in your favor!) But it is not entirely uncommon for waiters,

taxi drivers and shop owners to 'accidentally' give you 120 pesos when you're owed 220, or to give you change as if you'd paid with a 100 peso bill and not a 500 peso bill. The solution is to count your change right when you get it, before you leave the counter or the attendant helps the next person. If something's missing, say so right away.

DISABLED TRAVELERS

Few Latin American countries are well-suited for travelers with disabilities, and the Dominican Republic is no different. Travelers who are blind or in wheelchairs will have to negotiate narrow and often unkempt sidewalks, erratic traffic and restaurants, hotels and museums that were clearly not designed with disabled people in mind. On the other hand, all-inclusive resorts can be ideal for physically challenged travelers, as your room, meals and day- and night-time activities are all within close physical proximity, and there are plenty of staff members to help you navigate the occasional set of stairs or stretch of sand. Some resorts have a few wheel-chair friendly rooms, with larger doors and handles in the bathroom; others can at least make your stay easier by placing you in a room with easier access to the buffet or swimming pool. And because the Dominican Republic has so many all-inclusive resorts, all over the country and in all price ranges, disabled travelers will not want for variety or selection. And, it should be said, Dominicans tend to be extremely helpful and accommodating people. Disabled travelers should expect some long and curious stares, but also quick and friendly help from perfect strangers and passers-by.

NO RIDE IN THE PARK

Probably the single biggest danger tourists face in the Dominican Republic is getting hurt while riding on a *motoconcho* (motorcycle taxi). Cheap and convenient, *motoconchos* are often the best way to get around town, but scores of tourists and locals are hurt or killed on them every year. A common and extremely painful injury is burning your leg on the muffler while getting on or off the bike. (If you do get burned, be careful of infection as burns heal very slowly in tropical climates.) While many *motoconcho* drivers are conscientious, enough are maniacs to warrant caution – do not hesitate to ask the driver to go more slowly (¡*Más despacio por favor!*) or to simply stop and get off if you're nervous. Be sure you have your feet on the rests and that you have a good grip on the side-handles before setting off. Never ever have two passengers on a bike – not only is the price the same as taking separate bikes, the extra weight makes most scooters much harder to control. And since helmets are unheard of, even a small accident can be serious or fatal. For longer trips, or if you have any sort of bag or luggage, just take a cab.

DIRECTORY

EMBASSIES & CONSULATES
Dominican Embassies & Consulates

The Dominican Republic has embassies and consulates in most of the countries that send large number of tourists here. For the complete list of Dominican embassies and consulates and their contact information, check out the website of the **Secretaría de Estado de Relaciones Exteriores** (www.serex.gov.do, in Spanish). When it's functioning, it's a good resource.

Australia (☎ 02-9363 5891; 343a Edgecliffe Rd, NSW, Sydney, 2027)

Canada (☎ 613-569-9893; www.drembassy.org; 130 Albert St, Suite 418, Ottawa, Ontario KIP 5G4)

France (☎ 015 35 39 595; www.amba-dominicaine -paris.com; 45 Rue de Courcelles, Paris 75008)

Germany (☎ 228-364-956; embajada_dominicana@ hotmail.com; Burgstrasse 87, 53177 Bonn)

Haiti (☎ 509-257-9215; fax 509-257-0568; 121 Av Panamericaine, Pétionville, Puerto Principe)

Italy (☎ 63 200 441; embajadadominicanait@yahoo.it; Via Pisanelli No 1, Int 4, Rome 00196)

Jamaica (☎ 876-755-4154; domemb@cwjamaica.com; 32 Earls Court, Kingston 8, Kingston)

Japan (☎ 03-499 6020; fax 03-499 2627; Kowa 38, Bldg Rm 904, 4-12-24 Nishi-Azabu Minato-Ku 106-0031, Tokyo)

Netherlands (☎ 020 647 1062; Terschellingerstraat 6, 1181 HK, Amsterdam)

Spain (☎ 944 276 388; consul@repdom.euskalnet.net; José Mª Escuza 20-6A, 48013 Bilbao)

UK (☎ 020 7727-6285; www.dominicanembassy.org.uk; 139 Inverness Terrace, Bayswater, W2-6JF, London)

USA (☎ 202-332-6280; embassy@us.serex.gov.do; 1715 22nd St NW, Washington, DC 20008)

Embassies & Consulates in the DR

Countries that send the most tourists to the Dominican Republic also have embassies or consulates there. Embassies vary greatly in terms of the services they offer to their citizens. Some field questions and concerns of all sorts while others – the United States most notably – make it clear they provide assistance only in very serious legal or medical emergencies. That said, citizens should not hesitate to contact their embassy for help resolving large legal, medical or business-related matters. At the very least, they can direct you to appropriate third-party agencies or services. All of the following are located in Santo Domingo.

Canada (Map pp66-7; ☎ 809-685-1136; Av Eugenio de Marchena 39)

Cuba (Map pp66-7; ☎ 809-537-2113; Calle FP Ramírez 809)

France (Map pp72-3; ☎ 809-687-5270; Calle Las Damas 42 btwn Luperón & El Conde)

Germany (Map pp66-7; ☎ 809-542-8949; Torre Piantini, 16th fl Av Gustavo A Mejía Ricart at Av Abraham Lincoln)

Haiti (Map p78; ☎ 809-686-5778; Calle Juan Sánchez Ramírez 33 at Av Máximo Gómez)

Netherlands (Map pp66-7; ☎ 809-565-5240; Mayor Enrique Valverde)

Italy (Map p78; ☎ 809-682-0830; Calle Rodríguez Objío 4)

Japan (Map pp66-7; ☎ 809-567-3365; Torre BHD office Bldg, 8th fl, Calle Luís Thomen at Av Jiménez Moya)

Spain (Map pp66-7; ☎ 809-535-6500; Torre BHD office Bldg, 4th Flr, Calle Luís Thomen at Av Jiménez Moya)

UK (Map pp66-7; ☎ 809-472 7111; Av 27 de Febrero 233 at Av Máximo Gómez)

USA (Map p78; ☎ 809-221-2171; Av César Nicolás Penson at Av Máximo Gómez)

FESTIVALS & EVENTS

If there's any generalization to be made about Dominicans, it is that the people take holidays and celebrations very seriously. Here are some of the more notable events throughout the year.

February
CARNIVAL

Carnival (or Carnaval, in Spanish) is celebrated with great fervor throughout the country every Sunday in February, culminating in a huge blow out in Santo Domingo on the last weekend of the month or first weekend of March. Almost every major city (and many minor ones) has Carnival celebrations, each lending unique twists and traditions to the event. Masks and costumes figure prominently in all – Santiago even hosts an international *caleta* (Carnival mask) competition, and the craftsmanship is truly astounding. The largest and most traditional Carnivals outside of Santo Domingo, all of which are held in February or March, are celebrated in Santiago, Cabral, Monte Cristi and La Vega. See the respective city sections for further details.

INDEPENDENCE DAY

The Dominican Republic declared its independence from Spain in November 1821, but only a year later submitted to Haitian rule to avert reinvasion by Spain (or else Haiti itself). February 27 is the day, in 1844, that the Dominican Republic regained independence from its neighbor, making it the only Latin American country whose independence celebration does not mark a break from European colonial rule. The day is marked by street celebrations and military parades.

March
SEMANA SANTA
Any place that has access to water – mainly the beach towns, but also those near lakes, rivers or waterfalls – is thoroughly inundated with Dominican vacationers during 'Holy Week,' the biggest travel holiday in the country and much of Latin America. Many foreign travelers, with visions of deserted beaches and tranquil tropical nights, may find the crowded beaches, innumerable temporary food stands, and loud music day and night, a bit off-putting. Others, including most Dominicans, revel in the lively atmosphere. Inland is somewhat less crowded than the beaches, but make reservations early, no matter where you end up.

June
LATIN MUSIC FESTIVAL
This huge, annual three-day event – held at the Olympic Stadium in Santo Domingo – attracts the top names in Latin music, including jazz, salsa, merengue and *bachata* players. Enrique Iglesias, salsa king Tito Rojas and merengue legend Fernando Villalona are all regulars.

PUERTO PLATA CULTURAL FESTIVAL
This weeklong festival brings merengue, blues, jazz and folk concerts to the Puerto Plata's Fuerte San Felipe at the end of the Malecón. Troupes from Santo Domingo perform traditional songs and dances, including African spirituals and famous salsa steps.

July–August
SANTO DOMINGO MERENGUE FESTIVAL
Santo Domingo hosts the country's largest and most raucous merengue festival. For two weeks at the end of July and beginning of August, the world's top merengue bands play for the world's best merengue dancers. While the Malecón is the center of the action, you'll find dance parties in hotel ballrooms and private terraces, on city squares and public parks, in restaurants and makeshift bars throughout town.

October
PUERTO PLATA MERENGUE FESTIVAL
The country's other merengue festival is held in Puerto Plata during the first week of October. The entire length of Puerto Plata's Malecón is closed to vehicular traffic. Food stalls are set up on both sides of the boulevard and famous merengue singers perform on a stage erected for the event. This festival is different from the one in Santo Domingo in that it also includes a harvest festival and an arts-and-crafts fair.

FOOD
Food prices vary considerably in the Dominican Republic, from expensive in heavily touristed areas (comparable to US and European prices) to very cheap in small towns and isolated areas. Where there are many options, the listings in this book are divided into budget, midrange and top end, though many restaurants have a range of options, from cheap pizza and pasta plates to pricey lobster meals. In general, main dishes average US$1 to US$6 at budget eateries, US$7 to US$15 at midrange places, and US$16 and up at top-end restaurants. Travelers on a budget can save money by avoiding sit-down restaurants and instead going to informal food stands and small cafeteria-style eateries. Another way to save a little money is by buying food at a grocery store and making some of your own meals. Certain foods lend themselves well to simple meals on the go, including sardines, tuna, crackers, drinkable yogurt, pastries and more, all readily available in most Dominican markets. With a fresh tomato or cucumber to slice on top, you can eat quite nicely for a fraction of what you pay at a restaurant. This book includes food shacks and/or grocery stores for almost every town. For more information on food and drink in the DR, see p57.

GAY & LESBIAN TRAVELERS
As a whole, the Dominican Republic is quite open about heterosexual sex and sexuality, but still fairly close-minded about gays and lesbians. Gay and lesbian travelers will find the most open community in Santo Domingo, though even there the gay clubs are relatively discreet. Santiago, Puerto Plata, Bávaro and Punta Cana also have gay venues, catering as much to foreigners as to

DIRECTORY

locals. Everywhere else, open displays of affection between men or women are rare and quite taboo. Two men may have trouble getting a hotel room with just one bed, even though you'll pay more for a room with two. Two good websites with gay-specific listings and information for the Dominican Republic are www.guiagay.com and www.planetout.com.

HOLIDAYS

Of all the holidays celebrated in the Dominican Republic, Semana Santa is by far the one most likely to impact your travel plans. Right before Easter, it is the main vacation holiday for Dominicans and anyplace with water – beaches, lakes, waterfalls or rivers – is likely to be very crowded. At the same time, most water sports are prohibited during Semana Santa, including scuba diving and windsurfing. Hotels, tour operators and car rental agencies raise their prices, but are still booked solid. If you'll be in the DR during Semana Santa, definitely plan ahead; if you don't care for the crowds, consider using that week to explore more out-of-the-way destinations. Most other holidays should not disrupt your travel plans much – banks, government offices and some museums and galleries may be closed, and parades (especially on Independence Day) can block traffic. Carnival processions are held every weekend in February and are a highlight of any trip to this holiday-happy island.

New Year's Day January 1
Epiphany/Three Kings Day January 6
Our Lady of Altagracia January 21
Duarte Day January 26
Independence Day, Carnival February 27
Semana Santa March/April
Pan-American Day April 14
Labor Day May 1
Foundation of Sociedad la Trinitaria July 16
Restoration Day August 16

Our Lady of Mercedes September 24
Columbus Day October 12
UN Day October 24
All Saints' Day November 1
Christmas Day December 25

INSURANCE

Travelers insurance is always something worth considering, though relatively few tourists actually utilize it. Policies vary widely, but can include compensation for lost, damaged or stolen luggage, for cancelled or delayed trips (a concern mostly for cruise ship passengers) and even for bad weather. Some include coverage for medical treatment or evacuation, or for car rental. Travelers insurance makes the most sense for families spending a week or more at an all-inclusive resort – that is, if you're spending a significant amount of money in one place. Independent travelers may be interested in theft or damage insurance, and a plan with medical care and evacuation may be a good idea if you'll be doing any adventure activities.

INTERNET ACCESS

The Dominican Republic has no shortage of Internet cafés, where broadband connections are increasingly the norm, as well as CD burners, high-speed USB compatibility, even web cams for phone and chat programs. Most cafés charge US$0.75 to US$1.50 per hour to access the Internet, more for additional services like printing or burning CDs. In resort areas, rates jump to US$3 to US$6 per hour. Verizon, the country's main telephone service provider, has call centers throughout the country, many of which have computers with Internet access as well. The price is always US$1.50 per hour.

As more and more travelers bring their laptops along with them, many top-end hotels and resorts (and even some midrange places, especially those operated by expats) have begun providing in-room Internet

---

INTERNET ACCESS

Most travelers make constant use of Internet cafés and free Web-based email such as Yahoo (www.yahoo.com) or Hotmail (www.hotmail.com). If you're traveling with a notebook or handheld computer, be aware that your modem may not work once you leave your home country. The safest option is to buy a reputable 'global' modem before you leave home, or buy a local PC-card modem if you're spending an extended time in any one country. For more information on traveling with a portable computer, see www.teleadapt.com.

access. There is sometimes a per-minute or one-time connection fee – and in some cases you also need your own ISP – but more often than not the hotel offers free access through its own service provider, as long as you have your own computer and cables. This is still the exception as opposed to the rule, but the trend is definitely growing.

LAUNDRY

Most laundromats in the DR charge per piece, which adds up very fast. Expect to pay from US$0.75 to US$1.25 per piece, even underwear and T-shirts. For the ones that don't typically charge by the load (as opposed to the pound or kilo) it's a good idea to bring clothes that can all be washed together. A load is usually up to 14lb (sometimes 18), and can range from US$1.50 to US$6. Same-day service is usually available if you drop your clothes off early. You may have luck asking at your hotel, although they typically charge per piece as well.

LEGAL MATTERS

The Dominican Republic has two police forces – the Policía Nacional (National Police) and the Policía Turística (Tourist Police, commonly referred to by its abbreviation 'Politur'). The National Police are not as corrupt and unreliable as their counterparts in other Latin American countries, but you still want to have as little interaction with them as possible (and they feel pretty much the same way). If a police officer stops you, be polite and cooperate. They may ask to see your passport – you're required to have it with you, but it's always a good idea to have a photocopy of your passport on you at all times. But this is very rare, especially if you've really done nothing wrong.

Politur officers, on the other hand, are generally very friendly men and women whose job is specifically to help tourists. Many speak a little bit of a language other than Spanish. They wear white shirts with blue insignia and can usually be found near major tourist sights and centers. You should contact Politur first in the event of theft, assault or if you were the victim of a scam, but you can equally ask them for directions to sights, which *gua-gua* (minibus used for local public transport) to take etc. Many cities have a Politur station, which you will find listed in this book.

Prostitution is big business in the Dominican Republic, and it is not entirely clear if it is legal or not. Tourists picking up willing men or women is common and there is evidently no law that makes it illegal, even if money changes hands. But there is no law expressly legalizing prostitution, either. It is definitely illegal to have sex with anyone under the age of 18, even if the offender didn't know the prostitute's real age. Encouraging or aiding prostitution is illegal, and the law, while targeted at pimps or brothel owners, is obviously open for some interpretation. In fact, the Dominican consulate will tell you that prostitution in all forms is illegal. In any case, walking the line between what is legal and not legal, especially as a foreigner and given the corruption within the Dominican police force and judicial system, is definitely risky.

MAPS

If you rent a car, it is worth buying a good map to the area you'll be driving in, and/or the whole country. Road signs can be missing or unreliable, and a map can save you a lot of back and forth. You should also get in the habit of asking directions frequently, especially if you're headed to an isolated town or sight. Not only will this prevent you from getting off track, but is also a good time to ask about road conditions – in some cases rain or construction have made the roads very difficult to pass, especially if you're driving a compact car. The easiest way to ask directions if you are going to, say, Punta Rusia is to ask *¿Para Punta Rusia?*, literally 'For Punta Rusia?' To ask about conditions, you can say *¿El camino está bien o malo?* (Is the road good or bad?) or *¿Se puede pasar mi carro?* (Will my car be able to pass?). Of course, understanding the directions you're given is half the battle; some key words to listen for are *derecho* (straight), *derecha* (right), *izquierdo* (left), *desvío* (turnoff), *letrero* (sign), *mucho pozo* or *mucha olla* (lots of potholes or holes), and *vaya preguntando* (ask along the way).

In Santo Domingo, **Mapas GAAR** (Map pp72-3; ☎ 809-688-8004; www.mapasgaar.com.do; Espaillat; 🕙 8:30am-5:30pm Mon-Fri), near El Conde publishes and sells the most comprehensive maps of cities and towns in the DR. For a frame-quality map, head to the **Instituto**

DIRECTORY

Geográfico (Map pp72-3; ☎ 809-682-2680; El Conde btwn Las Damas & Av del Puerto; 8am-6pm Mon-Fri) where a great five-panel, 1m-by-1.5m map sells for US$35.

MONEY

The Dominican monetary unit is the peso, indicated by the symbol RD$ (or sometimes just R$). Though the peso is technically divided into 100 centavos (cents) per peso, prices are usually rounded to the nearest peso. There are one- and five-peso coins, while paper money comes in denominations of 10, 20, 50, 100, 500 and 1000 pesos. Many tourist-related businesses list prices in US dollars, but accept pesos at the going exchange rate.

ATMs

Automatic cash machines are common in the Dominican Republic and are, without question, the best way to obtain Dominican pesos and manage your money on the road. Banks with reliable ATMs include Banco Popular, Banco Progreso, Banco de Reservas, Banco León and Scotiabank. As in any country, be smart about where and when you take out cash – at night on a dark street in a bad part of town is not the ideal spot. Most ATMs are not in the bank itself, but in a small booth accessible from the street (and thus available 24 hours); in some cases the booth has a latching door, which gives you some added security. If there's no booth and the machine is right on the street, be extra cognizant of your surroundings. None of this is to say that taking out money from an ATM is inherently unsafe, even at night. But a few precautionary measures will give you peace of mind and keep you from being an easy target.

Cash

Credit and debit cards are becoming more common among Dominicans (and more widely accepted for use by foreigners) but the great majority of transactions are still conducted in cash. Travelers to the Dominican Republic will encounter less theft and trickery when it comes to exchanging or obtaining cash here than in their countries, though caution is always a good idea. Some merchants will 'accidentally' give you less change that you are due (see Scams, p263), so be sure to always count your change.

Credit Cards

Visa and MasterCard are accepted widely, especially in areas frequented by tourists. Some but not all businesses add a surcharge for credit card purchases (typically 16%). The surcharge will likely be even more common by the time you read this, as a new federal policy of withdrawing sales tax directly from credit card transactions means merchants will simply add the cost directly to the bill.

Moneychangers

Moneychangers will approach you in a number of tourist centers, with huge wads of cash asking 'change money, change money?' They can be quite aggressive in some places, including Sosúa and Cabarete, but you get equally favorable rates and a much securer transaction at an ATM, bank or exchange office.

Taxes & Tipping

There are two taxes on food and drink sales: a 12% to 16% value-added tax and a 10% service tax. The latter is supposed to be divided among the wait and kitchen staff, but it is customary to leave an additional 10% tip if you are happy with the service. There's a 23% tax on hotel rooms – ask whether the listed rates include taxes. It's customary to tip bellhops for carrying your bags and to leave US$1 to US$2 per night for the housecleaner. You should also tip tour guides, some of whom earn no other salary.

Travelers' Checks

With the advent of reliable ATM networks, travelers' checks have lost much of their usefulness and many travelers (including these writers) have stopped using them altogether. That said, travelers checks can be exchanged at most banks and *casas de cambio* (exchange booths) in tourist centers. You may be required to show your passport and, in some cases, the receipt from when you purchased the checks.

PHOTOGRAPHY & VIDEO
Film & Equipment

Film and camera equipment are available in the Dominican Republic, but the selection tends to be limited and the prices steep. Your best bet is to bring everything you'll want or need with you from home, including batteries.

TAKING GREAT PHOTOS

Bright tropical light can fool even the most sophisticated light-metering systems, digital or standard, and many travelers end up with washed-out pictures. Consider purchasing a polarizing filter, which will enrich pale blue skies and remove reflections from glass and water. Some digital cameras have functions that mimic polarizing filters, which may need to be manually initiated.

If most of your pictures will be taken outside during daylight hours – usually the case in the Caribbean – consider purchasing a 'slow' film, which will provide the best color rendition. For prints, 100 ISO film takes great day-time pictures; for slides, Fujichrome Velvia is the pro's choice, followed closely by Kodachrome 25 and 64. However 100-speed film doesn't do well in low-light situations, including sunsets – for more versatility, a 200 or 400 speed film is best.

Most travelers are now using digital cameras, and the problem of finding a place to buy or develop film has been replaced with the problem of downloading and saving pictures from your memory card. Many Internet cafés (but not all) have the necessary hardware and software to download pictures from your camera and burn them to a CD or (less commonly) DVD. You should bring your USB cable and plenty of blank CDs – in some cases, the CD burning software used 'closes' the CD after burning it, rather than allowing you to save several batches of photos to the same disc. You can also usually purchase blank CDs at the Internet café itself or from an electronics store. Lonely Planet's *Travel Photography* provides an extensive guide on taking great holiday snaps.

Restrictions

It is illegal to take pictures inside the DR's airports, or of police stations or penal institutions. Also, many police officers do not like having their pictures taken, and they have the authority to arrest you for photographing them without authorization.

Airport Security

Avoid sending your film through airport X-ray machines. Most won't damage your film – and newer machines are supposedly safe even for high speed film – but there's no point in taking the chance. Most security personnel will hand-inspect your film if you ask them to, removing the necessity of having it X-rayed. Don't forget to have your camera hand-inspected if it has film inside.

POST

There are post offices in every town and hours are typically 8am to noon and 2pm to 5pm Monday to Friday, and 8am to noon only on Saturday. It costs about US$0.75 to send a postcard to North and Central America, slightly more for Europe. Service is relatively reliable – postcards are more likely to arrive than letters – but by no means foolproof. For important documents and packages, definitely go with an international courier such as UPS, DHL or Federal Express. They each have stand-alone offices in Santo Domingo; in smaller towns, they are usually affiliated with Metro Pac or another local delivery agency, which will have all the packaging and tracking materials.

SHOPPING

There are a number of things unique to the Dominican Republic that make nice mementos or keepsakes.

Dominican amber is among the best in the world, both for its variety of color and the high number of 'inclusions' (insects, plant material and other things trapped inside). The quality of the jewelry made from amber varies widely, but if you look around enough you can find an excellent piece that's in your price range. Larimar is another beautiful material – a blue mineral with white streaks – and is found only in the Dominican Republic. Amber and larimar are typically sold together, so a shop that's good for one will likely be good for the other. You can also find objects made of horn, wood and leather.

You can't possibly miss the Haitian-style paintings that are for sale in great numbers at virtually every tourist destination in the country. Though most are very formulaic in their composition and style, they are also colorful and fanciful and many people find them to be nice souvenirs. If you like the style but are looking for a more professional piece, the country's best shop is the Haitian Caraibes Art Gallery in Las Terrenas (p165) and there are a number of excellent galleries in Santo Domingo (p94).

Many souvenirs sold in the Dominican Republic are made from endangered plant and animal species, and you should avoid buying them. All species of sea turtles are endangered, so steer clear of any item made of turtle shell – typically combs and bracelets – or food dishes made from *carey* (turtle meat). The same goes for products made from American crocodiles and black or white coral products, despite what some store owners say. You should also avoid buying products made from conch shell, though *lambí* (conch meat) is served in restaurants around the country.

SOLO TRAVELERS

The Dominican Republic is a perfectly fine place to travel alone, even for women. Solo travelers of both sexes may get more unwanted attention than they would if they were traveling as a couple or a group. Women traveling alone will get more ogling and whistling from Dominican men than they would if they were with a man or even another woman. Solo men (and even men traveling together) will get approached more frequently by prostitutes than if they were traveling with a woman.

Unlike some countries, most hotels in the Dominican Republic do not give discounts for single travelers as opposed to a couple. Rooms are priced according to the number of beds, so a solo traveler will pay the same as a couple and both pay less than two people wanting a room with separate beds. There are no hostels and very few rooms with a shared bath, which in other countries are a way for solo travelers to save on lodging.

The lack of hostels can also make meeting other travelers more challenging. However outgoing solo travelers should be able to meet other travelers in other ways, especially at popular hotels, on buses, at major sights and on guided excursions. There is also a rich foreign and expat community in many Dominican cities; this book indicates bars and other venues where foreigners tend to congregate.

Finally, while it is relatively rare to see solo travelers staying at all-inclusive resorts,

it certainly would not be hard to meet other people there, with the myriad programs and activities offered to guests.

TELEPHONE & FAX

The easiest way to make phone calls in the Dominican Republic is to use a Verizon Comunicard, available at many hotels and minimarkets. Dial ☎ 611 for English or ☎ 311 for Spanish from any residential or public telephone, enter the card number after the tone, and then dial the phone number you wish to reach. Remember that you must dial 1 + 809 for all calls within the DR, even local ones. Local calls cost US$0.14 per minute and national calls are US$0.21 per minute. Toll-free numbers have 200 for their prefix (not the area code).

The country code for the Dominican Republic is ☎ 809. However, you do not need to use the country code, or any other additional numbers when dialing to or from the USA or Canada – simply dial 1, the area code and the number, just as you would if you were there. The cost is around US$0.30 per minute. For calls to Europe (US$0.75 per minute) dial ☎ 011, then the country code, and then the number you are trying to reach.

For directory information, dial ☎ 1411 from a residential phone. If you're using a payphone, follow the instructions for making a call using a Comunicard and then dial ☎ 1411 – there is a minimal charge.

Mobile phones are very popular in the Dominican Republic and travelers with global-roaming enabled phones can often receive and make cell phone calls. It is worth checking with your mobile phone carrier for details on rates and accessibility – be aware that per-minute fees can be exorbitant. It is also possible to buy a phone locally (or bring one from home that's not currently in use) and have it activated to use with pre-paid cards. The most popular pre-paid card provider is Orange, which has offices throughout the country.

Fax service is available at many Internet cafés, and costs around US$0.75 per page to the USA and US$1.50 to Europe. Most cafés will also receive faxes for you and hold it under your name – the cost is lower, around US$0.35 per page typically. That said, not all Internet cafés have the same level of service - if the fax is especially important, choose the most established shop you can find and check back frequently.

TIME

The DR is four hours behind Greenwich Mean Time. In autumn and winter, it is one hour ahead of New York, Miami and Toronto. However, because the country does not adjust for daylight saving time as do the USA and Canada, it's in the same time zone as New York, Miami and Toronto from the first Sunday in April to the last Sunday in October.

TOILETS

There are very few good public toilets in the Dominican Republic. Your best bet, outside of your hotel room, is to use the toilets at transportation centers, like airports and large bus terminals. Large hotels will occasionally have toilets in the lobby area. Restaurants usually have toilets and washbasins, but they vary considerably in agreeableness. It is always a good idea to carry toilet paper with you.

TOURIST INFORMATION

Almost every city in the Dominican Republic that's frequented by tourists has a tourist information office, and a number of less-visited towns do as well. Whether they are actually helpful – well, that's another question entirely. There is no relation between the size or popularity of a town and the quality or helpfulness of its tourist office. Even within an office are staff members who take their job more or less seriously, so you never really know if stopping in will be an eye-opening experience or a complete waste of time. In general, treat the information you get at tourist offices the same way you treat information you get at your hotel or from other travelers – some of it is definitely correct and useful, but a certain amount will be wrong or misleading. Don't be afraid to ask to speak to another person at the tourist office if you feel the person helping you doesn't have the answers you're looking for. Some tourist offices have maps, bus schedules or a calendar of upcoming events, which can be handy.

The national tourist office is the **Secretaría de Estado de Turismo** (☎ 809-221-4660; www .dominicana.com.do; Oficinas Gubernmentales, Bloque D, Av México at Av 30 de Marzo) but it is primarily administrative. A more service-oriented branch is located in the heart of the Zona Colonial, on Calle Isabel La Católica beside Parque Colón. See the Information section (p68) of the Santo Domingo chapter for more details. The location and business hours of tourist offices throughout the country, where they exist, are listed in the appropriate information section.

There are also information counters at Aeropuerto Internacional Las Américas and at Aeropuerto Internacional Gregorio Luperón near Puerto Plata.

VISAS

The majority of would-be foreign travelers in the Dominican Republic do not need to obtain visas prior to arrival. Tourist cards, available upon arrival for US$10, are issued upon arrival to visitors from Australia, Austria, Belgium, Brazil, Canada, France, Germany, Greece, Ireland, Italy, Mexico, Netherlands, Spain, Sweden, Switzerland, the UK and USA, among many others.

Note that US citizens may now be required to have passports to reenter the USA from the Dominican Republic and elsewhere in the Caribbean. New anti-terrorism laws enacted after the September 11 attacks are tightening rules that for many years have enabled Americans to travel throughout North America and the Caribbean without a passport. These laws have been hotly contested, so it is of course possible they will have been revoked by the time you read this, or amended to exempt certain countries. Indeed, the DR, with such a large emigrant community in the US, would be a likely candidate for such an exemption. If you don't have one, definitely check the current regulations before buying your tickets – any travel agency or airline serving the DR should be able to give you the latest info.

Tourist Card Extensions

A tourist card is good for up to 90 days from the date of issue, though the exact length depends on what the officer writes on the card when you enter. If you need just a little time extra, it is usually not necessary to extend – instead you'll be charged a 'fine' of about US$2 for every month you overstayed when you leave. Another easy way to extend your time is to leave the DR briefly – mostly likely to Haiti – and then return, at which point you'll be issued a brand new tourist card. (You may have to pay entrance and departure fees in both countries, of course.)

To extend your tourist card the official way, you must apply in Santo Domingo at the **Dirección General de Migración** (☎ 809-508-2555; Av George Washington at Héroes de Luperón; ☽ 8am-2:30pm Mon-Fri) at least two weeks before your original one expires. You'll be required to fill out a form – usually available in Spanish only – and to present your passport, a photocopy of your passport's information page(s) and two passport-size photos of yourself. The fee is US$10; your passport and new tourist card will be ready for pickup at the same office two weeks later. The process takes you to at least two different offices, and it behooves you to do as the Dominicans do and be assertive – sitting and waiting to be called upon is a good way to blow an entire day.

WOMEN TRAVELERS

Women traveling without men in the Dominican Republic should expect to receive a fair amount of attention, usually in the form of stares and admiring comments like 'Hola, preciosa' (Hello, beautiful). Dominican men are also consummate butt-lookers, no matter what the age, size, shape or nationality of the woman passing by. Then again, women's fashion in the Dominican Republic is all about accentuating what you've got and having their backside checked out by men is clearly more bothersome to foreign women than it is to Dominicans. Indeed, much of what female travelers experience as unwanted attention is fairly ordinary male-female interaction among Dominicans. Many Dominicans, male and female, are somewhat baffled by the strong negative reaction some foreign women have to men's 'appreciation.'

But that is not at all to say that women travelers should not take the same precautions they would in other countries, or ignore their instincts about certain men or situations they encounter. Robbery and assaults, though rare against tourists, do occur and women are often seen as easier targets than men. In much the same way, it is not a good idea to flash money, jewelry or electronics. Foreign women who do not want extra male attention should avoid dressing in a way that especially attracts it. You don't have to dress dowdy – with the way Dominicans dress, that's liable to attract just as much attention! – but be realistic about the message your clothes are likely to send.

Beyond that, simply follow basic commonsense precautions when traveling by yourself; avoid isolated streets and places, especially at night, and don't hitchhike or camp alone.

WORK

The Dominican government frowns upon foreigners working in the DR, unless they're working for free or are hired by a recognized company or running a registered business. There's an assumption here that most any foreigner working in the DR is earning money that a resident Dominican should be earning. As a result of this logic, the government makes it very costly for a foreigner to work here by requiring that you obtain an expensive work permit.

In addition, any foreigner who doesn't have residency status must leave the country every six months for a period of no less than one week. Obtaining residency status is time-consuming, usually requires a lawyer and can cost US$10,000. However, a lawyer with the right connections can sometimes lower the expense and shorten the process, which averages about one year.

Transportation

THINGS CHANGE...

The information in this chapter is particularly vulnerable to change. Check directly with the airline or a travel agent to make sure you understand how a fare (and ticket you may buy) works and be aware of the security requirements for international travel. Shop carefully. The details given in this chapter should be regarded as pointers and are not a substitute for your own careful, up-to-date research.

GETTING THERE & AWAY

ENTERING THE COUNTRY

The vast majority of tourists entering the Dominican Republic (DR) arrive by air. Independent travelers typically arrive at the main international airport outside of Santo Domingo, Aeropuerto Internacional Las Américas. Flights from New York, Miami, San Juan (Puerto Rico) and various European countries arrive there daily. Passing through immigration is a relatively simple, though sometimes time consuming, process. Once disembarked, you are guided by a maze of tunnels to the immigration area where you must buy a tourist card (US$10) at one of the windows along the side. Once you've filled it in, join the queue in front of one of the immigration officers. They will often assume you are visiting for two weeks or less, and give you just 15 days, so if you plan on staying longer, let the officer know this right away – he is allowed to give you up to 90 days on a tourist card. In general, neither immigration nor customs officials pay much attention to tourists carrying an ordinary amount of luggage, and entering is pretty much a breeze. The procedure is the same if you arrive by charter plane to one of the smaller airports like La Romana or Punta Cana, used primarily by guests going to all-inclusive resorts. Officers are even less scrutinizing there, but the queues may be as long or longer. Hang onto your tourist card – you will need to turn it in when you leave the country.

Immigration officials at Dominican Republic–Haitian border crossings may ask you more questions, not so much because they suspect you of anything but because it is so rare to see foreign tourists crossing in or out of Haiti. Officially, you are supposed to pay US$20 to leave the DR, which gives you the right to reenter at the same point for no extra charge. However, border officials may charge you an extra US$5 to US$10 to leave, and the full US$10 to reenter for no other reason than they can. There isn't much point in arguing, though you can politely ask why you are being charged more.

Passport

All foreign visitors must have a valid passport to enter the DR. Be sure you have room for both an entry and exit stamp, and that your passport is valid for at least six months beyond your planned travel dates. See (p271) for information on visas.

AIR
Airports & Airlines

The DR has nine international airports, though at least three of them receive only a handful of international flights and serve primarily as domestic and air-taxi hubs.

Aeropuerto Internacional Arroyo Barril (ABA; ☎ 809-248-2718) West of Samaná, a small airstrip used mostly during whale-watching season (January to March).

TRANSPORTATION

Aeropuerto Internacional Cibao (STI; ☎ 809-581-8072) Serves Santiago and the interior.

Aeropuerto Internacional El Portillo (EPS) Tiny airstrip near Las Terrenas that gets busiest during whale watching season. Used mostly for domestic flights, but gets an occasional international arrival.

Aeropuerto Internacional Gregorio Luperón (POP; ☎ 809-586-1992) Serves Playa Dorada and Puerto Plata.

Aeropuerto Internacional La Herrera (HEX; ☎ 809-701-6457) On Santo Domingo's west side, this busy airport is the hub for all of the DR's domestic carriers.

Aeropuerto Internacional La Romana (LRM; ☎ 809-689-1548) Near La Romana.

Aeropuerto Internacional Las Américas (SDQ; ☎ 809-549-0081) 20km east of Santo Domingo. The country's main international airport.

Aeropuerto Internacional María Montez (BRX; ☎ 809-524-4144) Near Barahona; does not have a regular commercial passenger service.

Aeropuerto Internacional Punta Cana (PUJ; ☎ 809-959-2473) Serves Bávaro and Punta Cana.

International carriers with services to the Dominican Republic include:

Air Canada (AC; ☎ 809-541-2929; www.aircanada.ca; Toronto)

Air France (AF; ☎ 809-686-8432; www.airfrance.com; Paris)

Air Jamaica (JM; ☎ 809-872-0080; www.airjamaica.com; Kingston)

American Airlines (AA; ☎ 809-542-5151; www.aa.com; NYC/JFK)

Continental Airlines (CO; ☎ 809-262-1060; www.continental.com; Newark)

COPA Airlines (CM; ☎ 809-472-2672; www.copaair.com; Panama City)

Cubana de Aviación (CU; ☎ 809-227-2040; www.cubana.cu; Havana)

Delta (DL; ☎ 809-227-0672; www.delta.com; Atlanta)

Dutch Caribbean Air (K8; ☎ 809-541-5566; www.flydce.com; Amsterdam)

Iberia (IB; ☎ 809-508-7979; www.Iberia.com; Madrid)

Jet Blue (B6; ☎ 809-549-1793; www.jetblue.com; NYC/JFK)

Lan Chile (LAN; ☎ 809-689-2116; www.lan.com; Santiago)

LTU (LT; ☎ 809-586-4075; www.ltu.com; Dusseldorf)

Lufthansa (LH; ☎ 809-689-9625; www.lufthansa.com; Frankfurt)

Martinair Holland (MP; ☎ 809-621-7777; www.martinair.com; Amsterdam)

Mexicana de Aviación (MX; ☎ 809-541-1016; www.mexicana.com; Mexico City)

Spirit Airlines (NK; ☎ 809-381-4111; www.spiritair.com; Fort Lauderdale)

Swissport (☎ 809-508-2277; www.swissport.com) Handles ticketing and other ground services of various airlines and charters.

US Airways (US; ☎ 809-540-0505; www.usair.com; Philadelphia)

Varig (RG; ☎ 809-563-3434; www.varig.com; Sao Paolo)

Tickets

It goes without saying that, for independent travelers, the Internet has most of the best travel deals. The best sites include www.travelocity.com, www.expedia.com, www.qixo.com and www.ortbiz.com (for flights originating in USA only). Flying Monday to Thursday is generally cheaper. If you're interested in an all-inclusive resort vacation, travel agents often have good deals that include airfare, ground transportation and of course lodgings and all meals (some even throw in free long-term parking at your home airport). More importantly, though, travel agents are able to tell you which resorts receive the best reviews from previous clients for service, room quality etc. The Internet has some good all-inclusive deals, too, but be sure you're clear on all the fine print and definitely do some research on a given resort before booking there.

Canada

Travel Cuts (☎ 800-667-2887; www.travelcuts.com) is Canada's national student travel agency. For online bookings try www.expedia.ca and www.travelocity.ca.

France

Anyway (☎ 08 92 89 38 92; www.anyway.fr)

Lastminute (☎ 08 92 70 50 00; www.lastminute.fr)

Nouvelles Frontières (☎ 08 25 00 07 47; www.nouvelles-frontieres.fr)

OTU Voyages (☎ 05 61 12 18 88; www.otu.fr) This agency specializes in student and youth travelers.

Voyageurs du Monde (☎ 01 40 15 11 15; www.vdm.com)

Germany

Expedia (☎ 01805-900-560; www.expedia.de)

Just Travel (☎ 089-747-3330; www.justtravel.de)

Lastminute (☎ 01805-284-366; www.lastminute.de)

STA Travel (☎ 01805-456-422; www.statravel.de) For travelers under the age of 26.

Italy

CTS Viaggi (☎ 06-462-0431; www.cts.it) specializes in student and youth travel.

eViaggi (☎ 848-782-230; www.eviaggi.com) Specializes in travel from Italy to the Caribbean and elsewhere.
Expedia (☎ 899-234-500; www.expedia.it) Maintains an Italian website and service number.

Spain
Barceló Viajes (☎ 90 211 62 26; www.barceloviajes.com)
Nouvelles Frontiéres (☎ 90 217 09 79; www.nouvelles-frontieres.es).

UK & Ireland
Discount air travel is big business in London. Advertisements for many travel agencies appear in the travel pages of the weekend broadsheet newspapers, in *Time Out*, the *Evening Standard* and in the free online magazine *TNT* (www.tntmagazine.com).
Bridge the World (☎ 0870-444-7474; www.b-t-w.co.uk)
Flight Centre (☎ 0870-890-8099; http://flightcentre.co.uk)
Flightbookers (☎ 0870-814-4001; www.ebookers.com)
North-South Travel (☎ 01245-608-291; www.northsouthtravel.co.uk) North-South Travel donate part of their profit to projects in the developing world.
Quest Travel (☎ 0870-442-3542; www.questtravel.com)
STA Travel (☎ 0870-160-0599; www.statravel.co.uk) For travelers under the age of 26.
Trailfinders (www.trailfinders.co.uk)
Travel Bag (☎ 0870-890-1456; www.travelbag.co.uk)

USA
Discount travel agents in the USA are known as consolidators (although you won't see a sign on the door saying 'consolidator'). San Francisco is the ticket consolidator capital of America, although some good deals can be found in Los Angeles, New York and other big cities. The following agencies are recommended for online bookings:
www.cheaptickets.com
www.expedia.com
www.itn.net
www.lowestfare.com
www.orbitz.com
www.sta.com for travelers under the age of 26
www.travelocity.com

LAND
There are three points where you can cross between Haiti and the DR. The most trafficked is at the Jimaní/Malpasse crossing in the south, on the road that links Santo Domingo and Port-au-Prince. Also busy is the northern crossing at Dajabón/Ouanaminthe, which is on the road between

---

DEPARTURE TAX

For those leaving by air, the Dominican Republic levies a departure tax of zero to US$20, depending on your length of stay and whether you were charged an entrance fee. Those leaving by land or sea are routinely charged US$20. Only US dollars are accepted for this transaction. Note: this tax is not included in the price of plane tickets, as is customary elsewhere. You won't be able to clear immigration unless you've paid the tax at the check-in counter.

Santiago and Cap-Haïtien. The third border crossing is at Comendador (aka Elías Piña) and Belladere which sees few foreign travelers. Only Haitians and Dominicans are permitted to use other border crossings, including the one at Pedernales in the far south. Immigration offices on the Dominican side are usually open 8am to 5pm, and 9am to 6pm on the Haitian side. It is always a good idea to arrive as early as possible, so you are sure to get through both countries' border offices and onto a bus well before dark. When deciding between either crossing in the late afternoon or staying an extra night and crossing in the morning, choose the latter. (Also, long lines and immigration officials who leave early or take long lunch breaks can cause delays at the border)

Tourists leaving the DR will be asked to produce their passports and their tourist cards, and to pay US$20. Theoretically, you shouldn't have to pay anything when you reenter the DR, though some officials will charge US$10 for a new tourist card anyway – unfortunately you don't have much choice but to pay it.

When you enter Haiti, you pay a US$10 fee. Leaving Haiti, you must present your passport and yellow entry card, but are not supposed to have to pay anything. That said, it's wise to have small bills on hand (US cash is always best) to smooth your passage if need be. As with Dominican officials, you don't have much recourse if they decide to charge you extra 'fees'. Unless the fees are exorbitant, the best thing to do is simply pay up and move on.

Rental vehicles are not allowed to cross from one country into the other, and you need special authorization to cross the

TRANSPORTATION

border with a private vehicle. For specific information about the border facilities and services in individual towns, look to the relevant regional chapters in this book.

SEA

There is only one regularly scheduled international ferry service to and from the DR, and it is from Puerto Rico.

Puerto Rico

Ferries del Caribe (Santo Domingo ☎ 809-688-4400; Santiago ☎ 809-724-8771; Mayagüez, Puerto Rico ☎ 787-832-4400; San Juan, Puerto Rico ☎ 787-725-2643) offers a passenger and car ferry service between Santo Domingo and Mayagüez, Puerto Rico. The trip takes about 12 hours, and departs three times per week. See Santo Domingo (p96) for details.

GETTING AROUND

AIR
Airlines in the Dominican Republic

The DR is so small that most people simply take the bus from place to place, even all the way across the country. Still, if time is very short, flying is always an option. It is more expensive than buses of course, but not prohibitively so, with most one-way flights costing US$55 to US$85. All based at Aeropuerto LaHerrera, the main domestic carriers and air taxi companies include:

Aerodomca (☎ 809-567-1195; www.aerodomca.com)

Caribair (☎ 809-542-6688; www.caribair.com.do)

Take Off (☎ 809-552-1333)

BICYCLE

The DR's under-maintained highways are not well suited for cycling, and Dominican drivers are not exactly accommodating to people on bikes, passing at high speed and at very close quarters. Add to that the high number of motorcycles (who move faster than bikes but slower than cars), and *gua-guas* (minibuses) and *públicos* (private cars operating as taxis) making frequent unannounced stops, and the situation on the side of the road is hectic to say the least. However, mountain biking on the DR's back roads and lesser-used highways can be very rewarding, and a number of recommended tours are available from Jarabacoa and Cabarete for just that (p55).

Rental

There are very few places where you can rent a bike, and none are for long-distance travel. If you are planning a multi-day ride, definitely consider bringing your own bike. If you are joining a bike tour, most tour operators will provide you with a bike as part of the price, but of course it may or may not suit you as well as your own. A bike can be handy for tooling around some of the DR's beach towns, especially if you're there for a while. You'll find bike rental outfits in Las Terrenas, Las Galleras and at some of the resort areas. (A number of resorts and a few independent hotels offer bicycles for guest's use.) Expect to pay around US$5 to US$10 per day. There are, however, a few agencies that offer multi-day mountain bike tours; see Cabarete (p195) and Jarabacoa (p228).

BOAT

There is only one regular domestic passenger boat route in the DR; the one connecting Samaná and Sabana de la Mar, on opposite sides of the Samaná Bay in the northeastern part of the country. This route is typically served by a car ferry – making the same trip by road involves a time consuming loop through the DR's farm country – but the car ferry sank shortly before Lonely Planet passed through. (It was carrying supplies for a hotel being built on an island there.) Passenger services continue on small boats, but the car ferry service was interrupted indefinitely. It is possible it will have resumed by the time you read this, but definitely call one of the hotels or tour operators in Samaná (p150) to check.

BUS

The DR has a great bus system, with frequent service throughout the country. And since it is a relatively small country, there are none of the epic overnight journeys travelers often encounter in places like Mexico or Brazil. There are two classes of bus service in the DR: First class *(primera)* utilizes large air-conditioned buses similar to (but usually tidier than) Greyhound buses in the US. Virtually all first class buses have toilets in the back and TVs in the aisles showing movies en route. Fares are low – the most expensive first-class ticket is less that US$10. Second class service is on minibuses known as *gua-guas*, which are more frequent than first-class buses but go much more slowly as they stop to pick up and drop off passengers all along the way. *Gua-guas* are divided into two types - the majority are *caliente* (literally, 'hot') which don't have air-conditioning, naturally. For every four or five *caliente* buses there is usually an *expreso*, which typically has air-conditioning, makes fewer stops and costs slightly more.

First Class

First-class buses leave from designated terminals and almost never stop along the road to pick up passengers. Drivers are often willing to drop passengers off at various points along the way, but they will not open the luggage compartment at any point other than the actual terminal. If you plan on getting off early, bring your bags onboard with you. This is actually a very good idea, as you generally don't have to worry about your bag being stolen or accidentally unloaded along the way. (Even at the terminal, the luggage compartments are not opened until everyone is off the bus.) That said, there are sometimes unplanned intermediate stops, and it is a good idea at those times to check that your bag did not get removed.

FIRST CLASS CARRIERS

Caribe Tours (Santo Domingo ☎ 809-221-4422; Av 27 de Febrero at Av Leopoldo Navarro) The most extensive busline, with service everywhere but the south east.

Metro (Santo Domingo ☎ 809-566-7126; Calle Francisco Prats Ramírez) Located beside Plaza Central Mall in Santo Domingo, Metro serves nine cities, mostly along the Santo Domingo–Puerto Plata corridor.

Expreso Santo Domingo Bávaro (Santo Domingo ☎ 809-682-9670; Juan Sánchez Ruiz at Máximo Gómez) Connects Santo Domingo and Bávaro with a stop in La Romana.

El Canario (☎ 809-291-5594; US$7; 3½-4hrs) Not exactly first class, but the only daily direct service between Puerto Plata and Samaná, with stops in Nagua and Sánchez.

Terra Bus (☎ 809-531-0383; Plaza Lama, Av 27 de Febrero at Av Winston Churchill) Aircon service from Santo Domingo to Port-au-Prince, Haiti.

Gua-Guas

Wherever long-distance buses don't go, you can be sure a *gua-gua* does. *Gua-guas* are typically mid-size buses holding around 25 to 30 passengers. They rarely have signs, but

the driver's assistant (known as the *cobrador*, or 'charger' since one of his jobs is to collect fares from passengers) will yell out the destination of the bus to potential fares on the side of the road. *Gua-guas* pick up and drop off passengers anywhere along the route – to flag one down simply hold out your hand – the common gesture is to point at the curb in front of you (as if to say 'stop right here') but just about any gesture will do. *Gua-guas* rarely have signs, so you may have to flag down a couple before it's the one you actually want. Don't hesitate to ask a local if you're unsure which one to take – there are almost always other people waiting along the road to catch *gua-guas* as well. Most *gua-guas* pass every 15 to 30 minutes and cost US$1 to $2.

Costs

First class buses are quite affordable – one of the longest trips is the five hour trek from Dajabón to Santo Domingo which costs just US$7.50. *Gua-guas* are even cheaper – a half-hour ride costs around US$1. For first-class buses, you must buy your ticket at the ticket window before boarding. On *gua-guas*, simply climb onboard and the *cobrador* will eventually come around to get your money.

Reservations

Reservations aren't usually necessary and rarely even taken, even on first-class buses. The exceptions are the international buses to Port-au-Prince, Haiti, operated by Caribe Tours and Terra Bus. During Dominican holidays you can sometimes buy your ticket a day or two in advance, which assures you a spot and saves you the time and hassle of waiting in line at a busy terminal with all your bags. Finally, there are a few routes where you should arrive early to secure a spot, either because the bus fills up or because it may leave early. Those cases are noted in the appropriate chapters.

CAR & MOTORCYCLE

Though the DR's bus and *gua-gua* system is excellent, having your own car is invariably faster and more convenient. Even if renting a car isn't in your budget for the entire trip, consider renting one for a select couple of days, to reach sights that are isolated or not well-served by public transportation.

TRANSPORTATION

TRANSPORTATION

Driver's License

For travelers from most countries, your home country driver's license allows you to drive in the DR. Be sure it is valid.

Fuel & Spare Parts

Most towns have at least one gas station, typically right along the highway on the outskirts of town. There are a couple of different companies, but prices are essentially the same at all. The base price of gasoline is regulated by the federal government, but has fluctuated wildly in recent years, wreaking havoc not only on drivers but for those who rely on gas-powered generators for electricity (which is just about everyone). At the time of research, gas prices had just been hiked to US$3.35 per gallon of standard unleaded.

Play it safe and always keep your gas tank at least half full. Many *bombas* (gasoline stations) in the Dominican Republic close by 7pm, and even when they are open they don't always have gasoline. If you're traveling on back roads or in a remote part of the country, your best bet is to buy gas from people selling it from their front porch. Look for the large pink jugs sitting on tables on the side of the road.

The most common car trouble is a punctured or damaged tire caused by pot holes, speed bumps and rocks or other debris in the road. The word for tire is *goma* (literally 'rubber') and a tire shop is called a *gomero* which are even more common than gas stations. If you can make it to one on your busted tire, the guys there can patch a flat (US$5 to US$8), replace a damaged tire (US$10 to US$50 depending on type of

tire and whether you want a new or used replacement), or just put the spare on for you (US$1 to US$2).

Car Rental

There are dozens of car rental agencies in the DR. Prices range from US$40 to US$100 per day. Motorcycles can also be rented, but only experienced riders should do so because of poor road conditions.

Familiar multinational agencies like Hertz, Avis, Europcar, Alamo and Dollar all have offices at Aeropuerto Internacional Las Américas (and other airports like Punta Cana and Gregorio Luperón in Puerto Plata) as well as in Santo Domingo and other cities. Their prices tend to be higher than local or national agencies, although their service is usually more extensive and reliable, and you can sometimes find good deals on the Internet.

Insurance

The multinational car rental agencies typically offer comprehensive, non-deductible collision and liability insurance. Smaller agencies usually offer partial coverage, with a deductible ranging from US$100 to US$2000. US citizens with platinum level Visa or MasterCard credit probably have coverage through their credit card, thanks to a special agreement in the DR – double check before you leave, as this can save you 10% or more.

Road Conditions

Roads in the DR range from excellent to awful, sometimes along the same highway over a very short distance. The *autopista*

SIGN ON THE DOTTED LINE

Whether you rent a car from a well-known multinational agency or a small local shop, take the time to be sure you are 100% clear on the terms of the contract and any hidden costs. Some things to ask about are: Does the price include taxes and insurance? What is the deductible amount on the insurance policy? Are tires, windshield and windows covered? If you're quoted a price in dollars, what exchange rate do they use if you pay with credit card or pesos? Is there a 24-hour emergency and service number? Does the car have aircon? Does the agency offer hotel pick-up and drop-off? None of these questions have a right or wrong answer per se, but each should be part of your consideration when choosing if, and where, to rent a car. Most agencies allow you to extend your rental mid-trip, but you must call to let them know – if you simply show up late, you'll be charged a late fee (usually US$10 per hour) and not the regular daily rate. Lastly, don't let the agent rush you through the paperwork. While everything may be perfectly clear to him, what matters is that it all makes sense to you.

POLICE ETIQUETTE

Though having any interaction with Dominican traffic police is rare – you're more likely just to see them directing traffic during rush hour – encounters do occasionally occur. And it's best to be prepared when you do.

Typically, traffic police are waiting by the side of the road and when they see your car, they'll step in front of your vehicle and wave for you to stop. As soon as you do, the officer will come over and tell you why you've been flagged down – speeding is a common reason, though failing to stop fast enough or driving a dirty car are reasons sometimes given as well.

Don't argue with the police officer. And never be impolite or hostile. Instead, apologize for breaking the law and say that you didn't realize you were doing anything wrong. Tell him that you'd like to resolve the problem as soon as possible so that you can continue with your vacation.

The officer will typically tell you that you can pay the fine to him instead of going to the station. If you keep only a few Dominican pesos in a wallet and the rest of your money elsewhere, you can withdraw the small sum and give it to the officer. Make sure he sees you've got nothing left in your wallet. He'll typically take the cash and let you go.

And don't worry if you don't speak Spanish; police officers often know enough English to communicate exactly what they want!

(freeway) between Santo Domingo and Santiago has as many as eight lanes and is fast-moving and in excellent condition. However on the rest of the highways be alert for potholes, speed bumps and people walking along the roadside, especially near populated areas. On all roads, large or small, watch for slow moving cars and especially motorcycles. Be particularly careful when driving at night, as potholes and speed bumps are harder to spot and many motorcycles and pedestrians don't have lights or reflectors. One funny note: speed bumps in the DR are known here as *policía acostada,* or sleeping policemen.

Road Hazards

In large cities, especially Santo Domingo, the sheer number of cars, trucks, buses and motorcycles makes for hectic and sometimes hazardous driving. You should drive defensively at all times, though you may feel like you are the only one doing do so! Be aware that some of Santo Domingo's main thoroughfares have 'express' and 'local' lanes – the express lanes use tunnels and overpasses to speed through intersections. It can be dangerous to switch suddenly from a local to an express lane or vice versa, simply because the difference in speed in so great. Plan ahead, and try switching lanes well in advance. On highways, especially the secondary ones, roads may be unpaved for long sections and often have large potholes.

Road Rules

Road rules in the DR are the same for most countries in the Americas, and the lights and signs are the same shape and color you find in the US or Canada. Seatbelts are required at all times. That said, some people follow the traffic rules more faithfully than others, and you should anticipate other drivers passing suddenly or running through yellow lights (and even a car or two sneaking through the red). In small towns, traffic lights are frequently ignored, though you should always plan to stop at them. Watch what other drivers are doing – if everyone is going through, you probably should too as it can be even more dangerous to stop if the cars behind you aren't expecting it.

HITCHHIKING

Though hitchhiking is never entirely safe anywhere in the world, Dominicans hitch all the time, both men and women, especially in rural areas where fewer people have cars and *gua-gua* service is sparse. And the *motoconcho* (motorcycle taxi) and *público* systems in cities of all sizes is itself essentially hitchhiking, since there is little formal regulation. That said, it is extremely rare to see foreigners hitchhiking, and doing so (especially if you have bags) carries a greater risk than for locals. Travelers who decide to hitchhike should understand that they are taking a small but potentially serious risk.

LOCAL TRANSPORTATION
Bus

Large cities like Santo Domingo and Santiago have public bus systems that operate as they do in most places around the world. Many of the larger city buses are imported from Brazil, and are the kind in which you board in the back and pay the person sitting beside the turnstile. Other city buses are more or less like *gua-guas*, where you board quickly and pay the *cobrador* when he comes around. In general, you will probably take relatively few city buses, simply because *públicos* (see below) follow pretty much the same routes and pass more frequently.

Motoconcho

Cheaper and easier to find than taxis, *motoconchos* (motorcycle taxis) are the best, or only, way to get around in some towns. However, a shockingly high number of riders have been injured or killed in *motoconcho* accidents; use them only when necessary. (See the boxed text on p263 for more details.)

Públicos

These are banged-up cars, minivans or small pickup trucks that pick up passengers along set routes, usually main boulevards. *Públicos* (also called *conchos* or *carros*) don't have signs but the drivers hold their hands out the window to solicit potential fares. They are also identifiable by the crush of people inside them – up to seven in a midsize car! To flag one down simply hold out your hand – the fare is US$0.30. If there is no one else in the car, be sure to tell the driver you want *servicio público* (public service) to avoid paying private taxi rates.

Taxi

Dominican taxis rarely cruise for passengers – instead they wait at designated *sitios* (stops) which are located at hotels, bus terminals, tourist areas and main public parks. You also can phone a taxi service (or ask your hotel receptionist to call for you). Taxis do not have meters – agree on a price beforehand.

Health

CONTENTS

> **MEDICAL CHECKLIST**
> - Antibiotics
> - Antidiarrheal drugs (eg loperamide)
> - Acetaminophen (Tylenol) or aspirin
> - Anti-inflammatory drugs (eg ibuprofen)
> - Antihistamines (for hay fever and allergic reactions)
> - Antibacterial ointment (eg Bactroban) for cuts and abrasions
> - Steroid cream or cortisone (for poison ivy and other allergic rashes)
> - Bandages and adhesives
> - Scissors, safety pins and tweezers
> - Thermometer
> - Pocket knife
> - Insect repellent containing DEET for the skin
> - Sun block
> - Oral rehydration salts
> - Water purification tablets (if you will be hiking or camping)

From a medical standpoint, the Dominican Republic (DR) and most Caribbean islands are generally safe as long as you're reasonably careful about what you eat and drink. The most common travel-related diseases, such as dysentery and hepatitis, are acquired by consumption of contaminated food and water. Mosquito-borne illnesses are not a significant concern, though there was a minor malaria outbreak (since controlled) in the southeastern part of the country in late 2004. Travelers who receive the recommended vaccines and follow common-sense precautions usually come away perfectly healthy or with nothing more than a little diarrhea.

BEFORE YOU GO

Since most vaccines don't provide immunity until at least two weeks after they're given, visit a physician four to eight weeks before departure. Ask your doctor for an International Certificate of Vaccination (otherwise known as the yellow booklet), which will list all the vaccinations you've received, and it's a good idea to carry it wherever you travel.

INSURANCE

Many health insurance plans provide coverage while you are traveling abroad, but it is important to check with your provider before leaving home. Some travel insurance policies include short-term medical and life insurance, even emergency evacuation, in addition to the standard trip-cancellation and lost-luggage coverage. Ask your travel agent or current insurance provider about travel insurance plans, or check the Internet for providers in your area. As always, spend some time reading the fine print to be sure you are clear what the plan does (and does not) cover. Scuba divers should consider obtaining dive insurance from **DAN** (Diver Alert Network; www.diversalertnetwork.org); many standard insurance plans do not cover diving accidents, and even when they do, cannot compare to the specialized coverage and experience DAN offers.

INTERNET RESOURCES

There is plenty of travel health advice on the Internet. For further information, the Lonely Planet website at www.lonelyplanet.com

RECOMMENDED VACCINATIONS

No vaccines are required for the Dominican Republic, but a number are recommended.

Vaccine	Recommended for	Dosage	Side effects
Hepatitis A	All travelers	One dose before trip; booster 6-12 months later	Soreness at injection site; headaches; body aches
Typhoid	All travelers	Four capsules by mouth, one taken every other day	Abdominal pain; nausea; rash
Hepatitis B	Long-term travelers in close contact with the local population	Three doses over 6 month period	Soreness at injection site; low-grade fever
Rabies	Travelers who may have contact with animals and may not have access to medical care	Three doses over 3-4 week period	Soreness at injection site; headaches; body aches; Expensive
Tetanus-diphtheria	All travelers who haven't had booster within 10 years	One dose lasts 10 years	Soreness at injection site
Chickenpox	Travelers who've never had chickenpox	Two doses 1 month apart	Fever; mild case of chickenpox

HEALTH

is a good place to start. The World Health Organization (WHO) publishes a superb book, called *International Travel and Health,* which is revised annually and is available online at no cost at www.who.int/ith/. Another website of general interest is MD Travel Health at www.mdtravelhealth.com, which provides complete travel health recommendations for every country, updated daily and is also free.

It's usually a good idea to consult your government's travel health website before departure, if one is available:
Australia www.dfat.gov.au/travel/
Canada www.TravelHealth.gc.ca
UK www.doh.gov.uk/traveladvice/index.htm
United States www.cdc.gov/travel/

IN TRANSIT

DEEP VEIN THROMBOSIS

Blood clots may form in the legs (deep vein thrombosis) during plane flights, chiefly because of prolonged immobility. The longer the flight, the greater the risk. Though most blood clots are reabsorbed uneventfully, some may break off and travel through the blood vessels to the lungs, where they could cause life-threatening complications.

The chief symptom of deep vein thrombosis is swelling or pain of the foot, ankle or calf, usually but not always on just one side. When a blood clot travels to the lungs, it may cause chest pain and difficulty breathing. Travelers with any of these symptoms should immediately seek medical attention.

To prevent the development of deep vein thrombosis on long flights you should walk about the cabin, perform isometric compressions of the leg muscles (ie contract the leg muscles while sitting), drink plenty of fluids and avoid alcohol.

JET LAG & MOTION SICKNESS

Jet lag is common when crossing more than five time zones, resulting in insomnia, fatigue, malaise or nausea. To avoid jet lag try drinking plenty of fluids (non-alcoholic) and eating light meals. Upon arrival, get exposure to natural sunlight and readjust your schedule (for meals, sleep, etc) as soon as possible.

Antihistamines such as dimenhydrinate (Dramamine) and meclizine (Antivert, Bonine) are usually the first choice for treating motion sickness. Their main side effect is drowsiness. An herbal alternative is ginger, which works like a charm for some people.

IN THE DOMINICAN REPUBLIC

AVAILABILITY & COST OF HEALTH CARE

Medical care is variable in Santo Domingo and limited elsewhere. A private nationwide ambulance service called **Movi-med** (Santo Domingo ☎ 809-532-0000, all other areas ☎ 809-200-0911) operates in Santo Domingo, Santiago, Puerto Plata and La Romana. Movi-med expects full payment at the time of transport. There is also an emergency 911 service within Santo Domingo, but this is less reliable.

In Santo Domingo, acceptable medical care is available at these facilities:

Centro de Medicina Avanzada Abel González (☎ 809-227-2235; Av Abraham Lincoln 953)
Centro de Obstetricia y Ginecología (☎ 809-221-7100; Av Independencia 51 at José Joaquín Pérez)
Clínica Abreu (☎ 809-688-4411; Calle Beller 42 at Av Independencia)
Corazones Unidos (☎ 809-567-4421; Fantino Falco 21)
UCE University Hospital (☎ 809-221-0171; Máximo Gómez at Pedro Henríquez Ureña)

In La Romana, emergency and specialist care can be obtained at **Centro Medico Doctor Canela** (☎ 809-556-3135; Av Libertad 44 at Restauración). In Bávaro, you can go to **Centro Médico Punta Cana** (☎ 809-552-1506) or **Hopitén Bávaro** (☎ 809-686-1414) in Punta Cana. In Santiago, go to **Centro Médico Semma** (☎ 809-226-1053; Pedro Francisco Bonó) between Sánchez and Cuba. In Puerto Plata, the best clinic is the **Centro Médico Dr Bournigal** (☎ 809-586-2342; Antera Mota) between Doctor Zafra & Virginia Ortega.

Many doctors and hospitals expect payment in cash, regardless of whether you have travel health insurance. If you develop a life-threatening medical problem, you'll probably want to be evacuated to a country with state-of-the-art medical care. Since this may cost tens of thousands of dollars, be sure you have insurance to cover this before you depart. You can find a list of medical evacuation and travel insurance companies on the US State Department website at http://travel.state.gov/travel/tips/health/health_1185.html.

Pharmacies are denoted by green or red crosses. Most are well-supplied, though it is always preferable to bring along an adequate supply of any medications you may need.

INFECTIOUS DISEASES
Hepatitis A

Hepatitis A is the second most common travel-related infection (after travelers' diarrhea). It occurs throughout the Caribbean, particularly in the northern islands. Hepatitis A is a viral infection of the liver that is usually acquired by ingestion of contaminated water, food or ice, though it may also be acquired by direct contact with infected persons. Symptoms may include fever, malaise, jaundice, nausea, vomiting and abdominal pain. Most cases will resolve without complications, though hepatitis A occasionally causes severe liver damage. There is no treatment.

The vaccine for hepatitis A is extremely safe and highly effective. If you get a booster six to 12 months later, it lasts for at least 10 years. You really should get it before you go to the Dominican Republic or any other developing nation. Because the safety of the hepatitis A vaccine has not been established for pregnant women or children under age two, they should instead be given a gammaglobulin injection.

Hepatitis B

Like hepatitis A, hepatitis B is a liver infection that occurs worldwide but is more common in developing nations. Unlike hepatitis A, the disease is usually acquired by sexual contact or by exposure to infected blood, mainly through blood transfusions or contaminated needles. The vaccine is recommended only for long-term travelers (on the road more than six months) who expect to live in rural areas or have close physical contact with the local population. Additionally, the vaccine is recommended for anyone who anticipates sexual contact with the local inhabitants or a possible need for medical, dental or other treatments while abroad, especially if a need for transfusions or injections is expected.

The hepatitis B vaccine is safe and highly effective. However, a total of three injections are necessary to establish full immunity.

HEALTH

Several countries added hepatitis B vaccine to the list of routine childhood immunizations in the 1980s, so many young adults are already protected.

Typhoid fever

Typhoid fever is caused by ingestion of food or water contaminated by a species of Salmonella known as *Salmonella typhi*. Fever occurs in virtually all cases. Other symptoms may include headache, malaise, muscle aches, dizziness, loss of appetite, nausea and abdominal pain. Either diarrhea or constipation may occur. Possible complications include intestinal perforation, intestinal bleeding, confusion, delirium or (rarely) coma.

Unless you expect to take all your meals in major hotels and restaurants, typhoid vaccine is a good idea. It's usually given orally, but is also available as an injection. Neither vaccine is approved for use in children under age two. If you get typhoid fever, the drug of choice is usually a quinolone antibiotic such as ciprofloxacin (Cipro) or levofloxacin (Levaquin), which many travelers carry for treatment of travelers' diarrhea.

Dengue fever

Dengue fever is a viral infection found throughout the Caribbean. Dengue is transmitted by Aedes mosquitoes, which bite preferentially during the daytime and are usually found close to human habitations, often indoors. They breed primarily in artificial water containers, such as jars, barrels, cans, cisterns, metal drums, plastic containers and discarded tires. As a result, dengue is more common in densely populated urban environments.

Dengue usually causes flu-like symptoms, including fever, muscle aches, joint pains, headaches, nausea and vomiting, often with a rash following. The body aches may be quite uncomfortable, but most cases will resolve uneventfully in a few days. Severe cases usually occur in children under age 15 who are experiencing their second dengue infection.

There is no treatment for dengue fever except to take analgesics such as acetaminophen/paracetamol (Tylenol) and drink plenty of fluids. Severe cases may require hospitalization for intravenous fluids and supportive care. There is no vaccine. The cornerstone of prevention is insect protection measures, described in the Mosquito Bites section on p286.

Rabies

Rabies is a viral infection of the brain and spinal cord that is almost always fatal. The rabies virus is carried in the saliva of infected animals and is typically transmitted through an animal bite, though contamination of any break in the skin with infected saliva may result in rabies. Rabies occurs in several of the Caribbean islands, including the Dominican Republic. Most cases in the Dominican Republic are related to bites from street dogs or wild animals, particularly the small Indian mongoose.

The rabies vaccine is safe, but a full series requires three injections and prices range from being free to staggeringly expensive. Public hospitals in the Dominican Republic give the vaccine (and post-infection treatment) for no charge, including to tourists; however, if the nearest public facility doesn't have the vaccine on hand, a private facility can charge up to US$350 per injection. Those at high risk for rabies, such as animal handlers and spelunkers (cave explorers), should certainly get the vaccine. In addition, those at lower risk for animal bites should consider asking for the vaccine if they might be traveling to remote areas and might not have access to appropriate medical care if needed. The treatment for a possibly rabid bite consists of a vaccine with rabies immune globulin. It's effective, but must be given promptly. Most travelers don't need rabies vaccine.

All animal bites and scratches must be promptly and thoroughly cleansed with large amounts of soap and water and local health authorities contacted to determine whether or not further treatment is necessary (see Animal Bites p286).

Malaria

In the Dominican Republic, malaria occurs chiefly in the western provinces near the Haitian border, but was also reported in late 2004 in the Punta Cana area and San Francisco de Macorís. Malaria is transmitted by mosquito bites, usually between dusk and dawn. The main symptom is high spiking fevers, which may be accompanied by chills, sweats, headache, body aches, weakness, vomiting or diarrhea. Severe cases may involve the central nervous system and lead to seizures, confusion, coma and death.

At the time of publication, malaria pills were recommended for travelers to La Altagracia Province (including Punta Cana), Duarte Province and all rural areas in the Dominican Republic. The first-choice malaria pill is chloroquine, taken once weekly in a dosage of 500 mg, starting one-to-two weeks before arrival and continuing through the trip and for four weeks after departure. Chloroquine is safe, inexpensive and highly effective. Side effects are typically mild and may include nausea, abdominal discomfort, headache, dizziness, blurred vision or itching. Severe reactions are uncommon.

Protecting yourself against mosquito bites is just as important as taking malaria pills (see p286), since no pills are 100% effective.

If you may not have access to medical care while traveling, you should bring along additional pills for emergency self-treatment. If you were taking malaria pills when you were infected, you should switch to a different medication for treatment, as it is likely you were infected with a resistant strand. Since you will likely be taking chloroquine as a preventative pill, one treatment option is to take four tablets of Malarone once daily for three days. You should begin self-treatment if you can't reach a doctor and you develop symptoms that suggest malaria, such as high spiking fevers. However, professional medical attention is much preferred, and it is unlikely you will be out of reach of a hospital considering the relatively small size of the Dominican Republic. If you do start self-medication, you should try to see a doctor at the earliest possible opportunity.

Remember to continue taking malaria pills for four weeks after you leave an infected area. If you develop a fever after returning home, see a physician, as malaria symptoms may not occur for months.

Other infections

Wound infections caused by *Mycobacterium abscessus*, a relatively rare organism distantly related to tuberculosis, have been reported in those having cosmetic surgery in Santo Domingo. A number of different hospitals and a variety of procedures have been involved.

A small outbreak of poliomyelitis occurred between July 2000 and January 2001, resulting in a total of 13 cases before the outbreak was brought under control by a mass vaccination campaign. All cases occurred in people who were either unvaccinated or incompletely vaccinated. There is no risk of polio at this time.

Leptospirosis may be acquired by exposure to water contaminated by the urine of infected animals. Outbreaks often occur at times of flooding, when sewage overflow may contaminate water sources. The initial symptoms, which resemble a mild flu, usually subside uneventfully in a few days, with or without treatment, but a minority of cases are complicated by jaundice or meningitis. There is no vaccine. You can minimize your risk by staying out of bodies of fresh water that may be contaminated by animal urine. If you're visiting an area where an outbreak is in progress, you can take 200 mg of doxycycline once weekly as a preventative measure. If you actually develop leptospirosis, the treatment is 100mg of doxycycline twice daily.

Brucellosis is an infection of domestic and wild animals that may be transmitted to humans through direct animal contact or by consumption of unpasteurized dairy products from infected animals. In the Dominican Republic, most human cases are related to infected cattle. Symptoms may include fever, malaise, depression, loss of appetite, headache, muscle aches and back pain. Complications may include arthritis, hepatitis, meningitis and endocarditis (heart valve infection).

Leishmaniasis has been reported in the eastern part of the island. The infection is transmitted by sandflies, which are about one-third the size of mosquitoes. Most cases are limited to the skin, though symptoms are often diffuse. Leishmaniasis may be particularly severe in those with HIV. There is no vaccine. To protect yourself from sandflies, follow the same precautions as for mosquitoes (p286), except that netting must be finer-mesh (at least 18 holes to the linear inch).

Schistosomiasis, which is a parasitic infection acquired by skin exposure to contaminated fresh water, occurs mainly in the eastern lowlands and as far west as Jarabacoa.

HEALTH

The parasite can be contracted while swimming, wading, bathing or washing in bodies of fresh water, including lakes, ponds, streams and rivers. That said, the overwhelming majority of travelers do not get infected from the many water-activities around Jarabacoa. Salt water and chlorinated pools carry no risk of schistosomiasis.

HIV/AIDS has been reported from all Caribbean countries. Be sure to use condoms for all sexual encounters.

TRAVELERS' DIARRHEA

To prevent diarrhea, avoid tap water; only eat fresh fruits or vegetables if cooked or peeled; be wary of dairy products that might contain unpasteurized milk; and be highly selective when eating food from street vendors.

If you develop diarrhea, be sure to drink plenty of fluids, preferably with an oral rehydration solution containing lots of salt and sugar. A few loose stools don't require treatment but, if you start having more than four or five stools a day, you should start taking an antibiotic (usually a quinolone drug) and an antidiarrheal agent (such as loperamide). If diarrhea is bloody or persists for more than 72 hours or is accompanied by fever, shaking chills or severe abdominal pain, you should seek medical attention.

ENVIRONMENTAL HAZARDS
Animal Bites

Do not attempt to pet, handle, or feed any animal, with the exception of domestic animals known to be free of any infectious disease. Most animal injuries are directly related to a person's attempt to touch or feed the animal.

Any bite or scratch by a mammal, including bats, should be promptly and thoroughly cleansed with large amounts of soap and water, followed by the application of an antiseptic such as iodine or alcohol. Go to the nearest hospital or clinic for possible post-exposure rabies treatment, whether or not you've been immunized against rabies. It may also be advisable to start an antibiotic, since wounds caused by animal bites and scratches frequently become infected. One of the newer quinolones, such as levofloxacin (Levaquin), which many travelers carry in case of diarrhea, would be an appropriate choice.

Snakes are a minor hazard in the Dominican Republic. In the event of a venomous snake bite, place the victim at rest, keep the bitten area immobilized and move the victim immediately to the nearest medical facility. Avoid tourniquets, which are no longer recommended. Spiny sea urchins and coelenterates (coral and jellyfish) are a hazard in some areas.

Mosquito Bites

If visiting areas where malaria occurs, or if a dengue fever outbreak is in progress, you should keep yourself covered (wear long sleeves, long pants, hats and shoes rather than sandals) and apply a good insect repellent, preferably one containing DEET, to exposed skin and clothing. Do not apply DEET to eyes, mouth, cuts, wounds or irritated skin. Products containing lower concentrations of DEET are as effective, but for shorter periods of time. In general, adults and children over 12 should use preparations containing 25% to 35% DEET, which usually lasts about six hours. Children between two and 12 years of age should use preparations containing no more than 10% DEET, applied sparingly, which will usually last about three hours. Neurological toxicity has been reported from DEET, especially in children, but appears to be extremely uncommon and generally related to overuse. DEET-containing compounds should not be used on children under age two.

Insect repellents containing certain botanical products, including oil of eucalyptus and soybean oil, are effective but last only 1½ to two hours. Products based on citronella are not effective.

For additional protection, you can apply permethrin to clothing, shoes, tents and bed nets. Permethrin treatments are safe and remain effective for at least two weeks, even when items are laundered. Permethrin should not be applied directly to skin.

Sun

Along with diarrhea, sunburn is the most common travelers' health concern. To protect yourself from excessive sun exposure, you should stay out of the midday sun, wear sunglasses and a wide-brimmed sun hat, and apply sunscreen with SPF 15 or higher, with both UVA and UVB protection. Sunscreen should be generously applied to all exposed parts of the body approximately 30 minutes before sun exposure and should be reapplied after swimming or vigorous activity. Travelers should also drink plenty of fluids and avoid strenuous exercise when the temperature is high.

Water

Tap water in the Dominican Republic is not reliably safe to drink. Bottled water is preferable and widely available. Untreated river and lake water should also be avoided.

If you need to drink tap water or river or lake water, vigorous boiling for one minute is the most effective means of purification. Another option is to use iodine-based water purification pills. Instructions are usually enclosed and should be carefully followed. Pregnant women, those with a history of thyroid disease and those allergic to iodine should not drink iodinated water.

A number of water filters are on the market. Those with smaller pores (reverse osmosis filters) provide the broadest protection, but they are relatively large and are readily plugged by debris. Those with somewhat larger pores (microstrainer filters) are ineffective against viruses, although they remove other organisms. The manufacturers' instructions must be carefully followed.

TRAVELING WITH CHILDREN

In general, it's safe for children to go to the Dominican Republic. When traveling with children, make sure they're up to date on all routine immunizations. It's sometimes appropriate to give children some of their vaccines a little earlier before visiting a developing nation. You should discuss this with your pediatrician.

If you're traveling with children, Lonely Planet's *Travel with Children* may be useful. The *ABC of Healthy Travel*, by E Walker et al, is another valuable resource.

WOMEN'S HEALTH

The Dominican Republic is generally a safe place for travelers. However, because some of the vaccines listed above are not approved for use in children and pregnancy, these travelers should be particularly careful

ALTERNATIVE MEDICINE	
Problem	**Treatment**
Jet lag	Melatonin
Motion sickness	Ginger
Mosquito bite prevention	Oil of eucalyptus Soybean oil

not to drink tap water or consume any questionable food or beverage.

Pads, panty-liners, tampons and other women's sanitary products are generally available in the Dominican Republic. Large pharmacies and supermarkets tend to have the best selection, including a number of internationally recognized brands. Of course, there is no guarantee that you'll find the particular brand that you prefer; if you are especially attached to one, consider packing a supply from home.

The same applies for contraceptives. Although readily available at large pharmacies, you may not be able to find the birth control pills or condoms that you prefer – most travelers bring enough to last their entire trip. Abortion is illegal in the Dominican Republic, though there is growing support for legalizing the procedure.

If pregnant, you should bear in mind that should a complication such as premature labor develop while abroad, the quality of medical care may not be comparable to that in your home country.

Malaria is a high-risk disease in pregnancy. Advice from WHO recommends that pregnant women do not travel to areas with chloroquine-resistant malaria. None of the more effective antimalarial drugs are completely safe in pregnancy. That said, the risk of contracting malaria in the DR is quite low, and the malaria parasite there is not known to be chloroquine-resistant.

Traveler's diarrhea can quickly lead to dehydration and result in inadequate blood flow to the placenta. Many of the drugs used to treat various diarrhea bugs are not recommended in pregnancy. Azithromycin is considered safe.

HEALTH

Language

CONTENTS

The official language of the Dominican Republic is Spanish, and it's spoken by every Dominican. Some English and German are also spoken by individuals in the tourist business.

Dominican Spanish is much like Central America's other varieties of Spanish. One notable tendency is that Dominicans swallow the ends of words, especially those ending in 's' – *tres* will sound like 'tre' and *buenos días* like 'bueno día'. For some other regionalisms, see the box opposite.

If you don't already speak some Spanish and intend to do some independent travel outside Santo Domingo or Puerto Plata, you'd be well advised to learn at least some basics in the lingo. For a more detailed guide, get a copy of Lonely Planet's compact *Latin American Spanish Phrasebook*.

PRONUNCIATION

Pronunciation of Spanish isn't difficult. Many Spanish sounds are similar to their English counterparts, and the relationship between pronunciation and spelling is clear and consistent. Unless otherwise indicated, the English examples used below take standard American pronunciation.

Vowels & Diphthongs

a	as in 'father'
e	as in 'met'
i	as in 'police'
o	as in British English 'hot'
u	as in 'rude'
ai	as in 'aisle'
au	as the 'ow' in 'how'
ei	as in 'vein'
ia	as the 'ya' in 'yard'
ie	as the 'ye' in 'yes'
oi	as in 'coin'
ua	as the 'wa' in 'wash'
ue	as the 'we' in 'well'

Consonants

Spanish consonants are generally the same as in English, with the exception of those listed below.

The consonants **ch**, **ll**, **ñ** and **rr** are generally considered distinct letters, but in dictionaries **ch** and **ll** are now often listed alphabetically under **c** and **l** respectively. The letter **ñ** still has a separate entry after **n** in alphabetical listings.

TALKING LIKE A REPUBLICAN

Here are some Dominicanisms you should wrap your head (and tongue) around ...

apagón	a power failure
apodo	nickname
bandera dominicana	rice and beans (lit: Dominican flag)
bohío	a thatch hut
bulto	luggage
carros de concho	routed, shared taxi
chichi	a baby
colmado	a small grocery store
fucú	a thing that brings bad luck
guapo	bad-tempered
guarapo	sugarcane juice
gumo	a drunk
hablador	a person who talks a lot
papaúpa	an important person
pariguayo	foolish
pín-pún	exactly equal
una rumba	a lot
Siempre a su orden.	You're welcome.
tiguere	a rascal
timacle	brave

b	similar to English 'b,' but softer; referred to as 'b larga'
c	as in 'celery' before e and i; elsewhere as in 'cot'
ch	as in 'choose'
d	as in 'dog'; between vowels and after l or n, it's closer to the 'th' in 'this'
g	as the 'ch' before e and i ('kh' in our pronunciation guides); elsewhere, as in 'go'
h	invariably silent
j	as the 'ch' in the Scottish loch ('kh' in our pronunciation guides) or, often, the 'h' in 'how'
ll	as the 'y' in 'yellow'
ñ	as the 'ni' in 'onion'
r	as in 'run,' but strongly rolled
rr	very strongly rolled
v	as for b; referred to as 'b corta'
x	as English 'h' when it follows e or i, otherwise like 'taxi'; in some place-names it can also be pronounced as the 'sh' in 'ship'
z	as the 's' in 'sun'

Word Stress

In general, words ending in a vowel, an n or an s are stressed on the second-last syllable, while those with other endings stress the last syllable. Thus vaca (cow) and caballos (horses) are both stressed on the next-to-last syllable, while ciudad (city) and infeliz (unhappy) are stressed on the last syllable.

Written accents generally mark stress on words that don't follow these rules, eg sótano (basement), América and porción (portion).

GENDER & PLURALS

In Spanish, nouns are either masculine or feminine, and there are rules to help determine gender (there are, of course, some exceptions). Feminine nouns generally end with -a or with the groups -ción, -sión or -dad. Other endings typically signify a masculine noun. Endings for adjectives also change to agree with the gender of the noun they modify (masculine/feminine singular -o/-a). Where both masculine and feminine forms are included in this language guide, they are separated by a slash, with the masculine form first, eg perdido/a (lost).

If a noun or adjective ends in a vowel, the plural is formed by adding s to the end. If it ends in a consonant, the plural is formed by adding es to the end.

ACCOMMODATIONS

I'm looking for ...

Estoy buscando ...		e-stoy boos-kan-do ...
Where is ...?		
¿Dónde hay ...?		don-de ai ...
a hotel	un hotel	oon o-tel
a boarding house	una pensión	oo-na pen-syon
a youth hostel	un albergue juvenil	oon al-ber-ge khoo-ve-neel

Are there any rooms available?

¿Hay habitaciones libres?	ay a-bee-ta-syon-es lee-bres

I'd like a ... room.	Quisiera una habitación ...	kee-sye-ra oo-na a-bee-ta-syon ...
single	individual	een-dee-bee-dwal
double	doble	do-ble
twin	con dos camas	kon dos ka-mas

How much is it per ...?	¿Cuánto cuesta por ...?	kwan-to kwes-ta por ...
night	noche	no-che
person	persona	per-so-na
week	semana	se-ma-na

private/shared bathroom	baño privado/ compartido	ba-nyo pree-va-do/ kom-par-tee-do
full board	pensión completa	pen-syon kom-ple-ta
too expensive	demasiado caro	de-ma-sya-do ka-ro
cheaper	más económico	mas e-ko-no-mee-ko
discount	descuento	des-kwen-to

MAKING A RESERVATION

(for phone or written requests)

To ...	A ...
From ...	De ...
Date	Fecha
I'd like to book ...	Quisiera reservar ... (see the list under 'Accommodations' for bed and room options)
in the name of ...	en nombre de ...
for the nights of ...	para las noches del ...
credit card ...	... tarjeta de crédito
number	número (de)
expiry date	fecha de vencimiento (de)
Please confirm ...	Puede confirmar ...
availability	la disponibilidad
price	el precio

LANGUAGE

Does it include breakfast?

¿Incluye el desayuno?   een·kloo·ye el de·sa·yoo·no

May I see the room?

¿Puedo ver la   pwe·do ver la
   habitación?   a·bee·ta·syon

I don't like it.

No me gusta.   no me goos·ta

It's fine. I'll take it.

OK. La alquilo.   o·kay la al·kee·lo

I'm leaving now.

Me voy ahora.   me voy a·o·ra

CONVERSATION & ESSENTIALS

Hello.	Hola.	o·la
	Saludos.	sa·loo·dos
Good morning.	Buenos días.	bwe·nos dee·as
Good afternoon.	Buenas tardes.	bwe·nas tar·des
Good evening/ night.	Buenas noches.	bwe·nas no·ches
Bye/See you soon.	Hasta luego.	as·ta lwe·go
Yes.	Sí.	see
No.	No.	no
Please.	Por favor.	por fa·vor
Thank you.	Gracias.	gra·syas
Many thanks.	Muchas gracias.	moo·chas gra·syas
You're welcome.	De nada.	de na·da
Pardon me.	Perdón.	per·don
Excuse me.	Permiso.	per·mee·so

(used when asking permission)

Forgive me.   Disculpe.   dees·kool·pe

(used when apologizing)

How are you?

¿Cómo está usted? (pol)   ko·mo es·ta oos·ted
¿Cómo estás? (inf)   ko·mo es·tas

What's your name?

¿Cómo se llama? (pol)   ko·mo se ya·ma
¿Cómo te llamas? (inf)   ko·mo te ya·mas

My name is ...

Me llamo ...   me ya·mo ...

It's a pleasure to meet you.

Mucho gusto.   moo·cho goos·to

The pleasure is mine.

El gusto es mío.   el goos·to es mee·o

Where are you from?

¿De dónde es? (pol)   de don·de es
¿De dónde eres? (inf)   de don·de e·res

I'm from ...

Soy de ...   soy de ...

Where are you staying?

¿Dónde está alojado/a? (pol)   don·de es·ta a·lo·kha·do/a
¿Dónde estás alojado/a? (inf) don·de es·tas a·lo·kha·do/a

May I take a photo (of you)?

¿Puedo sacar una foto   pwe·do sa·kar oo·na fo·to
   (de usted)?   (de oos·ted)

DIRECTIONS

How do I get to ...?

¿Cómo puedo llegar a ...?   ko·mo pwe·do ye·gar a ...

Is it far?

¿Está lejos?   es·ta le·khos

Go straight ahead.

Siga derecho.   see·ga de·re·cho

Turn left.

Voltée a la izquierda.   vol·te·e a la ees·kyer·da

Turn right.

Voltée a la derecha.   vol·te·e a la de·re·cha

Can you show me (on the map)?

¿Me lo podría indicar   me lo po·dree·a een·dee·kar
   (en el mapa)?   (en el ma·pa)

SIGNS

Entrada	Entrance
Salida	Exit
Información	Information
Abierto	Open
Cerrado	Closed
Prohibido	Prohibited
Comisaria	Police Station
Servicios/Baños	Toilets
Hombres/Varones	Men
Mujeres/Damas	Women

---

north	norte	nor·te
south	sur	soor
east	este	es·te
west	oeste	o·es·te
here	aquí	a·kee
there	allí	a·yee
avenue	avenida	a·ve·nee·da
block	esquina	es·kee·na
street	calle	ka·ye

HEALTH

I'm sick.

Estoy enfermo/a.   es·toy en·fer·mo/a

Where's the hospital?

¿Dónde está el hospital?   don·de es·ta el os·pee·tal

I'm pregnant.

Estoy embarazada.   es·toy em·ba·ra·sa·da

I've been vaccinated.

Estoy vacunado/a.   es·toy va·koo·na·do/a

I'm allergic to ...	Soy alérgico/a a ...	soy a·ler·khee·ko/a a ...
antibiotics	los antibióticos	los an·tee·byo·tee·kos
nuts	las fruta secas	las froo·tas se·kas
penicillin	la penicilina	la pe·nee·see·lee·na

EMERGENCIES

Help!	¡Socorro!	so·ko·ro
Fire!	¡Incendio!	een·sen·dyo
I've been robbed.	Me robaron.	me ro·ba·ron
Go away!	¡Déjeme!	de·khe·me
Get lost!	¡Váyase!	va·ya·se
Call ...!	¡Llame a ...!	ya·me a
an ambulance	una ambulancia	oo·na am·boo·lan·sya
a doctor	un médico	oon me·dee·ko
the police	la policía	la po·lee·see·a

It's an emergency.
Es una emergencia. es oo·na e·mer·khen·sya
Could you help me, please?
¿Me puede ayudar, por favor? me pwe·de a·yoo·dar por fa·vor
I'm lost.
Estoy perdido/a. (m/f) es·toy per·dee·do/a
Where are the toilets?
¿Dónde están los baños? don·de es·tan los ba·nyos

I'm ...	Soy ...	soy ...
asthmatic	asmático/a	as·ma·tee·ko/a
diabetic	diabético/a	dee·ya·be·tee·ko/a
epileptic	epiléptico/a	e·pee·lep·tee·ko/a
I have ...	Tengo ...	ten·go ...
a cough	tos	tos
diarrhea	diarrea	dya·re·a
a headache	un dolor de cabeza	oon do·lor de ka·be·sa
nausea	náusea	now·se·a

LANGUAGE DIFFICULTIES
Does anyone here speak English?
¿Hay alguien que hable inglés? ai al·gyen ke a·ble een·gles
Do you speak (English)?
¿Habla (inglés)? a·bla (een·gles)
I speak a little Spanish.
Hablo un poco de español. a·blo oon po·ko de es·pa·nyol
I (don't) understand.
(No) Entiendo. (no) en·tyen·do

Could you please ...?	¿Puede ..., por favor?	pwe·de ... por fa·vor
repeat that	repetirlo	re·pe·teer·lo
speak more slowly	hablar más despacio	a·blar mas des·pa·syo
write it down	escribirlo	es·kree·beer·lo

How do you say ...?
¿Cómo se dice ...? ko·mo se dee·se ...
What does ... mean?
¿Qué quiere decir ...? ke kye·re de·seer ...

NUMBERS
0	cero	ce·ro
1	uno/a	oo·no/a
2	dos	dos
3	tres	tres
4	cuatro	kwa·tro
5	cinco	seen·ko
6	seis	seys
7	siete	sye·te
8	ocho	o·cho
9	nueve	nwe·ve
10	diez	dyes
11	once	on·se
12	doce	do·se
13	trece	tre·se
14	catorce	ka·tor·se
15	quince	keen·se
16	dieciséis	dye·see·seys
17	diecisiete	dye·see·sye·te
18	dieciocho	dye·see·o·cho
19	diecinueve	dye·see·nwe·ve
20	veinte	vayn·te
21	veintiuno	vayn·tee·oo·no
30	treinta	trayn·ta
31	treinta y uno	trayn·tai oo·no
40	cuarenta	kwa·ren·ta
50	cincuenta	seen·kwen·ta
60	sesenta	se·sen·ta
70	setenta	se·ten·ta
80	ochenta	o·chen·ta
90	noventa	no·ven·ta
100	cien	syen
200	doscientos	do·syen·tos
1000	mil	meel

SHOPPING & SERVICES
I'd like to buy ...
Quisiera comprar ... kee·sye·ra kom·prar ...
I'm just looking.
Sólo estoy mirando. so·lo es·toy mee·ran·do
May I look at it?
¿Puedo mirarlo? pwe·do mee·rar·lo
How much is it?
¿Cuánto cuesta? kwan·to kwes·ta
That's too expensive for me.
Es demasiado caro para mí. es de·ma·sya·do ka·ro pa·ra mee
Could you lower the price?
¿Podría bajar un poco el precio? po·dree·a ba·khar oon po·ko el pre·syo

I don't like it.
No me gusta.   no me *goos*·ta
I'll take it.
Lo llevo.   lo *ye*·vo

Do you accept ...?	¿Aceptan ...?	a·sep·tan ...
credit cards	tarjetas de crédito	tar·*khe*·tas de kre·*dee*·to
traveler's checks	cheques de viajero	*che*·kes de vya·*khe*·ro

less	menos	*me*·nos
more	más	mas
large	grande	*gran*·de
small	pequeño	pe·*ke*·nyo

I'm looking for (the) ...	Estoy buscando ...	es·toy boos·*kan*·do ...
ATM	el cajero automático	el ka·*khe*·ro ow·to·*ma*·tee·ko
bank	el banco	el *ban*·ko
bookstore	la librería	la lee·bre·*ree*·a
embassy	la embajada	la em·ba·*kha*·da
exchange office	la casa de cambio	la *ka*·sa de *kam*·byo
general store	la tienda	la *tyen*·da
laundry	la lavandería	la la·van·de·*ree*·a
market	el mercado	el mer·*ka*·do
pharmacy	la farmacia	la far·*ma*·sya
post office	los correos	los ko·*re*·os
supermarket	el supermercado	el soo·per·mer·*ka*·do
telephone centre	el centro telefónico	el *sen*·tro te·le·*fo*·nee·ko
tourist office	la oficina de turismo	la o·fee·*see*·na de too·*rees*·mo

What time does it open/close?
¿A qué hora abre/cierra?   a ke o·ra a·bre/sye·ra
I want to change some money/traveler's checks.
Quiero cambiar dinero/   kye·ro kam·byar dee·ne·ro/
cheques de viajero.   che·kes de vya·khe·ro
What's the exchange rate?
¿Cuál es la taza de   kwal es la *ta*·za de
cambio?   *kam*·byo
I want to call ...
Quiero llamar a ...   kye·ro ya·mar a ...

airmail	correo aéreo	ko·*re*·o a·e·re·o
stamps	estampillas	es·tam·*pee*·yas

TIME & DATES

When?	¿Cuándo?	*kwan*·do
What time is it?	¿Qué hora es?	ke o·ra es

It's (one) o'clock.	Es la (una).	es la (*oo*·na)
It's (seven) o'clock.	Son las (siete).	son las (*sye*·te)

midnight	medianoche	me·dya·*no*·che
noon	mediodía	me·dyo·*dee*·a
half past two	dos y media	dos ee *me*·dya
now	ahora	a·*o*·ra
today	hoy	oy
tonight	esta noche	es·ta *no*·che
tomorrow	mañana	ma·*nya*·na
yesterday	ayer	a·*yer*

Monday	lunes	*loo*·nes
Tuesday	martes	*mar*·tes
Wednesday	miércoles	*myer*·ko·les
Thursday	jueves	*khwe*·ves
Friday	viernes	*vyer*·nes
Saturday	sábado	*sa*·ba·do
Sunday	domingo	do·*meen*·go

January	enero	e·*ne*·ro
February	febrero	fe·*bre*·ro
March	marzo	*mar*·so
April	abril	a·*breel*
May	mayo	*ma*·yo
June	junio	*khoo*·nyo
July	julio	*khoo*·lyo
August	agosto	a·*gos*·to
September	septiembre	sep·*tyem*·bre
October	octubre	ok·*too*·bre
November	noviembre	no·*vyem*·bre
December	diciembre	dee·*syem*·bre

TRANSPORT
Public Transport

What time does ... leave/arrive?	¿A qué hora ... sale/llega?	a ke o·ra ... sa·le/ye·ga
the bus	el autobus	el ow·to·boos
the plane	el avión	el a·vyon
the ship	el barco	el bar·ko

airport	el aeropuerto	el a·e·ro·pwer·to
bus station	la estación de autobuses	la es·ta·syon de ow·to·boo·ses
bus stop	la parada de autobuses	la pa·ra·da de ow·to·boo·ses
luggage check room	guardería/ equipaje	gwar·de·ree·a/ e·kee·pa·khe
ticket office	la boletería	la bo·le·te·ree·a

I'd like a ticket to ...
Quiero un boleto a ...   kye·ro oon bo·le·to a ...
What's the fare to ...?
¿Cuánto cuesta hasta ...?   kwan·to kwes·ta a·sta ...

LANGUAGE

student's (fare)	de estudiante	de es·too·*dyan*·te
one-way	ida	ee·da
return	ida y vuelta	ee·da ee *vwel*·ta

Private Transport

pickup (truck)	camioneta	ka·myo·*ne*·ta
truck	camión	ka·*myon*
hitchhike	hacer dedo	a·ser *de*·do

I'd like to	Quisiera	kee·*sye*·ra
hire a/an ...	alquilar ...	al·kee·*lar* ...
bicycle	una bicicleta	oo·na bee·see·*kle*·ta
car	un auto/	oon *ow*·to/
	un coche	oon *ko*·che
4WD	un todo terreno	oon *to*·do te·*re*·no
motorbike	una moto	oo·na *mo*·to

Is this the road to ...?
¿Se va a ... por esta carretera?   se va a ... por *es*·ta ka·re·*te*·ra
Where's a gas/petrol station?
¿Dónde hay una bomba?   don·de ai oo·na *bom*·ba
I've run out of gas/petrol.
Me quedé sin gasolina.   me ke·*de* seen ga·so·*lee*·na
Please fill it up.
Lleno, por favor.   ye·no por fa·*vor*
I'd like (20) liters.
Quiero (veinte) litros.   kye·ro (vayn·te) lee·tros

ROAD SIGNS

Acceso	Entrance
Ceda el Paso	Give Way
Dirección Única	One-Way
Mantenga Su Derecha	Keep to the Right
No Adelantar/ No Rebase	No Passing
Peligro	Danger
Prohibido Aparcar/ No Estacionar	No Parking
Prohibido el Paso	No Entry
Pare	Stop
Salida de Autopista	Exit Freeway

---

diesel	diesel	*dee*·sel
leaded (regular)	gasolina con plomo	ga·so·*lee*·na kon *plo*·mo
gas/petrol	gasolina	ga·so·*lee*·na
unleaded	gasolina sin plomo	ga·so·*lee*·na seen *plo*·mo

(How long) Can I park here?
¿(Por cuánto tiempo) Puedo aparcar aquí?   (por kwan·to tyem·po) pwe·do a·par·kar a·kee

Where do I pay?
¿Dónde se paga?   don·de se pa·ga
I need a mechanic.
Necesito un mecánico.   ne·se·*see*·to oon me·*ka*·nee·ko
The car has broken down in ...
El carro se ha averiado en ...   el *ka*·ro se a·ve·*rya*·do en ...
The motorbike won't start.
No arranca la moto.   no a·*ran*·ka la *mo*·to
I have a flat tyre.
Tengo una goma pinchada.   ten·go oo·na go·ma peen·*cha*·da
I've had an accident.
Tuve un accidente.   too·ve oon ak·see·*den*·te

TRAVEL WITH CHILDREN

I need ...
Necesito ...   ne·se·*see*·to ...
Do you have ...?
¿Hay ...?   ai ...
  a car baby seat
  un asiento de seguridad para bebés
  oon a·*syen*·to de se·goo·ree·*da* pa·ra be·*bes*
  a child-minding service
  un servicio de cuidado de niños
  oon ser·*vee*·syo de kwee·*da*·do de *nee*·nyos
  (disposable) diapers/nappies
  pañales (de usar y tirar)
  pa·*nya*·les (de oo·*sar* ee tee·*rar*)
  infant formula (milk)
  leche en polvo para bebés
  le·che en *pol*·vo *pa*·ra be·*bes*
  a highchair
  una trona
  oo·na *tro*·na
  a potty
  una pelela
  oo·na pe·*le*·la
  a stroller
  un cochecito
  oon ko·che·*see*·to

Also available from Lonely Planet:
Latin American Spanish Phrasebook

Glossary

For common expressions and useful phrases, see p288. For lists of common food names and food-related expressions, see p61.

acuario – aquarium
apagón – power outage
avenida – avenue

bachata – Dominican 'country' music and dance style
bahía – bay
balneario – swimming hole, usually one created by blocking a river
barca – a large boat
bien-bienes – souls of dead African slaves, said to live along Haitian border
bohío – thatch hut
botánica – shop where religious articles can be found
bracero – Haitian sugarcane cutter
buscando – a freelance tour guide

cabaña turística – motel used by adulterers
calle – street
campesino – a peasant
capilla – chapel
carretera – highway
casa – house
casa de cambio – currency-exchange business
casa de huéspedes – an inn
casita de cita – a brothel
catedral – cathedral
cerveza – beer
club gallístico – a venue for cockfights
colmado – small grocery store
comedor – family-run restaurant serving simple Dominican cuisine
comida criolla – Dominican cuisine
Colón, Cristóbal – Christopher Columbus
Cuba libre servicio – a bottle of rum, a bucket of ice and two Cokes
cuero – prostitute

Dímelo? – How's it going?

fiesta patronal – patron saint festival
fortaleza – fortress
galería – gallery
gomero – a tire repair shop
guapo – bad tempered (the same word means 'handsome' in many other countries)
gua-gua – small bus providing low-cost local transport

hato – a huge cattle ranch
hostal – inn
¡Huepa! – Hello!

iglesia – church

jonron – home run

la bandera dominicana – national dish of beans and rice (literally, 'the Dominican flag')
la frontera – the border with Haiti
lago – lake
larimar – semiprecious blue stone found only in the Dominican Republic
lavandería – laundry

Malecón – literally 'sea wall,' refers to any seaside boulevard
mamacita – sexy woman
mercado – market
merengue – the national dance music
monasterio – monastery
motoconcho – motorcycle taxi
muelú – a male flirt
museo – museum
muy chulo – very handsome

oro – gold

pájaro – literally 'bird,' refers to a gay man
palacio – palace
parque – park
parque central – central park or plaza
pensión – an inn; traditionally, a home with rooms to rent
peso – monetary unit of the Dominican Republic
plata – silver
playa – beach
público – privately owned minivan or pickup truck that picks up passengers on major city streets
puerta – gate, door
puerto – port

¡Que chulo! – how nice

ruínas – ruins

son – form of Cuban guitar music often heard in the Dominican capital

todo incluido – an all-inclusive resort

yola – boat for smuggling people into the USA from the DR

Behind the Scenes

THIS BOOK
This is the third edition of *Dominican Republic*. The first edition of *Dominican Republic & Haiti* was written by Scott Doggett and Leah Gordon. The second edition was updated by Scott Doggett and Joyce Connolly. Gary and Liza Prado Chandler updated this edition.

THANKS from the Authors
Thank you, first and foremost, to the hundreds of Dominicans and expats we met along the way who contributed in big ways and small to the research and writing of this book. From taxi drivers and police officers, to shop owners and passers-by, we received a tremendous amount of friendly assistance and sound advice from people whose names we often never learned, but without whom this assignment would have been impossible to complete.

Extra special thanks go to Doña Agustina for her warm Valentine's Day welcome in Santo Domingo, to the friendly folks at El Colibrí Resort in Sosúa, Mark at Rocky's Rock & Blues Bar Hotel in Sosúa, Andy from samanaonline.com in Las Galeras, Walter Brandle from Rancho La Cueva in Playa Limón, Rosanna Selman de León from Paraiso Caño Hondo in Sabana de la Mar, Doña Rita and the staff at El Refugio in Boca Chica, Chris from Chris & Mady's restaurant in Cofresí, Mark McEachron at Gri-Gri Divers in Río San Juan, Noëlle Gillin at Sofy's Bed & Breakfast in Puerto Plata, and the staff at the tourism offices in Jarabacoa and Constanza for their help and information.

Lonely Planet does a terrific job of supporting and guiding its authors. Thank you (and good luck apple-picking) to Alex Hershey who got us started,

to Erin Corrigan who saw us through to the end, to Alison Lyall, Jolyon Philcox and everyone in cartography for the great maps, and to Craig Kilburn for the fine and friendly edits. Travel writing can be a lonely career, believe it or not, so we are extremely lucky to be able to do it together – thank you to everyone at Lonely Planet for helping make that possible.

We are also blessed with wonderful, loving and supportive families. Thank you to Mom and Dad Chandler, Ellen, Elyse, Joey, Sue, Katy and Kyle, and to Mom and Dad Prado – who visited us in Bávaro and opened our eyes to ocean aerobics and the joys of the lobby bar – and to Javier, Deb, Sammy, Owen and David. Together with our friends, they make coming home one of the best parts of traveling abroad.

CREDITS
Commissioning Editor Erin Corrigan
Coordinating Editor Craig Kilburn
Coordinating Cartographer Jolyon Philcox
Coordinating Layout & Color Designer David Kemp
Cover Designer Candice Jacobus
Managing Editor Bruce Evans
Managing Cartographer Alison Lyall
Assisting Editors Trent Holden, Holly Alexander, Sasha Baskett, Andrea Dobbin
Assisting Cartographer David Connolly
Project Manager Eoin Dunlevy
Language Content Coordinator Quentin Frayne

Thanks to Alex Hershey, Alan Murphy, Korina Miller, Marcel Gaston

THE LONELY PLANET STORY
The story begins with a classic travel adventure: Tony and Maureen Wheeler's 1972 journey across Europe and Asia to Australia. There was no useful information about the overland trail then, so Tony and Maureen published the first Lonely Planet guidebook to meet a growing need.

From a kitchen table, Lonely Planet has grown to become the largest independent travel publisher in the world, with offices in Melbourne (Australia), Oakland (USA) and London (UK). Today Lonely Planet guidebooks cover the globe. There is an ever-growing list of books and information in a variety of media. Some things haven't changed. The main aim is still to make it possible for adventurous travelers to get out there – to explore and better understand the world.

At Lonely Planet we believe travelers can make a positive contribution to the countries they visit – if they respect their host communities and spend their money wisely. Every year 5% of company profit is donated to charities around the world.

THANKS from Lonely Planet

Many thanks to the following travelers who used the last edition and wrote to us with helpful hints, useful advice and interesting anecdotes.

A John Adams, Paul Alper, Jorge Alvar Villegas, Fabian Andersson, Juha Asikainen **B** Hauke Baeumel, Emilio Baldi, Gabriele Bapst, Claudia Barchiesi, Dyanne Bax, Rosemary Beattie, Johannes Beck, Philippe Bélisle, Jorg Beyeler, Leander Bindewald, Linda Gray Biok, Dan Broockmann, Heather Buck **C** Andrew Campbell, Andrew & Barb Campbell, Robert Carbo, Bonnie Carpenter, Olivia Carrescia, Robert Chaleff, Karen Cheung, David Church, Ann Cleary, James Cocks, Jeffrey Cohen, H Crighton, Michael Critchley, Margaret Cunningham **D** Edward Dadswell, Robert d'Avanzo, Susan Davis, Chad de Groot, Ruud Dirksen, Daniel Dolan, Faye Donnaway, Joseph Dragon, Sheila Duncan **E** Frank Ehrlicher, Nils Elvemo, Patricia Erickson, Dimos Ermoupolis, Ana Escorbort, Rhian Evans **F** Maria Falgoust, Hanne Finholt, Jude Fish, Muriel Foucher, Eric Franco, Jonathon Frisbee **G** Jean Marc Gaude, Mordechai Gemer, Mylene Gibbs, Stephan Gorthner, Maarten Gresnigt **H** Ronald Hakenberg, David Hall, Jean-Lou Hamelin, Thomas Hill, Caroline Houde, Frans Huber, Olivia Hung, Maggie Hurchalla **I** John Ide **J** Ellen James, Volkmar Janicke, Fausto Jimenez, Neysha Jimenez, Joey Johnson **K** Linda Karlbom, Kevin Keller, Lisa Kirkman, Toni Klein, Cara & Sam Kolb, Richard Kowalczyk, Jack Kravitz, Dennis Kroeger, Irina Kuha **L** Andy Lam, Michelle Lewis, Paul Luchessa **M** Fulvio Maccarone, Andre Marcil, Anna Marfitt, Judit Marothy, Volker Maschmann, Sara Mason, Nick Massey, Michael Mayan, Liam McKnight, Theresa McDonald, John McEnroe, Jeanette McGarry, Iris Metawi, Ryan Miller, Helen Miner, Landon Modien, Denise Molina, Dennis Mooij **N** Akanksha Naik, Peter Necas, Leah Nichols, Sally Nowlan **O** Marielle Ogor, Rob Ostrowski, Todd Owens **P** Rolf Palmberg, Wolfgang Pannocha, Carlos Paz-Soldan, Muriel Peretti, Johnathan Pierce, Tom Pisula, Sonya Plowman, Sergio Prescivali, Sylvie Proidl, Peter Puranen **R** Helen Raynor, Ken Reed, Riikka Reunanen, Eddie Reynoso, John Riley, Bruce Rumoga **S** Loeve Saint-Ourens, Michelle Salazar, Gabriele Schenk, Beate Schmahl, Mark Schuler, Sheila Sedgwick, Brigitte Seidel, Travis Smith, Karen Söderberg, Ioannis Sofilos, Gordon Stewart, Ben Stubenberg **T** Gerard Tarly, Erin Taylor, Helen Temple, Suzanne Teune, Rosalie Thanh, Peter Theglev, Betty Theriault, Heather Thoreau, David Thornton, Armin Timmerer, Patrick Traynor, S. P. Tschinkel, Le Tu, Leo Tucker, Jack Tyler **V** Adrie van Sorgen, Monika Vetsch, Eric Viel **W** Eunice Walaska, Clive Walker, Richard Walton, Garth Ward, Doug Wilkins, E Winmill, Ruth Wise, Swiatoslaw Wojtkowiak, Ute Wronn **Y** Elaine Yong **Z** Karen Zabawa, Harald Zahn, Ondrej Zapletal, Marc Zieltjens, Baerbel Zimmer, Marshall Zipper, John Zubatiuk

ACKNOWLEDGMENTS

Globe on back cover © Mountain High Maps 1993 Digital Wisdom, Inc.

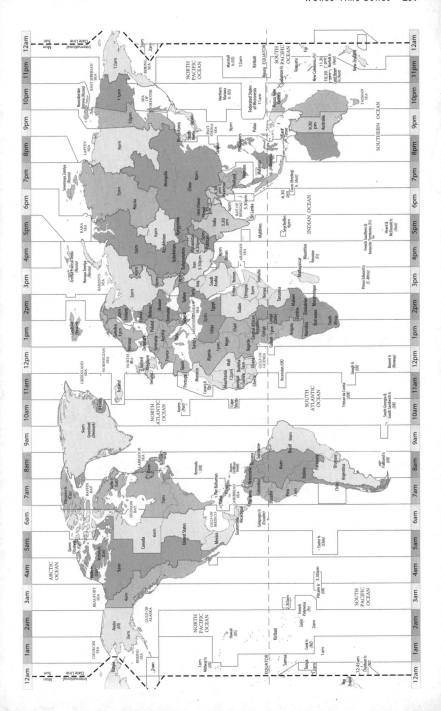

Index

000 Map pages
000 Location of color photographs

INDEX

000 Map pages
000 Location of colour photographs

INDEX

MAP LEGEND

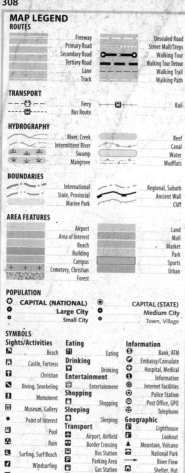

ROUTES

Freeway
Primary Road
Secondary Road
Tertiary Road
Lane
Track

Unsealed Road
Street Mall/Steps
Walking Tour
Walking Tour Detour
Walking Trail
Walking Path

TRANSPORT

Ferry
Bus Route

Rail

HYDROGRAPHY

River, Creek
Intermittent River
Swamp
Mangrove

Reef
Canal
Water
Mudflats

BOUNDARIES

International
State, Provincial
Marine Park

Regional, Suburb
Ancient Wall
Cliff

AREA FEATURES

Airport
Area of Interest
Beach
Building
Campus
Cemetery, Christian
Forest

Land
Mall
Market
Park
Sports
Urban

POPULATION

⊙ CAPITAL (NATIONAL)
● Large City
○ Small City

◉ CAPITAL (STATE)
◉ Medium City
○ Town, Village

SYMBOLS

Sights/Activities

Beach
Castle, Fortress
Christian
Diving, Snorkeling
Monument
Museum, Gallery
Point of Interest
Pool
Ruin
Surfing, Surf Beach
Windsurfing
Zoo, Bird Sanctuary

Eating

Eating

Drinking

Drinking

Entertainment

Entertainment

Shopping

Shopping

Sleeping

Sleeping

Transport

Airport, Airfield
Border Crossing
Bus Station
Parking Area
Gas Station
Taxi Rank

Information

Bank, ATM
Embassy/Consulate
Hospital, Medical
Information
Internet Facilities
Police Station
Post Office, GPO
Telephone

Geographic

Lighthouse
Lookout
Mountain, Volcano
National Park
River Flow
Shelter, Hut
Waterfall

LONELY PLANET OFFICES

Australia

Head Office
Locked Bag 1, Footscray, Victoria 3011
☎ 03 8379 8000, fax 03 8379 8111
talk2us@lonelyplanet.com.au

USA

150 Linden St, Oakland, CA 94607
☎ 510 893 8555, toll free 800 275 8555
fax 510 893 8572, info@lonelyplanet.com

UK

72-82 Rosebery Ave,
Clerkenwell, London EC1R 4RW
☎ 020 7841 9000, fax 020 7841 9001
go@lonelyplanet.co.uk

Published by Lonely Planet Publications Pty Ltd
ABN 36 005 607 983

© Lonely Planet 2005

© photographers as indicated 2005

Cover photographs: Isla Saona (p123-4), Ludovic Maisant/APL Corbis (front); Friendly faces, Andrew Marshall & Leanne Walker/Lonely Planet Images (back). Many of the images in this guide are available for licensing from Lonely Planet Images: www.lonelyplanetimages .com